# AMNESTY INTERNATIONAL

---

## The 1993 Report on Human Rights Around the World

This report covers the period
January to December 1992

Hunter House

© 1993 Amnesty International Publications

Hunter House Inc., Publishers
P.O. Box 2914
Alameda, CA 94501-0914

Series ISSN 1070–0781
ISBN 0-89793-140-8 (soft cover)
ISBN 0-89793-141-6 (hard cover)
AI Index: POL 10/01/93
Original language: English

Typesetting and page makeup by Accent on type, London, England
Manufactured in the United States of America

**This report documents Amnesty
International's work and its
concerns throughout the world
during 1992.** The absence of an
entry in this report on a particular
country does not imply that no
human rights violations of concern to
Amnesty International have taken
place there during the year. Nor is
the length of a country entry any
basis for a comparison of the extent
and depth of Amnesty International's
concerns in a country. Regional maps
have been included in the report to
indicate the location of countries and
territories cited in the text and for
that purpose only. It is not possible on
the small scale used to show precise
political boundaries, nor should the
maps be taken as indicating any view
on the status of disputed territory.
Amnesty International takes no
position on territorial questions.
Disputed boundaries and cease-fire
lines are shown, where possible, by
broken lines. Areas whose disputed
status is a matter of unresolved
concern before the relevant bodies of
the United Nations have been
indicated by striping only on the
maps of the country which has *de
facto* control of the area.

# CONTENTS

# CONTENTS

# CONTENTS

## APPENDICES

# INTRODUCTION

# Playing politics with people's lives

Appalling human rights catastrophes shocked the world in 1992. In the former Yugoslavia and in Somalia, the carnage was on a terrifying scale, with thousands of men, women and children tortured, killed or unaccounted for. In countries such as Chad, China, Iraq, Liberia, Peru and Sri Lanka, human rights violations and abuses continued at horrifying levels. The scale of these crises, and others that barely made the news, was almost beyond comprehension and seemingly beyond control.

So how have governments around the world responded to such atrocities? Most are quick to proclaim that human rights must be defended and in 1992 international action in response to some human rights crises was at a high level. Despite this, politically motivated selectivity has continued to be the norm for governments when dealing with human rights issues, and international treaty obligations have been cynically ignored when convenient. In short, the response by governments to human rights crises in other countries has been marked by a conspicuous lack of political integrity.

© Reuters

**In the growing human rights nightmare in Bosnia-Herzegovina, a uniformed policeman forces a suspected sniper down a street in the town of Brcko. Seconds after this photograph was taken, the policeman fired a bullet into the back of the man's head.**

Self-interest has guided governments' responses to human rights crises and has prevented or hindered action in many countries where it is desperately needed. The world has witnessed human rights violations of allies being greeted with silence while those of declared enemies were met with public condemnations, sometimes backed with action. Such hypocrisy has led to a lack of public confidence in the way governments deal with human rights at home and abroad, in their relations with other governments or through international institutions.

This report is a grim testament to a lack of consistent commitment to fundamental human rights standards, laying bare the abject failure of governments to protect basic rights. It records the violent suppression of dissent – and of human rights – by governments in every region in the world. It shows that governments, which are increasingly bringing their laws into line with human rights standards and making public pronouncements of those rights, are through their actions exposing those laws and words as cynical gestures.

In the human rights records of the 161 countries that follow, the results of this double standard can be seen. In dozens of countries people are still being put behind bars because they speak out against their government, or because of their political affiliation or family ties. The report exposes scores of governments that let their police and soldiers get away with beating, inflicting electric shocks or raping prisoners just to humiliate them or force them to sign false confessions. There are descriptions of gruesome torture sometimes leading to death. There are stories of some of the thousands of people who have

Mother and son of Victor Pineda Henestrosa, a Zapoteco indigenous leader from Juchitán de Zaragoza in Mexico, who "disappeared" after he was abducted, allegedly by soldiers, in 1978. His was one of many cases highlighted by Amnesty International during a year-long campaign in 1992 to call attention to the continuing human rights violations against indigenous peoples in the Americas.

Tens of thousands of people died in Somalia in 1992, either in fighting between rival political groups or through starvation. The country's civil war prevented the distribution of relief supplies to many areas hit by famine. In the picture, bodies are being loaded into a Somali Red Crescent truck in Baidoa, one of the towns in which hundreds of people died of starvation every week in the second half of the year.

"disappeared" or were brutally murdered at the hands of security forces or government-linked "death squads" – all because governments wanted to stamp out their opposition for good.

This report also shows that armed political and opposition groups commit sickening abuses, including torture, mutilation, deliberate and arbitrary killing and hostage-taking. These have been recorded in places such as India, Israel and the Occupied Territories, Peru and Sri Lanka. Amnesty International urges all such armed groups to live up to international humanitarian standards which forbid torture and deliberate and arbitrary killings of civilians at all times.

There are glaring examples of double standards being applied by the international community in relation to human rights. For example, by the end of 1992 there had still been no serious international attempt to address the widespread torture, executions or administrative detention in China, despite the outcry following the 1989 massacres in Beijing. The worldwide pressure to stop human rights violations in South Africa eased up as the political reform process began – even though black South Africans were still being tortured in police cells and massacred in their

4

townships. That pressure only picked up again in the wake of atrocities that hit the international headlines and the collapse of political negotiations.

There is ample evidence of the blatant disregard so many governments show for human rights in their own countries. For example, executions continued to spiral in the USA, with 31 prisoners killed by the state in 1992 — more than double the number in the previous year. In Turkey, the government claimed that the walls of its police stations would be "made of glass" as part of its commitment to end torture, yet the number of people who died from torture rose in 1992 and new patterns of political killings by the security forces emerged in the southeast. In Mexico, torture continued virtually unchecked even though the country has strong commitments to human rights in its laws.

At the heart of this report is the cumulative failure of nations to make the protection of human rights a genuine priority of government at home or abroad. When governments knowingly shirk their obligation to protect rights themselves and to hold other states to their international commitments, their seeming indifference becomes complicity. When the international community remains silent, it provides a shield behind which governments believe they can order the secret police, the torturers and state assassins into action with impunity.

In 1993 the human rights records of governments around the world are under scrutiny in the context of the UN World Conference on Human Rights and the UN International Year for the World's Indigenous People. It is also the year of a special Amnesty International campaign against extrajudicial executions and "disappearances". Amnesty International is challenging governments to back words about human rights with concrete action as part of its continuing campaign to enhance respect for human rights worldwide.

All governments should ensure that their laws and practices respect international human rights standards. In 1993 Amnesty International is calling on all governments to initiate a national review to be carried out by an independent body on the extent to which all international human rights standards – civil, political, economic, social and cultural – have been implemented in practice. In each country domestic and international protection of human rights must be given the same priority as other essential functions of government, including by strengthening appropriate government machinery at the executive level.

Governments must make sure the citizens of their countries know about basic human rights and how to complain if those rights are violated. They should also use their influence to promote human rights internationally and raise questions about the human rights practices of other governments.

© Times of India

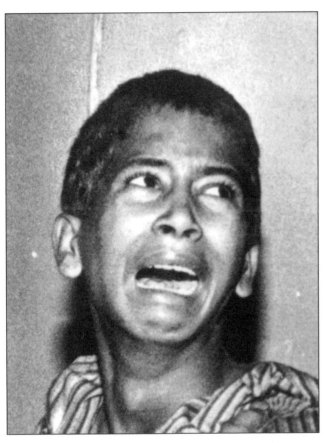

Torture victim Manoj Singh, aged 12, was arrested in August 1991 on suspicion of stealing a purse. His father, Jairam Singh, accompanied the boy to a New Delhi police station and was allegedly tortured to death. This case featured in an Amnesty International report, *India: Torture, Rape and Deaths in Custody*, which was published in March 1992 to launch a major international campaign on custodial violence in the country.

It is also essential that all governments train their police, military forces, diplomats and other public servants to protect human rights at home and in other countries. When government agents do violate human rights, they should be subject to independent investigation and brought to justice.

Governments should also ensure in their relations with other countries that there is impartial and objective scrutiny of and action on human rights violations wherever they occur.

To some, these goals may seem unrealistic in the present world climate. But, after all, Amnesty International was dismissed as "one of the larger lunacies of our time" when its founder suggested that prisoners of conscience could be freed by raising public awareness on their behalf. We believe that if people around the world force their governments to take up these challenges, human rights can be defended honestly, vigorously and successfully.

# The formidable spirit of human solidarity

Investigators exposing human rights crimes committed during eight years of brutal dictatorship in Chad discovered piles of letters and postcards sent by Amnesty International members around the world. There were over 50,000 of them in all. Each one appealed to Chadian officials at the highest level to end the torture and executions in Chad's jails: an official commission estimated that 40,000 people, out of a total population of some five million, had been killed between 1982 and 1990. Amnesty International members wrote from as far away as Finland and New Zealand, and from within Africa itself, from Côte d'Ivoire, Egypt and Mauritius. The commission concluded: "Thanks to its formidable spirit of human solidarity, Amnesty International gave back hope to thousands of prisoners and their families."

Amnesty International was born in the 1960s as a movement of ordinary people who did not want to watch in silence while fellow human beings were imprisoned and persecuted for their beliefs, colour or identity. Amnesty International's ever-growing army of volunteers remains the backbone of the international campaign. Numbering more than a million, these are the activists who mobilize their communities, put pressure on governments, support the victims and their families, lobby for legal reform, and raise public awareness through the press and human rights education work.

During 1992, Amnesty International volunteers around the world took on many fresh challenges. They worked on over 3,000 cases of torture, arbitrary imprisonment, "disappearance", political killing and the death penalty.

The Amnesty International group in Salamanca, Spain, has been working since 1990 on a case involving the persecution of a Guatemalan family by the Guatemalan armed forces. Four members of the Chitay-Camey family were murdered in separate incidents between 1988 and 1990; two more "disappeared" after being abducted. Surviving members of the extended family received repeated death threats. The Amnesty International group helped 23 members of the family, 17 of them children, to leave Guatemala. They now live in Spain, where group members have assisted them to be financially self-sufficient and visit them regularly.

To draw public attention to their case and increase the pressure on the Guatemalan Government to take action, the group held a press conference in March to mark the anniversary of one of the "disappearances". Two members of the family attended. The next day, a theatre group performed *¿Dónde Están?* (Where Are They?) in Salamanca's historic main square. After the performance, group members collected signatures on a petition calling for action and gave out cards featuring the case to members of the audience. A major national newspaper covered the story and local newspapers have also reported on the issue. Interviews with members of the family and local Amnesty International group members were broadcast on two national radio stations. The group says: "Despite the fact that we have not received any responses from the Guatemalan authorities yet – notwithstanding our sending letters and cards every month to several government officials – we will not give up working on this distressing case until the perpetrators of these outrageous human rights violations are brought to justice and the families are awarded compensation for their suffering. We are optimistic and hope this case will be successfully resolved because only pressure from the international community will bring about justice for these families. We have had the chance to meet personally members of the Chitay-Camey family, and such an extraordinary experience has helped strengthen our struggle for human rights."

The Chitay-Camey family came originally from a predominantly Indian area of Guatemala, but were forced to flee from there in 1982 at the height of the army's counter-insurgency operations. Members of the family attended a press conference in Spain in October 1992 as part of a major Amnesty International campaign to persuade governments throughout the Americas to stop turning their backs on the human rights of indigenous peoples. In the 500th anniversary year of the arrival of Europeans in the region, Amnesty International supporters all over the

**Amnesty International members in Nepal campaigning on Human Rights Day in Bhaktapur Square near Kathmandu. The children in the square had participated in a painting competition to promote awareness of human rights.**

8

Morocco's three longest-serving prisoners of conscience, Ahmed Aitbennacer (shown right), Ahmed Rakiz and Abdallah Harif, were released on 15 January 1992 from Kenitra Central Prison. They had been held since the mid-1970s and sentenced in 1977 to between 20 and 32 years' imprisonment after an unfair trial of 178 left-wing activists. The three men had featured in several major Amnesty International campaigns.

world chose their own ways to mark the survival and courage of the indigenous peoples of the Americas. Prisoners in six jails in Ireland constructed different sections of a totem pole to express their solidarity with indigenous prisoners in the Americas. In Norway torch-lit processions were held throughout the country to mark a day of mourning for all the indigenous victims who have died since European colonization.

The campaign was launched in Mexico City with the publication of Amnesty International's report on human rights violations against the indigenous peoples of the Americas, which analyses the contexts which give rise to violations – land and resource disputes, repression of indigenous activism, the so-called "war against drugs" and internal conflicts. The report found that although the manifestations of abuse differ – for example, discrimination in the judicial system in Canada and the USA, torture in Mexico, massive extrajudicial executions in Peru – the root causes are the same throughout the region, lying in the discrimination, deprivation and marginalization to which indigenous peoples have been subjected. Amnesty International called on governments in the Americas to carry out effective investigations into abuses against indigenous peoples and bring to justice those responsible; it also called on them to resolve justly land disputes that all too often lead to abuses.

Amnesty International launched other major international campaigns in 1992. During a campaign against deaths, torture and rape of prisoners in India, thousands of copies of a newly published Amnesty International report on India were sent to police officials, judges and civil rights workers throughout the vast country. The report

stimulated a national debate about the state of human rights protection in India. Much of the public discussion took place in the Indian press, which despite some criticisms of Amnesty International, overwhelmingly endorsed the view that the Indian Government could no longer be excused for failing to take effective action to stop violence in custody. The Indian Government began by denying that the violations reported by Amnesty International had taken place – a minister commented that the report was based on "mere hearsay" – but later responded by giving details on over 200 cases listed in the report. In November Amnesty International took up its first invitation to India for government discussions since 1978, and the authorities proposed strengthening legal safeguards for detainees and promised to set up a Human Rights Commission.

Groups of Amnesty International volunteers in 45 countries took part in the campaign against torture in India. Some were in the former Soviet Union and other countries of Eastern and Western Europe; others were in South, Central and North America, Africa, the Middle East and Asia and the Pacific. An Indian human rights lawyer toured Australia. In Belgium an exhibition of tapestries by Indian women was displayed and paper boats containing flowers and candles were floated on a pond near the European Community buildings; 415 in all, one for every detainee whose death was described in the report. In Brazil, police units were asked to write to their Indian counterparts and

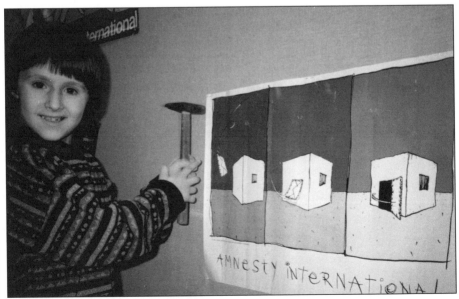

Mihai Crişan, the son of an Amnesty International member in Romania, helping to set up an exhibition to promote human rights and the organization's work. The event was staged in March in a students' club in Cluj.

Nayef 'Ali Nayef Sweitat, a Palestinian journalist from the West Bank, who was arrested in April by Israeli border police and later served with a six-month administrative detention order. This was reduced to two and a half months on appeal in June and he was released in July. The appeal judge referred to Amnesty International's adoption of him as a prisoner of conscience in his ruling.

in Guyana exhibitions were held on a university campus and at an open-air market. In Japan "curry and rice" evenings accompanied the writing of letters to Indian officials, and the Japanese Section of Amnesty International section organized a symposium on human rights violations against women in India.

During 1992 Amnesty International members also undertook special activities to highlight the human rights situation in 19 other countries which were of particular concern. The issues highlighted included torture and ill-treatment in prisons and police stations in Greece; killings and torture by the security forces in South Africa; arbitrary detention and ill-treatment of prisoners by the Chinese authorities in Tibet; a campaign of terror and violence by Myanmar's ruling military council against the country's Muslims and other minorities; and killings and "disappearances" in Peru perpetrated by government forces as well as by the armed opposition.

In the Philippines, where hundreds of people had been brutally killed by government and government-backed forces between 1988 and 1992, an international Amnesty International delegation launched a campaign in Manila in February. The organization challenged all candidates in the forthcoming elections to take a stand on human rights issues, and succeeded in raising the profile of human rights on the election agenda.

In August Amnesty International appealed to all Somali political leaders for action to end the severe human rights abuses – including massacres of civilians – which characterized the civil wars raging in Somalia.

Special campaigns on the plight of specific groups included worldwide calls for an end to a particularly abhorrent form of abuse – the sexual torture of women.

Often human rights emergencies arise which require immediate action, rather than the months of careful planning that lie behind campaigns. Amnesty International supporters mobilized within hours to take action on emergencies in nine countries, including the forcible return of Haitian asylum-seekers from the USA in January; a sharp deterioration in human rights under a state of emergency in Algeria in February; the dissolution of democratic institutions leading to suspension of constitutional rights in Peru in April; the deliberate killing of demonstrators in Thailand in May; and widespread arbitrary killings, hostage-taking and detentions by warring sides in the internal conflict in Liberia in November.

In September Amnesty International learned of mass detentions and killings in the southern Sudanese town of Juba over the previous three months. Immediate action, which captured widespread media coverage, and intensive lobbying of home governments alerted the international community to what had been a hidden human rights crisis. Although the Sudanese Government denied that the abuses had taken place, in November it announced that a committee chaired by a High Court judge would investigate incidents in Juba. In December the UN General Assembly adopted a resolution expressing deep concern about serious human rights violations in the Sudan.

Video footage of atrocities in Bosnia and eye-witness testimonies formed the basis of a television news release prepared by Amnesty International in October. The film was shown worldwide by all the major international television news organizations.

Near the end of the year, within hours of learning of the forcible deportations of over 400 Palestinians, Amnesty

**An Amnesty International group in Taipei, Taiwan, staging a public exhibition in October on prisoners of conscience around the world.**

International had launched appeals to the Israeli authorities to protest against the deportations and call for the deportees to be allowed to return.

Amnesty International's campaigns depend on its members and supporters – the people from all walks of life who write reminding governments of the depth of feeling that exists around the world about human rights and who mobilize the media and politicians in their own countries to take up human rights issues. Many of Amnesty International's supporters are members of local groups, which meet regularly in over 70 countries around the world. In 48 countries Amnesty International sections coordinate the work of the local groups and organize campaigns, national publicity and fund-raising.

While many Amnesty International activists work on long-term cases which may require sustained efforts over a number of years, participants in the Urgent Action Network respond to the immediate risk of torture, execution or other serious abuse. Over 50,000 people in 75 countries used their telephones, fax machines and telegraph lines to intervene urgently on behalf of hundreds of individuals whose cases were featured in more than 580 "Urgent Action Appeals" issued throughout the year.

There are other groups of people who participate in Amnesty International's work in special ways. Amnesty International often asks for support from doctors, lawyers, police officers, trade unionists and others, many of whom will contact their counterparts in other countries or appeal for members of their own profession who have become victims of human rights violations.

Amnesty International local groups do their best to brief themselves on the countries on which they work. A group

# A tribute in memory of Anette Fischer

Anette Fischer, Chairperson of Amnesty International's governing International Executive Committee (IEC) was killed in a car crash on 11 July 1992 in Italy. She was on her way home from a holiday with her husband, Carl Eli Fischer, who also died in the accident.

Anette Fischer was elected Chairperson of the IEC in 1991, after serving on the Committee since 1989. A librarian by profession, she had been a human rights activist for more than 20 years. She was a member of the board of the Danish Section of Amnesty International for six years from 1983, serving as its Chairperson from 1986 to 1989.

"The movement has lost a dedicated campaigner against human rights violations," said Ross Daniels, Vice-Chairperson of the IEC. "We shall all miss her courage and her commitment to human rights."

in Costa Rica, working on behalf of a Shi'a Muslim imprisoned in Saudi Arabia apparently because of his views, contacted a university professor of Arabic to translate some of their letters into Arabic. Now the group dedicates some time in each meeting to learning about the culture and history of Saudi Arabia. More than half the local groups participate in special Regional Action Networks, working on cases from a particular group of countries. A group in Mexico which participates in the Southern African Network writes: "On becoming part of the network we started to study the geography, history and culture of each of the countries in it. We submerged ourselves in encyclopedias and dived into every bookshop we passed. Each member was put in charge of keeping up-to-date files on one or two countries, so that when a call for action arrives from the International Secretariat we can design a strategy for work that corresponds to the characteristics of the country."

The International Secretariat in London gathers and analyses the information on which Amnesty International's activities are based. Its main task is to ensure that Amnesty International members and supporters in over 150 countries around the world receive accurate and timely information for effective human rights action. Research teams covering all regions investigate reports of human rights violations, cross-checking and corroborating information from a wide variety of sources and contacts. The International Secretariat also communicates with government authorities and opposition groups in countries where abuses have taken place. It submits information to the United Nations and other intergovernmental organizations. Amnesty International representatives are sent to various countries to discuss concerns with governments and collect information.

The International Secretariat produces a monthly summary of human rights news and cases of concern in the *Amnesty International Newsletter*. Many Amnesty International supporters write letters to the governments responsible about cases featured in the newsletter. For example, the case of a Tibetan Buddhist appeared in the June issue, and a supporter from Albania wrote the following to the government of the People's Republic of China: "I am an Albanian engineer deeply concerned about the case of Dorje Wangdu. As I understand it, he is detained in the Rawa 're-education through labour' camp for peacefully expressing support for Tibet's leader in exile, the Dalai Lama. He is punished for reasons of belief, and this violates Article 18 of the Universal Declaration of Human Rights. Being an electrical engineer myself, I urge you to release the electrician from Lhasa."

Albania was just one of the countries where new Amnesty International groups developed during 1992. The network of members and supporters has continued to spread in all parts of the globe, where people have joined

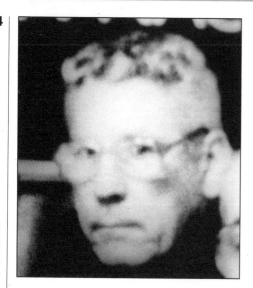

Prisoner of conscience Esteban González González was freed in April 1992 from prison in Cuba, five years before his sentence expired. He was convicted in 1990 of "rebellion" and his case was highlighted by Amnesty International during the organization's 30th anniversary campaign in 1991.

in the fight for universal human rights. There are now Amnesty International members in 24 out of the 25 countries of Eastern and Central Europe and the former Soviet Union: the sole exception is Tadzhikistan. Groups were also formed in countries as far apart as Mongolia, South Africa and Bolivia. Groups in Jordan were granted legal registration by the Jordanian Government during a visit by Amnesty International representatives in September. A representative also attended, with the Queen of Jordan, the opening session of a meeting organized by Amnesty International members in Jordan on the rights of the child. At the same time, a police helicopter showered the surrounding area with copies of the Convention on the Rights of the Child.

Amnesty International members themselves decide the policies and overall strategies of the organization, through democratic internal structures. During 1992, special meetings were held where members from different countries discussed key issues and directions for the future.

The world is changing very rapidly, and Amnesty International has to respond to those changes. A group from South Korea writes: "Looking back on the tumultuous 1970s and 1980s, when hundreds of riot police surrounded our regular meeting place to 'protect' us, when our human rights campaign was labelled as 'impure' and when Amnesty International groups had to be closed when members were arrested, now we feel we need to adapt ourselves to the new environment, globally as well as domestically. One thing is clear: the very existence of an Amnesty International group in this society has to some extent been a symbol of the value of human rights and the importance of international cooperation."

# The death penalty: a gross human rights violation

Amnesty International is unconditionally opposed to the death penalty and works for its worldwide abolition. Through its constant campaigning against this violation of fundamental human rights, the organization seeks to save the lives of those facing the ultimate form of cruel, inhuman and degrading punishment. It also works strenuously to educate both politicians and the general public about the arbitrary and irrevocable nature of the death penalty – emphasizing how it is often used as a tool for political repression or disproportionately imposed on the poor and powerless. In its campaigns and publications, Amnesty International exposes the bankruptcy of the argument that application of the death penalty has any real deterrent effect on rates of crime or political violence in a society. The organization monitors death sentences and executions around the world and appeals for clemency whenever it learns of an imminent execution.

© Pascal G/Agence Vie

A mass execution in Chengdu city, Sichuan province, July 1989. Amnesty International recorded more than 1,000 executions in China in 1992, although the true figure was believed to be far higher.

AMNESTY INTERNATIONAL REPORT 1993

Countries undergoing substantial political change often provide critical openings for the abolition of the death penalty. Two such openings arose in 1992. In Paraguay, a new Constitution introduced in June abolished the death penalty for all peacetime offences, although the penalty was retained for use in time of war. In Angola, the National Assembly approved a constitutional amendment in August making the country completely abolitionist; however, the amendment apparently required the approval of a new National Assembly elected in September. Elsewhere, Switzerland joined the list of completely abolitionist countries in March, when the Swiss Council of States abolished the death penalty for offences committed in time of war.

These positive developments, reinforcing a worldwide trend towards abolition, must unfortunately be placed alongside less encouraging events witnessed in 1992. Executions resumed in Pakistan, and by the end of the year 19 people had been hanged there. Public executions were staged in Afghanistan, Albania and Saudi Arabia. In the United States of America, 31 people were executed – the highest number of death sentences carried out in a single year since the reintroduction of the death penalty in 1976.

Amnesty International responded to all these developments, including the announcement that executions were to resume shortly in Belize and in Trinidad and Tobago after seven and 13 years respectively. The organization also expressed concern about the strong support by the government in the Philippines for legislation aiming at the reintroduction of the death penalty: the country's 1987 Constitution had abolished the death penalty for all offences. Similarly, Amnesty International expressed concern at statements made by President Alberto Fujimori of Peru, who signalled his intention to extend the scope of the death penalty to strengthen the government's campaign against armed opposition groups. Such a move would violate Article 4.2 of the American Convention on Human Rights, which Peru has ratified: the Article states in part that the death penalty "... shall not be extended to crimes to which it does not presently apply".

During 1992 Luxembourg and the Federal Republic of Germany ratified the Second Optional Protocol to the International Covenant on Civil and Political Rights (ICCPR), and the Czech and Slovak Federal Republic and Hungary ratified the Sixth Protocol to the European Convention on Human Rights. In March the European Parliament passed a resolution calling on all member states of the European Community to abolish the death penalty if they had not already done so, and to ratify the Sixth Protocol to the European Convention on Human Rights and the Second Optional Protocol to the ICCPR – both of which provide for the abolition of the death penalty for all peacetime offences. The resolution stated that "no state, and in particular no democratic state, may dispose of the lives of

*"My dear ones, I don't know how to express my gratitude to you ... Of course, I do not justify my son's actions, and he is gravely guilty with regard to his victims. However, my son has grown extremely weak after three years in solitary confinement in a death row cell ... I send a photo which comes from Alexander ... Once more I thank you for your campaign to save the life of my sinful son ..."*

**The mother of Alexander Grigorievich Dryndin of Saratov in the Russian Federation, who wrote to Amnesty International after her son's death sentence was commuted to 15 years' imprisonment by presidential decree in August 1992.**

its citizens or other persons on its territory by having its law impose the death penalty".

In August the Working Group on Detention of the 44th United Nations Sub-Commission on Prevention of Discrimination and Protection of Minorities decided to publish periodically a list of abolitionist and retentionist countries. The list will be broken down into four categories: countries which have abolished the death penalty under all circumstances; countries which have abolished the death penalty for all peacetime offences; countries which are abolitionist in practice, having not used the death penalty for an extended period; and countries which retain the death penalty. This last category will also indicate which countries carry out death sentences against juvenile offenders, as well as which countries are referred to in the report of the Special Rapporteur on Summary or Arbitrary Executions.

By the end of the year, 44 per cent of countries in the world had abolished the death penalty in law or practice. Forty-seven countries had abolished the death penalty for all offences and 16 for all but exceptional offences, such as wartime crimes. A further 20 countries and territories, while retaining the penalty in law, had not carried out any executions for at least 10 years.

During 1992, 1,708 prisoners are known to have been executed in 35 countries and 2,697 people were sentenced to death in 62 countries. These figures include only cases known to Amnesty International: the true number is certainly higher. As in previous years, a very few countries accounted for the majority of executions recorded.

# Protecting refugees

The number of refugees around the world reached crisis proportions in 1992. Millions of people were forced to abandon their homes, their land and often their families and friends. Some had witnessed the most appalling human rights atrocities and feared they would be next on the list. Others belonged to religious, ethnic or other groups that had been singled out for persecution. Many were individually targeted by their government because of their political activities or opposition to the government. Yet others had escaped from civil war and hunger.

In Europe, the horrendous human rights abuses being committed in the former Yugoslavia, particularly in Bosnia-Herzegovina, led to hundreds of thousands of people seeking protection in neighbouring countries and elsewhere in Europe.

In Asia, over a quarter of a million Burmese Muslim

© Popperfoto

**Port-au-Prince, Haiti: this group of 272 asylum-seekers were intercepted in May by the US Coast Guard and returned directly to Haiti without examination of their asylum claims. An Amnesty International delegation to Haiti in March found extensive evidence that the security forces were committing grave human rights violations against civilians, including torture and extrajudicial executions. Yet the US authorities turned away tens of thousands of Haitians who had fled their country in the hope of finding sanctuary.**

refugees had fled to Bangladesh by the end of 1992, escaping a campaign of repression which had started in early 1991. Thousands of Vietnamese asylum-seekers remained detained in Hong Kong.

In Africa, the widespread human rights abuses taking place in the continuing civil war in Somalia led to the flight of over 300,000 refugees into Kenya, and thousands more fled by boat to Yemen. Other civil wars and human rights crises on the continent had caused millions of people to flee their homes in Liberia, Mozambique, Sierra Leone, Sudan and elsewhere.

In the Americas, the September 1991 coup in Haiti and the subsequent and continuing widespread repression against perceived supporters of the overthrown government led tens of thousands of Haitians to board fragile boats in search of asylum in the United States of America (USA) or Caribbean countries.

In the Middle East, thousands of refugees who feared to return to their homes in Iraq following the uprisings of March 1991 and the subsequent repression remained in camps in Saudi Arabia facing an uncertain future. The failure to implement the 1991 UN-sponsored peace settlement in the Western Sahara has meant that tens of thousands of Sahrawis still remain, after 17 years, in refugee camps in Algeria.

Many refugees consider themselves fortunate, for at least they are still alive. Yet after their escape, they often find themselves suffering not only the pain of dislocation and exile, but also humiliation, degradation, and the risk of being returned to the dangers they have fled.

## The international system
The international system established to protect refugees and asylum-seekers depends on governments being willing to live up to their obligations not to return people forcibly to countries where they risk serious human rights violations. However, this obligation was seriously undermined in May 1992 when the US Government decided to return all Haitian asylum-seekers intercepted at sea directly to Haiti without giving them any opportunity to apply for asylum. The international system was also threatened when, in Europe, member states of the European Community (EC) adopted proposals designed to obstruct asylum-seekers from gaining access to full asylum procedures in the member states. It is feared that these proposals will be followed in other European states and even outside Europe.

As the numbers of refugees increased, the Office of the United Nations High Commissioner for Refugees (UNHCR) started to undertake new tasks. For a number of years the UNHCR had been debating the merits of taking a more preventive approach to refugee crises by tackling their "root causes". The apparent willingness of the UN as a whole to become more involved in political negotiations and actions aimed at resolving long-standing conflicts and humanitarian emergencies has established a framework within which it has become more acceptable for the UNHCR to undertake such preventive activities inside refugees' countries of origin.

The most dramatic example of this was in the territories of the former Yugoslavia, where the UNHCR was requested by the UN Secretary-General in late 1991 to act as the lead UN agency for the delivery of humanitarian relief. As the conflict escalated in 1992 the UNHCR found itself simultaneously charged with activities inside Bosnia-Herzegovina designed to alleviate the causes of flight, and intervening with European governments on behalf of the hundreds of thousands who had fled.

The changing nature of the UNHCR's role was welcomed by Amnesty International, insofar as it could lead to a greater effort by the UN to address the systematic human rights violations which are so often the "root cause" of refugee movements. In a letter sent in August 1992 to more than 20 governments worldwide, Amnesty International argued against the forcible return of Burmese Muslim refugees to Bangladesh unless the UNHCR monitored both the repatriation process itself and the situation of the refugees in Myanmar (Burma) after their return. Amnesty International called on the international community to press the government of Myanmar to accept an effective UNHCR monitoring role, and to help the Bangladeshi Government provide protection to the Burmese Muslim refugees until they could safely return to Myanmar.

However, Amnesty International was concerned that in some instances UNHCR involvement inside refugees' countries of origin might preclude opportunities for individuals at risk to flee abroad and could be used by potential asylum countries as a reason to refuse protection to those who ask for it. In a statement issued at the time of the International Meeting on Humanitarian Aid for Victims of the Conflict in the Former Yugoslavia, convened by the UNHCR in Geneva in July 1992, Amnesty International argued that the right of each individual to seek asylum abroad must not be undermined. The organization also called on all states to recognize that people fleeing the territories of the former Yugoslavia were in need of protection against forcible return, and condemned narrow national efforts by some European governments to restrict access to their territory through such measures as the imposition of visa requirements.

Amnesty International also raised refugee protection issues in intergovernmental forums which had not traditionally focused on such issues. At the fourth Follow-Up Meeting of the Conference on Security and Co-operation in Europe (CSCE – "Helsinki II"), Amnesty International urged CSCE member states to reaffirm their existing obligations not to return people to countries where they risk serious

Some of more than a quarter of a million Muslims who fled Myanmar (Burma) in 1991 and 1992 for the refugee camps in Bangladesh, one of the poorest countries in the world. As the richer nations increasingly closed their doors to refugees, so more and more of the responsibility fell on those countries which could least afford to help the millions of people seeking sanctuary from terror and persecution.

human rights violations. It also called on participating states which had not yet done so to accede to the 1951 Convention and 1967 Protocol relating to the Status of Refugees. For the first time, the final document at Helsinki II brought refugee issues into the so-called "human dimension" of the CSCE, and the participating states expressly reaffirmed the importance of international standards and instruments related to the protection of refugees.

## Amnesty International's concerns

Amnesty International's policy on refugees arises directly from its mandate, which focuses on the release of prisoners of conscience, fair trials for political prisoners, and an end to torture, "disappearance" and all forms of execution. It opposes any person being returned against their will to a country where they risk such violations, and seeks to ensure that states provide refugees with effective and durable protection against return to a country where they would be at risk. It also opposes asylum-seekers being sent to any other country unless the government sending them there has ensured that in that country they will be granted effective and durable protection, which should normally include legal protection against return to any country where they risk serious human rights violations. This aspect of Amnesty International's work is based on the

© Ben Bohane

principle of *non-refoulement*, which is recognized as a norm of international law binding on all states, according to which states are obliged not to send people to any country where they would be at risk of serious human rights violations.

To ensure that refugees are identified and given the protection which governments are obliged to provide, asylum-seekers must have access to asylum procedures which are fair and impartial.

While Amnesty International recognizes that governments are entitled to control immigration and entry to their territory, it nevertheless calls on them to ensure that asylum-seekers have effective access to their asylum procedures and that any restrictions on entry, such as visa requirements or other restrictive measures, do not obstruct that access. For example, Amnesty International strongly condemned the US Government's policy of intercepting Haitians at sea and returning them to Haiti without any attempt being made to identify those who would be at risk of human rights violations after return. This policy was a flagrant breach of international law.

Amnesty International has set out certain essential principles and safeguards which must be included in asylum procedures to ensure they are fair and impartial. These are based on international standards such as the International Covenant on Civil and Political Rights and the Conclusions adopted by the more than 40 government members of the Executive Committee of the Programme of the UNHCR. Such principles include that asylum claims should be thoroughly examined by an independent and specialized authority; that decision-makers should have expertise in international law relating to human rights and refugees, and should take full account of human rights information drawn from the widest possible range of independent sources; that asylum-seekers should be able to appear in person before decision-makers, and be entitled to legal counsel at all stages in the procedure; and that applicants must be given written reasons for any refusal of their claim and have the right to appeal before being expelled. These principles should form the basis of all states' asylum procedures.

## Amnesty International's work

In addition to monitoring developments at an international level, Amnesty International also monitors closely the actions of individual governments with regard to refugees and asylum-seekers. A great deal of this work is done by Amnesty International's sections based in the countries where people seek protection. They provide information about human rights violations in asylum-seekers' countries of origin to governments, to those who make decisions on asylum claims, and to lawyers and others working on behalf of asylum-seekers. Amnesty International also monitors governments' asylum policies and practices to ensure that they are adequate to identify and protect those at risk. In some cases, Amnesty International intervenes directly with the authorities in an effort to prevent a particular asylum-seeker being forcibly returned.

In 1992 Amnesty International's Austrian Section continued to raise concerns with the Austrian Government about inadequate safeguards for ensuring that asylum-seekers, particularly those who are detained, have the opportunity to lodge an asylum claim. Sections, for example in Australia, Belgium, Canada, France, Greece, the Netherlands, New Zealand and the United Kingdom, raised concerns with their governments on proposed amendments to national legislation which would affect the protection of asylum-seekers and refugees. The Japanese Section participated in an Amnesty International research visit to Japan to examine policies and practices in that country regarding refugees and asylum-seekers.

Amnesty International's Irish Section launched a national campaign calling on the Irish Government to adopt legislation which would formally establish the rights of refugees and asylum-seekers. Currently, asylum claims are dealt with entirely on the basis of administrative procedures, which has led to inadequate legal protection for those seeking asylum – particularly for those who apply immediately on their arrival in Ireland. The US Section undertook a number of public initiatives to highlight the organization's concerns about the US Government's policy of forcibly returning all Haitian asylum-seekers to Haiti.

European governments, particularly those of the EC, continued to move towards closer cooperation on matters affecting asylum-seekers (see *Amnesty International Report 1992*). Amnesty International sections in Europe lobbied their governments about the organization's concerns on these matters, focusing particularly on regional agreements affecting asylum-seekers which were being drafted and adopted by EC governments. Amnesty International believed that these agreements did not include satisfactory safeguards for the protection of asylum-seekers and refugees and that, in many cases, they would make it more difficult for asylum-seekers to seek and obtain protection in EC countries. These concerns were intensified at the end of 1992 when EC governments adopted a number of resolutions at the EC Summit in Edinburgh for dealing with certain types of asylum claims in "accelerated" procedures or, in some cases, for excluding some claims and sending people back to supposedly "safe" third countries. Amnesty International's sections in EC member states jointly issued a report in November 1992 which set out the organization's concerns. They urged EC member states to adopt an international agreement on the minimum standards for asylum procedures and proposed essential principles and safeguards which should be included in any such agreement.

# Working with international organizations

### The United Nations (UN)

At the beginning of 1992 the UN appeared poised to fulfil the role originally envisaged for it. It convened its first ever summit meeting of Heads of State or Government of the Security Council; East-West antagonism seemed to be over as the Russian Federation smoothly took over the former USSR's permanent seat on the Security Council; and serious plans were being made for a restructured and more relevant UN.

However, the dissipation of superpower control combined with an upsurge in nationalism, ethnic hatred and violent conflict confronted it with an ever-growing range of crises. By the end of the year the UN was looking severely under-resourced and overwhelmed. In the words of the Secretary-General, the UN could not "afford to become a victim of its own popularity, suffering from a crisis of expectations".

In March the UN launched two of its largest-ever operations. The United Nations Transitional Authority in Cambodia (UNTAC) was charged with a complex set of civilian and military tasks, with the ultimate goal of organizing free and fair elections in 1993. The civilian operation, which included extensive supervision and control of the civil administration, incorporated a specific role in human rights protection and education. In the territory of the former Yugoslavia, the UN's peace-keeping operation known as UNPROFOR rapidly evolved from supervision of UN Protected Areas in Serb-dominated Croatian territories to a much larger operation, including securing humanitarian relief and monitoring the "no-fly" zone in Bosnia-Herzegovina.

Both operations raised the UN's visibility and fuelled expectations that it could and should intervene in almost every conflict. Despite attempts in some situations to share the burden of peace-keeping with regional organizations, these organizations have not so far generally proved politically or financially capable of effectively tackling emerging conflicts. Since the UN's perceived strengths are its credibility, its humanitarian approach and its moral authority, the crisis of expectations is a real one.

The Security Council became a new focus for human rights in 1992, with some of its members showing greater readiness to bring human rights considerations into its role in maintaining peace and security. The Declaration of the Security Council's first summit, convened in January, recognized that "non-military sources of instability in the economic, social and humanitarian fields have become threats to peace and security". It also welcomed the fact that human rights verification was among the elements which had "in the settlement of some regional conflicts, at the request or with the agreement of the parties concerned, been integral parts of the Security Council's effort to maintain international peace and security".

Throughout the year the Security Council addressed a number of situations which raised human rights concerns. For example, in Resolution 726 the Council condemned Israel's decision to resume deportations of Palestinian civilians and, in Resolution 799, demanded that Israel ensure their immediate return; in Resolution 772 the Council authorized the Secretary-General to deploy UN observers in South Africa; in Resolution 780 the Council requested the Secretary-General to establish an impartial Commission of Experts to provide conclusions on the evidence of war crimes committed in the territory of the former Yugoslavia; and in Resolution 798 it condemned the systematic detention and rape of Muslim women in Bosnia-Herzegovina and demanded that all detention camps be closed. Evidence of human rights violations gathered by the UN Special Rapporteur on Iraq was put before the Security Council in August and November. Subsequently the United States of America (USA), the United Kingdom and France declared a mandatory "no-fly" zone over the southern marshes of Iraq and the Security Council refused to lift the sanctions on that country.

In his report in September 1992 on the work of the UN, the Secretary-General pinpointed the inability of the UN "to act effectively to bring to an end massive human rights violations". He proposed that the UN explore ways of empowering the Secretary-General and expert human rights bodies to bring such violations to the attention of the Security Council with recommendations for action. The increased use by the Secretary-General of fact-finding missions such as those sent to Georgia, Latvia, Moldova, Tadzhikistan, Uzbekistan and to Nagorno-Karabakh was a further step towards an early-warning procedure, which might enable the UN to act more expeditiously to defuse and contain conflict. However, at the end of the year the results of these visits and the intended follow-up still remained unclear.

Nevertheless, in some cases the UN instigated innovative human rights operations, often with unprecedented powers, when deploying peace-keepers. The UN's operation in El Salvador known as ONUSAL, established in 1991 with the task of monitoring a specific agreement on human rights between the parties, was the forerunner of these. In 1992 its mandate was expanded to include a Military Division and a Police Division in accordance with the agreements signed in Mexico City at the beginning of the year. In

Cambodia the UN operation, UNTAC, included a specific human rights component with the possibility of taking corrective action in the case of violations. UNTAC's civilian control and supervision of the administrative structures, such as the police, also had considerable potential to assist in the protection of human rights. However, the human rights components of peace-keeping operations tended to be subordinate to the political and military objectives which sometimes compromised their effectiveness. In other operations, such as that in Angola, human rights issues were not at all adequately addressed. Furthermore, there remained a conspicuous lack of involvement of the UN's human rights bodies in the planning and implementation of the human rights components of these operations. Nor did the operations generally include any plans for the longer-term institutionalization of human rights protection or for continued UN monitoring after the departure of the peace-keepers.

In respect of a number of such operations which had a specific human rights component or objective, Amnesty International provided information about its concerns in the country and made recommendations about ways in which the human rights elements might address these. These included the operations in Angola, Cambodia, El Salvador, Western Sahara and the former Yugoslavia as well as those in the planning stages in respect of Liberia, Mozambique and Somalia. Amnesty International also participated in two human rights seminars organized by the UN operations in Angola in August and in Cambodia in November.

At the end of 1992 the UN faced difficult questions about its future role with regard to peace and security. Its operation in Cambodia was in jeopardy, largely owing to the non-cooperation of the *Partie* of Democratic Kampuchea ("Khmer Rouge"). The El Salvador operation was behind schedule with the government refusing to demobilize according to the timetable and senior military officers disputing the conclusions of the *ad hoc* commission which evaluated the past performances of members of the armed forces and recommended the removal of a number of officers on grounds of human rights violations.

In the former Yugoslavia gross human rights violations continued unchecked, while in Somalia the Security Council authorized, by Resolution 794, a military coalition of UN member states to intervene to establish a secure environment for providing humanitarian relief.

On the eve of 1992, the Secretary-General's suggestions outlined in his June report to the Security Council, *An Agenda for Peace*, were no longer academic and there was a real debate as to whether UN forces could be authorized to carry out "peace enforcement". Similarly, although a UN standing army still seemed rather remote, the Secretary-General's proposal that the member states should supply stand-by rapid response forces, whose deployment could be authorized by the Security Council under the Secretary-General's command, seemed to be gaining some acceptance. Even though no decision was taken on whether to arm UN forces heavily and authorize them to use greater force, by the end of 1992 the UN had undergone a radical change of image. In conflict situations such as Bosnia-Herzegovina and Cambodia, UN personnel were seen to be under fire yet powerless to go beyond a neutral peace-keeping role. This left some member states impatient to use force outside the multilateral framework of the relevant UN peace-keeping operations. The possibility of peace-keeping being complemented by peace enforcement leaves unanswered the crucial question of how the human rights of men, women and children can actually be protected while avoiding the situation where human rights are either marginalized or exploited.

### The World Conference on Human Rights

Preparations for the 1993 UN World Conference on Human Rights, to be held in Vienna, gathered momentum but continued to be beset by tensions and deep divisions. The second and third sessions of the Preparatory Committee did not progress beyond procedural issues and could not even agree on the agenda for the Conference, which was only finally adopted in December by the General Assembly. Two regional preparatory meetings were postponed and only the Regional Meeting for Africa took place during the year. The Preparatory Committee did finally resolve the contentious issue of the role of non-governmental organizations (NGOs) in the World Conference. In addition to the participation of NGOs in consultative status with the Economic and Social Council (ECOSOC), it was agreed, although subject to certain conditions, that a potentially wide range of other national and regional NGOs could attend the regional meetings and thereby the Conference itself.

The objectives of the World Conference include a review of the UN's mechanisms and procedures in the field of human rights and the formulation of concrete recommendations to improve their effectiveness. Amnesty International, which attended both sessions of the Preparatory Committee and the Regional Meeting for Africa, submitted a paper to the preparatory process in December – *Facing up to the Failures: Proposals for Improving the Protection of Human Rights by the United Nations*. It called for the establishment of a Special Commissioner for Human Rights to function as a new high-level authority in the UN, with a mandate covering the full spectrum of human rights. The Special Commissioner should be able to take speedy and more effective action in urgent situations of grave violations, coordinate the UN's human rights activities, integrate human rights more fully into other areas of the UN's work, and generally give greater weight and political authority to the human rights program. Amnesty International also called for measures to strengthen existing human rights mechanisms, particularly the theme mechanisms of the Commission on Human Rights and the bodies set up to monitor the implementation of international human rights treaties.

### UN action on the human rights situation in individual countries

The Commission on Human Rights ("the Commission"), enlarged to 53 members in 1992, made historic progress during the year. It held its first ever special sessions in response to the emergency situation in the former Yugoslavia. ECOSOC had agreed in 1990 that the Commission could meet exceptionally outside its regular annual six-week meeting if a majority of its members agreed. Although a request in June for a special session on the Israeli-Occupied Territories failed to secure the required majority, two special sessions on the former Yugoslavia were held in August and November.

At the first session, in a resolution condemning human rights violations in the former Yugoslavia in the strongest terms, the Commission appointed a Special Rapporteur to investigate the human rights situation in the territory. In a departure from the usual practice, it also urged the Special Rapporteur to work closely with other appropriate human rights mechanisms of the Commission. The Special Rapporteur carried out two visits to the former Yugoslavia in 1992, accompanied on one or both by the Special Rapporteur on summary or arbitrary executions (who subsequently made a third visit), the representative of the Secretary-General on internally displaced persons, the Chairman of the Working Group on arbitrary detention, and the Special Rapporteur on torture. The Special Rapporteur on the former Yugoslavia forwarded his reports to the Commission on an ongoing basis. He also submitted an interim report to the General Assembly and appeared before the Security Council, thereby informing the wider discussions on the investigation of war crimes, the development of safe zones, as well as the deployment of peacekeeping troops and human rights monitors in Bosnia-Herzegovina, Croatia, Macedonia and Kosovo.

In an equally condemnatory resolution adopted at its second special session, the Commission called for adequate staff and resources for the Commission of Experts examining war crimes and consideration of the extent to which the acts committed in Bosnia-Herzegovina and Croatia constitute genocide. It also endorsed the concepts of safe areas and the importance of humanitarian relief corridors. It called on the Special Rapporteur to continue his investigations, assisted by the other human rights mechanisms. It urged that his reports continue to be made available to the Security Council and that his request for

UN staff to be based in the territory of the former Yugoslavia be met, although by the end of the year only one monitor was based in the territory.

Amnesty International made oral statements at both special sessions and addressed an open letter to all governments participating in the International Conference on the former Yugoslavia and other intergovernmental organizations involved in the situation in the territory. Amnesty International called for a substantial on-site human rights monitoring presence, including in territories such as Kosovo, Sandžak and the Vojvodina where it was feared the conflict would intensify. It called for much closer cooperation among the various intergovernmental initiatives relevant to human rights protection, for the involvement of all appropriate human rights mechanisms and for states to ensure that refugees from the conflict were given adequate protection and were not obstructed in seeking asylum. It stressed the need for the Special Rapporteur to play a central coordinating role by documenting the human rights situation and making recommendations about preventive measures.

At its regular session in February, the Commission took a number of important steps in respect of other serious human rights situations. Myanmar (Burma) was finally moved from the confidential 1503 procedure to the public agenda and a Special Rapporteur was appointed to report to both the General Assembly and the next session of the Commission, with a specific mandate to establish direct contacts with the government and the people of Myanmar. It was regrettable that the Special Rapporteur was able to visit the country only after his report was presented to the General Assembly, but the Assembly's firm resolution sent a clear message to the government of its grave concern about the human rights situation there, calling for the release of political prisoners and the restoration of democracy and respect for the results of the 1990 election. Amnesty International continued to raise its concerns about Myanmar, including in an oral statement to the Sub-Commission.

The Commission took action on two serious situations not formally on its agenda, although both were the subject of a report by one of the theme mechanisms following an on-site visit. This action, on East Timor and Sri Lanka, fell short of a resolution and instead consisted of a statement by the Commission's Chairman on each situation, with the result that both will be considered by the Commission at its 1993 session.

On East Timor, the Chairman's statement was regrettably weak in its response to the November 1991 Santa Cruz massacre in Dili, merely welcoming the government's steps to investigate the killings and the appointment of the personal envoy of the Secretary-General who visited East Timor while the Commission was in session. It did, however, request the Secretary-General to report back to the next session of the Commission on the human rights situation in East Timor and urged the government to grant access to the country to humanitarian and human rights organizations. The subsequent August session of the Sub-Commission on Prevention of Discrimination and Protection of Minorities ("the Sub-Commission") adopted a stronger resolution on East Timor, deploring the massacre and inviting the Secretary-General to release the full report of the visit by his Special Envoy. In a statement to the General Assembly's Special Committee on Decolonization in July, Amnesty International detailed its continuing concerns in the country, particularly regarding the failure of the Indonesian authorities to investigate properly the Santa Cruz massacre or to bring those responsible to justice.

In respect of Sri Lanka, the Working Group on Enforced or Involuntary Disappearances submitted a strong report on its visit to the country. A statement by the Chairman of the Commission, which expressed grave concern about the situation, took note of the government's agreement to a second visit by the Working Group, which subsequently took place in October. Amnesty International had submitted hundreds of cases in Sri Lanka to the Working Group during the year.

The Expert on Haiti, who had been appointed in 1991 seven months before the Haitian Government was overthrown in a coup, presented a report detailing the continuing grave human rights situation in the country. The Commission took up the Expert's recommendation to take stronger measures and appointed a Special Rapporteur to report to its next session and to the General Assembly. The later session of the Sub-Commission also adopted a strong resolution on Haiti. The General Assembly in its resolution requested the Secretary-General to take measures to assist the Organization of American States, which has deployed human rights monitors in the country, to find a solution to the crisis in Haiti.

Action on Iran was much stronger in 1992, reversing the trend in recent years to tone down concern about continuing violations. A tougher resolution by the Commission also renewed the mandate of its Special Representative on Iran for a further year and reinstated the Representative's interim report to the General Assembly. The Sub-Commission also adopted a much stronger resolution on Iran at its session and the General Assembly's condemnatory resolution noted in particular its concern about the use of death penalty and urged the government to resume co-operation with the Special Representative. Amnesty International raised its serious concerns in Iran in an oral and a written statement to the Commission.

The first report of the Special Rapporteur on Iraq to the Commission strongly condemned a wide range of grave human rights violations. Calling it an exceptional situation that demanded an exceptional response, the Special Rapporteur recommended that a team of on-site human rights monitors be established in the country. Although it adopted a tough resolution and renewed the Rapporteur's mandate, the Commission took no action on this recommendation beyond requesting that it be developed in his interim report to the General Assembly. The General Assembly welcomed this proposal but sent it back to the 1993 Commission to be followed up. Although the Memorandum of Understanding between the Iraqi Government and the UN relating to the provision of humanitarian assistance was renewed eventually, it did not provide for a UN presence in the south and the government remained resolutely opposed to what it saw as further intrusion in its territory. Amnesty International continued to vigorously support on-site monitoring in Iraq and reiterated its grave human rights concerns in oral and written statements to the Commission and Sub-Commission.

In light of the wide-ranging human rights work being carried out by ONUSAL, the Commission finally terminated the mandate of one of its longest-standing mechanisms – the Special Representative on El Salvador. However, he was replaced by an independent expert to act as a much-needed link between the Commission and ONUSAL. The expert's task is to consider the human rights situation and the effects of the Peace Agreements and to investigate implementation of recommendations by the former Special Representative, by ONUSAL and by the committees established during the negotiating process. The expert was requested to report to the General Assembly as well as to the Commission, which decided to move El Salvador to the advisory services program in 1993 if the human rights situation improved substantially.

UN action on Guatemala was disappointing, although it continued to be an observer to the peace talks between the government and the *Unidad Revolucionaria Nacional Guatemalteca* (URNG), Guatemalan National Revolutionary Unity. Yet again, the Commission took no decisive step to move Guatemala from the advisory services program and place it under more effective scrutiny, although it renewed the mandate of the Expert, requesting him to assess the extent to which Guatemala had complied with the recommendations made to it. The Sub-Commission's 1992 resolution on Guatemala expressed deep concern over the persistence of human rights violations in the country. Amnesty International, which again strongly urged that Guatemala be moved from the advisory services program, highlighted its concerns in a written statement to the Commission and an oral statement to the Sub-Commission.

Expectations that the Commission might finally adopt a resolution on Tibet, following the 1991 Sub-Commission resolution requesting the Secretary-General to transmit to the Commission information on the situation there, were dashed. The Commission decided to take no action on a draft resolution on Tibet following disagreements as to whether the resolution should refer only to Tibet or also to the People's Republic of China. The later session of the Sub-Commission also took no further action on China or Tibet. Amnesty International had submitted information for the Secretary-General's report and referred to its concerns in China and Tibet in oral statements to the Commission and Sub-Commission.

While the UN sought to support the process of political negotiations in South Africa, resolutions of the General Assembly, Commission and Sub-Commission continued to express human rights concerns, including in relation to the role of the security forces in political violence. In August the Security Council called for the deployment of some 50 UN observers in the country to work in coordination with the structures of the National Peace Accord. Amnesty International raised its concerns in an oral statement to the Commission and at sessions of the Special Committee Against Apartheid and the *Ad Hoc* Working Group of Experts on southern Africa.

In addition to the Security Council's condemnation of the deportation of Palestinians, a range of human rights violations in the Israeli-Occupied Territories was highlighted in various resolutions of the General Assembly, Commission and Sub-Commission. Amnesty International drew attention to its continuing concerns in an oral statement to the Commission.

Although the Commission terminated the mandates of its Special Rapporteurs on Occupied Kuwait and Romania, it maintained its consideration of a number of other countries on its agenda. The mandate of the Special Rapporteur on Afghanistan was renewed. The Commission designated the Special Representative of the Secretary-General on Cuba as a Special Rapporteur of the Commission, who was also to submit an interim report to the General Assembly. In a stronger resolution on Equatorial Guinea, the mandate of the Expert was renewed and the Commission decided to take the country out of advisory services in 1993 unless there was significant improvement in the human rights situation. The Secretary-General was again requested to report on Albania in 1993. In its main oral statement to the Commission, Amnesty International highlighted the challenge of protecting human rights during internal conflicts. Amnesty International recognized the grave abuses frequently committed by armed opposition groups and explained its policy of working to oppose specific abuses which are contrary to minimum standards laid down by humanitarian law. The statement emphasized that abuses by opposition groups should never be used as a means to divert attention from, still less to justify, human rights violations by governments.

Under the confidential 1503 procedure, it was indicated

in March that Bahrain, Chad, Myanmar, Somalia, Sudan, Syria and Zaire had been considered by the Commission and all except Syria and Myanmar (the latter transferred to the public agenda) were kept pending for further examination at the next session. Subsequently in April, in the annual cycle of this procedure, Amnesty International submitted communications for consideration on Bahrain, Chad, China, Morocco, Sudan, Syria, Tunisia, Turkey and Uganda.

In an unusual move, the General Assembly adopted a resolution in December on Sudan. Its resolutions on the human rights situation in individual countries are generally confined to those on which reports are submitted to it by the Commission's country rapporteurs. The Assembly expressed deep concern at the serious human rights situation in Sudan and invited the Commission to give this urgent attention.

Resolutions on two situations not previously on the UN agenda – Peru and the island of Bougainville in Papua New Guinea – were adopted by the Sub-Commission in August, but neither urged follow-up action by the Commission. The resolution on Peru was extremely weak, supporting the restoration of democracy without mentioning the human rights violations occurring there.

### Progress on standard-setting

Two important new human rights texts were adopted by the General Assembly in December, having been transmitted by the Commission earlier in 1992. These were the Declaration on the Protection of All Persons from Enforced Disappearance and the Declaration on the Rights of Persons Belonging to National or Ethnic, Religious and Linguistic Minorities. They are the first international instruments on these topics and have been long awaited.

A Working Group of the Commission on Human Rights, which Amnesty International again attended, completed the first reading of the draft Declaration on the Rights and Responsibilities of Individuals, Groups and Organs of Society to Promote and Protect Universally Recognized Human Rights and Fundamental Freedoms, commonly referred to as the draft Declaration on Human Rights Defenders. The Commission also decided to establish an inter-sessional working group to elaborate an Optional Protocol to the Convention against Torture and Other Cruel, Inhuman or Degrading Treatment or Punishment aimed at establishing a system of preventive visits by UN experts to any places of detention in a State Party to the Protocol. In an oral statement to the Commission, Amnesty International emphasized the importance of a universal preventive mechanism as a demonstration of the international community's determination to eradicate torture. The organization also attended the first session of the drafting Working Group in October.

### Other action by the Commission on Human Rights

Other developments at the Commission included a stronger resolution on the work of its theme mechanisms, such as those dealing with "disappearances", summary or arbitrary executions, torture and arbitrary detention, to which Amnesty International continued to submit a large number of individual cases and country information throughout the year. The mandates of these mechanisms were renewed for three years for the first time despite some member governments raising objections, including the financial implications and the possible overlap with treaty monitoring bodies. The resolution called for prompt responses by governments to requests by the thematic mechanisms for information, urged governments to extend invitations for on-site visits and follow-up visits and to inform the thematic mechanisms on the progress made in the implementation of recommendations following a visit. It also called for the necessary resources for the theme mechanisms to carry out their tasks. In another resolution, the Commission called for the creation of a standing team of forensic and other appropriate experts. Regrettably, this only referred to providing such assistance to governments in the forensic documentation of human rights violations.

The newest theme mechanism, the Working Group on arbitrary detention, established in September 1991, submitted its first report to the Commission. This indicated that it had taken significant steps towards defining its mandate broadly and had adopted sound working methods. It had also started investigating a number of cases.

The Commission considered a proposal submitted by Austria to establish an emergency mechanism which could be invoked in any situation of gross human rights violations. Upon written request of any member state to the Secretary-General, and with the agreement of a majority of members of the Commission, a panel of experts would be asked to produce a report and recommendations, which would be submitted to the government concerned for comments. The report would remain confidential until it was considered either in an exceptional meeting of the Commission or, if such a session were not convened, by the next regular session of the Commission or the General Assembly. However, no final agreement was reached on the proposal and it was kept pending for further consideration in 1993.

On the recommendation of the Sub-Commission, the Commission called on all states which had not already done so to establish a procedure such as *habeas corpus* by which anyone deprived of his or her liberty by arrest or detention would be entitled to institute proceedings before a court in order that the court may decide on the legality of the detention. It called on all states to ensure that such procedures are maintained at all times, including during a state of emergency.

The Commission also adopted a resolution on civil defence forces, following the concern raised by the Working Group on Enforced or Involuntary Disappearances that the activities of such forces are on the increase, particularly in areas of conflict, and are reportedly involved in many cases of "disappearance" and other abuses. The resolution asked the UN Secretary-General to collect information on this phenomenon for a report to the next session of the Commission.

The Commission continued its discussion of the situation of internally displaced people on the basis of a report from the UN Secretary-General. It called on the Secretary-General to designate a representative to gather information on human rights issues related to the internally displaced and for the Secretary-General to prepare a comprehensive study for the Commission identifying existing laws and mechanisms for their protection as well as possible additional measures.

### The work of the Sub-Commission

Work on studies at the Sub-Commission was hindered by an overloaded agenda and because the session was somewhat disrupted by the convening of the first special session of the Commission on the former Yugoslavia. The final report on freedom of opinion and expression, including the Special Rapporteurs' conclusions and recommendations, was barely debated and no resolution was adopted on this topic. Two Sub-Commission experts were requested to prepare a study on the impunity of perpetrators of human rights violations, although the experts' recommendation that a Special Rapporteur on this subject be appointed was not taken up. In an oral statement on widespread human rights violations during states of emergency, Amnesty International called for the work of the Special Rapporteur on states of emergency to develop his work further.

Some procedural progress was achieved by the adoption of a set of Guidelines which should help streamline the work of the Sub-Commission. A number of studies, including that on youth and human rights, were concluded at this session. Further progress was made on important studies on the right to a fair trial and the independence and impartiality of the judiciary. The Sub-Commission decided to ask one of its members to prepare a working paper on a draft declaration defining gross and large-scale violations of human rights as an international crime. This is to be discussed at the next session.

The sessional Working Group on Detention, which has been studying the death penalty with special reference to its imposition on people aged under 18, decided to draw up annually a list of abolitionist countries (categorized as abolitionists for all crimes; for crimes committed in normal times; and *de facto*) and retentionist countries, distinguishing between those countries that do and those that do not impose the death penalty on minors.

In an oral statement to the pre-sessional Working Group on Indigenous Populations, Amnesty International drew attention to grave violations suffered by indigenous peoples, highlighting its concerns in various countries of the Americas.

### The Commission on Crime Prevention and Criminal Justice

In April the first session of the new Commission on Crime Prevention and Criminal Justice took place. This Commission replaces the former expert body – the Committee on Crime Prevention and Control – and is part of a reorganization and upgrading of the UN's crime prevention program. However, the new Commission appeared reluctant to tackle the issue of human rights directly and did not identify this as among its priorities in the immediate term. In particular, the Commission was reluctant to address the question of monitoring implementation of important international standards which have been adopted over the years in the field of criminal justice, many of which are aimed at protecting human rights, although a standing agenda item on norms and standards was finally agreed. The Commission did not set up any expert bodies to assist it in this or any other area of its work. Amnesty International, which attended this session, urged the Commission in an oral statement to set up some form of expert body, particularly to examine the implementation of standards.

### Ratification of human rights treaties

Some progress was made on ratification of or accession to international human rights standards during the year (see Appendix VI). Fifteen states became party to the International Covenant on Civil and Political Rights (ICCPR) and 14 to the International Covenant on Economic, Social and Cultural Rights (ICESCR). By 31 December, there were 115 States Parties to the ICCPR and 118 to the ICESCR. Seven States Parties to the ICCPR ratified the first Optional Protocol, bringing the total number of ratifications to 67 and two ratified the Second Optional Protocol, bringing the total number to 12. Seven countries ratified or acceded to the Convention against Torture, bringing the total number of States Parties to this treaty to 71.

Although these figures represented a considerably higher rate of ratification than in previous years, the overall situation remained unsatisfactory. Nine members of the 1992 Commission on Human Rights had not ratified or acceded to any of the standards listed above; indeed, only two of its members were States Parties to all five of these instruments.

In an oral statement to the Sub-Commission, Amnesty International expressed its concern that international human rights standards are still not universally accepted. It urged that states ratify or accede to international human rights instruments without limiting reservations, since these undermine the guarantees contained in the treaties and call into question the willingness of a state to comply fully with the international obligations contained in the treaties. It highlighted in particular its concerns about the extensive reservations by the USA, including to some non-derogable rights, on its ratification of the ICCPR and also drew these concerns to the attention of other States Parties to the ICCPR and to the Human Rights Committee which monitors implementation of this treaty.

### The United Nations Educational, Scientific and Cultural Organization (UNESCO)

Amnesty International continued to submit information during the year, including new cases from China and Peru, to the Committee on Conventions and Recommendations which examines human rights violations against writers, teachers and others within UNESCO's mandate.

### The International Labour Organisation (ILO)

As in past years, Amnesty International attended the ILO's International Labour Conference in Geneva in June as an observer. It followed the proceedings of the Committee on the Application of Conventions and Recommendations, which forms part of the ILO's supervisory mechanism for the implementation of its conventions. Amnesty International raised concerns about human rights violations relevant to the Committee's work in Colombia and Syria, both of which were taken up by the Committee, and in Peru.

### The Organization of American States (OAS)

In September Brazil acceded to the American Convention on Human Rights, bringing the total number of States Parties to 24. In November Uruguay became the 12th state to ratify the Inter-American Convention to Prevent and Punish Torture (see Appendix VII).

Amnesty International continued to submit to the Inter-American Commission on Human Rights (IACHR) information relating to its concerns in member states of the OAS, including Colombia, Guatemala, Haiti and Peru. In May Amnesty International again attended the OAS General Assembly held in Nassau, Bahamas, as a "special guest", together with other NGOs. A Working Group of the Permanent Council of the OAS finished the first reading of a draft Inter-American Convention on Enforced Disappearance of Persons and presented it to the General Assembly for consideration and for approval of an extension of the Working Group's mandate to continue work on the text. The draft text contains several serious weaknesses, including a "due obedience" provision, which would exonerate those who commit "disappearances" while obeying orders, and the omission of any reference to "disappearances" as constituting a "crime against humanity". Furthermore, the text would not provide for the operation of special emergency procedures by the IACHR in cases involving "disappearances". Other necessary measures regarding the investigation of complaints and the protection of complainants are omitted.

Prior to the General Assembly, Amnesty International wrote to the representatives of all member states urging that the draft Convention should not fall below emerging international standards, such as the draft UN Declaration on the Protection of All Persons from Enforced Disappearance. It set out what it considered to be the essential principles which should be incorporated in the text. Amnesty International also urged the OAS to establish an *ad hoc* consultative mechanism whereby international and regional NGOs and organizations of relatives of "disappeared" people could contribute to the drafting process.

The proposal to involve NGOs in the drafting of this Convention was put before the General Assembly by Chile and provoked a general debate on the role of NGOs within the OAS. However, when the General Assembly renewed the Working Group's mandate on the draft convention it authorized it to consult studies and reports prepared by NGOs only when it deems it necessary.

In February the IACHR formally submitted to the Inter-American Court of Human Rights a case against Peru, concerning the killing of at least 31 people by the army in Cayara region, Ayacucho, in May 1988. Amnesty International and Americas Watch had presented the case to the Commission as co-complainants and had requested that it be submitted to the Court. The first hearing by the Court was held in June and dealt with 12 preliminary objections raised by the Peruvian Government. Staff members of Amnesty International were appointed advisers to the Commission and attended the hearing in this capacity. A decision by the Court on the preliminary objections was expected in January 1993.

### The Organization of African Unity (OAU)

Seven member states ratified the African Charter on Human and Peoples' Rights – Côte d'Ivoire, Kenya, Lesotho, Madagascar, Mauritius, Namibia and Seychelles. This left only two of the 51 member states – Ethiopia and Swaziland – who were not yet parties to this treaty (see Appendix VII). With almost universal ratification, the OAU Assembly of Heads of State and Government adopted a resolution at its June to July session calling on States Parties which had not yet done so to submit their initial reports under Article 62 of the African Charter on steps taken to implement that treaty as soon as possible and to reflect the rights guaranteed by the African Charter in their law and practice.

The African Commission on Human and Peoples' Rights – the monitoring body for the African Charter – continued to suffer from significant shortages of funding and professional personnel. Amnesty International participated in both its regular sessions in 1992. At the first session in Tunis, Tunisia, in March, the African Commission considered the periodic reports of Egypt and Tanzania and adopted resolutions on the right to freedom of association and fair trial. It also completed the adoption of an ambitious program of activities including sponsorship of seven seminars in 1992 and 1993. It established a working group to act on communications and other business between sessions. In April three members of the African Commission went as observers to monitor the elections in Mali at the invitation of the government.

At the second session in Banjul, Gambia, in October, the African Commission considered the periodic reports of Gambia, Senegal and Zimbabwe. It requested the intersessional working group to propose improvements in the Rules of Procedure governing communications and a stronger and more comprehensive resolution on the right to fair trial. In a significant departure from past practice, it made its first public statements critical of situations in States Parties. It expressed concern about the death in October of Orton Chirwa, a long-term prisoner of conscience in Malawi, while a communication was pending concerning his and his wife's detention. It also condemned mass expulsions of Nigerian nationals from Gabon.

The Attorney-General of Gambia addressed the session and stated that the situation in Africa meant a fresh look at the African Charter was needed. This was the latest in a series of calls by drafters of the treaty, African legal scholars and others for the Charter's human rights guarantees and implementation procedures to be strengthened. In October and November the African Commission sponsored its first seminars – on implementation of the African Charter in national law and practice, and on the role of the media in promoting human rights in Africa.

Amnesty International submitted three communications under Article 55 of the African Charter concerning human rights violations in Burundi, Malawi and Tunisia, although by the end of the year the African Commission had not reached a decision on the merits of any of the 74 communications submitted during its first five years. Amnesty International urged it to act on these communications promptly and to make public as much information as possible concerning this procedure.

Amnesty International attended the pre-session conferences for NGOs organized by the International Commission of Jurists in cooperation with the African Centre for Democracy and Human Rights Studies. The conferences discussed ways to strengthen the effectiveness of the African Commission and made detailed recommendations to the African Commission.

Amnesty International also continued to monitor the work of the OAU's Co-ordinating Committee on Assistance to Refugees in Africa, of which it is a member.

## The Council of Europe

The Council of Europe faced significant challenges to its traditional role, character and working methods, including the implications of a potential increase in size from 23 members in 1989 to perhaps 40 or more as eastern and central European states seek to join. It also had to reassess its role in the face of a reformed and expanded Conference on Security and Co-operation in Europe (CSCE).

Both the Czech and Slovak Federal Republic and Hungary ratified the European Convention for the Protection of Human Rights and Fundamental Freedoms and its Protocol No. 6 concerning abolition of the death penalty. Only one state – Bulgaria – became a full member of the Council of Europe in 1992, when it also signed the European Convention for the Protection of Human Rights and Fundamental Freedoms. This brought the total number of members to 27. Nine other countries have applied to join and five have applied for Special Guest status with the Parliamentary Assembly, regarded as the first step to full membership. Only "European" states are admitted as members and the Council continued to debate this definition, in particular, whether the three Caucasian states of Armenia, Azerbaydzhan and Georgia and the five Asian republics of Kazakhstan, Kyrgyzstan, Tadzhikistan, Turkmenistan and Uzbekistan could in principle be considered for membership.

The question of minority rights highlighted diverging views about the Council's role. At the direction of the Committee of Ministers, the Steering Committee for Human Rights began work on developing legal standards on minority rights. Meanwhile, the Parliamentary Assembly urged that the Council should also act as a mediator in cases of urgent minority disputes, notwithstanding that the CSCE is developing a role in this regard.

The European Committee for the Prevention of Torture entered its third year of operation. The Committee increased the number of periodic visits from six in 1991 to eight in 1992 covering Cyprus, Finland, Italy, Luxembourg, the Netherlands, Portugal, San Marino and Turkey. In 1992 it also carried out its second *ad hoc* visit to Turkey and made a public statement – its first on any country – after the visit highlighting the continuing widespread use of torture in the country. Sweden and Malta agreed to the public release of reports of the Committee's earlier visits to these countries, which would otherwise remain confidential.

As part of its function to prevent torture and other ill-treatment, the Committee started to elaborate safeguards it considers all states should observe. In regard to police custody, the Committee highlighted the importance of the right of a detainee to have a third party such as a relative or friend informed of the detention, the right of access to a lawyer and the right to request a medical examination by a doctor of the detainee's choice.

Amnesty International continued to contribute as an observer to the biannual meetings of the Council of Europe's Steering Committee for Human Rights. It also attended a meeting in December of a subordinate committee which is elaborating a draft Protocol to the European Convention for the Protection of Human Rights and Fundamental Freedoms on the rights of people deprived of their liberty and submitted recommendations regarding essential principles which should be reflected in the Protocol. Amnesty International continued to attend the parliamentary Committee on Migration, Refugees and Demography and provided information to the Committee's members about its concerns.

## The European Community (EC)

New references to human rights as general principles of EC law and as objectives of EC foreign and development policy were included in the Treaty on European Union signed by EC member states in Maastricht, the Netherlands, in February. However, human rights policy and action by the EC institutions continued to lack a firm basis in the EC legal order and were dealt with primarily through intergovernmental cooperation. EC governments increased their efforts to implement a more coherent and consistent human rights policy as part of their aid and trade relations with third countries. In light of the November 1991 Resolution on human rights, democracy and development, the EC Commission drafted new proposals on programs of cooperation in support of democracy, human rights and the rule of law in developing countries.

The EC took a number of initiatives on human rights issues at the legislative and operational level to bring about a solution to the conflict in the former Yugoslavia. EC governments also sent observers and experts to South Africa in October to assist in investigating human rights violations and to monitor relations between the police and residents of black communities. Human rights were an important item on the agenda of a number of EC Council of Ministers meetings, in particular those which reviewed EC relations with countries of the Association of Southeast Asian Nations (ASEAN), and with Turkey, the Maghreb and Central and Latin America.

The European Parliament (EP) adopted a report on the death penalty, reiterating its position in favour of total abolition and calling on retentionist states to take effective measures to abolish this punishment in law and practice. It also adopted reports on the situation of the Kurds, on the conflict in the former Yugoslavia, on relations between the

EC and Turkey, and between the EC and ASEAN countries. The continuing human rights violations in East Timor were the subject of a public hearing organized by the EP in April, and were also raised by its delegation for relations with ASEAN states when it visited Jakarta, Indonesia, in September. Other inter-parliamentary meetings which debated human rights issues were held with parliamentarians from China, Turkey and Central America. Important human rights resolutions adopted by the EP included those on East Timor, Malawi, Myanmar, the Philippines, Sudan, Syria and the USA. Early in the year the EP refused to approve financial protocols on EC assistance to Morocco and Syria, because of its concern for continuing human rights violations in these countries. Later, it lifted its reservations with regard to the protocol on Morocco and one of the two agreements with Syria.

The Joint Parliamentary Assembly, comprising 69 EP members and an equal number of representatives from African, Caribbean and Pacific (ACP) states, held a substantial debate on the interrelationship of human rights, democracy and development cooperation at its September session. However, it failed to take any further steps owing to major differences of opinion on how this interrelationship should be reflected in development co-operation programs.

EC governments took further steps to harmonize certain procedural and substantive questions relating to their asylum legislation. Important policy documents outlining a common approach to manifestly unfounded claims and to the principles of host third country and "safe" country of origin were adopted by EC governments in December (see **Refugees**, pages 18 to 23). The EP adopted a report on these and other aspects of the process of harmonization of EC member states' asylum policies.

Amnesty International continued to bring to the attention of EC governments, the EC Commission and members of the EP its concerns and recommendations on a number of human rights issues and on the situation in individual countries. These included further proposals for a fair and satisfactory EC asylum policy, and observations on the need for coherent and consistent action on human rights as an essential element of EC development co-operation. The organization also submitted a memorandum to the EC on a draft EC directive on data protection. In its original form the directive would seriously undermine the effectiveness of the work of human rights organizations, including Amnesty International.

## The Conference on Security and Co-operation in Europe (CSCE)

With the rise of violent conflicts in Europe, the CSCE has attempted to reform itself and find a new and credible role as peace-maker, peace-keeper and protector of human rights. Following the break-up of both the USSR and the former Yugoslavia, the CSCE also dramatically increased in size from 38 to 52 participating states, bringing with it new tensions as the organization tried to redefine its European character. Armenia, Azerbaydzhan, Belarus, Kazakhstan, Kyrgyzstan, Moldova, Tadzhikistan, Turkmenistan, Ukraine and Uzbekistan were admitted in January; Croatia, Georgia and Slovenia in March; and Bosnia-Herzegovina in April.

The conflict in the former Yugoslavia dominated many of the CSCE meetings in 1992, often preventing states from focusing on plans for long-term reform. The CSCE largely supported initiatives taken by other intergovernmental organizations on the former Yugoslavia. From July the Federal Republic of Yugoslavia was excluded from all CSCE meetings, pending regular review. The organization sent several fact-finding teams to the region and established a long-term monitoring mission in Kosovo, Sandžak and the Vojvodina.

During the three-month Follow-Up Meeting (known as Helsinki II), which opened in March, member states reviewed the CSCE's role in human rights, security, environmental and economic issues. They introduced a new CSCE peace-keeping role, paved the way for small, *ad hoc* steering groups to respond to crises by seeking a negotiated settlement, and strengthened the use of "early warning" techniques.

In a document entitled *Human Rights in the New Europe: the CSCE in Search of a Role*, Amnesty International made a number of proposals for institutional reform of the CSCE human rights process. Among them were ways to improve monitoring of the implementation by all member states of the wide range of CSCE human rights commitments; to improve openness and access to information; and to develop a meaningful role for NGOs. The organization raised these concerns directly with governments throughout the Helsinki II meeting.

Amnesty International welcomed some of the reforms and commitments agreed in Helsinki, such as the creation of a High Commissioner on National Minorities to investigate and conciliate minority conflicts at an early stage, and a commitment to deal with the growing problem of refugees and displaced people. However, Helsinki II failed to strengthen significantly the CSCE human rights process. The biennial human rights implementation meeting set up by Helsinki II has no power to make binding decisions or even send experts to investigate a situation. The work of the CSCE remains largely shrouded in secrecy and Helsinki II failed to develop a more open and substantive working relationship with NGOs.

The CSCE Parliamentary Assembly met for the first time in Budapest, Hungary, in July, although its role and relationship with the CSCE intergovernmental structure is still to be worked out. The CSCE office in Warsaw, Poland, was upgraded into a new Office for Democratic Institutions and Human Rights. It will act as a clearing house for assistance programs for eastern and central Europe and will organize future CSCE expert seminars.

### Inter-Parliamentary Union (IPU)

The Inter-Parliamentary Union, an NGO composed of members of parliament from 118 countries, maintains a special Committee on the Human Rights of Parliamentarians. During 1992 Amnesty International submitted information to this Committee on parliamentarians from Colombia, Côte d'Ivoire, Equatorial Guinea, Honduras, Indonesia, Jordan, Maldives, Myanmar, Togo, Turkey and Uzbekistan. Amnesty International delegates attended the September session of the Inter-Parliamentary Conference in Stockholm, Sweden.

# COUNTRY
# ENTRIES

# AFGHANISTAN

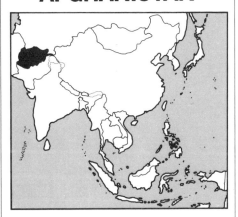

**Thousands of political prisoners were released in April when a new government, composed of armed Mujahideen groups formerly in opposition, took office. However, the fate of hundreds of political prisoners held in prisons controlled by some Mujahideen groups remained unknown. Cruel, inhuman or degrading punishments were introduced such as the severing of hands or feet, flogging and stoning to death. Some extrajudicial executions were reported. Mass graves containing the bodies of thousands of people apparently extrajudicially executed in previous years were discovered. At least 20 people were sentenced to death after apparently unfair trials and at least 12 of them were publicly executed.**

United Nations (UN) proposals for a transitional government acceptable to all parties in the Afghan conflict were abandoned as armed Mujahideen groups converged on the capital, Kabul, resulting in the resignation of President Najibullah on 16 April. Professor Sibghatollah Mojaddedi, former head of the Afghan Interim Government based in Pakistan, became President of the renamed Islamic State of Afghanistan on 28 April. Under an agreement signed earlier by the Mujahideen groups, this interim government was replaced after two months by another transitional government headed by Burhanuddin Rabbani, leader of the *Jamiat-e-Islami*, Society of Islam, one of the Mujahideen groups. On 30 December an assembly representing various Mujahideen groups elected Burhanuddin Rabbani as President for a two-year term. However, five of the nine major Mujahideen groups

boycotted the elections.

Both before and after the change of government only part of the country, centred on Kabul, was under government control – the rest was controlled by various Mujahideen groups. In the second half of the year there was fierce fighting between different Mujahideen groups and between the forces of the new government and the Mujahideen *Hesb-e-Islami*, Party of Islam, led by Gulbuddin Hekmatyar. At least 2,500 people reportedly died during the fighting in Kabul alone, and thousands of people again sought refuge in Pakistan which in September reportedly denied access to new arrivals. Earlier in the year about one million refugees were reported to have returned to Afghanistan from Pakistan.

In May all laws not in conformity with Islamic precepts were declared void. Islamic courts were set up and reportedly passed at least 20 death sentences. By October at least 12 people had been publicly executed.

Under new government policies, several fundamental freedoms such as the rights to freedom of expression, religion and association were severely curtailed. In May "anti-religious" books were seized and in June non-Islamic parties were banned. Participation in congregational prayers and the adoption of an Islamic dress code for women became mandatory in May.

In late April all prisoners, including between 2,000 and 3,000 political prisoners, hundreds of whom were prisoners of conscience, were released from Pul-e-Charkhi, Kabul's largest prison. Many had been sentenced at unfair trials by special courts or held without charge or trial for up to 10 years. Similar releases reportedly took place in other towns. However, the fate of hundreds of political prisoners reportedly held in Mujahideen prisons in Afghanistan and border areas of Pakistan remained unknown.

Before the change of government, torture was reported to have been practised in several detention centres.

After April several Mujahideen groups reportedly imprisoned political rivals as hostages and there were unconfirmed reports of killings and ill-treatment of prisoners in Mujahideen detention centres. It was not known whether the new government imprisoned political opponents.

Judicial punishments were introduced

**48**

which Amnesty International considers constitute cruel, inhuman or degrading treatment or punishment and are prohibited by international law. The Deputy Minister of Justice declared in May that people convicted of adultery would be stoned to death and those convicted of theft would have a hand or a foot severed. He said that people convicted of consuming alcohol would be punished with 80 lashes and those who traded in alcohol would receive the death penalty. It was not known if any of these punishments were imposed. However, vigilante groups were reported to have carried out such punishments, apparently believing they were acting according to official policies. By the end of May they had reportedly executed 66 of some 120 people allegedly caught looting in Kabul. Members of Mujahideen groups were also reported to have ill-treated alleged criminals. In April a man caught looting a private house in Kabul was reportedly arrested by Mujahideen, bound and beaten, and then paraded through the streets with a sign around his neck identifying him as a thief.

A general amnesty for former government and ruling party members was declared on 26 April. Although the amnesty was generally respected, several people who should have been protected by it were extrajudicially executed. In late April a man believed to be a member of the former ruling party was summarily executed by a member of the militia. He was seized during a search of a government building in Kabul, tied up, kicked down a flight of stairs, clubbed with a rifle butt and finally shot dead. In May the former Chief Justice, Abdul Karim Shadan, was reportedly abducted, tortured and killed, apparently in reprisal for his activities as a member of the former government.

After the change of government in April, mass graves of thousands of people allegedly extrajudicially executed under previous governments were discovered in various locations. The remains of several thousand bodies were reportedly found near Kabul in May and of about 2,000 in Herat in September. However, no official investigation was initiated into the mass killings.

At least 20 people were sentenced to death by Islamic courts after apparently unfair trials on criminal charges. None of those convicted reportedly had the right to appeal to a higher court or to seek clemency. The trials appeared to have been concluded within a few days and to have been held *in camera*.

By early October, 12 of those sentenced to death by Islamic courts had been publicly hanged. In June four militia members were publicly hanged in Kandahar after they were convicted of breaking into a house, raping a young woman and killing two Mujahideen who tried to arrest them. In September three men in Kabul were publicly hanged for robbery, looting and murder. In Jalalabad a public execution was reportedly carried out in September by the brother of a murder victim. In a public hanging of four men in Kabul on 30 September, guards reportedly pulled at the bodies of the convicts to bring about asphyxiation.

In April Amnesty International appealed to the new government in Kabul and Mujahideen groups in control of other areas of Afghanistan to ensure the safety of all prisoners, both those still detained under orders of the former government and those held by Mujahideen groups. Amnesty International was particularly concerned that during the political upheaval related to the change of government, prisoners held by Mujahideen groups might be tortured or summarily executed.

In May Amnesty International detailed its concerns in a report, *Afghanistan: reports of torture, ill-treatment and extrajudicial executions of prisoners, late April – early May 1992*. The government of President Mojaddedi responded to Amnesty International by reiterating its commitment to observance of the civil and political rights of all Afghans. It said that the human rights violations reported by Amnesty International were acts of individuals and contrary to government policies.

In September Amnesty International published a report, *Afghanistan: New forms of cruel, inhuman or degrading punishment*, which expressed concern that the death penalty might be extended to more offences and that forms of punishment might be imposed which Amnesty International considers constitute cruel, inhuman or degrading treatment or punishment. The organization urged the government to halt executions and to ensure that trial procedures, particularly those involving offences punishable by death, strictly conform to international standards for fair trial.

# ALBANIA

**A student died reportedly as a result of ill-treatment by police. Fourteen people were sentenced to death and seven of them were executed.**

Elections were held in March and won by the Democratic Party. Its leader, Sali Berisha, was elected state President by the People's Assembly in April. In May Albania's first Constitutional Court was sworn in. In October a special commission, formed to identify people from the Shkodër area who had allegedly been killed for political reasons by security forces during the years of communist rule from 1944 to 1991, produced its first report. It stated that it had so far discovered six common graves in Shkodër and had succeeded in identifying 40 victims, although it believed the total to be some 2,000.

Leonard Arapi, a student at Shkodër university, died two days after being arrested by officers of a police unit known as the Rapid Deployment Forces. He had reportedly been seized from a bus near Sukth on 27 February. Albanian radio reported that he had been beaten so severely that he died from his injuries two days later in Tirana hospital. In December five police officers convicted of responsibility for the deaths of four men during demonstrations in Shkodër in April 1991 (see *Amnesty International Report 1992*) were imprisoned for between 15 and 20 years.

Eleven offences were punishable by death, including embezzlement, theft of state property, treason, espionage and murder. Fourteen men were sentenced to death for murder or other offences resulting in death. Three death sentences were commuted to imprisonment. Seven men were

executed, among them Ditbardh and Josif Çuko. They had been sentenced to death for acts of looting which led to the deaths of five members of a family. On 25 June they were hanged in the early hours of the morning in a square in the town of Fier, where they were exposed to public view for the rest of the day.

Amnesty International called on the authorities to commute death sentences and urged an immediate moratorium on the passing and carrying out of death sentences, with a view to the eventual abolition of the death penalty.

# ALGERIA

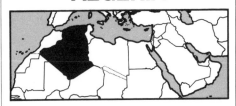

**Thousands of supporters of Islamic opposition groups were arrested, most following mass demonstrations in January and February. Among them were possible prisoners of conscience. Over 10,000 of those arrested were administratively detained without charge or trial in internment camps for several months: conditions in some camps were harsh. Hundreds of other government opponents were sentenced to prison terms after trials before military and civil courts, some of which fell short of international fair trial standards. Torture and ill-treatment of detainees by the security forces became widespread during the year. Over 100 people, most of them supporters of Islamic groups, were killed by the security forces during clashes and raids: some may have been victims of extrajudicial executions. At least 19 people were sentenced to death, but no executions were carried out.**

In January President Chadli Benjedid resigned following major gains by the *Front Islamique du Salut* (FIS), Islamic Salvation Front, in the first round of multi-party elections held in late 1991 (see *Amnesty International Report 1992*). The government cancelled the second round of elections scheduled for January, provoking widespread protests. Mohamed Boudiaf returned from 27 years of exile to head a five-man *Haut Comité d'Etat*, Higher Council of State, which served as a collective presidency. Over 100 civilians and members of the security forces were killed during demonstrations and violent clashes, and there were mass arrests of demonstrators and suspected members of the FIS and other Islamic opposition groups.

On 9 February a 12-month state of emergency was declared. This empowered the authorities to place under administrative detention or house arrest anyone whose activities were deemed likely to threaten public order. It also empowered them to ban meetings and demonstrations likely to disturb public order, and suspend or dissolve local assemblies. Under state of emergency regulations, the FIS was dissolved by a court ruling in March.

On 29 June President Boudiaf was assassinated by a member of the security forces. Ali Kafi, a member of the *Haut Comité d'Etat*, replaced him as President. In September the government introduced an anti-terrorist legislative decree which increased the scope of the death penalty. The decree also instituted special courts for "terrorist" crimes, lowered the age of criminal responsibility in such cases to 16, limited the right of appeal and broadened the definition of terrorist acts. The law is retroactive insofar as any case under instruction may be transferred to the special courts and defendants sentenced to increased penalties which did not apply at the time of the offence.

Throughout the year armed Islamist opposition groups and unknown individuals carried out violent attacks on the security forces and public places in which over 200 police and security officers and some civilians were killed.

More than 10,000 people arrested in January and February, including possible prisoners of conscience, were administratively detained without charge or trial. They were initially held in seven internment camps in the desert, between 800 and 3,000 kilometres south of Algiers, including at Reggane and Ain M'Guel near Tamanrasset. Families and lawyers of the detainees were not informed of their whereabouts for up to several weeks. The distant location of the camps and administrative delays in issuing visiting permits made it difficult for families to visit the camps.

The detainees were held under state of emergency regulations which allow administrative detention without charge or trial for up to 12 months. Groups of detainees were released from internment camps after March, and more than half were released within eight months of being arrested. However, arrests and internments continued and new camps were opened in Tiberghamine, Wad Namous and other locations. Some camps, including those at Reggane and El Homr, were reportedly closed and the inmates transferred to other camps. In August the authorities announced that the internment camps would be closed and that all detainees would be brought to trial or released. However, over 3,000 detainees remained in administrative detention without charge or trial at the end of the year.

Conditions in some camps were harsh. There were reports of overcrowding and lack of hygiene and medical facilities, resulting in a high incidence of illness. At the end of March a 60-year-old detainee was shot dead by security forces in the camp at Reggane: no public investigation into his death was known to have been held.

Torture of detainees, which had been rare since 1988 (see *Amnesty International Report 1989*), became widespread during the year. Most reported cases took place in pre-trial incommunicado (*garde à vue*) detention, which was frequently prolonged beyond the 12-day limit permitted under the anti-terrorist decree. Methods of torture included beatings, often with sticks, wires, belts or broom-handles on all parts of the body; burning with cigarettes; pulling out finger- and toe-nails; insertion of bottles and other objects into the anus; the "*chiffon*" (cloth), whereby the victim is tied to a bench and partially suffocated with a cloth soaked in dirty water and chemicals; and electric shocks. For example, Nadir Hammoudi, who was arrested in November and held in *garde à vue* detention for 25 days, alleged that he was tortured in Bab El Oued Police Station and in an unknown place to which he had been taken while hooded. He said he was beaten, kicked, burned with a cigarette and then tortured by the "*chiffon*" method by being forced to swallow water and chemicals while police officers sat on his feet and held his nose.

Over 100 protesters and supporters of Islamic opposition groups were killed by the security forces during demonstrations and clashes, some in circumstances suggesting they were victims of extrajudicial executions. According to official sources, between 12 January and 14 March over 70 civilians died as a result of shootings by law enforcement officials. Scores more were killed in April and later in the year in clashes and during raids on houses where armed government opponents were thought to be hiding. Bystanders and civilians passing through police barricades were also killed and injured in circumstances which violated international standards for the use of firearms by law enforcement officials. In one case, for example, security forces killed an unarmed man in February while searching a building for armed government opponents. According to his family, the man was made to lie face down on the floor by police and was shot dead when he lifted his head abruptly after gunfire was heard. The authorities said internal inquiries by the security forces were held into cases of death by shooting by the security forces, but no result of any investigation was made public.

Hundreds of people were tried by military and civil courts without legal representation in breach of international standards for fair trial. Under the state of emergency, those accused of serious crimes and felonies against state security may be tried before military courts whose procedures lack some of the safeguards provided in civil courts. In July Abbas Medani and Ali Belhadj, two leading FIS members who were arrested in June 1991 (see *Amnesty International Report 1992*), were sentenced by a military court to 12 years' imprisonment after being convicted of offences against state security, undermining the national economy and distributing subversive literature. They were acquitted on charges including kidnapping and torturing members of the security forces. The trial appeared to fall far short of international standards for fair trial. Defence lawyers complained of breaches of procedure in the pre-trial and trial proceedings, and said that they were unable to prepare an adequate defence because they had not been given full access to their clients' case files. The trial proceedings were boycotted by the defendants and their lawyers in protest at the court's failure to meet defence demands and to admit international observers and foreign media.

At least 19 people were sentenced to death for participating in armed attacks against the security forces resulting in fatalities. The cases of four people sentenced to death in 1991 for financial crimes (see *Amnesty International Report 1992*) were sent back for retrial. Over 100 people remained on death row at the end of the year, but no executions were reported.

At least 10 Tunisian asylum-seekers were expelled to Libya in May, despite the risk that they would be returned to Tunisia where they might face serious human rights violations. Some were returned by the Libyan authorities to Tunisia where they were reported to have been detained and tortured. During the year, four Tunisians and one Iraqi were expelled to other third countries. Amnesty International wrote to the Algerian Government reminding it of its obligation under international law not to send asylum-seekers to third countries without ensuring that they would be granted effective protection against *refoulement*.

New information was received about detainees who were held in camps and allegedly tortured and ill-treated by the *Frente Popular para la Liberación de Seguia el-Hamra y Rio de Oro*, Popular Front for the Liberation of Seguia el-Hamra and Rio de Oro (Polisario Front), in an area of southern Algeria controlled by the Polisario Front and known as the Sahrawi Arab Democratic Republic (SADR). Some detainees were said to have been held incommunicado for several years in the camps, which are located around Tindouf. Those detained were believed to have been imprisoned as a result of political disputes within the Polisario Front: there appeared to be no legal basis for their detentions.

In January Amnesty International wrote to the Algerian Minister of Human Rights urging him to issue the security forces with strict guidelines concerning the use of firearms and providing him with the United Nations (UN) Basic Principles on the Use of Force and Firearms by Law Enforcement Officials. The ministry responded by emphasizing that human rights were respected in Algeria and promising to send copies of the UN Basic Principles to security authorities. In March and December Amnesty International delegates visited Algeria and met government ministers and other officials to discuss the organization's human rights concerns. In June Amnesty

**52**

International delegates were refused permission to observe the trial of the FIS leaders or to see copies of the trial documents.

In May Amnesty International sent a memorandum to the government expressing its concern about the fatal shooting of unarmed civilians, ill-treatment of detainees, administrative detention without charge or trial, and death sentences. No response had been received by the end of the year.

In November Amnesty International wrote to President Mohammad 'Abdul 'Aziz of the SADR raising its concerns about reported torture in camps holding detainees.

# ANGOLA

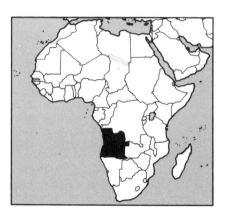

**Despite further releases of political prisoners under the 1991 Peace Accords, the fate and whereabouts of hundreds of prisoners remained unknown. There were new political arrests and reports of torture and ill-treatment: at least one detainee died in police custody, apparently as a result of torture. Government forces committed scores of extrajudicial executions of suspected political opponents. The death penalty was abolished. The main armed opposition group, the *União Nacional para a Independência Total de Angola* (UNITA), National Union for the Total Independence of Angola, and armed factions of the *Frente da Libertação do Enclave de Cabinda* (FLEC), Enclave of Cabinda Liberation Front, were also responsible for gross human rights abuses, including executions and other deliberate and arbitrary killings.**

The Peace Accords agreed in 1991 by the government and UNITA were repeatedly undermined by political violence and human rights violations. They had not been fully implemented before national elections were held in September under United Nations (UN) supervision. The elections, won by the *Movimento Popular para a Libertação de Angola* (MPLA), People's Movement for the Liberation of Angola, led by President José Eduardo dos Santos, were declared by international observers to have been generally free and fair, but Jonas Savimbi, UNITA's leader, rejected the results, alleging they were fraudulent. He withdrew his troops from the new national army and UNITA forces occupied many towns and villages. Fierce fighting broke out in Luanda and other towns in late October. By the end of the year thousands of people had died: a large proportion were victims of deliberate revenge killings carried out by both sides. UN and diplomatic efforts to break the deadlock continued, unsuccessfully, to the end of 1992.

The timetable set out in the Peace Accords for the demobilization of troops, the formation of police monitoring groups and the extension of the central administration was not observed. The implementation of the accords was the responsibility of the *Comissão Conjunta Político-Militar* (CCPM), Joint Political-Military Commission, comprising equal numbers of government and UNITA representatives and observers from the governments of Portugal, the Russian Federation and the United States of America. The CCPM, in which each side had a veto over decisions, failed to investigate violations of human rights, allowing politically motivated killings and other abuses to be committed with impunity. The accords also provided for the government's administrative structures to be extended to UNITA-controlled areas, but in practice UNITA retained control over a large part of the country.

Violence continued in Cabinda, an oil-rich Angolan enclave between Zaire and the Congo, where separatist groups fought for independence.

Angola abolished the death penalty in August. No executions had been carried out for over four years. Earlier, in January, Angola acceded to the International Covenant on Civil and Political Rights and its Optional Protocol, and to the International Covenant on Economic, Social and

Cultural Rights.

Under the Peace Accords, all prisoners detained in the context of the conflict were to be released by August 1991. By the start of 1992 the government had released over 900 prisoners (see *Amnesty International Report 1992*) and in April it released a further three. UNITA said that it had released over 3,000 prisoners by February, but that most had chosen to remain in UNITA-controlled areas. It released more prisoners in March, May and July. However, according to reports, at the end of the year other prisoners were still being held or had been coerced into staying in UNITA-controlled areas.

In early July, the CCPM ruled that all remaining prisoners should be released by the end of the month. This followed claims by UNITA that the government had failed to release 400 of its members and by the government that UNITA was still holding some 4,000 prisoners. However, there were no further releases, and thousands of prisoners remained unaccounted for. They included many hundreds of people, including suspected UNITA supporters, who "disappeared" in government custody in the late 1970s. The fate and whereabouts of scores of government soldiers and civilians taken prisoner by UNITA, as well as UNITA members detained by the organization for opposing its policies or leadership, also remained unclear.

Prisoners still held by the government at the start of the year included José Alberto Ferreira Pinto "Zeca Siberia", who had been convicted of diamond smuggling and plotting against the government in an unfair trial and sentenced to 16 years' imprisonment in 1984. He was released from prison in August.

There were new political arrests. In June over 40 people, most of them UNITA supporters, were detained in Luanda during the visit of Pope John-Paul II. They were all subsequently released uncharged. In July Manuel Matias, nine other former UNITA soldiers and three civilians were arrested by government soldiers: they were held for over a month and then released uncharged. At least a dozen other UNITA members were reportedly detained for political reasons during the elections in September. They were subsequently released. In the violence which followed the elections, hundreds of UNITA members and others suspected of sympathizing with UNITA were arrested in

Luanda. Over 70 of them were released in December.

Political detainees and criminal suspects were reported to have been beaten or ill-treated in custody as common practice: others were tortured during interrogation. Francisco dos Santos Queirós, who was arrested on suspicion of theft, died in police custody in Luanda in May. An autopsy reportedly revealed that he had been beaten around the head, his genitals had been mutilated and he had been shot. Paulo Godinho and David Pedro Chiovo, two UNITA supporters who were detained in Luanda shortly before the elections, were also reported to have been badly beaten in police custody. There were further reports of ill-treatment and torture following the violence in Luanda in late October and early November. No further investigation concerning these cases was known to have occurred.

There were new reports of extrajudicial executions both before and after the elections. At least 10 people were extrajudicially executed in Cabinda, where armed FLEC factions continued to fight for the territory's independence. In early September government troops took violent reprisals against the local population. At least six people, all civilians, were killed. They included a woman who was shot as she swept her doorstep and João "Incumbio" Macaia, a civil servant, who was burned to death by soldiers – they placed a tyre round his neck, doused it with petrol and set it alight. The four others were killed later in the month: João Maria Taty, an electricity company worker, and his three companions were reported to have been detained by soldiers and then summarily executed by firing-squad. No action was known to have been taken by the authorities to investigate these killings.

During the violence which erupted in Luanda after the elections hundreds of suspected UNITA sympathizers were extrajudicially executed by government police or by civilians supporting them to whom the authorities had distributed arms. Some eye-witnesses reported that they had seen bodies with the hands or ankles bound, indicating that they had been captured and then killed. The authorities broadcast appeals to people not to carry out revenge killings but these had little effect. The government failed to take other action to stop the killings and by the end of the year had

**54**

taken no steps to bring those responsible to justice.

UNITA was also responsible for gross human rights abuses, including executions and other deliberate and arbitrary killings. In March four government air force officers were deliberately killed, two of whom were apparently buried alive. The same month, UNITA admitted that two of its former leading officials – Pedro "Tito" Chingunji and Fernando Wilson dos Santos – had been executed in the latter half of 1991 together with at least three members of their families (see *Amnesty International Report 1991*). Defecting UNITA officials claimed the victims had been executed on the direct orders of UNITA's leader Jonas Savimbi but UNITA blamed one of the defectors. Other internal dissidents within the organization continued to be held by UNITA, including Nelson Malaquias and his daughters, Germana "Tita" and Bela. Bela Malaquias, a journalist, had been working for UNITA in Luanda but was forced to return to Jamba, UNITA's headquarters in southeastern Angola, in May. She was not allowed to leave Jamba although it was not clear whether or not she was held in a prison.

Following the election, UNITA forces were reported to have committed deliberate and arbitrary killings of suspected government supporters in areas which they seized. However, it was difficult to obtain information from these areas.

FLEC factions also carried out deliberate and arbitrary killings of suspected government supporters. In December, one faction – it was not clear which – ambushed four vehicles carrying oil company employees and killed four of the workers, all apparently targeted because they were Angolans but not from Cabinda.

Amnesty International representatives visited Angola for the first time in March. In May the organization published *Angola: An appeal for prompt action to protect human rights*, which reported that both sides were responsible for politically motivated killings and other abuses and that these were not being adequately investigated by the mechanisms set up under the Peace Accords. Amnesty International appealed to both sides and the international observers to ensure that the human rights provisions of the Peace Accords were upheld. In August Amnesty International published *Angola: Will the new government protect human rights?*, which

updated the previous report and outlined a framework of reforms to prevent further human rights violations in Angola. Following the elections Amnesty International urged the parties to the conflict to take action to prevent extrajudicial executions and other deliberate and arbitrary killings and abuses.

# ARGENTINA

**There were new allegations of torture and ill-treatment by the police and one person died in police custody, reportedly as a result of torture. One person in police custody allegedly "disappeared". A new commission was set up to investigate the fate of hundreds of children who "disappeared" during the years of military rule. A draft law to reintroduce the death penalty was presented to Congress.**

In January the government passed a law giving financial compensation to detainees held during the years of military rule from 1976 to 1983. Political prisoners who were detained "at the disposal of the Executive Power" and civilians detained by order of military courts are entitled to compensation, which is increased for detainees who suffered "very serious injuries".

There were new allegations of ill-treatment and torture of detainees held as criminal suspects in police units in the federal capital, Buenos Aires, and the provinces. According to the authorities, between 1989 and 1991 there had been 773 complaints of unlawful coercion, which includes ill-treatment of detainees, by police in different units in Buenos Aires. Only one person had been prosecuted as a result of these complaints.

Among the cases of torture reported during 1992 was that of Ramón María Centurión, who was arrested in January on suspicion of theft in the city of Corrientes, Corrientes Province, by police from Chaco Province. He was taken to the Investigations Department of Chaco Province Police Force, where he was allegedly tortured with electric shocks to the testicles and by having one of his hands burned with hot paraffin. He was released after a few days and was subsequently rearrested several times. He was reportedly tortured again when detained in June. To Amnesty International's knowledge, none of those allegedly responsible for the torture of Ramón María Centurión was brought to justice.

In May around 30 youths who were trying to attend a rock concert in Lanús, Buenos Aires Province, were detained near Lanús stadium. They were taken to a police station where they were allegedly beaten. Most of the youths were released a few hours later. However, according to reports, nine of them, including Diego Dotro, were detained for up to five days without access to their relatives and without being brought before a judge. Two days later another group of about 50 youths, who were trying to see the same rock group in Lanús stadium, were chased and beaten by the police. The youths were marched through the streets of Lanús while being hit and verbally abused. Judicial inquiries were initiated into both incidents.

Seventeen-year-old Sergio Gustavo Durán died in police custody in Morón, Buenos Aires Province. He had allegedly been taken into custody to check his police record on 6 August but the following morning was taken to hospital, where he was pronounced dead on arrival. The Juvenile Court was reportedly not notified of his detention until 10 hours after his death. Although a police doctor's certificate stated that at the time of his detention Sergio Gustavo Durán had no signs of cuts or bruises, a post-mortem examination showed that he had cuts on his upper lip and tongue, and severe bruises, consistent with blows, on his body, including his testicles. A judicial inquiry was opened into Sergio Gustavo Durán's death.

One person in police custody was alleged to have "disappeared". In May Pablo Cristian Guardatti was reportedly detained at gunpoint in the city of Men-

doza, Mendoza Province, by a man believed to be a policeman wearing civilian clothes whom he had accidentally hit with a stone. Pablo Cristian Guardatti was allegedly taken by the man to the nearby "La Estanzuela" police unit. However, the police denied having detained Pablo Cristian Guardatti and a writ of *habeas corpus* filed on his behalf was rejected. In September witnesses identified the man who reportedly detained Pablo Cristian Guardatti as a police officer from "La Estanzuela" police unit. The police officer and three other officers from "La Estanzuela" police unit were then detained and charged with kidnapping following a judicial investigation. However, the whereabouts of Pablo Cristian Guardatti remained unknown. The investigation was continuing at the end of the year.

Judicial investigations failed to clarify the fate of three people who reportedly "disappeared" in 1990 (see *Amnesty International Report 1992*). Adolfo Argentino Garrido and Raúl Baigorria "disappeared" in April 1990 after allegedly being detained by uniformed police in General San Martín park, Mendoza city. Andrés Alberto Nuñez "disappeared" in September 1990 after reportedly being taken into custody by the Investigations Force of La Plata, Buenos Aires Province (see *Amnesty International Report 1991*). In all three cases the police denied arresting the men or having any record of their detention, despite evidence to the contrary.

The governor of the Federal Penitentiary System was charged with unlawful coercion for his part in the ill-treatment of detainees belonging to the *Movimiento Todos por la Patria* (MTP), All for the Fatherland Movement, who were involved in an armed attack on La Tablada army barracks in 1989 (see *Amnesty International Reports 1990* to *1992*). However, the case was dismissed by a judge who ruled that the criminal action was inadmissible because the judicial investigation had taken over three years to complete. Investigations were still not completed into the allegations that two MTP prisoners were extrajudicially executed after they surrendered and that three others "disappeared" after giving themselves up to military personnel on the day of the attack.

In November a new commission was set up within the Sub-Secretariat of Human Rights of the Ministry of the Interior to

**56**

investigate the fate of hundreds of children who "disappeared" during the "dirty war" of the 1970s and 1980s. Only 53 of the "disappeared" children had been traced by the end of 1992.

In March the Vice-President of the Chamber of Deputies presented draft legislation to Congress to reintroduce the death penalty for certain crimes including rape and kidnapping resulting in death, acts of terrorism, subversion, sabotage resulting in death, and drug-trafficking. The draft bill was being considered by the Commission for Penal Legislation of the Chamber of Deputies.

During the year Amnesty International called on the authorities in various provinces to thoroughly and impartially investigate reports of torture and ill-treatment in police custody and to take steps to prevent such abuses. It also urged the authorities to investigate the "disappearance" of Pablo Cristian Guardatti.

In October Amnesty International told the government of its concern that in the past decade very little progress had been made in clarifying the fate of thousands of people who "disappeared" during the years of military rule. The organization welcomed President Carlos Menem's pledge in 1992 to track down any information on the "disappeared" and asked the authorities to take all necessary measures to disclose the information on the "disappeared" allegedly available in police and military archives.

In April Amnesty International expressed concern at the proposal to reintroduce the death penalty and stressed that its reintroduction would be in breach of Argentina's obligations under the American Convention on Human Rights.

# ARMENIA

**The death penalty was abolished for two offences. The status of three prisoners sentenced to death in 1990 remained unclear.**

Armenia gained independence after the break-up of the Soviet Union. Headed by President Levon Ter-Petrosyan, Armenia joined the Conference on Security and Co-operation in Europe in January and became a member of the United Nations in March.

The political situation continued to be

influenced by armed conflict in the disputed region of Nagorno-Karabakh, situated in the neighbouring republic of Azerbaydzhan but populated mainly by ethnic Armenians. Parliament postponed discussion of a draft law which would have provided a civilian alternative to military service for conscientious objectors, although no one was known to have been imprisoned for refusing call-up on these grounds during the year.

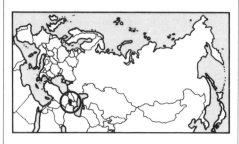

In March, for the first time, the authorities provided Amnesty International with statistics on the recent use of the death penalty. In 1989 four people were sentenced to death: in subsequent years two had their sentences commuted and two were executed. Three people sentenced to death in 1990 were still awaiting the outcome of petitions for clemency in May and their status was unclear at the end of the year. On 11 May parliament abolished the death penalty for two economic offences: "violation of rules for currency transactions" and "large-scale theft of state and social property".

Amnesty International urged that the three death sentences be commuted, and that parliament consider the total abolition of the death penalty.

Following allegations of hostage-taking, ill-treatment and deliberate and arbitrary killing of non-combatant civilians by ethnic Armenian paramilitary forces in Nagorno-Karabakh (see **Azerbaydzhan** entry), the organization also urged the authorities to exert all influence possible to ensure that international human rights and humanitarian principles were observed by all those associated with the conflict.

# AUSTRALIA

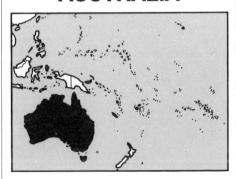

**The government published its response to the findings and recommendations of the Royal Commission into Aboriginal Deaths in Custody (RCIADC).**

In March the Australian Government published a three-volume response to the findings and recommendations of the RCIADC (see *Amnesty International Report 1992*). The response, comprising the responses of federal and state governments to the RCIADC report, endorsed the majority of the 339 recommendations of the RCIADC covering areas in law and criminal justice and social and economic development. The response authorized the Aboriginal and Torres Strait Islander Commission (ATSIC) to monitor the implementation of the RCIADC recommendations at all government levels. A Social Justice Unit within the Human Rights and Equal Opportunity Commission (HREOC) was created to produce an annual State of the Nation Report on the human rights situation of the Aboriginal and Torres Strait Islander peoples.

At least four Aboriginal people died in custody during 1992, despite the government's moves to address the issue of Aboriginal deaths in custody. The coroner's inquest into the death in custody of Darryl Leedham Cameron, an Aboriginal, in December 1991 returned an open verdict. This meant the inquest was unable to determine the precise circumstances of his death. Darryl Cameron was found hanged in a cell in the Greenough Regional Prison in Geraldton, Western Australia. He had been arrested six days earlier on an assault charge. His brother, Edward, had died in a similar way while in custody in Geraldton police lock-up in 1988 (see *Amnesty International Report 1989*). Edward Cameron's

death was investigated by the RCIADC.

In April Amnesty International representatives visited 24 police lock-ups, juvenile detention centres and prisons located in the Northern Territory, and in the states of Western Australia, Queensland and New South Wales. The representatives met federal and state level officials including the Federal Minister for Aboriginal and Torres Strait Islander Affairs, and representatives of non-governmental organizations. Amnesty International's representatives found that conditions in certain detention facilities, such as Alice Springs Prison, most of whose inmates were Aboriginal, were so overcrowded and harsh they amounted to cruel, inhuman or degrading treatment. The representatives also found that the criminal justice system functions in such a way as to make Australia's Aboriginal people a group distinctly vulnerable to highly disproportionate levels of incarceration and to ill-treatment in custody.

In January Amnesty International asked the federal government and state authorities in Western Australia to conduct full and impartial investigations into the death of Darryl Leedham Cameron and expressed regret that such deaths were continuing despite the recommendations of the RCIADC. In response, the state authorities informed Amnesty International in March that a public inquest would be held, but that the findings of an internal inquiry by the Department of Corrective Services on Darryl Cameron's death would not be made public "for security reasons", the nature of which was not made clear.

In March Amnesty International sent a memorandum to the federal and state governments expressing concern about the high incidence of Aboriginal deaths in custody, some of which may have resulted, at least in part, from ill-treatment. It asked the state and federal authorities for information about all deaths in custody since 31 May 1989, the cut-off date of the RCIADC investigations, including the nature of official investigations into the deaths and their findings in each case. Some but not all state and federal territory governments had responded to the memorandum by the end of the year.

In July Amnesty International wrote to the Tasmanian state government to urge the repeal of sections of the Tasmanian Criminal Code Act which allow for the prosecution and imprisonment of

**58**

consenting adults who engage in homosexual acts in private.

In an oral statement to the United Nations Sub-Commission Working Group on Indigenous Populations in July Amnesty International included reference to its concerns in Australia.

# AUSTRIA

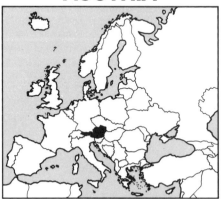

**There were new allegations that detainees were ill-treated in police custody, although these were fewer in number than in previous years.**

In February the Tyrol Independent Administrative Tribunal concluded that Werner Nosko's constitutionally guaranteed right not to be subjected to inhuman or degrading treatment had been infringed. Press photographer Werner Nosko had been arrested and handcuffed while taking pictures at a demonstration near Innsbruck. The handcuffs were fastened in such a way as to cause bruising and swelling to his left wrist. The tribunal also concluded that since his injuries must have been visible, the entry on the police arrest card which stated that the detainee had suffered no injuries had been falsely made.

In March Werner Hirtmayr submitted a complaint to the Vienna Independent Administrative Tribunal alleging that he had been ill-treated by two police officers in February when he was arrested outside his home for a speeding offence. Werner Hirtmayr alleged that he was kicked in the right knee by one of the officers, causing him to fall to the ground. He further alleged that both officers continued to kick him as he lay on the ground until he lost consciousness. According to a medical report issued by the hospital where he was

later treated, Werner Hirtmayr had suffered badly torn ligaments to his right knee, abrasions to his buttocks and right hand, bruising to his right calf, and a broken nose. The following day he underwent an operation lasting several hours on his leg. A complaint was lodged against Werner Hirtmayr by the Vienna Public Procurator accusing him of attempting to resist arrest and of causing serious injury to a police officer whom he was alleged to have struck in the face with his elbow and fist.

In June Amnesty International asked the Austrian authorities what efforts had been made by the police authorities, in the light of the decision by the Tyrol Independent Administrative Tribunal, to identify the officer who ill-treated Werner Nosko. The organization also inquired whether disciplinary action had been taken against the officer who had made a false entry on the police arrest card. In December the authorities informed Amnesty International that a judicial inquiry into the allegations of ill-treatment had been carried out by the Innsbruck Public Procurator. The inquiry concluded that there was insufficient evidence to show that the injury sustained by Werner Nosko had been the result of police negligence or had been caused intentionally. A separate inquiry concluded that the false entry on the arrest card was the result of a mistake on the part of the officer concerned.

In November Amnesty International asked the Austrian authorities to inform it about steps taken to investigate Werner Hirtmayr's allegations of ill-treatment by the police. No reply had been received by the end of the year.

# AZERBAYDZHAN

**Scores of people, including possible prisoners of conscience, were held as hostages on grounds of their ethnic origin. Many alleged they were tortured or ill-treated in detention. Hundreds of non-combatant civilians were deliberately and arbitrarily killed in the disputed region of Nagorno-Karabakh, according to reports. At least 18 people were sentenced to death and one death sentence was commuted.**

Azerbaydzhan was recognized as an independent state after the break-up of the

Soviet Union. It joined the Conference on Security and Co-operation in Europe in January and became a member of the United Nations in March. President Abulfaz Elchibey came to power following elections in June. Armed conflict in the disputed region of Nagorno-Karabakh, an area populated mainly by ethnic Armenians who had declared their own republic, continued and claimed hundreds of lives during the year.

In August Azerbaydzhan acceded to the International Covenant on Civil and Political Rights and the International Covenant on Economic, Social and Cultural Rights.

Scores of people said to be non-combatant civilians, including women and children, were detained as hostages solely on grounds of their ethnic origin. They appeared to be held for the purpose of future prisoner exchanges by the Azerbaydzhani authorities, ethnic Armenian paramilitary forces and private individuals. For example, two ethnic Armenian citizens of the Republic of Georgia, Vilik Oganasov and Artavaz Mirzoyan, were arrested by Azerbaydzhani police in April at Baku airport in Azerbaydzhan while in transit from Russia to Georgia. At the end of the year they still had not been charged with any criminal offence, and unofficial sources claimed their ethnic origin was the sole ground for their detention. Ethnic Azeri Saltanat Zulal gyzy Mamedova was reportedly detained by Armenian paramilitary forces together with two of her daughters and three grandchildren, the youngest aged four, in late February, while they were attempting to flee the site of an alleged massacre at Khodzhali. They were said to have been seen six weeks later held as hostages in the village of Venk. Their situation had not been clarified by the end of the year.

Many of those detained alleged they were tortured or ill-treated. Ethnic Armenian Eleanor Grigoryan, for example, was said to have been bleeding from multiple wounds when released in March after a month's detention together with her four-year-old son. She alleged she had been repeatedly raped by Azeri military units, and that her son had had his hand burned with cigarettes. Ethnic Azeri women detained in late February and early March said that they had been beaten and raped by ethnic Armenian forces.

Hundreds of non-combatant civilians were said to have been deliberately and arbitrarily killed as a result of the conflict in Nagorno-Karabakh. In April, 45 non-combatant Armenian inhabitants of Maraga, including women and children, were reportedly extrajudicially executed after Azerbaydzhani army units entered the village. Over 300 Azeri non-combatants, including women and children, were said to have been killed by ethnic Armenian paramilitary forces while attempting to leave the scene of fighting around the town of Khodzhali at the end of February.

Official statistics on the death penalty were released for the first time in October. Seventy-six people had been sentenced to death since 1986, including 18 people in the first half of 1992. All but two convictions were for premeditated, aggravated murder. The exceptions were for sabotage and the attempted murder of a police officer. Thirty-four people were executed between 1986 and 1990, all for premeditated, aggravated murder, but no executions were reported to have been carried out since then. One death sentence was commuted. Lieutenant Yevgeny Lukin, an ethnic Russian army officer, was sentenced to death for murder in August but pardoned and returned to Russia at the end of December.

Throughout the year Amnesty International urged all parties to the conflict in Nagorno-Karabakh to ensure that no non-combatants were detained as hostages, or otherwise held solely on the grounds of their ethnic origin. The organization also appealed to all sides to protect non-combatants from all acts of reprisal and violence and to treat prisoners in their custody humanely. It called for all alleged abuses within its mandate to be investigated fully and impartially, with the results made public and the perpetrators brought to justice.

Amnesty International continued to urge the authorities to commute all pending death sentences and to take concrete steps towards abolition of the death penalty.

60

# BAHAMAS

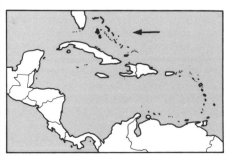

At least two people were sentenced to death; there were no executions. At the end of the year some 25 people were on death row.

The Free National Movement won the general election in August, replacing the People's Liberation Party which had been in power for 25 years. The manifesto of Hubert Ingraham, the new Prime Minister, included a commitment to promote and protect human rights and to consider the United Nations human rights covenants "with a view to early ratification".

Cyril James Darville was sentenced to death in August for a murder committed in March 1990. Michelle Woodside was sentenced to death in November for a murder committed in October 1991.

In February the Supreme Court dismissed a motion challenging the constitutionality of executions (see *Amnesty International Report 1992*). An appeal lodged in the Court of Appeal was still pending at the end of the year. Executions remained suspended pending a final decision on this appeal.

Amnesty International wrote to Prime Minister Ingraham in September to express its concern about the death penalty and corporal punishment. It urged the government to commute all current death sentences, abolish the death penalty and repeal legislation allowing for the use of corporal punishment, including flogging. A reply from the Prime Minister's Office in October stated that "the issues raised ... are under consideration by the appropriate policy making bodies".

# BAHRAIN

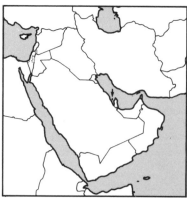

Approximately 70 political prisoners, including possible prisoners of conscience, who had been sentenced after unfair trials in previous years remained in prison throughout 1992. Three people accused of membership of an unauthorized political organization were sentenced to prison terms by the Supreme Civil Court of Appeal, whose procedures fall short of international human rights standards. Scores of Bahraini nationals were forcibly exiled, apparently for exercising their right to freedom of opinion and expression, although restrictions preventing the return of more than 120 others were lifted.

The State Security Measures of 1974, which permit administrative detention without charge or trial for renewable periods of up to three years (see *Amnesty International Report 1990*), remained in force. However, they were rarely applied in 1992. Several members of the majority Shi'a Muslim community were detained under this law, but in contrast to previous years they were released within several days and no reports of torture were received.

About 70 political prisoners, including possible prisoners of conscience, who had been sentenced after unfair trials in previous years remained in prison throughout 1992. Almost all were held in connection with banned Islamic groups such as *Hizbollah*, Party of God, and the Islamic Front for the Liberation of Bahrain. Among them were Salah al-Khawaja, serving a seven-year sentence, who was arrested in Saudi Arabia in 1988 and handed over to the Bahraini authorities; and Mohammad Jamil 'Abd al-Amir al-Jamri and 'Abd al-

Jalil Khalil Ibrahim, who were sentenced in March 1990 to 10 and seven years' imprisonment respectively (see *Amnesty International Reports 1989* to *1991*). Charges against all three included membership of an unauthorized organization. About 50 of the long-term political prisoners were serving 15 or 25 years' imprisonment, imposed after an unfair trial, in connection with an alleged coup attempt in 1981 (see *Amnesty International Reports 1989* to *1991*).

The trial of 11 alleged members of the banned Islamic Front for the Liberation of Bahrain resumed in February (see *Amnesty International Report 1992*). Hearings took place before the Supreme Civil Court of Appeal, whose procedures allow for convictions based solely on defendants' confessions and provide for no right of appeal. The group on trial were arrested in June 1990; most were reportedly tortured or ill-treated to make them confess while held in prolonged incommunicado detention. In October 1991 all were released on bail. The prosecution reportedly demanded the death penalty for Sadiq Ja'far Mohammad 'Ali. In December the court sentenced him to three years' imprisonment on charges of membership of an unauthorized political organization and inviting others to join it. Two others were sentenced to one year's imprisonment; the remaining eight defendants were acquitted.

In May Dr 'Abd al-Latif Mahmoud Al Mahmoud, a Sunni scholar and associate professor of Islamic studies, was acquitted of charges related to a lecture about the Gulf Cooperation Council which he had given in Kuwait (see *Amnesty International Report 1992*). He had been detained for two weeks in December 1991 on his return to Bahrain.

Scores of Bahraini nationals resident abroad were refused entry when attempting to return to Bahrain. Following interrogation on arrival at the airport, they were forcibly exiled from the country. They included Dr 'Abd al-Hadi Khalaf, a research fellow at the Human Rights Program of the University of Lund in Sweden. However, two amnesties were declared by the Amir of Bahrain, al-Sheikh 'Isa Bin Sulman Al Khalifa, in April and June, allowing the return of a total of 121 Bahraini nationals living abroad, although the identities of those concerned were not made public. Following these amnesties, those who were allowed to return to Bahrain included

some of the families of 73 political prisoners sentenced in connection with an alleged coup attempt in 1981, many of whom had fled to Iran or Syria at the time.

Amnesty International expressed concern to the government about cases of detentions and forcible exile. It welcomed the government's decision to permit some Bahraini exiles to return but remained concerned about the continuing forcible exile of others. The Interior Minister responded on most cases, providing details and offering assurances of Bahrain's commitment to human rights.

At the end of 1991 Amnesty International had been planning to send a delegation to Bahrain early in 1992 in response to an invitation from the Minister of the Interior (see *Amnesty International Report 1992*). However, the Minister indicated that it was not convenient for the visit to take place in January, as proposed, and that he would "be in touch . . . concerning the matter in due course". No further communication on this was received from the government and the proposed visit, to discuss Amnesty International's concerns, had not taken place by the end of the year.

In April Amnesty International submitted information about its concerns in Bahrain for United Nations review under a procedure, established by Economic and Social Council Resolutions 728F/1503, for confidential consideration of communications about human rights violations.

# BANGLADESH

**Hundreds of prisoners of conscience and other political prisoners were among over 1,700 people illegally detained under the Special Powers Act (SPA). Torture continued to be widespread, resulting in at least 12 deaths in police custody. At least six people were reportedly extrajudicially executed by the paramilitary Bangladesh Rifles (BDR). In the Chittagong Hill Tracts, over 100 tribal civilians were reported to have been extrajudicially executed in April by the security forces. At least 66 people were sentenced to death between early 1991 and September 1992. Four people were executed during 1992.**

Political and criminal violence continued at a high level throughout the year.

More than 25,000 people were arrested during an anti-crime campaign called "Operation August 92", but about 22,000 were released within days for lack of evidence.

The trials on criminal charges of former President Hossain Mohammad Ershad and several other former government ministers and officials continued. A parliamentary standing committee reviewed charges brought against political activists during the nine-year rule of President Ershad, most of whom had been freed on bail. The committee recommended withdrawing charges in 103 cases, and by September 91 cases had been withdrawn. Home Ministry sources said in March that over 6,000 people could benefit from the continuing review process.

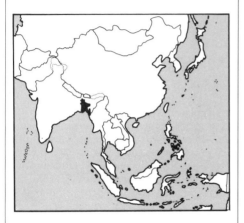

In July the Presidential Security Force Ordinance (Amendment) Act was passed, granting legal immunity to security personnel if they shoot to kill anyone believed to endanger the security of the prime minister.

In September President Abdur Rahman Biswas promulgated the Curbing of Terrorist Activities Ordinance, which extended the use of the death penalty. It also provided for the establishment of special tribunals which can impose the death penalty in trials that fall short of international standards in several respects, including restrictions on the rights of the defence. The offences listed as "terrorist" which the tribunals are to try and which carry the death penalty include obstructing or diverting traffic and damaging vehicles or property. In September, 65 courts were set up, but no death sentences were known to have been passed by them during 1992.

Parliament passed a bill based on the Ordinance in November.

The government of Prime Minister Begum Khaleda Zia appointed a committee in July to negotiate a political solution in the Chittagong Hill Tracts. In August the *Shanti Bahini* (Peace Force), the armed group seeking autonomy for the area, declared a unilateral cease-fire. Talks between the government and tribal representatives began in November. Abuses of human rights by *Shanti Bahini* forces were reported during the year.

Members of the Rohingya minority group continued to flee widespread human rights violations in Myanmar, and by December the number of refugees in Bangladesh exceeded 260,000. In April an agreement was signed with Myanmar providing for the safe and voluntary return of refugees, but refugees resisted repatriation and insisted that the United Nations High Commissioner for Refugees (UNHCR) should monitor the repatriation process. From September onwards, over 2,000 refugees were repatriated to Myanmar, many of them reportedly against their will and without UNHCR involvement.

The SPA was used extensively to detain suspected government opponents, including hundreds of prisoners of conscience. The SPA empowers the authorities to detain without charge or trial for an indefinitely renewable period anyone suspected of committing a "prejudicial act" likely or intended "to endanger public safety or the maintenance of public order". The Home Minister stated in June that 5,120 people had been detained under the SPA since July 1991, of whom 2,538 were still in detention. Between August 1991 and July 1992, the High Court ruled that SPA detention orders were illegal in 1,742 cases. At least four detainees reportedly continued to be held by the authorities despite High Court orders for their release.

Torture in police and military custody continued to be reported. At least two journalists were beaten by riot police when they took photographs during a demonstration in July. About 50 other journalists were injured, some seriously, when police broke into the National Press Club in Dhaka, the capital, on the same day and opened fire. A commission of inquiry identified seven police officials responsible for the incident, and recommended that they be given exemplary punishment. It was not known if any criminal proceedings were initiated against them.

At least 12 people were reported to have died as a result of torture, among them Mominuddin Ahmed who was arrested on 18 August by police in Rangpur. During a court hearing the next day he told his wife that he had been severely kicked in the chest and stomach. He died on 1 September in Rangpur Medical College Hospital. A post-mortem established that he had died of "shock as a result of perforation [of the stomach] ... and intracranial haemorrhage". No investigation into his death was known to have been initiated.

At least six people were reportedly extrajudicially executed by the paramilitary BDR in three separate incidents. On 10 July a BDR party seized cattle in Ramchandrapur which they claimed were smuggled. When the owners protested, the BDR opened fire and killed Monirul Islam, aged 16, and wounded a bystander.

Tribal people in the Chittagong Hill Tracts continued to be subjected to torture, illegal detention under the SPA and extrajudicial executions. On 10 April over 100 tribal people were reportedly killed in Logang, apparently in reprisal for the killing of a Bengali boy by *Shanti Bahini* fighters. Paramilitary security forces reportedly set fire to the village and shot dead those attempting to escape. The BDR arrived later, but reportedly did not attempt to stop the killing. The government later admitted that 12 tribal villagers were killed and 13 injured in the incident by paramilitary forces acting together with Bengali civilians. An official inquiry confirmed these figures. Some of those apparently responsible for the extrajudicial executions were said to be in custody but it was not known whether any of them had been prosecuted by the end of 1992.

According to official sources, 114 people were on death row in September, of whom 66 had been sentenced to death since early 1991. Four people were reportedly executed, three of them for murder.

In March Amnesty International was informed by the government that arrest warrants against eight police officers had been issued in connection with the death of a prisoner in police custody in Mymensingh in 1990.

Amnesty International expressed its concern to the government in January and May about the renewed use of the death penalty. In a report published in April, *Bangladesh: Reports of torture and possible extrajudicial executions*, Amnesty International described how in 1991 at least 10 people died and more than 100 were injured as a result of unlawful or unnecessary use of force by security personnel. In May Amnesty International published a report, *Bangladesh: Reprisal killings in Logang, Chittagong Hill Tracts, in April 1992*, and called for a full and impartial inquiry into the incident. Amnesty International repeatedly urged the government to ensure that none of the Rohingya refugees in Bangladesh would be forcibly returned to Myanmar, and that effective international monitoring of returning refugees would be provided. In July the organization urged the government to investigate the ill-treatment of journalists in the Dhaka Press Club.

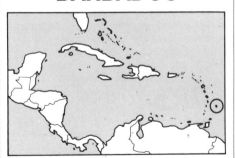

# BARBADOS

**One person died apparently as a result of ill-treatment in police custody. At least one person was sentenced to be flogged but corporal punishment was declared unconstitutional by the Court of Appeal. Two prisoners had execution dates set but they were granted stays of execution. At least three death sentences were passed during the year. Sixteen people were under sentence of death at the end of the year.**

In April 17-year-old Ryan Jordan died three days after being arrested by police on suspicion of theft. He died in hospital as a result of injuries allegedly sustained while under interrogation in police custody. Information from various sources, including a post-mortem report, pointed to a severe beating while in detention as the most likely cause of the injuries leading to his death. Officials stated that his death

**64** would be investigated, but little or no progress appeared to have been made by the end of the year.

A man convicted of rape was sentenced in April to 28 years' imprisonment and the maximum 24 strokes with the cat-o'-nine-tails (a device of nine knotted cords or hide thongs attached to a handle). However, in August the Appeal Court upheld the appeals of two men who had been sentenced to flogging with the cat-o'-nine-tails in 1991. The court ruled that flogging constituted "inhuman and degrading punishment", in contravention of Barbados' Constitution. The prison sentences of the two men were increased by five years to 15 and 20 years instead.

Peter Bradshaw and Denzil Roberts, sentenced to death in 1985 and 1986 respectively, were scheduled to be executed on 25 May. There had been no executions since 1984. Lawyers submitted a constitutional motion on their behalf and they were granted a stay of execution at a rare Sunday sitting of the High Court. The constitutional motion was dismissed in September and the court granted a six-week stay of execution pending further appeals to the Court of Appeal. Appeals were still pending at the end of the year.

Three people were sentenced to death in May on conviction of a murder committed in 1991.

In May Amnesty International wrote to the Minister of Justice and Public Safety about the death of Ryan Jordan. It called for a thorough, independent and impartial investigation and for those responsible for the death to be brought to justice. In June the Minister replied stating that "in this case as in all others in Barbados, the law will take its course with thoroughness, independence and impartiality".

Amnesty International wrote to the Governor General, Dame Nita Barrow, and the Prime Minister, Erskine Sandiford, in June. It expressed its grave concern at the attempt to resume executions. It welcomed the stays granted to Peter Bradshaw and Denzil Roberts and urged the government to introduce legislation to narrow the use of the death penalty as a first step towards abolition. It also urged that all death sentences be commuted. Acknowledgements were received from the Governor General's and Prime Minister's offices in June; Amnesty International was informed that its concerns were receiving consideration.

# BELARUS

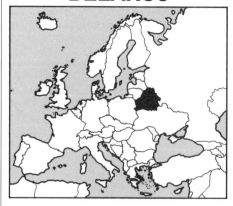

**Belarus retained the death penalty for 16 peacetime offences. Twenty-four people were sentenced to death. Three death sentences were commuted and 28 people were executed.**

Belarus became an independent state, headed by Supreme Soviet Chairman Stanislav Shushkevich, following the break-up of the Soviet Union. The country, already a member of the United Nations, joined the Conference on Security and Co-operation in Europe in January.

By the end of the year parliament had still not debated proposed revisions to the criminal code which would reduce the scope of the death penalty to four offences: premeditated, aggravated murder; aggravated rape; kidnapping of a child; and acts of terrorism with aggravated circumstances.

Twenty-four people were sentenced to death during the year and 28 executions were carried out. Three death sentences were commuted. All death sentences and executions were believed to be for premeditated, aggravated murder.

Amnesty International repeatedly urged the authorities to take steps towards abolition of the death penalty, and to impose a moratorium on death sentences and executions.

# BELIZE

**Two people were sentenced to death and two others remained under sentence of death. In two cases death sentences were overturned on appeal. No executions were carried out.**

Francisco Conorquie was sentenced to death for murder in May and lodged an appeal with the Court of Appeal.

In September the Court of Appeal set aside the death sentences of two people convicted of murder in April, Abel Martinez and Roberto Galeano Aguilar, on the grounds that the trial judge had misdirected the jury. The court ordered a retrial in the case of Abel Martinez and Roberto Galeano Aguilar was freed.

Catalino O'Niel and Dean Vasquez had been sentenced to death for murder in 1991. An appeal to the Judicial Committee of the Privy Council (JCPC) in London, the final court of appeal for Belize, was submitted on behalf of both men, after all other legal avenues had been exhausted (see *Amnesty International Report 1992*). Leave to appeal was first denied by the JCPC in both cases, but this decision was later reversed and the two prisoners were granted leave to appeal only days before the scheduled execution in October of Dean Vasquez. The appeals were still pending at the end of the year.

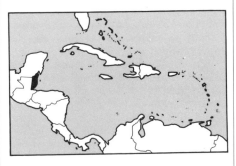

In September the Court of Appeal dismissed an appeal by Ellis Taibo, convicted and sentenced to death in August for rape and murder. Ellis Taibo applied for commutation of his sentence to the Advisory Council, which advises the Governor General on the exercise of the prerogative of mercy.

In October Amnesty International wrote to the Governor General, Dr Dame Minita E. Gordon, urging that the death sentences on Dean Vasquez and Catalino O'Niel be commuted. Amnesty International also called for the commutation of all death sentences and the abolition of the death penalty in Belize.

# BENIN

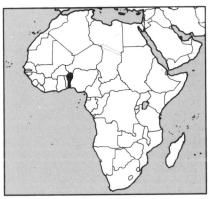

**At least 18 government opponents, including students, were detained for short periods and several received suspended prison sentences. Among them were possible prisoners of conscience. A group of soldiers were detained without charge for over six months in connection with an alleged coup attempt. One detainee died in custody reportedly as a result of torture.**

Benin acceded to the International Covenant on Economic, Social and Cultural Rights in January and in March to both the International Covenant on Civil and Political Rights and the Convention against Torture and Other Cruel, Inhuman or Degrading Treatment or Punishment.

The government of President Nicéphore Soglo made no attempt to investigate or bring to justice officials who had been responsible for human rights violations while former President Mathieu Kérékou was in power between 1972 and 1990 (see previous *Amnesty International Reports*). However, 10 associates of the former head of state were tried on corruption charges and convicted. Amadou Mohammed Cissé, a Malian religious figure who had been a close adviser to President Kérékou and was widely seen as having influenced his government's repressive policies, was sentenced to 10 years' imprisonment for embezzlement. Seven of the 10 received prison sentences of between two and eight years, and the remaining two were given suspended prison sentences and released.

Two former senior security officials associated with President Kérékou's government were detained throughout the year but were not brought to trial. Jean N'Tcha

**66**

and Fousséni Seïdou Gomina had been arrested in August 1991. It had initially appeared that their arrest was connected to a formal complaint about the death of a prisoner in 1984 (see *Amnesty International Report 1992*). However, in 1992 it became clear that both faced charges of murder and theft in connection with other offences allegedly committed in 1984 while they were security officials. Jean N'Tcha faced additional charges of carrying out illegal arrests, and Fousséni Seïdou Gomina was also apparently suspected of organizing, while in jail, an alleged coup attempt in May 1992.

The authorities faced widespread opposition during the year, including demonstrations against taxes, student unrest, and an army mutiny in August which was rapidly quashed. Most of those arrested in connection with the protests were referred promptly for investigation by the procuracy and most of those convicted received suspended prison sentences. However, there were important exceptions.

François Comlan, a journalist, was sentenced in May to six months' imprisonment after writing an article alleging financial irregularities in President Soglo's 1991 election campaign. He lodged an appeal against his conviction and remained free on bail pending appeal. If imprisoned he would be a prisoner of conscience.

Student unrest led to the arrest and conviction of students, some of whom may have been prisoners of conscience. In March a meeting of university students in Cotonou was broken up by the police on the grounds that it was unauthorized. Four students addressing the meeting were arrested. They were held for three days before being released pending trial. In April they were convicted of various acts of violence and received three-month suspended prison sentences. It was unclear if they had in fact used or advocated violence. Another student from Cotonou, Benoît Sossou, was detained for two months before being given a six-month suspended prison sentence for acts of violence. Again, it was not clear if he had used or advocated violence. One other student was held for three weeks from March and charged with assaulting an official. He was released on bail and had not been tried by the end of the year.

A group of military officers arrested in May in connection with an alleged coup attempt the same month were still held without charge at the end of the year. However, seven of those arrested escaped from Ouidah barracks during the army mutiny in August.

Three people arrested in May 1991 (see *Amnesty International Report 1992*) on suspicion of distributing a tract criticizing divisions between the north and the south of the country were tried in May. All received suspended prison sentences. An appeal against their conviction had not been heard by the end of the year.

The two remaining prisoners still held in connection with protests during the March 1991 presidential election (see *Amnesty International Report 1992*) were brought to trial in mid-1992. They were each sentenced to 20 years' imprisonment after being convicted of organizing acts of violence. The sentence was reduced to 10 years in a general measure of clemency.

Célestin Ongala, a Zairian refugee, was arrested in May and held incommunicado for two months without charge. He was apparently suspected of involvement in the bombing of an aircraft in neighbouring Niger several years earlier. Although not formally charged, he was released provisionally in July while inquiries into his case continued.

One prisoner died in detention reportedly as a result of torture. Gbea Orou Sianni was among at least seven people arrested in March and taken to the central police station in Kandi, in the north of the country, after participating in a demonstration against police corruption during which a police officer was injured. Others were arrested and taken to the gendarmerie offices in Segbane. Gbea Orou Sianni died shortly afterwards allegedly as a result of torture. No investigation was believed to have been carried out into his death. Two of the seven were held briefly and released; two were tried and received 10-month prison sentences for injuries caused to the police officer; and the others remained held awaiting trial on similar charges.

Amnesty International sought clarification of the legal basis for the continued detention without charge of those suspected of involvement in the alleged May coup attempt and urged that any who did not face criminal charges should be released without delay. It also urged the authorities to initiate an independent inquiry into the death in custody of Gbea Orou Sianni.

# BHUTAN

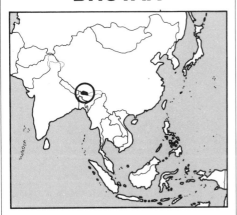

A prisoner of conscience, a former adviser to the King, remained in detention throughout the year. Around 150 political detainees, all Nepali-speaking people arrested in 1992 and previous years, remained held without charge or trial at the end of the year. Thirty-two others, all suspected of violent "anti-national" activities, were convicted of treason and jailed after a trial which may have been unfair. At least one detainee died in custody owing to inadequate medical treatment. There were reports of torture, ill-treatment and generally harsh prison conditions. The government took a number of steps to improve human rights.

Unrest continued in southern parts of the country, where groups of Nepali-speaking people continued to oppose the government policy of national integration on the basis of *driglam namzha* (northern Bhutanese traditions and culture), the application of the 1985 Citizenship Act and the carrying out of a census (see previous *Amnesty International Reports*). By the end of the year, more than 70,000 Nepali-speaking people had fled to Nepal. Among them were many who had been classified as illegal immigrants during the census. Many refugees said that they had been forced to leave by local officials or that they had left out of fear of falling victim to human rights violations by government security forces. Certain opposition groups, including the Bhutan People's Party (BPP), were allegedly responsible for torturing, killing and kidnapping civilians, including government officials and people suspected of being government informers.

Towards the end of the year, the government took a number of steps to improve the human rights situation. A new National Security Act, replacing the Law of Treason, made the death penalty an optional rather than a mandatory punishment for crimes against the state. The government also banned the use of shackles in prisons, gave relatives access to prisoners and invited the International Committee of the Red Cross to visit Bhutan periodically.

Tek Nath Rizal, one of six prisoners of conscience arrested in late 1989 for allegedly initiating unrest among the Nepali-speaking population (see *Amnesty International Report 1992*), continued to be detained without trial. On 29 December he was charged with nine offences, including acts against national security, although the real reason for his detention appeared to be his non-violent opposition to government policies. His trial was due to begin in January 1993. The two others who remained held without charge or trial at the start of the year, Jogen Gazmere and Sushil Pokhrel, were among 313 political prisoners released in an amnesty announced by King Jigme Singye Wangchuck in February. By the end of the year, the King had ordered the release of 530 detainees in amnesties.

Scores of people of Nepali origin were arrested during 1992 on suspicion of supporting or sympathizing with southern opposition groups engaged in violent activities. In May, 41 prisoners were brought to trial before the Thimphu High Court on charges of treason, including four *in absentia*. One of them was sentenced to life imprisonment, 31 were sentenced to prison terms ranging between nine months and just over 10 years, and five were acquitted after a trial which may have been unfair. The four tried *in absentia* had not been sentenced by the end of the year. Around 150 political detainees remained held without charge or trial at the end of 1992, about half of whom had been detained for more than two years. The large majority of them were detained at Chemgang detention camp near Thimphu; the place of detention of others remained unknown. Deo Datta Sharma, who had been detained at Wangdi Phodrang prison, was transferred to another place of detention on 31 December 1991. The government has since refused to reveal his precise whereabouts.

Torture, ill-treatment and generally poor

**68**

conditions in prison camps were reported. Several former prisoners alleged that conditions at Chemgang detention camp were particularly harsh. They said that all prisoners there were forced to do hard labour, even when ill, and that guards routinely beat prisoners. In early January one political prisoner, H.P. Sapkota, was seen being taken to Thimphu Hospital in shackles and in a very weak condition. After several months of conflicting reports as to his fate, the government finally confirmed in July that H.P. Sapkota had died from typhoid. An independent doctor who studied the medical records for Amnesty International concluded that inadequate diet or poor prison conditions may have contributed to his illness and that H.P. Sapkota appeared to have been given "inappropriate and ineffectual medical care". The government admitted that normal procedures for informing the next of kin of his death had not been followed.

An Amnesty International delegation visited Bhutan for the first time in January. The delegates met the King and government officials to discuss human rights. They also visited Samchi District in southern Bhutan but were not permitted to go to Chirang District for "security reasons". The delegates were also refused permission to visit places of detention. They met former prisoners of conscience and other victims of human rights violations, as well as people affected by opposition violence. In June the government refused Amnesty International permission to observe the trial of 41 political prisoners charged with treason.

During the year Amnesty International called for the release of prisoner of conscience Tek Nath Rizal and urged the authorities to try or release other political detainees. It also urged the government to introduce safeguards to prevent torture and ill-treatment in prison camps. Amnesty International welcomed the steps taken by the government to improve human rights.

In December Amnesty International published a report, *Bhutan – Human rights violations against the Nepali-speaking population in the south*, which documented the organization's concerns since 1990 and made several concrete recommendations for safeguarding human rights.

# BOLIVIA

**There were new allegations of torture and ill-treatment of political detainees by the police. Some peasants and indigenous leaders were reported to have been arbitrarily detained and ill-treated by the narcotics police. Two people were alleged to have been extrajudicially executed by police. The trial of a former president for past human rights violations continued. No official investigations were carried out into alleged torture and extrajudicial executions in previous years.**

There were hunger-strikes and long-running work stoppages in the first half of the year to protest against the privatization of the country's mines and the government's announcement that it would use the army to control coca leaf growing areas. Miners, trade unionists and university students were arrested in January and April for short periods, following demonstrations that were violently dispersed by the police. In May the police forcibly dispersed a peaceful demonstration in the capital, La Paz, called to mark the World Week on Forcible Disappearances by mothers and relatives of people who had "disappeared" during past military governments.

Dozens of people were arrested and some allegedly tortured by police in the context of a police offensive against the armed group, *Ejército Guerrillero Tupaj Katari* (EGTK), Tupaj Katari Guerrilla Army. No official investigation was opened into the allegations of torture. The EGTK admitted responsibility for several bomb attacks on economic targets around the country, in which three civilians were killed.

Among those arrested on suspicion of supporting the EGTK and allegedly tortured were Silvya María Renée De Alarcón and her husband José Raúl García Linera. They were arrested by security agents in La Paz in March, handcuffed, hooded and taken to police installations where they were held incommunicado for 17 days. According to their testimonies, they were kept in separate rooms and forced to stand for several hours in a contorted position known as the "pig", while being beaten on the hips and buttocks. They were both threatened with their partner's torture and José Raúl García Linera was threatened with the rape of his wife and himself. They both stated that a state prosecutor was present during most of the interrogation and torture.

Another couple, Alvaro García Linera and his Mexican wife, María Raquel Gutiérrez Aguilar, were arrested in April in La Paz. In her testimony María Raquel Gutiérrez Aguilar stated that after her arrest she was taken to Ministry of the Interior premises where for about four days she was kept hooded, handcuffed and, for several hours at a time, made to stand in the "pig" position while being whipped, subjected to electric shocks in the genitals, neck and ears and threatened with her husband's torture. While still in incommunicado detention and the day before she was presented to a judge, María Raquel Gutiérrez Aguilar tried to commit suicide. Alvaro García Linera stated that he was kept hooded and handcuffed in Interior Ministry premises, where he was beaten, given electric shocks on the genitals and limbs for several hours at a time, and had nails driven into his toes and finger-nails.

Victor Ortiz, also detained in April in La Paz, testified that he was tortured while kept in incommunicado detention for three days at police installations controlled by the Ministry of the Interior. He was beaten all over his body while in the "pig" position, beaten on the soles of his feet while suspended by his legs and arms, and subjected to electric shocks on his testicles. Victor Ortiz' pregnant wife, four children and father-in-law were held under house arrest by the police in El Alto, a poor area of La Paz, for 14 days.

All those arrested in connection with the activities of the EGTK were charged with armed rebellion and terrorism. None had been tried by the end of the year.

Human rights violations against peasants and indigenous leaders committed by members of the *Unidad Movil de Patrulla Rural* (UMOPAR), Mobile Rural Patrol, a specialized narcotics branch of the police force, continued to be reported. In May Emilio Flores Corpa, a young coca leaf grower, was shot dead by members of the UMOPAR during a raid near Eterazama, Cochabamba Department, in circumstances suggesting he had been extrajudicially executed. Another peasant, Mario Ovando García, was reportedly seriously injured during the same raid. Dozens of peasants were arrested and released without charge a few days later. Officials stated that the shootings had taken place during a confrontation with drug-traffickers in the area. Leaders of the *Federación Especial de Trabajadores Campesinos del Trópico*, Tropical Peasant Workers' Union, denied the official version and alleged that members of UMOPAR had fired at the peasants as they ran off. The leaders demanded an investigation into the killing. By the end of the year, Amnesty International was not aware that any investigation had been initiated.

In June Aniceto Ervin and Adrian Nogales, two indigenous leaders of the Yuracaré ethnic group, were arrested by UMOPAR agents in Beni Department. Both men were taken to the army barracks at Chimoré, Cochabamba Department. The authorities stated that Aniceto Ervin had not been arrested but "invited for a talk" at the barracks, and that Adrian Nogales was being held in incommunicado detention until investigations were completed. Several days later the two men were released and returned to their communities. UMOPAR denied allegations that Adrian Nogales had been ill-treated by having his face drenched in kerosene to force him to confess to alleged links with drug-trafficking.

A man killed by the police in Santa Cruz in August was alleged to have been extrajudicially executed. According to official statements, Juan Carlos Melgar Estertary was killed in an armed confrontation with members of the police. His family publicly challenged the authorities' version after the official forensic certificate stated that the victim had been hit by eight bullets, some of them shot at close range, and that his body showed injuries consistent with torture. The family asked for an investigation into the killing but, as far as Amnesty International was aware, no investigation was opened.

The trial of former President General Luis García Meza and 54 co-defendants,

**70** known as the *Juicio de Responsabilidades* (responsibilities trial), continued in the Supreme Court. The charges against the accused include killing and torturing government opponents during the military government between July 1980 and August 1981 (see *Amnesty International Reports 1981* to *1983*). The trial was initiated in 1984. Following protracted delays, threats to the prosecution lawyers, the escape of General García Meza and the extradition to the United States of America of his Minister of the Interior, Luís Arce Gómez, the trial reached the stage of evaluation of the evidence (see *Amnesty International Report 1991*).

The government again failed to investigate allegations that political detainees had been tortured and extrajudicially executed in previous years. Amnesty International urged the government in July to initiate thorough and impartial investigations into all allegations of torture by the police and security forces, including those from 1989 and 1990 (see *Amnesty International Reports 1989* to *1992*). The organization also expressed concern about reports of torture and ill-treatment of detainees arrested in 1992 in connection with alleged links to armed groups.

The government told Amnesty International in September that complaints made by the independent Permanent Assembly of Human Rights that political detainees had been tortured were unreliable, as some of the detainees were also members of the human rights organization. All allegations of torture and ill-treatment of detainees were denied by the authorities.

In September Amnesty International sent an observer to attend hearings in the trial of former President General García Meza and 54 co-defendants.

In October Amnesty International published *Human rights violations against the indigenous peoples of the Americas*, which included concerns in Bolivia.

# BOSNIA-HERZEGOVINA

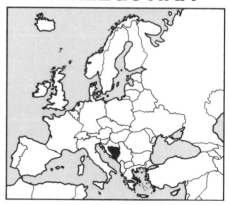

**Hundreds, probably thousands, of civilians and captured or wounded combatants were deliberately and arbitrarily killed in the course of armed conflict. Tens of thousands of people were detained in connection with the fighting, in most cases solely because of their ethnic origin, sometimes as hostages for exchange. Torture or other ill-treatment of detainees, including rape, was common. Although all sides in the conflict were responsible for abuses, the majority of victims were Muslims and the main perpetrators were local Serbian armed forces.**

Ethnic tensions increased in Bosnia-Herzegovina with the break-up of the Socialist Federal Republic of Yugoslavia following declarations of independence by the Republics of Slovenia and Croatia in June 1991, and subsequent armed conflict, largely on Croatian territory. Bosnia-Herzegovina's Serbian communities sought to remain within a Yugoslav federation while its Muslim and Croatian communities demanded independence. At the beginning of March open conflict flared up when a referendum, supported by Muslim and Croatian communities but largely boycotted by Serbian communities, favoured independence for the republic. By mid-March serious fighting had broken out. On 7 April the European Community (EC) and the United States of America recognized Bosnia-Herzegovina's independence. The same day, Serbian political leaders proclaimed the independence of "the Serbian Republic of Bosnia-Herzegovina" (areas of the republic under Serbian control). Fighting spread rapidly throughout Bosnia-Herzegovina. In April the Republic of Bosnia-Herzegovina was accepted as a participatory state in the Conference on Security and Co-operation in Europe and in May it became a member of the United Nations (UN).

Numerous members of the Yugoslav National Army (JNA) of Bosnian origin, as well as JNA supplies and arms, remained in the republic after the official withdrawal of the JNA in May. By December, together with mobilized local Serbian reservists and Serbian irregulars, they had occupied some 70 per cent of the republic's territory. Local Croatian forces, aided by forces of the Croatian Army and Croatian irregulars from the Republic of Croatia, established control over much of Herzegovina, proclaimed as the "Croatian Community of Herceg-Bosna". This led to sporadic clashes with Bosnian government forces, although the two were supposedly allied. The area of the republic over which the Bosnian Government had effective control declined throughout the year.

Vast numbers of civilians fled their local communities to escape the conflict; many were deliberately intimidated by their opponents into leaving. This was particularly evident in areas under Serbian control, where many Muslims and Croats were rounded up and forcibly expelled. The scale of human rights abuses and the obstacles to collecting evidence made it difficult to substantiate allegations of atrocities. The difficulty was compounded by media reports in which all sides sought to minimize abuses committed by their own forces and maximize those of their opponents. While all parties to the conflict committed abuses, it was clear that the Serbian side was responsible for the majority of atrocities committed and that Muslims were the chief victims. In August the UN Commission on Human Rights appointed a Special Rapporteur to investigate the human rights situation in former Yugoslavia, and in particular in Bosnia-Herzegovina. At the end of August a joint UN-EC International Conference on the former Yugoslavia was established, which tried to achieve a cessation of hostilities in Bosnia-Herzegovina and to bring the parties together to negotiate a new constitutional arrangement for the country. In October the UN Security Council set up a Commission of Experts to investigate war crimes committed in former Yugoslavia.

There were many reported incidents in which civilians and unarmed or wounded combatants were deliberately and arbitrarily killed. The Yugoslav news agency *Tanjug* reported that 15 members of five Serb families had been massacred by Croatian troops on the night of 26 to 27 March in the village of Sijekovac near Bosanski Brod. A Muslim fighting with Croatian forces who claimed to have taken part in this massacre and others described in a statement video-recorded while he was held prisoner in Yugoslavia how he and other soldiers had killed over 30 elderly villagers in their homes and had abducted and raped young women.

On 16 May at least 83 Muslims, including men, women and children, were massacred in the village of Zaklopača, near Vlasenica. According to eye-witnesses, the massacre was carried out by local uniformed Serbs who had previously surrounded the village. Some surviving eye-witnesses believed that as many as 105 people were killed.

In the town of Mostar on 13 June, according to the account of a surviving witness (a Muslim), Serbian forces rounded up some 150 people in his neighbourhood. After separating out the women, children and Serbs, they took the remaining men to the morgue at Sutina cemetery. While the witness was waiting to be questioned, he heard bursts of gunfire. After interrogation he and another prisoner were forced to carry the corpses of seven or eight men to a rubbish dump near the banks of the river Neretva. Their captors then fired on his companion; he himself escaped by throwing himself down an embankment. In August the police chief of the town of Mostar announced that 150 bodies had been found in mass graves, one of them in the Sutina quarter of town; a pathologist stated they had almost all been killed at close range.

At least 30 Muslim civilians were reportedly deliberately and arbitrarily killed in Bosanski Petrovac between 19 and 24 September when local Serbian soldiers returning to the town apparently took revenge for losses they had suffered on the front. On 22 October, 16 Muslims, including one woman, from Sjeverin village in the Sandžak region of Serbia were abducted by armed men while travelling to

**72**

work by bus across Serbian-held Bosnian territory. Another Muslim man from Sjeverin had been abducted the previous night. *Borba*, a Belgrade newspaper, citing military sources in Serbia, reported that they had been killed the same day by Serbian forces near Višegrad in Bosnia-Herzegovina. This was never confirmed. Two Serbian irregulars, described by Serbian military sources in Bosnia-Herzegovina as volunteers fighting under the command of the Višegrad brigade, were arrested in Serbian territory four days later but were soon released. By the end of the year the fate of the 17 remained unknown, despite the creation of a Yugoslav state commission to investigate their "disappearance".

Released Muslim prisoners stated that Serbs had deliberately and arbitrarily killed large numbers of prisoners, including civilians, detained in camps in Bosnia-Herzegovina. Not all these reports could be confirmed, but accounts from many former detainees agreed that in June and July prisoners were killed almost every night in Omarska camp. Many died after being clubbed to death by guards or by local Serbs who entered the camp at night. According to these accounts, on some nights as many as 30 men were killed. Detainees were also reportedly killed in other camps, including Keraterm, Manjača and Trnopolje. There were also allegations that Serbian prisoners had been killed by their captors. Serbian sources alleged that at least five men held by Bosnian government forces in a place of detention near Konjic died as a result of beatings between mid-June and late July.

Thousands of non-combatants, the majority Muslims, were arbitrarily detained in connection with the conflict, in most cases solely because of their ethnic origin, sometimes as hostages for exchange. In May all parties agreed to give the International Committee of the Red Cross (ICRC) access to detention centres, but there continued to be unacknowledged places of detention, ranging from cellars in private houses to factories and school-halls. From September onwards considerable numbers of detainees were released, mostly under the supervision of the ICRC. Arbitrary detention was sometimes accompanied by forced expulsion, particularly in areas under Serbian control. For example, on 26 June local Serbs and irregulars from Serbia detained Muslim families in the village of Kozluk

and forced them at gunpoint to board a convoy of lorries which took them to Loznica in Serbia. From there they were taken by train to the Hungarian border, where Serbian police issued them with passports before they crossed into Hungary.

Many detainees were tortured or ill-treated in detention centres, and conditions often amounted to cruel, inhuman or degrading treatment. In June large numbers of Muslim and Croat civilian men were detained by Serbian forces in the area of Bosanski Novi; witnesses believed that prominent and better-educated members of the local community had been targeted for detention and interrogation. Villagers from Blagaj were rounded up and transported en masse: women, children and men over 60 were subsequently expelled into Muslim-controlled territory. Several hundred men were held in a football stadium at Mlakve, and individuals were held in Bosanski Novi town, in places such as the police station and a hotel. All witnesses reported that detainees were routinely beaten with truncheons and rifle butts. Former detainees often reported that prisoners were not only beaten, but were also deliberately humiliated and degraded in other ways. For example, prisoners detained by Serbian forces in Keraterm, a ceramics factory near Prijedor, in June and July, alleged that men were forced to perform sexual acts with each other. Almost all accounts indicated that prisoners were severely underfed in camps, and that in some cases, for instance at Omarska, Manjača and Trnopolje, this amounted to near-starvation. Serbs held by Muslim forces similarly reported that they were subjected to regular beatings and other cruel, inhuman or degrading treatment. Among them was Milan Šobić, a Serbian journalist, who in July was reportedly severely beaten by Muslim irregulars and military police in Zenica. The available evidence indicated that all sides to the conflict raped female prisoners, including young girls, and in some cases kept selected women prisoners in conditions amounting to brothels for the use of the military and police, but the majority of victims were Muslim women held by local Serbian armed forces.

Amnesty International repeatedly called on all parties to the conflict to release all civilians detained solely because of their national origin, and for an end to deliberate and arbitrary killings and the torture and ill-treatment of detainees. It urged all parties to provide information to relatives and international organizations on the whereabouts and fate of people who "disappeared" after being detained by military, paramilitary or police forces. Amnesty International also urged that full and impartial investigations into human rights abuses be carried out and that the perpetrators be brought to justice. In oral statements to the first and second special sessions of the UN Commission on Human Rights in August and November, Amnesty International urged that a substantial on-site human rights investigative and monitoring operation be established. In October the organization published a report, *Bosnia-Herzegovina: Gross abuses of basic human rights*.

# BOTSWANA

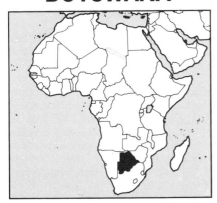

**Government officials allegedly tortured members of the Basarwa (Bushman) ethnic group who were detained unlawfully for poaching.**

The Basarwa are the aboriginal inhabitants of large areas of Botswana and other parts of southern Africa. Their economy is based on hunting and gathering and they are socially disadvantaged compared with the majority Batswana, who are settled agriculturalists.

In March the Botswana Christian Council reported that Basarwa men who were alleged to have poached wild animals had been victims of widespread torture by officials of the Department of Wildlife and National Parks (DWNP). The officials were said to have routinely placed a rubber ring tightly around each prisoner's testicles and

a plastic bag over the head. The pain would cause the victim to excrete involuntarily and the prisoner would then be beaten. It was alleged that Basarwa arrested by DWNP officials were detained without charge, unlawfully, for periods of up to two weeks, before being brought before a magistrate and charged with poaching.

In September Amnesty International wrote to the authorities calling for an independent investigation into allegations of torture and unlawful detention of Basarwa and for those responsible to be brought to justice. The government replied in November, saying that investigations had been held but had found no evidence of discrimination or torture against Basarwa.

# BRAZIL

**Military police killed 111 prisoners while quelling a disturbance in a São Paulo prison: many were apparently extrajudicially executed. Hundreds of street children were killed and others ill-treated by death squads and the police. There were new reports of torture and ill-treatment of people in police custody, in some cases leading to death. Human rights workers and others received death threats. Rural leaders, peasants and members of indigenous communities continued to suffer death threats and attempts on their lives and some were ill-treated by the police.**

In December President Fernando Collor de Mello resigned shortly before he was impeached by the Senate on grounds of corruption. Vice-President Itamar Franco was then appointed President: he had been acting President since early October when President Collor was suspended from office pending impeachment proceedings.

In January Brazil acceded to both the International Covenant on Civil and Political Rights and the International Covenant on Economic, Social and Cultural Rights, and in September to the American Convention on Human Rights.

On 2 October 111 prisoners were killed and 35 others wounded at the House of Detention in São Paulo, after military police were called in to quell a disturbance in Block 9. Evidence from prison staff suggested that the police invasion was ordered before negotiations with the prisoners had been attempted. The then Secretary of

**74**

Public Security reportedly told the press that in cases of such disturbances, police are ordered to shoot to kill and that there was nothing absurd about police using machine-guns against prisoners. Police alleged that the prisoners had guns, but this was denied by inmates. A Ministry of Justice investigation into the killings suggested that firearms later found in the prison had been "planted" by military police.

An Amnesty International delegation, including a forensic doctor, interviewed and examined surviving prisoners and inspected cells in Block 9. They found considerable evidence to suggest that the majority of prisoners had been extrajudicially executed after surrendering. The evidence was also consistent with survivors' testimonies that their cell-mates had been killed while lying or sitting down with hands on or behind their heads. Survivors

said they had been forced to strip and run a gauntlet of police, who beat them. Some had also been bitten by police dogs. A number of the wounded were allegedly told they were being taken for treatment and were then extrajudicially executed. Some survivors hid among the dead bodies: police bayoneted the bodies and allegedly shot those who cried out. Some prisoners who were ordered to collect the bodies from the cells were allegedly executed subsequently.

Several official inquiries were set up to investigate the massacre. An investigation by the Federal Ministry of Justice's Human Rights Council concluded in December that "the military police killed 111 people in state custody without any justification". It said this was "a natural result of the violent public security policy of the government of

São Paulo" in which summary executions, arbitrary aggression and torture were part of police working methods. The São Paulo state legislature concluded that there were some "excesses" by the military police, but no massacre. However, military police, who are answerable only to special military courts, have rarely been successfully prosecuted for fatal shootings. Official figures reported 1,264 fatal shootings by military police in São Paulo in the first nine months of 1992. Amnesty International was concerned about reports that many of these killings may have been extrajudicial executions. A number of the officers commanding the police operation at the House of Detention had reportedly been implicated in previous multiple summary killings on the streets and in detention centres without being convicted or losing rank. The use of lethal force to quash prison disturbances is common practice in Brazil and Amnesty International was not aware of any cases where those responsible for death in such circumstances had been convicted.

In February, seven prisoners were killed by military police shock troops at the Aníbal Bruno prison in Recife, Pernambuco, during a police operation to regain control of the prison from rioting inmates who had killed a hostage. At least some of the seven prisoners were killed in circumstances suggesting that they may have been extrajudicially executed after surrender.

Hundreds of street children were killed by the police or by death squads which often included off-duty police officers. Hundreds of others were ill-treated. A report by a Parliamentary Commission of Inquiry of the Federal Chamber of Deputies stated that civil and military police participation in the killing of children and adolescents was "far from exceptional".

The authorities indicated that between January and July, 667 children and adolescents were killed in the states of São Paulo and Rio de Janeiro alone. During the year the Federal Police reported that 4,611 children and adolescents had been killed between 1988 and 1990, of whom 82 per cent were black. In many cases no police inquiry was completed or sent to the judiciary.

On 5 May Erivan José da Silva, aged 14, and José Fernandes de Almeida, aged 15, were forced off their bicycles and into a car in the town of Lagarto, Sergipe, by three men, two of whom were allegedly military police officers. Witnesses said that one of the abductors shouted that this was the last time the children would be seen alive. The bodies of Erivan José da Silva and José Fernandes de Almeida were found the following evening under a bridge on a road between Lagarto and São Domingos. Their hands were tied behind their backs and both had been shot three times. One of the military police officers allegedly involved was detained shortly afterwards, but later escaped. Another officer and a civilian were detained and remained in police custody awaiting trial at the end of the year.

In April Roberto Carlos da Costa, aged 18, was detained by a military police patrol in São Paulo city, on suspicion of robbery. He was reportedly beaten and given electric shocks in the patrol car to make him reveal the whereabouts of goods he had allegedly stolen. The beatings lasted for several hours. He was then taken to Police District 70, where he was allegedly subjected to further beatings and electric shocks. The day after his release, Roberto Carlos da Costa denounced the torture and beatings to the Public Prosecutor for Children and Adolescents of São Paulo, and was medically examined. A police inquiry into the incident was opened but no progress was reported. In August Roberto Carlos da Costa told a human rights worker that he had been shot at from an unidentified black car. On 10 September he went missing together with a friend, 16-year-old Natalino José Batista. Neither was seen again. Their relatives searched for them in hospitals, police stations and relatives' homes without success.

On 11 November, 13-year-old Jean Alves da Cunha, a local leader in the National Movement of Street Boys and Girls in Espirito Santo, and other street children were detained by four Justice Officers attached to the Juvenile Court. All were questioned and released that afternoon. Jean Alves da Cunha, however, was reportedly rearrested the same evening. Two days later his body was found dumped on a hill in the city, with two gunshot wounds in the head. A few weeks before his killing, Jean Alves da Cunha had expressed fear for his life after he had publicly accused the police of forcing street children to commit crimes and share the proceeds with them. A police inquiry into his death was initiated in late 1992.

Deaths, torture and ill-treatment of people in police custody were reported. In April Luiz Alexandre da Silva, a builder, was detained by the São Paulo state military police near his home in Itapevi. Three hours later he was taken to the Itapevi police station, which is run by civil police, where he later died. An autopsy by the official Legal Medical Institute reportedly found multiple bruises, superficial injuries to the limbs and extensive internal bleeding caused by the rupture of the heart and major blood vessels. A police inquiry was opened into the case.

Human rights workers and people who denounced human rights violations were repeatedly threatened with death. In January the mothers of some of the 11 people, including six minors, who had been abducted in July 1990 from a farm in Magé, Rio de Janeiro (see *Amnesty International Report 1991*), reportedly received death threats from some of the military police officers alleged to have been involved in the abduction. The women had been campaigning for an investigation into the case. Between April and June human rights workers from the Dom Maximo Biennes Human Rights Centre in the city of Cáceres, Mato Grosso, were allegedly subjected to repeated death threats and intimidation. The centre was broken into and documents were stolen. Members of the centre were reportedly followed by armed people in cars and the centre's secretary was forced into a car and then beaten and threatened.

In September Caco Barcellos, a journalist and author, reportedly received death threats from members of the São Paulo military police after publishing a book denouncing killings by members of the military police in the city. On 31 August around 15 military police officers named in the book reportedly threatened Caco Barcellos and guests attending the book's launch. Later that day Caco Barcellos was reportedly followed by some of the same officers in two police vehicles. Following further threats after he made a broadcast about the House of Detention massacre, Caco Barcellos left the country temporarily fearing for his safety.

Peasants, rural leaders and members of indigenous communities continued to suffer killings, assaults, threats and attempts on their lives by private gunmen. The persistent failure of the authorities to identify those responsible for such abuses and bring

**76**

them to justice helped to create a climate of impunity that encouraged further violations of human rights. Cases of ill-treatment by the police were also reported. In January two peasants, Domingos Mendes Cardoso and a man known as João reportedly "disappeared" in the region of Pimenteira, near Marabá, Pará. Local people reported that they had seen armed guards from a nearby estate detaining two peasants, tying them up and taking them to another estate. Other people living in the vicinity reported hearing two gunshots and later seeing two bodies being taken away by gunmen. Police reportedly refused to act for two days and had failed to find the bodies of the alleged victims by the end of 1992.

In April José Alves de Souza, a member of the Rural Workers' Union of Sitio Novo, was shot at by an unknown gunman and seriously wounded in the neck and chest. It was the third time an attempt on his life had been made. To Amnesty International's knowledge no one had been brought to justice for the attack.

On 29 January Damasceno Segundo, a Macuxí Indian, was detained during an unauthorized police raid on Gavião village near Normandia, Roraima. He was reportedly beaten, handcuffed and taken to a land claimant's house, where he was chained to a beam. He escaped and went into hiding for two weeks. When he reappeared he was reportedly still bruised and one of his ear-drums had been perforated. The incident occurred during a raid on five Macuxí villages in the Raposa-Serra do Sol area by a joint force of military and civil police officers, accompanied by land claimants with whom the Macuxí were in dispute.

During the year Amnesty International urged the federal authorities and various state authorities to investigate reports of torture and ill-treatment of people in police custody, death threats against human rights workers and attempted killings of rural leaders. In April and July Amnesty International published reports on the killing of street children in Rio de Janeiro and Sergipe and urged the national and state authorities to investigate fully the killings and to implement effective measures to end such abuses. In October Amnesty International published *Human rights violations against the indigenous peoples of the Americas*, which included concerns in Brazil. The same month the organization

called on the authorities to undertake a thorough and impartial investigation into the killings in the House of Detention and to bring to justice those responsible.

In an oral statement to the United Nations Sub-Commission Working Group on Indigenous Populations in August, Amnesty International included reference to its concerns in Brazil.

# BRUNEI DARUSSALAM

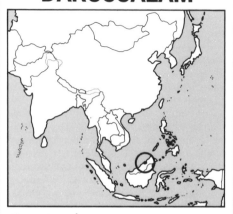

**Three suspected government opponents detained without trial since 1990 were released.**

The authorities informed Amnesty International in October that three political prisoners – Garip bin Timpus, Garip bin Mangool and Omar bin Tamin – had been released. The date of release was not given. The three had been held in the Jerudong Detention Centre under the Internal Security Enactment of 1982, which allows for indefinite detention without charge or trial (see *Amnesty International Report 1992*). The authorities did not make public the reasons for their detention but it appeared that they were suspected of having links with the *Partai Rakyat Brunei* (PRB), Brunei People's Party. The PRB was banned after an abortive armed rebellion in 1962.

The authorities also informed Amnesty International in October that all restrictions imposed at the time of his release in March 1990 on Abdul Latif Chuchu, a former prisoner of conscience, had been lifted in March 1991. Amnesty International welcomed the releases of the three political detainees and the lifting of all restrictions on Abdul Latif Chuchu.

# BULGARIA

**Police officers allegedly tortured and ill-treated members of the Roma community in Pazardjik. One death sentence was passed.**

Bulgaria became a member of the Council of Europe in May. It ratified the European Convention for the Protection of Human Rights and Fundamental Freedoms in September and declared that it recognized both the right of individual petition and the compulsory jurisdiction of the European Court of Human Rights.

In April four former officials of the Lovech and Skravena labour camps, where political prisoners were detained from 1944 to 1962, were charged with killing inmates. Todor Zhivkov, former General Secretary of the Bulgarian Communist Party, was charged in June, together with four other former officials, with incitement to racial and national hatred for initiating the assimilation campaign against Bulgaria's ethnic Turkish minority (see *Amnesty International Reports 1986* to *1991*). He was also awaiting trial for ordering the creation of a network of forced labour camps.

In June police officers allegedly tortured and ill-treated members of the Roma community in Pazardjik. Policemen surrounded the Romany neighbourhood in order to search the houses for arms and check identification documents. They allegedly used truncheons and sticks to beat indiscriminately men, women and children. The inhabitants of one house were reportedly taken outside, made to stand against the wall and were told by policemen that they would be shot. Nasko Iliev Angelov's leg was allegedly broken with a hammer.

Georgi Assenov Yurtov was reportedly tied and beaten in the street.

One person was sentenced to death in February for murder. This was the first death sentence passed since the introduction of a moratorium on executions in July 1990, which remained in force.

In April Amnesty International urged the authorities to abolish the death penalty. In September it called for a full and impartial investigation into the alleged torture and ill-treatment of Roma in Pazardjik and for those responsible to be brought to justice. It also called for the adoption of legislation providing an alternative service for conscientious objectors to military service.

In July President Zhelyu Zhelev wrote to Amnesty International concerning the death penalty. He stated, "[W]e are doing our best to abolish this anti-human measure ... and align with the majority of European states where this has long been a fact".

In October the Minister of Justice, replying to Amnesty International's September letter concerning the alleged torture and ill-treatment of Roma, wrote that "[T]he Ministry of the Interior has initiated a prompt and impartial investigation of the minority situation here in Bulgaria".

# BURKINA FASO

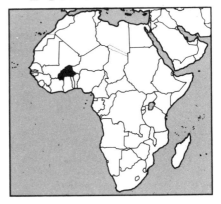

**Over 80 people were assaulted and severely beaten by soldiers in June; nine soldiers were subsequently sentenced to short prison terms. A commission of inquiry into the killing of an opposition leader in December 1991 had not reached any conclusions by the end of the year. The government made no efforts to**

**78**

investigate the "disappearance" of two prisoners of conscience who were believed to have died in detention in 1989 and 1990 as a result of torture.

The first multi-party parliamentary elections since 1978 were held in May and contested by over 20 political parties. The ruling *Organisation pour la démocratie populaire/Mouvement du travail*, Organization for Popular Democracy/ Labour Movement, won an outright majority of seats. In June President Blaise Campaoré appointed Youssouf Ouedraogo as Prime Minister and the latter formed a new government.

In June over 80 people were reportedly injured, four seriously, in Fada N'Gourma, when soldiers rounded up residents in the town centre and beat them with belts and chains, apparently in reprisal for a dispute between a local resident and a soldier. In July over 32 soldiers were tried on various charges in connection with this incident. Nine of them were sentenced to between three and 10 months' imprisonment for assault and battery, theft, looting and destruction of private property; 23 others were fined and received suspended prison sentences.

A commission of inquiry set up at the end of 1991 to investigate the killing of opposition leader Clément Oumarou Ouedraogo and the attempted murder of another opposition activist in December 1991 (see *Amnesty International Report 1992*) had not announced any conclusions by the end of the year. It comprised representatives of the government, opposition political parties and human rights groups, who reportedly met several times during the year and interviewed over 50 people in the course of their inquiries. An armed forces sergeant was reportedly detained for investigation by the procuracy in connection with these cases.

The government made no attempt during 1992 to investigate the "disappearance" of two prisoners of conscience who were believed to have died in detention as a result of torture (see *Amnesty International Reports 1990* to *1992*). Guillaume Sessouma, a university lecturer, was arrested in 1989 in connection with an alleged conspiracy to overthrow the government. He allegedly died less than 24 hours after his arrest as a result of injuries sustained during torture. Medical student Boukary Dabo was arrested in 1990 with over 40 other

students. He reportedly died several hours after his arrest after losing consciousness as a result of severe beating and torture. Amnesty International continued to receive further information about the torture and ill-treatment of the two "disappeared" prisoners of conscience and other political detainees arrested in 1989 and 1990.

No death sentences or executions were reported during the year. Although the transitional government informed Amnesty International in January that it was seriously considering the question of the death penalty, no steps were taken to abolish it in law.

Amnesty International again urged the government to investigate the "disappearance" of prisoners of conscience Guillaume Sessouma and Boukary Dabo. Amnesty International also called on the government which took power in June to ratify international human rights treaties and take steps to abolish the death penalty.

# BURUNDI

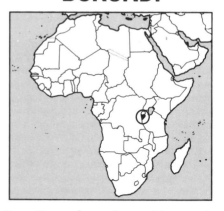

Over 20 members of opposition parties who were briefly detained were prisoners of conscience. Two prisoners of conscience served prison sentences during the year. Hundreds of suspected supporters of an armed opposition group arrested in 1991 remained in detention without trial. Others were tried, but their trials were unfair: 84 people, some of whom were possible prisoners of conscience, were sentenced to prison terms and five to death, although they were not executed. New evidence emerged of torture of political detainees in 1991 and ill-treatment continued to be reported. The authorities rejected calls for an inquiry into the alleged extrajudicial execution by the security forces of at least 1,000 people in late 1991 and failed to clarify the fate and whereabouts of 35 people who "disappeared" at the same time.

Relations between the majority Hutu ethnic group and the politically dominant Tutsi minority remained tense in the wake of armed insurgency and mass reprisal killings in late 1991. Insurgents carried out armed attacks in Cibitoke province in April, but the violence was on a lesser scale than in 1991. The government of President Pierre Buyoya attributed the attacks to the banned *Parti pour la libération du peuple Hutu* (PALIPEHUTU), Hutu People's Liberation Party. PALIPEHUTU insurgents were reported to have arbitrarily and deliberately killed civilians during the year, mostly Tutsi, but also some Hutu who refused to support them.

In March an apparent attempt to overthrow President Buyoya and replace him with the Minister of Foreign Affairs, Cyprien Mbonimpa, was foiled and about 150 soldiers, mainly Tutsi, were arrested. In April the minister and his alleged accomplices were detained. Cyprien Mbonimpa and one of his alleged accomplices were still held without trial at the end of the year, but the other alleged accomplices were released without trial in December.

A new Constitution adopted by referendum in March ended the one-party state. At least seven new political parties were recognized during the year. The Constitution guarantees a number of internationally recognized human rights, such as the right to life and not to be tortured. However, mechanisms to ensure that they are respected in practice were not established. The Constitution does not prohibit prolonged detention without charge or trial, nor does it give detainees the right to challenge their detention in a court of law.

In July the Burundi Government said it had ratified the United Nations (UN) Convention against Torture and Other Cruel, Inhuman or Degrading Treatment or Punishment, but by the end of the year the UN had not received the instruments of ratification.

At least 20 opposition party supporters were detained briefly in February, all of whom were prisoners of conscience. They included 18 members of the *Parti royaliste parlementaire* (PRP), Royalist Parliamentary Party (later renamed the *Parti pour la réconciliation du peuple*, People's Reconciliation Party), who were held for three days for criticizing the new Constitution. They were fined although they did not appear in court and were then released. Several members of the *Front pour la démocratie au Burundi* (FRODEBU), Front for Democracy in Burundi, were also briefly detained.

Emile Ruvyiro (see *Amnesty International Report 1992*) was convicted in April of inciting the public to disobey orders and sentenced to four years' imprisonment. A prisoner of conscience, he had been arrested in March 1991 after encouraging farmers to reclaim land taken by officials. Ephrème Ndabwarukanye, another prisoner of conscience who had been sentenced to a 16-month prison term in 1991, was released around May after completing his sentence.

About 500 Hutu who had been arrested in late 1991 were held throughout 1992, mostly without trial. They included about 70 suspected supporters of PALIPEHUTU who had been arrested before the rebel attacks in November 1991. The others had been arrested during or after the attacks. Most were held incommunicado on the blanket charge of "jeopardizing the security of the state". About 200 other Hutu from neighbouring Rwanda who had been detained in December 1991 were released uncharged and deported to Rwanda in the first half of the year.

Over 100 Hutu were brought to trial during the year for alleged involvement in the 1991 violence or as alleged supporters of PALIPEHUTU. The trials, which began in April, each lasted only a few hours and were unfair in many respects. The first trial took place before the High Court and the others before the Criminal Chamber of the Court of Appeal. In court, most defendants alleged that they had been beaten or ill-treated in custody but in no case was any investigation initiated, and confessions and other statements allegedly extracted under duress were apparently accepted as evidence. Defendants in the first three trials had no legal representation. In all, five people were sentenced to death and 84 to prison terms ranging from one year to life imprisonment. Some appeared to be prisoners of conscience.

At the first trial in April six of the eight defendants, who had been arrested in July 1991, were sentenced to 20-year prison terms after being convicted of disturbing public order, subversion and collusion with insurgents. A seventh defendant received a two-year sentence and the other was acquitted.

At the second trial, which was held in July, 12 people were convicted on the day of the trial: two were sentenced to death and the others received sentences of between five years' and life imprisonment.

At the third trial, also held in July, Antoine Ntirabampa, Vice-President of PALIPEHUTU, and two others were sentenced to death and 55 defendants received prison terms ranging from 10 years to life. Antoine Ntirabampa, who was not permitted by the court to cross-examine prosecution witnesses, was convicted of attempting to overthrow the government and inciting others to kill.

A fourth trial of 18 defendants was repeatedly postponed because they demanded legal counsel. It resumed in September with defence lawyers present, but the presiding judge then ruled that the court would sit for only half a day a week. This trial, the only one in which defendants had legal representation, resulted in lighter sentences than the previous three. Six defendants were acquitted, six were sentenced to one-year prison terms and released because they had spent a year in custody, and six were sentenced to two years' imprisonment.

New information received in 1992 indicated that torture and ill-treatment of political detainees were widespread both before and after the violent events of late 1991. Suspects were commonly beaten at the time of arrest, particularly by the gendarmerie, and tortured in detention by being made to kneel for long periods on sharp bottle tops and pebbles, assaulted with bayonets, pipes, truncheons and machetes, or by having their arms tied so tightly behind their backs as to cause severe injury. Some were reported to have died as a result of torture. For example, in December 1991 a teacher named Byibuza died reportedly after being gagged and hit on the forehead with a piece of piping in Bubanza Gendarmerie Brigade. The main purpose of torture appeared to be to extract confessions. Emile Ruvyiro, for example, had been taken to Bubanza Gendarmerie Brigade in December 1991 and beaten with truncheons for several hours in an attempt to force him to admit to involvement in the November 1991 insurgency.

Many of those held as suspected PALIPEHUTU supporters were held incommunicado for long periods in conditions so cramped as to amount to cruel, inhuman or degrading treatment. For example, at Bujumbura's Mpimba Prison, each isolation cell, measuring less than four square metres, was used to confine four prisoners.

The government persistently resisted calls for an inquiry into the alleged extrajudicial executions of at least 1,000 mostly Hutu civilians by the security forces in November and December 1991 (see Amnesty International Report 1992). The government denied that extrajudicial executions had occurred, despite the emergence of new evidence to the contrary, including eye-witness testimonies and reports by national and international observers which were publicized by human rights activists. The authorities failed to take any steps to identify the victims, many of whose bodies had been taken away by the security forces before relatives could identify or bury them. A government press release in May stated that insurgents had killed 551 people in late 1991 and 61 in April 1992. It did not refer to killings by the security forces. In one exceptional case, however, a gendarmerie commander and several soldiers were arrested in February and accused of killing about 10 Hutu in December 1991. They were still untried at the end of 1992.

The fate of at least 35 people who "disappeared" following their arrest by members of the security forces in 1991 remained unknown. There was no established procedure for discovering the whereabouts of people unaccounted for after arrest. The missing detainees included Obedi Bambanze and Saïdi Hussein, who had been shown on Burundi television in late 1991 "confessing" to being accomplices of the insurgents. There were fears that they might have been secretly executed. Renovat Ndikumana, a journalist working for the Burundi Press Agency, also remained "disappeared": he was reported to have been arrested by soldiers at the end of November 1991.

Amnesty International repeated its call for a full, impartial and independent inquiry into the mass extrajudicial executions and "disappearances" of late 1991 and urged the government to take steps to stop torture. The organization also called for the release of Emile Ruvyiro and for all political trials to be conducted in accordance with international standards for fair trial. Amnesty International representatives visited Burundi in February and met the Ministers of Justice, External Relations and the Interior, and other government and security officials. The organization published two reports on Burundi: in May, *Appeals for an inquiry into army and gendarmerie killings and other human rights violations*; and in November, *Sectarian security forces violate human rights with impunity*. It appealed for the five death sentences imposed to be commuted. In October an Amnesty International representative observed one of the trials of alleged PALIPEHUTU insurgents.

In an oral statement to the UN Commission on Human Rights in February Amnesty International included reference to its concerns in Burundi. Amnesty International also submitted a communication under the African Charter on Human and Peoples' Rights concerning "a series of serious and massive violations" of human rights guaranteed by the Charter.

# CAMBODIA

**At least seven political prisoners remained held without charge or trial at the end of 1992, although hundreds of others were released. Prisoners were tortured and ill-treated, and some were reportedly executed extrajudicially. Members of legal opposition parties were killed in what appeared to be extrajudicial executions. Forces of the *Partie* of Democratic Kampuchea (PDK or Khmer Rouge) killed at least 39 Vietnamese civilians during armed attacks, and 11 others "disappeared" while in their custody.**

In March the United Nations Transitional Authority in Cambodia (UNTAC) began to oversee the country's administration in the run-up to internationally supervised multi-party elections scheduled for May 1993. UNTAC's role was mandated by the 1991 Paris Peace Agreement (see *Amnesty International Report 1992*) which was signed by the State of Cambodia (SOC) Government and the three other main political factions – the PDK; the National United Front for an Independent, Neutral, Peaceful and Co-operative Cambodia (FUNCINPEC); and the

Khmer People's National Liberation Front (KPNLF). However, cease-fire violations between SOC and PDK forces continued throughout the year, increasing in November, and the last two months of the year saw a sharp increase in politically motivated killings by both SOC and PDK forces. The Supreme National Council (SNC), created to embody Cambodian sovereignty during the transitional period, and comprising the four factions, continued to meet throughout 1992 in the presence of UNTAC. The UNTAC human rights unit opened offices in almost all of Cambodia's 21 provinces by the end of the year. In September UNTAC human rights monitors began work in zones controlled by FUNCINPEC and the KPNLF. However, the PDK denied UNTAC officials access to territory it controlled and refused to cooperate with the disarmament program. In October UNTAC began registering voters for the 1993 elections.

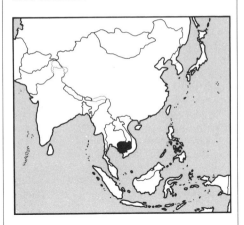

Some legal reforms were introduced during the year. The SNC adopted a new penal code drafted by UNTAC to be enforced by the four main factions. The code provides for the establishment of a new court structure and requires detainees to be given access to a lawyer and to be brought before a judge within 48 hours. However, it was unclear whether SOC laws which contravene the penal code were still being enforced.

In May the SNC acceded to the International Covenant on Civil and Political Rights and the International Covenant on Economic, Social and Cultural Rights. In October the SNC also acceded to the Convention against Torture and Other Cruel, Inhuman or Degrading Treatment or

Punishment, and the 1951 Convention and the 1967 Protocol Relating to the Status of Refugees. From January the SOC Government allowed the International Committee of the Red Cross (ICRC) access to prisons in its territory to supervise the release of political prisoners and prisoners of war.

Hundreds of political prisoners were released, including possible prisoners of conscience Kang Tong Heang and Kuch Siek, who had been held without charge or trial since October 1991. Seven KPNLF members arrested in 1990 remained in detention without charge or trial at the end of 1992. In June the SOC Government stated that all political prisoners had been freed. However, it did not provide a comprehensive list of all political prisoners released.

In August UNTAC closed Tasang and T-6, two secret military prisons in Battambang province, freeing 12 prisoners, four of whom had reportedly been held for political reasons. Sang Seth, a common criminal, was believed to have been taken from Tasang Prison and killed by prison guards on 30 June. Prisoners at T-6 were reportedly routinely beaten, kicked and deprived of food. A few hours before UNTAC entered T-6, prison guards reportedly removed three prisoners and one guard from the prison and shot them dead. Their bodies were later discovered buried in shallow graves.

Prisoners were tortured and ill-treated in Battambang provincial prison and Poipet police lock-up, as well as in the Ministry of National Security compound. There were continued reports of prisoners being shackled in dark cells, but the practice appeared to have ceased by the end of 1992. In July the Ministry of National Security established a commission to investigate prison conditions.

In Battambang provincial prison common criminals were beaten with axes, pistol butts and sticks, and severely burned. In Poipet police lock-up prisoners were reportedly beaten with chains, bamboo and wooden sticks, and fists. In September a man apparently arrested solely for his alleged political affiliation was severely beaten in the Ministry of National Security compound; he was later released and treated in hospital for two broken ribs, a fractured sternum and severe bruising.

Several people were killed in circumstances suggesting they may have been extrajudicially executed. Tea Bun Long, an SOC official who had spoken out against SOC corruption, was found shot dead in January after being abducted by two men in a jeep of a type driven by SOC security forces. Also in January an attempt was made to assassinate Ung Phan, leader of the newly formed Liberal Social Democracy Party and a former prisoner of conscience; he was hit three times by gunmen but survived. At least three Buddhist Liberal Democratic Party (BLDP) activists, including Ath Sodhan, and four FUNCINPEC members, including In Dar and his 12-year-old son, Vun Thom Dar, were apparently extrajudicially executed. During November and December at least eight FUNCINPEC offices and one BLDP office were attacked with grenades or bombs, injuring at least 20 people. In November UNTAC discovered five bodies buried in Battambang province: the five victims had all been arrested by SOC forces a few days previously. The circumstances of their deaths remained unclear.

SOC security forces violently dispersed several demonstrations, killing at least three people. In February military police opened fire on families protesting against their forcible eviction from land on the outskirts of Phnom Penh. A woman street vendor was reportedly killed and five others were injured. In April SOC police allegedly opened fire on villagers demonstrating in connection with a land dispute: one person was reportedly killed and another seriously injured. UNTAC investigators were turned away at gunpoint by local police from the scene, but the SOC Government later cooperated with UNTAC in an investigation. In December SOC forces opened fire on a group of squatters near Phnom Penh, after reportedly being attacked with knives. One woman was killed.

PDK forces killed at least 39 ethnic Vietnamese civilians and 11 others "disappeared" while in PDK custody. In April PDK troops reportedly killed seven Vietnamese men in Kompong Chhnang province. In July PDK troops shot dead or disembowelled eight Vietnamese men and women, including a week-old baby, in Kampot province. On 3 October PDK forces shot dead 11 Vietnamese fishermen, and three others "disappeared" in their custody. In September eight Vietnamese fishermen and women "disappeared" while in PDK custody in Kompong Chhnang province. In December the bodies of three ethnic Vietnamese were discovered in the Mekong river by UNTAC personnel, apparently victims of deliberate killings by PDK forces. The same month PDK forces shot dead 13 ethnic Vietnamese civilians and two Cambodians in Kompong Chhnang province; 13 other civilians were injured in the attack. In December PDK forces took prisoner four groups of UNTAC military personnel; all were released unharmed after a few days.

In April Amnesty International published a major report, *Cambodia: Human Rights Developments, 1 October 1991 to 31 January 1992*. This and a further report, *Cambodia: Update on Amnesty International's concerns*, published in October and previously submitted as a Memorandum to the SOC Government, drew attention to the continued detention without charge or trial of political detainees, harassment and intimidation of government opponents, and the lack of an independent judiciary. Amnesty International also criticized the authorities' failure to ensure independent investigation of killings by SOC forces. In May and June, an Amnesty International delegation visited Cambodia to discuss these and other concerns with Prince Norodom Sihanouk, SOC Government ministers and UNTAC officials. The delegation also met FUNCINPEC and KPNLF representatives, but could not gain access to zones controlled by the PDK. Three Amnesty International representatives visited Cambodia in late 1992 to investigate human rights violations in the context of the election campaign.

# CAMEROON

**Hundreds of government opponents were detained as prisoners of conscience and possible prisoners of conscience. Most were held without charge or trial after a state of emergency was imposed in one province in October. There were new reports of torture and ill-treatment of political detainees; one detainee died from his injuries. Prison conditions were harsh and at least 17 prisoners under sentence of death were reported to have died from malnutrition and medical neglect. At least 130 other prisoners were reportedly under sentence of death but no new death sentences or executions were reported.**

President Paul Biya was re-elected in October, narrowly defeating his main rival, John Fru Ndi of the Social Democratic Front (SDF), whose party had boycotted in March the first multi-party legislative elections since 1964. Amid reports of widespread electoral fraud, the SDF declared that it would not accept the results. Following rioting in Bamenda, the provincial capital, in which at least three people died, the government imposed a state of emergency in North-West Province on 27 October. Hundreds of people, most of them SDF supporters, were then detained without charge or trial in Bamenda and other towns. Under heavy international pressure, the government lifted the state of emergency in late December and released over 170 detainees and 150 people restricted to John Fru Ndi's compound (see below).

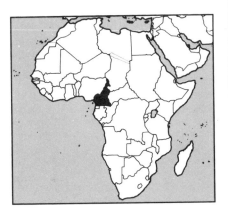

In February President Biya inaugurated a human rights monitoring body, the *Comité national des droits de l'homme et des libertés* (CNDHL), the National Commission on Human Rights and Freedoms. Set up by decree in November 1990, its members – representatives of governmental and non-governmental bodies – were appointed by President Biya, to whom the Commission reports. On at least two occasions the work of the Commission was blocked. In early May the head of the Commission was refused access to a political detainee (see below), was himself briefly detained and had documents confiscated. In November it visited detainees in Bamenda held by the *Brigade Mixte Mobile* (BMM), the security police, and found evidence of systematic torture. It was refused permission to visit detainees restricted under house arrest. Its reports, which condemned what it had

**84**

found but made no concrete recommendations, were not published but were leaked to the national press. The Commission undertook other investigations but did not make its reports public.

There were intercommunal disturbances in several parts of the country which resulted in deaths. Two died in the capital, Yaoundé, in January. The same month intercommunal fighting in Kousséri in the far north of the country left as many as 300 dead, including six executed extrajudicially by the armed forces. Further fighting in the north in November left about 10 dead. Intercommunal disturbances in Meïganga in April also resulted in killings.

Critics and opponents of the government were detained and tortured or ill-treated. Those detained included four members of the banned *Comité d'action populaire pour la liberté et la démocratie* (CAP *Liberté*), Popular Action Committee for Liberty and Democracy, who were arrested in the first weeks of 1992. All were prisoners of conscience. Jean-Michel Nintcheu was arrested on 3 January at his printing works in Douala, which police reportedly ransacked. He went on hunger-strike after being denied hospital treatment for injuries allegedly caused by police beatings, particularly on the soles of his feet. All four detainees were released uncharged by March, but Jean-Michel Nintcheu and another of them, Gabriel Wato, who had also been beaten in police custody, were again briefly detained several times in the following months. On 20 July both men and one of the others detained in January were charged with incitement to revolt and criticizing the government in the name of a banned organization. The case had not been heard by the end of the year.

At least three of some 40 people arrested in Bamenda on 11 February were prisoners of conscience. The arrests followed a peaceful demonstration, one of several held in western Cameroon before the elections calling for greater autonomy for the English-speaking region. Three leading members of the Cameroon Anglophone Movement were charged with organizing an unauthorized public meeting and released on bail in March. Two of them, Dr Zama Kimbi Ndefru and Blaise Berinyuy, were beaten and trampled on at the gendarmerie headquarters in Bamenda at the time of their arrest. All 40 detainees were reportedly held in cramped and filthy cells

and were given insufficient food and water. When Dr Ndefru requested medical attention he was beaten again and drenched with cold water. He needed hospital treatment on his release. Most of the other detainees were released without charge after short periods. Dr Ndefru was detained again on 13 November under the state of emergency (see below) and was held until the end of the year.

Student leader and prisoner of conscience Senfo Tonkam was released in April after serving a five-month prison term for carrying false identity papers. He appeared to have been prosecuted because of an open letter he had sent to President Biya (see *Amnesty International Report 1992*).

The authorities misused administrative detention powers aimed at preventing "banditry" to imprison their opponents. In May at least 16 SDF members were detained without charge in Nkambe, North-West Province, on the basis of administrative detention orders. They were accused of holding illegal political rallies and inciting violence – but not of "banditry". It was not known whether they had been released by the end of the year. In October the Minister of Territorial Administration (Interior) claimed publicly that administrative detention was needed to maintain public order.

Following the imposition of the state of emergency, hundreds of people, mostly SDF supporters, were detained or restricted without charge or trial both in North-West Province and in other parts of the country where no emergency was in force. The authorities said that only about 50 people had been arrested and accused opposition leaders of inciting violence. Those detained included Nyo Wakai, a former President of the Supreme Court, who was beaten after his arrest. Victorin François Hameni Bielu, the SDF campaign manager and leader of another opposition party, was detained on 3 November after visiting 50 opposition supporters detained without charge in Nkongsamba, Coastal Province, for a month from 28 October.

On 25 October the Bamenda compound of John Fru Ndi was surrounded by armed gendarmes and police. He and about 150 supporters were restricted there, effectively detained without charge or trial. Several became ill after initially being denied food and medical care, and owing to lack of adequate shelter and clothing.

Detainees in North-West Province were held under the provisions of the state of emergency which permitted the Minister of Territorial Administration to impose administrative detention without charge or trial for up to four months and Provincial Governors and Senior Divisional Officers to authorize such detentions for up to 15 and seven days respectively. On 23 December the High Court in Bamenda ordered the release of over 170 detainees held under state of emergency provisions by the security police in Bamenda. The government challenged this decision, saying the court did not have the powers to release administrative detainees. The Bamenda detainees were transferred to Yaoundé and were released on 31 December after their cases were reviewed by the State Security Court. It appeared that some other detainees held under the emergency provisions had not been released by the end of the year. Following mass demonstrations in Bamenda by SDF supporters and under increasing international pressure, the state of emergency was lifted and John Fru Ndi and his supporters were released from house arrest.

In Douala, outside the area under the state of emergency, about 50 opposition supporters were detained for 24 hours following a demonstration on 26 October. Some were reported to have been severely beaten, including SDF member Moukouri Manga Bell. At the end of the year, at least 13 people were reportedly still detained incommunicado at the palace of the traditional ruler of Rey Bouba, Northern Province. They were among about 70 opposition supporters illegally detained before and after the presidential elections, apparently with the knowledge of the local government authorities.

There were also reports of torture and ill-treatment of political detainees by gendarmes and police before the elections. Supporters of opposition parties, including the *Union nationale pour la démocratie et le progrès*, National Union for Democracy and Progress, were among over 50 people detained without charge following election disturbances on 1 March in Balikumbat, North-West Province. They were said to have been badly beaten following their arrest and held in harsh conditions at the gendarmerie in Bamenda. Some appeared to be prisoners of conscience. More than 30 were believed still held at the end of the year.

On 6 May some 50 students at the University of Yaoundé were briefly detained and reportedly tortured and ill-treated by soldiers. They were publicly stripped, beaten with rifle butts and had their heads shaved with broken bottles. One student leader was reportedly stripped in public before being led to the local gendarmerie where the head of the CNDHL was denied access to her. The students were commemorating the deaths of two students in disturbances in May 1991 (see *Amnesty International Report 1992*). There had also been arrests of students in March and April after violent protests over the authorities' failure to pay study grants.

In response to the refusal of some communities to pay taxes, in continuance of the 1991 civil disobedience campaign, the gendarmerie launched a series of mass operations in opposition strongholds, during which they committed systematic violations of human rights. For example, for six days from 29 May, gendarmes reportedly made repeated assaults on the town of Bali in North-West Province, raping women and looting and destroying property after the local population protested against extortion by gendarmes at road-blocks.

At Ndu, North-West Province, on 6 June, gendarmes fired into a crowd which had attacked them after they arrested suspected tax-defaulters. At least four civilians were shot. Three days later gendarmes ransacked Ndu on the pretext of recovering unpaid taxes, assaulting anyone who resisted. Some women were reportedly raped. They arrested up to 100 people, including children, reportedly kicking and beating them with gun butts. Many of the detainees were SDF supporters. Most were released the same day after further beatings and ill-treatment, including sexual humiliation. However, Mary Biena Kimbi, an SDF member, and six men were detained for several weeks under administrative detention orders for political reasons.

Detainees held under the state of emergency were beaten at the gendarmerie headquarters and by the security police in Bamenda. One detainee died as a result of torture. Ghandi Che Ngwa, an accountant detained on 9 November, was suspended by his arms and legs from a metal bar and beaten severely by security police. Four days later he was transferred to the military hospital: his body was bruised and swollen

**86**

and some of his toe-nails were missing. He died a week later. Other detainees transferred to the military hospital included a 17-year-old youth detained on 8 November, who had also been suspended from a bar and beaten. An officer was reported to have subsequently jumped on his stomach and kicked him while he was lying on the ground. He received no medical treatment at the military hospital and required major surgery after being transferred to a civilian hospital on 20 November. At Kumba, South-West Province, dozens of opposition supporters were allegedly tortured at the palace of a traditional ruler after the presidential elections, reportedly with the knowledge of gendarmes guarding the building.

At least six people killed by security forces during intercommunal fighting appeared to have been extrajudicially executed. In January, during clashes in Kousséri in northern Cameroon, the armed forces were reported to have detained six people allegedly involved in the fighting and executed them without any form of trial.

Prison conditions generally remained harsh, particularly at Tcholliré prison camp in Northern Province. Inmates there were held naked in overcrowded cells, without being allowed out for exercise, and were given inadequate food and water. No medical care was available and any medicines prisoners managed to obtain were confiscated by prison guards. Prisoners who complained about conditions were beaten and held in dark punishment cells for up to seven days. In May a delegation from the CNDHL visited the prison and reported that 40 prisoners under sentence of death had died there, apparently from malnutrition and medical neglect, since May 1990, including 17 between January and May 1992. It reported that over 130 death row prisoners were held in chains day and night and no medical care was available: prisoners either recovered without treatment or died. The Commission found approximately 30 prisoners in critical condition.

At least 130 prisoners were believed to be on death row but no further death sentences were known to have been imposed during 1992, nor executions carried out: the last was in 1987. On 28 December the government announced that it had commuted the death sentences on some

categories of prisoners convicted of aggravated theft, but provided no details of the prisoners concerned

Amnesty International appealed to the government to release all prisoners of conscience and to either try other political detainees fairly and promptly, or release them. It called on the authorities to take urgent action to safeguard detainees against torture and ill-treatment, and for independent investigations into all allegations of torture and unlawful killings. However, no action was known to have been taken by the government to safeguard prisoners or to bring those responsible to justice. Amnesty International also criticized the authorities' misuse of their administrative detention powers to detain political opponents.

In April Amnesty International called for immediate steps to be taken to prevent further deaths at Tcholliré prison camp. It also called for an independent judicial inquiry into the deaths and for those responsible to be brought to justice. In response, the head of the prison service publicly denied that there were food shortages at Tcholliré prison. The Minister for Territorial Administration stated that six prisoners only had died there, in a recent dysentery epidemic.

# CANADA

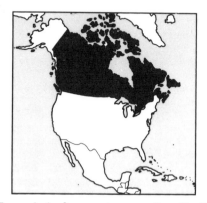

**Two criminal suspects were allegedly ill-treated during a police raid on their house.**

Two men, both Chinese immigrants, alleged they were ill-treated by members of a police Emergency Response Team (ERT) in Vancouver, British Columbia (BC), during a raid on their house in February. A videotape showed officers kicking and punching one of the men as he lay on the ground. A police internal inquiry and an investigation by the Regional Crown Counsel considered that the force used against the two occupants was reasonable and none of the officers involved was charged or disciplined for his actions.

Amnesty International wrote to the BC Police Commission in September expressing concern that the degree of force described was considered reasonable when it included kicking a man who was apparently offering no resistance, stating that such action may amount to cruel, inhuman or degrading treatment. Amnesty International drew attention to international standards on police use of force, including the United Nations (UN) Code of Conduct for Law Enforcement Officials and the UN Basic Principles on the Use of Force and Firearms, urging that these be incorporated into police guidelines.

The Police Commission replied stating that the man on the ground had been struck once on each side in order to release his arms for handcuffing and that no further force had been used. The Commission stated that it had reviewed the inquiries into the incident and concurred with the finding that the force used was reasonable. Both men, it added, had been advised of their right to request a public inquiry by the police board but had not done so. The Commission also informed Amnesty International that the BC Attorney General had ordered an independent inquiry into municipal policing which would include a review of ERT procedures.

Allegations of ill-treatment of Mohawk Indians in 1990 remained unresolved. The Quebec Ministry of Justice replied in May to Amnesty International's call for a thorough and independent inquiry into allegations that several Mohawks had been ill-treated by police during a land dispute in 1990 (see *Amnesty International Report 1992*). The Ministry said that four of the six cases named by Amnesty International were being investigated internally by the Quebec Police, but the results were still pending. A fifth case, that of Ronald Cross, was investigated by the police ethics commissioner under new procedures introduced for complaints occurring after 1 September 1990, but a final decision by the police ethics committee was still pending. Amnesty International was unaware of any further developments by the end of 1992.

In July Amnesty International included reference to its concerns in Canada in an oral statement to the UN Sub-Commission Working Group on Indigenous Populations. In October Amnesty International published *Human rights violations against the indigenous peoples of the Americas*, which included concerns in Canada.

# CENTRAL AFRICAN REPUBLIC

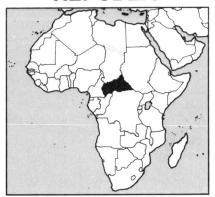

**Two prisoners of conscience were tried and convicted; both had been released by the end of the year. In August a prominent political activist died after being severely beaten by gendarmes.**

The government of President André Kolingba continued to face pressure from opposition parties and trade unions to allow a sovereign National Conference to debate the country's future. Most of the pressure came from a coalition of political parties and trade unions known as the *Concertation des forces démocratiques* (CFD), Coalition of Democratic Forces. The President refused to convene a National Conference but instead held a *Grand débat national*, Grand National Debate, to discuss political issues. Only government supporters participated in the "debate", which began in August, as it was boycotted by opposition parties. The "debate" concluded in early September and President Kolingba announced that delegates had adopted recommendations for democratic reforms and had set up a committee to monitor their implementation by the government. Presidential and parliamentary elections were announced for October but were suspended following reports of

**88** widespread irregularities and violence, and later rescheduled for 1993.

The authorities used the security forces to prevent or disperse meetings and press conferences organized by the opposition to call for a National Conference. In one case a prominent government opponent died from injuries inflicted when gendarmes violently dispersed a CFD demonstration.

Two prisoners of conscience were tried, one in May and the other in July, and sentenced to prison terms. Joseph Bendounga, President of the *Mouvement démocratique pour la renaissance et l'évolution de Centrafrique*, Democratic Movement for the Rebirth and Development of the Central African Republic, was arrested in May after writing an open letter to the President demanding a sovereign National Conference. He was tried five days later, found guilty of insulting the Head of State and sentenced to eight months' imprisonment. He was acquitted on appeal and freed in October. He had previously been arrested and convicted in similar circumstances in 1991, when he received a one-year suspended sentence (see *Amnesty International Report 1992*), which he was not made to serve.

In June Bachir Walidou, a member of the *Association pour la démocratie et le développement*, Association for Democracy and Development, was arrested for writing an open letter critical of the President. In it he alleged that the government was inciting violence against certain nomadic communities in the country (one of them his own ethnic group), which were widely rumoured to be responsible for a series of robberies and murders of travellers. He alleged that these communities had been victimized as a result of government incitement. He was tried in July, found guilty of insulting the Head of State, and sentenced to eight months' imprisonment. He was released on 1 December following a presidential amnesty.

A prominent government opponent died in hospital after being assaulted and arrested by gendarmes during a demonstration on 1 August. Dr Claude Conjugo, leader of an opposition party, the *Alliance pour le progrès*, Alliance for Progress, and a former prisoner of conscience, was assaulted by gendarmes during an opposition demonstration to protest at the opening of the Grand National Debate. The gendarmes reportedly singled out a group of demonstrators which included Dr Conjugo, apparently because, as editor of an opposition journal, *Le Progrès*, he was known to have published articles criticizing the government. Dr Conjugo and five other demonstrators were beaten with rifle butts during their arrest and taken to a gendarmerie post. Dr Conjugo was later transferred to hospital, where he died as a result of the beatings. The government initially claimed that he had died as a result of inhaling teargas. It later announced an inquiry to establish the cause of his death. However, it was unclear at the end of the year whether any inquiry had been held or any action taken against the gendarmes responsible for his death. Dr Conjugo had been one of several dozen members of the *Comité de coordination pour la convocation de la conférence nationale*, Coordination Committee for the Convening of the National Conference, detained between September 1990 and early 1991 for holding political meetings (see *Amnesty International Report 1992*).

Amnesty International appealed for the immediate and unconditional release of prisoners of conscience Joseph Bendounga and Bachir Walidou. The organization also urged the authorities to order an independent inquiry into the death of Dr Conjugo. The government did not respond to the appeals.

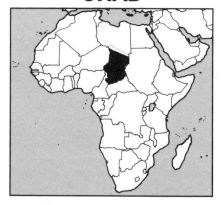

# CHAD

Hundreds of unarmed civilians and prisoners were victims of extrajudicial executions by government security forces. More than 400 opponents of the government, including prisoners of conscience, were detained; most were released by the end of the year. Although some were charged, none was brought to trial. **Most detainees were held incommunicado: many were tortured or ill-treated and several dozen died as a result. Some detainees who "disappeared" in security force custody remained unaccounted for. Two people were sentenced to death.**

Gross human rights violations occurred during sporadic fighting between forces loyal to President Idriss Déby and armed opposition groups. Armed clashes between government forces and the opposition *Mouvement pour la démocratie et le développement* (MDD), Movement for Democracy and Development, which had begun in late 1991, continued intermittently in the Lake Chad region. The MDD was reportedly composed of fighters loyal to former President Hissein Habré, who was overthrown in 1990. An agreement between the government and the MDD to end hostilities, signed in June, did not hold and fighting resumed in October.

There was also fighting with former government supporters who resorted to armed opposition after being accused of disloyalty or failing in their political objectives. Early in the year there were armed clashes in Guéra prefecture between government forces and an armed group loyal to Maldom Bada Abbas, former Vice-President of the ruling *Mouvement patriotique du salut* (MPS), Patriotic Movement for Salvation. He had been detained in October 1991 with several dozen members of his Hadjeraï ethnic group and accused of mounting a coup attempt (see *Amnesty International Report 1992*). Maldom Bada Abbas and most of the others were released in January and he was then appointed President of an interim legislative body known as the Provisional Council of the Republic.

In February Lieutenant Moïse Nodji Ketté, a senior member of the MPS, led a group of soldiers into armed opposition, initially in the capital, N'Djamena, and later in southern Chad. A peace accord signed in July broke down in August when government troops killed about 150 civilians around the southern town of Doba (see below), but in September Lieutenant Ketté's group reached a peace agreement with the government.

In June Abbas Kotti, a government minister, left the government and his supporters fought with government troops in western Chad before he left the country. In mid-December he and three of his Chadian supporters were detained in Cameroon after the reported discovery of an arms cache near the border with Chad. They were still held without charge or trial in Cameroon at the end of the year.

The government also faced non-violent opposition. A series of strikes was organized by trade unions protesting at unpaid salaries and redundancies, and by political parties calling for a National Conference to debate Chad's political future and introduce a multi-party system. Nearly 30 political parties had been formed by the end of the year.

In May a Commission of Inquiry into crimes committed by the former government of President Habré, including human rights violations, published its findings. The Commission concluded that some 40,000 people had been victims of extrajudicial execution or "disappearance" during President Habré's eight years in power. The report described how prisoners were tortured, shot, burned alive, poisoned or starved to death in detention. The Commission identified some of those responsible and recommended their dismissal from similar posts and their prosecution. However, no dismissals or prosecutions had occurred by the end of the year.

Several hundred people were extrajudicially executed during the year in various parts of the country by members of the security forces. Some of those killed, for example, in Ouaddaï region, were apparently executed because they refused to hand over their property to soldiers. In January several dozen civilians in Guéra prefecture were reported to have been executed extrajudicially by soldiers because they failed to disclose the whereabouts of rebels loyal to Maldom Bada Abbas.

About 100 people were executed extrajudicially by the security forces in the N'Djamena area in January and February. The victims included Joseph Behidi, a lawyer and Vice-President of the Chadian Human Rights League. Joseph Behidi was apparently targeted because of his criticism of the government's human rights record and because he was defending a newspaper in a defamation case brought by the army. Those responsible for his death were not identified, despite substantial evidence that they were linked to the armed forces. No progress in police investigations into his death had been reported by the end of the year.

**90**

In February several dozen civilians in N'Djamena and about 50 soldiers awaiting demobilization at Boudouloum, south of N'Djamena, were executed extrajudicially by members of the Republican Guard. They were apparently killed as a reprisal for an attack by rebel soldiers loyal to Moïse Ketté on Chagoua police station in N'Djamena.

Seven people, including Faky Ahmat Ali, a Quranic teacher, were killed and about 14 others wounded on 1 August when gendarmes opened fire on members of the Ouaddaï community in a mosque at Diguel-Est, north of N'Djamena. Faky Ahmat Ali was being sought for arrest in connection with a land dispute. The gendarmes fired tear-gas into the mosque and shot down people, including children, as they ran out. The authorities claimed that the victims had tried to attack the gendarmes, but this was denied by other sources.

In mid-August more than 100 unarmed civilians were executed extrajudicially during reprisals taken against southern Chadians by members of the Republican Guard in the town of Doba in the south. The killings took place after clashes between rebels loyal to Moïse Ketté and government troops, in which about 20 government soldiers were reportedly killed.

The security forces were not held accountable for any of the extrajudicial executions committed during the year and were in effect allowed to kill with impunity. The government did not respond to appeals to launch independent public inquiries following any of the incidents. In some cases it claimed killings were justified, but in most cases it said that the killings were not condoned by the government and were the work of undisciplined soldiers. However, it took no steps to discipline them.

Hundreds of suspected government opponents, including prisoners of conscience, were imprisoned early in the year, but most of them were released by August. In January eight members of the opposition *Rassemblement pour la démocratie et le progrès* (RDP), Rally for Democracy and Progress party, were held for several weeks in N'Djamena on unsubstantiated suspicion of supporting the MDD. They appeared to be prisoners of conscience. They were reportedly arrested by armed members of the security police known as the *Centre de recherche et de coordination de renseigne-* *ments* (CRCR), Centre for Research and Co-ordination of Intelligence, and by agents of other branches of the security forces. Three RDP members were killed at the time of the arrests, including Bisso Mamadou, former director general of Chad's water and electricity company. The killings, which appeared to be extrajudicial executions, were not independently investigated. The eight detainees were released without charge at the end of January, together with most other political detainees held since October 1991, although some remained unaccounted for. Fifteen detainees who had been arrested at the end of 1991 and severely ill-treated were released in February.

Two journalists, Samba Aiwo Akonso and Makaila ka Yamarke, both leaders of the *Syndicat des professionnels de la communication*, Communication Professionals' Union, were detained for two days in September by members of the CRCR. They were released after the Procuracy declared their detention illegal. There was, however, no procedure for reviewing detentions systematically and checking on their legal basis.

Some of the hundreds of political detainees were accused of fighting for or supporting one or other armed opposition group. However, many were detained without any evidence or investigation. More than 200 Chadian nationals living in Nigeria's northwest Borno State were forcibly returned to Chad and handed over to the Chadian authorities in February. They included members of the MDD. They were held incommunicado in military barracks without charge or trial, together with about 60 MDD combatants captured in Chad. They were first held in N'Djamena and later transferred to Iriba and Abéché in the northeast. The captured combatants were released at the beginning of July under an agreement between the MDD and the government; the others were released at the end of the month following intervention by a representative of the Paris-based *Fédération internationale des droits de l'homme* (FIDH) International Federation for Human Rights, and an emissary of the French Government.

More than 100 civilians and soldiers suspected of supporting Lieutenant Moïse Ketté because they came from southern Chad were arrested in February. The arrests took place after an armed attack on Chagoua police station in N'Djamena. The detainees were apparently charged with endangering the security of the state but not tried. They were released in July.

More than 40 soldiers, including Captain Amine Youssouf Oumar, deputy commander of the Republican Guard, and several civilians were arrested in June on suspicion of supporting Abbas Kotti. Two civilians, Ibrahim Kossi and Bichara Doudoua, were held at the headquarters of the *Renseignements généraux* intelligence service until November, when they were released without charge or trial. They appeared to be prisoners of conscience. The soldiers were first detained at the *Camp des martyrs* military barracks in N'Djamena. In September the authorities said the detainees had been transferred to Faya detention centre in northern Chad. However, there were fears for the lives of Amine Youssouf Oumar and at least four others.

Torture and ill-treatment of detainees, most of whom were held incommunicado, were widespread, leading to deaths and "disappearances". None of these incidents was independently investigated. Reports from former detainees and other sources indicated that most detainees were routinely beaten at the time of their arrest and while being interrogated. For example, some of the people forcibly returned from Nigeria were reportedly given electric shocks and had their arms tied tightly behind their backs and two sticks tied tightly on both sides of their heads. Both methods of torture had been used extensively in the 1980s when President Habré was in power. At least two of these detainees, Issa Gorane and Goukouni Guet, who were held at the Presidential Palace, reportedly died there from torture. A third, Mahamat Saker, was reportedly tortured and then executed extrajudicially at the headquarters of the CRCR.

There were reports of detainees dying from starvation, thirst, asphyxiation and exhaustion. More than a dozen suspected members of the MDD died at the former Presidential Palace in March and April. Others died at Iriba and Abéché.

Several detainees "disappeared" in the custody of the security forces, including Assali Adil, a computer scientist employed by the Chadian Water and Electricity Company.

Two members of the security forces were convicted of murder in August by a special military court set up in 1991. The killings had not been committed in the course of military or security operations. The two soldiers were sentenced to death, with no right of appeal. However, no executions were announced during the year.

Amnesty International called for a full, impartial and independent inquiry into alleged extrajudicial executions and "disappearances" and urged the government to take steps to end incommunicado detention without charge or trial, and torture. It appealed for the two death sentences imposed to be commuted. Amnesty International representatives visited Chad in September and discussed the human rights situation in the country with the President and other government and security officials. In October Amnesty International published a report entitled: *Chad: Extrajudicial executions in Doba*.

In an oral statement to the United Nations (UN) Commission on Human Rights in February Amnesty International included reference to its concerns in Chad. In April Amnesty International submitted updated information about its concerns in Chad for UN review under a procedure, established by Economic and Social Council Resolutions 728F/1503, for confidential consideration of communications about human rights violations.

# CHILE

**At least 50 cases of torture and ill-treatment by the security forces were reported. Two journalists were briefly detained for publishing articles accusing the police of corruption. Dozens of political prisoners arrested under the former military government were released, but more than 10**

**92** remained in prison at the end of the year. The Supreme Court continued to approve the transfer of investigations into past human rights violations to the military courts; most cases remained unresolved and none of those responsible was convicted. At least three people died in circumstances suggesting they may have been extrajudicially executed. Five people were sentenced to death but their sentences were commuted; one political prisoner remained under a recommended death sentence.

In February a law was passed creating the *Corporación Nacional de Reparación y Reconciliación*, National Corporation for Reparation and Reconciliation, and providing compensation for relatives of people "disappeared" or killed as a result of human rights violations under the former military government. The role of the Corporation, which was set up in July, included investigating 641 cases about which the *Comisión Nacional de Verdad y Reconciliación* (CNVyR), National Commission for Truth and Reconciliation, could reach no conclusions; opening investigations into hundreds of new complaints of past human rights violations; and promoting recommendations in the CNVyR's 1991 final report (see *Amnesty International Report 1992*).

A proposal to extend the scope of the death penalty was introduced by the Senate in January and was still being considered in Congress at the end of the year.

The *Movimiento Juvenil Lautaro*, Lautaro Youth Movement, an armed opposition group, claimed responsibility for the killing of three police officers in the capital, Santiago, in September. The killing of Senator Jaime Guzmán in 1991 remained unresolved (see *Amnesty International Report 1992*).

In May Chile acceded to the first Optional Protocol to the International Covenant on Civil and Political Rights.

At least 50 cases of torture by the security forces were reported, more than twice the number in 1991. Mirentchu Vivanco Figueroa was arrested without warrant in March by uniformed police. She was reportedly held incommunicado in a Santiago police station for three days, deprived of sleep, threatened with death and forced to remain standing for long periods. Those allegedly responsible remained at large by the end of the year.

In April, 15-year-old Germán Andrés Vargas Armijo was arrested by uniformed police in Santiago, charged with attacking police officers. He was reportedly hit with rifle-butts while being arrested, then beaten, given electric shocks and nearly drowned in custody. Those responsible had not been brought to justice by the end of the year.

Evaristo Godoy, a member of the Socialist Party and former political prisoner, was arrested in September by members of the criminal investigations police in Santiago. He was reportedly beaten by police, given electric shocks and threatened with death. He was released without charge a week later. An investigation into his complaints had not concluded by the end of the year.

Those responsible for the death under torture of Ricardo Parra Flores in October 1991 (see *Amnesty International Report 1992*) remained at large at the end of the year.

In November Andrés Lagos, director of *El Siglo* magazine, and Francisco Herreros, a journalist on the magazine, were detained for one day in Santiago on the orders of a military court. They were charged with "inciting sedition" because of an article published in 1991 accusing the uniformed police of corruption. They were released and were awaiting trial at the end of the year.

Dozens of political prisoners were released, but more than 10 were still imprisoned at the end of the year, despite repeated announcements that the authorities intended to resolve the cases of those arrested under the former government, whose trials were marred by serious irregularities. In September, nine political prisoners in Santiago began a 40-day hunger-strike to demand the release of those still imprisoned.

No one was convicted during the year for past human rights violations. The military courts continued to claim jurisdiction over human rights cases in civilian courts and to close cases covered by the 1978 Amnesty Law (see *Amnesty International Report 1992*). The Supreme Court continued to support the transfer of investigations from civilian courts to military courts. For example, an investigation by a civilian judge into the 1974 abduction, torture and "disappearance" of Alfonso Chanfreau Oyarce was halted after being transferred to military jurisdiction in November. The Supreme Court upheld this decision, claiming that the case had occurred at a time of internal war.

Progress was reported in some cases of past human rights violations not covered by the 1978 Amnesty Law. In May Alvaro Corbalán, former operations chief of the disbanded *Central Nacional de Informaciones* (CNI), state security police, was arrested in connection with the killings of union leader Tucapel Jiménez in 1982 (see *Amnesty International Report 1983*) and of carpenter Juan Alegría in 1983. He remained in detention at the end of the year. In November General Manuel Contreras and Brigadier Pedro Espinoza, director and chief of operations respectively of the disbanded *Dirección de Inteligencia Nacional* (DINA), Directorate of National Intelligence, were formally indicted with having planned the murder of Orlando Letelier in 1976, the only case to be exempted from the 1978 Amnesty Law. Both defendants remained free on bail at the end of the year (see *Amnesty International Report 1992*). In November the Supreme Court dropped the charges against General César Mendoza Durán, former director of the CNI, who had been indicted by a lower court for covering up the abduction and killing of three communist leaders in 1985 (see *Amnesty International Report 1986*). However, nine members of the security forces remained in prison awaiting trial in this case at the end of the year. The judge in charge of the case reportedly received repeated death threats.

Investigations to establish the identity of 127 bodies exhumed in 1991 in a Santiago cemetery were still continuing at the end of the year (see *Amnesty International Report 1992*).

At least three people died in circumstances suggesting that they may have been extrajudicially executed. On 30 January Alexis Muñoz and Fabián López, members of the *Frente Patriótico Manuel Rodríguez Autónomo*, Autonomous Manuel Rodríguez Patriotic Front, were reportedly killed after surrendering to police in Santiago. Although the police claimed they died during a shoot-out, a forensic report established that Alexis Muñoz died 50 minutes after the alleged shoot-out. On 12 October 17-year-old Rodrigo Briones was reportedly killed by uniformed police. According to witnesses, he was beaten during his arrest in the streets of Santiago and was shot at close range while he lay wounded crying for help. An investigation into his death had not concluded by the end of the year.

Five people were sentenced to death, four of whom later had their sentences commuted to life imprisonment by President Patricio Aylwin. Three Peruvian citizens convicted of murder had their sentences commuted in August and a political prisoner sentenced to death in August for kidnapping had his sentence commuted in November. Juan Domingo Salvo Zúñiga, whose death sentence for murder was confirmed on appeal by the Supreme Court in November, remained on death row at the end of the year awaiting presidential clemency. A recommendation for the death sentence by the prosecution continued to stand against Hugo Gómez Peña (see *Amnesty International Report 1992*).

Amnesty International continued to call for full investigations into human rights violations and for those responsible to be brought to justice. The organization also continued to call for the abolition of the death penalty.

In July the organization published *Chile: "Extreme Cruelty": the plight of the Mapuche Indians during the years of military rule* to highlight the human rights violations suffered by indigenous peoples under the military government. In October Amnesty International published *Human rights violations against the indigenous peoples of the Americas*, which included concerns in Chile. In an oral statement to the United Nations Working Group on Indigenous Populations of the Sub-Commission on Prevention of Discrimination and Protection of Minorities in July, Amnesty International included reference to its concerns about past human rights violations against indigenous peoples in Chile and the lack of accountability of those responsible.

# CHINA

**Thousands of political prisoners were held, including hundreds of prisoners of conscience. Scores of prisoners of conscience were serving prison sentences but others were detained without charge or trial. Political activists, religious leaders and members of ethnic groups continued to be arrested and held without charge or**

**94**

trial or sentenced to terms of imprisonment after unfair trials. Administrative detention continued to be used on a large scale to hold political prisoners without charge or trial. Torture and ill-treatment were frequently reported. The death penalty continued to be used on an extensive scale: 1,891 death sentences were recorded and 1,079 executions, but the true figures were believed to be much higher.

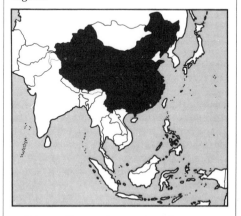

The police and security forces continued to exercise extensive powers of arbitrary arrest and detention. Political dissidents and others were detained for prolonged periods without trial or sentenced to lengthy terms of imprisonment for "crimes of counter-revolution". There was still no public inquiry into the killings of over 1,000 civilians by government forces in Beijing during the 1989 pro-democracy protests.

In August the government issued a "white paper" entitled *The Reform of Criminal Offenders in China*, but this failed to acknowledge or take into account the frequency of human rights violations in Chinese prisons and the need for urgent measures to remedy such violations. In September another government "white paper", *Tibet – Its Ownership and Human Rights Situation*, made clear that activities considered to be detrimental to "stability and unity" in Tibet – such as peaceful political demonstrations – would be "cracked down on relentlessly".

Hundreds of prisoners of conscience arrested in connection with the 1989 pro-democracy protests remained in prison; the fate of thousands of others remained unknown (see *Amnesty International Reports 1990 to 1992*). Many prisoners of

conscience were serving prison sentences imposed after unfair trials; others were held without charge or trial.

Arrests of people suspected of involvement in political activities continued during the year. In June several dozen people were arrested in Beijing and elsewhere during a crackdown on pro-democracy activists. They included Chen Wei, a former student, and Wang Guoqi, a printer, both of whom had been arrested three times since 1989. Also detained were at least six members of the China Progressive Alliance, a newly formed non-violent political organization. The same month Wang Wanxin was arrested in Tiananmen Square, Beijing, for unfurling a banner commemorating the massacre of 4 June 1989. In July it was reported that he had been confined to a mental hospital and forcibly given drugs. Several other political activists were arrested in September. Two of them were released without charge a few weeks later, but the others were believed to be still detained at the end of the year.

Hundreds of people were arrested because of their religious activities or for their membership of ethnic or other groups. Some were released but others remained in detention without charge or trial. Early in the year at least 30 members of the "New Birth" Christian Church were arrested in Henan, Shanxi and Liaoning provinces: 20 of them were later sentenced administratively to three years' detention, known as "re-education through labour". In the same period some 160 other Christians were arrested in Henan, Jiangsu and Shanxi provinces. In September a further 160 Christians were reportedly arrested in Henan Province. In January it was reported that Pei Ronggui, a Trappist priest from Hebei Province, had been sentenced to five years' imprisonment: he was arrested in 1990 while administering the last rites to a dying man.

The same month Zhang Weiming, a Catholic intellectual from Baoding, Hebei Province, was sentenced administratively to two years of "re-education through labour" because of his religious activities. He had been held incommunicado in Baoding for over a year following his arrest in December 1990. He was moved to a labour camp in Shijiazhuang after being sentenced and released in November.

Some 60 Roman Catholic clergy and lay members remained held, including

76-year-old Bishop Yang Libo. However, several others were released. James Xie Shiguang, the 74-year-old bishop of Xiapu in Fujian Province, and two priests from Fujian who were arrested in July 1990 during a religious meeting, were freed in January. Among others reported released were Li Side, Roman Catholic bishop of Tianjin, and Liu Guangdong, bishop of Yixian in Hebei Province. All belong to the "underground" church which remains loyal to the Vatican.

Members of ethnic groups in the Autonomous Regions of Inner Mongolia and Xinjiang were arrested and accused of instigating "separatist activities". Others arrested in previous years remained in prison. In Inner Mongolia, those still held, apparently without charge or trial, included Huchin Togos, a teacher, and Wang Manglai, a linguist, both of whom had been arrested in May 1991 for founding two cultural organizations. In Xinjiang several political activists were reportedly detained in and around Kashgar at the beginning of the year. Scores of others who had been arrested in 1991 or before remained in prison throughout 1992. Kajikhumar Shabdan, a 62-year-old ethnic Kazakh writer and poet, was believed to be still serving a sentence of 12 years' imprisonment. He was reported to have been arrested in 1988 with about 10 other people following peaceful demonstrations in Tacheng, northern Xinjiang. He had previously been arrested in 1958 and jailed for 18 years for allegedly "opposing socialism".

Arrests of Tibetan political activists continued. Over 200 political prisoners, including at least 100 prisoners of conscience, remained held in Tibet. They included Buddhist monks and nuns detained for peacefully advocating Tibetan independence, and lay Tibetans allegedly found in possession of Tibetan nationalist material. Some were serving prison terms imposed after unfair trials, others terms of "re-education through labour" imposed without formal charge or trial. Among the latter was Dawa Kyizom, a student, who was serving a three-year term imposed in October 1990 after she reportedly gave a Tibetan flag to a monk. She was held in Gutsa Detention Centre. Several Tibetan prisoners of conscience were released during the second half of the year after completing their sentences.

Trials continued to fall far short of inter-national standards for fairness. Minimum standards for fair trial are not provided for in Chinese law, such as the right to have adequate time and facilities to prepare a defence, the right to be presumed innocent until proven guilty, and the right to call defence witnesses. In practice, the verdict and sentence are often decided by the authorities before trial. Other major obstacles to fair trial include extreme limitations on the role of defence lawyers and the use of torture to extract "confessions".

Prisoner of conscience Qi Lin, a journalist with the Beijing Daily newspaper, was tried in secret in Beijing and sentenced in April to four years' imprisonment on charges of "leaking state secrets". He was accused of telling a Taiwanese newspaper about political sanctions imposed on a member of China's National People's Congress. Qi Lin is diabetic and his health seriously deteriorated in prison. He was released on bail on medical grounds in June but his sentence remained in force.

Two prominent prisoners of conscience were convicted, after more than three years' detention without trial, for their activities during the 1989 protests. Bao Tong, a senior official of the Chinese Communist Party (CCP) and close associate of former CCP leader Zhao Ziyang, was sentenced to seven years' imprisonment in July for "leaking state secrets" and "counter-revolutionary propaganda and incitement". In a related trial, Gao Shan, a researcher in a CCP institute headed by Bao Tong, was sentenced to four years in prison in August for "leaking state secrets". Both trials were held in secret before the Beijing People's Intermediate Court and lasted only a few hours. The court's verdict against Bao Tong indicated that the charge of "leaking state secrets" was based solely on a private conversation between him and Gao Shan. An appeal by Bao Tong was rejected in August by Beijing Municipal High People's Court.

New information was received in 1992 about unfair trials of political prisoners in previous years. For example, information was received that Hu Hai, a peasant from Liuzhuang township in Henan Province, had been sentenced to three years' imprisonment in November 1991 for taking part in peaceful petitions by peasants against local taxes. He was convicted by a local court in Weihui city of "disturbing social order".

**96**

The authorities restricted the freedom of movement, association and other fundamental human rights of released prisoners of conscience. Restrictions on freedom of movement included being forced to live in specific isolated areas, house arrest, and regular mandatory reporting to local Public Security offices. Relatives of former political prisoners were also harassed and subjected to restrictions.

Torture and ill-treatment of prisoners were common. The methods most frequently cited were severe beatings, shocks with electric batons and the use of shackles. Deprivation of sleep or food, exposure to extremes of cold or heat, and being forced to adopt exhausting postures were also reported to be common during interrogation. Such torture and ill-treatment of prisoners were said to be particularly severe in Liaoning, Shaanxi and Hunan provinces and in the Tibet Autonomous Region.

Political prisoners in Lingyuan No. 2 Labour Reform Camp in Liaoning Province were repeatedly beaten and given electric shocks with high-voltage batons. As a result, several reportedly needed hospital treatment. However, despite international appeals on behalf of the victims, no investigation was known to have been initiated by the authorities and allegations of torture continued to be received. The victims included Liu Gang, who had been a student leader in Beijing during the 1989 protests.

Political prisoners reportedly tortured in Hunan Province included Yu Dongyue, Yu Zhijian and Lu Decheng, who were sentenced in 1989 to long prison terms after being convicted of defacing a portrait of Mao Zedong and distributing political leaflets. By early 1992 they had been held continuously in solitary confinement in extremely harsh conditions for more than two years in Hunan Provincial No. 3 Prison in Lingling; two of them were reported to be in poor health.

Torture and ill-treatment of prisoners also reportedly continued in Tibet. Tane Jigme Sangpo, a primary teacher detained since 1983, and three others remained in solitary confinement: they had been put in solitary confinement in December 1991 after one of them shouted slogans supporting Tibetan independence. There were fears for the health of Tane Jigme Sangpo, who had spent a total of 25 years in prison since 1960. Information was received that Laba Dunzhu, a Tibetan political detainee, had died at the People's Hospital in Lhasa in November 1991 after being transferred there from Gutsa Detention Centre. He had been arrested in 1989 and was reportedly tortured in detention, suffering a ruptured spleen and other injuries.

Han Dongfang, a former prisoner of conscience and a prominent labour activist during the 1989 protests, was reportedly beaten, kicked and stunned with electric batons by court officials in May when he appeared before the Dongcheng District People's Court in Beijing on a matter related to his housing.

During the year the authorities revealed that 407 cases of "torture to extract confessions" had been investigated and prosecuted by the procuracy in 1991 – a figure believed to represent only a fraction of actual cases.

Prison conditions were often harsh and many prisoners were reported to have fallen ill as a result. Prisoners faced prolonged periods in solitary confinement as punishment, often resulting in physical or psychological disorders. Medical care was frequently inadequate. Ren Wanding, a prisoner of conscience held in Beijing since 1989, was reported to be in danger of losing his sight and to have numerous other health problems. Li Guiren, an editor from Xi'an in Shaanxi Province held since 1989, became severely ill in prison in late 1991 but was still reportedly being denied adequate medical care in July. Several hunger-strikes were held by prisoners to protest against prison conditions, including one begun in August in Yang Qing Prison by Wang Juntao, a writer and political activist who had been sentenced to 13 years' imprisonment in 1991 for his involvement in the 1989 protests (see *Amnesty International Report 1992*).

The dramatic increase in the use of the death penalty which began in 1990 (see *Amnesty International Report 1991*) continued, particularly during an anti-drug campaign in the first half of the year. At least 1,891 death sentences and 1,079 executions were recorded by Amnesty International, but the actual figures were believed to be far higher. Many of those executed were tried under legislation which allows for summary procedures.

Throughout the year Amnesty International urged the authorities to release prisoners of conscience, ensure fair trials for all political prisoners and commute all death sentences. The government did not respond directly to any of these appeals and did not allow Amnesty International representatives to attend political trials or visit the country.

In oral statements to the United Nations (UN) Commission on Human Rights in February and to its Sub-Commission on Prevention of Discrimination and Protection of Minorities in August, Amnesty International included reference to its concerns in China.

In April Amnesty International submitted information about its concerns in China for UN review under a procedure, established by Economic and Social Council Resolutions 728F/1503, for confidential consideration of communications about human rights violations.

The organization published several reports about human rights violations in China including: in January, *Amnesty International's Concerns in Tibet*; in February, *Drugs and the Death Penalty in 1991*; in May, *Continued Patterns of Human Rights Violations in China* and *Repression in Tibet, 1987-1992*; in November, *Secret Violence: Human Rights Violations in Xinjiang*; and in December, *Torture in China*.

# COLOMBIA

At least 1,000 people were extrajudicially executed by the armed forces or paramilitary groups operating with their support or acquiescence. Many of the victims had been tortured before being killed. "Death squad"-style killings of "social undesirables" in urban areas continued to be reported. Over 100 people "disappeared" after detention by the security forces or paramilitary groups. In several cases disciplinary sanctions were imposed on police and army personnel for human rights violations but little progress was reported in judicial inquiries. Several hundred people were held hostage by armed opposition groups and scores more were deliberately and arbitrarily killed.

Peace talks resumed in March between the government and the coordinating body of armed opposition groups, the *Coordinadora Nacional Guerrillera* (CNG) – representing the *Fuerzas Armadas Revolucionarias de Colombia* (FARC), Revolutionary Armed Forces of Colombia; the *Ejército de Liberación Nacional* (ELN), National Liberation Army; and a faction of the *Ejército Popular de Liberación* (EPL), Popular Liberation Army. The talks were adjourned in May and indefinitely suspended after the insurgents launched a major offensive in the second half of the year resulting in heavy casualties on both sides. The government responded to the guerrilla offensive by imposing a nation-wide 90-day state of "internal commotion" in November and issuing a series of emergency decree laws. These included constraints on media coverage of guerrilla activities, penalized the failure to pass to the authorities information about insurgent activities and empowered the armed forces to carry out judicial investigations and press charges against civilian suspects.

Throughout the year there were intense counter-insurgency activities in several areas of the country, particularly the central Magdalena Medio region and Meta department. In this context government forces and paramilitary groups operating under their control or with their support were responsible for serious human rights violations, including the extrajudicial execution, "disappearance" and torture of non-combatant civilians in conflict areas. Serious abuses were also committed by the FARC, ELN and EPL who held hundreds of hostages and, in some cases, carried out deliberate and arbitrary killings of civilians, including hostages.

At least 1,000 people were extrajudicially executed during the year. Victims of human rights violations by government forces were mainly peasant farmers in conflict zones, but included students, teachers, trade unionists, members of legal left-wing political associations and human

**98**

rights defenders. Leading members of human rights organizations were publicly accused by senior military commanders of being members of guerrilla organizations or collaborators. In some cases accusations were followed by attacks on their lives. Members of the Magdalena Medio-based *Comité Regional para la Defensa de los Derechos Humanos* (CREDHOS), Regional Human Rights Committee, were particularly targeted. In January CREDHOS secretary Blanca Valero de Durán was killed outside the Committee's offices in Barrancabermeja, Santander department, by gunmen in civilian clothes. Three policemen who witnessed the attack reportedly ignored her cries for help and made no attempt to pursue her assailants. During the first few months of the year CREDHOS repeatedly protested at the severe escalation of abuses against civilians by the army, police and paramilitary forces in the Magdalena Medio region. Following statements by local military commanders in February accusing CREDHOS of links with guerrilla organizations, threats from army-backed paramilitary forces against CREDHOS members increased. In June CREDHOS worker Julio Berrio was killed by unidentified gunmen. In July Ligia Patricia Cortez, a student who was working on an educational project for CREDHOS, was shot dead together with trade unionists Parmenio Ruíz Suárez and René Tavera by unidentified gunmen in a restaurant in Barrancabermeja. Only days before, Parmenio Ruíz and another trade unionist, Gustavo Chinchilla Jaimes, had lodged a complaint with the Regional Procurator's office after receiving death threats. Gustavo Chinchilla was abducted and killed in Bogotá in October as he made preparations to leave the country. His body was found with signs of torture.

Oscar Elías López Muñoz, a lawyer, was killed in May in Santander de Quilichao, Cauca department, by unidentified armed men. Oscar López worked as legal adviser to the *Consejo Regional Indígena del Cauca* (CRIC), Regional Indigenous Council of Cauca. He had received death threats which he believed were connected to his representation of the Paez indigenous community, 20 of whose members were massacred in December 1991. The Indians, who had been occupying a property called "El Nilo" near Caloto, were attacked by some 40 heavily armed and hooded men – some dressed in military uniforms – who burst into a building where they were holding a meeting. Among those killed were four children. Before the massacre the Paez had made repeated official complaints to the authorities about harassment and threats by armed gunmen believed to be acting for a would-be owner of the farm. However, no action was taken by the authorities to investigate the allegations or to protect the community. In March the Procurator General announced that his office was investigating whether senior Cauca police officials had participated in the massacre. In November lawyers who took over the case following Oscar López' death reported receiving repeated death threats.

Members of the legal left-wing political alliance *Unión Patriótica* (UP), Patriotic Union, continued to be particular targets for political killings. Among those killed were elected local government officials: in June William Ocampo, recently elected mayor of El Castillo in Meta department, outgoing mayoress María Mercedes Méndez, municipal treasurer Rosa Peña Rodríguez, her husband Ernesto Serralde and their driver Pedro Agudelo were killed when the car in which they were travelling was attacked with hand grenades and submachine guns by men in military uniforms at Caño Sibao near El Castillo. Only days before the massacre María Méndez had reported to local police and military authorities the presence of paramilitary groups in the area and had asked for protection. In November her husband, José Rodrigo García Orozco, vice-president of the departmental Assembly of Meta, was killed by unidentified gunmen. An official bodyguard, assigned to him after the murder of his wife, had been withdrawn two days earlier.

According to an official report produced in October by the People's Defender, political violence against the UP is particularly concentrated in regions where they receive most electoral support. The report documents 717 killings of UP members between January 1985 and September 1992: in only four cases have those responsible been convicted. The People's Defender concluded: "One of the most horrifying forms of violence that UP activists have suffered has been the massacres. Innumerable deaths, a complete lack of security prior to the events – in spite of their being 'pre-announced' in many cases – and irregularities in the investigations are factors contributing to impunity in these cases."

Paramilitary forces, declared illegal by the government in 1989, continued to engage in counter-insurgency operations with the armed forces, to forcibly recruit civilians, including children, and to commit widespread human rights violations, including torture, extrajudicial execution and "disappearance". Among the areas most severely affected by paramilitary abuses was the municipality of Carmen de Chucurí, Santander department. In June Juan de Dios Gómez, a 70-year-old peasant farmer, was killed when a group of armed and hooded men burst into his home in the community of Los Aljibes and shot him repeatedly. Shortly before his murder, Juan de Dios Gómez had denounced paramilitary and army abuses against the civilian population in a sworn statement before officials of the Procurator General's office and in declarations to the press and television.

In November the Procurator Delegate for the Armed Forces brought disciplinary charges against the head of military intelligence, General Carlos Gil Colorado, and six other army officers. They were accused of organizing, arming and conducting joint operations with illegal paramilitary groups responsible for the murder of community leaders and suspected guerrilla sympathizers in Santander department. However, efforts to hold members of paramilitary groups in Santander department criminally liable for gross human rights violations were obstructed by army personnel. In March a civilian public order judge, accompanied by judicial police, tried to enforce arrest warrants against 26 people implicated in paramilitary activities in Carmen de Chucurí, including the mayor. Local officials and army personnel based in the town intervened and only one person was arrested. In June the mayor surrendered to the authorities. Members of another paramilitary organization sentenced to 30 years' imprisonment in 1991 for a series of massacres in the Urabá region of Antioquia in 1988 were still at large at the end of 1992 (see *Amnesty International Reports 1989* and *1992*).

Killings of "social undesirables" by "death squads" backed by the police in major cities and towns continued to be reported. Vagrants (including children), homosexuals and petty criminals were gunned down in the streets at night or were seized and driven away in unmarked cars. Their bodies, which were rarely identified, often bore signs of torture. Community leaders, students and unemployed youths in shanty towns surrounding major cities were also frequently threatened and killed by shadowy "death squads". In July heavily armed men entered the neighbourhood of Juan Pablo II in Ciudad Bolívar on the southern outskirts of Bogotá and opened fire on a group of teenagers leaving a birthday party: six were killed. Rosabel Jiménez, the grandmother of one of the victims, was shot dead as she attempted to apprehend one of the killers. A police cap was found beneath her body.

Over 100 "disappearances" were reported. Gustavo Salgado Ramírez, a biologist and project consultant for the French development agency *Terres des Hommes* and a collaborator with the *Liga Internacional de Mujeres por la Paz y la Libertad*, International League of Women for Peace and Freedom, was last seen in Bogotá on 4 November. Some two months earlier an unidentified man had threatened him with death because of his human rights activities.

Two members of the judicial police were arrested in September in connection with the "disappearance" of lawyer Alirio Pedraza Becerra in July 1990 (see *Amnesty International Report 1991*). His whereabouts remained unknown.

In several cases the Procurator General's Public Ministry opened disciplinary investigations and imposed sanctions on members of the army and police for human rights violations. In August disciplinary charges were brought against four officers from Bogotá's Metropolitan Police for their part in the "disappearance", torture and death of university student Alvaro Moreno Moreno in January 1991 (see *Amnesty International Report 1992*). Also in August, the Procurator General formally requested the dismissal from the armed forces of three army officers for the massacres of banana plantation workers in the Urabá region in March 1988. According to the ruling, one of the three army officers, then a major (since promoted to Lieutenant-Colonel), paid the hotel bills for the paramilitary agents who carried out the massacres and identified 20 plantation workers who were to be killed as "guerrilla suspects". No information was made available about criminal proceedings

**100**

against the army officers after the case was taken over by the military courts in 1991.

The judiciary failed to bring to justice those responsible for the vast majority of human rights violations, although in exceptional cases civilian judges made significant progress in their investigations. In August a civilian judge ordered the arrest of a former mayor of Arauca and an army colonel implicated in the killing by two soldiers of journalist Henry Rojas Monje in December 1991. The colonel's lawyers immediately asked for the case to be passed to the military justice system. Military tribunals investigating human rights violations by army personnel have persistently failed to bring those responsible to justice and have routinely released army personnel facing trial. In March it became apparent that at least one of the soldiers whose arrest had been ordered by a military court judge in 1991 in connection with the killing of five members of the Palacios family in August 1991 (see *Amnesty International Report 1992*) was no longer in detention. He was rearrested in March and charged with the killing, days before, of a further three people, including a 17-year-old pregnant woman, in Bogotá.

Victims of deliberate and arbitrary killings by the FARC, ELN and EPL armed opposition groups included people suspected of being informers for the armed forces, petty criminals, members of rival groups and local government officials believed to be collaborating with paramilitary organizations. Several hundred people were believed to have been kidnapped and held hostage by guerrilla organizations. Many, including landowners, industrialists and business people, were held for ransom. Several hostages were killed or died while in captivity. Argelino Durán Quintero, a 77-year-old former cabinet minister, died in March of a heart attack while being held hostage by the EPL. He had been kidnapped in January. Other hostages were seized and held for propaganda purposes or to force local government officials to adopt policies favoured by the insurgents.

Amnesty International repeatedly urged the government to ensure effective and impartial investigations into all reported extrajudicial executions, "disappearances" and torture cases, and called for those responsible to be brought to justice. It urged the government to dismantle para-

military forces and to take measures to ensure that human rights monitors and others are able to carry out their legitimate activities without fear of reprisal.

Amnesty International investigated and expressed concern about abuses by armed opposition groups.

In oral statements to the United Nations Commission on Human Rights in February and the Working Group on Indigenous Populations of its Sub-Commission on Prevention of Discrimination and Protection of Minorities in August, Amnesty International included reference to its concerns about extrajudicial executions, "disappearances" and torture committed by the armed forces and paramilitary groups in the course of counter-insurgency operations. In October Amnesty International published *Human rights violations against the indigenous peoples of the Americas*, which included concerns in Colombia.

# COMOROS

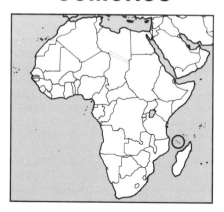

**About 30 soldiers and civilians arrested during and after a coup attempt in September were still held without trial at the end of the year. Among them were possible prisoners of conscience. Some of the detainees were reportedly tortured and all were held incommunicado in harsh conditions. Several civilians were killed during the coup attempt and there were reports that some were extrajudicially executed by loyalist forces.**

Following a national reconciliation pact between President Saïd Mohamed Djohar and opposition political parties at the end of 1991, a new government led by a former opposition leader, Mohamed Taki, was formed in January. Mohamed Taki is leader of the *Union nationale pour la démocratie aux Comores* (UNDC), National Union for Democracy in the Comoros, whose supporters had been arrested and accused of an attempted coup in 1990 (see *Amnesty International Report 1992*).

A National Conference to discuss the country's political future started in January and ended in April. Conference delegates drafted a new federal Constitution which was adopted by referendum in June.

The National Conference was followed by a period of political instability. In May the President appointed a new government, again headed by Mohamed Taki. In July President Djohar accused Mohamed Taki of appointing a former French mercenary to a government post and dismissed him and the government. The UNDC and other opposition parties accused the President of violating the national reconciliation pact and called for his resignation. In early September the government announced that legislative elections would be held in October. In mid-September members of the gendarmerie used violence to disperse demonstrators in Moroni demanding the President's resignation. The first round of legislative elections on 22 November was marred by violence and gross irregularities, and some opposition parties boycotted them. The second round passed more peacefully and a number of National Assembly members were elected.

On 26 September about 100 soldiers took control of the national radio and announced that they had deposed President Djohar. They were led by two sons of former President Mohamed Abdallah, who was assassinated in November 1989 and succeeded by President Djohar (see *Amnesty International Report 1990*). Forces loyal to the government thwarted the coup and about 10 soldiers involved in the revolt, including former President Abdallah's sons, were captured.

In the aftermath of the coup attempt more than 20 civilians were detained, including Omar Tamou, a former Minister of the Interior and member of the Udzima political party, and M'Tara Maecha, a former Minister of Foreign Affairs. They were apparently detained because they had expressed support for the overthrow of President Djohar. None had been tried by the end of the year, although the author-

ities said in October that they would soon be brought to trial. A few were released without charge by mid-October, including Djamal Edine Salim, a former Minister of Justice and Public Service. At least five people, including Loutfi Adenane, President of the *Parti comorien pour la démocratie et le progrès* (PCDP), Comorian Party for Democracy and Progress, were charged with complicity in the coup attempt but released provisionally. Omar Tamou, M'Tara Maecha and about 20 other civilians remained in custody at the end of the year. Some of them appeared to be prisoners of conscience detained solely on the basis of their non-violent opposition to President Djohar. On 6 October the 10 detained soldiers appeared before an examining magistrate who remanded them in custody in a civilian prison. However, military officials transferred them instead to Kandani military barracks, despite protests by judicial officials and defence lawyers.

Some of the detainees were reportedly tortured. One of them, Hassan Arouna, was said to have been severely beaten while in police custody for eight days in October, with resulting damage to one of his eyes and paralysis of the right side of his face. He was subsequently transferred to prison where he received medical treatment, but no action appeared to have been taken against those who tortured him. The detained soldiers were kept incommunicado in harsh conditions: each was held in a separate cell with no furniture and only straw to sleep on.

At least six civilians were killed in mid-October during and after an attack on Kandani barracks by armed government opponents who were apparently trying to free the 10 imprisoned soldiers. Opposition sources and the Comorian Human Rights Association claimed that some of those killed were executed extrajudicially by government troops on suspicion of supporting the armed opponents. Among those killed were Ahmed Abdallah Djida, an aide to Mohamed Taki, and two former soldiers who were said to have been extrajudicially executed at a private house where they were staying overnight. These claims could not be confirmed; however, no investigations were undertaken by the authorities to indicate the exact circumstances in which the killings occurred.

During the year Amnesty International learned that four supporters of the UNDC

**102**

who had been held since 1990 in connection with an alleged coup attempt had been freed at the end of 1991 (see *Amnesty International Report 1992*). None had been brought to trial. They included Ali Soihili, a journalist, and Abdou Bakar Boina, a former secretary general of the UNDC.

After the coup attempt Amnesty International urged the government to investigate reported killings of civilians by government soldiers in the aftermath of the coup attempt and to bring to justice anyone responsible for committing extrajudicial executions. Amnesty International also called for the release of those against whom there was no evidence of involvement in the coup attempt and for those accused of involvement to be tried in accordance with international standards for fair trial. It urged the authorities to end the use of prolonged incommunicado detention.

# CONGO

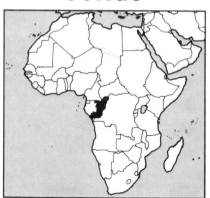

A journalist detained for several days appeared to be a prisoner of conscience. Five people killed by soldiers in January appeared to be the victims of extrajudicial executions. Allegations of gross human rights violations, including torture and extrajudicial executions, committed under former governments remained uninvestigated. At least four people remained under sentence of death but there were no reports of executions.

A multi-party political system was established and elections brought a new government and head of state to power, despite a threatened military coup against the transitional government of Prime Min-

ister André Milongo early in the year.

A new Constitution containing a number of human rights safeguards and institutionalizing a multi-party system was adopted by referendum in March (see *Amnesty International Report 1992*). Local and municipal elections were held in May.

National Assembly elections in July brought to power the *Union panafricaine pour la démocratie sociale* (UPADS), Pan-African Union for Social Democracy, led by Pascal Lissouba, a former Prime Minister and prisoner of conscience. It won a third of the seats in the National Assembly. Pascal Lissouba was subsequently elected President in August. Former President Sassou-Nguesso was defeated in the first round.

On 15 January about 100 soldiers occupied television and radio stations in the capital, Brazzaville, for several hours. They broadcast a communique demanding the dismissal of the newly appointed Secretary of State for Defence, Michel Gangouo. He had announced changes in the army's command structure, which would have had the effect of weakening the influence of officers loyal to the then President, Denis Sassou-Nguesso. On 18 January another group of soldiers prevented Prime Minister Milongo from leaving Brazzaville: two days later soldiers fired on some of his supporters who had gathered outside his residence to prevent the possibility of his being seized by mutinous soldiers. Five people were killed and dozens injured. The mutinous soldiers demanded Prime Minister Milongo's resignation and imposed a curfew in the capital, but the crisis was defused three days later through the intervention of the *Conseil supérieur de la République* (CSR), High Council of the Republic, the transitional legislative body. This persuaded Prime Minister Milongo to reshuffle the cabinet, effectively removing Michel Gangouo. No subsequent action, however, was taken against the soldiers responsible for the killings on 20 January.

On 21 May Durcil Pambou, a television journalist, was arrested in Brazzaville. He was accused of "inciting civil war" after he read out on a television news program anonymous protests against the CSR's request that Prime Minister Milongo reshuffle the cabinet. He was released without charge several days later. He appeared to be a prisoner of conscience arrested for pursuing his professional duties.

The new Constitution prohibits human rights violations including torture. However, the new government took no steps to establish any inquiry into gross human rights violations which had occurred in previous years or into the killings of demonstrators in January. On the contrary, at his inauguration ceremony in August, President Lissouba announced that he would submit to the National Assembly a general amnesty bill, apparently intended to protect the country's past leaders from prosecution for offences including human rights violations committed while they were in power. However, no such bill was presented to parliament during the year.

Four people convicted of criminal offences in 1989 remained under sentence of death. No new death sentences or executions were reported.

Amnesty International remained concerned by the failure of the authorities to investigate past human rights violations, including torture and extrajudicial executions, and the possible introduction of legislation providing immunity against prosecution for senior government officials and others implicated in human rights violations.

# COSTA RICA

**Three long-term political prisoners were released on bail pending trial. Two men were extrajudicially executed and two indigenous women were reportedly raped by the Rural Assistance Guard during an anti-narcotics operation. Other instances of torture and ill-treatment by police were reported.**

Livia Cordero Gené, Bolívar Eduardo Díaz Rojas and Domingo Solís Solís were released in July after being detained for 29 months without trial. Charges against them included illegal association, aggravated explosion and aggravated robbery, but there were allegations that they were held on account of their left-wing ideas. In July a court upheld only the charge of illegal association and all three were released on bail. No trial date had been set by the end of 1992. Twelve others who had been arrested with them were released in 1990.

In February Rolando Watson Sáenz and Julio Trejos Obando were beaten, slashed and shot dead by members of a special command of the *Guardia de Asistencia Rural* (GAR), Rural Assistance Guard, during an anti-narcotics operation in an area of Talamanca, Limón province, populated by indigenous people. In the same operation, GAR agents also reportedly raped two Guaymi indigenous women, one of them aged 15, and beat a five-year-old girl to force her mother to reveal the location of a marijuana plantation. At least one other person was beaten, and several houses raided or burned. Twelve GAR members were arrested and charged with aggravated homicide, aggravated deprivation of liberty, causing concussion, illegal entry, rape and aggravated theft. At the end of 1992 three remained in pre-trial detention.

At least seven transvestites were reportedly arrested by police agents in San José, held for several hours and subjected to torture or cruel, inhuman or degrading treatment. One of them, Manuel Horacio Guevara Albornoz, was reportedly arrested in April wearing women's clothes. He was taken to the radio patrol unit, where policemen reportedly mocked him and fondled his buttocks. He was rearrested in May, taken to the same radio patrol unit, made to strip and subjected to mockery. Jorge Enrique Vargas González was arrested in May by two policemen, driven to the ruins of a house, and reportedly forced at gunpoint to have oral sex with one of the officers. Investigations into these cases were carried out by the Ministry of the Interior.

In December Amnesty International wrote to the government of President Rafael Calderón Fournier to express concern about the extrajudicial executions, torture and ill-treatment by GAR agents and police officers, and to urge it to take measures to investigate such abuses and bring those responsible to justice. The organization also raised its concern about the

**104**

torture or cruel, inhuman or degrading treatment of transvestites and asked to be informed about the methods and findings of the investigations into the reported cases.

# CÔTE D'IVOIRE

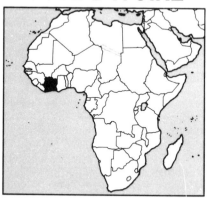

**More than 250 people, including opposition party leaders, were arrested in February following demonstrations: over 80 of them, all prisoners of conscience, were sentenced to between three months' and three years' imprisonment. However, all those still held in late July were released under an amnesty law. Five journalists also appeared to be prisoners of conscience: they too were released under the amnesty law. One person reportedly died in custody as a result of torture. Conditions in at least one prison were extremely harsh, resulting in a large number of deaths.**

For the first time in many years a large number of prisoners of conscience were detained when the government put the blame on its opponents for damage to property which occurred during riots in February. The rioting took place after demonstrations called by opposition parties to protest against President Félix Houphouët-Boigny's refusal to accept the findings of a commission of inquiry into a military raid on Yopougon university campus in May 1991 (see *Amnesty International Report 1992*). The commission had concluded that members of the security forces had beaten and raped students during the raid. It held the army chief of staff responsible and called for him to be punished. President Houphouët-Boigny rejected the criticism of the chief of staff

and reaffirmed his confidence in him.

In March Côte d'Ivoire acceded to the International Covenant on Civil and Political Rights; the International Covenant on Economic, Social and Cultural Rights; and the African Charter on Human and Peoples' Rights.

More than 250 people were arrested in February after two demonstrations in the capital, Abidjan. Most were prisoners of conscience. The demonstrations started peacefully but were followed by rioting. Some sources alleged this was provoked by government agents, although this could not be confirmed. The government accused the political leaders who had organized the demonstrations of responsibility for damage caused by the rioting. Most of those arrested were released without charge after about two months in prison, or released on the orders of investigating magistrates, but 85 people were convicted at a series of trials and sentenced to between three months' and three years' imprisonment. They were found guilty of "sharing responsibility" for the violence and damage which followed the demonstrations. However, no evidence was produced in court to show that any of those convicted had been responsible for acts of violence or vandalism: some had not even been present during the demonstrations.

An appeal was heard in June. At its conclusion the President of the Appeal Court, Judge Yanon Yapo, announced that the court's decision would be delayed. This gave rise to speculation that the government was putting pressure on the Appeal Court not to acquit the defendants. This speculation in turn led the Public Prosecutor to file a formal request to the Supreme Court for the removal of the Appeal Court President who, he suggested, was unfairly favourable to the defendants. The Supreme Court apparently deliberately failed to meet the deadline for its decision in order to avoid becoming involved, but Judge Yapo was later removed from his post and given no other posting. Independent observers who attended the appeal hearing reported that the judge had in fact been both independent and impartial.

Those arrested included four opposition members of parliament. One was released but three were convicted, including Laurent Gbagbo, leader of the opposition *Front populaire ivoirien* (FPI), Ivorian Popular Front. In protest, all other opposition members of parliament withdrew from the National Assembly until the release of their colleagues. Because the authorities said the three had been caught while in the act of committing an offence, they were imprisoned without their parliamentary immunity being formally lifted.

Also convicted were René Dégni Ségui, President of the *Ligue ivoirienne des droits de l'homme*, Ivorian Human Rights League, and Martial Ahipeaud, President of the *Fédération estudiantine et scolaire de Côte d'Ivoire*, Ivorian Federation of Students and School Pupils, which had been banned in 1991. Among others convicted were teachers, trades unionists, students and journalists.

Some of those convicted were released after serving their three-month prison sentences. On 31 July, two days after the National Assembly unanimously passed an amnesty law following months of protest against the trials and convictions, the 77 people who remained in prison in connection with the demonstrations were released. The amnesty law also ruled out the possibility of legal proceedings being brought as a result of the May 1991 incident at Yopougon university campus: in effect, it conferred immunity on the security forces responsible for beating and raping students.

At the same time, a new law was also adopted which provides for the prosecution and imprisonment for up to 20 years of anyone who calls or leads a gathering that becomes violent, whether or not they are personally responsible for inciting or perpetrating violence. Similar legislation had been proposed in February, but in the event the existing penal code was used to prosecute Laurent Gbagbo and others as it provides for prosecution for shared responsibility.

Some prisoners of conscience were injured at the time of their arrest. They included Simone Gbagbo, an FPI activist and the wife of Laurent Gbagbo, and Georges Coffy, a journalist and former prisoner of conscience (see *Amnesty International Report 1992*). Simone Gbagbo was arrested by gendarmes as she sought refuge in a building. She was beaten on the head and knocked unconscious, requiring hospital treatment. She spent one month in a surgical collar as a result of the assault, but no action was taken against those responsible.

Five journalists who were sentenced to prison terms because of articles they had written appeared to be prisoners of conscience. In February three journalists working on the independent bi-weekly, *Le Jeune Démocrate*, were each sentenced to 18 months' imprisonment and a fine, and the newspaper was banned from publishing for three months. Ignace Dassohire, the director, Jean-Sylvestre Lia, the editor, and Emmanuel Koré, the deputy director, were convicted of insulting the Head of State and inciting the military to revolt. The newspaper had compared President Houphouët-Boigny to President Bourguiba of Tunisia and also referred to him as "rubbish". In early March two other journalists – Norbert Gnahoua and Konan Yao, of the weekly *L'Oeil du peuple* – were sentenced to 18 months in prison on charges of insulting the head of state. All five were released under the amnesty law.

One prisoner reportedly died as a result of torture. Désiré-Lazare Abané died in Divo hospital in May after being taken into police custody in Divo the previous day, apparently on suspicion of criminal offences. He was sent to hospital reportedly because he had taken medication, but his body was apparently severely swollen and his neck fractured. It was not clear what steps were taken, if any, by the procuracy to establish if he had been tortured.

Criminal prisoners at the *Maison d'Arrêt et de Correction d'Abidjan*, the main prison in Abidjan, were reportedly held in extremely harsh conditions, leading to scores of deaths in custody. Lack of hygiene, inadequate medical attention and insufficient nutritious food accounted for over 100 deaths between February and July alone. The prison was holding around 4,600 prisoners, about a third of whom were awaiting trial.

Amnesty International expressed concern to the government about the mass arrests of political activists who had not used or advocated violence, and called for the immediate, unconditional release of all prisoners of conscience. It also urged the government to ensure that the new law introduced to punish people who organize demonstrations which result in violence should not be used to imprison peaceful demonstrators or to limit peaceful exercise of the rights to freedom of expression and association. Amnesty International also protested against the government's

**106**

decision to grant immunity to members of the security forces responsible for human rights violations and called for all perpetrators of human rights violations to be brought to justice.

# CROATIA

**Thousands of people, the majority of them Serbs, were charged with armed rebellion or seeking to undermine the territorial unity of Croatia by force; they included some prisoners of conscience detained on account of their ethnic origin. There were reports of extrajudicial executions by members of the Croatian Army. In areas under Serbian control, "special police units" were linked to the extrajudicial execution of over 50 people. Many people were beaten and ill-treated in custody by civilian or military police and at least three people died in Split as a result. People detained in areas under Serbian control were also reportedly beaten and ill-treated in custody, as a result of which at least four died.**

The conflict in Croatia largely ended with the signing of a cease-fire agreement which came into effect in January and allowed the establishment of a United Nations (UN) peace-keeping force in areas of Croatia under Serbian control. These areas, amounting to almost one third of the territory of Croatia, were named United Nations Protected Areas (UNPAs). In May Croatia became a member of the UN.

As a result of the conflict in the former Yugoslavia, there were over 750,000 displaced persons in Croatia, including at least 450,000 refugees from Bosnia-Herzegovina.

According to official Croatian figures,

military courts passed judgment in 423 cases of war crimes and crimes against humanity. The conviction rate was 91 per cent and most of those convicted were Serbs. In several cases, members of the Croatian Army who had been charged with the murder of Serbian civilians or captured soldiers were released, either after acquittal or pending further trial proceedings. The military public prosecutor of the Federal Republic of Yugoslavia stated in November that proceedings had been started there against 125 members of the Croatian Army accused of war crimes and crimes against humanity; 60 had been indicted and 12 convicted. Most, however, had already been released in prisoner exchanges with Croatia in August.

According to official Croatian figures, some 20,000 people were charged between August 1990 and June 1992 with armed rebellion, many of whom were tried *in absentia*. Over 70 per cent of those charged were Serbs. Among these were people who appeared to have been prosecuted solely because of their ethnic origin. For example, a Serb from the Split area arrested in June and charged together with 44 others with "armed rebellion" was detained in prison for two months, despite lack of evidence against him. He was then, against his will, offered in an exchange of prisoners with the Federal Republic of Yugoslavia. In August he refused to be exchanged and returned to Split, where he was rearrested and held for 24 hours before finally being released.

Proceedings against many people charged with "armed rebellion" were discontinued under an amnesty granted in September. In December, 94 prisoners were pardoned. Among them were 38 Serbs from the village of Budimci who had been arrested in April and convicted on charges of preparing or taking part in armed rebellion in November 1991. According to the Croatian Vice-Premier, members of the Yugoslav National Army (JNA) had distributed arms to them, but they had not used the arms. Also pardoned were members of the Croatian Army, among them 11 men variously convicted of murder, attempted murder and assault and battery.

In areas under Croatian Government control, there were reports of extrajudicial executions committed by members of the Croatian Army. In November a government official stated that the "Croatian police will do everything they can to ensure that the Croatian state becomes as soon as possible a legal state in which peace and protection will be provided for all citizens, regardless of their religion, race or nationality". However, in certain areas local authorities sometimes appeared unwilling or unable to take effective action against extrajudicial executions or to bring their perpetrators to justice. According to the military prosecutor of Osijek, in the first nine months of the year, members of the Croatian Army had been responsible for 72 killings in the Osijek area alone and there had been 14 convictions. Those killed included Serbs, among them four elderly people in Markušica in August.

In the UNPAS, particularly in eastern Slavonia and the Knin area, local Serbian authorities largely failed to implement the UN peace plan's demilitarization program; Serbian irregulars, including refugees from Bosnia-Herzegovina, were absorbed into units, described as "special police units", which retained their military weaponry. In October a senior UN official reportedly linked these "special police units" to the murders of some 50 non-Serbs in eastern Slavonia between April and October. Among the victims were an elderly Croatian couple from Branjin Vrh. By the end of the year reports indicated that the security of remaining non-Serbs in eastern Slavonia had improved. Serbian authorities in the UNPAS pointed to numerous violations of the cease-fire by Croatian forces in which they claimed civilians as well as members of Serbian forces had been killed. In December a UN Commission of Experts investigating war crimes in former Yugoslavia found evidence of a mass grave in a field near Vukovar alleged to contain the bodies of up to 300 men extrajudicially executed by JNA units, together with Serbian irregulars, in November 1991.

A number of people died after being tortured or otherwise ill-treated in custody by Croatian military or civilian police. At least three reportedly died as a result of torture by the military police in Split. They included Nenad Knežević, a Serb, who was arrested at home in Kaštel Lukšić on 13 June by five Croatian military police officers. A day later he was taken to hospital in Split in a coma. A certificate issued by the hospital stated that he was being treated for injuries to the liver, bruising of the body and head, four broken ribs and

gunshot wounds. He died on 23 June. In August Dalibor Sardelić, a Croat, died following arrest; in September criminal proceedings were started against four military police officers in connection with his death, but by the end of the year they had not been brought to trial.

In June Serbian authorities in Knin handed over to the Croatian authorities the bodies of two soldiers and three civilians (two of them women) from Bosnia-Herzegovina. The five had reportedly died in Knin prison on various dates in April and May. Autopsies carried out in Split hospital concluded that four had died as a result of injuries inflicted by beatings. The cause of death of the fifth could not be established because of putrefaction.

After tens of thousands of people fleeing Bosnia-Herzegovina had been admitted to Croatia, the Croatian Government announced that it could not accept any more refugees. From July onwards, there were several reports that people fleeing Bosnia-Herzegovina without proper documents were being refused entry at the Croatian border, in violation of international standards. In August, dozens of men of military age were forcibly returned from Croatia to Bosnia-Herzegovina; after protests from UN officials, the government reportedly agreed to halt such returns. However, in November there were further reports that refugees had been forcibly sent back to Bosnia-Herzegovina from Croatia.

In January Amnesty International wrote to the Croatian authorities expressing concern about reports of the arrest or "disappearance" in the previous months of a number of Serbs. The organization asked about the reason for their arrest and called for the release of any who had not been charged with a recognizably criminal offence, and for all others to be granted proper legal safeguards. Amnesty International also urged the authorities to take effective action to ensure that law enforcement officers implemented international standards for law enforcement. The organization subsequently learned of the release of several people about whom it had inquired, but the fate of others remained unknown. In October Amnesty International called on the Croatian authorities not to return people against their will to Bosnia-Herzegovina, since they risked becoming victims of human rights abuses.

In November Amnesty International

**108** wrote to the government expressing concern about human rights abuses committed by all parties to the conflict in Bosnia-Herzegovina (see **Bosnia-Herzegovina** entry). It said that the governments of the Federal Republic of Yugoslavia and of Croatia shared a heavy responsibility for abuses to the extent that they had supported politically and materially the various forces operating in Bosnia-Herzegovina. Amnesty International called on all parties to ensure respect for international human rights and humanitarian standards.

# CUBA

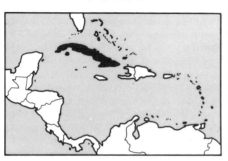

**Between 300 and 500 prisoners of conscience and possible prisoners of conscience were believed to be in detention. Peaceful opponents of the government were frequently taken in for questioning by the security forces or harassed by government-sponsored gangs. Trials in political cases fell far short of international fair trial standards. Reports of ill-treatment, in isolated cases amounting to torture, increased and several prisoners died in custody, allegedly as a result of ill-treatment. Prison conditions were harsh. At least three people were executed.**

The government of President Fidel Castro responded swiftly to two alleged "counter-revolutionary" incidents near the start of the year. On 29 December 1991 three Cuban residents of the United States of America were captured as they landed on the Cuban coast, reportedly carrying weapons and incendiary devices. On 9 January 1992, nine people were arrested and accused of killing four security officials during an attempt to flee Cuba. In response to the two incidents, which coincided with a wave of arrests of leading dissidents, senior government officials suggested that harsher measures should be introduced to

deal with "counter-revolutionary" crime. No such new measures were introduced but three of those detained in connection with the two incidents were executed (see below) and peaceful government opponents continued to face harassment and arrest throughout the year. Attacks by members of the *Destacamentos Populares de Respuesta Rápida*, People's Rapid Response Detachments, which had been set up by the authorities in 1991 to counter signs of dissent (see *Amnesty International Report 1992*), became more frequent.

Freedom of expression, association and assembly, including independent monitoring of human rights, continued to be severely limited. No independent international human rights monitors were known to have been allowed to visit the country. Despite such restrictions, there were grounds to believe that political prisoners numbered at least 600 and possibly 1,000 or more.

In March the United Nations (UN) Commission on Human Rights designated the Special Representative appointed in 1991 by the UN Secretary-General as its Special Rapporteur to review and report on the situation of human rights in Cuba. The Cuban Government refused to co-operate in any way with the Special Rapporteur.

Reforms to the 1976 Constitution which were introduced in July included the removal of all references to the former Soviet Union while retaining a commitment to communism. New paragraphs guaranteeing religious freedom and prohibiting discrimination on the grounds of religious belief were introduced and new constitutional powers were granted to the President, including the right to declare a state of emergency.

There were believed to be between 300 and 500 prisoners of conscience in detention, possibly more, at the end of 1992. Dozens of prisoners of conscience were detained during the year because of their activities as members of unofficial political, trade union, religious or human rights groups. They were most commonly charged with offences such as "enemy propaganda", "disrespect" and "illegal association". Scores of others were imprisoned for trying to leave the country illegally.

Prisoner of conscience Sebastián Arcos Bergnes, Vice-President of the unofficial *Comité Cubano Pro Derechos Humanos* (CCPDH), Cuban Committee for Human

Rights, was arrested with two other leading members of the committee, including his brother Gustavo, in January. Their addresses were prominently displayed during a television program purporting to link them with the three Cuban exiles who had entered the country illegally in December 1991. Crowds of government supporters went to their homes, where the three were arrested by police. While the other two were released with an official warning after 24 hours, Sebastián Arcos Bergnes was kept in detention by the *Departamento de Seguridad del Estado* (DSE), Department of State Security, initially on a charge of "rebellion", later changed to the lesser offence of "enemy propaganda". He was tried in October and sentenced to four years and eight months' imprisonment on the grounds that he had disseminated abroad information about human rights abuses which the authorities said was false.

José Luis Pujol Irizar, President of the unofficial *Proyecto Apertura de la Isla* (PAIS), Project for Opening Up the Island, was arrested while a pro-government crowd besieged his home in March. Two other leading dissidents – Elizardo Sánchez Santa Cruz, President of the unofficial *Comisión Cubana de Derechos Humanos y Reconciliación Nacional*, Cuban Commission of Human Rights and National Reconciliation, and Lázaro Loreto Perea, acting President of the *Asociación Defensora de los Derechos Políticos*, Association for the Defence of Political Rights – were also arrested on their way to his house. The three were led by police through the hostile crowd which attacked them, causing minor injuries to Elizardo Sánchez. He and Lázaro Loreto were released the next day, but José Luis Pujol was kept in detention and sentenced in September to three years' imprisonment for "disrespect" on the grounds that he had criticized President Castro in a letter sent abroad.

Dozens of other political and human rights activists were arbitrarily arrested for short periods or harassed. In Havana on 10 December, the anniversary of the Universal Declaration of Human Rights, and for several days after that, several people were arrested or harassed. For up to 10 days, crowds of pro-government supporters besieged the homes of at least six people belonging to different organizations. Elec-

tricity and water supplies were cut off in some cases. On 15 December Rolando Prats, a leading member of the *Corriente Socialista Democrática Cubana* (CSDC), Cuban Social-Democratic Current, was beaten up in the street by three civilians. He was taken to hospital by police and then transferred to a police station before being released on payment of a fine for disrupting public order. Four days earlier he had been stopped by five people who threatened him with death if he did not give up his activities and leave the country.

Several activists were arrested during this period, including Elizardo Sánchez and Rodolfo González, a leading member of the CCPDH. Elizardo Sánchez, who was beaten almost unconscious at the time of arrest, was released on bail on 28 December pending trial on a charge of "disrespect". Rodolfo González reportedly remained in detention at the Havana headquarters of the DSE at the end of the year under investigation on a charge of "enemy propaganda".

Prisoners of conscience Marco Antonio Abad Flamand and Jorge Crespo Díaz, who had been detained since November 1991 for making a film that insulted President Castro and which had been shown abroad, were both sentenced in November to two years' imprisonment on charges of "enemy propaganda" and "disrespect".

Politically motivated arrests were reported throughout the country. Although in most cases information was scant, many of those arrested were thought to be prisoners of conscience. For example, three members of the unofficial *Movimiento Cristiano "Liberación"*, "Liberation" Christian Movement, who had been gathering signatures for a petition to change the Constitution, were arrested in Santiago in early 1992 and charged with "enemy propaganda". One was sentenced to six years' imprisonment and the other two to five years each.

Scores of people, possibly 200 to 300, who were believed to be prisoners of conscience, were reported to have been imprisoned for trying to leave the country without permission. Most were arrested after putting out to sea in small boats or on home-made rafts. Detailed information was available on only a few such cases. They included Michael Pérez Pérez and 10 others picked up from a raft near Mariel in March. In May Humberto Colón and several others were intercepted by coastguards in a boat off the coast of Matanzas; at least one man is said to have died after the authorities opened fire on the vessel.

Several prisoners of conscience were released during the year. Esteban González, Manuel Pozo Montero and Manuel Regueiro, who had been convicted in 1990 (see *Amnesty International Report 1991*), were released in April but only on condition they left Cuba. Arturo Montané Ruiz, whose sentence was due to expire in September, refused to accept such conditions but was released in July. Three members of the *Movimiento Pacifista Solidaridad y Paz*, Solidarity and Peace Pacifist Movement (see *Amnesty International Report 1992*), were released either upon or shortly before expiry of their sentences.

Trials in political cases and in cases involving the possible application of the death penalty continued to fall well short of international standards of fairness, particularly with regard to the right of defence. Prisoners of conscience Yndamiro Restano Díaz, President of the unofficial *Movimiento de Armonía* (MAR), Harmony Movement (see *Amnesty International Report 1992*), and MAR member María Elena Aparicio were sentenced to 10 years' and seven years' imprisonment respectively on a charge of "rebellion" at their trial in May. They reportedly had only limited access to lawyers shortly before the trial took place.

The number of reports of ill-treatment at the time of arrest or while in police or prison custody increased. In isolated instances, the reported treatment amounted to torture. For example, in Alambradas de Manacas Prison in June, Bienvenido Martínez Bustamante, a possible prisoner of conscience, was reportedly beaten unconscious by three guards while his hands were tied. He was said to have received no immediate medical attention. Reports were received in November that two prisoners were in poor health. Luis Alberto Pita Santos (see *Amnesty International Report 1992*), a prisoner of conscience serving a five-year prison sentence for "disrespect", "illegal association" and "clandestine printing", and political prisoner Arturo Suárez Ramos had reportedly been beaten by guards while on hunger-strike in Boniato Prison.

Several deaths in detention were reported as the apparent result of medical neglect, hunger-strikes or ill-treatment. Political prisoner Alain Hermida Oviedo, aged 17, was said to have died in Combinado del Este Prison in the first half of the year after being beaten by a prison guard while handcuffed. Francisco Díaz Mesa reportedly died in Alambradas de Manacas Prison in February after being beaten by guards because he had banged on his cell bars seeking medical attention.

General prison conditions were said to have seriously deteriorated during the year, in part owing to the grave economic situation facing the country. Serious shortages of food, medicines and other necessities were reported in many prisons. In some cases political prisoners were apparently transferred unnecessarily to prisons far from their families, where transport shortages made it extremely difficult for relatives to visit and take additional supplies. In some cases prisoners were reportedly deprived of food and medicines as a form of punishment. Several prisoners with AIDS were said to have been held in punishment cells where their food quota was cut and the diet and treatment recommended by doctors withdrawn.

At least three executions took place during the year, after trials which fell far short of international standards for fair trial. The trials, concerning the two incidents around the start of the year, took place very shortly after arrest in a highly charged political atmosphere. Access to defence lawyers was reported to have been extremely limited. Eduardo Díaz Betancourt, who had been captured on the coast, allegedly carrying weapons, was executed on 20 January after being convicted of planning acts of terrorism and sabotage. The entire process from arrest through trial and appeals procedures to execution took only 23 days. Two others convicted with him had their death sentences commuted to 30 years' imprisonment. In February Luis Miguel Almeida Pérez and René Salmerón Mendoza were executed after being convicted of killing four security officials, apparently after capturing them and tying them up, when they were attempting to leave the country illegally.

Throughout the year Amnesty International appealed to the authorities to release prisoners of conscience and sought further information about other concerns. In January the organization expressed concern at the execution of Eduardo Díaz Betancourt and publicly urged the government to halt further executions. In July Amnesty

International sought permission to visit Cuba. No response was received to the request or to other communications sent during the year. In December the organization sent a series of recommendations to the government. These included the immediate and unconditional release of all prisoners of conscience, adherence to international standards pertaining to trials and prison conditions, the protection of human rights monitors, the disbandment or strict regulation by law of the People's Rapid Response Detachments, impartial investigations of allegations of unlawful killings, ill-treatment and deaths in custody, the introduction of legislation to abolish the death penalty, and access to political prisoners by appropriate international humanitarian monitoring bodies.

# CYPRUS

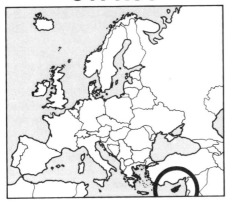

**There were at least 15 prisoners of conscience, all Jehovah's Witnesses who had refused on conscientious grounds to perform military service or reservist exercises. Some detainees alleged they were tortured or ill-treated by the police.**

In January the House of Representatives passed legislation, recognizing for the first time the right to have conscientious objections to military service and providing for "unarmed military service" inside and outside military camps. However, its provisions fall short of international standards in several respects. It was unclear whether the service outside the military camps would be completely civilian; its length – 42 months as against the 26 months of ordinary military service – is punitive, particularly since conscientious objectors have to perform supplementary service equiva-

lent to periods of reservist exercises; it was not clear whether it would be open to conscientious objectors on grounds other than religious; and the right to transfer to alternative service from military service would be suspended during periods of emergency or general mobilization. No conscientious objectors were known to have been offered the option of "unarmed military service" by the end of the year.

In April Cyprus ratified the first Optional Protocol to the International Covenant on Civil and Political Rights.

Conscientious objectors were imprisoned for periods of up to 15 months. Among them was Christakis Ionathan Christoforou, who was sentenced to one year's imprisonment in November for refusing to perform military service. Athinakis Zinonos was sentenced to 15 months' imprisonment in December on the same charge. It was the second time in two years that both men had been sentenced to terms of imprisonment for refusing to perform military service.

Several detainees in police custody alleged that they had been tortured or ill-treated. For example, Mehmet Canbulut, a Turkish Cypriot, was allegedly threatened, slapped, punched, beaten on the soles of his feet, burned with a cigarette and verbally abused by members of the Special Branch in April. He had voluntarily gone to Limassol Central Police Station to report his arrival in the Republic from the northern part of the island (under the control of the Turkish armed forces and the Turkish Cypriot administration). The Attorney General reportedly rejected a complaint on his behalf saying that according to information submitted by the police, it could not be substantiated. In July Dimos Dimosthenous, mistakenly detained by police in Limassol for a bank robbery, said four or five police officers blindfolded him, beat him all over, gave him electric shocks and hung him upside-down. Following an investigation, in October two police officers were indicted for trial on charges of ill-treating Dimos Dimosthenous and causing bodily harm. Their trial, which was scheduled for December, was postponed until 1993.

Amnesty International called for the release of all imprisoned conscientious objectors. It repeatedly urged the government to bring the new legislation on conscientious objection into line with

**112**

international standards. In March President George Vassiliou informed Amnesty International that an entirely civilian service would be available for objectors on a variety of grounds but that the authorities did not consider the length of the alternative service to be punitive, nor would they permit conscripts who developed conscientious objections during periods of emergency or mobilization to switch to alternative civilian service.

Amnesty International expressed its concern to the government about allegations of torture and ill-treatment. The government informed Amnesty International that the trial of the police officers indicted for ill-treating Andreas Zinonos in May 1991 (see *Amnesty International Report 1992*) was still pending. It had not responded to Amnesty International's other concerns with regard to torture and ill-treatment by the end of the year.

In October Amnesty International sent an appeal to the heads of both the Greek Cypriot and the Turkish Cypriot communities prior to their meeting that month in New York under United Nations auspices. The organization called on them to ensure that the subject of people who had gone missing in Cyprus between 1963 and 1964 and in 1974 would be put on the agenda of their talks and urged that full investigations into the fate of all those who had "disappeared" should be carried out.

# CZECH AND SLOVAK FEDERAL REPUBLIC

**Police officers allegedly ill-treated members of the Roma community, and spectators at a football match.**

The Civic Democratic Party and the Movement for a Democratic Slovakia won elections in June for the Federal Assembly and two republican parliaments. Vaclav Klaus became Prime Minister of the Czech Republic and Vladimir Mečiar, whose party campaigned for an independent Slovakia, became Prime Minister of the Slovak Republic. In July President Vaclav Havel failed to be re-elected as President by the Federal Assembly when Slovak parliamentarians did not give him a majority in their side of the Upper Chamber. Two weeks

later when the Slovak National Council adopted a Declaration of Sovereignty, he submitted his resignation. Three subsequent attempts failed to elect a new President.

Vaclav Klaus and Vladimir Mečiar agreed in August that the Czech and Slovak Federation should split into two separate states by 1 January 1993. A constitutional amendment to this effect was adopted by the Federal Assembly in November. The two states would preserve economic ties through a customs and monetary union.

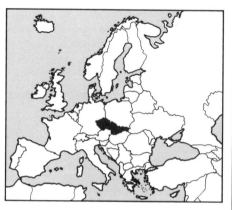

In March the Czech and Slovak Federal Republic ratified the European Convention for the Protection of Human Rights and Fundamental Freedoms, and its Sixth Protocol which provides for the abolition of the death penalty for peacetime offences. It declared that it recognized both the right of individual petition to and the compulsory jurisdiction of the European Court of Human Rights.

In May police officers in Eastern Slovakia reportedly ill-treated members of the Roma community. Following a dispute in a bar, a police officer and two other people assaulted František Oračko, a Rom from Lomnička. That night 40 police officers went to Lomnička and broke into the house where František Oračko lived together with 20 other people. The police allegedly beat everyone there indiscriminately with truncheons and shouted: "All of you will die. Heil Hitler! All Gypsies are to be shot." Ľudovita Oračka, a 10-year-old child, was reportedly held by the neck by a police officer and thrown against the wall. Some other children who crawled under a bed were dragged out and thrown on to the floor. Anna Oračkova, who was ill in bed, was forcibly removed from her bed by police and put on the floor. Ľudovit Oračko Sr was kicked in the head and beaten. František Oračko, Ľudovit Oračko Sr, Ľudovit Oračko Jr and Martin Mirga were taken into custody. They were reportedly beaten in the car on the way to the police station.

In September, following disturbances at a football match in Bratislava, it was alleged that the police beat scores of spectators with truncheons, including some not involved in the disturbances. At least 16 people required hospital treatment for injuries resulting from police beatings.

Amnesty International called for a full and impartial investigation into the alleged torture and ill-treatment of Roma in Lomnička and for those responsible to be brought to justice. It also asked the Slovak authorities whether a full and impartial investigation had been carried out into the use of force by the police at Bratislava football stadium, urging them to establish procedures which would prevent ill-treatment in such situations.

In November the Slovak authorities denied that members of the Roma community in Lomnička had been ill-treated. An investigation reportedly concluded that police used force only to apprehend criminal offenders. Amnesty International asked the Slovak authorities for full details of the investigation.

# DENMARK

**The government published in March the report of a judicial inquiry into the treatment of asylum-seekers in prisons in Copenhagen, the capital. The report included the inquiry's findings into allegations of ill-treatment made by two foreign visitors.**

Babading Fatty and Himid Hassan Juma both alleged that they had been ill-treated by prison guards in 1990 while in custody (see *Amnesty International Report 1992*). The inquiry found that the treatment of the two detainees was mistaken, largely on account of the police officers' relative youth, inexperience and lack of training. In the case of Himid Hassan Juma, the police officer responsible for the case had had an insufficient knowledge of the basic regulations governing arrest procedures.

In the case of Babading Fatty the inquiry

accepted that the detainee had experienced both physical and mental distress while in custody, but rejected any assertion that he had been deliberately ill-treated in order to frighten him, or that his treatment had been an expression of racial discrimination.

The report expressed concern about the degree of force which had been used in both cases to restrain the detainees but it did not accept that it constituted cruel, inhuman or degrading treatment.

Amnesty International wrote to the government in August expressing concern that the report had not accepted that the force used against the detainees constituted cruel, inhuman or degrading treatment. The organization noted that ill-treatment of a detainee can qualify as cruel, inhuman or degrading treatment whether or not that treatment is deliberate or intended to frighten or coerce the detainee.

# DJIBOUTI

**Several government opponents and human rights activists who were detained for periods of days or weeks appeared to be prisoners of conscience. Eleven prisoners of conscience held since January 1991 were convicted and sentenced to terms of imprisonment after an unfair trial. The security forces reportedly carried out dozens of extrajudicial executions in areas affected by fighting with rebel forces. One prisoner remained under sentence of death.**

A new Constitution introduced in September after a referendum ended 11 years of one-party rule. It allowed a maximum of

**114**

four political parties, including the ruling *Rassemblement pour le progrès populaire* (RPP), Rally for Popular Progress, and strengthened the independence of the judiciary. In the parliamentary elections on 18 December, which were boycotted by many government opponents, the RPP won all 65 seats.

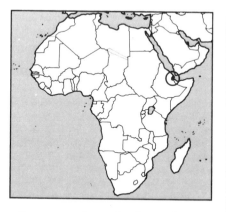

Government forces faced armed opposition in the north and southwest of the country from the *Front pour la restauration de l'unité et de la démocratie* (FRUD), Front for the Restoration of Unity and Democracy. Government control over both areas was disrupted by fighting, although a cease-fire lasted from late February until July.

A partial amnesty for opponents of the government was declared on 29 June and led to the release of several captured FRUD fighters. The FRUD freed 25 captured government soldiers in November, but continued to hold 29 others. Several people facing charges or suspended prison terms on political grounds had the cases against them dropped as a result of the government amnesty.

Leaders of new human rights organizations, as well as other government opponents, were arrested and held for several days or weeks for criticizing President Hassan Gouled Aptidon's government. Several appeared to be prisoners of conscience. Mohamed Houmed Souleh, President of the *Association pour la défense des droits de l'homme et des libertés* (ADDHL), Association for the Defence of Human Rights and Liberties, was arrested in April and accused of forming an illegal association. He was released after three days but was later charged with publishing false reports. He was tried and given a three-month

suspended prison sentence in June.

Hassan Ali Mohamed ("Dalga"), President of the *Comité de soutien pour la libération des détenus politiques à Djibouti*, Support Committee for the Release of Political Detainees in Djibouti, was arrested three times during 1992 for criticizing human rights violations. He was arrested in June but the case against him was dropped under the terms of the 29 June amnesty. He was rearrested a week later after organizing a protest demonstration at the trial of Ali Aref (see below). The security forces fired on demonstrators outside the court, wounding several, and arrested at least seven, whom they detained throughout the seven-day trial. Hassan Ali Mohamed's own arrest took place inside the courtroom as he was about to appear as a defence witness. He too was released when the trial ended on 11 July but was rearrested eight days later. He was convicted in October of insulting the Head of State and sentenced to three months' imprisonment, but was released as he had already spent three months in detention.

Another government opponent, Abbate Ebo Adou, a doctor who had been arrested in December 1991, was still detained at the beginning of 1992. He had been appointed by the FRUD to represent the organization in negotiations with the Djibouti Government, with the mediation of the French Government. He was released on 28 February, without being tried, when a cease-fire was announced. Rearrested on 13 April and charged with insulting the Head of State by criticizing political repression, he was released under the June amnesty after three months in detention. He was nevertheless put on trial in July, but fled the country before any verdict was announced.

Twenty-nine people were tried from 5 to 11 July by a special security court, 15 of them *in absentia*, on charges of subversion. Ali Aref, former head of Djibouti's pre-independence administration up to 1977, and the 13 others in court with him, had been arrested in January 1991 (see *Amnesty International Report 1992*). They were accused of responsibility for an attack on a military barracks and conspiring to overthrow the government. Most of the judges at their trial before the Security Tribunal of the Republic were government officials and the trial proceedings were marred by serious irregularities. The prosecution case was based mainly on statements obtained by torture or threats of torture, which were admitted as evidence by the court without any scrutiny of the torture allegations. One defendant, lawyer Aref Mohamed Aref, was acquitted. Ali Aref and 12 others, along with the 15 tried *in absentia*, were all convicted and sentenced to prison terms of five or 10 years. Their appeals to the Supreme Court had not been heard by the end of the year. Ali Aref, who was sentenced to 10 years' imprisonment, and 10 others appeared to be prisoners of conscience.

One man accused of planting a bomb at an army barracks in mid-1990 was still held awaiting trial at the end of 1992 (see *Amnesty International Report 1991*).

Extrajudicial executions of dozens of civilians were reported in February during fighting between government forces and the FRUD. In Yoboki village in the southwest, some 50 civilians were reportedly extrajudicially executed by government troops on 11 and 12 February, after a FRUD force which had occupied the village withdrew. In the nearby village of Garabous, 10 people were reportedly executed in similar circumstances.

The authorities failed to bring to justice those responsible for human rights violations in previous years. Four police officers charged after a judicial investigation into the deaths of at least 10 prisoners in September 1991 (see *Amnesty International Report 1992*) were provisionally released in 1992. The result of a police investigation into shootings by police of at least 30 unarmed civilians in the Arhiba quarter of the capital in December 1991 (see *Amnesty International Report 1992*) was not published and no action was announced by the authorities against those responsible.

The only prisoner under sentence of death, Adouani Hamouda Ben Hassan (see *Amnesty International Report 1992*), had his appeal to the Supreme Court rejected in June. At the end of the year he was awaiting the outcome of an appeal for presidential clemency.

Amnesty International appealed for the release of prisoners of conscience and the fair trial of other political prisoners. An Amnesty International representative observed the trial of Ali Aref and others in July. In a report published in December, *Djibouti: Prisoners of conscience – an unfair security trial*, Amnesty International appealed for the release of 11 prisoners of conscience and for the fair retrial of two others. It repeated earlier calls for an impartial inquiry into allegations of torture, and urged abolition or thorough reform of the special security court, as its composition and procedures are incompatible with international standards for fair trial. Amnesty International also called for independent inquiries into the reports of extrajudicial executions by the security forces, and appealed for the commutation of the one death sentence.

# DOMINICAN REPUBLIC

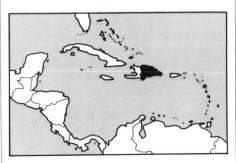

**A detainee was reported to have been tortured. Two political prisoners were held in detention despite judicial orders for their release. Police reportedly killed one person and wounded two others during a demonstration.**

Felipe de Jesús Medrano García, a university professor, was allegedly tortured on 16 January at the National Police headquarters after being arrested by members of the Forgery Investigation Department of the National Police. He said he was beaten on the buttocks and lower back with a wooden bat and around the left ear with a piece of rubber. He was subsequently released. According to a medical certificate, Felipe Medrano suffered severe injuries to the buttocks and lower back. In July two police captains were reportedly tried before a police tribunal for their alleged involvement in the torture, but it appeared that no one had been convicted by the end of the year.

In June an investigating judge in Barahona recommended that an army and a police officer be tried before a criminal court for the death in custody in February 1991 of Julio (José) Samboy (see *Amnesty*

**116** *International Report 1992*). A 1991 investigation commission, comprising an army general, a police general and a navy admiral, had found that Julio Samboy had died as a result of beatings. It recommended that the two officers be dismissed and that legal proceedings be initiated against them. However, it appeared that neither officer had been brought to trial by the end of 1992.

No judicial proceedings were initiated in the case of Haitian national Joubert Pierre, who died in April 1991 reportedly as a result of beatings by the security forces (see *Amnesty International Report 1992*). In the case of the killing of Jesús Diplán Martínez after his arrest in 1990 (see *Amnesty International Reports 1991* and *1992*), seven members of the security forces were reported to have been tried before a military tribunal in February. In spite of strong evidence indicating their involvement, all were subsequently acquitted.

Two political prisoners were held in detention despite judicial orders for their release. Teudo Mordán Gerónimo was held in the National Penitentiary of La Victoria for over a year. He was arrested in June 1991, reportedly accused of being a guerrilla and of instructing peasants to overthrow the government. Despite court orders for his release in November 1991 and May 1992, and a similar order in June by the Attorney General to the Chief of the National Police, the police authorities refused to free him. He was, however, released in July. The police continued to refuse to comply with two 1989 court orders for the release of Luis Lizardo Cabrera, who was arrested in 1989 for alleged involvement in a bombing (see *Amnesty International Reports 1990* to *1992*).

On 20 September the police were reported to have shot dead Rafael Efraín Ortiz, a lawyer who headed the Dominican Committee of Human Rights, and wounded Pedro Juan Reynoso and trade union leader Flavio Sánchez, during a demonstration against the celebrations planned to mark the 500th anniversary of Columbus' arrival in the Americas. Ten policemen were reportedly detained in connection with the incident, pending a police investigation. To Amnesty International's knowledge, no one had been brought to justice for these shootings by the end of the year.

Amnesty International urged the government of President Joaquín Balaguer to initiate investigations into the alleged torture of Felipe Medrano García and the death in custody of Julio Samboy. The organization sought clarification from the government about the continued imprisonment of Luis Lizardo Cabrera and Teudo Mordán Gerónimo and urged that they be released if no legal basis existed for their detention. In September Amnesty International wrote to the Minister of the Interior urging that the investigation into the shooting of Rafael Efraín Ortiz, Flavio Sánchez and Pedro Juan Reynoso be thorough and impartial, and that those responsible be brought to justice. No response was received to any of these appeals.

# ECUADOR

**Dozens of cases of torture and ill-treatment by members of the security forces were reported and one person allegedly died under torture. A juvenile was reported to have "disappeared" following his detention by members of the security forces.**

There were widespread protests against government policies during the year. In January President Rodrigo Borja ordered the mobilization of troops in the province of Guayas following a wave of street violence in Guayaquil in protest at the municipal authorities' decision to dismiss thousands of municipal employees. Sixto Durán Ballén, of the *Partido Unidad Republicana*, Republican Unity Party, became President in August after elections. In September the government issued Decree Law 86, mobilizing the army and the police in anticipation of street demonstrations protesting at economic austerity measures imposed by the incoming government. In October thousands of members of Indian communities from all over the country met in Quito, the capital, to protest against the economic measures and against celebrations marking the 500th anniversary of Columbus' arrival in the Americas. Also in October, more than 1,000 members of the Huahorani Indian community marched from the Amazon region to Quito to protest against a road construction project which would penetrate the territory where they live.

By the end of the year the judicial police force whose creation was announced in 1991 had not begun to operate (see *Amnesty International Report 1992*).

A number of detainees were reportedly tortured by members of the *Oficina de Investigación del Delito* (OID), Office of Criminal Investigation, the police unit which replaced the disbanded *Servicio de Investigaciones Criminales* (SIC), Criminal Investigation Service (see *Amnesty International Report 1992*). Víctor Hugo Cadena was detained in July by the police in a street in Quito on suspicion of theft. He was taken, hooded, to the Pichincha offices of the OID. He was held for three days and was reportedly suspended from a rope with his arms tied behind his back, beaten and given electric shocks. A medical certificate issued by the public prosecutor's office certified that his body was bruised. In an official reply to a complaint presented by a human rights organization, the OID denied that he had been detained.

Five young artists taking part in a peaceful public protest against the celebrations to mark Columbus' arrival in the Americas were detained in Quito by members of the army in October. Andrea Stark, Susana Tapia, Amparo Ponce, Joan Bagué and Jean Marc Duray were reportedly tortured with electric shocks at the Pichincha Battalion army base, and were threatened with being thrown out of an army helicopter. They were transferred to the custody of the OID, and again threatened with death by members of the police. The artists were released three days later without charge.

One detainee died in custody, allegedly as a result of torture. Felipe Moreira Chávez was detained on 20 August and taken to the OID office in Quevedo, province of Los Ríos. Two days later, his body was taken by the police to the local morgue. Although the police claimed he died after a fall while attempting to escape, his family claimed that he died under torture.

The authorities failed to conduct thorough investigations into many of the torture cases reported during 1991, including that of José María Cabascango (see *Amnesty International Report 1992*). An inquiry into the death under torture of Mayer Yoncer Mina Montaño in July 1991 (see *Amnesty International Report 1992*) was reported to have been initiated by the military judiciary, but by the end of 1992 it was not known whether the investigation had been completed. In August the *Tribunal de Garantías Constitucionales*, Tribunal of Constitutional Guarantees, urged the public prosecutor to initiate criminal proceedings against the police officers allegedly responsible for the torture of Edison Roberto Sarasti and Eddy Pablo Rivadeneira Muñoz (see *Amnesty International Report 1992*). However, by the end of December judicial proceedings were not known to have been initiated.

One person "disappeared" from police custody. On 24 February, 16-year-old Marco Antonio Romero Carrasco was detained by police at a bus stop in the city of Esmeraldas, in the presence of numerous witnesses. He then "disappeared". When questioned by a public prosecutor, the police denied having detained him. A judicial investigation into the "disappearance" was initiated but produced no results by the end of the year.

In October the public prosecutor issued his final report on the "disappearance" in 1988 of the Restrepo brothers (see *Amnesty International Report 1992*). The report recommended that the police officers believed to be responsible for the "disappearances" be brought to trial. The file on the case was subsequently referred to the Supreme Court. Two days after the prosecutor's announcement, retired police general Gilberto Molina, the former director of the SIC who was alleged to be responsible for the "disappearances", escaped from detention and fled to Colombia. The Ecuadorian authorities announced that they would request his extradition. The case of Consuelo Benavides who was killed in 1985 (see *Amnesty International Reports 1987, 1990* and *1991*) was also passed to the Supreme Court, where new witnesses were summoned.

Colombian political refugee Oscar

**118**

Amaris was detained in October on suspicion of "subversion", and it was feared that he would be forcibly returned to Colombia, where he would be at risk of human rights violations. The Ecuadorian authorities granted Oscar Amaris a limited period to find a third country of asylum.

Amnesty International called on the government to investigate reported cases of torture and death in custody. In October Amnesty International appealed against the possible *refoulement* (forcible return) of Colombian refugee Oscar Amaris. In November Amnesty International wrote to the Minister of Government and Police calling for an investigation into the torture of the five artists detained in Quito. The organization urged the government to clarify the fate of Marco Antonio Romero Carrasco.

In an oral statement to the Working Group on Indigenous Populations of the United Nations Sub-Commission on Prevention of Discrimination and Protection of Minorities in July, Amnesty International included reference to its concerns about human rights violations against indigenous peoples in Ecuador. In October Amnesty International published *Human rights violations against the indigenous peoples of the Americas*, which included concerns in Ecuador.

# EGYPT

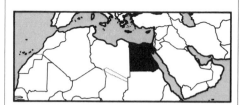

Thousands of suspected opponents of the government, including possible prisoners of conscience, were arrested and detained without charge or trial under state of emergency legislation. Political detainees were reportedly tortured in security police custody. At least 45 people were sentenced to death and at least five, sentenced to death in previous years, were executed. At the end of the year dozens of prisoners remained under sentence of death.

The state of emergency, reintroduced in 1981 and extended for a further three years in 1991, remained in force (see previous *Amnesty International Reports*). Emergency legislation empowers the Minister of the Interior to order the administrative detention without charge or trial of political suspects and to contest court decisions to release untried political detainees. Amendments to the Criminal Procedure Code, introduced in July, give the police additional powers of arrest and increase the length of time a detainee may be held by the police before referral to the procuracy. These measures, introduced in the absence of new safeguards, increased the likelihood of the torture of detainees. Amendments to the Penal Code promulgated at the same time increased the number of offences punishable by death for "terrorism", although the exact nature of "terrorist" offences was not defined.

Throughout the year increasingly violent clashes took place between Islamic militant groups and the security forces, especially in Asyut, Dayrut, Sanabu and Fayoum, resulting in deaths on both sides. There were also violent attacks by Islamic groups on Christians. In one incident, 13 Christians and one Muslim were killed in Sanabu in May. During the second half of the year there were several armed attacks by Islamic militant groups on foreign tourists in Upper Egypt, in which one tourist was killed and five others were injured.

During the year thousands of people were arrested for political reasons under the emergency legislation. Most were members or sympathizers of banned Islamic militant groups such as *al-Gama'a al-Islamiya* (Islamic Group) and *Gihad* (Holy War). The authorities made public only limited details about arrests and detentions, although in late November the Minister of the Interior indicated that 1,123 people were being detained at that time under emergency provisions.

In February the owner and two employees of a Cairo-based computer company were arrested. They were accused of being members of the Muslim Brothers, a banned but tolerated organization, and of preparing to overthrow the government. They denied the charges against them and claimed they had been arrested for their non-violent beliefs or activities. Shortly after their arrests the authorities claimed to have uncovered a conspiracy to establish an Islamic state. In September a Cairo court ordered the detention of the three men for a further 45 days while investigations into their case continued. All three had been released by the end of December. Sixteen others, however, who were arrested in connection with the same case in late October, were still held without charge or trial at the end of the year.

In March a former Ambassador and Commander of the Egyptian armed forces, Sa'd al-Din al-Shazli, was arrested on his return to Egypt after 14 years in self-imposed exile. He had been tried *in absentia* in 1983 and sentenced to three years' imprisonment for disclosing military secrets about the Arab–Israeli War of October 1973 in a book published in 1981. His whereabouts remained unknown for several weeks after his arrest. In August the (Emergency) Supreme State Court ruled that the sentence imposed in 1983 should be suspended. However, within days of this decision the Supreme Military Court upheld the three-year prison sentence. At the end of the year the Higher Constitutional Court was still examining the two conflicting verdicts and Sa'd al-Din al-Shazli remained held in isolation in the hospital of a military prison near Cairo.

Suspected opponents of the government, including possible prisoners of conscience, were rounded up and arrested on numerous occasions during the year, often after clashes between the security forces and Islamic militant groups. For example, nearly 150 members of Islamic groups were arrested following the assassination in March of a State Security Intelligence officer in Fayoum. Nine of those detained were on trial at the end of the year; the rest were released shortly after arrest.

Forty alleged members of the Muslim Brothers were arrested in Zagazig in June while attending a meeting with 'Abd al-Rahman al-Rasad, a former member of the People's Assembly. They were initially accused of membership of an illegal organization but were reportedly released uncharged in August.

There were also mass arrests in June of members and sympathizers of banned Islamic groups following the killing of the writer Farag Foda, allegedly by two members of *al-Gama'a al-Islamiya* (see below). Large demonstrations in Cairo followed these arrests, during which at least 13

others were detained. During one week in December more than 700 suspected members of Islamic groups were arrested in Imbaba, a district of Cairo. At the end of December at least 145 others were arrested in 'Ain Shams, another Cairo district.

The role and independence of the judiciary continued to be undermined by the executive authorities. There were many reports that courts' decisions were not respected, particularly those ordering the release of political detainees held under emergency legislation. In many reported cases, detainees whose release had been ordered by the courts were transferred to remote police stations or detention centres, held for several days or even weeks, then served with new detention orders and transferred to other places of detention. This practice resulted in some detainees being held for up to three years without charge or trial.

Major political trials continued before (Emergency) Supreme State Security Courts whose verdicts are not final until approved by the Prime Minister and which provide for no right of appeal. Among defendants still being tried at the end of the year were those accused of the murder of Dr Rifa'at al-Mahgoub, former Speaker of the People's Assembly (see *Amnesty International Report 1992*).

On 3 December a military court in Alexandria sentenced eight alleged members of *Gihad* to death after an unfair trial. Seven of the eight were tried *in absentia*; only al-Sharif Hassan Ahmed was present. Thirty-one co-defendants received sentences ranging from life imprisonment to one-year prison terms. Nine were acquitted. Charges against the defendants included membership of an underground organization which calls for the overthrow of the government, possession of weapons and theft. The court apparently applied for the first time the new amendments to the Penal Code, and there was no right to appeal against the sentences. At least five defendants – Ahmed Ibrahim 'Abd al-Galil, Qassim Ibrahim Qassim Qettish, al-Sharif Hassan Ahmed, Mohammad Sa'id Mohammad 'Abdu and 'Ala' al-Din Isma'il 'Abbas Ramadhan – said they were tortured after arrest: official forensic medical doctors who examined the defendants found physical scars consistent with the alleged torture.

The cases had been referred to a military

court in October by a presidential decree. On 8 December, five days after the defendants had been sentenced, the Higher Administrative Court ruled that the presidential decree was invalid as the cases had no connection with the armed forces and that the defendants should be tried before a state security court. On 10 December the government challenged this ruling.

The eight-year prison sentences imposed by the (Emergency) Supreme State Security Court in December 1991 on the novelist 'Ala' Hamed and two co-defendants (see *Amnesty International Report 1992*) had still not been approved by the Prime Minister by the end of the year. In June 'Ala' Hamed was sentenced to a further one-year jail term by a court in Cairo, following publication of his novel, *al-Firash* (The Bed), which discusses sex. He was released pending an appeal.

Political detainees continued to be tortured. The most common methods reported were beatings, suspension, burning with cigarettes, electric shocks and psychological torture. For example, Mahmoud Guhayni al-Sa'dawi, an office employee at the University of Asyut, was reported to have died as a result of torture in the Lazoghly Square headquarters of the security police in May, five days after his arrest. An inquiry by the procuracy established that his death was due to circulatory and respiratory depression, but apparently did not shed light on the circumstances surrounding his death.

'Amer 'Abd al-Mun'im, a journalist working for the opposition *al-Sha'b* newspaper, was arrested in July and detained for a month. He was accused of possessing anti-government leaflets and was reportedly tortured at the Lazoghly Square headquarters of the security police. He alleged that he had been beaten and subjected to electric shocks on different parts of his body, in particular his left hand. A forensic doctor reportedly confirmed that his scars were consistent with the methods of torture he described. His lawyer lodged an official complaint of torture with the procuracy but by the end of the year no investigation was known to have been carried out.

At least 45 people were sentenced to death. Eight were sentenced to death for political reasons in Alexandria (see above). Nineteen, including 15 foreign nationals, were convicted in separate cases of drug smuggling into the country. One death sentence was passed for selling drugs. All the others were found guilty of murder. At least five people, sentenced to death in previous years, were hanged, including two in Tanta Prison in September and one in al-Hadhra Prison in Alexandria in July.

On 8 June Farag Foda, a writer and vocal opponent of Islamic militant groups, was shot dead by two men: responsibility for the killing was claimed by *al-Gama'a al-Islamiya*. Two other people were wounded in the attack, including the writer's 15-year-old son. Amnesty International condemned the assassination as a deliberate killing by an armed opposition organization. It also urged that those arrested following the murder be humanely treated in custody.

Amnesty International repeatedly called for an end to the widespread practice of torture of detainees. The organization urged the authorities to conduct prompt, thorough and impartial investigations into allegations of torture, and to end the long-term detention without charge or trial of government opponents, particularly when their imprisonment was unlawful or contrary to court orders.

During the year Amnesty International appealed on several occasions to President Hosni Mubarak to commute death sentences. It also urged that Egypt ratify the Optional Protocol to the International Covenant on Civil and Political Rights.

In January Amnesty International published a report, *Egypt: Security police detentions undermine the rule of law*, which focused on the long-term pattern of arbitrary detentions. In May the organization called for a retrial of General Sa'd al-Din al-Shazli in accordance with internationally recognized fair trial procedures.

In May Amnesty International representatives visiting Egypt were received by President Mubarak and also discussed human rights concerns with the President and ministers. The President expressed Egypt's commitment to human rights and stated that Amnesty International was welcome in Egypt as long as its work was fair and non-partisan. Shortly afterwards the government sent a 20-page response to recent Amnesty International reports on human rights violations in Egypt, which failed to allay the organization's human rights concerns. Amnesty International continued to raise its concerns, particularly torture, prolonged detention and the death penalty. Throughout the year the authorities responded to inquiries on specific cases.

In oral statements to the United Nations (UN) Commission on Human Rights in February and to its Sub-Commission on Prevention of Discrimination and Protection of Minorities in August, Amnesty International included reference to its concerns about torture and prolonged detention under the state of emergency in Egypt.

In March Amnesty International submitted information about its concerns regarding torture in Egypt to the UN Committee against Torture, pursuant to Article 20 of the UN Convention against Torture and Other Cruel, Inhuman or Degrading Treatment or Punishment.

# EL SALVADOR

**Extrajudicial executions and "death squad"-style killings continued, despite the end of the civil war. Members of the political opposition were subjected to death threats and armed attacks. The torture of political detainees appeared to cease, but there were many allegations of ill-treatment of criminal suspects and others by police. Further evidence came to light of gross human rights violations by government forces during the civil war, but the failure to bring to justice those responsible for recent and past abuses continued.**

On 16 January the government and the armed opposition *Frente Farabundo Martí para la Liberación Nacional* (FMLN), Farabundo Martí National Liberation Front, signed a definitive peace accord in Mexico City, following 12 years of armed conflict and 21 months of United Nations (UN)-mediated negotiations. The accord set a timetable for a cease-fire, the gradual

demobilization of the FMLN and the implementation of numerous military, judicial and other reforms agreed in previous rounds of negotiations (see *Amnesty International Report 1992*).

On 15 December the armed conflict was formally ended, three months later than originally scheduled because of repeated setbacks in implementing agreements on land tenure, military and police reform and other issues. By the end of the year the FMLN had demobilized and reorganized as a political party, but several other aspects of the agreements remained to be implemented.

As a result of the accords, the National Civil Police was set up to replace the three existing police forces, two of which were disbanded in the course of the year. Certain military and paramilitary units were also gradually disbanded. The *Ad Hoc* Commission, created by the accords, presented confidential recommendations to President Alfredo Cristiani in September for purging the army, based on its evaluation of the professional and human rights records of military officers. However, the government had not implemented the recommendations by the end of the year, despite commitments to do so.

A National Counsel for the Defence of Human Rights was appointed in February and his office set up in July. Despite broad powers, his office suffered numerous setbacks, including covert threats and inadequate resourcing, and took few effective steps to ensure alleged abuses were clarified. Days after its creation in July, a prominent member of staff was left paralysed after an attack by two unidentified gunmen.

The Truth Commission, mandated under the accords to investigate "exceptionally important acts of violence" committed by government or FMLN forces since 1980, began operation in July (see *Amnesty International Report 1992*). The Commission, made up of three prominent non-Salvadorians assisted by a team of lawyers and human rights experts, took testimony from hundreds of people. It was due to present its findings and recommendations in January 1993.

These efforts to hold accountable those responsible for past abuses were undermined by the Law of National Reconciliation, passed in January, which granted amnesty to those who committed political or related common crimes and crimes in connection with the armed conflict. The law effectively shielded perpetrators of human rights violations from prosecution, although it excluded those who may eventually be named in the Truth Commission's report. Thirty-six political prisoners were released under the amnesty in March, but prisoners convicted by a jury were excluded under the terms of the law.

Implementation of the Agreement on Human Rights signed in July 1990 by the government and FMLN continued to be monitored by the Human Rights Division of the UN Observer Mission in El Salvador (ONUSAL – see *Amnesty International Reports 1991* and *1992*). The Division continued to investigate human rights abuses and to make recommendations to both parties for human rights protection. Threats and accusations against ONUSAL were made in the press by clandestine groups allegedly linked to the armed forces.

Despite the advent of peace, there was an apparent increase in the number of violent deaths over 1991. The majority were not effectively investigated by the authorities, making it difficult to ascertain whether the armed forces were directly involved. In a few cases extrajudicial executions were carried out by uniformed members of the armed forces. For example, on 22 October six unidentified armed men in uniforms went to the home of Miguel Angel Alvarado, treasurer of an agricultural co-operative in Zacatecoluca, searching for weapons. When he denied possessing any, they shot him dead. Uniformed members of the *Policía Nacional*, National Police, had previously searched a nearby co-operative for arms, and armed men in uniform and in plain clothes had been patrolling neighbouring communities. Miguel Angel Alvarado had also reportedly been threatened by landowners during a dispute over ownership of the co-operative. By the end of the year few steps appeared to have been taken to identify those responsible for the killing.

At least 35 killings bore the hallmarks of the so-called "death squads", believed to be intimately linked to the armed forces, which murdered hundreds of suspected government opponents during the civil war. As in previous years, mutilated corpses were found dumped in public places. Other possible "death squad" victims were seen being detained or abducted by unidentified armed groups. Some victims appeared to have been targeted on suspicion of links to the FMLN. On 2 March Nazario de Jesús Gracias, nightwatchman and union activist for the Federation of Independent Salvadorian Trade Unions and Associations (FEASIES), was hacked to death with a machete at the FEASIES offices by unknown assailants. Five months earlier he had been detained by the National Police, accused of being an FMLN member, and threatened. Preliminary official investigations, described by ONUSAL as "entirely inadequate", yielded no results and the killing had not been clarified at the end of the year.

Many trade union members were attacked and threatened with death by unidentified individuals. The attacks and threats often coincided with public accusations by the authorities that certain unions were fomenting unrest and jeopardizing the peace process by undertaking strike action in protest at the government's economic program. On 17 September, four armed men in plain clothes opened fire on the FEASIES offices in San Salvador, killing a passer-by. The offices had been under surveillance for several days and had received numerous anonymous death threats by telephone.

Several FMLN leaders were wounded in separate attacks by unidentified gunmen. Eight uniformed men, believed to be members of the Belloso battalion, shot at José Mario Moreno Rivera, local FMLN leader in Sonsonate, in October. José Moreno, who escaped injury, claimed to have been harassed on several occasions since April by members of the local police and military.

Threats against FMLN leaders and others were sometimes broadcast publicly. A communique by the clandestine *Brigada Maximiliano Hernández Martínez*, Maximiliano Hernández Martínez Brigade, appeared in the press in October threatening to kill 16 named FMLN commanders and warning "front organizations, terrorist collaborators and all supporters of the accords".

Reports of the arrest and torture of political detainees decreased sharply following the accords and the disbanding of the security force units notorious for the widespread use of torture in the past. However, cases of torture and ill-treatment of non-political detainees continued to be reported. At least three criminal suspects died from injuries allegedly sustained in the custody of the Municipal Police. Seventeen-year-old Juan Antonio Turcios Mejía was detained with a friend by Municipal Police in Soyapango in June and taken to the *Alcaldía Municipal* (mayor's office), accused of theft. Juan Antonio Turcios was allegedly beaten on the chest and throat, then kicked repeatedly in the stomach and testicles, causing fatal injuries. His friend was beaten unconscious when he protested. Local police and officials reportedly threatened Juan Antonio Turcios' father with "disappearance" if he continued to denounce the death of his son.

The police were also accused of ill-treatment in the context of land evictions and political demonstrations. Riot police allegedly beat Elías Romero Villalta, an employee of the *Consejo de Comunidades Marginales* (CCM), Council for Marginal Communities, during a demonstration in June. A forensic pathologist recorded severe bruising and a large wound on his forehead. The court receiving Elías Romero Villalta's complaint reportedly refused to process it because he could not name the individual riot police officers concerned.

Proceedings continued against several prisoners accused of being members of the FMLN who were charged with murder in previous years on the basis of confessions obtained under duress. In March Jorge Miranda was sentenced to 30 years' imprisonment for the 1987 killing of human rights worker Herbert Anaya, despite evidence that the security forces may have carried out the killing (see *Amnesty International Report 1992*). Adolfo Aguilar Payés, who went on hunger-strike in October to protest at having been held without trial since 1989, was released in December after a jury found him not guilty of the 1989 murder of two ruling party officials. In both cases the evidence against the defendants appeared to be based almost exclusively on confessions extracted under torture which they had since retracted.

No new cases of "disappearance" by government forces were reported. However, the "disappearance" of hundreds of people in previous years remained unresolved, including previously unreported cases which came to light after the signing of the accords.

Very few official investigations into past abuses made any progress through the courts. In the only case where senior army officers were held to account, a colonel and lieutenant were sentenced in January to 30 years' imprisonment for the killing of six Jesuits, a cook and her daughter in November 1989 (see *Amnesty International Report 1992*). Amnesty International remained concerned that irregularities and obstacles throughout the proceedings had prevented clarification of the full extent of the involvement of senior officers.

In September the courts authorized the exhumation, under the supervision of international forensic experts, of remains believed to be those of at least 800 victims of an army massacre in El Mozote, Morazán, and neighbouring villages in 1981. By December 143 skeletons, mostly of children, had been exhumed. Preliminary forensic examinations supported claims by a witness that the victims had been herded into a local church building and summarily executed. Government assertions that the victims might have been killed in cross-fire during combat were refuted in the forensic team's report to the Truth Commission.

Several deliberate and arbitrary killings by the FMLN were reported. The FMLN reportedly admitted killing Carlos Nuñez Membreño, a farmer who had deserted from the FMLN and had served temporarily with the armed forces, at his home in Guatajiagua, Morazán, on 26 March. Several other army and security force members were killed by unidentified individuals. Some cases, such as the abduction and murder in September of former military intelligence lawyer, José Mauricio Quintana Abrego, were alleged to have been the work of members of the army opposed to the military reforms resulting from the peace process.

In March two FMLN members accused of killing United States military advisers David Pickett and Ernest Dawson in January 1991 turned themselves over to the Salvadorian judicial authorities (see *Amnesty International Report 1992*). The FMLN had previously sought to try the suspects in an FMLN tribunal, claiming that a fair trial could not be guaranteed until agreed judicial reforms had been implemented.

Amnesty International repeatedly called on the government to investigate possible extrajudicial executions and death threats and to take effective measures to eradicate abuses. In an oral statement to the UN

**124**

Commission on Human Rights in February, Amnesty International included reference to its concerns in El Salvador. In June Amnesty International presented documentation on hundreds of cases of killings, "disappearances" and torture since 1980 to the government, FMLN and Truth Commission, urging them not to restrict unduly the scope of the commission's investigations and presenting further recommendations for the protection of human rights. Amnesty International also expressed concern that the Law of National Reconciliation could grant immunity from prosecution to human rights violators.

# EQUATORIAL GUINEA

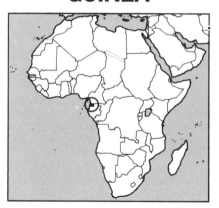

**Four opposition party supporters were detained without trial but released before the end of the year: all were prisoners of conscience. Four other prisoners of conscience serving sentences imposed after an unfair trial in 1988 were released under an amnesty in January, as were several possible prisoners of conscience who had been imprisoned or restricted. Hundreds of new arrests of opposition activists were reported but virtually all those held, most of whom appeared to be prisoners of conscience, were released within weeks. Most were reported to have been tortured or ill-treated. Two people were sentenced to 12 years' imprisonment by a military court after an unfair trial. At least two people were sentenced to death and one was executed.**

Several laws were passed in January to give effect to the amended Constitution, approved in 1991, which introduced a multi-party political system. However, the new Law on Political Parties initially placed opposition parties at a disadvantage by requiring them to pay a substantial amount, equivalent to 2,000 times the average annual salary, to obtain legal recognition while President Obiang Nguema's ruling *Partido Democrático de Guinea Ecuatorial* (PDGE), Equatorial Guinea Democratic Party, was automatically recognized under the law. Following criticism, the new law was amended in October and its most restrictive clauses deleted. By the end of the year six opposition political parties had obtained recognition.

The Law on Freedom of Assembly and Demonstration requires that official permission is obtained in advance for any gathering of more than 10 people in a public place and provides that those organizing such meetings or demonstrations are to be held accountable for the actions of those present. The Law on the Exercise of Freedom of Religion retained various restrictive clauses including six forbidding criticism of government actions or policy by ministers of religion.

In January the government granted an amnesty for all political offences committed before December 1991. Among the prisoners freed were four prisoners of conscience – Pedro Bacale Mayé, Joaquín Elema Borengue, Gaspar Mañana Okiri and Francisco Bonifacio Mba Nguema – who were serving sentences imposed after an unfair trial in September 1988 (see *Amnesty International Reports 1989* to *1992*). Several possible prisoners of conscience held in prison or restricted to their villages since 1990 were also released. However, some of those released from prison were apparently required to return to and remain in their home villages. Ricardo Nvumba Bindang, who had been restricted to his village in March 1991 after he sent a letter to the Gabonese President Omar Bongo asking him to promote democracy in Equatorial Guinea (see *Amnesty International Report 1992*), apparently remained restricted to his village until late July 1992.

Information was also received in 1992 that another prisoner of conscience, Antonio Ebang Mbele Abang (see *Amnesty International Reports 1991* and *1992*), had been released in late 1991.

Four opposition party supporters were

detained without trial for between two and four months. All were prisoners of conscience. Plácido Mikó Abogo, a leader of the *Convergencia para la Democracia Social* (CPDS), Convergence for Social Democracy, was arrested in February in Malabo after security officials at the airport intercepted party documents and letters which were being taken to Spain. He was arrested in the street at gunpoint, beaten and then tortured in police custody. He was charged with insulting the Head of State and with resisting arrest and held incommunicado for four months until June, when he was released under a presidential pardon issued to mark the Head of State's birthday. Four other CPDS members evaded arrest by temporarily seeking refuge in foreign embassies. However, two of them, Celestino Bacale and José Luis Nvumba Mañana, were arrested in April after charges of insulting the Head of State were brought against them. Both prisoners of conscience, they too were released untried in June under the presidential pardon. Celestino Bacale was rearrested for political reasons on 10 December. Before being released without charge on 29 December, he was tortured so severely he sustained serious kidney injuries and broken teeth.

Several possible prisoners of conscience were also freed under the presidential pardon in June, including Andrés Abaga Ondo Mayé. He was serving a three-year sentence imposed by a military court in 1991 after being convicted of defaming the authorities by complaining that his family had received death threats (see *Amnesty International Report 1992*).

In June Pilar Mañana, José Luis Nvumba Mañana's aunt, was arrested apparently for being in possession of the CPDS newspaper. She was held incommunicado until late July when she was charged with insulting the Head of State and resisting arrest. However, she was released untried a month later.

Scores of other suspected government opponents were arrested and detained without trial for exercising their right to freedom of expression. At least 40 members of the *Unión Popular* (UP), Popular Union, which had been officially recognized as a political party in May, were arrested in June after holding a meeting in Bata. All were released except José Martínez Bikie, a possible prisoner of conscience who was tried in October on charges of insulting the Head of State and sentenced to six months' imprisonment.

In September, 30 supporters of the *Partido del Progreso de Guinea Ecuatorial* (PPGE), Equatorial Guinea Progress Party, were arrested in Malabo: they were detained without charge or trial for between one and seven weeks and then released. They included Felipe Ndong Ecua, a former sergeant in the customs police who had previously been detained as a suspected PPGE supporter. He and seven others were tried in December on charges of public disorder: four were given prison sentences ranging from two to four months and four were acquitted.

Many of those detained were reportedly tortured or ill-treated in detention. For example, Plácido Mikó Abogo was allegedly tied up, suspended and then beaten. Other prisoners were reportedly beaten on the soles of their feet with truncheons, batons or whips. In another case, a prisoner was reportedly tied up for hours under a tap from which water was dripped on to his head.

Forty students were reportedly tortured after they were arrested in late November in Bata for participating in a peaceful demonstration. The victims included an eight-months pregnant woman. A male student apparently lost consciousness as a result of torture. The female students were said to have been made to dance naked in front of security officers.

Over 100 people were beaten severely or tortured in Malabo after their arrests following a reportedly peaceful student demonstration in December. The students were protesting against the rearrest of Celestino Bacale (see above). Most of those arrested were teachers and students, but priests and members of opposition parties who had not taken part in the demonstration were also held. Some of those detained were tortured with particular brutality. Among them were two Roman Catholic priests, Father Luis María Ondó Mayé and Father Pedro Ncogo, both well known government critics, who sustained serious injuries. Following international pressure, all the detainees were released by the end of December, although none was given permission by the government to go abroad for medical treatment.

In November two Spanish nationals, Salvador Vilarrasa and Santiago Hanna,

**126**

were tried by a military court and convicted of conspiring to overthrow the government. They had been arrested in October after they imported surplus Dutch military vehicles and other equipment for use in their timber business. Both were sentenced to 12 years' imprisonment and a fine. Their trial was unfair: in particular, they were denied adequate access to defence counsel. They were released from prison a few days after they were sentenced following the intervention of the Spanish Government, but were told they could not leave the country until the fines were paid. The restrictions were later lifted and both left the country in December.

At least two people were sentenced to death for murder and one was executed. Angel Marcos Asumu Esono, a member of the security forces, was executed in December two hours after he was sentenced without having the right to appeal to a higher court against his conviction and sentence.

Amnesty International appealed for the release of prisoners of conscience and for the introduction of effective safeguards against torture and ill-treatment of prisoners. An Amnesty International representative visited Malabo in June to observe the trial of Plácido Mikó Abogo and four others (two *in absentia*), but the trial did not take place as the defendants were released under the presidential pardon.

# ESTONIA

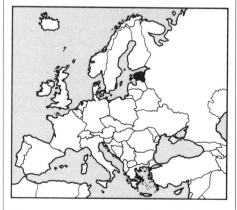

One person was sentenced to death and was later granted clemency. At least two other people were believed to be under sentence of death at the end of the year.

Following parliamentary and presidential elections in September, Lennart Meri replaced Arnold Rüütel as President and Mart Laar was confirmed as Estonia's new Prime Minister.

In June a new criminal code entered into force. The death penalty was retained for three crimes: aggravated murder, acts of terrorism and assassination. Under the new code homosexual acts between consenting adult males are no longer criminal offences punishable by imprisonment. In July the new Constitution of the Republic of Estonia came into effect. In August the length of military service was reduced from 18 to 12 months. The length of alternative service remained unchanged at 24 months. In October the procedure for appealing for clemency, the final stage of the judicial process for capital offences, was amended. Petitions for clemency are now heard by the President.

One person sentenced to death during the year was granted clemency. At least two other people – one sentenced to death in June 1991 and the other in December 1992 – were believed to be still under sentence of death at the end of the year. All three men had been convicted of aggravated murder.

In May Amnesty International asked the Minister of Justice whether anyone had been imprisoned for engaging in consensual homosexual acts at the time the new criminal code came into force, and if so whether they had subsequently been released. No reply had been received by the end of the year.

In July the authorities informed Amnesty International that Rein Oruste's execution (see *Amnesty International Report 1992*) had been carried out by firing-squad. However, the organization continued to receive reports that the prisoner had been shot by prison guards in the washroom or sauna, allegedly in retaliation for an earlier altercation.

In December Amnesty International wrote to the Minister of the Interior and asked for an inquiry to be conducted into the circumstances surrounding the killing of Rein Oruste. The organization also urged that the regulations on the procedures for executions be made public.

In August Amnesty International raised again its concern about the punitive length of alternative service (see *Amnesty International Report 1992*). A senior official in the

Ministry of Defence told the organization in October that military service was of shorter duration than alternative service because the conditions under ·which it was performed were considerably harsher. There were no reports of people imprisoned for refusing conscription on grounds of conscience.

In October Amnesty International delegates visited Estonia to collect information on human rights issues. This was the first research visit by Amnesty International to the country.

Amnesty International appealed for commutation of the three death sentences during the year and urged the authorities to consider the complete abolition of the death penalty.

# ETHIOPIA
# (AND ERITREA)

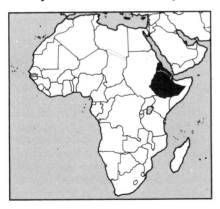

Almost 20,000 suspected supporters of the Oromo Liberation Front (OLF) and dozens of other government opponents were detained in Ethiopia. Some 2,000 senior members of former President Mengistu Haile-Mariam's government and armed forces arrested in mid-1991 remained in detention without charge or trial, accused of human rights violations and other offences. There were reports of torture and ill-treatment of prisoners and of extrajudicial executions by government forces. Armed opposition groups, including the OLF, were also reported to have carried out deliberate and arbitrary killings. In Eritrea, 900 former officers of the Ethiopian armed forces who had been captured in May 1991 were handed over

to the Ethiopian authorities and detained. **127** Over 200 Eritreans accused of human rights violations or criminal offences under the previous Ethiopian government remained in detention in Eritrea without charge or trial, and some opponents of the new Eritrean government were reportedly detained.

The former state of Ethiopia continued to be administered by two separate provisional governments, one in Ethiopia and one in Eritrea. Both were scheduled to hold office for a two-year transitional period following the overthrow of former President Mengistu's government in May 1991.

The Transitional Government of Ethiopia under President Meles Zenawi was headed by the Ethiopian People's Revolutionary Democratic Front (EPRDF). The leading member of the EPRDF, the Tigray People's Liberation Front (TPLF), formed the new government security forces from its former guerrilla force. The EPRDF and its allied political groups in the Council of Representatives (parliament) were opposed by other political groups, which were also mostly ethnic-based. Some of these groups had their own armed forces which clashed with the government's forces sporadically throughout the year, notably the OLF.

Elections for 14 new regional assemblies in Ethiopia were held in June. International observers criticized electoral irregularities and arrests of government opponents in some regions. Four political parties, including the OLF, boycotted the elections, which in two regions were postponed until later in the year because of fighting and general insecurity. There were widespread arrests during the regional elections campaign, particularly of OLF members. Hundreds of OLF supporters, many of them unarmed activists, were reportedly detained and scores of others were allegedly killed by government or pro-government forces. OLF armed units were also reportedly responsible for deliberate killings of civilians. Immediately after the elections, the OLF withdrew from the government coalition and most of its leaders went into self-imposed exile. OLF armed units, which had clashed sporadically with government troops earlier in the year, opposed government forces in some rural Oromo-populated areas which the OLF claimed to control. Government forces detained almost 20,000 OLF personnel but continued talks with the OLF, which prevented any

**128**

major escalation of the conflict. A high level of insecurity in the south and east disrupted relief operations for victims of drought and famine, as well as for hundreds of thousands of refugees from civil wars and famine in Somalia and Sudan.

The Provisional Government of Eritrea began preparations for a 1993 referendum on independence with United Nations and other international observers. The Central Committee of the Eritrean People's Liberation Front (EPLF), which formed the provisional government and was the only permitted political party, assumed legislative powers. Some armed clashes were reported early in the year in western border areas between EPLF forces and an opposition Eritrean Liberation Front-Revolutionary Council (ELF-RC) force.

In Ethiopia, thousands of government opponents were arrested and held outside any legal framework. These new detainees, as well as others arrested in 1991, were held without charge or trial and without any safeguards for their basic rights.

A Special Prosecutor's Office was established in August to investigate and institute criminal proceedings against people accused of abusing their positions in the former government or ruling Workers' Party of Ethiopia. The right to *habeas corpus*, which was already ineffective, was formally suspended for six months from August onwards, and no limit was set on the time detainees could be held without charge. The Vice-Minister of Justice was appointed Special Prosecutor. No detainees had been charged by the end of the year.

After the regional assembly elections in June, the EPRDF security forces detained almost 20,000 suspected OLF armed personnel. It did not disclose their identities but some, including women and children, were believed to be unarmed civilians. They were held in three military camps at Dedessa near Gimbi, Blatta in Sidamo region, and Hurso in Hararghe region. The government said it had detained them in order to disarm and "re-educate" them politically, but few had been released by the end of the year. Arrests of OLF political activists were reported throughout the year, but none was charged or tried.

Between February and May, 11 former army officers and civilians were arrested in the capital, Addis Ababa. The authorities said that they had plotted armed insurrection. Two of them publicly admitted this,

possibly under duress, but all 11 reportedly remained in detention without charge or trial at the end of the year.

Kaafi Yusuf Ali, a prominent member of the Ogaden National Liberation Front (ONLF), which had called for a referendum on independence for Ethiopia's southeastern Ogaden area, was arrested in Kebre Dahar in eastern Ethiopia in January. He died in detention in July, reportedly as a result of beatings and ill-treatment. Several other ONLF supporters were believed to be in custody at the end of the year.

In June over 20 suspected members of the opposition Ethiopian People's Revolutionary Party (EPRP) were arrested in Gedaref in eastern Sudan, where most had lived for several years as refugees. They were immediately forcibly returned to Ethiopia. Tadelle Demeke, who was visiting Sudan for academic research while a refugee in the United Kingdom, denied that she was an EPRP member and was released six weeks later. Most of the others were released shortly afterwards, but four EPRP members remained in detention without charge or trial at the end of the year. Four EPRP leaders including Tsegay Gebre-Medhin, who were detained in August 1991 when EPRP armed opposition collapsed, remained in detention throughout 1992.

Some 2,000 officials of the former government, armed forces and ruling party in Ethiopia remained in detention throughout the year without charge or trial. They had been arrested in 1991 and accused of human rights violations, war crimes or abuse of power (see *Amnesty International Report 1992*). They were mostly detained in Sendafa Police College and Holeta military academy near Addis Ababa, and Tolay military camp in Wollega region. They were allowed to receive visits from relatives. In August the final 900 former Ethiopian armed forces officers who had been captured in Eritrea in May 1991 were handed over to the Ethiopian Government and joined the others who had been detained.

It appeared that a number of opponents of the EPRDF or TPLF who had been detained by them before May 1991 were still held throughout 1992, although there was no official confirmation of this. They included Hagos Atsbeha, brother of a prominent defector from the TPLF, who had been abducted from Sudan in 1988 by the TPLF and detained in TPLF-held territory in Ethiopia. Brigadier-General Beretta Germamew and Colonel Getahun Wolde-Ghiorgis, who were captured in 1989 by the TPLF and later fought with it against the government, were allegedly kept in secret detention from May 1991 onwards for opposing the new EPRDF government.

In January three leaders of the National Democratic Union (NDU) who had been arrested in Addis Ababa in November 1991 (see *Amnesty International Report 1992*) were released without charge.

There were reports of torture and ill-treatment of some prisoners, in particular of OLF members.

Many areas were affected by political violence and government soldiers reportedly extrajudicially executed scores of unarmed civilians. In the east, EPRDF soldiers shot dead two leading ONLF members in January: Mohamed Sheikh Mohamoud Iraad, a member of the ONLF central committee, in Dega Bur; and Abdirashid Sulub Anshur, editor of an ONLF magazine, in Kebre Dahar. In the regional elections campaign, some people were reportedly killed for supporting the OLF. In Watar, a town near Dire Dawa, EPRDF troops shot dead scores of OLF supporters in March during a demonstration. In April OLF troops killed over 150 OLF opponents in Bedeno town near Dire Dawa; their bodies were later recovered from a ravine. Ethnic and religious tensions led to intercommunal killings as well as killings of members of ethnic minorities in some areas. In Harar and Dire Dawa in the east, dozens of members of the Amhara minority were killed in early 1992, allegedly by OLF supporters. In Arba Gugu village in Arsi region, armed militias of the Oromo People's Democratic Organization (OPDO), part of the coalition government, allegedly killed scores of Amhara civilians in June.

Inquiries into some of these killings were carried out by the Council of Representatives. Its inquiry into the killings in Watar called for clearer guidelines on the use of lethal force by EPRDF soldiers, noting though that they had faced violence from anti-government demonstrators. The Council's inquiry into the killings in Bedeno urged the OLF to punish its members who were responsible, but no such action was known to have been taken by the OLF.

Groups opposed to the government coalition were also responsible for human rights abuses, including torture and deliberate killings of scores of unarmed civilians. In an OLF camp in the east, several opponents were reportedly tortured or killed in early 1992. OLF armed units were also alleged to have deliberately killed unarmed members of ethnic minorities in predominantly Oromo areas. Three other opposition groups, including the Islamic Front for the Liberation of Oromia (IFLO), also reportedly committed deliberate and arbitrary killings of suspected opponents.

The bodies of thousands of people who "disappeared" or were extrajudicially executed under the Mengistu government were discovered and exhumed for proper burial. They included several detained former officials summarily executed in November 1974; former Emperor Haile Selassie, killed in custody in his palace in 1975; Patriarch Tewoflos, former head of the Ethiopian Orthodox Church, the Reverend Gudina Tumsa, former head of the Ethiopian Evangelical Mekane Yesus Church, and Kassa Wolde-Mariam, a former university president and government minister, all of whom "disappeared" from detention in 1979; and thousands of students, workers and farmers who were extrajudicially executed during the "Red Terror" campaign in the late 1970s (see *Amnesty International Report 1978*).

In Eritrea, over 200 people, including opponents of the provisional Eritrean government, were detained without charge or trial, and without reference to the law. Information about them was particularly difficult to obtain, as the authorities disclosed no details. Many of the detainees had been arrested in mid-1991 because they were alleged to have violated human rights or committed criminal offences as employees or supporters of the former Mengistu government. Ali Higo Mohamed, a former regional governor, remained in detention after having been abducted from Addis Ababa in May 1991, although the government denied holding him. Other detainees were also believed to be held in secret, such as Tekle-Berhan Gebre-Tsadik and Wolde-Mariam Bahibi, officials of the armed opposition ELF-RC, who were alleged to have been abducted from Kassala in eastern Sudan in April 1992, forcibly returned to Eritrea and secretly detained there. In October the government announced the release of 90 detainees, but disclosed no details about them or the

**130** reasons for their imprisonment.

Secret burial grounds of execution victims were also discovered in Asmara and other places in Eritrea, where thousands of Eritreans suspected of supporting the EPLF's armed struggle for Eritrea's independence from Ethiopia had been extrajudicially executed during the previous two decades or more.

There were no reports of any death sentences passed by courts or judicial executions during 1992 in either Ethiopia or Eritrea.

Amnesty International continued to appeal to the Ethiopian authorities to end the arbitrary detention of officials of the previous government and opponents of the present government, and to ensure that they were formally charged with recognizably criminal offences and given fair and prompt trials within a reasonable time, or released. It called for independent inquiries into reports of torture and extrajudicial executions and for steps to be taken to prevent extrajudicial executions. The organization criticized human rights abuses by the OLF and other opposition groups.

Amnesty International also appealed to the Eritrean authorities to ensure that detainees held for offences under the former Ethiopian government or for their opposition to the EPLF received fair and prompt trials or were released.

# FIJI

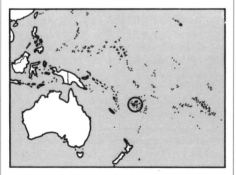

Sedition charges against seven civil rights activists were dropped. There were allegations that six people sentenced to jail terms for obstructing the police had been ill-treated in custody.

Former Major-General Sitiveni Rabuka became Prime Minister after national elections in May. The elections were held under the 1990 Constitution which guarantees power for indigenous Fijians. Prime Minister Rabuka, leader of the *Soqosoqo Ni Vakavulewa Ni Taukei* (SVT), Fijian Political Party, the dominant party in the ruling coalition government, had led two military coups in 1987 (see *Amnesty International Reports 1988* and *1989*).

Sedition charges against seven civil rights activists who had participated in non-violent protests against the country's new Constitution in October 1990 were dropped (see *Amnesty International Reports 1991* and *1992*). The seven included Dr Anirudh Singh, who had been abducted and tortured by army officers in October 1990.

Six miners who were sentenced to jail terms for obstructing police officers and damaging police vehicles were reportedly ill-treated in custody. They said they had been beaten and punched by police officers. The miners also alleged that they were not given adequate time to consult their lawyers before the trial. They had been arrested in February during a clash between police and striking miners at a gold mine in Vatukoula town which resulted in the death of a court official trying to enforce an eviction order.

An Amnesty International representative visited Fiji in May to discuss the organization's concerns with government officials, including Solicitor-General Filimone Jitoko.

# FINLAND

**One conscientious objector was imprisoned for refusing to perform military service. Three conscientious objectors were released after serving their sentences. All four were considered prisoners of conscience.**

Marko Ulvila, a conscientious objector to military service, began serving a 75-day prison sentence in September. He had been convicted under a temporary law on alternative service which was in force from 1987 to the end of 1991.

Three conscientious objectors were released after serving sentences imposed in 1991: Janne Mäkinen, Timo Tapani Karjalainen and Kari Hämäläinen (see *Amnesty International Report 1992*).

A new law on alternative service took effect on 1 January. According to the law, a conscript who refuses to perform military service for reasons of conscience will be exempted from it during peacetime and will be allowed to perform alternative civilian service. The length of alternative service was reduced from 16 to 13 months.

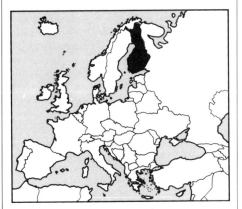

Amnesty International welcomed the new law insofar as it offered an alternative service of comparable length to military service, which is between eight and 11 months' duration. The organization was concerned, however, that alternative service is available to conscientious objectors only during peacetime. Amnesty International believes that it is of particular importance that individuals are able to exercise their right to freedom of conscience at a time of actual military conflict. The organization urged the government, therefore, to allow conscientious objectors to perform alternative service during military conflicts as well as in peacetime.

Amnesty International urged the immediate release of the detained conscientious objectors because it considered the length of the alternative service under the previous law (twice the length of ordinary military service) to have been punitive.

# FRANCE

**Hundreds of conscientious objectors to the national service laws were considered prisoners of conscience. There were allegations of ill-treatment in police custody.**

The alternative civilian service available to recognized conscientious objectors remained twice the length of ordinary military service. Conscientious objectors refusing to conform to the national service laws received sentences of up to 18 months' imprisonment.

All but four of the known imprisoned conscientious objectors were Jehovah's Witnesses. According to unofficial estimates, between 700 and 1,000 Jehovah's Witnesses were imprisoned during the year for refusing military service; they had not applied for conscientious objector status because they also rejected the option of civilian service.

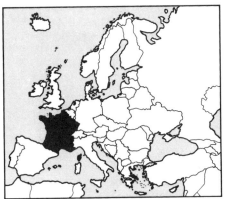

Among them was Jérémy Bernardi who had already spent over seven months in prison during 1991 under judicial investigation for insubordination. This had resulted from his refusal to put on military uniform after reporting to an army barracks, as ordered, to commence military service. He was released in January, pending trial, but because he remained liable for military service he immediately reported back to barracks where he again refused to put on military uniform. He was detained under investigation on a second charge of insubordination and in February was sentenced to 15 months' imprisonment. In June he was sentenced to 18 months' imprisonment on the first charge of insubordination, reduced on appeal to 15 months' imprisonment, to run concurrently

**132** with the sentence imposed in February. He was released in July.

There were allegations of ill-treatment in police custody, often concerning immigrants and French citizens of North African origin.

Jacques Cherigui, of Franco-Algerian parentage, claimed that police officers who arrested him in Argenteuil in June, apparently in the course of a criminal investigation, threw him to the floor, kicked and punched him and subjected him to racial abuse. On his release some 19 hours later he was charged with insulting the police and resisting arrest. A medical certificate issued within hours of his release and subsequent photographs recorded multiple cuts and bruises to his body. He made two criminal complaints of ill-treatment against the police in June but was informed verbally by the prosecutor's office that they had been declared inadmissible; he was not given the reasons for these decisions. In October the criminal court due to hear the charges against him decided to await the report of an internal police inquiry into his allegations of ill-treatment and adjourned the trial until March 1993. Jacques Cherigui also announced his intention of making a civil complaint against the police.

A judicial inquiry into the circumstances surrounding the detention and death in police custody of Aïssa Ihich in May 1991, following an asthma attack (see *Amnesty International Report 1992*), led in February to a charge of involuntary homicide against a forensic doctor attached to Versailles appeal court. Aïssa Ihich had allegedly been beaten by police officers on arrest and deprived of medication to alleviate his chronic asthma during his detention. The doctor had issued a medical certificate some 18 hours after the arrest stating that the detainee's state of health was compatible with a 24-hour extension of his preventive detention; he had also recorded injuries caused by blows to his body. He failed to make any reference to the detainee's asthma and gave no instructions to the police regarding his treatment. By the end of the year the judicial inquiry had still not established which police agency had carried out the arrest and alleged ill-treatment of Aïssa Ihich.

A judicial inquiry into Lucien Djossouvi's allegations of ill-treatment by police in 1989 (see *Amnesty International Reports 1990* to *1992*) had still not concluded.

Amnesty International considered that the length of the civilian service for conscientious objectors, twice that of military service, was punitive. It therefore considered those imprisoned as a result of rejecting both military and civilian service to be prisoners of conscience and appealed for their release. It sought information from the authorities about the steps taken to investigate allegations of ill-treatment in police custody.

# GAMBIA

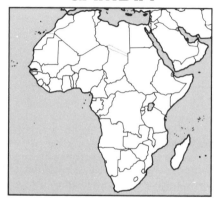

**Sixteen possible prisoners of conscience were detained for several weeks. Three police officers were tried and two convicted in connection with the death of a detainee in 1991. Five people were sentenced to death; there were no executions.**

Presidential and parliamentary elections in April returned President Dawda Jawara to office for a fifth term. The President publicly reiterated his commitment to human rights and democracy. On 11 May he announced an amnesty for most of those who had participated in an unsuccessful coup attempt in 1981. As the last of the prisoners sentenced in connection with the coup attempt had been released in 1991, this opened the way for the return of those who had gone abroad to escape prosecution. However, the amnesty apparently excluded Kukoi Samba Sanyang, the leader of the 1981 coup attempt, for whom a new arrest warrant had recently been issued.

Sixteen suspected government opponents who were detained, some for nearly six weeks, appeared to be prisoners of conscience. On 31 March it was announced

**133**

that seven people had been arrested in connection with a new plot by Kukoi Samba Sanyang against the government. During April at least nine others were arrested because of their suspected involvement with the banned Movement for Justice in Africa (MOJA), some of whose members had been implicated in the 1981 coup attempt. All 16 were charged with "managing an unlawful society" (MOJA) and were released on bail on 11 May at the time of the presidential amnesty. They appeared in court on 26 May and were discharged, apparently for lack of evidence. Before the court hearing, one prisoner publicly alleged that he had been tortured in detention; it was not clear whether the authorities carried out any investigation into his allegation. In November President Jawara lifted the ban on MOJA, allowing it to function openly.

Two police officers were found guilty of ill-treating a prisoner who died in custody. They and another police officer were brought to trial before the Supreme Court in October 1991. They were charged with assault and murder in connection with the death in custody in August 1991 of Mamadu Jarju, a criminal suspect (see *Amnesty International Report 1992*). In February the court ruled that Mamadu Jarju had died as a result of torture and convicted two of the three police officers of "assault occasioning grievous bodily harm". Both were sentenced to three years' imprisonment. The third officer was acquitted. Following the judgment, the Director of Public Prosecutions filed an appeal against the acquittal of one officer and the court's failure to convict the other two of murder, a more serious offence punishable by a mandatory death sentence. In December the Appeal Court ruled that the two officers should have been convicted of murder and sentenced them to death. The acquittal of the third officer was confirmed.

The first death sentences since 1987 were imposed. Two men were sentenced to death by the Supreme Court in January and a third man was sentenced to death in March. All three had been convicted of murder. Their appeals had not been heard by the end of the year. On 31 December the two death sentences passed in January were commuted to life imprisonment. One execution only is known to have been carried out since Dawda Jawara became President in 1970.

During the year Amnesty International appealed to President Jawara to commute all death sentences.

# GEORGIA

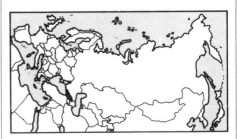

**In the disputed region of Abkhazia scores of people, including possible prisoners of conscience, were reportedly held as hostages on grounds of their ethnic origin. Many alleged that they were tortured or ill-treated in detention. Dozens of non-combatant civilians were said to have been deliberately and arbitrarily killed. Elsewhere, dozens of political prisoners alleged that they were beaten while in short-term detention.**

Georgia received international recognition as an independent state following the break-up of the Soviet Union. In March it joined the Conference on Security and Co-operation in Europe and in July became a member of the United Nations. President Zviad Gamsakhurdia was deposed in January and replaced by a Military Council. In March this body handed power to a State Council headed by Eduard Shevardnadze, who became Chairman of a newly elected parliament in October.

Armed clashes between government forces and supporters of the ousted president claimed scores of lives during the year. Hundreds were also said to have died after Georgian troops entered Abkhazia, a region in the northwest of the country seeking greater autonomy, in August. The confused situation made it difficult to corroborate allegations of deliberate and arbitrary killings and hostage-taking by both government and opposition forces.

The death penalty was abolished for all offences when the 1921 Constitution was restored in February. Nine prisoners awaiting execution when the death penalty was abolished were officially reported to have had their sentences commuted.

**134**

All public meetings were banned in January after rallies protesting against the ousting of President Gamsakhurdia led to deaths. Scores of his supporters were placed under administrative arrest for up to 30 days for taking part in later demonstrations which were said to have been peaceful. Dozens claimed that they were beaten while in the custody of law-enforcement officials. Valeriya Novodvorskaya, for example, reported that she was beaten unconscious when detained on 7 October in the capital, Tbilisi, at a rally calling for a boycott of parliamentary elections.

In Abkhazia, Georgian armed forces were reportedly involved in the arbitrary detention of non-combatants, including the taking of hostages, on the grounds of ethnic origin. They were also implicated in rape, beatings and ill-treatment of detainees and extrajudicial executions. M. K. Dzhindzholiya, for example, an ethnic Abkhazian, said that he was walking in Sukhumi on 17 August with his uncle when they were detained by the Georgian National Guard solely because of their ethnic origin. He alleged that they were beaten, kicked and subjected to a mock execution before being taken to Dranda prison. There, they and about 40 other detainees were reportedly forced to pass between two lines of Georgian guardsmen who beat them severely. Murman Zadrovich Kvitsiniya, who alleged that his skull was fractured in a similar assault at Dranda prison on 27 August, said that the previous day a man detained with him near the Kodor river was shot dead by Georgian troops for answering "Republic of Abkhazia" when asked where he lived.

Similar allegations were made against forces under Abkhaz control, although specific information on concrete incidents was difficult to obtain.

At least 14 people were executed in Abkhazia, some after what were reported to be summary military proceedings, despite the fact that the death penalty had been abolished. Vitaly Gladkikh, for example, an ethnic Russian accused of sabotage, was said to have been sentenced to death in Sukhumi on 10 November by a Georgian court-martial and executed five days later. Twelve people were reportedly executed for looting by Abkhazian military units in Gagra in October.

After numerous detentions of demonstrators from January onwards, Amnesty International asked the government to clarify what steps it was taking to ensure that citizens were able to exercise peacefully their rights to freedom of association and expression, and urged that all complaints of beatings in custody be investigated fully and impartially. The organization urged that all alleged abuses in Abkhazia within its mandate be investigated fully and impartially, with the results made public and the perpetrators brought to justice.

Amnesty International expressed regret at the executions in Abkhazia and asked for a full and impartial investigation to be carried out into the circumstances of the deaths. It also asked for confirmation that the nine death sentences pending had been commuted.

# GERMANY

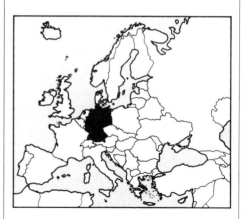

**At least one conscientious objector served a prison sentence for refusing to perform military service; he was released in January. He was considered a prisoner of conscience. Allegations were received concerning the ill-treatment of asylum-seekers and other foreign nationals.**

The Federal Republic of Germany ratified in August the Second Optional Protocol to the International Covenant on Civil and Political Rights aiming at the abolition of the death penalty.

In January the first of a number of trials of former East German border guards ended (see *Amnesty International Report 1992*). They had been charged with the manslaughter of Chris Gueffroy, who was shot dead trying to cross the Berlin Wall in February 1989. One of the former guards was sentenced by the Berlin Regional Court to three and a half years' imprisonment; another was given a two-year suspended prison sentence. The two other guards were acquitted.

In November the trial of former East German leader Erich Honecker began in Berlin. Erich Honecker, who was returned to Germany in July after spending seven and a half months sheltering in the Chilean Embassy in Moscow, was charged with the manslaughter of 13 defectors at the East German border. Similar charges were also brought against other former high-ranking East German government officials.

Thomas Biskupek served almost three months in detention between October 1991 and January 1992 for refusing to perform military service on grounds of conscience. On 29 October 1991 Thomas Biskupek's application to perform alternative service, submitted some 12 weeks earlier, was rejected. He appealed against this decision and was finally recognized as a conscientious objector on 27 January, having spent a total of 81 days in detention for refusing to put on his uniform.

Ill-treatment of asylum-seekers and other foreign nationals by police was reported on several occasions. In March an asylum-seeker, a 14-year-old Turkish Kurd, was stopped by police officers near the main railway station in Bremen. He attempted to flee but was caught by police officers and thrown roughly to the ground. His arms were reportedly bent backwards and he was struck when he cried out in pain. He later underwent an operation on a fracture to his arm.

During a trial in August allegations were made that police officers had failed to intervene in an attack by right-wing extremists on an Angolan immigrant worker. Amadeu Antonio Kiowa was kicked and beaten to death in November 1990 in Eberswalde, a town 45 kilometres northeast of Berlin. Three men who participated in the attack were found guilty of inflicting grievous bodily harm on Amadeu Antonio Kiowa resulting in his death. During the trial it was alleged that police officers had shadowed the attackers but had failed to come to the Angolan's rescue when he was attacked.

In August the Bavarian Ministry of Justice rejected Amnesty International's recommendation that *Haus III*, the secure psychiatric unit attached to Straubing prison, be re-established as an independent and separate clinic. Amnesty International had expressed concern that the close link between the prison and psychiatric facility tended to result in the placing of prison objectives before patients' needs (see *Amnesty International Report 1992*). The Ministry denied this and stated that the integration of the psychiatric unit into the prison brought considerable advantages to the prisoners detained there.

Amnesty International wrote to the German authorities expressing concern about Thomas Biskupek's imprisonment. The organization urged the authorities to consider the adoption of a procedure to ensure the automatic suspension of call-up once an application to perform alternative service is submitted. In April the Ministry of Defence replied that the Law on Conscientious Objection allowed for such a suspension, provided that an application to perform alternative service was submitted before call-up papers were issued. Amnesty International wrote again to the Ministry of Defence in August emphasizing its belief that conscientious objectors should be allowed to claim conscientious objector status at any time.

In May Amnesty International asked the German authorities whether charges had been brought against the police accused of ill-treating the 14-year-old Turkish Kurd. In October the Minister of Justice in Bremen replied that a judicial investigation into the allegations was still continuing.

In August and October Amnesty International wrote to the authorities asking to be informed of the outcome of an investigation reportedly launched into the behaviour of the police officers who allegedly stood by and watched the attack which resulted in the death of Amadeu Antonio Kiowa. In November Amnesty International was informed by the Ministry of the Interior of the State of Brandenburg that a judicial investigation into the allegations was currently in progress. An earlier decision by the relevant police authorities not to take any action against the officers would be reassessed in the light of any new information which emerged.

**136**

# GHANA

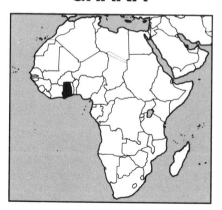

One prisoner of conscience was held throughout the year and over 50 other government opponents arrested in 1992 may have been prisoners of conscience. Some 37 long-term political prisoners, including prisoners of conscience, were released. At least three people were sentenced to death, but no executions were reported.

The ruling Provisional National Defence Council (PNDC) set out a timetable for a return to civilian rule by early 1993. In April a new Constitution, due to come into force on 7 January 1993, was approved by referendum, despite controversy over provisions granting immunity from prosecution to all PNDC members and appointees for their actions while in power. It will effectively abolish the National Public Tribunal, the highest in a system of special courts created in 1982 which are not independent of the executive and whose procedures do not guarantee a fair trial. The new Constitution will also give a right of appeal from lower Public Tribunals to the higher courts in the ordinary court system. Public Tribunal chairpersons will have to have the same qualifications as High Court judges and the judiciary will be given the main responsibility for their appointment.

In September two laws providing for indefinite administrative detention without charge or trial were repealed: the Preventive Custody Law, PNDC Law 4 of 1982; and the Habeas Corpus (Amendment) Law, PNDC Law 91 of 1984. They were replaced by the Public Order (No. 2) Law, PNDC Law 288 of 1992, which allows the Secretary (Minister) of the Interior to order 28 days'

administrative detention without charge or trial of any person whose actions he considers are likely, among other things, to foment ethnic conflict or violence. After 14 days the detention must be reviewed by a panel of three judges, which may approve the detainee's continued detention. The courts are specifically excluded from challenging such detentions.

In May the ban on political parties was lifted. On 3 November, in the first multi-party elections since 1979, the PNDC Chairman, Flight-Lieutenant J.J. Rawlings, who had been Head of State since 1981 and who retired from the armed forces to stand for election, was elected President. Opposition parties accused the government of electoral malpractices and vote-rigging, and boycotted legislative elections in December.

At least one prisoner of conscience remained in prison. George Naykene, editor of the *Christian Chronicle* newspaper, had been detained in late 1991 (see *Amnesty International Report 1992*). He was sentenced in April to 18 months' imprisonment for libel by the Circuit Court in Accra, the capital. He had published a letter which alleged that all members of the former Armed Forces Ruling Council (AFRC) – the military government headed by Flight-Lieutenant Rawlings from June to September 1979 following a coup – had profited from an illegal foreign loan. The court ruled that he had not proved that *every* AFRC member had profited from the loan, although evidence before the court showed that some members had. Kwesi Armah, a lawyer and former government minister also detained in late 1991 in connection with the same case, was released uncharged on 5 April. He had apparently been detained because he refused to testify for the prosecution.

In April four pro-democracy demonstrators, including government critic and former prisoner of conscience Kwesi Pratt (see *Amnesty International Report 1992*), were arrested and detained for a few days after peacefully demonstrating against the immunity granted to the PNDC in the new Constitution. They were charged, although not subsequently prosecuted, with public order offences.

At least 21 people were arrested by the security police – the Bureau of National Investigation (BNI) – following several bomb attacks in Accra and the port of Tema after the November elections. They were suspected of involvement in the attacks or of having connections with Al-haji Tahidu Braimah Damba, who had been detained without charge or trial for two years from December 1984 on suspicion of plotting to overthrow the government. Those detained included Johnny Hansen, a former government minister and opposition leader; seven relatives of Alhaji Damba; and several soldiers. Five of Alhaji Damba's relatives were released by December and one apparently escaped and fled abroad. The seventh, Hadi Tahidu Damba, was charged before the National Public Tribunal on 7 December, with Alhaji Damba and two others *in absentia*. They were charged with conspiracy, abetment and causing criminal damage. Johnny Hansen was released from detention after testifying in court in December. Some of those detained may have been prisoners of conscience, held because of their criticism of government policies or their relationship to a government opponent. On 17 December Kwesi Pratt (see above) and Professor Albert Adu-Boahen, leader of the New Patriotic Party (NPP), were charged with obstructing the court for refusing to testify on the grounds that they did not consider the court to be independent of government influence. The case had not been completed by the end of the year.

On 5 and 6 December more than 35 people in the Ashanti Region, an opposition stronghold, were detained in Kumasi and Obuasi. Among them were at least 15 leading NPP members and supporters, including Nana Yaw Boakye, who is over 70 years old. It was not known whether they had been released at the end of the year.

In March Flight-Lieutenant Rawlings announced that security agencies had been instructed to review the cases of all those detained on grounds of national security with a view to releasing prisoners "where appropriate". Later that month the government announced the release of the first 17 prisoners. They included at least 15 political prisoners: 14 untried detainees and one serving a prison sentence. Several were prisoners of conscience, including Major Courage Quarshigah, detained without charge or trial on suspicion of conspiring to overthrow the government (see *Amnesty International Reports 1990 to 1992*), and Jacob Jabuni Yidana, a former Chief Super-intendent of Police (see *Amnesty International Report 1992*). Other political

prisoners released included Andrew Kwame Pianim, as well as Bombardier Mustapha Mohamed, who had been detained without charge or trial since 1982, and four other members of the armed forces held without charge or trial since 1983.

At least 22 other political detainees were among about 60 detainees released without announcement, mostly during April and May. Little information was available about the reasons for their detention and it was difficult to determine how many had been held for political reasons. Among those released were prisoners of conscience Edward Akakpo, Joy Cudjoe and Simon Sablah, who had been arrested in September 1989 in connection with the same alleged coup attempt as Major Courage Quarshigah and held without charge or trial. Also released was Corporal Moses Harlley, who had allegedly been tortured after his arrest in 1985 in an attempt to coerce him to give evidence in an unfair political trial.

Seven other political prisoners convicted in connection with alleged conspiracies were still serving prison sentences. All had been tried before Public Tribunals.

At least three people were sentenced to death. Kwaku Duroh and Kofi Ntorie were sentenced to death by firing-squad for murder in separate trials in January before Public Tribunals. In April Bukari Musah was sentenced to death by hanging following conviction for murder by the High Court, Tamale. No executions were reported.

Amnesty International called for the immediate and unconditional release of all prisoners of conscience, and the release of other political suspects held in administrative detention if they were not to be promptly charged and brought to trial. It welcomed the releases of prisoners of conscience and detainees held without charge or trial as well as the repeal of laws which allowed unlimited detention without charge or trial. However, the organization expressed concern that the new detention law still allows prisoners of conscience and others to be detained without recourse to the courts. It appealed on behalf of the prisoners sentenced to death, urging that their sentences be commuted, and called for abolition of the death penalty.

**138**

# GREECE

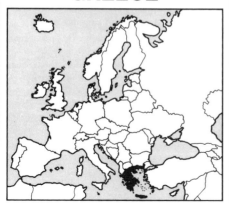

**There were about 400 prisoners of conscience, all of them conscientious objectors to military service. Reports of torture and ill-treatment in police custody and prisons continued.**

There is no alternative civilian service for conscientious objectors to military service. Some 400 conscientious objectors, most of them Jehovah's Witnesses, were in prison. Most were serving four-year sentences which they could reduce to about three years by working while in prison.

The military authorities continued to imprison Jehovah's Witness ministers (see *Amnesty International Reports 1990* to *1992*). Anastasios Georgiades, a Jehovah's Witness minister, was jailed in January after refusing to perform military service on conscientious grounds. The military authorities refused to grant him the exemption enjoyed by ministers of other religions on the grounds that they considered that the Jehovah's Witness faith was not a recognized religion under Greek law. He was acquitted of insubordination on two separate occasions, but following both trials he was immediately recalled to the army and reimprisoned. He was finally released in July after the Council of State ruled he was a minister of a recognized religion eligible for exemption from military service.

A number of people were prosecuted for peacefully exercising their right to freedom of expression. Stratis Bournazos, Maria Kalogeropoulou, Vangelio Sotiropoulou and Christina Tsamoura were each sentenced to 19 months' imprisonment in May for a statement they had made advocating peace in the Balkans and opposing government foreign policy and domestic policy regarding Greece's ethnic minorities. They remained free pending appeal. In a separate case, Christos Sideropoulos and Anastasios Boulis were prosecuted for stating in a magazine interview that there was a Macedonian minority in Greece and criticizing the government's foreign policy. Their trial, which was postponed twice during the year, was rescheduled for 1993. There was no indication that any of these people had advocated violence and if imprisoned they would be prisoners of conscience.

Reports of torture and ill-treatment in police stations and prisons continued. For example, in February police in Patras allegedly slapped and punched Youssef Akroumi, a Moroccan asylum-seeker detained on criminal charges, until he lost consciousness and suffered temporary hearing loss in his left ear. He was subsequently treated for a ruptured ear-drum in hospital. He reportedly informed the examining magistrate about his ill-treatment, but no action appeared to have been taken to investigate his allegations.

Several conscientious objectors alleged they had been ill-treated by military personnel in the initial detention period. For example, in March military policemen at Kozani Army Camp kicked and punched Dimitris Tsironis, threatened him with loaded weapons and made obscene remarks insulting to his religious beliefs.

In June prison staff allegedly beat Ibrahim Lumwe before he was held for 10 days in isolation in Patras Closed Prison. Fellow prisoners said that when Ibrahim Lumwe was released from isolation he had severe bruising on his body, legs and arms. In July Georgios Avgoustidis, also held in Patras Closed Prison, alleged that he was punched and kicked by the chief guard and director of the prison after he questioned them about a punishment.

In September Manolis Tsapelis died one month after police in Hydra had allegedly headbutted him in the chest and punched him in the stomach following an argument. An autopsy report recorded the cause of death as an embolism following an operation on an injured spleen resulting from a fall or beating. An investigation into the allegations of ill-treatment, which was initiated by the Public Prosecutor's Office, had not concluded by the end of the year.

Amnesty International appealed repeatedly for the release of all imprisoned conscientious objectors and for the government to introduce alternative civilian service of non-punitive length. It urged that all charges against people ·prosecuted for peacefully exercising their right to freedom of expression be dropped and that all convictions in such cases be quashed. Amnesty International urged that all allegations of torture and ill-treatment be investigated promptly and impartially and that those responsible be brought to justice. In December an Amnesty International observer travelled to Greece to attend the trial of Christos Sideropoulos and Anastasios Boulis which was postponed.

In June Amnesty International published a report, *Greece: Torture and ill-treatment*, which drew attention to the many cases of torture and ill-treatment reported in recent years. The report made specific recommendations for safeguards to protect detainees, including an effective and impartial complaints mechanism.

In August the Minister of Public Order commented on cases mentioned in Amnesty International's report. One of these concerned Süleyman Akyar, who died in police custody in January 1991 (see *Amnesty International Report 1992*). In his case the Minister stated that disciplinary measures had not been taken pending the outcome of the judicial inquiry. In another case, he said disciplinary measures had been taken against a policeman. In four cases, including the alleged ill-treatment of Dimitris Voglis and Stella Evgenikou, a judicial inquiry was pending (see *Amnesty International Reports 1990 to 1992*). The case against police officers alleged to have tortured Vasilis Makrinitsas, Vasilis Makripoulias and Argyris Kavatas was dropped following a decision by the Council of Judges (see *Amnesty International Report 1992*). The Minister's response contained virtually no information on the methods used to investigate allegations of torture and ill-treatment, although Amnesty International had asked for full details of the methods and findings of each investigation. The government made no substantive comment on the allegations Amnesty International had received regarding ill-treatment of people in prison, nor did it respond to Amnesty International's proposals regarding the protection of police detainees and prisoners from abuse.

In September the government informed Amnesty International that it was unable to introduce alternative civilian service because, according to a decision by the Legal State Council (which does not have binding authority), such a service would be unconstitutional.

# GRENADA

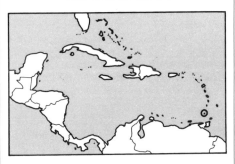

There were concerns for the health of Phyllis Coard, the only female prisoner in Richmond Hill Prison, who had spent much of the past six years in solitary confinement. No new death sentences were passed and there were no executions.

Phyllis Coard, one of 14 former members of the People's Revolutionary Government whose death sentences were commuted to life imprisonment in 1991 (see *Amnesty International Report 1992*), was reportedly suffering from severe depression and in August began a hunger-strike. Later that month, the Prison Commissioner reportedly expressed concern that she might be suicidal and two prison doctors recommended that she be examined by a qualified outside psychiatrist. Such treatment was withheld, however, until October, when she was allowed to see a psychiatrist of her choice. She then ended her hunger-strike.

There had been reports of the deteriorating health of Phyllis Coard for a number of years, owing in part to the long periods she had spent in solitary confinement since 1983 (see *Amnesty International Reports 1985, 1986, 1988 and 1991*). However, her prison conditions improved in 1992 and, according to the authorities, she was allowed to work daily with other inmates, attend communal religious services and participate in games and occasional cultural events.

Amnesty International wrote to Prime

**140**

Minister Nicholas Brathwaite and the Minister of Health in September, urging that Phyllis Coard be examined by an independent psychiatrist without delay and receive all appropriate psychiatric and medical care.

# GUATEMALA

**At least 200 people were alleged to have been extrajudicially executed by the security forces and their civilian agents. Death threats and harassment increased dramatically, and several people were abducted by unidentified armed men believed to belong to the security forces. There were a number of "disappearances". Torture and ill-treatment by police officers and civilians apparently acting in connivance with them were widely reported.**

Talks between the government and representatives of the armed opposition coalition *Unidad Revolucionaria Nacional Guatemalteca* (URNG), Guatemalan National Revolutionary Unity, continued without reaching agreement. A preliminary agreement not to create new *Patrullas de Auto-Defensa Civil*, civil defence patrols, unless specifically requested by the population, was reached in August. The Human Rights Attorney was given responsibility for verifying whether patrols were voluntary.

Armed conflict continued despite the peace talks. The army's counter-insurgency tactics included aerial bombings and attacks on *Comunidades de Población en Resistencia* (CPRs), Communities of People in Resistance, which led to civilians being injured. The CPRs are communities which fled army counter-insurgency operations in the early 1980s and refused to live in areas controlled by the army. A commission to investigate their situation, including church representatives, local human rights and grassroots groups and the Human Rights Attorney, described them as civilian non-combatants and produced evidence of army bombings.

In May Guatemala acceded to the International Covenant on Civil and Political Rights.

In July Human Rights Attorney Ramiro de León Carpio was re-elected by Congress for a further five years.

In September Congress passed a law which provides the death penalty for drug-trafficking acts resulting in death. This contravenes the American Convention on Human Rights, to which Guatemala is party, which states that the application of the death penalty shall not be extended to crimes to which it did not apply at the time of the ratification of the Convention. Congress also adopted a new code of penal procedure, to become effective in 1993, which provides for trials in the defendant's own language, makes the Public Ministry responsible for criminal investigations, and grants the Human Rights Attorney and relatives of victims special facilities to conduct their own investigations into alleged extrajudicial executions and "disappearances".

In October the government and Guatemalan refugees in Mexico reached an agreement guaranteeing some 45,000 returning refugees physical safety, the rights to freedom of movement, association and organization, and access to land. It also provided for their return to be monitored by United Nations (UN) and other international observers.

Human rights violations by military personnel and their civilian agents, sometimes acting in the guise of "death squads", continued unabated throughout 1992. The victims, often indigenous people, included the displaced, human rights activists, trade unionists, suspected members of the armed opposition, members of popular movements, journalists and judges.

Members of the *Consejo de Comunidades Etnicas "Runujel Junam"* (CERJ), Council of Ethnic Communities "We are all Equal", an organization working for indigenous peoples' rights, continued to suffer abuses. CERJ President Amílcar Méndez Urízar received repeated death threats and in May a grenade exploded outside his home. CERJ member Esteban Tojín from Cruzché II, El Quiché department, reportedly "disappeared" in Guatemala City in

May. He had received repeated death threats from local civil patrollers because of his opposition to civil defence patrols.

Others opposed to civil defence patrols were singled out for abuse. In April Pedro Raguez, who had refused to participate in patrols, was stabbed and shot dead, reportedly by two patrol leaders in Xoljuyú, San Pedro Jocopilas, El Quiché. In August Catarino Chanchavac Larios from San Pablo hamlet, San Pedro Jocopilas, was stabbed to death. He had received numerous death threats because he would not participate in patrols.

Human rights monitors came under attack. In January Rosa Pú Gómez, a member of the *Coordinadora Nacional de Viudas de Guatemala* (CONAVIGUA), National Coordination of Guatemalan Widows, was threatened at gunpoint by a man who asked her about several grassroots leaders and her "disappeared" husband. A police officer made no effort to arrest the man. CONAVIGUA members received numerous death threats accusing them of links with the armed opposition. In May José Nerio Osorio of the *Centro de Investigación, Estudio y Promoción de los Derechos Humanos* (CIEPRODH), Centre for the Investigation, Study and Promotion of Human Rights, was stabbed by two men after CIEPRODH staff had received death threats. The car driving indigenous leader Rigoberta Menchú to Quetzaltenango in July was rammed by men in another car and she suffered further harassment and death threats during her visits to Guatemala.

In October a bomb exploded near the entrance of the *Grupo de Apoyo Mutuo por el Aparecimiento con Vida de Nuestros Familiares* (GAM), Mutual Support Group for the Appearance of Our Relatives Alive. Days later Kakchikel indigenous teenagers Cristina Par and Matea Par, members of the *Coordinadora Maya Majawil Q'ij*, Mayan Coordination "The New Dawn", were beaten and stripped naked in the street by two men and a woman who accused them of being guerrillas because they were wearing indigenous clothes. The assailants had identified them at the march celebrating Rigoberta Menchú's Nobel Peace Prize award.

Trade unionists were also targeted for attack. In March, at a time of industrial conflict within the government-owned electricity industry, Perfecto Us, of the *Sindicato de Trabajadores del Instituto Nacional de Electrificación* (STINDE), Electrical Workers' Union, was abducted by armed men who threatened to kill him if he continued his union activities. He was beaten and left tied up beside a road. In May the 10- and 13-year-old sons of STINDE conflict secretary Víctor Hugo Alvarez were abducted by two unidentified men while walking home after school in Chimaltenango. They were forced into a van and released about 36 kilometres away.

Also prominent among the victims of human rights abuses were the internally displaced and peasants. José Jiménez, leader of the *Consejo Nacional de Desplazados de Guatemala* (CONDEG), National Council for the Displaced in Guatemala, in Huehuetenango department, reported receiving threats from a civil patrol leader in February. In August CONDEG member Marco Antonio Díaz was killed in Crique Grande, Izabal department, by unidentified civilians. Witnesses accused local military commissioners – civilian army representatives.

Attacks on the University of San Carlos (USAC) continued. Bombs exploded in the offices of the *Asociación de Estudiantes Universitarios* (AEU), University Students' Association, of USAC in January, after two AEU-sponsored seminars on peace talks, and in October after death threats to those involved in a lawsuit against the *Hunapú* security force unit (see below). There were at least three other bomb attacks on USAC premises.

At least five students and four academics were apparently extrajudicially executed and many others were subjected to death threats and intimidation. In February professor Manuel Estuardo Peña, who had worked with the displaced and was well known for his left-wing ideas, was shot dead outside his home by two men in plain clothes. On 10 April student Julio Cuc Quim was killed and seven others wounded by members of the security force unit *Hunapú*, made up of the National Police, the Treasury Police and the Military Police. He was shot dead when *Hunapú* agents opened fire on unarmed students after an argument. Legal proceedings were brought against 31 *Hunapú* agents but students involved in the case and their relatives received death threats warning them to stop. In November six *Hunapú* agents from the National and Treasury Police were convicted for the killing and wounding and

**142**

each sentenced to 12 years six months' imprisonment. *Hunapú* agents from the Military Police were tried in a military court, which had not given its verdict by the end of 1992.

Members of the press were also attacked and threatened. Radio journalist Ricardo Castro, producer of a current affairs program, was shot and wounded by a man in plain clothes driving a maroon pick-up van. In October a bomb exploded at the offices of *Tinamit* magazine, which had published articles critical of the government. Many others received death threats.

Members of the armed opposition, and suspected members, were targeted for abuse. Teacher Maritza Urrutia was abducted in July by armed men who she said were military agents. She said she was interrogated about her activities and threatened with the abduction of her son, aged four. She was released a week later. Maritza Urrutia said she had been warned that her family would suffer if she complained about her abduction.

Some active members of the armed opposition were killed in circumstances suggesting they may have been extrajudicially executed. In September the army announced the death in combat of three guerrillas in Sacatepéquez department. Photographs of the bodies, however, showed that all three had been killed by a single shot to the head.

Torture and ill-treatment by the police were widely reported. Several secondary students, many of them minors, were tortured or ill-treated by police in April after demonstrations demanding better conditions in schools. After the demonstrations, National Police agents entered two schools, arresting some 170 students. Among those reportedly tortured was 13-year-old Amado López Hernández, who was forced by a police officer to drink bleach. In July a peaceful march by peasants from Cajolá, Quetzaltenango, was violently dispersed by anti-riot police. Several peasants, including a pregnant woman, were beaten. Several weeks later, uniformed policemen reportedly tried to abduct two Cajolá peasants in Guatemala City.

Street children and those working on their behalf continued to be shot at, beaten and threatened, both by uniformed policemen and by civilians apparently working with them.

Most human rights violations, including thousands of extrajudicial executions and "disappearances" over the previous 15 years, remained uninvestigated and unpunished. However, in a few cases investigations or criminal proceedings were pursued. In April the four policemen convicted of the murder of 13-year-old street child Nahamán Carmona López, whose convictions had been overturned (see *Amnesty International Reports 1991* and *1992*), were retried and again found guilty. In July the Supreme Court set all their sentences at 12 years six months' imprisonment. A private police agent accused of murdering street child Francisco Chacón in 1991 was sentenced to 10 years' imprisonment.

Criminal proceedings in human rights cases were generally flawed and subject to long delays, and judicial officials reported receiving death threats. Among them were appeal judges Mario Guillermo Ruiz Wong, Napoleón Gutiérrez Vargas and Héctor Hugo Pérez Aguilera, who stated in July that they had been receiving threats, in part because of their involvement in judicial proceedings against the military. Two civil patrollers accused of killing Juan Perebal Xirum and Juan Perebal Morales and wounding Diego Perebal León (see *Amnesty International Report 1992*) were acquitted despite ample evidence against them. The trial of an army sergeant for the killing of anthropologist Myrna Mack in 1990 reached the sentencing stage in October, but no sentence was pronounced in 1992.

Cases where evidence reveals the involvement of active military personnel are referred to military courts. However, in the few cases investigated by military courts, investigations and proceedings appeared to be irregular or delayed. In September, five soldiers were sentenced to 30 years' imprisonment for the 1990 killing of United States citizen Michael Devine in El Petén department but the chief of intelligence at a nearby army base was acquitted despite consistent court testimony that he had ordered the killing. The Attorney General appealed against the official's acquittal. In August the Supreme Court confirmed the death sentences imposed by a military court on soldiers Nicolás Gutiérrez Cruz and Eliseo Suchité Hernández for the murder of a displaced family in Ciudad Peronia, Solalá. The two escaped in June, but Nicolás Gutiérrez was later recaptured.

The sentence had not been carried out by the end of 1992.

There were allegations that opposition URNG forces were responsible for the deliberate and arbitrary killing of Ernesto Rivera, military commissioner of La Primavera, El Petén department, in May. He was reportedly taken from his house, forced to reveal the addresses of other local military commissioners and then taken to a URNG public meeting and accused of being an army informant. He was then released, but as he was walking away he was shot dead.

Throughout the year Amnesty International repeatedly called on the government to investigate the many reported incidents of human rights violations and to bring those responsible to justice. In September Amnesty International representatives visited Guatemala and held talks with government officials, human rights groups and others.

In oral and written statements to the UN Commission on Human Rights in February and to the Working Group on Indigenous Peoples of its Sub-Commission on Prevention of Discrimination and Protection of Minorities in August, Amnesty International included reference to its concerns about human rights violations in Guatemala and the government's failure to end the abuses. In October Amnesty International published *Human rights violations against the indigenous peoples of the Americas*, which included concerns in Guatemala.

# GUINEA

**Dozens of students, an opposition leader and a journalist were detained, some for up to six weeks, and appeared to be prisoners of conscience. Some were tortured or ill-treated. New legislation broadened the application of the death penalty but no death sentences were passed.**

In April a law permitting political parties came into effect; at least 40 parties had been set up and legalized by the end of the year. President Lansana Conté, who remained head of state and government during a transitional period until presidential and parliamentary elections, rejected opposition demands for a National Conference to discuss the country's political future. The first round of parliamentary elections due to take place in December was delayed but President Conté announced it would take place during 1993.

In May a new law increased the number of offences punishable by death to include murder committed during demonstrations or attacks on buildings. It also made organizers of public meetings responsible for the actions of all those attending such meetings and punishable by imprisonment for any violence or damage caused at the time of the meetings. In September the government stipulated that all public meetings and marches must have a five-person organization committee, which would be held responsible for any breaches of public order committed during such events. The government also assumed the power to ban any meetings deemed likely to threaten public order.

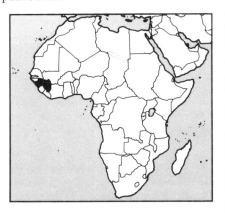

Political violence continued throughout the year resulting in several deaths. In the run-up to the elections scheduled for December, the clashes took on an increasingly ethnic character, with members of the Soussou ethnic group generally supporting the government and sometimes working closely with the security forces during attacks on other ethnic groups.

Between January and April there was violent conflict between students and the security forces in which at least two students died. Dozens of students were arrested and many of them appeared to be prisoners of conscience. Some were ill-treated in custody.

In mid-January a student strike was launched in many parts of the country when the government failed to respond to student demands for better conditions. At first the strikes and protest marches took place without incident, but on 27 January a

**144**

special "anti-gang" police unit opened fire on students demonstrating peacefully in the capital, Conakry, injuring at least five. Several students were arrested and held for two days, during which they were beaten. A few days later, the governor of Conakry, who was apparently responsible for the police intervention, was appointed Minister of Higher Education.

In February one student was killed and at least 50 others were arrested and ill-treated during a security raid on a university campus in Conakry. In other incidents one other student died and others were seized by groups of pro-government students working with members of the "anti-gang" police unit. For example, Mamadou Moustapha Diallo, the press officer of the students' coordinating committee, was arrested in April by a group of unidentified people armed with knives and handed to the "anti-gang" police for interrogation. He was tortured by the "anti-gang" police at their office on the university campus while being questioned about political documents found in his possession. He was detained incommunicado in a police infirmary until June, when he was released to receive medical treatment on the understanding that he would return to custody if required.

More than 200 women were arrested during a peaceful demonstration on 27 August to commemorate the 15th anniversary of a protest by market women in 1977. They were released the same day; many bore injuries as a result of ill-treatment by the security forces. Later that day, the security forces reportedly destroyed market stalls and the following day angry demonstrators burned property in protest: two people died, apparently as a result of action by the security forces.

No official investigations were opened into these killings or that of the students in February, with the result that the security forces were not held accountable for their use of lethal force. There was also no further news about two inquiries which the government had said it had established in previous years into the killings of at least five students in late 1990 and at least three demonstrators in October 1991 (see *Amnesty International Report 1992*). It was unclear whether either of these inquiries had actually taken place.

An opposition leader was detained for a few days in October and appeared to be a prisoner of conscience. The authorities claimed that Amadou Oury Bah, Secretary General of the *Union des forces démocratiques* (UFD), Union of Democratic Forces, and founding member of the *Organisation guinéene des droits de l'homme* (OGDH), Guinean Human Rights Organization, was suspected of involvement in an attempt to assassinate President Conté earlier in October, but the real reason appeared to be his peaceful political activities. He was released following a mass strike organized by government opponents.

One journalist was imprisoned as a prisoner of conscience. Foday Fofanah, a Sierra Leonean national, was arrested in October and tried on charges of libel and working without official accreditation. The libel charge related to a report in which he claimed that hundreds of Liberians opposed to the control of most of Liberia by the National Patriotic Front of Liberia were receiving military training in Guinea. The prosecution pressed for a two-year prison sentence, but on 25 November he was acquitted on both charges and released.

Amnesty International appealed to the government for the release of prisoners of conscience including Amadou Oury Bah and Foday Fofanah. It also urged the government to establish thorough and impartial investigations into the killings by security forces in 1992 and previous years, but received no response.

# GUINEA-BISSAU

**One person died in custody after being badly beaten; security officials were arrested in connection with the death. There were several other reports of torture and ill-treatment of prisoners by members of the police and security forces.**

New political parties were legalized in accordance with the May 1991 constitutional amendments introducing a multi-party political system (see *Amnesty International Report 1991*). In August President João Bernardo Vieira empowered a Transitional Multi-Party Commission to propose further legal changes including additional human rights guarantees.

People were able to exercise new freedoms, including the right to strike and demonstrate, but not without some problems. Security officials continued to harass suspected opponents of the ruling *Partido Africano de Independência da Guiné e Cabo Verde* (PAIGC), African Party for the Independence of Guinea and Cape Verde. The Guinea-Bissau Human Rights League, a non-governmental organization founded in 1991, carried out visits to a number of prisons and reported numerous instances of torture and ill-treatment of prisoners: its president received anonymous telephone calls, believed to be from security officials, threatening him with death if the League maintained its activities.

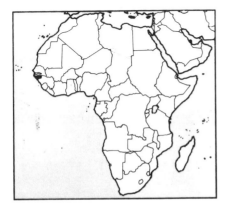

In February nine people, members of two political parties, were severely beaten in police custody. They had been arrested in the streets of Bissau, the capital, while they were announcing a demonstration planned for a few days later in defiance of an Interior Ministry ban on demonstrations during the carnival period. They were beaten while held for about an hour in the prison known as *Segunda Esquadra* (Second Squadron). Some required medical treatment.

In August police in the town of Bafatá who were checking identity cards and tax receipt forms stopped 10 people who failed to produce their documents and severely beat them. In September police in Bissau charged a crowd of Bissau Municipality workers who were planning a strike. They grabbed hold of some of them on an apparently arbitrary basis and beat them repeatedly with truncheons. The police accused the workers of holding an illegal gathering, although the latter said they had followed official procedures. After both incidents victims required medical treatment.

Ussumane Quadé, a soldier suspected of arms trafficking, died in custody two days after his arrest in September. The authorities announced that he had committed suicide but they refused to return Ussumane Quadé's body to his relatives for burial. The Guinea-Bissau Human Rights League made inquiries and subsequently seven police and security officials were detained, apparently in connection with the death. They had not been charged or brought to trial by the end of 1992.

Amnesty International expressed concern about the ill-treatment of prisoners in February and urged the introduction of safeguards against torture and ill-treatment. It repeated its concerns and appeals in November, and called for an inquiry into the death of Ussumane Quadé and for anyone responsible to be brought to justice. No response had been received by the end of the year.

# GUYANA

**Allegations of torture and ill-treatment of people by the police continued. At least three people were sentenced to death for murder and some 25 people were under sentence of death at the end of the year. No executions were carried out.**

The People's Progressive Party (PPP) came to power after winning a general election in October, defeating the People's National Congress (PNC) which had governed the country since 1964. The PPP leader Dr Cheddi Jagan became President.

There were several reports of torture and other ill-treatment by the police. Hardath Ramdass, a PPP supporter, was arrested in January and allegedly tortured while being questioned about an alleged plot to overthrow the PNC government and about armed robberies. In an affidavit he alleged that he was blindfolded, shackled, stripped and beaten repeatedly about the head, body and soles of his feet, was kicked in the groin and had a gun placed in his mouth and a liquid resembling methylated spirits poured into his ears. His lawyer who saw him in custody four days after his arrest said that he saw "marks of violence" on his body. Hardath Ramdass was released without charge after eight days in custody. A 13-year-old boy arrested with him was held for four days in police custody with adult prisoners and allegedly threatened into signing a statement before being released without charge.

The wife of a murder suspect alleged that five plainclothes police officers assigned to search her house raped her on a public road in July and that she was raped again by both police and prisoners while detained at a police lock-up. The Police Commissioner announced in September that an investigation into the allegations had been completed but the results were not made public. The woman's lawyer was reported to be considering a private prosecution against the officers allegedly involved.

There was no information regarding the outcome of police investigations into the alleged ill-treatment of suspects in police custody in June and July 1991 and threats made against human rights worker Shirley Howells, who was briefly kidnapped by unidentified men in October 1991 (see *Amnesty International Report 1992*).

The trial was still pending in the case of several people charged with treason, which carries a mandatory death penalty on conviction (see *Amnesty International Report 1991*).

At least three people were sentenced to death for murder. However, no executions were carried out for the second consecutive year.

Amnesty International wrote to the Minister of Home Affairs in May expressing concern at the alleged torture of Hardath Ramdass and urging that a full, impartial inquiry be held. The Minister replied that the case had been referred to the Attorney General for action.

In October Amnesty International wrote to the Police Complaints Authority about alleged police abuses during the past two years, including the case of Hardath Ram-

dass and several fatal police shootings of unarmed suspects who appeared to offer no immediate threat of deadly resistance. Amnesty International asked whether the cases it mentioned had been reviewed by the Authority or passed to the police for investigation and for the results of any such inquiries. No response was received.

In December Amnesty International wrote to President Jagan, welcoming the fact that there had been no executions for two years and urging the government to take steps to abolish the death penalty. It also asked about the outcome of investigations into police torture and ill-treatment, including the rape case cited above and cases involving questionable shootings. The organization called for the United Nations Code of Conduct for Law Enforcement Officers and the Basic Principles on the Use of Force and Firearms to be incorporated into police codes and practice.

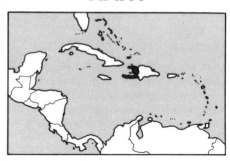

# HAITI

**Hundreds of prisoners of conscience were detained, the majority for brief periods after which they were released without charge. Most detainees were tortured or ill-treated, and at least 10 people allegedly died as a result of torture. Prison conditions continued to be extremely harsh. At least 100 people were killed in circumstances suggesting they had been extrajudicially executed, and at least 10 "disappeared".**

In February an agreement brokered by the Organization of American States (OAS) was reached between deposed President Jean-Bertrand Aristide and representatives of the National Assembly. The accord recognized President Aristide, who had been deposed in 1991 (see *Amnesty International Report 1992*), as the legitimate president. It agreed on a new Prime Minister and set the basis for a return to the constitutional order, although it did not fix a date for President Aristide's return to Haiti. In March, however, the agreement was declared unconstitutional by the Supreme Court on the grounds that the National Assembly had no authority to sign such an agreement. In June President Joseph Nérette and Prime Minister Jean-Jacques Honorat resigned. Marc Bazin, who had been a minister in the former government of Jean-Claude Duvalier, became Prime Minister but the presidency was still vacant at the end of the year.

The OAS continued to mediate in negotiations between deposed President Aristide and the *de facto* authorities. In September an OAS delegation arrived in Haiti to monitor the human rights situation and the distribution of humanitarian aid, and to evaluate the progress of negotiations. However, by the end of 1992 no agreement had been reached and President Aristide was still in exile.

At least 800 people, most of them prisoners of conscience, were arrested without warrant, apparently for political reasons, by the military, the police, rural police chiefs or by civilians acting in connivance with the security forces. Many were held without charge for longer than the 48-hour limit laid down by the Constitution. The majority were released without charge or any form of judicial proceedings. The length of their detention generally did not exceed one month. Often the authorities asked prisoners or their relatives to pay money to secure their release, to avoid ill-treatment or to obtain better prison conditions. Prominent among the victims were President Aristide's supporters and former officials in his government, residents of poorer urban and rural areas, journalists, members and leaders of grassroots organizations, peasants, trade unionists and members of the Roman Catholic Church.

In March Dully Oxéva and Dérose Eranor, two members of the *Mouvement paysan de Papaye* (MPP), Papaye Peasant Movement, were arrested without warrant by the military in Mirebalais, Centre Department, where they had been in hiding since September 1991. The two men, who both appeared to be prisoners of conscience, were badly beaten upon arrest at the Mirebalais military barracks where they were held until their release without

charge in April. Their families had reportedly paid 250 gourdes (US$31) to secure their release.

Also in March Harry Nicolas, a plumber and an active member of his local literacy movement and neighbourhood committee, was arrested without warrant in Cap Haïtien by soldiers. He had returned to his home town only days earlier after several months in hiding. He was released without charge about one month later.

Members of the clergy, nuns and religious workers were targeted for arrest because of their role in protecting human rights. In April Venezuelan nun Clemencia Ascanio and two Dominican women, Sunilda Altagracia Céspedes and Bienvenida Valdés, were arrested when soldiers found calendars bearing President Aristide's photograph in the bus in which they were travelling. The three women were released uncharged after five days in custody.

Priests and members of churches were arrested and harassed throughout the year. During a three-week period in May and June, at least seven priests were arrested by the police or the army. All were released uncharged, but some were held for several days. For example, Father Denis Verdier, director of the regional office of Caritas, a Roman Catholic charity, Father Sony Decoste and Brother Jean-Baptiste Casséus were arrested in the South Department, apparently in reprisal for the burning of a military outpost by unidentified civilians. Father Marcel Bussel, a Belgian citizen, was arrested without warrant after his rectory in Ballan, North Department, was searched and ransacked by soldiers. French priest Gilles Danroc, co-ordinator of the Haitian Justice and Peace Commission, was arrested without warrant during a catechism class in his parish in La Chapelle, in the central Artibonite valley. Fourteen of his parishioners, including a pregnant woman, were arrested with him and beaten. They were all released uncharged in the days following their arrest.

A prisoner of conscience, Aldajuste Pierre, the president of an MPP co-operative, was released in February. He had been arrested in October 1991 and badly beaten (see *Amnesty International Report 1992*). To obtain his release, his family reportedly raised 9,000 gourdes (about US$1,100) from relatives and friends and the sale of most of their possessions.

Torture and ill-treatment of detainees

continued to be widely reported and at least 10 people died allegedly as a result of torture. Methods of torture included beatings with fists, sticks and rubber hoses, kickings and a technique known as the *djak* – a baton is wedged under the knees and over the arms of a prisoner, who is then repeatedly beaten all over the body. The *kalot marassa*, a twin slap on the side of the head that can cause severe damage to the ears, was also used. Many victims were refused medical attention in custody.

Roosevelt Charles, an official of the *Parti national progressiste révolutionnaire Haïtien* (PANPRA), National Progressive Revolutionary Party of Haiti, was arrested without warrant by the military in Limbé, North Department, in February after a dispute with another individual. He had stones thrown at him, and was beaten during the arrest and again in custody. On one occasion he was reportedly beaten 250 times with a stick. He was released after eight days. Roosevelt Charles was hospitalized for approximately a month following his release, and required a skin graft.

Wilcéna Dorléus, a teacher, was arrested in May as he was entering a football stadium in the capital, Port-au-Prince, apparently because he was carrying a pro-Aristide leaflet. He was beaten on the head, stomach, waist and ribs, handcuffed and taken to a police station known as the "Cafeteria". There he was beaten with rifle butts and his hand was crushed. He was later transferred to the National Penitentiary, where ill-treatment continued. He was released about two weeks later, after his family reportedly paid about US$450 to the authorities.

In late September five-year old Daniel Raymonvil was among several people beaten by soldiers in the Jubilé slum area of Gonaïves, Artibonite Department. The soldiers had apparently gone to Jubilé to prevent the population demonstrating its support for deposed President Aristide on the first anniversary of the coup.

At least 10 people died allegedly as a result of torture. In January school teacher Jean-Claude Museau died shortly after being released from one week's detention. He had been arrested in late December 1991 in Les Cayes, South Department, reportedly because he was sticking up posters of President Aristide. He was badly beaten on his head and body, slashed with a blade in the buttocks, and made to swallow the posters he had with him. Also in January Jacquelin Louis, a member of a neighbourhood committee, was reportedly arrested by two armed civilians and badly beaten. He reportedly continued to be ill-treated in prison at Cap Haïtien, and subsequently died. Woodly Gérard Jacques, a Haitian citizen normally resident in the United States of America (USA), died in March reportedly as a result of torture in the military barracks of Arcahaie. His body had a broken finger, cuts and bruises on the face, and signs of blows on the abdomen. His left ear was partly mutilated from burns, and one of his buttocks had a large wound and severe bruising.

Conditions in prisons and detention centres throughout the country were extremely harsh. Beatings and other forms of ill-treatment were frequent, as was the practice of demanding money in exchange for better prison conditions or to avoid ill-treatment. Most prisoners suffered from malnutrition and a lack of medical treatment, and several reportedly died in custody as a result.

At least 10 people "disappeared" during 1992 and could not be traced, despite efforts by their relatives and human rights groups to find them. The number of "disappearances" was probably much higher, but it was not possible to establish the precise figure because of the difficulties of monitoring human rights in Haiti. One of the "disappeared" was Fritz Dérose, a member of *Comité opération délivrance* (CODEL), Operation Deliverance Committee, a local grassroots organization. He was reportedly arrested without warrant in April in Cité Soleil, a poor suburb of Port-au-Prince, by the police and accused of agitation against the government. According to witnesses, he was beaten upon arrest and taken to the local police station. His family later found out that he had been transferred, but despite their efforts to locate him, his whereabouts remained unknown.

At least 100 people were killed in circumstances suggesting that they had been extrajudicially executed. In late May, at a time of repeated popular protests against the government, uniformed military and police forces, as well as heavily armed men in civilian clothes apparently working with the security forces, made nightly incursions into poor districts in Port-au-Prince, killing at least 17 civilians and wounding many more. In one such incident, an unarmed civilian, Rodolphe Lominy, was reportedly shot dead in his home in Port-au-Prince by a group of uniformed soldiers. There was no investigation into his killing. Three members of the military, at least one of whom was a known supporter of President Aristide, were shot dead by unidentified, heavily armed men in late May, shortly before a public radio appeal by soldiers for the resignation of the *de facto* President.

Also in May, Georges Izméry, the brother of an outspoken supporter of ousted President Aristide, was shot dead by an unidentified man near the shop he owned with his brother, Antoine. Antoine Izméry was believed to have been the target of the attack. After the shooting, Georges' stepmother was prevented from approaching him by uniformed police and the family doctor was also prevented by soldiers from seeing him at the morgue.

In August Robinson Joseph, director of the Haiti branch of World Concern International, a US-based organization, and former director of a Protestant radio station, was driving home when he was ordered to stop at a military road-block in Port-au-Prince. He apparently attempted to park his car on the side of the road when several shots were fired at him from the road-block. He was killed instantly. His secretary, who was with him, was detained for a few hours.

Throughout the year Amnesty International made public its concerns, including the lack of investigations into human rights violations, and called on the government to investigate effectively and put an end to such abuses. In January Amnesty International published *Haiti: The Human Rights Tragedy*, detailing the gross human rights violations since the military coup of September 1991.

Amnesty International representatives visited Haiti in March and held talks with Prime Minister Honorat and military officials, as well as with private individuals and human rights groups. In August Amnesty International made public the findings of this visit in another report, *Haiti: Human Rights Held to Ransom*.

# HONDURAS

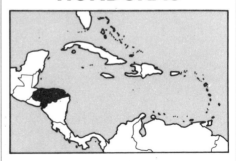

**Reports of torture and ill-treatment of detainees in police custody continued; most of the victims were criminal suspects. At least one person was killed in circumstances suggesting he had been extrajudicially executed for political reasons. The judiciary made little progress in investigating human rights violations and no one was brought to justice for past abuses. The government again failed to initiate a full inquiry into "disappearances" in the early 1980s.**

A law was promulgated in May creating the Office of the National Commissioner for the Protection of Human Rights, attached to the President's office. The office's functions were to include monitoring respect for human rights and investigating allegations of human rights violations. A commissioner with ministerial status was appointed in November. The law also expanded the mandate of the National Reconciliation Commission which was to work closely with the new office. The National Reconciliation Commission had been set up in 1987 to provide a forum for debate and to make proposals about human rights and other issues, but had eventually ceased to operate. The Commission was re-appointed in August 1992.

In spite of assurances by the Office of the Presidency in October 1991 that the National Congress was soon to ratify international treaties related to refugees, torture and the death penalty, no such measures had been taken by the end of 1992.

Violence by armed opposition groups resurfaced in August when the *Frente Patriótico Morazanista* (FPM), Morazanist Patriotic Front, claimed responsibility for the murder of a man it accused of being a member of the former 3-16 Battalion involved in the murder and "disappearance"

**150**

of grassroots leaders in the early 1980s.

Two leaders of right-wing organizations were killed in July: Rigoberto Borjas of the parallel electricity workers' union, and Cayo Eng Lee of the *Frente Unido Universitario Democrático*, United Democratic University Front. The government attributed their deaths to inter-organizational disputes but in neither case did investigations lead to the identification of those responsible.

Reports of torture and ill-treatment continued. While most of the victims were criminal suspects, five men and a woman arrested in May in the capital, Tegucigalpa, said they were interrogated about their suspected involvement in an opposition group by members of the *Fuerza de Seguridad Pública* (FUSEP), Public Security Force. All but one were released within three days. They said that they had been hooded and subjected to beatings with batons covered in sponge to prevent marks.

Marco Rivera, arrested in July in San Pedro Sula by FUSEP agents, claimed that he was beaten and subjected to the "helicopter" technique: his hands and feet were tied behind his back and he was suspended from a beam and spun around until he fell to the ground. Four others accused of robbery were arrested in May in Intibucá by agents of the *Dirección Nacional de Investigaciones* (DNI), National Investigations Directorate, and illegally held incommunicado for between five and six days. They alleged they had been hooded and beaten and said they had been threatened with death if they complained about their treatment to human rights groups. Three men arrested in Intibucá in December reported similar treatment.

In November, a university student was knocked unconscious in Tegucigalpa after being thrown against a wall and then to the ground by a group of uniformed military personnel, including an officer. She had protested when soldiers tried to seize her cousin without explanation outside his home. The soldiers fled, apparently fearing that the young woman had died. Following national and international press reports about the case, the head of the DNI and other army officials reportedly apologized to the two victims and their families and said that they would investigate who was responsible.

At least one person was killed in circumstances suggesting that he had been extrajudicially executed for political reasons. In July the mutilated body of Juan Humberto Sánchez was found near his home in Colomoncagua. He had been abducted 13 days earlier by a group of armed men wearing camouflage headgear of the type used by the *Fuerzas Territoriales*, Territorial Forces, which patrol the border with El Salvador. He was abducted only hours after being released from a day in military custody. Army officials accused him of being a member of the armed opposition in El Salvador and threatened him on his release. Investigations were initiated into the killing but no one had been arrested by the end of the year. To Amnesty International's knowledge, no autopsy was carried out.

In March witnesses disarmed a gunman who reportedly threatened to kill Antonio Zelaya Reyes, president of the Olancho branch of the *Comité para la Defensa de los Derechos Humanos en Honduras* (CODEH), Committee for the Defence of Human Rights in Honduras. The gunman, alleged to be a DNI collaborator, broke into a radio studio where Antonio Zelaya was preparing a human rights program.

There was limited or no progress in the investigation of human rights abuses in previous years. In the case of Riccy Mabel Martínez (see *Amnesty International Report 1992*), the judge announced in January that forensic examinations by the United States Federal Bureau of Investigations (FBI) showed that pubic hair found in Riccy Mabel Martínez' underwear matched that of Colonel Castillo, who remained in detention on charges of rape and murder. At the same time the judge ordered the release of an army captain detained in connection with the case, for lack of evidence. A low-ranking soldier also accused of participating in the killing remained in prison. In December two army colonels reportedly refused to go to court to give statements on the case. The case had not been concluded by the end of the year.

Investigations into other possible extrajudicial executions were again subject to long delays and irregularities. Not one case being monitored by Amnesty International was fully resolved and none of those responsible was brought to justice. No progress was reported in investigations into the killing of indigenous leader Vicente Matute Cruz (see *Amnesty International Report 1992*). Dario Urbina, mayor of

Yoro, who had reportedly publicly accused a local cattle farmer and military personnel of masterminding the killing of Vincente Matute, was himself murdered in December, but the full circumstances surrounding his death were unclear. Investigations into the killing of five peasants in Agua Caliente (see *Amnesty International Report 1992*) were paralysed throughout the year because of the Supreme Court's failure to rule on whether the case should be handled by a military or civilian court. Human rights workers in Honduras alleged that an army colonel accused of participating in the killings who was supposed to be in military detention was in fact carrying out his normal duties.

In the case of Manuel Guerra, assistant secretary of the *Central Nacional de Trabajadores del Campo* (CNTC), the National Union of Rural Workers, who was killed in December 1991, the court failed to pursue important information indicating police involvement in his death. Officials initially claimed that Manuel Guerra had died in a car accident, but an autopsy established that he had been killed by a single bullet fired at close range. A former police collaborator, who subsequently left the country because of fears for his safety, testified to CODEH that his cousin, a DNI agent, had admitted being involved in the killing together with three other DNI agents. He said his cousin had told him that two DNI agents had forced Manuel Guerra to take them in his car, followed by another car carrying two DNI agents. One of the men in Guerra's car subsequently fired a shot at him, killing him instantly. The judge, who has the power to initiate his own investigations, refused to accept the former police collaborator's statement, on the grounds that it had not been presented by the prosecuting or defence attorneys. The DNI initially denied that the men named in the statement were police agents, but the agents themselves later contradicted these official claims at a press conference. They stated, however, that the agency's records showed that they had not left the police station on the night of the killing.

CNTC Secretary General Angel Gutiérrez was arrested in June. He alleged that police used psychological pressure to try to make him confess to killing Manuel Guerra. He later lodged a formal complaint against the police on the grounds of illegal arrest and death threats. Honduran human rights groups concluded that his arrest was an attempt to divert attention away from possible police involvement by presenting the case as the result of an internal organizational dispute. Angel Gutiérrez was released without charge after several days in police custody.

The government again failed to initiate a full inquiry into "disappearances" in the early 1980s. It also continued to refuse to pay the full damages ordered by the Inter-American Court of Human Rights to the families of "disappeared" prisoners Saul Godínez and Manfredo Velásquez. In unprecedented rulings in 1988 and 1989 the court had found the Honduran Government responsible for the two "disappearances" in 1981 and 1982.

Amnesty International issued a report in May, *"Disappearances" in Honduras: A Wall of Silence and Indifference*, which documented the long campaign of relatives to clarify the fate of those who "disappeared" following arrest in the early 1980s, and the failure of successive governments to fulfil their obligation to carry out effective investigations. The report was sent, together with a letter requesting information about cases and issues included in it, to the president of the official Inter-Institutional Human Rights Commission but no reply was received.

Amnesty International was also still waiting for information the government had said it would provide about cases included in the organization's 1991 memorandum (see *Amnesty International Report 1992*). The organization continued to press for thorough and impartial investigations into possible extrajudicial executions and allegations of torture and the bringing to justice of those responsible. It also called for an inquiry into the attack on Antonio Zelaya Reyes. In response, a FUSEP official claimed that investigations into the incident were inconclusive, and the allegations against police "unfounded and irresponsible".

In October Amnesty International published *Human rights violations against the indigenous peoples of the Americas*, which included concerns in Honduras.

# HONG KONG

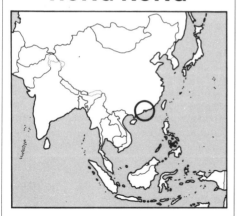

A draft bill for the abolition of the death penalty was introduced. The screening process to determine the refugee status of Vietnamese asylum-seekers detained in Hong Kong continued to have shortcomings.

In a policy statement before the opening session of the Legislative Council in October, Governor Christopher Patten outlined proposals for major changes in the structure of Hong Kong's government and announced his intention to submit a draft bill aiming at the abolition of the death penalty to that session of the Council. The abolitionist legislation was tabled in November but no vote had taken place by the end of the year. The Legislative Council had called in 1991 for abolition of the death penalty, mandatory for murder but systematically commuted since 1966 (see *Amnesty International Report 1992*).

Governor Patten proposed that a majority of the Legislative Council's members be elected either directly or indirectly by a broad electoral base. He also proposed to resign from the chairmanship of the Legislative Council to allow the Council to elect its own chair. The Governor's proposals were broadly endorsed by the Legislative Council in November, pending detailed discussion due in 1993. However, the authorities of the People's Republic of China sharply criticized Governor Patten's proposals, arguing in particular that they would alter the Hong Kong Basic Law adopted by China in 1991 and due to come into force in 1997 when sovereignty over Hong Kong reverts to China (see *Amnesty International Report 1992*). These criti-

cisms increased the uncertainty about the future course of Chinese policy towards Hong Kong. In March the Chinese Public Security Minister confirmed press reports that his ministry had collected information on Hong Kong residents, including political activists, suspected of opposing the Chinese Government. He stated that reports that such people would risk arrest after 1997 were "inaccurate".

At the end of the year around 43,000 Vietnamese asylum-seekers remained in detention, of whom more than 27,000 had been "screened out" (denied refugee status). The rest were awaiting a decision on their claim for refugee status. Over 300 asylum-seekers who had been "screened out" were forcibly returned to Viet Nam under an agreement signed in 1991 with the Vietnamese Government (see *Amnesty International Report 1992*). A further agreement between the governments of Hong Kong and Viet Nam signed in May 1992 opened the way for the eventual forcible return of all "screened out" asylum-seekers. There were still shortcomings in the screening process: in particular, asylum-seekers did not have the right to appear in person when appealing against refusal of refugee status.

In July the Hong Kong authorities decided that two asylum-seekers should be returned to China despite fears that they would be liable to imprisonment there on account of their peaceful political activities. Liu Yijun, a poet, and Lin Lin, a university graduate, had left China for Hong Kong in December 1991, when they feared they faced imminent arrest. Amnesty International was concerned that the two women would be at risk of imprisonment as prisoners of conscience if forcibly returned to China and appealed to the Hong Kong authorities not to take such a step. In the event, the authorities permitted them to remain in Hong Kong pending a judicial review of their case, but before this took place the two women were accepted as refugees by Canada and allowed to travel there.

In October a representative of Amnesty International met government officials during a visit to Hong Kong. He reiterated the organization's concerns about the screening procedures and raised questions about the government's policy of detaining Vietnamese asylum-seekers.

Amnesty International representatives

met Governor-designate Christopher Patten shortly before he took office in July. They urged him to introduce as a matter of urgency legislation to abolish the death penalty.

# HUNGARY

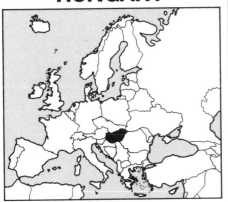

**There were reports of ill-treatment of foreign nationals in detention. The police reportedly failed to protect members of the Roma community from racially motivated violence.**

In November Hungary ratified the European Convention for the Protection of Human Rights and Fundamental Freedoms and its Sixth Protocol, which provides for the abolition of the death penalty for peacetime offences. It declared that it recognized both the right of individual petition and the compulsory jurisdiction of the European Court of Human Rights.

Foreign nationals in the Kerepestarcsa detention camp near Budapest were reportedly ill-treated by the police. The alleged incidents involved people who were staying in the country without authorization and were in some cases awaiting deportation. In one case, in January, a Chinese man was reportedly hit about the face and head until he lost consciousness, and then kicked. Following pressure from fellow inmates he was taken to hospital. Beatings were reported to have occurred often in the camp. For example, on 25 April inmates were beaten after they protested against what they considered to be unacceptably poor hygiene and other conditions. A unit of the Budapest police intervened using truncheons, police dogs and tear-gas in confined spaces.

Police reportedly failed to protect mem-

bers of the Roma community in Ketegyhaza from violent attacks. On 8 September a dozen men deliberately drove a truck into the home of Peter Csurar, a Rom, injuring one person and destroying the house and furniture. A police unit failed to detain those responsible for the attack even though they were known to the victims. Only four policemen remained in the village in spite of mounting anti-Roma tensions. At around midnight, other Roma homes were attacked and two houses were set on fire with petrol bombs.

Amnesty International wrote to the government of Prime Minister Joszef Antall in February urging it to investigate reports of ill-treatment of foreign nationals detained in the Kerepestarcsa camp. As many of those detained in Kerepestarcsa were asylum-seekers and following reports that people attempting to enter Hungary, some of whom may have been asylum-seekers, had been summarily expelled, Amnesty International sought assurances from the authorities that all asylum-seekers would be granted access to a fair and satisfactory asylum procedure. The government replied in March that official inquiries had not produced evidence to suggest any unlawful action on the part of the authorities and that all asylum-seekers in Hungary were treated in accordance with international standards. Amnesty International asked the authorities for full details of this inquiry, particularly the methods used in the investigation.

In September Amnesty International urged the Minister of the Interior to investigate allegations concerning police behaviour in Ketegyhaza. The authorities denied that the attack in Ketegyhaza was racially motivated and stated that an inquiry had established that the police took appropriate steps to "restore and maintain public order". Amnesty International asked the authorities for full details of this inquiry.

# INDIA

**Thousands of political prisoners, including several prisoners of conscience, were held without charge or trial under special or preventive detention laws. Torture and ill-treatment of detainees were widespread throughout the country and the perpetrators operated with virtual**

impunity. Torture was practised systematically in Jammu and Kashmir and Punjab, where its occurrence was facilitated by illegal, incommunicado and secret detentions. Dozens of people died in police custody. "Disappearances" of scores of suspected political activists were reported from Jammu and Kashmir and Punjab, and hundreds of political activists were allegedly extrajudicially executed. At least four prisoners were executed after being sentenced to death by the courts: two of them had been convicted of a politically motivated murder. Armed opposition groups committed numerous arbitrary killings of civilians, including hostages in their custody.

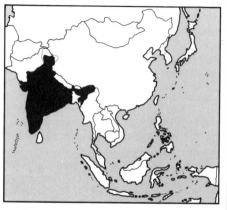

The government of Prime Minister Narasimha Rao faced a crisis after Hindu nationalists attacked and destroyed the Babri Masjid – a mosque – at Ayodhya in Uttar Pradesh on 6 December. The Uttar Pradesh state government, ruled by the Hindu nationalist Bharatiya Janata Party (BJP), was dismissed after it allowed work to start on building a Hindu temple at the site, which many Hindus claim is the birthplace of the Hindu god Ram. It had previously undertaken to abide by a Supreme Court ruling prohibiting any construction work at the site. Over 1,200 people were shot dead by police or killed in violence between Hindus and Muslims in the days that followed. Most of the victims were Muslims. In Bombay, where over 200 people died, there were reports that police sided with Hindus and fired indiscriminately at crowds of Muslim protesters. Five extremist groups were banned, including *Rashtriya Swaymsevak Sangh* (RSS), National Service Organization, and *Vishwa Hindu Parishad* (VHP), World Hindu Council,

both linked to the Hindu nationalist BJP. State governments in Madhya Pradesh, Rajasthan and Himachal Pradesh, which were controlled by the BJP, were dismissed for failing to implement the ban. The BJP's national leader, Lal K. Advani, was among over 1,300 people arrested in the days after the destruction of the mosque. He was charged with inciting communal violence.

In February a Congress party administration was elected in Punjab, which since May 1987 had been ruled directly by the central government in New Delhi. Elections were also promised for Jammu and Kashmir, but at the end of the year the state remained under direct rule by central government, as did the four states formerly ruled by the BJP, Manipur and Nagaland.

Armed opposition groups continued to commit human rights abuses, notably in Jammu and Kashmir, Punjab, Andhra Pradesh, Assam and the northeast states. Among the victims of hundreds of deliberate and arbitrary killings were political figures and civilians, including women and children.

Many thousands of political prisoners were held without trial under special laws. At least 400 petitions challenging the constitutionality of the broad powers of the Terrorist and Disruptive Activities (Prevention) Act (TADA) remained pending before the Supreme Court, despite widespread concern among lawyers and human rights activists; some petitions had been pending for eight years. Its sweeping provisions were frequently misused to detain innocent people or to deny to suspects the safeguards normally available in Indian law. According to the government, in October 16,925 people were being held under the act nationwide, including 8,768 in Punjab and 1,452 in Gujarat, a state where no armed opposition to the government was reported. In Bihar, the Chief Minister admitted that innocent people had been detained under the TADA and in Tamil Nadu the law was abused to detain people for pasting up posters supporting a Sri Lankan armed opposition organization. Among those detained during the year were a former High Court judge, Ajit Singh Bains, who was held for more than four months under the TADA for advocating separatism in Punjab, and Shabir Ahmed Shah, leader of the People's League, which advocates the right to self-determination in Kashmir. Amnesty International appealed for the release of both men. Shabir Ahmed Shah had been held without trial since September 1989 under both the TADA and the Public Security Act, a preventive detention law often used to detain political activists, with provisions similar to the National Security Act (NSA). The NSA was also used to detain political suspects without trial. In October 2,369 people were officially reported to be held under the NSA.

Torture of suspects in custody was routine throughout the country. Women were often raped in police cells and in army custody. Most of the victims were poor, often illiterate people from among the most underprivileged and vulnerable sections of society: the scheduled castes and tribes. Such individuals were usually detained illegally and tortured by being beaten, suspended by their wrists or ankles, or subjected to electric shocks to extract confessions or information. In Jammu and Kashmir, torture reportedly included burning with hot irons and electric shocks. One doctor in the state said in October that he had treated 36 cases of renal failure caused by torture in that month alone: four of the victims had died.

Senior officials participated in routine cover-ups by police of deaths under torture and police acted with virtual impunity: only in six out of 415 cases of custodial deaths known by Amnesty International to have occurred between 1985 and March 1992 were police officers known to have been tried and convicted in connection with the deaths of detainees in their custody. Although an investigation by a magistrate is obligatory under section 176 of the Code of Criminal Procedure, such inquiries were often not held. With some notable exceptions, the reports of investigations were not published and relatives were often denied copies of post-mortem and other reports, preventing them from taking effective legal action for redress. Only in 14 of the 415 cases was compensation known to have been paid.

At least 65 more cases of torture and deaths in custody were reported to Amnesty International between March and November. One victim was a man named Nandagopal, a university employee belonging to the scheduled castes, who died on 3 June in the Annamalainigar police station, Chidambaram, Tamil Nadu. The post-mortem report listed 21 wounds on his body. He had been arrested a few days ear-lier on suspicion of theft together with his wife, Padmini, who was alleged to have been repeatedly raped in her husband's presence. Two detainees testified that Nandagopal was tortured to death, but the doctor carrying out the post-mortem examination was reportedly threatened by police who wished him to report that the victim had committed suicide. The state government eventually ordered a judicial inquiry – the outcome of which was not known – and five police officers were reportedly arrested.

Towards the end of the year, there were increasing reports that dozens of people had "disappeared" after arrest in Jammu and Kashmir, and that others had been summarily executed within hours of arrest and their bodies dumped on the road. Human rights activist H.N. Wanchoo, who had frequently represented the families of people who had "disappeared" before the Jammu and Kashmir High Court, may himself have been a victim of extrajudicial execution: he was killed by unidentified gunmen in Srinagar on 5 December. In Punjab dozens of people "disappeared" after arrest even though their relatives had located some of them in detention. Harjit Singh of Buttar Kalan village was located in detention by his father and a judicial officer, but still "disappeared".

Hundreds of political activists were alleged to have been deliberately killed in "encounters" staged by the police in Punjab. Such killings were also reported from Andhra Pradesh. Extrajudicial executions were also reported from other states: at least 16 tribal trade union workers demonstrating peacefully for better working conditions were shot dead by the Madhya Pradesh police on 1 July, reportedly without provocation. The government ordered a judicial inquiry and small *ex gratia* payments to the victims' families. However, at least 200 people were arbitrarily detained after the incident and held without being produced in court for several weeks.

At least four people were executed. Sukhdev Singh and Harjinder Singh were executed in October after being convicted of the murder of General A.S. Vaidya, a senior army officer, in 1986. They were tried *in camera* under the special procedures of the TADA, even though they had been acquitted of all charges under that act.

Armed opposition groups committed numerous human rights abuses, including

**156**

hostage-taking, torture and deliberate and arbitrary killings. Reports of such abuses were mainly received from Jammu and Kashmir, Punjab, Andhra Pradesh, Assam and the northeast states. In Punjab, relatives of police officers were targeted for summary killings by armed opposition groups: according to the government, 1,415 people were killed by such groups in the first nine months of the year. In Andhra Pradesh, members of the Naxalite People's War Group, banned by the government in May, were reportedly responsible for numerous killings of people whom they suspected of being police informers. Armed groups in Assam, Andhra Pradesh and particularly in Jammu and Kashmir and Punjab were reported to have taken hostages to press their demands for a separate state or greater autonomy, or to obtain the release of captives.

In June Amnesty International urged all armed opposition groups in India to stop deliberate and arbitrary killings of civilians and to respect basic humanitarian standards. It specifically condemned the killing of the Acting Director of All India Radio in Patiala, Punjab, who was beheaded after he was reportedly taken prisoner by the Babbar Khalsa International, a Sikh militant group.

Amnesty International called on the government to release prisoners held for the non-violent exercise of basic human rights and for all political prisoners to be charged with a recognizably criminal offence, or released. The organization called for a judicial inquiry into the killing of H.N. Wanchoo, but the government said an inquiry would be conducted by the Central Bureau of Investigation.

In March Amnesty International released a report, *India: Torture, Rape and Deaths in Custody,* marking the start of a campaign to halt custodial violence in India. Amnesty International said that hundreds if not thousands of men, women and children had died from beatings and other forms of torture in recent years. Amnesty International said that torture was practised throughout the country under successive governments, regardless of the political party in power, and whether there was organized armed opposition or not.

Initially, the government dismissed the report, which was based on information in the Indian press, judgments of the Supreme Court and official reports of the National

Police Commission, as "conjectures and general allegations" and based on "mere hearsay". However, many Indian civil liberties groups and newspapers challenged the government's response. In June the government decided to investigate the specific allegations made in the report, a decision welcomed by Amnesty International. By the end of the year responses had been received on 230 cases. Despite strong evidence to the contrary in most cases, the government claimed that 153 were "unsubstantiated" without, however, providing post-mortem or inquiry reports by magistrates to substantiate its conclusions. The government's response showed that compensation had been paid in a further eight cases. It also reinforced Amnesty International's concern about the lack of official determination to bring the perpetrators of custodial crimes to justice: although the government found Amnesty International's allegations to be substantiated in at least 77 cases, no more than six had resulted in convictions of the police officers responsible, confirming the pattern of impunity described. In many cases, magisterial inquiries, although obligatory, were not known to have been held.

State governments in Kerala and Assam announced specific investigations into the report's allegations, and in June the Calcutta High Court ordered a judicial inquiry into all deaths in custody reported in West Bengal since 1977, although the state government contested the judgment.

For the first time since 1978 an Amnesty International delegation was permitted to visit India to discuss its human rights concerns with the government. In November the delegation met the Home Minister and the Human Resources Development Minister, as well as Secretaries and other officials of relevant ministries. Amnesty International welcomed the commitment expressed by the Prime Minister that human rights violations would not be tolerated and that the perpetrators would be brought to justice. It also welcomed proposals put before state Chief Ministers to strengthen legal safeguards against torture of detainees and to enhance investigation procedures in cases of deaths in custody. A number of the proposals reflected recommendations Amnesty International had made in a 10-point program to prevent torture in India, published in its report. Amnesty International urged the government to make judicial inquiries into custodial deaths mandatory, to provide statutory compensation to victims of custodial violence, to make reports of inquiries and post-mortem reports publicly and readily available and to strengthen legal safeguards on arrest. It put forward standards for the effective functioning of human rights commissions, in response to the government's own proposals to establish such a body. It stressed the need for human rights commissions to be independent from government and to have effective powers to investigate alleged human rights violations whether committed by the army, paramilitary forces or the police.

Amnesty International renewed its longstanding request to visit various Indian states, including Jammu and Kashmir, Punjab and the northeast states. However, by the end of the year, official authorization for such access had not been granted, although the Home Minister promised that Amnesty International's requests would be actively considered.

# INDONESIA AND EAST TIMOR

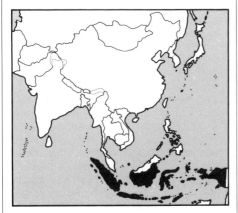

More than 180 suspected government opponents were prisoners of conscience or possible prisoners of conscience, including some 30 sentenced during the year. At least 300 other political prisoners continued to serve lengthy sentences imposed after unfair trials. Hundreds of others were arrested and held without trial for up to two years as suspected opponents of the government and scores were feared to have "disappeared".

Torture and ill-treatment of political detainees, peaceful demonstrators and criminal suspects were common and resulted in some deaths. Government forces extrajudicially executed scores of alleged supporters of independence in Aceh and East Timor. At least two people were sentenced to death and one person was executed for murder; at least 33 prisoners remained on death row.

The government won a substantial majority in general elections tainted by fraud and the intimidation and arrest of government opponents. Following the elections President Suharto was nominated to stand for his sixth consecutive term as president; as in previous years no other candidates were put forward. The government continued to face both armed and peaceful opposition from groups seeking independence for Aceh, East Timor and Irian Jaya. The leader of the resistance movement in East Timor was arrested in November. He and scores of suspected supporters and relatives arrested in a subsequent crackdown were held incommunicado for more than two weeks, and some were tortured.

A personal envoy of the United Nations (UN) Secretary-General visited East Timor in February to obtain information about the November 1991 massacre in which more than 100 people were killed (see *Amnesty International Report 1992*). A consensus statement of the UN Commission on Human Rights in March, and a resolution of the UN Sub-Commission on Prevention of Discrimination and Protection of Minorities in August, expressed concern about continuing human rights violations in East Timor and urged the government to facilitate access to the territory by humanitarian and human rights organizations. A report by the UN Special Rapporteur on Torture said that Indonesian government forces practised torture routinely.

The government said it would seek to implement the human rights recommendations of various UN bodies, and took some initiatives aimed at improving its human rights image, but there was no fundamental change in its repressive posture toward political dissent. In August the national legislative body established a human rights committee and in December the government announced plans to establish an independent human rights commission. However, the government continued to

**158**

restrict access to East Timor and parts of Indonesia, making effective human rights monitoring almost impossible. Some government officials expressed support for the principle of political "openness" while others, including the President and the Armed Forces Commander, warned that "foreign ideologies", such as communism and liberalism, threatened national security. Human rights organizations which expressed concern about the November 1991 massacre in East Timor were accused of serving the interests of foreign powers and some were threatened with legal penalties. At least 33,000 people remained on an official government blacklist restricting entry and exit to the country, and a new immigration law included provisions preventing the return to Indonesia of citizens deemed to have tarnished the government's image while abroad. Hundreds of thousands of former members of the Indonesian Communist Party (PKI), banned since 1965, remained subject to restrictions affecting their freedom of movement and civil rights.

Prosecutions for human rights violations continued to be the exception rather than the rule. Following official inquiries into the November 1991 massacre, 10 military officials were tried before a military tribunal for breach of discipline, and received prison sentences of between eight and 18 months. Despite at least 100 killings during and after the massacre, none of the 10 was charged with murder. One other military official was tried in connection with the March 1990 torture and killing of Candido Amaral in East Timor (see *Amnesty International Reports 1991* and *1992*); he was sentenced to two months in jail. A small number of police officers were convicted of killing or torturing criminal suspects but most received short prison sentences.

At least 180 suspected government opponents were prisoners of conscience or possible prisoners of conscience, of whom some 30 were sentenced during the year. They included advocates of independence for East Timor, Aceh and Irian Jaya, as well as Islamic activists, former members of the PKI, university students and human rights workers.

At least 13 of the scores of East Timorese arrested at the end of 1991 were believed to be prisoners of conscience. Four were sentenced to prison terms ranging from nine years to life imprisonment

for subversion and nine others received lesser sentences for "publicly expressing hostility" towards the government. Francisco Maria Branco and Gregorio da Cunha Saldanha were sentenced to 15 years' and life imprisonment respectively for organizing a peaceful pro-independence demonstration in Dili in November 1991. Two East Timorese political prisoners sentenced in unfair trials in 1984 were released in September but three others sentenced at the same time remained in prison in Jakarta.

In Aceh and North Sumatra, more than 20 alleged supporters of *Aceh Merdeka*, an armed opposition group seeking independence for Aceh and parts of Sumatra, were sentenced to prison terms of up to 20 years for subversion. Some appeared to be prisoners of conscience, including police sergeants M. Yacob and Idris Ahmad, who were each sentenced to 11 years' imprisonment for copying and distributing "illegal pamphlets on religious issues". Thirty-two other alleged *Aceh Merdeka* supporters, sentenced after unfair trials in 1991, continued to serve prison sentences of between four years and life.

More than 100 political prisoners from Irian Jaya, at least 70 of them prisoners of conscience, remained in jail for advocating Irian Jaya's independence. Most were held in East Java, more than 2,500 kilometres away, making it difficult for their relatives to visit them. Twenty-three had been released by the end of the year, including 12 who were believed to be prisoners of conscience.

At least 50 of an estimated 300 Islamic activists imprisoned for subversion, and serving sentences up to life imprisonment, were also believed to be prisoners of conscience. They included Abdul Fatah Wiranagapati, who was sentenced to eight years' imprisonment in June for "undermining the state ideology", *Pancasila*, and attempting to establish an Islamic state. Seven Islamic activists were released during the year, including four who were believed to be prisoners of conscience.

At least 30 prisoners sentenced in the 1960s after unfair trials for alleged involvement in a 1965 coup attempt or for PKI membership remained in prison. Seven of them were on death row. Most were believed to be prisoners of conscience. One such prisoner, Sanusi bin Haji Muhammad Ibrahim, was released from prison in

August after serving a life sentence; another, Johannes Sucipto, died in custody during the year after 26 years in prison.

Two university students, Bambang Wahya Nirbita and Ambar Widi Atmoko, were jailed in June for two and a half years for blasphemy; they were prisoners of conscience. The two were arrested following complaints that a comedy routine they had performed in late April had offended Islam. Two other students were charged with political crimes in May but had not been tried by the end of the year. Six students sentenced in February 1990 for insulting the Minister of Home Affairs at a demonstration in Bandung were released in February (see *Amnesty International Reports 1990* to *1992*).

A human rights lawyer, Dadang Trisasongko, was arrested in October and accused of subversion, incitement and "expressing hostility toward the government". The precise allegations against him were not known but colleagues believed they were linked to his lawful activities on behalf of villagers in Singosari, East Java. Following protests from human rights organizations, the subversion charge was dropped and he was released from custody. However, other charges remained and he was due to stand trial in early 1993.

Political trials, particularly those held under the vaguely worded Anti-Subversion Law, did not meet international standards of fairness or conform with Indonesia's Code of Criminal Procedure. Defendants in political cases in Aceh and East Timor were frequently held incommunicado for several months, tortured, and denied access to legal counsel of their choice. Some defendants were convicted on the basis of uncorroborated confessions or testimony allegedly extracted under duress.

Hundreds of alleged government opponents were detained without charge or trial and denied access to relatives and lawyers; some had been held for more than two years before being formally charged. At least 45 of the scores of East Timorese arrested after the November 1991 massacre were held in Dili and Jakarta without charge or trial for more than three months. Hundreds of others were detained and held incommunicado in the weeks before the anniversary of the massacre and following the 20 November arrest of Xanana Gusmão, the leader of the East Timorese resistance movement. In Aceh and North Sumatra, military authorities released hundreds of alleged supporters of *Aceh Merdeka* who had been held in unacknowledged detention without charge for up to two years. Hundreds of others were believed to remain in unacknowledged police or military custody in Aceh at the end of the year. It was reported in June that three men, Hasan Tito, Slamet Suryadi and Jayus bin Karmo had been held incommunicado without charge or trial by military authorities in Lampung province for more than two years; all three had reportedly been tortured. In September, following protests from human rights organizations, two of the men were released without charge. The third, Jayus bin Karmo, was charged with subversion and brought to trial, but had not been convicted by the end of the year.

Scores of alleged government opponents were reported to have "disappeared" in Aceh and East Timor, and the whereabouts of many detained in previous years remained unknown. One of the "disappeared", Mohamad Jafar Abdurrahman Ed, had been arrested in August 1990 in North Aceh on suspicion of assisting *Aceh Merdeka*. Military authorities later denied having him in their custody and refused to provide any information about his fate. The government also failed to account for as many as 100 people reported missing after the November 1991 massacre in East Timor. Eye-witnesses and relatives of the "disappeared" believed that many had been killed and their corpses secretly buried.

Torture and ill-treatment of political detainees continued to be routine. Ismail bin Gani, a civil servant, was arrested in March, held incommunicado for two months, and tortured by military officials to force him to confess to supporting *Aceh Merdeka*. When his wife was allowed to visit him in May, he had to be carried by soldiers because his arms and legs had been broken. He told her that he had been beaten repeatedly and had not received any medical treatment.

In East Timor, military authorities reportedly tortured some of the hundreds of suspected government opponents detained in November. One man, Enrique Belmiro Guterres, was hospitalized after his finger-nails were pulled out and his hands broken by his captors. Another, Jorge Manuel Aranjo Serrano, was reported to have died in custody following torture.

Criminal suspects, strikers, peaceful protesters and members of the urban poor were also tortured and ill-treated, and some died as a result. Sofyan Lubis, a shoe-shine boy aged 16 accused of stealing clothes, died in the Tanjung Gusta Children's Prison in Medan in September. Prison officials claimed that he had suddenly become ill and had died on the way to hospital, but an autopsy concluded that his death had been "unnatural". According to relatives and lawyers, his corpse bore clear signs of torture; his stomach, chest and neck were severely bruised, two teeth were missing, and blood was coming from his mouth, nose, ears and genitals. An investigation by the Ministry of Justice concluded in November that Sofyan Lubis had not died of torture, but when challenged by doctors and relatives, the Ministry admitted that its report was "not accurate".

Scores of people were extrajudicially executed by government forces in counter-insurgency operations in East Timor, Aceh and Irian Jaya. The victims included elderly men such as Teungku Imam Hamzah, aged 80, who was reportedly shot dead without any apparent reason by security forces in April while walking down the road in Lhok Kruntjong, Aceh. At least 2,000 others, and possibly many more, were believed to have been extrajudicially executed in Aceh since 1989, but there had been no official investigations into any killings by the end of the year.

More than 30 criminal suspects were shot dead in Jakarta as part of a continuing "shoot-on-sight" policy instituted by the city's police chief in 1989. In September police authorities in Jakarta said they had been "forced" to shoot a robbery suspect, Heri Gunawan, when he tried to escape. They said he was shot first in the back and then twice in the head. Military authorities also threatened to shoot on sight anyone "causing trouble" during a summit meeting of the Non-Aligned Movement in Jakarta in September.

At least 33 people were on death row at the end of 1992, seven of them political prisoners. They included a former member of parliament, Sukatno, and six other elderly men sentenced for involvement in the 1965 coup attempt or PKI membership. At least two people were sentenced to death for murder during the year and one person, Sergeant Adi Saputro, was executed in

December for murder.

Amnesty International appealed throughout the year for the release of prisoners of conscience, for the fair trial or release of other political prisoners, and for urgent government action to halt torture, extrajudicial executions and "disappearances". In meetings and correspondence with representatives of the Indonesian Government, the organization reiterated its request to visit Indonesia and East Timor. The government responded by asserting that it observed the rule of law and said Amnesty International should not interfere in Indonesia's domestic affairs.

In a report issued in February, *Santa Cruz: The Government Response*, Amnesty International criticized the government's response to the November 1991 massacre, and reiterated its appeal for an impartial international investigation into the incident and its aftermath. In July the organization published a report, *Indonesia/East Timor: The Suppression of Dissent*, summarizing its human rights concerns. In an oral statement to the UN Special Committee on Decolonization in August, Amnesty International outlined its concerns about the imprisonment, after unfair trials, of East Timorese political and human rights activists.

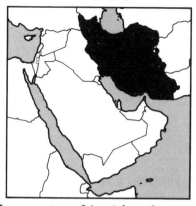

# IRAN

Mass arrests, unfair trials and summary executions took place following riots and demonstrations in several towns. Hundreds of political prisoners, including prisoners of conscience, were among those detained during the year. Torture of prisoners continued to be reported. At least 330 people, including dozens of political prisoners, were executed. Two government opponents were abducted outside Iran and at least four others were killed outside the country in circumstances suggesting that they may have been extrajudicially executed.

The government of President 'Ali Akbar Hashemi Rafsanjani faced renewed opposition from the People's Mojahedin Organization of Iran (PMOI), based in Iraq, which was responsible for a number of bomb attacks, including one on the tomb of the late Ayatollah Ruhollah Khomeini, the founder of the Islamic Republic. The authorities stated that three people were killed during these attacks. No further information was available.

Over 500 people were arrested following demonstrations and violent protests in Shiraz, Arak and Mashhad in April and May. Further mass arrests were carried out in June following violent demonstrations in Bukan, west Azerbaijan, and other protests in Tehran and Tabriz. The protests were apparently sparked by discontent over the government's social and economic policies and incidents such as attempts by municipal authorities to destroy illegally constructed buildings and forcibly evict their inhabitants.

At least eight of those arrested in connection with the demonstrations were executed within days of their arrest after summary trials. Five others were sentenced to death. Unofficial sources claimed the true total was much higher. Others were sentenced to long prison terms and floggings following unfair trials, or were held without charge or trial in circumstances that facilitated torture and ill-treatment.

People detained and held as prisoners of conscience during the year included Naser Arabha, the editor-in-chief of a science magazine, and three of his colleagues. They were arrested in Tehran in April and held incommunicado in Evin prison for printing a cartoon considered to be insulting to the late Ayatollah Ruhollah Khomeini. In September Naser Arabha became the first journalist to be tried by a jury for violating press laws: he was sentenced to a six-month prison term. One of his colleagues, identified as Karimzadeh, was tried by an Islamic Revolutionary Court and sentenced to one year in jail and a fine of 500,000 rials. At the end of the year the fate of the other two journalists still remained unclear.

Tension between the government and Sunni Muslims belonging to the Naroui tribe in the Baluchistan-Sistan region of southeast Iran resulted in a number of armed clashes and scores of arrests and detentions of Narouis: some of those detained were ill-treated; others were sentenced to death or prison terms after unfair trials. Many of those arrested were reported to be still detained without charge or trial at Zahedan prison at the end of 1992.

Hundreds of government opponents arrested in previous years, including prisoners of conscience, remained in prison, and some former political prisoners were reportedly rearrested in Tehran in May and June. Those held throughout 1992 included at least 50 followers of Dr 'Ali Shari'ati. One of them, Mohammad Baqer Borzoui, had been held at Evin prison since 1982, having apparently been sentenced to a long prison term after an unfair trial in the early 1980s. Dozens of others, known as the "Mohajerin group", had been arrested in 1990 and sentenced to between five and 15 years' imprisonment on arms charges. Their trials too were believed to have been unfair. Three members of this group, 'Ali Reza Hamidabad, Hamid Kord and Gholam Reza Sagvand, were reportedly executed in Dezful prison in September after having spent around two years in the prison. The authorities denied that any followers of Dr Shari'ati had been imprisoned since the Islamic Republic was founded in 1979.

Other political prisoners held in 1992 included alleged members of opposition groups such as Forghan; the People's Fedaiyan Organization of Iran (Minority); the PMOI; Rah-e Kargar, Sazeman-e Vahdat-e Kommunisti; members of Kurdish organizations such as the Communist Party of Iran (CPI), and the Kurdistan Democratic Party of Iran (KDPI); and members of ethnic-based groups including Arab and Baluchi organizations. Among them were a number of Kurdish workers who had been arrested in 1990 and 1991 for having taken part in a May Day rally in Sanandaj (Kurdistan) in 1989. They too were serving sentences imposed after unfair trials and were held at Sanandaj prison. They included Zahed Manouchehri, a member of the Tailors' Syndicate who was reportedly released at the end of 1992, and Arasto Shabani, who had reportedly been held in solitary confinement for over a year after his arrest in April 1990. However, Sa'id Sa'idi, a

**162**

member of the Metalworkers' Union held since July 1991, was believed to have been released during the first half of 1992.

Mehdi Dibaj, a possible prisoner of conscience held since 1984 who had converted from Islam to Christianity many years previously, was among those who remained in prison throughout 1992. It was not clear whether he had been tried and he has reportedly never been given any reason for his arrest and continued detention.

Some political prisoners, including prisoners of conscience, were among those released during the year, although many were required to "repent" and sign undertakings that they would not again engage in political activities as a condition of their release. Others were released on temporary leave. Almost all former political prisoners were required to report back to the authorities at regular intervals.

Those freed included nine elderly prisoners of conscience who had been jailed since 1990 because of their membership of the Association for the Defence of Freedom and Sovereignty of the Iranian Nation or for signing an open letter to President Hashemi Rafsanjani calling for reforms (see *Amnesty International Reports 1991* and *1992*). They were among 108 prisoners pardoned and released to mark the 13th anniversary of the establishment of the Islamic Republic. Approximately 3,500 prisoners were pardoned or had their sentences reduced on the occasion of religious festivals, including 53 members of the clergy. Those released may have included prisoners of conscience.

Trials before Islamic Revolutionary Courts continued to fall far short of internationally recognized standards for fair trial. Hearings were usually held *in camera* inside prisons. Proceedings were summary, often lasting only a few minutes, and defendants had no access to legal counsel and no right of appeal. In October 1991 new legislation had been introduced to permit defendants the right to appoint a defence lawyer, but during 1992 no defendants in political trials before Islamic Revolutionary Courts were known to have received legal assistance. Moreover, no provision appeared to have been made to allow those previously without the benefit of legal counsel to seek fair retrial.

Torture of prisoners was reported to remain common throughout the country. The most frequently used methods, according to former prisoners, were beatings with cables and rifle butts on the back and the soles of the feet, suspension for long periods in contorted positions and burning with cigarettes. They said torture was used primarily to extract confessions and obtain information about political opposition activities.

At least 330 people were executed, although unconfirmed reports suggested that the actual number of executions may have been considerably higher. The Iranian press reported over 120 executions of prisoners sentenced for drugs offences.

Two alleged members of *Komala*, Towfiq Aliasi and Rahman Aliasi, were executed in Sanandaj in June and August 1992 respectively. No information was available as to their trials. Televised "confessions" by Towfiq Aliasi, apparently given under physical or psychological pressure, were reported to have been broadcast on local television in Sanandaj in August. At least 48 Baluchis were executed during the year, many of them hanged in public. The majority were members of the Naroui tribe, although executions of Barahouis (another Baluchi tribe) were also reported. Dr 'Ali Mozaffarian, a possible prisoner of conscience and a leading member of the Sunni community in the southern Iranian province of Fars, was executed in Shiraz at the beginning of August. He had been charged with spying for the United States of America and Iraq and also accused of adultery and homosexuality. His video-taped "confessions", apparently obtained as a result of physical or psychological pressure, were broadcast on television in Shiraz. He had been held in Evin prison since his arrest at the end of 1991. On 18 March Bahman Samandari, a businessman and member of a prominent Baha'i family, was summarily executed in secret in Evin prison after he had been summoned there to sign some documents. Two other Baha'is were reported to have been sentenced to death.

Several government opponents were either abducted or killed outside Iran in circumstances suggesting that Iranian officials or people acting on their behalf may have been responsible. In June 'Ali Akbar Ghorbani, also known as Mansour Amini, a PMOI member, was abducted in Istanbul by persons unknown. His mutilated body was discovered several months later in Turkey. Several bomb attacks were carried out on vehicles belonging to the PMOI at the same time. The Iranian Government denied involvement in his abduction. In December Abbas Gholizadeh, a member of *Derafsh-e Kaviani*, Flag of Freedom Organization, a monarchist opposition group, was abducted near his home in Istanbul. At the end of the year no news of him was available.

In September Dr Sadegh Sharafkandi, Secretary General of the KDPI, and two other KDPI leaders were among four Iranians who were shot dead in a restaurant in Berlin. Two weeks earlier, Iran's Minister of Intelligence, Hojatoleslam 'Ali Fallahian, had spoken on television of the government's success in striking at opponents outside the country: "We have been able to deal blows to many of the mini-groups outside the country ... as you know, one of the active mini-groups is the Kurdistan Democratic Party ... we were able to deal vital blows to their cadres last year." In October the German authorities arrested two Lebanese nationals and an Iranian national in connection with the killings, but the Iranian Government denied any involvement.

Amnesty International continued to press for the release of all prisoners of conscience. It appealed throughout the year for an end to executions and expressed grave concern about the continuing use of the death penalty and the large number of executions. It urged the government to introduce appropriate safeguards to ensure political detainees received a fair trial, particularly those facing charges punishable by death. The organization also continued to call for the lifting of the *fatwa* (religious edict) issued in 1989 against the British novelist, Salman Rushdie (see *Amnesty International Report 1990*).

The government responded to certain inquiries, particularly with regard to the nine prisoners of conscience released in April. However, many of the organization's requests for clarification of reported human rights violations remained unanswered, including requests for information on a number of cases of prisoners of conscience and political prisoners. The authorities denied allegations of involvement in extrajudicial executions and made statements on defendants' access to legal counsel which conflicted with other official statements.

Amnesty International published three reports about its concerns in Iran: in January, *Imprisonment, torture and execution of political opponents*; in July, *Unfair trials of political detainees*; and in October, *Executions of prisoners continue unabated*. In March the Iranian authorities responded to the January report, but no new safeguards for human rights appeared to have been introduced.

In a written statement to the United Nations Commission on Human Rights in February, Amnesty International described its concerns in Iran, including mass executions, unfair trials, torture and the detention of prisoners of conscience.

# IRAQ

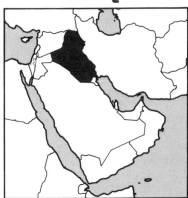

**Thousands of suspected government opponents and their relatives were detained during the year and tens of thousands of others continued to be held. Many of them were prisoners of conscience. Torture continued to be common and widespread. Hundreds of detainees "disappeared" and new information was received about thousands of detainees who "disappeared" in previous years. An unknown number of judicial and extrajudicial executions were carried out. Armed opposition groups committed abuses, including torture and executions.**

Economic sanctions against Iraq imposed by a United Nations (UN) Security Council cease-fire resolution in April 1991 remained in force. A 1991 agreement imposing an "air exclusion zone" over northern Iraq, forbidding Iraqi fixed-wing aircraft and helicopters from flying north of the 36th parallel, was renewed in June and December, each time for a further six months. In August a similar "air exclusion zone" came into effect in southern Iraq south of the 32nd parallel. Both operations

**164**

were enforced by United States (US), British and French forces, and were aimed at protecting Iraq's Kurdish and Arab Shi'a Muslim populations respectively. A UN-sponsored Memorandum of Understanding, which expired in June, was renewed in October after its terms were amended.

In May the government declared an amnesty for Iraqi army deserters and defaulters held in Rafha and Artawiyya camps in Saudi Arabia. There was no independent confirmation of government claims in June that some 210 refugees had returned to Iraq to benefit from the amnesty. In September the government declared a general amnesty for army deserters and "misguided military personnel" from several southern provinces. Government claims in September that 3,212 people from the southern provinces had surrendered to the authorities under the amnesties could not be confirmed.

In December Iraq's Revolutionary Command Council issued a decree which forbids the arrest, interrogation and bringing to justice of law enforcement officials who kill or injure criminal suspects, security offenders or army deserters in the course of their duty. It was feared that the decree would give officials a free hand to adopt a "shoot-to-kill" policy against both criminal suspects and political opponents.

Kurdish opposition groups retained control of parts of the northern provinces of Duhok, Arbil, Sulaimaniya and Kirkuk following the withdrawal of Iraqi government forces and the imposition of an economic blockade by the Iraqi Government in October 1991. In January the Iraqi Kurdistan Front (IKF), representing all the main Kurdish opposition groups, suspended negotiations with the government about greater autonomy for Kurds in Iraq. In May elections were held under the auspices of the IKF to elect a 105-member Kurdistan National Assembly for a three-year term, replacing the former (government-created) Legislative Assembly of the Autonomous Region of Kurdistan. The Patriotic Union of Kurdistan (PUK) and the Kurdistan Democratic Party (KDP) each received 50 seats, with five seats allocated to two Christian parties. In July a Council of Ministers for Iraqi Kurdistan was formed, which effectively administered IKF-held territory.

In March the IKF established a Special Court of the Revolution, which replaced the Revolutionary Court set up by the IKF in 1991. Both courts applied existing Iraqi legislation, namely the Penal Code and the Code of Criminal Procedure, but their proceedings fell far short of international standards and their decisions were not subject to appeal. In November the Kurdistan National Assembly abolished the Special Court and in December a Court of Cassation was set up, to sit in Arbil. In October and November the death penalty was introduced for two offences: premeditated murder of foreigners and using explosives to carry out acts of sabotage against the Kurdish people.

Several thousand Arab Shi'a Muslims were arrested by Iraqi government forces in southern Iraq. Most arrests were said to have begun after the imposition of the "air exclusion zone" in August and to have continued into December. Those detained were largely non-combatant civilians, including whole families, taken from their homes and public places and transferred to unknown destinations. In October random and widespread arrests of unarmed civilians were carried out in al-'Amara by the army and security forces as part of the officially-named "punitive campaign". Most were held at the 4th Army Corps' headquarters in al-'Amara city; many of them were reportedly held for short periods and tortured, and in some cases released only after making cash payments. Others were reported to have "disappeared" and there were fears that they were extrajudicially executed (see below). The government publicly denied reports of a renewed crackdown on the Shi'a Muslim population, but in September President Saddam Hussein declared that attempts by saboteurs and infiltrators to "terrorize civilians and assassinate government officials" had been crushed.

Scores of military personnel, including army officers, were reportedly arrested during the year. At least 47 of them, arrested between May and July, were said to have been involved in military attacks against suspected Shi'a Muslim opponents in the southern marshes (al-Ahwar). Others were arrested after allegedly failing to comply with military orders. The fate and whereabouts of those detained remained unknown; among them were Brigadier Anwar Isma'il Hantush and Major Ghaffuri Ahmad Isma'il.

At least 12 foreign nationals were arrested and accused of illegal entry into Iraq, of whom 11 remained held at the end of 1992. They included two Britons arrested in April and August and sentenced to 10 and seven years' imprisonment respectively, and three Swedish telephone engineers arrested in September and sentenced to seven years' imprisonment each. The other six still held were two Bangladeshis, one Filipino, one Pakistani and two Romanians, but no further details about their cases were known. All were held in Abu Ghraib Prison near Baghdad. Two US nationals and a Filipino arrested for illegal entry in December 1991 were released in January. They were reportedly ill-treated (see below).

Thousands of government opponents arrested in previous years continued to be held throughout 1992, including prisoners of conscience. Among them were hundreds of Arabs and Kurds detained during the mass uprisings in April 1991, including at least 106 Shi'a Muslim religious scholars and students arrested in al-Najaf (see *Amnesty International Report 1992*) and at least 76 Kurds arrested in the Arbil region. The Kuwaiti Government said an estimated 870 Kuwaitis taken prisoner after the Iraqi invasion were still held in Iraq; the Iraqi Government continued to deny holding Kuwaiti detainees. Also still held was 'Aziz al-Sayyid Jassem, a Shi'a Muslim from al-Nasiriyya and former editor of the government magazine *Al-Ghad*. He was arrested in April 1991, apparently for his failure to write articles in support of the government following Iraq's invasion of Kuwait. Until January he was believed to be held in *Mudiriyyat al-Amn al-'Amma* (General Security Directorate) in Baghdad, but thereafter his fate and whereabouts remained unknown.

Reports of torture and ill-treatment of detainees continued to be received. Two Shi'a Muslims released in June from al-Radwaniyya garrison, southwest of Baghdad, stated that they had been repeatedly beaten and subjected to electric shocks during their four months' detention. They also stated that a fellow detainee died from severe burns after being tied to a skewer and "roasted" over a flame. David Martin, a US national, and Joseph Ducat, a Filipino, stated upon their release in January that they had been thrown naked into a cell, forced to sleep on a concrete floor while blindfolded, and deprived of food and water for several days. They reported that detainees held with them, including

Egyptians, Syrians and Iranians, had been beaten and subjected to electric shocks, and that they had heard the screams of others being tortured. Several Iraqi merchants and businessmen arrested in July were also reportedly tortured before being executed. In June and September further details were revealed of the torture of US and British military prisoners of war during the Gulf War (see *Amnesty International Report 1992*). Torture methods reportedly used included severe beatings with truncheons and rubber hoses, electric shocks, prolonged isolation, mock executions, threats of dismemberment, and sexual abuse of a woman US army officer.

New information was received from documents obtained from areas under Kurdish control and other sources about some of the estimated 100,000 Kurds who "disappeared" in Iraqi government custody after being detained in 1988 during the "Anfal operations" (see *Amnesty International Report 1992*), including details of over 5,000 people who "disappeared" from Kalar in Sulaimaniya province. Further details were also received about 60 Shi'a Muslim Arabs who "disappeared" between 1979 and 1985, although their fate and whereabouts remained unknown.

Scores of executions were carried out during the year, although in many cases it was not possible to determine whether these were judicial or extrajudicial. The death penalty continued to be imposed for criminal offences, including rape and murder, but no overall figures for the year were available. On 26 July at least 42 merchants, traders and businessmen were executed in Baghdad: they were accused of profiteering. They were among several hundred members of prominent Sunni and Shi'a families who were detained that month in a wave of arrests. The government stated that those executed had been tried and convicted, but reports indicated that several were shot dead upon being apprehended. Among those executed was Salim 'Abd al-Hadi Hamra, former head of the Baghdad Chamber of Commerce. Unconfirmed reports suggested that 25 other merchants and traders may have been executed in September. Also in September Iraqi television broadcast details of the trials of seven Iraqis who were executed that month following their conviction for premeditated murder. In October there were unconfirmed reports of the execution of at least

**166**

30 military personnel following an alleged military coup attempt in July.

An unknown number of unarmed civilians were extrajudicially executed in the southern marshes region, where thousands of suspected government opponents and army deserters remained in hiding. In February President Hussain said that Shi'a Muslims who participated in the March 1991 uprising should be machine-gunned for treason. In April the government ordered villagers living in the marshes region to resettle in purpose-built camps outside the area. Between April and August, government forces, including the Republican Guards, launched repeated military attacks on the marshes region using helicopter gunships and fighter aircraft. The extent and persistence of the bombardment of civilian targets, which intensified in July, heightened fears that the government had adopted a policy of deliberately targeting non-combatant civilians. In one incident in May, 13 civilians, among them women and children, were reportedly killed after helicopter gunships attacked a wedding ceremony in the village of al-Agir in al-'Amara province. Scores of others were killed in similar attacks in the province in July and August. No aerial attacks were reported following the imposition of the "air exclusion zone". However, ground attacks intensified and were accompanied by widespread arrests and the torture or execution of detainees. Earlier, hundreds of Shi'a Muslim detainees arrested after the March 1991 uprising were reportedly extrajudicially executed at al-Radwaniyya garrison between March and June.

Information was received about extrajudicial executions perpetrated by government forces in northern Iraq in previous years. Several mass graves were found near Arbil, Sulaimaniya and other areas, each containing the remains of scores of Kurdish civilians and combatants who had "disappeared" in custody. One mass grave outside Arbil contained the remains of 107 Kurdish villagers killed in 1987: they were among a group of some 360 people who had survived chemical weapons attacks and were arrested after seeking medical treatment in Arbil's hospitals. They had been moved to an unknown location and in 1988 were reported to have been killed (see *Amnesty International Report 1989*). A Kurdish doctor who worked at the deten-

tion centre in Arbil where the victims had been held told Amnesty International that he had been prevented by Iraqi security personnel from providing them with medical treatment, and that they were left to die and then buried. He added that 15 men who survived had been shot dead and then buried with the others.

Human rights abuses were committed by Kurdish opposition groups and the Kurdish authorities in control of northern Iraq, including torture and execution. Several hundred people were held in detention centres and prisons in Arbil, Sulaimaniya, Duhok and other places under the jurisdiction of the IKF, Kurdish political parties and, after July, police and security personnel of the Kurdish Ministry of the Interior. Some were Iraqi Arabs accused of espionage, but the majority were Kurds arrested at various times since the 1991 uprising on charges including murder, robbery and security offences. Scores of those detained, including young people, were reported to have been tortured to extract "confessions" which were later used to convict them. Among them were 13 political detainees, four of them women, arrested during a demonstration in Arbil in August and charged with the murder of two members of *Pesh Merga* (armed Kurdish units). Other detainees were sentenced to death and executed by firing-squad, but it was not known how many prisoners in all were sentenced to death or executed. Scores of people were also reported to have "disappeared" during the year after being picked up by members of armed Kurdish groups or to have been killed for political reasons. However, in most cases there was insufficient information to identify the perpetrators.

An IKF investigation into the killing of some 60 unarmed Iraqi soldiers by *Pesh Merga* forces in October 1991 (see *Amnesty International Report 1992*) identified 14 Kurds, most of whom were affiliated to the PUK and Kurdistan Socialist Party-Iraq (KSP-I), suspected of having carried out the killings. However, the suspects were released during the year in accordance with an IKF decision not to pursue the investigation.

Amnesty International continued to appeal to the Iraqi Government to halt human rights violations, including politically motivated arrests, unfair trials, "disappearances" and executions, but without response. In September and November Amnesty International publicly expressed its concern about extrajudicial executions in the southern marshes, and reiterated its call to the UN to press ahead and undertake direct monitoring of human rights throughout Iraq.

In May and December Amnesty International delegations visited northern Iraq and held discussions with Kurdish political leaders, officials and members of the judiciary about its concerns regarding human rights abuses perpetrated in territory effectively under the control of the IKF and the Council of Ministers. Amnesty International urged, among other things, that steps be taken to protect detainees from torture and that death sentences be commuted. During the year, Amnesty International obtained further government documents seized by Kurds during the 1991 uprising from security and intelligence offices in northern Iraq. Many of the documents confirmed the pattern of gross human rights violations committed by Iraqi government forces in previous years, including arbitrary arrests, "disappearances" and executions which had been reported by Amnesty International.

In a written statement to the UN Commission on Human Rights in February, Amnesty International drew attention to its grave concerns in Iraq, and in an oral statement urged the Commission to take up the recommendation of the UN Special Rapporteur on Iraq that a human rights monitoring operation be established in the country. The Special Rapporteur, who visited Iraq in January, detailed gross and widespread human rights violations in Iraq in his report to the Commission, and stated that "this exceptionally grave situation demands an exceptional response". The Commission adopted a resolution extending the Special Rapporteur's mandate for a further year and requested him "to develop further his recommendation for an exceptional response". In August, in an oral statement to the UN Sub-Commission on Prevention of Discrimination and Protection of Minorities, Amnesty International drew attention to continuing human rights violations in Iraq.

In December the UN General Assembly adopted a resolution endorsing the UN Special Rapporteur's proposal to establish a human rights monitoring operation in Iraq.

# IRELAND

**Three former prisoners continued to press for the re-examination of allegations that they had been ill-treated in police custody.**

Ireland signed the Convention against Torture and Other Cruel, Inhuman or Degrading Treatment or Punishment in September, but had not yet ratified it by the end of the year.

Nicky Kelly was given a government pardon in April. He had been convicted in 1978, along with Osgur Breatnach and Brian McNally, of involvement in the 1976 Sallins mail train robbery, solely on the basis of confessions allegedly obtained by ill-treatment during incommunicado detention (see Amnesty International Reports 1990 to 1992). In 1980 the Court of Criminal Appeal ruled that the confessions of Osgur Breatnach and Brian McNally had been involuntary and quashed their convictions. Nicky Kelly was released on "humanitarian grounds" in 1984. The three continued to press for re-examination, through civil proceedings, of their allegations that they had been ill-treated in police custody.

Amnesty International welcomed the pardon for Nicky Kelly, but continued to urge the government to establish an independent inquiry into all the allegations of ill-treatment in custody made in connection with the Sallins robbery case.

**168**

# ISRAEL AND THE OCCUPIED TERRITORIES

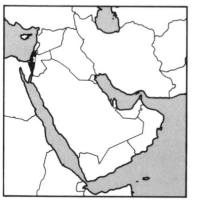

About 25,000 Palestinians were arrested in 1992 on security grounds, with more than 10,000 imprisoned at any one time. Most were serving sentences passed by military courts or were awaiting trial. Several hundred were administratively detained without charge or trial; over 500 of them were still held at the end of the year. There were Palestinian and Israeli prisoners of conscience, including conscientious objectors to military service. Palestinians under interrogation were systematically tortured or ill-treated. Four died in circumstances related to their treatment under interrogation. At least 120 Palestinians were shot dead by Israeli forces, often in circumstances suggesting extrajudicial executions or other unjustifiable killings. Investigations of abuses and subsequent measures appeared inadequate. One person remained under sentence of death. Members of Palestinian armed groups committed human rights abuses, including deliberate and arbitrary killings.

The Palestinian *intifada* (uprising) increasingly took the form of attacks with firearms or knives against Israelis. Twenty Israeli civilians and 18 soldiers and policemen were killed in these attacks. Over 200 Palestinians were also killed, mostly on suspicion of "collaborating" with the Israeli authorities (see below). Those who carried out the killings were believed to include members of the Palestine Liberation Organization (PLO) and the Islamic Resistance Movement (*Hamas*).

Following elections for the *Knesset* (Parliament) in June, a new government was formed under Prime Minister Yitzhak Rabin. The new government announced its intention to repeal 1986 legislation forbidding unauthorized contacts with organizations like the PLO, previously used to hold prisoners of conscience. In August it cancelled deportation orders issued in January against 11 Palestinians, who remained in custody in administrative detention. However, in December the government deported 415 Palestinians to south Lebanon following an upsurge in attacks against Israeli forces by *Hamas*. Lebanon did not accept the deportees, and by the end of the year they remained stranded in south Lebanon. In the Occupied Territories, the Israeli authorities continued to make extensive use of firearms, arrests and restriction orders.

Renewable administrative detention orders of up to six months were imposed on several hundred Palestinians. Appeals against such orders under a two-step process of judicial review usually took place several weeks after arrest. Almost always, detainees and their lawyers were not provided with crucial evidence about the reasons for detention, thus undermining existing legal safeguards. Almost all administrative detainees were held in the Ketziot detention centre in Israel.

Prisoners of conscience among the administrative detainees included political activists Nayef Sweitat, arrested in April, and Walid Zaqut, arrested in June. They were issued with detention orders of six and four months respectively, reduced on appeal to two and a half months. Sami Abu Samhadanah, another prisoner of conscience, was held for four months after a deportation order issued against him in January was cancelled in August.

Israeli prisoners of conscience included Abie Nathan, released in March, and David Ish Shalom, released in July (see *Amnesty International Reports 1990* to *1992*). Both were granted presidential pardons after undertaking not to break legislation forbidding unauthorized contacts with the PLO. Other prisoners of conscience included conscientious objectors to military service. For example, Yonatan Ben Efrat was sentenced in September to 56 days' imprisonment for refusing to serve on the West Bank.

At least 14 Lebanese nationals apprehended in Lebanon between 1986 and 1989 remained held under deportation or administrative detention orders. They included Shi'a Muslim leader Shaikh 'Abd al-Karim 'Ubayd and three others, who were abducted in Lebanon by Israeli forces in 1989, and 10 held after the expiry of prison sentences. The Israeli authorities said the 14 were held "in accordance with the law" but did not disclose the legal basis for these detentions. Ten others, including Lebanese and other foreign nationals, who had been held since 1985, were released and deported in June. The authorities gave no information about six Lebanese Shi'a Muslims arrested in Lebanon by the Lebanese Forces militia in 1987 and held in Israel after having been secretly moved there in 1990.

About 200 detainees were held without charge or trial at any one time in the Khiam detention centre in an area of south Lebanon controlled by Israel and the South Lebanon Army (SLA) (see **Lebanon** entry).

Some 14,600 Palestinians were tried by military courts on charges including acts of violence. Adults were commonly held for up to 18 days before being brought before a judge and longer without access to lawyers and relatives. The maximum period of detention without judicial review was reduced from 18 to eight days for detainees aged 16 or below. Confessions were often obtained during these periods of incommunicado detention. Although improvements appeared to have been made in some military court procedures, defendants continued to be put under undue pressure to enter into plea bargains. Several hundred prisoners were pardoned and released during the year.

Palestinian detainees continued to be systematically tortured or ill-treated, mostly during interrogation. Methods included beatings, hooding with dirty sacks, sleep deprivation, and confinement in small, dark cells known as "closets" or, when cold, "refrigerators". Ahmad Qatamesh said he was hooded, deprived of sleep, and shackled in painful positions while held under interrogation by the General Security Service (GSS) for more than 12 weeks. He had been arrested in September on suspicion of being a senior official of the Popular Front for the Liberation of Palestine, a faction of the PLO. In October Palestinian prisoners went on hunger-strike to protest against ill-treatment and prison conditions.

A police unit operating in the West Bank since 1990 was said to have specialized in interrogating detainees at night with methods including severe beatings with wooden sticks and electric shocks. The results of an official investigation into this unit, which started in February, were not known at the end of the year.

Three Palestinians died in detention and another died shortly after release after interrogations which reportedly included hooding, beating and sleep deprivation. They included Mustafa 'Akkawi, who died in custody in February. According to a pathologist who attended the autopsy on behalf of the victim's family, death was caused by a heart attack triggered by emotional and physical pressure, and exposure to the cold, with medical negligence a contributory factor. Mustafa Barakat died in August some 36 hours after arrest. A pathologist representing the victim's family found that he had died due to an acute asthma attack brought about by conditions in detention, and also that he could have been subjected to "severe mistreatment".

Mordechai Vanunu, a former nuclear technician, remained held in solitary confinement for the sixth consecutive year (see *Amnesty International Reports 1988* to *1992*). Amnesty International continued to appeal for his isolation to be ended as it believes it constitutes cruel, inhuman and degrading treatment.

At least 120 Palestinians were shot dead by Israeli forces, including undercover police and army units. Some were shot in the context of armed clashes, others in circumstances suggesting that they were the victims of extrajudicial executions or other unjustifiable killings. In some cases medical help was not given or was hindered. In March Jamal Ghanem was playing football in Tulkarem when four undercover police chased him on the pitch and shot him dead. An ambulance was reportedly not allowed to enter the football pitch. In May Anton al-Shumali was shot at point-blank range with rubber bullets by one of two border policemen who stopped him on a road in Beit Sahur. They left him dying by the roadside. Official investigations into these killings were not known to have been completed by the end of the year.

Thirty-four members of the Israeli forces were prosecuted for offences including

**170**

illegal use of force and theft. In July, the commander of the "Shimshon" undercover army unit operating in the Gaza Strip received a suspended sentence of one month's imprisonment and was later demoted. He was tried in connection with the killing of a Palestinian in 1989 and found guilty after appeal of exceeding his authority by ordering his subordinates to fire at a suspect's body rather than the legs, in violation of standing orders. Also in July, an army colonel was reprimanded in connection with punitive beatings of Palestinians in 1988.

In June the Jerusalem District Court acquitted a Border Police officer who had been charged with manslaughter following the death of Fadi Zabaqli, a Palestinian killed in Bethlehem in December 1989. Television footage of the incident showed the officer firing towards Fadi Zabaqli as he was running away. An army investigation had found in 1990 that the officer had violated standing orders for opening fire. The court ruled that there was insufficient evidence linking the officer's shooting to Fadi Zabaqli's death. An appeal by the prosecution against the court's verdict was pending at the end of the year.

It was announced in June that responsibility for investigating alleged offences by the police had been transferred from the police to the Ministry of Justice, except for minor offences. In October a Ministry of Justice representative told the *Knesset* that her ministry would in future be responsible for investigating all complaints against members of the GSS. The findings of investigations by the GSS and the Ministry of Justice into allegations of torture or ill-treatment by the GSS, announced in May 1991, were not publicly known, although the authorities said that measures had been taken against a number of interrogators.

John Demjanjuk remained under sentence of death while his appeal before the Supreme Court continued. He had been convicted in 1988 of offences including crimes against humanity (see *Amnesty International Reports 1989* to *1992*).

Palestinians – members of armed groups and others – killed 20 Israeli civilians and over 200 Palestinians, many of them suspected of "collaborating" with the Israeli authorities. Some were interrogated and tortured before being put to death. Palestinian political leaders condemned the torture and wanton killing of suspected "collaborators". However, they seemed generally to endorse the view that "collaborators" could be punished with death if this was approved by the top Palestinian leadership. In December *Hamas* took hostage and then killed a Border Policeman, Nissim Toledano.

Amnesty International called for the immediate and unconditional release of prisoners of conscience and for all administrative detainees to be brought to trial promptly and fairly, or be released. It called for an end to interrogation practices amounting to torture or ill-treatment and for the impartial investigation of deaths in detention and killings by the security forces. It also called for the immediate return of the Palestinians deported in December.

In May Amnesty International published a report, *Israel/South Lebanon: The Khiam Detainees: torture and ill-treatment*. The organization called on the Israeli authorities to clarify the legal situations of the detainees and ensure the release of any held as a hostage. It also called for an end to all forms of torture and ill-treatment in the centre and for the detainees to have access to the International Committee of the Red Cross.

In an oral statement to the United Nations Commission on Human Rights in January, Amnesty International included reference to its concerns relating to torture and ill-treatment during interrogation and administrative detention in the Israeli Occupied Territories.

In correspondence and meetings with Amnesty International representatives, the Israeli authorities replied in detail on a number of individual cases and commented on the *Amnesty International Report 1992*. They provided information on cases of Druze objectors to military service, saying that their number was "minuscule" and that their objection rose often from socio-economic reasons rather than conscience. In April the Military Advocate General's Unit issued a 17-page response to a report on the military justice system published by Amnesty International in July 1991 (see *Amnesty International Report 1992*). The authorities criticized the report's methodology, arguing that it had arrived at "misleading and inaccurate conclusions". They said that progress had been made in areas including the prompt notification to families and lawyers of individuals' arrests and trial sessions. They also stated that although "the use of a certain degree of force is often necessary in order to obtain information, the disproportionate exertion of pressure on suspects (i.e. by torture or maltreatment) is strictly forbidden". With regard to the Khiam detention centre in south Lebanon, the authorities said that no Israeli personnel were stationed there and that they had no authority over the SLA, which staffed the centre.

Amnesty International called on the PLO and *Hamas* to prevent torture and deliberate and arbitrary killings. With regard to the killing of Jamal Faddah, an alleged "collaborator" taken prisoner and shot dead in December by a man who claimed to be an activist for *Fatah* (a faction of the PLO), the PLO told Amnesty International that it had "strongly condemned the acts of shooting that took place" in the Occupied Territories. In response to appeals by Amnesty International and its condemnation of the killing of Nissim Toledano, *Hamas* stated that "[m]ilitary operations against foreign occupation" were "legal" and "a natural human response".

Amnesty International expressed great concern to PLO Chairman Yasser Arafat about the execution in 1991 of Hamza Abu Zaid, who was alleged to have shot dead Salah Khalaf, a PLO leader, and others in Tunis in 1991 (see *Amnesty International Report 1992*). Hamza Abu Zaid was taken from Tunisia to Yemen where he was sentenced to death by a PLO court and executed. Amnesty International appealed to Yasser Arafat to commute any death sentences imposed by the PLO (see **Lebanon** entry).

# ITALY

**Allegations of torture and ill-treatment in police custody and prisons continued and were more frequent than in previous years; some appeared to have been inadequately investigated.**

Draft legislation reforming the existing system of conscientious objection to compulsory military service (see *Amnesty International Reports 1989* to *1992*) gained parliamentary approval in mid-January. However, it was rejected by the then President of the Republic, Francesco Cossiga, and returned to parliament for further consideration; this had not been completed by the end of the year.

There were numerous complaints of ill-treatment against the police, *carabinieri* and prison guards; many concerned immigrants from outside Europe and people held in connection with drugs-related offences.

Daud Addawe Ali, a Somali asylum-seeker, was arrested in March following a disturbance at the aliens' registration office attached to a Rome police station. Inside the station four police officers allegedly struck him to the ground, beat him with batons and knocked his head repeatedly against a wall until he lost consciousness. Members of the public reported hearing his cries for help. He was transferred to hospital, where doctors diagnosed a head injury and bruising to the left leg and chest. Some hours later he was taken to prison, accused of resisting arrest and of insulting and injuring a police officer. Shortly after his release into provisional liberty some 17 days later, a medical examination found injuries consistent with his allegations. Members of parliament called for an inquiry into his treatment and he reportedly made a judicial complaint. In April a government delegation told the United Nations Committee against Torture that he had been involved in a violent struggle with the police preceding arrest.

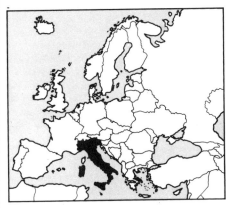

Carmelo La Rosa, a heroin addict, alleged that he and 17 fellow drug addicts in Gazzi prison were beaten by prison guards using batons. On 24 June, during Messina Appeal Court's hearing of his appeal against an eight-year prison sentence for possession of heroin, he removed

**172**

his clothing, claiming that the injuries visible on his body had been inflicted by prison guards. The court recorded that there were clear signs of violent blows caused by a blunt instrument on his chest and shoulders. It requested the Public Prosecutor to order his medical examination by the director of Gazzi prison clinic immediately on his readmission to prison. After receiving a two-year reduction in his sentence, Carmelo La Rosa returned to prison but the Public Prosecutor apparently neglected to order his medical examination. He was found dead during the night of 24 to 25 June, hanging by the neck from a belt tied to his cell window. His lawyer made a signed declaration to the Public Prosecutor describing his client's allegations of ill-treatment and his claim that, after his last beating prior to his court appearance, prison guards had threatened to hang him if he denounced them. The Public Prosecutor's office opened an investigation into the circumstances surrounding the death.

Numerous transfers of prisoners held in connection with Mafia-related offences took place from July onwards as part of a series of anti-Mafia measures launched by the government. Allegations of ill-treatment concerning several prisons affected by the transfers, including Poggioreale prison and the island prisons of Asinara and Pianosa, were made by inmates, their relatives and lawyers and several members of parliament.

It was reported that over 60 prisoners transferred to the "Agrippa" high security section of Pianosa prison during July and August were held under a provision of the so-called "anti-Mafia" law introduced in June by government decree and converted into law in August. This allows the Minister of Justice to suspend – for public order and security reasons – all or part of the normal prison rules regulating the treatment of prisoners for those held in connection with organized crime and terrorism. From mid-August onwards, when prisoners were allowed their first visits from lawyers and relatives since transfer, there were reports that many prisoners appeared dirty and undernourished and that they had been punched, kicked, subjected to arbitrary beatings with batons, repeatedly threatened and insulted, and had been forced to run continuously during exercise periods. The majority of prisoners' relatives making

such allegations did not identify themselves by name, saying that they feared retaliation against the prisoners concerned, although the wives and lawyers of two prisoners did make formal complaints to the judicial authorities.

In September the magistrate of surveillance responsible for monitoring the treatment of Pianosa inmates sent the Minister of Justice the findings of his August visit to the prison. His report appeared to lend credibility to a number of the allegations emanating from the "Agrippa" section. He concluded that criminal acts had possibly taken place there and also described several incidents involving "gratuitous and illegal brutality" against detainees in the ordinary sections of the prison.

Amnesty International made inquiries throughout the year about official steps taken to investigate allegations of torture and ill-treatment and the outcome of inquiries opened into such allegations. The Minister of Justice sent a partial response to a few of the cases of alleged torture and ill-treatment described in the memorandum which Amnesty International had presented to the government in October 1991 (see *Amnesty International Report 1992*). In March Amnesty International replied, requesting more comprehensive information on all the cases in its memorandum and expressing concern about several new cases of alleged ill-treatment reported during the first three months of 1992, including that of Daud Addawe Ali. Amnesty International also wrote to the Minister asking for details of the regime in force in the "Agrippa" section of Pianosa prison and of the steps taken as a result of the magistrate of surveillance's findings. The authorities did not respond to any of these inquiries.

# JAMAICA

**A law which created new categories of "capital" and "non-capital" murder was applied retroactively to more than 270 prisoners already under sentence of death. By the end of the year, at least 46 death sentences had been commuted under the new law and 83 prisoners (already on death row) had had their offences reclassified as "capital murder". At least 15 new death sentences were**

passed during the year but no executions were carried out. There were allegations of ill-treatment of prisoners, four of whom died while in police custody. A number of people were killed by police officers in circumstances suggesting they may have been extrajudicially executed.

Michael Manley, who had been Prime Minister since 1989 and between 1972 and 1980, resigned the leadership of the ruling People's National Party in March, a post he had held for 23 years. He was replaced in both posts by Percival J. Patterson.

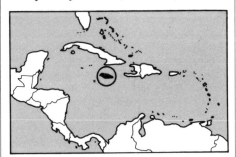

The Offences against the Person (Amendment) Act was passed by parliament and became law in October. It repealed legislation which had provided a mandatory death sentence in all cases of murder, and created new categories of "capital" and "non-capital" murder. Capital murder under the Act includes the killing of members of the security forces, judicial and correctional officers and witnesses in civil and criminal cases, and murders in the course of other crimes. The death sentence remains mandatory in such cases. Other murders carry a sentence of life imprisonment.

The law applied retroactively to more than 270 prisoners who were under sentence of death for murder in October 1992, and stipulated that such prisoners' offences would be reclassified as "capital" or "non-capital" by an appeal court judge. The law further stipulated that prisoners whose offences were reclassified as "capital murder" had 21 days in which to apply for a final review of their classification by three judges of the Court of Appeal, and the right to be represented by counsel.

The first reclassifications took place in December when at least 46 death row inmates had their death sentences commuted to life imprisonment and 83 had their offences reclassified as "capital murder". There were fears that prisoners whose offences had been reclassified as "capital murder" would not be able to obtain legal representation at their final review hearings, despite the provisions of the new law. Few of these prisoners had lawyers in Jamaica as there was no legal aid after the trial and direct appeal, and United Kingdom lawyers who represented Jamaican prisoners in appeals to the Judicial Committee of the Privy Council (JCPC) in London (the final court of appeal for Jamaica) had initially not been informed which prisoners' offences had been reclassified.

The situation was made even more serious by the Minister of Justice's announcement in December that executions would resume early the next year. At the end of 1992 lawyers were still seeking information on cases and appealing to the authorities for adequate time in which to provide legal representation.

There was concern that, without a thorough review process and adequate legal representation, many prisoners on death row who should benefit from the new law might not be identified. The new law stipulated, for example, that where two or more people were convicted jointly of murder, only the actual killer would receive the death sentence; others would be convicted of "non-capital" murder. Despite this provision, some prisoners whose offences were reclassified as "capital murder" were not the killers and in other cases the record was unclear.

There were serious concerns about the quality of the evidence in some cases. In 1989 the JCPC had quashed the convictions and death sentences of 10 Jamaican prisoners who had been sentenced solely on the uncorroborated identification testimony of a single witness, on the ground that the trial judges had failed to warn juries of the dangers of convicting on such evidence. Despite this ruling, a number of prisoners who had been convicted on similar evidence had their offences reclassified as "capital murder".

In six of the cases classified as "capital murder" under the new law – those of Paul Kelly, Ivan Morgan, Earl Pratt, Carlton Reid, Leroy Simmonds and Clifton Wright – the United Nations (UN) Human Rights Committee had recommended that the death sentences be commuted or the prisoners released because their rights under the International Covenant on Civil and Political Rights (ICCPR) had been violated.

**174**

However, the Jamaican Government had not acted on the recommendations.

In the case of Clifton Wright (sentenced to death in 1983) important forensic evidence had been overlooked at his trial. In July the UN Human Rights Committee adopted the view that his rights had been violated under Article 14 of the ICCPR (the right to a fair trial) and Article 6 (the right to life), since the death sentence had been imposed after judicial proceedings that fell short of international standards for a fair trial. The Committee concluded that he was entitled to "an effective remedy... entailing his release". (The Inter-American Commission on Human Rights had previously considered his case and in 1988 found a violation of Article 25 – the Right to Judicial Protection – under the American Convention on Human Rights.)

In October the UN Human Rights Committee adopted the view that Leroy Simmonds' rights had also been violated under Articles 14 and 6 of the ICCPR and concluded that he, too, was entitled to release. Similar views had been adopted in the cases of Carlton Reid in 1990 and Paul Kelly in 1991.

In the cases of Earl Pratt and Ivan Morgan (sentenced to death in 1979) the UN Human Rights Committee had recommended in 1989 that their death sentences be commuted on the ground, among other things, that a four-year delay in the issuing of a written appeal judgment had deprived them of the right to a fair trial without undue delay. However, they remained on death row. In June 1992 the Court of Appeal dismissed a constitutional motion in their cases, stating that "delay in execution cannot be regarded as inhuman and degrading punishment or other treatment". In July they were granted leave to appeal to the JCPC, which was still pending at the end of the year.

Glenford Campbell, Aston Little and Raphael Henry – who had also been recommended for release by the UN Human Rights Committee – were among those whose death sentences were commuted to life imprisonment under the new law.

At least 15 people were sentenced to death for murder during the year. There were no executions: the last had been carried out in 1988.

Three prisoners died from suffocation after being held with 16 other prisoners in a small, unventilated cell in the Constant Spring Police Station from 22 to 24 October. In December an inquest jury found the deaths were caused by criminal negligence amounting to manslaughter by the police although the verdict did not identify individual officers responsible. According to testimony at the inquest, the prisoners were given no food or water from around midday on 23 October until the three were found dead the following morning; some inmates had been forced through intense heat and thirst to drink their own sweat or urine; and no one had attended to calls for help during the night. A government pathologist found bodily injuries, including head injuries, on the three who died, which could have contributed to their deaths, although the cause of the injuries was not established. A decision on whether there was evidence to charge individual police officers was pending at the end of the year.

A decision was also pending in the case of John Headley, who died in the Ramble Police Station in November, allegedly after being beaten by police officers. Inmate witnesses alleged that John Headley was bleeding and unable to stand when he was placed in a police cell where he was found dead some hours later.

A number of people were shot and killed by police in circumstances suggesting that they may have been extrajudicially executed. Many people were reportedly killed during shoot-outs, while resisting arrest or during confrontations. However, some victims who were shot dead were unarmed or appeared to offer no immediate threat of deadly resistance. In some cases suspects had allegedly surrendered or were in police custody at the time they were shot. They included Fitzgerald Polson who was shot dead by a police officer in the street in September. Police claimed that he was shot when he tried to disarm an officer, but eye-witnesses disputed this; one eye-witness stated that he had his hands in the air at the time. The case was submitted to the Director of Public Prosecution for a ruling on possible action and a decision was pending at the end of the year.

In May Amnesty International wrote to the Governor General, Sir Howard Cooke, and Prime Minister P.J. Patterson welcoming the fact that there had been no executions since 1988, and expressing the hope that the moratorium would be maintained and that steps would be taken to abolish the death penalty. It also urged the Governor General to use his prerogative of mercy to commute all death sentences. Amnesty International also wrote to the government in May about the bill, which was then before parliament, to amend the Offences against the Person Act. While Amnesty International welcomed provisions to restrict the use of the death penalty, and to review the cases of all those on death row, it drew attention to concerns about the fairness of capital trials, lack of adequate legal representation and the poor quality of the evidence in many cases. It urged that these and other factors be taken into account in the review of cases and appealed for the commutation of the death sentences of all those on death row.

# JAPAN

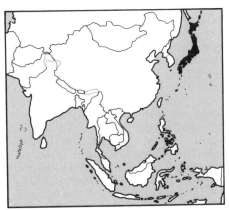

**For the third consecutive year there were no executions. However, five death sentences were finalized, bringing the total number of prisoners under final sentence of death to 56. There was concern about the lack of legal protection for refugees and asylum-seekers.**

The death penalty was the subject of public debate throughout the year. Among those supporting a growing campaign for abolition were a former Minister of Justice, a former Supreme Court judge, more than 230 members of the *Diet* (Japan's parliament), and members of the religious community. The Japan Federation of Bar Associations established a working group to study abolition of the death penalty. In August abolitionist groups organized a series of public events to mark 1,000 days

since the last execution in November 1989. This was the first time since the Penal Code was introduced in 1907 that no executions had taken place for such a long period.

At the start of 1992 some 90 prisoners convicted of murder were believed to be under sentence of death. During the year five sentences were finalized, bringing to 56 the number of prisoners under final sentence of death. They included the sentences imposed on Tetsuya Sasaki, Kosaku Nada and Tetsuyuki Morikawa, which were upheld by the Supreme Court. Twenty-six prisoners under sentence of death were reported either to have applied for a retrial or to be preparing to do so, claiming miscarriages of justice. Four prisoners had been held under sentence of death for over 20 years.

Further information was received about Lin Guizhen, an asylum-seeker from the People's Republic of China. She had been forcibly returned from Japan to China in August 1991 before the appeal against the refusal of her asylum request had been heard (see *Amnesty International Report 1992*). In April the Chinese authorities stated that Lin Guizhen was serving a term of "re-education through labour" without imprisonment, although her family reportedly stated that she had been imprisoned shortly after her return to China.

In October Amnesty International representatives met government officials and others to gather information on the protection of refugees and asylum-seekers and, in particular, to assess the extent to which Japanese law and practice conforms with Japan's international obligations. They found that asylum-seekers face difficulties in obtaining relevant information and exercising their right to apply for asylum; that procedures do not provide for a fair and satisfactory examination of individual claims; and that there is inadequate protection against forcible return for those at risk of serious human rights violations in their own countries.

Amnesty International urged the government to commute all death sentences and abolish the death penalty. In April the organization issued a report, *Japan: Debating Abolition of the Death Penalty*, which included information about the main arguments put forward by both abolitionists and retentionists in legal, political and academic circles in Japan.

176

# JORDAN

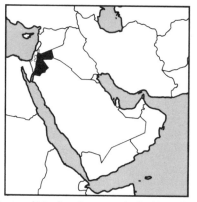

Most political prisoners, including about 50 prisoners serving sentences imposed after unfair trials and untried detainees, were released in November when over 1,480 prisoners were freed in a royal amnesty. Five prisoners of conscience were convicted and sentenced to prison terms but released after serving their sentence or being pardoned. Hundreds of other security detainees were arrested and held in incommunicado detention: some were tried by the State Security Court with no right of appeal; most were released without charge. There were new allegations of torture and ill-treatment but fewer than in previous years. No executions were carried out.

The state of emergency was lifted completely during the year. In March a new Defence Law was passed: although not in force, it can be introduced in the event of "an emergency threatening national security and public safety". It replaced legislation in force since 1939 which had given the authorities sweeping powers of arrest and detention. The new law still provides for the indefinite administrative detention of security suspects, but gives detainees a right of appeal to the High Court of Justice. In April martial law, in force since 1967, was lifted. As a result, the Martial Law Court was abolished and a Law on Lifting Responsibility as a Result of the End of Martial Law came into force. This grants immunity from prosecution to officials who had enforced martial law directives.

Other legislative changes were introduced. In February the 1953 Law on Resistance to Communism, under which prisoners of conscience were held in previous years, was repealed. In October a new Law on Political Parties was introduced, which recognizes the right to form political parties, although these must be authorized by the Ministry of the Interior. Political parties must be committed, among other things, to "protecting the independence and security of the nation and the preservation of national unity". They may not have any organizational, financial or other links abroad, and the Ministry of the Interior may request the High Court of Justice to dissolve any party.

Parliament resumed debating a new law on the State Security Court in December. The law had been proposed by the government in July 1991 and passed by Parliament but then vetoed by King Hussein bin Talal in November 1991. The King's objections included the introduction of the right of appeal to the Court of Cassation against verdicts of the State Security Court.

Five members of the Islamic Liberation Party in Jordan (LPJ) were held as prisoners of conscience. They had been arrested in October and November 1991 for speaking and distributing leaflets against peace negotiations with Israel. The main charge against them was membership of an illegal, violent organization. The State Security Court, however, found that neither the LPJ, which advocates the establishment of an Islamic state, nor its members on trial had used or advocated violence. It ruled that the LPJ was nevertheless an illegal organization and on those grounds convicted the defendants. In June Muhammad Abu Maidan and Tareq Qubi'ah were each sentenced to one and a half year's imprisonment; the other three received one-year prison sentences. Two of the three, Bakr al-Khawalidah and Muhammad al-Khabbas, were also tried with four others before the Criminal Court of Amman for the same offence of membership of the LPJ. They were convicted and sentenced in April to three months' imprisonment, confirmed by the Court of Appeal in May and commuted to a fine. All five prisoners had been released by November after serving their sentences or being pardoned.

The General Intelligence Department (GID) held over 520 security detainees, including some who may have been prisoners of conscience, mostly in incommunicado detention. About 400 were released without charge, trial or judicial review. They included Ramadan al-Battah, a member of *Fatah*, a faction of the Palestine Liberation Organization (PLO). He was held in June for over three weeks in the GID headquarters in Amman with no access to family or lawyers, apparently in connection with Palestinian attacks against Israel. He was then released uncharged. Khaled 'Ayed Abu Hudayb, a researcher at the Institute for Palestine Studies in Beirut, was arrested on arrival at Amman's main airport in August and held at the GID headquarters, apparently on suspicion of belonging to an illegal organization and of having written an article in an illegal newspaper. He was held in solitary confinement and only allowed access to a lawyer after four weeks. He was eventually released without charge in October.

Other political suspects were tried by the State Security Court, from which there is no right of appeal, contrary to international fair trial standards. They included Leith Shubeilat, a prominent member of Parliament; Ya'qub Qarrash, another member of Parliament; and two shop owners. All four were arrested in August and tried on charges including membership of an illegal, violent organization, *Harakat shabab al-nafir al-islami*, the Movement of the Youth of the Islamic Call to Arms, and possession of weapons and explosives. One session of the trial was held *in camera* and several witnesses gave testimony for the prosecution while they were still detained in the custody of the GID. Amnesty International delegates observed sessions of the trial. In November the defendants were sentenced to between 10 and 20 years' imprisonment. However, they were granted a royal pardon and released a few days later.

Over 1,480 prisoners, including about 50 political prisoners and detainees, were released under a royal general amnesty in November. They included 18 convicted members of *Jaysh Muhammad*, the Army of (the Prophet) Muhammad, who were tried by the State Security Court in 1991 (see *Amnesty International Report 1992*). A further 100 prisoners were amnestied and released in December. Musa Fadaylat and Maher Abu 'Ayyash, two political prisoners serving life sentences passed by the Martial Law Court, were pardoned and released in March and December respectively.

There were new allegations of torture and ill-treatment but on a lesser scale than in previous years. The victims reportedly included both political and criminal suspects who alleged in most cases that they had been tortured or ill-treated while detained incommunicado. Among them were nine suspected members of *Hamas* (an Islamic Palestinian group). They were arrested between October 1991 and January 1992 on suspicion of possessing weapons. They were allegedly tortured or ill-treated while held at the GID headquarters before being moved to Swaqa prison in March. They were released under the November amnesty. The GID denied that they had been ill-treated. It also informed Amnesty International that it had introduced routine medical examinations for detainees in its custody. In a case relating to forgery of real estate documents, Fawwaz al-Fa'uri was held incommunicado for 12 days in May by the Preventive Security (a special police force), during which he was allegedly deprived of sleep and subjected to beatings, including *falaqa* (beatings on the soles of the feet). He was released in December.

Amnesty International welcomed the releases of prisoners, the lifting of the state of emergency, other human rights initiatives such as the repeal of legislation which had led to the imprisonment of prisoners of conscience, and the reported absence of executions during the year. It remained concerned, however, about the continued use of incommunicado detention, which facilitates torture and ill-treatment, and about trials by the State Security Court in the absence of the right of appeal to a higher tribunal. The organization called for the release of prisoners of conscience and a review of the cases of political prisoners held after unfair trials.

In September Amnesty International representatives visiting Jordan were received by King Hussein and Crown Prince Hassan bin Talal, and held discussions with Prime Minister Sharif Zeid Ben Shaker and other cabinet ministers and officials, including some from the GID. Amnesty International welcomed King Hussein's call for an Arab human rights charter and the government's reiterated commitment to human rights protection and promotion. While welcoming the progress in human rights reforms, Amnesty International stressed the need to strengthen safeguards for detainees such as guaranteed access to lawyers, the introduction of the right of appeal before the State Security Court, and an end to all executions.

178

# KAZAKHSTAN

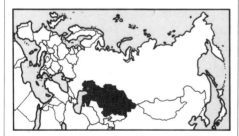

**One prisoner of conscience was detained on a charge of insulting the President. At least six people were sentenced to death and at least six executions were carried out.**

Kazakhstan's independence, declared in December 1991, was recognized internationally following the dissolution of the Soviet Union. Headed by President Nursultan Nazarbayev, Kazakhstan became a member of the Conference on Security and Co-operation in Europe in January and the United Nations in March.

Karishal Asanov, a writer and academic, was held in pre-trial detention from August to November after being charged under Article 170-3 of the criminal code with "infringement upon the honour and dignity of the President". The charge related to the publication in the opposition newspaper *Khak*, published in Moscow, of an article entitled "Don't believe the President's smile". He was released conditionally in November on the first day of his trial, which ended in his acquittal in December.

Reports indicated that at least six people were sentenced to death in 1992 and six executions were carried out; the true figure was believed to be much higher. Execution is by shooting. Although Kazakhstan retains the death penalty for 18 peacetime offences, statistics shown to Amnesty International by Justice Ministry officials in April indicated that between 1987 and 1991 the death penalty was applied for only four offences: premeditated, aggravated murder; rape; threatening the life of a police officer; and banditry. Between 1987 and 1990 a total of 165 people received death sentences, but at least 41 of them benefited from commutation or pardon. In 1991, 67 death sentences were passed, at least 26 of which were subsequently commuted.

Amnesty International appealed for the release of Karishal Asanov and expressed concern that legislation to protect the honour and dignity of the President and People's Deputies appeared to place unwarranted restrictions on freedom of expression.

In April Amnesty International representatives visited Kazakhstan for the first time. They had meetings with the Vice-President and other government officials at which they urged the abolition of the death penalty and discussed prospects for constitutional, legislative and penal reform.

# KENYA

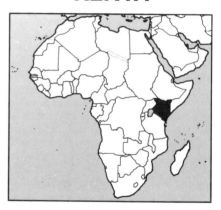

**Hundreds of government critics, many of them prisoners of conscience, were detained for short periods. Over 30 were charged with political offences and freed on bail. Four long-term prisoners of conscience and more than 20 other political prisoners were released. There were reports of torture by the police and beatings of peaceful demonstrators. Over 700 people were killed in ethnic clashes allegedly instigated or condoned by the government. Some 350 people were under sentence of death, including over 30 convicted during 1992, but no executions were reported.**

After 12 years of one-party rule, several opposition parties and human rights groups were allowed to campaign openly, but they still encountered considerable harassment. Elections in late December, which were marred by electoral irregularities, returned to power President Daniel arap Moi and the ruling Kenya African National Union (KANU), but opposition parties won almost half the seats in parliament.

Kenya became a party to the African Charter on Human and Peoples' Rights in February.

Hundreds of members of opposition parties, journalists and peaceful demonstrators were arrested during the year, including students and members of the Release Political Prisoners (RPP) campaign group. Many were prisoners of conscience. Most were soon released without charge, but at least 30 were charged with political offences and later released on bail. None had been tried by the end of the year.

Among those charged were 11 prominent members of the Forum for the Restoration of Democracy (FORD) party, who were arrested in January after giving a press conference in the capital, Nairobi, expressing fears that a pro-government military take-over was imminent and that government opponents would be assassinated. They were charged with "publishing false rumours", then released. Sheikh Khalid Salim Balala, an Islamic preacher and a leader of the prohibited Islamic Party of Kenya (IPK), was arrested in Mombasa in July after giving an open-air sermon. He was charged with treason, which carries a mandatory death penalty, for "imagining the death of the President". He was still awaiting trial at the end of the year.

Eleven journalists, all prisoners of conscience, were briefly detained and interrogated by police about articles critical of the government. Six staff of *Society* magazine, including its editor Pius Nyamora and his wife, were arrested in Nairobi in May and charged with sedition in connection with articles alleging government involvement in political killings. Njehu Gatabaki of *Finance* magazine, and the Reverend Jamlick Miano of a church magazine, *Jitegemea* (Self-Reliance), were also charged with sedition. None of the journalists, who were all released on bail within a few days, had been tried by the end of 1992.

All 22 known political prisoners serving prison terms imposed after unfair trials in previous years (see *Amnesty International Report 1992*) were released during the year. They included George Anyona, a former member of parliament, and three other prisoners of conscience serving seven-year sentences for sedition, who were freed on bail in February. The High Court, with the prosecution's consent, lifted the remaining part of their sentences in June. George Anyona later sued the state for wrongful imprisonment and ill-treatment.

Koigi wa Wamwere, a former member of parliament, remained in custody throughout the year without being tried, together with his relative Geoffrey Kuria Kariuki, a farmer, and Rumba Kinuthia and Mirugi Kariuki, both lawyers. They had been arrested in 1990 and charged with treason (see *Amnesty International Report 1992*). Four other co-defendants were released in June when the state withdrew charges. Koigi wa Wamwere and the other three appeared in court several times during the year to complain about torture after their arrests, subsequent ill-treatment in prison, and violations of their constitutional rights. A court ruled in November that Rumba Kinuthia, who doctors testified was too ill to stand trial, should be tried separately when he was medically fit, but it did not investigate his complaint of torture and ill-treatment.

Cases of torture and ill-treatment of prisoners in police custody, including rape of women, were reported during the year. Riot police in the General Service Unit severely beat peaceful demonstrators on several occasions. In February they assaulted women belonging to the Release Political Prisoners group who were demonstrating in a Nairobi park. They beat four women unconscious, including Professor Wangari Maathai, chairperson of the Green Belt Movement, an environmental pressure group. By the end of the year, none of these cases had been independently investigated.

Conditions in Kenyan prisons were generally harsh, particularly in Kamiti prison near Nairobi and Langata women's prison in Nairobi. Rumba Kinuthia, who was in hospital for most of the year with high blood pressure and other complaints, was kept chained to his bed for between 14 and 23 hours a day, in violation of the United Nations (UN) Standard Minimum Rules for the Treatment of Prisoners.

Hundreds of Somali refugees and asylum-seekers were arbitrarily detained in August. One reportedly died after being beaten by police. They were held for several days in makeshift camps without proper shelter, food or medical treatment and were denied access to relatives and officials of the UN High Commissioner for Refugees.

Political violence claimed the lives of

**180** some 700 people in western and central Kenya in inter-ethnic clashes in the first half of the year. Credible evidence was published following a church-sponsored investigation in June, and later in a parliamentary committee report, indicating that one group responsible for many of the killings was supported and financed by senior government and KANU officials. The group was nicknamed "Kalenjin warriors", Kalenjin being President Moi's ethnic group. However, the full parliament, composed solely of KANU members, voted in October to reject the committee report. No further action was taken by the authorities to bring to justice any government officials alleged to have been responsible for killings.

No judicial action was taken into the reportedly deliberate killing by police of three people at the time of a demonstration and rioting against arrests of IPK leaders in Mombasa in May. The three people killed were reportedly not involved in the rioting.

Further evidence emerged of high-level government involvement in the murder of former Foreign Minister Robert Ouko in 1990 (see *Amnesty International Report 1992*). After President Moi stopped a judicial inquiry in December 1991, Jonah Anguka, a former official, was charged with the murder. At his trial which started in November, the prosecution named as his accomplice the former head of the security service, who had died of natural causes earlier in 1992.

More than 30 people were sentenced to death for murder or armed robbery. A total of over 350 people, including seven women, were under sentence of death, but there were no reports of executions.

Amnesty International appealed for the release of prisoners of conscience and for other political prisoners to be brought to trial promptly and fairly. It called for impartial inquiries into allegations of ill-treatment or torture of prisoners and also into assaults on peaceful demonstrators. It called for independent investigations to establish responsibility for political killings where government involvement had been alleged, and appealed for commutation of all death sentences. In June Amnesty International representatives were able to visit Kenya for the first time since 1987. They discussed the organization's concerns with the Attorney General and met human rights activists, including lawyers.

# KOREA
## (DEMOCRATIC PEOPLE'S REPUBLIC OF)

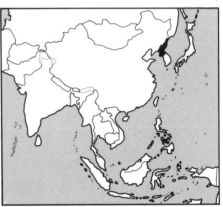

**New information emerged about political prisoners held in labour camps. One person was reported to have been publicly executed.**

In April the Supreme People's Assembly amended the 1972 Constitution and adopted a new Code of Criminal Procedure. The texts were not available outside the country. One of the constitutional amendments was said to remove "freedom of anti-religious propaganda" from the provision guaranteeing freedom of religious belief and to introduce a prohibition on religion being used to involve foreign powers in the country's affairs or to destroy the state or social order. However, this could not be confirmed.

Information about human rights concerns was severely limited and difficult to verify. Human rights issues were rarely reported in the media, which is controlled by the government of President Kim Il Sung, and there was no independent group in the country monitoring and recording human rights problems. Access to the country remained restricted and Amnesty International received no reply to its request to visit the country during the year.

New information became available during the year about political prisoners held in labour camps. In Japan, the media published interviews with relatives of Koreans and Japanese who had settled in North Korea in previous decades and had apparently been arrested for alleged espionage or other political reasons. They had reportedly been sent to labour camps, often with members of their families. In one case, three brothers were said to have been detained in labour camps from 1969 to 1977, although they consistently denied any involvement in espionage.

Further information on imprisonment in labour camps was provided in October by two North Koreans who had recently fled to South Korea. They said that they had been held in a labour camp in Yodok county, South Hamgyong Province. One reported that he had been held from 1977 to 1987 with members of his family because a relative was suspected of espionage. The other said that he had been held from 1986 to 1989 after returning from an unauthorized visit to China. Both named other people who were believed to be still held in the camp. Among them were relatives of a South Korean who, having moved to the north, later defected from there to Europe. They also named people held in the camp in previous years, including Japanese women who had settled in North Korea with their Korean husbands who were held in the 1970s, and former senior government officials who were held in the 1980s.

One person was reported to have been executed by shooting at a public rally in the northern city of Hamhung in November. According to eye-witnesses, the victim had been sentenced for desertion from the armed forces and murder. No statistics on the total number of executions were available. Reports during the year suggested that 13 army officers had been executed in June 1991 after they led a protest march in Pyongyang, the capital, to complain about shortages of food and building materials.

Amnesty International submitted a memorandum to the government in May and sought information about the protection of basic rights. The organization asked how many prisoners were being held for alleged "anti-state" crimes and whether they included several named individuals reported to have been arrested in previous years. There was no response by the end of the year.

# KOREA
## (REPUBLIC OF)

**Over 200 political prisoners were detained and charged or convicted for alleged national security offences and about 200 others imprisoned on similar grounds in previous years continued to be held. Some were prisoners of conscience, others were serving sentences imposed after trials which were believed to have been unfair. Dozens of prisoners were reportedly tortured or ill-treated by the police and the Agency for National Security Planning (ANSP). Nine people were executed and about 50 prisoners were believed to be under sentence of death.**

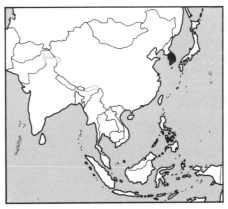

The Agreement on Reconciliation, Non-Aggression and Exchanges and Cooperation Between the South and the North came into force in February (see *Amnesty International Reports 1991* and *1992*). In September agreement was reached on its implementation, although practical arrangements for this had not been worked out and the government refused to revise or repeal the National Security Law (NSL) to reflect the changes in inter-Korean relations. A presidential election held in December was won by Kim Young-Sam of the Democratic Liberal Party.

The Constitutional Court made several rulings strengthening human rights protection. In January it ruled that law enforcement officials should not be present at or record conversations between prisoners and their lawyers. A ruling in February effectively reduced the scope of the Military Secret Protection Law: it said the law's definition of military secrets had been too broad and had possibly restricted freedom of information and expression. In April the court ruled that it was unconstitutional to detain suspects for interrogation under the NSL for up to 50 days before formal charges were brought (suspects under other laws may be held for up to 30 days before indictment). However, the court said that detention for 50 days should be allowed for

**182**

the most serious offences under the law, such as espionage or membership of an "anti-state" organization.

The government introduced to the National Assembly draft legislation to amend the Penal Code, which proposes to abolish the death penalty for 10 offences where death is caused unintentionally.

Hundreds of people were arrested during the year on account of their political activities, some of whom were prisoners of conscience. Over 200 people were arrested under the NSL which prohibits "anti-state" activities and contacts with "anti-state" organizations. Others were arrested for participating in unauthorized or violent demonstrations or for breaking restrictive trade union laws.

Those arrested included nine members of the preparatory committee of the Korea Labour Party, all of whom were prisoners of conscience. Four of them – Chu Dae-hwan, Lee Yong-son, Chun Song and Min Yong-chan – were arrested in January and charged under the NSL for attempting to form an "anti-state" organization "which praises and benefits North Korea". They were brought to trial but released in June and July after receiving suspended prison sentences.

Thirty-nine members of *Sanomaeng*, Socialist Workers' League, were arrested in April and charged under the NSL with belonging to an "anti-state" organization which seeks to establish a socialist government through armed uprising. Many of them were tortured or ill-treated during interrogation. The organization's leader, Baik Tae-ung, denied that *Sanomaeng* espoused an armed uprising. He was given a life sentence in October. At the end of the year some 100 members of *Sanomaeng* arrested since 1990 remained in prison (see *Amnesty International Report 1992*). They were possible prisoners of conscience.

In August and September, 62 people were arrested under the NSL for their alleged involvement in a spy-ring operated by the North Korean authorities. Charges against them included meeting and passing information to alleged North Korean spies, setting up or joining a South Korean chapter of the North Korean Workers' Party and failure to report alleged spies. Their trials had not concluded by the end of the year and it was not clear what evidence existed to support these accusations or whether some might be prisoners of conscience.

Former military conscript Yoon Sok-yang was arrested in September and sentenced the following month to three years' imprisonment for desertion. A possible prisoner of conscience, he had been in hiding since making a "declaration of conscience" in October 1990. In this he had made public his moral objection to the forced recruitment of students, including himself, by the military to inform on fellow student activists and had exposed the illegal surveillance of civilians by the army's intelligence wing, the Defense Security Command (DSC). Following a public outcry at these disclosures, the authorities had announced in 1990 that the DSC would in future refrain from collecting information on civilians. There were some 40 other army conscripts serving sentences on national security charges, some of whom also appeared to be prisoners of conscience.

Several leaders of various political and labour organizations who had been sentenced following anti-government protests in April and May 1991 remained in prison (see *Amnesty International Report 1992*). They included Hyon Ju-ok, acting Chairman of *Chonnohyop*, Korean Trade Union Congress, and Lee Su-ho, Vice-President of *Chunkyojo*, Korean Teachers' and Educational Workers' Union. Both were serving two-and-a-half-year prison terms and were possible prisoners of conscience. Im Su-kyong and Father Moon Kyu-hyun were the only prisoners of conscience released on parole in a presidential amnesty on 24 December. They were serving sentences of five years' imprisonment for an unauthorized visit to North Korea in 1989 (see *Amnesty International Report 1990*).

In July the Supreme Court upheld a three-year sentence passed in December 1991 on Kang Ki-hun, a staff member of *Chonminnyon*, National Democratic Alliance of Korea. He had been arrested in June 1991 and convicted of aiding and abetting the protest suicide of another *Chonminnyon* member, a charge which he denied. The evidence against him consisted exclusively of a contested analysis of the handwriting in the suicide note. Amnesty International believes that Kang Ki-hun was wrongly convicted after an unfair trial and is a prisoner of conscience.

In all, more than 200 prisoners convicted of national security offences in previous years remained in prison. Many had been sentenced to long prison terms for alleged contacts with North Korean agents or espionage. Some were prisoners of conscience; others appeared to have been convicted after unfair trials and claimed that they had been forced to confess under torture (see *Amnesty International Reports 1990* and *1991*). Some of these long-term prisoners were denied early release on parole because they refused to recant their political views.

Torture and ill-treatment of prisoners continued to be reported. In March several members of *Chunkyojo* reported that they had been tortured or ill-treated by police in custody. They had been arrested after a protest meeting on 2 March and taken to Yongdeungpo and Nambu police stations in Seoul. All were later released. Pae Choon-il, Vice President of *Chunkyojo*, stated that he had been beaten and threatened by police officers. Kim Sang-chol alleged that he had been beaten unconscious. Five *Chunkyojo* members filed official complaints with the police.

Some of the 62 prisoners arrested in August and September for involvement in an alleged North Korean spy-ring claimed they were tortured and ill-treated during incommunicado detention by the ANSP. Most prisoners were denied visits by their families for over 22 days, and lawyers had to obtain court orders to force the ANSP to allow them access to some of the prisoners. Many prisoners reported that they had been deprived of sleep for long periods and some said that they had been beaten, threatened, or forced to do repeated strenuous physical exercises. Song Hae-suk was said to have been beaten and threatened in front of her three-year-old son. Chun Hee-sik was held without warrant for 48 hours, during which he says he was beaten under interrogation and deprived of sleep. He filed a complaint about his ill-treatment.

Prosecutions of law enforcement officials for torturing or ill-treating political prisoners were rare: Amnesty International knew of only three cases between 1986 and 1992. In January a Seoul court awarded compensation to a former prisoner of conscience, Kim Keun-tae, for the torture he had suffered in 1985. Four police officers had been sentenced in 1991 to prison terms ranging from two to five years for their involvement in his torture.

Nine prisoners convicted of murder were executed in December. About 50 prisoners were said to be under sentence of death.

Amnesty International appealed for the release of prisoners of conscience and urged the government to bring the NSL and other laws used to hold political prisoners fully into line with international standards relating to basic human rights such as freedom of expression and association. The organization called for a review of the cases of political prisoners convicted after apparently unfair trials, urged that prisoners should be safeguarded against torture and ill-treatment and called for impartial investigations of all torture allegations. Amnesty International also appealed for the commutation of all death sentences and abolition of the death penalty.

In October Amnesty International delegates visited South Korea and discussed human rights concerns with Ministry of Justice officials. In December Amnesty International wrote to all presidential election candidates urging them to commit themselves publicly to the protection and promotion of human rights.

# KUWAIT

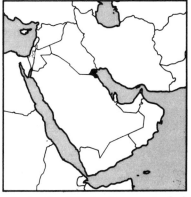

**Hundreds of political prisoners, including possible prisoners of conscience, who had been arrested in 1991 on charges of "collaboration" with Iraqi forces during the occupation of Kuwait, continued to be held throughout the year. At least 150 of them were brought before the State Security Court between April and December. Following unfair trials, 32 received prison sentences and six were sentenced to death, including one *in absentia*. Sixty-nine others continued to serve prison sentences imposed after unfair trials in 1991.**

**184**

There were new reports of torture and ill-treatment. The fate and whereabouts of at least 62 detainees who "disappeared" from custody in 1991 remained unknown.

On 5 October elections were held for the 50-seat National Assembly (parliament), which had been dissolved in 1986 by the Amir, Shaikh Jaber al-Ahmad al-Sabah. At least 30 seats were won by opposition candidates who had run broadly anti-government election campaigns. On 17 October a new ministerial cabinet was announced, which included for the first time six elected members of parliament.

Two journalists were arrested in October and briefly detained on charges of defamation. Muhammad al-Saqr, editor of the daily newspaper *al-Qabas*, and 'Abd al-Latif al-Du'aij, a journalist, were accused of writing and publishing articles critical of government policies and of the then Minister of Information, Badr Jassem al-Ya'qub. Both men were released on bail pending trial. If imprisoned they would be prisoners of conscience.

Hundreds of political prisoners, including possible prisoners of conscience, remained held following their arrest in 1991 on suspicion of "collaboration" with Iraqi forces during the occupation of Kuwait. Among them were Egyptians, Iraqis, Jordanians, Palestinians, Sudanese and members of Kuwait's *"bidun"* community (stateless Arabs), who had been held without trial for over a year.

Between April and December at least 150 of those held were brought before the State Security Court, the majority on charges relating to "collaboration with the enemy". The proceedings at the trials, most of which were held in public, fell short of international standards for fair trial. Some defendants were not permitted to see the evidence against them or to cross-examine prosecution witnesses. Others were convicted on the basis of "confessions" reportedly extracted under torture. Among those convicted were Khaled Salem al-'Asfour, a Kuwaiti who was sentenced to life imprisonment, and Bassem Muhammad al-Jame', a Syrian who was sentenced to four years' imprisonment. In all, six people were sentenced to death, including one *in absentia*; 32 received prison sentences ranging between three years and life; and 20 were acquitted. The trials of the other defendants had not been concluded by December. Defendants were permitted the right of appeal on points of law only. At least 32 cases were referred to the Court of Cassation, which upheld four of the sentences and had not ruled on the others by the end of the year.

Sixty-nine political prisoners, among them 12 women, continued to serve prison terms imposed by the Martial Law Courts in 1991 after unfair trials on charges of "collaboration" (see *Amnesty International Report 1992*). All had been denied the right of appeal and remained in Kuwait Central Prison. Among them were two Iraqi sisters, Sabiha and Intisar Rasan Khallati, each sentenced to 15 years' imprisonment, and Malek Sultan Murdhi, a *"bidun"* sentenced to life imprisonment.

New reports of torture and ill-treatment were received. In June a Sri Lankan national, Colompurage Asoka Pathmakumara, died on the way to al-Farwaniyya Hospital, apparently after being tortured at Jlaib al-Shuyukh police station. He had been arrested in May after being accused of robbery. A death certificate issued by the Ministry of Public Health gave the cause of death as "bruises on the back and foot and fractures in the right thigh, internal haemorrhage and shock". His wife pressed the authorities to clarify the circumstances of his death but without success. In another case, Hisham ben Soltana, an airline steward of dual British and Tunisian nationality, was reportedly tortured in July while held for over two weeks at Messila Civil Defence Centre. After his release he said he had been beaten repeatedly and burned with cigarettes while in custody, and denied access to British consular officials until the moment of his release. In November there were reports that detainees held at Talha deportation centre in al-Farwaniyya, including members of the *"bidun"* community, had been tortured or ill-treated. Several hundred *"bidun"* had by then been held there awaiting deportation for over eight months.

Testimonies from former detainees received during the year, many of them supported by medical evidence, provided further evidence of widespread and routine torture during the 1991 martial law period (see *Amnesty International Report 1992*). Methods of torture commonly alleged were repeated beatings, electric shocks, cigarette burns, suspension by the hands or feet for prolonged periods and mock execution. Among the victims were scores of Iraqi

Kurds who had been accused of "collaboration" with Iraqi occupation forces. One, 'Issam Rustum Mirza, had been held for over two months at al-Salhiyya police station and tortured so badly that he became semi-comatose.

The fate and whereabouts of at least 62 detainees who "disappeared" in custody between late February and June 1991 remained unknown at the end of 1992. It was feared that all or many of them, including Iraqis, Jordanians, Palestinians and others, had died under torture or been extrajudicially executed in 1991. They included Nuri 'Abd al-Karim Layedh Muhammad, an Iraqi driver who "disappeared" in March 1991 with his sons Sabah and 'Abd al-Karim; Haidar 'Enayat Sayyid, an Iraqi Kurd and former Ministry of Education employee who "disappeared" in April 1991; and George Victor Salsa, a Palestinian bank employee who "disappeared" in May 1991. During the year Amnesty International learned that 18 others who had apparently "disappeared" in the same period (see *Amnesty International Report 1992*) had in fact been expelled from Kuwait in 1991.

Between May and December, six death sentences were passed by the State Security Court, one of them *in absentia* (see above). All those sentenced were convicted on charges of "collaboration"; among them were Ghaleb Muhammad al-Turki and Muhsin Shawkat Hussain, both Iraqi nationals. No death sentences had been ratified by the end of the year, but one was upheld by the Court of Cassation in December.

In May an Amnesty International observer attended trial proceedings before the State Security Court and discussed the organization's concerns with government officials and members of the judiciary. During the visit Amnesty International again urged the authorities to set up thorough and impartial investigations into cases of "disappearance", torture and extrajudicial execution relating to the 1991 martial law period. The organization also reiterated its call for a judicial review of all sentences imposed after unfair trials by the Martial Law Courts in 1991.

During the year Amnesty International called for impartial and thorough investigations into allegations of torture and for those responsible to be brought to justice. It also sought information about the legal sta-

tus and whereabouts of people arrested in 1992. In November Amnesty International published *Kuwait: Cases of "disappearance", incommunicado detention, torture and extrajudicial execution*, and publicly urged the government to investigate the 79 cases highlighted in the report.

In January Amnesty International received information it had requested in November 1991 from the Ministry of the Interior about detainees held pending deportation. The same month the Ministry of Justice responded to two communications sent in 1991 about unfair trial proceedings, but failed to address the substance of Amnesty International's concerns. In October the Interior Ministry provided information on the cases of three detainees arrested in July, about whom the organization had sought information. In December the Justice Ministry told Amnesty International that the death of a Sri Lankan detainee in June (see above) was not unlawful and was the result of injuries sustained when he fell from a building while attempting to escape. The Ministry conceded that he had been beaten "lightly" during interrogation to extract a confession, and said that seven policemen had been referred to the Criminal Court on torture charges.

# KYRGYZSTAN

**One execution was reported and at least three people were under sentence of death at the end of the year.**

Kyrgyzstan's independence, declared in August 1991, was recognized internationally following the dissolution of the Soviet Union. Headed by President Askar Akayev, Kyrgyzstan became a member of the Conference on Security and Co-operation in Europe in January and the United Nations in March.

In September the Kyrgyzstan Supreme Soviet reduced the number of peacetime

**186**

offences punishable by death from 18 to six. One execution was reported in 1992 and at least three people were known to be under sentence of death at the end of the year. Figures given to Amnesty International by the Justice Ministry in April indicated that between 1987 and 1990, 31 people had been sentenced to death and all had been executed. Figures for 1991 indicated that 21 people were sentenced to death, of whom at least three had their sentences commuted. Kyrgyzstan was reportedly without facilities for carrying out executions, so people sentenced to death were transported to neighbouring republics of the former Soviet Union for execution by shooting. The Procurator General told Amnesty International in April that current practice was to pass death sentences only for premeditated, aggravated murder.

Amnesty International wrote in March to the Chairman of the State Committee for Defence Affairs recommending that draft legislation on compulsory military service should provide for an alternative civilian service for conscientious objectors. In reply, the State Committee Chairman wrote in April that draft alternative service provisions envisaged "optimum extension of freedom of choice for young people between military and alternative service", and that since 1991 people refusing military service for religious or any other reasons performed "extra-military service" in the national economy. Approval of the draft legislation was still awaited at the end of the year. There were no reports of people imprisoned for refusing conscription on grounds of conscience.

In April Amnesty International representatives visited Kyrgyzstan for the first time. They had meetings with government ministers and senior judiciary officials at which they urged abolition of the death penalty and discussed prospects for constitutional and legislative reform.

# LAOS

**Three prisoners of conscience detained since 1990 received 14-year prison sentences after an unfair trial. Criminal investigations were reportedly begun against two other prisoners of conscience and three other political detainees who had been held without trial for over 17 years. Eight possible prisoners of conscience were sentenced to between four and 10 years' imprisonment and three long-term political prisoners received life sentences after an unfair trial.**

President Kaysone Phomvihan died in November and Nouhak Phoumsavan was appointed as his successor.

Three prisoners of conscience, Thongsouk Saysangkhi, Latsami Khamphoui and Feng Sakchittaphong, were each sentenced to 14 years' imprisonment on 4 November by a tribunal in Sam Neua, in the northern province of Houa Phanh. They had been arrested in October 1990 (see *Amnesty International Reports 1991* and *1992*). They were officially reported to have been charged with "making preparations to stage a rebellion and for conducting propaganda against [the Lao Government], gathering groups of people to create disturbances and carry out slanderous charges against other people, and creating disorder in prison". However, they were believed to have actually been detained for advocating a multiparty political system. Their trial was attended by a few people selected by the authorities and appeared to have been unfair: the prisoners had no access to defence counsel prior to or during the proceedings. They were reportedly sent to Sop Hao Central Prison in Houa Phanh province to serve their sentences and held incommunicado.

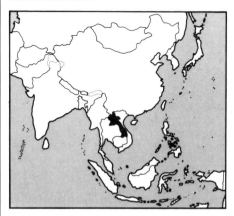

The same tribunal sentenced three other political prisoners to life imprisonment on 3 November. Pangtong Chokbengboun, Bounlu Nammathao and Sing Chanthakoummane were convicted of crimes related to events which took place in 1963 and 1975 while they held minor official positions. Before being brought to trial, they had been detained without charge for 17 years at a "re-education" camp in Sop Pan, also in Houa Phanh province. Their trial appeared to have been unfair: they had no access to a defence lawyer.

Five other prisoners, including two prisoners of conscience, all held without charge or trial since 1975, were apparently under police investigation. Thuck Chokbengboun, a prisoner of conscience and the brother of Pantong Chokbengboun, was questioned about alleged massacres of civilians in the town of Thalet between 1972 and 1975, while he was serving as a middle-ranking government official. He denied involvement in any killings, as did his brother. The other prisoner of conscience, Khamphan Pradith, was released in December.

In March the official Lao National Radio announced that eight "bad elements" had been sentenced to terms of imprisonment by a court in the province of Luang Namtha. They were accused of "setting up an underground unit to collaborate with foreigners to ... undermine and destroy local government, military and social institutions". Mai Thokeo, La Su, and Som La were sentenced to 10, nine and eight years' imprisonment respectively. Amnesty International was concerned that they might be prisoners of conscience. They appeared to have been held in detention without trial since 1988. Thao Puei, Thao Song, and Thao Litho were each sentenced to six years' imprisonment; Thao Gnoi and Thao Khamchan received four-year prison sentences.

In December Khamsone Vongnarath, a Lao student, was forcibly taken back to Laos by Lao officials after visiting the Lao Embassy in Moscow. He had been studying in the Ukraine. He was believed to have been suspected of opposing Lao Government policies and to have been detained in Laos after being returned.

In June the Lao authorities forcibly returned an asylum-seeker, Huang Guisheng, to the People's Republic of China (PRC), where he was at risk of detention as a prisoner of conscience. Huang Guisheng had sought protection against such return from the Vientiane office of the United Nations High Commissioner for Refugees. By the end of the year there was no information about his whereabouts in China.

Amnesty International continued to press for the immediate release of prisoners of conscience and the fair trial or release of other long-term political prisoners. In May Amnesty International wrote to President Kaysone Phomvihan to request information about the exact charges against the eight people sentenced in Luang Namtha and expressed concern about the fairness of their trials. No response had been received by the end of the year.

In December the organization wrote to the new President to urge the release of the prisoners of conscience sentenced in November. Amnesty International pressed the government to make public the exact charges on which other political prisoners had been tried, the evidence against them and to indicate what steps, if any, had been taken to ensure that the trials conformed with international fair trial standards. Also in December Amnesty International appealed to the authorities on behalf of Khamsone Vongnarath after he had been forcibly taken back to Laos: the organization was concerned that he was being held as a prisoner of conscience.

Earlier, in June, Amnesty International made an urgent appeal on behalf of asylum-seeker Huang Guisheng, urging the Lao authorities not to forcibly return him to the PRC. Subsequently, Amnesty International criticized the Lao authorities' action in returning him to China as a breach of their obligation under international law not to forcibly return anyone to a country where he or she risks serious human rights violations. By the end of the year there was no response from the Lao authorities.

# LATVIA

**Two people were executed. Three people were under sentence of death at the end of the year.**

In February the number of offences punishable by death was reduced to seven. Newly released statistics recorded that 16 executions had taken place during the period 1988 to 1991, five more than previously known (see *Amnesty International Report 1992*).

Also in February an amendment to Article 124 of the criminal code legalized consensual homosexual relations between adults.

The Republic of Latvia acceded to the International Covenant on Civil and Political Rights, the International Covenant on Economic, Social and Cultural Rights and the United Nations Convention against Torture and Other Cruel, Inhuman or Degrading Treatment or Punishment in April.

Two death sentences were carried out, one in January and one in May. Both of those executed had been convicted of premeditated murder under aggravating circumstances. Five death sentences were passed, of which two were commuted. At the end of the year the three people under sentence of death were still waiting to hear the outcome of their petitions for clemency.

During the year Amnesty International raised again with the authorities its concern at the length of the alternative service to military service – 24 months compared to 18 months (see *Amnesty International Report 1992*). The Minister of Defence informed Amnesty International that a new bill had been drafted by his ministry which would reflect the principle that military and alternative service should be the same length. There were no reports of people being imprisoned for refusing conscription on grounds of conscience.

In July the Minister of Justice informed Amnesty International, in response to a query from the organization, that people who had been imprisoned for homosexuality had been released from prison immediately after the change in the law.

In October Amnesty International representatives visited Latvia in order to collect information on human rights issues related to the organization's mandate. This was the first research visit by Amnesty International to the country.

During the year Amnesty International called for the commutation of all death sentences of which it learned. The organization also urged the authorities to consider the complete abolition of the death penalty.

# LEBANON

**Over 150 people, including possible prisoners of conscience, were arrested by government forces. Most of them were released by December, as were several detainees arrested in previous years. Allegations of torture and ill-treatment continued to be received. Scores of people were abducted during the year and the fate of thousands who were abducted in previous years remained unknown. There were numerous killings, apparently for political reasons, but there was insufficient information to attribute responsibility for these abuses. One death sentence was commuted.**

Following widespread protests about the economy in May, a new government was formed under Prime Minister Rashid al-Solh. Elections for the National Assembly, held between August and October, were boycotted by Christian political parties and others. The Christian parties, including the Phalange Party, the Lebanese Forces, the National Liberal Party and supporters of General Michel 'Aoun, later formed the Lebanese Opposition Front; which called for the elections to be declared null and void pending the withdrawal of all foreign forces from Lebanon. At the end of October, a new government was formed under Prime Minister Rafiq al-Hariri.

The Lebanese army continued to gain control of areas previously controlled by armed militias and place them under government jurisdiction. However, some groups, such as *Amal* and *Hizbullah*, retained control of parts of south Lebanon. The South Lebanon Army (SLA) retained control over the Jezzine region, and Israeli forces with the SLA maintained control of the so-called "security zone" along the Lebanese/Israeli border. Syrian forces withdrew from Beirut airport in April but remained deployed throughout most of the country.

The government announced on several

occasions releases of detainees under the 1991 general amnesty, which covered both criminal and political offences. The total number of detainees released was not known. In March the government published official statistics on people killed, wounded or "missing" between 1975 and 1990. Of 17,415 persons listed as "missing", 13,968 were Lebanese nationals said to have been abducted by various armed groups. Their fate remained unknown.

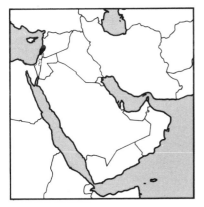

Over 150 people, including possible prisoners of conscience, were arrested by government forces. Among them were three supporters of former President Amin Gemayel, who were arrested in March. Two were soon released uncharged but the third, Ghassan al-Gemayel, was still held apparently without charge or trial at the end of the year.

Between July and November the military authorities arrested over 120 supporters of General Michel 'Aoun, whose forces were driven from East Beirut by Syrian forces and Lebanese army units in October 1990 (see *Amnesty International Reports 1991* and *1992*). The majority were believed to have been held in the Ministry of Defence building in Beirut. Some were allegedly tortured (see below). Most were released uncharged, but at least 22 were charged by the end of the year, of whom 11 were still detained. The charges included distribution of leaflets and acts of sabotage.

In October, 27 members of the Lebanese Forces were arrested by Lebanese army personnel in East Beirut. Seven were later released and the 20 others had their cases referred to the military prosecutor; they were accused of state security offences. Among those arrested were Joseph Maroun, Kivork Anshahalian and Tony Romanos.

It was not possible to confirm the continued detention of over 370 people arrested by the Lebanese army during 1991, the majority of whom were Palestinians arrested in Sidon in July following clashes with Palestine Liberation Organization (PLO) forces in the area (see *Amnesty International Report 1992*).

Reports of the torture and ill-treatment of detainees were received during the year. Three brothers arrested in June in connection with a murder were reportedly tortured in Rumieh Prison in Beirut. One of them, 'Adel Hawila, allegedly suffered spinal injuries as a result and was denied medical treatment. Reports were received of the torture of supporters of General 'Aoun arrested in July, August and November. A former detainee who was held for two days told Amnesty International that he and others were handcuffed and severely beaten during interrogation by military police, and that he witnessed some detainees having their heads immersed in water and being subjected to electric shocks.

In November the death sentence passed on Sam'an Habib al-Ahmar, a Lebanese national accused of committing murder in 1972, was commuted to life imprisonment by the Beirut Criminal Court in accordance with the provisions of the 1991 general amnesty.

The SLA held a number of prisoners throughout the year, some of whom may have been hostages. At any one time there were some 200 prisoners detained without charge or trial in the Khiam detention centre, which is run by the SLA. Most were suspected of belonging to armed groups engaged in conflict with Israel and the SLA. Many were believed to have been tortured during interrogation. Visits by families and the International Committee of the Red Cross (ICRC) were not allowed.

Over 60 members of the Fatah Revolutionary Council, a Palestinian group headed by Abu Nidal, were reportedly detained by *Fatah* (the main faction of the PLO), in a refugee camp near Sidon. Some were later released, while at least two were said to be awaiting trial by a PLO court and may have faced the death penalty.

Heinrich Strubig and Thomas Kemptner, two German nationals released in June after having been held captive since 1989, stated that they had been ill-treated, including by being handcuffed almost

**190**

continuously. A group calling itself the "Organization of Strugglers for Freedom" said it was responsible for their abduction.

During the year scores of people were victims of apparently politically motivated abductions, following which their fate and whereabouts remained unknown. They included four Christians who were abducted in Tibnin in south Lebanon in August. One of the four, Nasri al-Khoury, a lawyer, was released in November; the body of Maroun 'Atmeh was found shortly afterwards and the two others were still missing by the end of the year. Butros Khawand, a member of the Political Bureau of the Phalange Party, was abducted outside his home in East Beirut in mid-September. It was not possible to obtain further information on the fate of thousands of people, including Lebanese, Palestinians, Syrians and other nationals, who had been taken prisoner by armed groups in Lebanon since 1975.

Scores of people were deliberately killed, apparently for political reasons, outside the immediate context of armed conflict. However, there was insufficient information to attribute responsibility for these abuses. Among the victims were Mustafa Juha, a Lebanese journalist killed in January; Anwar Madhi, a senior *Fatah* commander in Lebanon killed in June; and Walid Khaled, official spokesperson of the Fatah Revolutionary Council killed in July.

Amnesty International sought information from the government about the arrest of political suspects and called for investigations into allegations of torture. It also sought information about individuals whose fate and whereabouts after they were detained or abducted in previous years remained unknown. In October the Minister of the Interior informed Amnesty International that the authorities had found no evidence to support the torture allegations of three brothers arrested in June (see above). In September the organization appealed to President Hrawi to ensure that Palestinians held by the PLO in Lebanon received a fair trial by an independent tribunal established by law and to prevent any executions. Amnesty International also appealed to PLO leader Yasser 'Arafat to commute any death sentences.

In May, Amnesty International published a report, *Israel/South Lebanon: The Khiam detainees; torture and ill-treatment* (see **Israel and the Occupied Territories** entry), calling on the SLA to release any

detainees being held as hostages, to end all forms of torture and ill-treatment and to allow detainees medical attention and visits by the ICRC and families . The SLA denied that torture took place and said that visits by the ICRC would be allowed only if Israeli and SLA personnel missing in Lebanon were granted such visits.

# LESOTHO

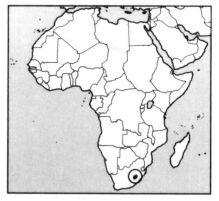

**Twenty-three political prisoners held after unfair trials in 1986 were released. The government stated publicly that it would investigate allegations of torture and extrajudicial executions, but had not apparently done so by the end of the year.**

Lesotho became a party to the International Covenant on Civil and Political Rights in September and the African Charter on Human and Peoples' Rights in February.

The military government had been due to hand over power to an elected civilian administration during 1992. The new Constitution was to include a Bill of Rights enforceable by the courts. However, elections scheduled for November were postponed until January 1993. In July 1992, after protracted negotiations with the government, King Moshoeshoe II, who had been ousted in 1990 and replaced by his son, returned to the country but was not allowed to reclaim his throne.

It was established that riots in May 1991 were not, as reported in the *Amnesty International Report 1992*, provoked by the actions of Asian shopkeepers. The shopkeepers who beat to death an African woman suspected of theft were themselves Africans of local origin.

During the course of the year 23 people

imprisoned at the time of the military coup in 1986 were released from custody, the last of them in October, just before the High Court was due to hear an application challenging the legality of their imprisonment (see *Amnesty International Report 1992*). The 23 were members of the army loyal to the ousted government of Chief Leabua Jonathan. They had been tried in 1986 by a military tribunal, some of whose members had taken part in a gun battle against the accused, which sentenced them to long terms of imprisonment. The 23 had been denied the right to lawyers of their choice or defence witnesses and had had no right of appeal to an independent tribunal.

Amnesty International published a report in June, *Lesotho: Torture, political killings and abuses against trade unionists*, which documented human rights violations since 1986 and urged the introduction of a number of safeguards for human rights. The government stated publicly that it would investigate the cases mentioned in the report, but had not initiated an independent and impartial investigation by the end of the year.

# LIBERIA

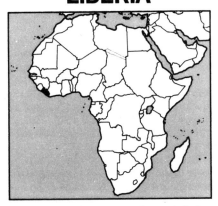

**Wide-ranging human rights violations and abuses were committed by various forces that controlled different parts of the country, including detention without charge or trial, torture and ill-treatment, deliberate and arbitrary killings and executions. It was extremely difficult to monitor the situation owing to restricted access in some areas.**

Armed conflict continued throughout 1992, intensifying in the second half of the year. At the end of 1992, the capital, Monrovia, remained in the hands of the Interim Government of National Unity (IGNU), led by Dr Amos Sawyer, and peace-keeping troops of the Economic Community of West African States (ECOWAS). Most of the rest of Liberia was controlled by the National Patriotic Reconstruction Assembly Government (NPRAG), a rival administration set up in 1990 by the rebel force, the National Patriotic Front of Liberia (NPFL), headed by Charles Taylor.

In April the Interim Government and NPRAG reached a peace agreement brokered in Geneva by ECOWAS heads of state. However, the NPRAG continued to refuse to disarm NPFL troops. In May troops of the ECOWAS Monitoring Group (ECOMOG) were deployed in NPFL-held territory but were withdrawn in September after they were briefly taken hostage by NPFL forces. In July and August the NPRAG lost control of areas between Sierra Leone and Monrovia to the United Liberation Movement for Democracy in Liberia (ULIMO), an armed group mostly comprising supporters of former President Samuel Doe, who was killed in 1990 (see *Amnesty International Report 1991*). In October NPFL forces attacked Monrovia, targeting ECOMOG troops and the Armed Forces of Liberia (AFL), the national army which had remained encamped in the capital since 1990. The attackers were joined by most members of the Independent National Patriotic Front of Liberia (INPFL), an armed group which had split from the NPFL in 1990 and subsequently supported the Interim Government. The INPFL leader, Prince Johnson, deserted by his supporters, sought refuge with ECOMOG forces. In December the United Nations (UN) Secretary-General, at the request of the UN Security Council, sent a Special Representative to Liberia. The UN also imposed an arms embargo on the country, exempting only the ECOMOG forces.

After the fighting resumed in August, thousands of displaced people from areas previously controlled by the NPRAG fled to Monrovia and other parts of the country. Aid agencies were forced to withdraw from NPRAG-held territory and nearly 100,000 refugees who had fled fighting in Sierra Leone were left in northern Lofa County without relief assistance.

While still formally allied to the Interim Government, the INPFL ill-treated and held two journalists – Isaac Bantu and Dan

**192**

Brown – for three days in harsh conditions in early January. The journalists had expressed concern about the detention of five boys at an INPFL camp near Monrovia. The five, all from an orphanage at the camp, included one 14-year-old. They were said to have confessed to spying for the AFL. However, they were later reported to have been released. The orphanage, which had apparently been sited within the camp to deter attack on the INPFL by ECOMOG forces, was evacuated in October by UN aid workers after an NPFL attack on the camp. In January the INPFL had executed at least three of their own soldiers at the camp for being in possession of new currency issued by the Interim Government.

In late October civilians in Monrovia were subjected to ill-treatment, harassment and looting by AFL and ULIMO troops. At least six people were reported to have been summarily executed by these forces on suspicion of being NPFL fighters. On 2 November ECOMOG forces threatened to shoot on sight any members of these forces who broke a night curfew in Monrovia. On 21 November an AFL soldier was publicly executed in the capital by the AFL the day after he was convicted of murder and robbery by an AFL court-martial.

In NPRAG-controlled areas, people suspected of opposing the NPFL were detained and in some cases tortured or ill-treated. Detailed information was scarce: most of that available concerned foreign nationals although Liberians were believed to be the majority of those held. Father Seraphino Dalpont, an Italian priest, was arrested in April for possessing Interim Government currency and a Roman Catholic newsletter, alleged to be seditious literature. He was released after paying a large fine, but re-arrested allegedly on suspicion of espionage. He was held in a police station in Gbarnga, where the NPRAG had its headquarters, until mid-May, when he was released and deported to Côte d'Ivoire. In October two groups of foreign nationals – one mostly of aid workers, the other of missionaries – were detained for several days accused of spying for the ECOMOG forces. They were released uncharged.

NPFL troops tortured and ill-treated civilians while looting their property and forcing them to work without pay. In April the NPFL announced that it was investigating such allegations, but the results of any investigation were not known. In Sept-

ember nearly 600 ECOMOG soldiers were taken prisoner by NPFL forces who severely beat some of them. Later that month Charles Taylor acknowledged that NPFL troops were "perpetrating atrocities" and said he would take "drastic military action" against those responsible for assaulting the ECOMOG troops. However, it was not clear what action, if any, was taken.

NPFL forces summarily killed scores, possibly hundreds, of people. In April the NPRAG authorities charged four senior NPFL officers with the murder of seven suspected ULIMO supporters in Buchanan. Three were later released and it was not known if the other was tried. In May NPFL troops seized six Senegalese members of the ECOMOG forces in Vahun, near the Sierra Leone border. They took them to Gbarnga and reportedly tortured and executed them. In July, when the NPFL was being pushed back by ULIMO forces, NPFL troops reportedly killed and robbed civilians indiscriminately. On 3 July, for example, NPFL fighters allegedly killed nine forestry workers at Jenimana. In late August, when ULIMO seized NPFL-controlled territory, both NPFL and ULIMO forces were alleged to have killed civilians suspected of supporting the other side in the fighting.

In October, during an attack on Monrovia, NPFL forces were reported to have deliberately killed civilians and taken others prisoner. NPFL troops reportedly abducted 50 people and killed others when they took control of Louisiana township near the capital. Two Roman Catholic nuns, both United States nationals, a Liberian man employed by the nuns' convent and two ECOMOG soldiers were killed in the nuns' car near Barnersville, a suburb of Monrovia, on 20 October, apparently by the NPFL. On 23 October six NPFL soldiers entered the nuns' convent in the suburb of Gardnersville, killed three other American nuns and a Lebanese businessman, and abducted the businessman's Liberian wife, two other Liberian women with their four children, and four Liberian novices. Those abducted were apparently later released. NPRAG officials denied that NPFL forces were responsible. Up to 300 orphans and a former government official were apparently taken away by NPFL forces on about 28 October from an orphanage near Gardnersville; orphans who escaped reportedly said that the NPFL was forcing the boys to fight for them. In late October the NPFL allegedly killed more than 25 people in Maryland County, apparently because they were suspected of supporting ULIMO.

The NPFL also executed people after summary trials before military courts. In February an NPFL commander was executed after being convicted by a military court of murdering an INPFL fighter. In August several dissident NPFL soldiers were reportedly executed by the NPFL for their involvement in an attempted assassination of Charles Taylor in which a bodyguard was killed.

In January Amnesty International appealed to the Interim Government to prevent abuses by INPFL forces. In November Amnesty International published a report, *Liberia: Risk of human rights violations as conflict increases*, which summarized recent abuses by various parties to the conflict. It called on all parties to ensure that their troops respected human rights, were accountable for their actions and observed basic international humanitarian standards. It also appealed to governments around the world to urge that all sides make every effort to prevent further human rights violations.

# LIBYA

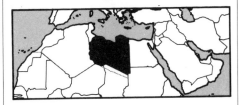

Five prisoners of conscience remained imprisoned throughout 1992. About 550 suspected government opponents, including possible prisoners of conscience, continued to be detained apparently without charge or trial. Seventeen political prisoners continued serving sentences imposed after unfair trials, and one remained in prison despite having been tried and acquitted. The fate and whereabouts of 16 Malian nationals, who had allegedly "disappeared" in custody in 1991, remained unclear. Six judicial executions were carried out – the first to be officially announced since 1987. Fourteen Tunisian nationals were forcibly repatriated despite fears that they would be at risk of imprisonment and torture.

In October the Basic People's Congresses approved a new administrative structure for the country, dividing it into 1,500 self-governing units and granting locally elected "Popular Committees" extensive administrative, economic and legal powers.

Five prisoners of conscience, all suspected members of the prohibited Islamic Liberation Party, continued to serve life sentences in Abu Salim Prison in Tripoli (see *Amnesty International Reports 1991* and *1992*). Among them was 'Ali Muhammad al-Qajiji, a student arrested in Tripoli in April 1973.

New information was received about at least 549 suspected government opponents, including possible prisoners of conscience, who had been arrested in previous years and were still held apparently without charge or trial at the end of 1992. Some 469 of them had been arrested between December 1989 and May 1991 during a crackdown on suspected members or sympathizers of banned Islamic groups (see *Amnesty International Report 1992*). The arrests took place in various towns and cities, particularly in Ajdabiya, Benghazi, Derna and Tripoli, and were mainly carried out by the security forces and members of the Revolutionary Committees (official bodies set up to enforce government policies). All had been held incommunicado since their arrest and their places of detention remained unknown. Among them were Ibrahim Saleh Marseet, an employee of the Agricultural Bank in Tripoli, who was arrested in January 1989, and Wanis al-Sharef al-Warfali, a legal consultant at the Secretariat of the People's Committee for Economy and Planning, who was arrested in April 1990 in Benghazi.

At least 80 other suspected government opponents arrested between 1974 and 1986 also remained in detention apparently without charge or trial. They had not benefited from the March 1988 amnesty in which 400 political prisoners, including prisoners of conscience, were released (see *Amnesty International Report 1989*). Most were arrested following an armed clash in May 1984 at Bab al-'Aziziya between the security forces and members of the opposition National Front for the Salvation of Libya (NFSL). They included 'Abdul-Mun'im Ibhiri al-Awjali, a professor of Economics at Gar-Yunis University in Benghazi, and Khamis al-Fayturi al-Jurnazi,

**194**

an employee of the Tripoli Postal Service. Both were believed to be held in Abu Salim Prison in Tripoli.

Seventeen government opponents sentenced after unfair trials in 1974 and 1987 remained in Abu Salim Prison serving life sentences. They had been convicted on charges including plotting to overthrow the government and membership of banned opposition groups (see *Amnesty International Reports 1991* and *1992*).

'Abdullah Menina, a political prisoner held since 1984 despite having been tried and acquitted in 1985, remained in detention, possibly in Abu Salim Prison (see previous *Amnesty International Reports*).

The fate and whereabouts of 16 Malian nationals who allegedly "disappeared" in custody in 1991 (see *Amnesty International Report 1992*) remained unclear. They were among hundreds of Nigerian and Malian workers who were held in custody and ill-treated before being deported. The cases of two NFSL leaders who "disappeared" after allegedly being handed over to the Libyan authorities by the Egyptian security forces in 1990 also remained unresolved (see *Amnesty International Report 1992*).

In November, six men were executed by hanging after being convicted of criminal offences including murder and rape. These were the first officially announced executions since 1987.

Fourteen Tunisian nationals were forcibly repatriated by the Libyan authorities during the year. All were suspected members of *al-Nadha*, a Tunisian opposition group banned in Tunisia. They were reportedly arrested on their arrival in Tunis and held in incommunicado detention for several months. At least two of them were allegedly tortured (see **Tunisia** entry).

During the year Amnesty International continued to appeal for the immediate and unconditional release of all prisoners of conscience. It expressed concern about the continued imprisonment of hundreds of other political prisoners without trial or after unfair trials. In October Amnesty International published a report, *Libya: further information on political detention*, which contained new information about political detainees received during the year.

Amnesty International sought clarification from the government about the fate and whereabouts of the two Libyans who

allegedly "disappeared" in 1990 and 1991, but without response. The organization also expressed regret at the executions of six people in November and urged Libyan leader Colonel Mu'ammar Gaddafi to commute any other pending death sentences. During the year Amnesty International urged the authorities not to forcibly repatriate suspected members of *al-Nahda* to Tunisia. In March the organization reiterated its request to Libya's Permanent Representative to the United Nations in Geneva to visit Libya to discuss its concerns with the relevant authorities.

# LITHUANIA

**One person was executed.**

In a referendum held in October a new constitution was approved. In November the former leader of the Lithuanian Communist Party, Algirdas Brazauskas, replaced Vytautas Landsbergis as President and Head of State. Bronislovas Lubys was chosen as Prime Minister in December.

In August Aleksandras Novadkis was executed by shooting. His petition for clemency had been rejected three months earlier. Aleksandras Novadkis had been sentenced to death for the murder of a young girl. He was the first person to have been executed in Lithuania since restoration of independence. One other death sentence passed during the year was commuted.

In July Amnesty International asked the Ministry of Justice how many people were currently detained under Article 122 of the criminal code which prohibits homosexual acts between males. The organization said that it considered people imprisoned solely because of consensual homosexual acts in private with other adults to be prisoners of conscience. In September the Ministry of Justice replied that since March 1990 two people had been convicted under the second part of Article 122 which concerns homosexual acts involving minors, violence or the threat of violence, or exploiting the dependent situation or helplessness of the victim. In a third case a minor had been sentenced to two and a half years' imprisonment, reduced from three and a half years after appeal, for engaging in consensual homosexual intercourse with another minor and had been released on probation before completion of sentence. However, according to figures provided by the Ministry of the Interior to the Lithuanian AIDS Prevention Centre in September, a total of 17 people had been convicted under Article 122 since the beginning of 1990, all under part two. At least one of these convictions dated from 1991. In December Amnesty International asked the Ministry of Justice for clarification of these figures.

In August Amnesty International wrote to the Minister of National Defence raising again its concern about the punitive length of the alternative service to military service – 24 months compared to 12 months (see *Amnesty International Report 1992*). No reply had been received by the end of the year. There were no reports of people being imprisoned for refusing to perform military service on grounds of conscience.

In October Amnesty International representatives visited Lithuania to collect information on human rights issues related to the organization's mandate. This was the first research visit by Amnesty International to the country.

Amnesty International appealed to the authorities for commutation of the death sentence passed on Aleksandras Novadkis and urged the complete abolition of the death penalty.

# LUXEMBOURG

**A number of prisoners were kept in prolonged isolation.**

In February Luxembourg ratified the Second Optional Protocol to the International Covenant on Civil and Political Rights, aiming at the abolition of the death penalty.

In July one prisoner was ordered to be held in isolation in Schrassig prison for 12 months. During the year a number of other prisoners spent between one and five months in isolation. Solitary confinement is imposed for disciplinary reasons or when prisoners are classed as dangerous. Prisoners placed in isolation spend 23 hours a day in their cells and exercise alone for one hour a day. During the year Amnesty International learned that until 1990 a number of prisoners had been held in isolation for periods of several years. One such prisoner, Jean-Marc Mahy, was held in isolation from April 1987 until March 1990. Amnesty International is concerned that prolonged isolation may have serious effects on the physical and mental health of prisoners and may constitute cruel, inhuman or degrading treatment or punishment.

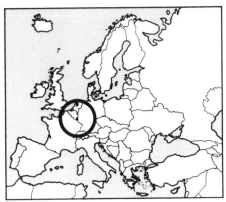

Amnesty International repeatedly expressed its concern about the use of prolonged isolation by the Schrassig prison authorities to the Minister of Justice. In particular, the organization asked whether it was still possible for prisoners to be placed in solitary confinement for several years.

In his replies the Minister of Justice rejected the term "prolonged isolation". He stated that Luxembourg legislation provided for solitary confinement in order to cut the prisoner off from the rest of the prison population for several months. The Minister informed Amnesty International that the prisoner placed in solitary confinement in July had repeatedly attacked prison guards and that his punishment would be suspended at the end of November, provided there had been no repetition of his previous behaviour. The Minister stated that it was not the current policy of those

**196**

responsible for punishing prisoners to impose periods of solitary confinement lasting several years. Amnesty International was still concerned, however, that the imposition of such long periods of isolation remained a possibility in Luxembourg, and that this punishment might be applied again in the future.

In October Amnesty International published a document entitled *Luxembourg: Prolonged isolation of detainees in Schrassig prison.*

# MACAO

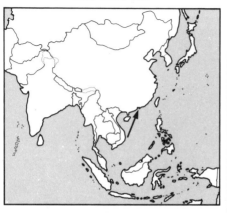

The draft of the Basic Law due to come into force when the territory reverts to administration by the People's Republic of China (PRC) in 1999 was revised, but continued to lack adequate human rights safeguards. The Drafting Committee rejected a proposal to amend the Basic Law so as to prohibit the future reintroduction of the death penalty.

The Basic Law of the Macao Special Administrative Region will come into force in 1999, when Portuguese administration of the territory ends. The first draft of the Basic Law was published in 1991 by the Basic Law Drafting Committee (BLDC), a body comprising representatives from Macao and the PRC. A revised draft was published in March 1992. It fails to guarantee that all human rights safeguards currently in force in Macao will be maintained, notably abolition of the death penalty. Publishing the revised draft, a spokesperson for the Committee said that the BLDC was not prepared to rule out the possible future reintroduction of the death penalty. The death penalty was last used in

Macao in the 19th century and is banned under the Portuguese Constitution.

The revised draft also lacks safeguards against torture and ill-treatment, guarantees of fair trial, guarantees to protect the exercise of all fundamental human rights, and safeguards against the curtailment of basic rights under a state of emergency.

Amnesty International had expressed concern about the draft Basic Law, and called for guarantees against the future reintroduction of the death penalty, in a report published in November 1991, *Macao: Strengthening Human Rights Safeguards – Memorandum from Amnesty International to the Basic Law Drafting Committee.* In August the organization renewed its call on the Portuguese Government to formally recognize that the International Covenant on Civil and Political Rights (ICCPR) and other international human rights treaties ratified by Portugal apply to Macao. It also urged the Chinese Government to ensure that these basic standards for human rights protection would continue to apply in Macao after 1999.

In September Portugal declared that the ICCPR fully applies in Macao due to its ratification by Portugal. While welcoming this decision, Amnesty International called on the BLDC to reconsider its refusal to include provisions to abolish the death penalty in the Basic Law.

# MADAGASCAR

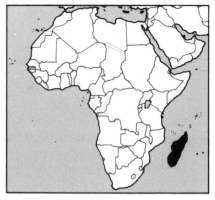

Government forces killed at least five people in a demonstration; it appeared they might have been extrajudicially executed.

There was conflict throughout the year between supporters of President Didier Ratsiraka, known as federalists, and his principal rival in the presidential elections, Albert Zafy. Several people were killed in the violence. President Ratsiraka, who came to power in 1975, had been deprived of all but titular powers in 1991 (see *Amnesty International Report 1992*), although he retained control of the Presidential Guard. Albert Zafy, leader of the political alliance *Hery Velona*, Active Forces Committee, headed the High State Authority, part of the interim government established in November 1991 to introduce a multi-party political system. He escaped an assassination attempt on 30 March.

A new Constitution, drafted in March by a National Forum which included opposition parties and the churches, was approved by referendum in August. The federalists wanted the referendum to offer the option of a federal as well as a unitary constitution and prevented voting in some provincial towns. In August and October they seized control of radio stations and administrative buildings in provincial capitals, declared the provinces of Antsiranana, Toamasina and Toliary to be "federal states", and cut off oil supplies and railway links from the port of Toamasina to the capital, Antananarivo. They also took captive members of *Hery Velona*.

The first round of presidential elections in November was won by Albert Zafy, with a further round and legislative elections planned for 1993.

In March the government became a party to the African Charter on Human and Peoples' Rights.

At least 14 people were detained after an armed group briefly seized control of the national radio station in Antananarivo in July and announced the dissolution of the government. They were reportedly members of an opposition group, the National Unity Rally, which had taken similar action in 1990 (see *Amnesty International Report 1991*). The detainees were charged in September with attempting to overthrow the government, taking hostages and disturbing the peace, and were released to await trial.

On 31 March, eight people were killed and 31 wounded when hundreds of federalists tried to force their way into the National Forum's debate on the new constitution. At least five unarmed federalist demonstrators, including Gaston Lahy, a former government minister, were shot dead by soldiers.

On 8 October troops shot dead eight people, including federalist leader Mohamed Koubessy and journalist Thérèse Bandrou, in clashes with armed federalists trying to close the airport at Antsiranana. Mohamed Koubessy had previously been arrested after political violence in June in which six people had died, but had escaped from custody with the assistance of some soldiers.

In August and October supporters of President Ratsiraka took captive several *Hery Velona* members in Antsiranana and reportedly beat some of them. Although some were released within days, others were apparently held for several weeks; they included Dr Jeanson Rakotoarinivo, a medical doctor, and Patricia Bardoux, a French sculptor. Also in August, federalists were reported to have killed a director of a sugar company in Ambilobe, northern Madagascar, who had been nominated to the post by *Hery Velona*.

Amnesty International called for an inquiry into the killings of the federalists in March and October and urged that, if they were found to be extrajudicial executions, those responsible should be brought to justice. No inquiries were opened into these killings, and there was still no indication that any inquiry had taken place into the extrajudicial execution of dozens of demonstrators by the Presidential Guard in August 1991 (see *Amnesty International Report 1992*).

# MALAWI

**Hundreds of people, including many prisoners of conscience, were held for weeks without charge, as the authorities attempted to suppress emerging political opposition. Some were tortured and most were held in deliberately harsh prison conditions. One long-term prisoner of conscience died in prison. Nearly 70 long-term political detainees were released during the year, including one man who had been held for 27 years. However, at least one long-term prisoner of conscience remained held in poor conditions. At least 45 people were believed to be under sentence of death and 36 death sentences were commuted to life imprisonment. It was not known if any executions were carried out.**

**198**

Unprecedented opposition to the one-party state headed by Life-President Dr H. Kamuzu Banda emerged during the year. In March the country's Roman Catholic bishops issued a pastoral letter in which they criticized aspects of the government's human rights record, corruption and the lack of popular participation in political life. The bishops were interrogated by the Inspector General of Police and held briefly under house arrest, and one was expelled from the country. The pastoral letter was declared seditious, making possession of it a criminal offence. A meeting of senior officials of the ruling Malawi Congress Party (MCP) openly discussed whether the bishops should be killed. After international appeals, the government gave public guarantees of the bishops' safety, although members of the paramilitary Malawi Young Pioneers harassed Roman Catholics and burned down the press where the pastoral letter had been printed. In the following months members of other denominations, notably the Church of Central Africa (Presbyterian), endorsed the position of the Roman Catholic bishops and were themselves harassed.

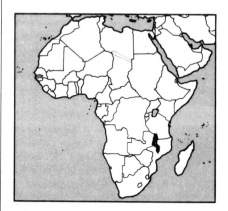

The pastoral letter sparked off widespread demonstrations in favour of a multiparty political system. These included protests at the University of Malawi, which resulted in the arrest of student leaders on public order charges. In May industrial and plantation workers started the first wave of strikes since the 1960s. More than 40 people were shot dead by police during riots in Blantyre, the main industrial centre.

In July President Banda announced reforms to the Preservation of Public Security Regulations, under which many government critics had been detained in the past,

introducing for the first time a Detainees' Review Tribunal chaired by a High Court judge to adjudicate the reasons for detention. However, in the second half of the year the authorities appeared to stop using these regulations, instead holding suspected opponents unlawfully for several weeks before releasing them without charge or charging them with sedition. The charge of sedition in Malawian law penalizes anyone found to have made "statements likely to undermine public confidence in the Government". Anyone imprisoned solely on such grounds would appear to be a prisoner of conscience.

Malawi's main aid donors suspended all non-humanitarian assistance in May for six months. Its resumption was to depend on significant improvements in respect for human rights. In August the International Committee of the Red Cross (ICRC) was allowed to begin visits to Malawian prisons. However, the suspension of aid continued as donors considered that there had not been sufficient progress on human rights.

On 31 December President Banda announced that there would be a referendum in March 1993 on whether to retain the one-party state or reintroduce a multi-party system.

Many hundreds of people, most of whom appeared to be prisoners of conscience, were arrested in the months after the bishops' pastoral letter was published. Many of them were office workers suspected of having duplicated and distributed the pastoral letter or other documents advocating a multi-party system. For example, in May more than 20 employees of the National Bank of Malawi were arrested after an industrial dispute because they were suspected of having leaflets advocating multi-party democracy. All the staff of the computer section at the Electricity Supply Commission of Malawi were arrested at about the same time, apparently on suspicion of having used office equipment to circulate opposition literature. Those arrested were all released after about three months, some without charge and some to face trial on charges of sedition, but none had been tried by the end of the year.

In April Chakufwa Chihana, an official with an international trade union body, was arrested at the airport in Lilongwe, the capital. He was held for three months without charge. The authorities failed to comply with repeated High Court orders for him to appear in court and for the legal basis for his detention to be clarified. In July he was charged with sedition in connection with speeches he had made calling for a multi-party political system. He was released on bail but rearrested two days later. He was later charged on further counts of sedition relating to comments he had made to the press after his release. He was released on bail for a second time in September. At his trial before the High Court, which began in November, he was sentenced to two years' imprisonment after being convicted of sedition. His appeal had not been heard by the end of 1992. Chakufwa Chihana had been a prisoner of conscience for five years during the 1970s when he was detained without charge for non-violent opposition to the government.

Church members were also vulnerable to arrest. There were dozens of reported arrests during the year of members of the Watchtower Bible and Tract Society – the Jehovah's Witnesses – which is illegal in Malawi and has been subject to persecution for many years. Jehovah's Witnesses refuse to join the ruling MCP: membership of the party is virtually compulsory. It appeared that many Jehovah's Witnesses were released before the August visit of the ICRC. The Reverend Aaron Longwe, minister of the Mzuzu Presbyterian congregation, was arrested in April after preaching a sermon which was deemed critical of the government. He was released the following day but rearrested shortly afterwards with an elder of the congregation, Steven Chenda Mkandawire. The next day two other elders of the congregation, Gift Kaunda and Jairos Beza, were also arrested. The Reverend Longwe and Steven Mkandawire were released in May but the other two were held without charge until July. The Reverend Longwe was briefly detained again at the end of August with other Presbyterian and Roman Catholic church members.

Krishna Achutan, the son-in-law of Aleke Banda, a prisoner of conscience released in July (see below), was arrested in May, the day after he had given an interview to a British radio station drawing attention to his father-in-law's poor health in prison. After being held for two months without charge and in defiance of High Court orders that he be produced, Krishna Achutan was released in July and charged

with publishing information "likely to be prejudicial to public security" and with making a broadcast "harmful to the interests or to the good name of Malawi". If convicted he faced a maximum penalty of life imprisonment. He had not been tried by the end of the year.

In December over 260 people were arrested in Blantyre at a peaceful demonstration against the imprisonment of Chakufwa Chihana. All were released within a few days but about 130 of them were charged with "unlawful assembly" or other offences and were due to be tried in early 1993.

There were frequent reports that many of those arrested for possession of multi-party leaflets were tortured by police. There were persistent allegations of prisoners being subjected to severe beatings. Women prisoners alleged that police interrogators used pliers to inflict sexual abuse on them. One woman was alleged to have been stripped naked, beaten and poked with an electric cattle prod. Two officials of the Blantyre Polytechnic student union, arrested in March after a demonstration in support of the Roman Catholic bishops, were alleged to have been tortured by having their genitals squeezed. There were repeated accounts of detainees being forced to clear human excrement out of cells with their bare hands.

Crowded and insanitary prison conditions appear to have been used as a form of deliberate ill-treatment. Many of those arrested for suspected involvement in the multi-party movement were taken to Chichiri Prison in Blantyre or Maula Prison in Lilongwe, which were already the most overcrowded in the country. Previously prisoners in Chichiri spent nights sitting back-to-back because there was insufficient room for them to lie down. After the new wave of arrests, prisoners were reportedly forced to stand through the night as there was not enough space for them to sit. One cell in Chichiri Prison, measuring about five metres by four metres, was reported to contain 285 prisoners. Former prisoners estimated that on average one prisoner in this cell died every two nights. When a prisoner died he was immediately replaced by another, suggesting that overcrowding was being used as a deliberate form of ill-treatment.

A total of about 70 long-term political detainees, including prisoners of conscience, were released in January, June and July. Among the prisoners of conscience were Aleke Banda, who had been held without charge since 1980 for criticizing President Banda's financial management of a parastatal company; Machipisa Munthali, detained for 27 years for political opposition; Danny (Goodluck) Mhango, whose brother was an opposition journalist murdered in an unexplained firebomb attack in Zambia in 1989; and Laurenti Phiri, who had been imprisoned because he had bought tobacco from tenant farmers on land owned by President Banda (see *Amnesty International Report 1992*).

However, other long-term prisoners of conscience remained in custody, notably Orton Chirwa and his wife, Vera Chirwa, who were reportedly abducted from Zambia in 1981 and then convicted of treason after an unfair trial in a "traditional court" (see previous *Amnesty International Reports*). They were sentenced to death but in 1984 President Banda commuted their sentences to life-imprisonment after international appeals. In September 1992 they received a visit from a delegation of British lawyers, their first outside visit for many years. It was also the first time since 1984 that they had been permitted to see each other. Both were in poor health, and Orton Chirwa died in October. Vera Chirwa was not allowed to attend his funeral and the authorities failed to comply with calls for an inquest into his death.

The authorities continued to fail to investigate the frequent instances of deaths in custody (see *Amnesty International Report 1992*). In April prisoner of conscience Frackson Zgambo died in custody. He had been held without charge since 1989. There were unsubstantiated reports that he had died as a result of poisoning or other ill-treatment. However, despite the requirements of the Inquests Act, there was no inquest or other impartial investigation into his death.

More than 40 protesters were shot dead in May, many of them allegedly by the "Red Army" – a newly organized paramilitary force incorporating members of the red-shirted Malawi Young Pioneers, who have powers of arrest. The shootings took place during violent protests by striking workers in Blantyre and Lilongwe – the first public demonstrations against the government since independence in 1964. The government did not respond to calls for an independent inquiry into the killings.

At least 45 prisoners were believed to be under sentence of death at Mikuyu and Zomba Prisons in mid-1992. It was not known if any executions were carried out during the year. Earlier in the year 36 prisoners under sentence of death were reported to have had their sentences commuted to life imprisonment by the National Traditional Court of Appeal. It was not known what offences these prisoners had been convicted of.

Amnesty International published two reports on its concerns: in March, *Malawi: Prison conditions, cruel punishment and detention without trial*; and in September, *Malawi: March to July 1992, mass arrests of suspected government opponents*. Amnesty International welcomed the release of prisoners of conscience and the decision to allow the ICRC access to political detainees. The organization called for the release of prisoners of conscience held because of their non-violent support for the multiparty movement and for the withdrawal of all criminal charges against them. Amnesty International publicized the death threats by senior ruling party officials against the Roman Catholic bishops and called for the government to guarantee their safety. It asked the government to establish an independent commission of inquiry into the deaths of more than 40 protesters in May. Representatives of Amnesty International held meetings with Malawian diplomats abroad and the organization asked in April and September to send a delegation to observe court proceedings involving Chakufwa Chihana. No formal reply was received from Lilongwe, but a Malawian diplomat indicated that Amnesty International would not be welcome in the country.

# MALAYSIA

**Over 80 political activists, including seven prisoners of conscience, continued to be detained without charge or trial under the Internal Security Act (ISA). Caning was imposed as a punishment for criminal offences. At least 28 people were sentenced to death. Some 200 Acehnese asylum-seekers were in danger of being forcibly returned to Indonesia where they**

**risked possible torture and extrajudicial execution.**

In September the government of Sabah state reimposed a rule requiring Malaysians from the rest of the country to carry passports when visiting Sabah. The measure was promptly opposed by the federal government which threatened to abolish it. This added to the continuing tension between the two governments.

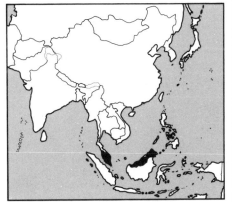

Seven prisoners of conscience remained in detention without charge or trial on suspicion of advocating the secession of Sabah state from Malaysia. All were said to be supporters of the main ruling party of Sabah, the *Parti Bersatu Sabah*, United Sabah Party. They were held under the ISA, which permits detention without charge or trial for up to two years, renewable indefinitely. The detention orders of four of the detainees who had been held since 1990 – Abdul Rahman Ahmad, Benedict Topin, Wencelous Damit Undikai and Albinus Yudah – were renewed during the year. The other three – Vincent Chung, Ariffin Haji Hamid and Jeffrey Kitingan – continued to be held under their initial detention orders issued in 1991.

In December the Home Ministry Parliamentary Secretary told parliament that a total of 126 people were in detention under the ISA. Their identities were not disclosed. Among them 74 were communists who had voluntarily renounced their involvement in armed opposition and surrendered to the authorities in December 1989.

Caning remained a supplementary punishment to imprisonment for dozens of crimes including drugs offences, rape and attempted rape, kidnapping, firearms offences, attempted murder, causing grievous injury, child abuse, robbery and theft.

Amnesty International believes that caning constitutes a cruel, inhuman or degrading punishment prohibited by international law. Shaari Abdullah, a fisherman, was sentenced in May to 10 years' imprisonment and 10 strokes of the cane on conviction of raping a 17-year-old girl. In August Lee Kim Sen, a welder, was sentenced to 10 years' imprisonment and six strokes of the cane after being convicted of causing grievous injury to a waitress.

At least 28 people were sentenced to death: 25 for drugs offences, two for murder and one for a firearms offence. The Supreme Court confirmed the death sentences on 12 people. Their last recourse was an appeal to the Pardons Board of the state where the offence was committed. Eight Filipinos and two Pakistanis remained under sentence of death (see *Amnesty International Report 1992*): they had reportedly been tortured in custody and convicted of drugs offences in Sabah state after unfair trials. It was not known whether any executions were carried out.

Some 200 Acehnese asylum-seekers were in danger of being forcibly repatriated to Indonesia where they would be at risk of serious human rights violations, including torture and extrajudicial execution. Deputy Prime Minister Abdul Ghafar Baba said in July that the Malaysian Government had received assurances from the Indonesian authorities that the asylum-seekers could return safely and that there was "no reason to believe that the situation is that bad in Indonesia". However, the Deputy Prime Minister added that the Acehnese would not be asked to leave the country immediately.

Amnesty International appealed throughout the year for the release of the seven prisoners of conscience from Sabah and called for the prompt trial or release of the political prisoners detained under the ISA. It called for the commutation of all death sentences and urged the government not to forcibly return the Acehnese asylum-seekers to Indonesia.

# MALDIVES

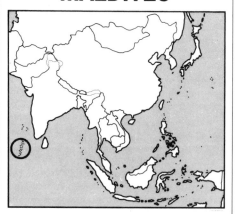

**A journalist was sentenced to six months' imprisonment; he was a prisoner of conscience. Four other prisoners of conscience were serving sentences of banishment for periods ranging between four and seven years. A group of political prisoners arrested on criminal charges were sentenced to long terms of imprisonment or banishment after trials which fell short of international standards for fair trial. There were reports of ill-treatment at Dhoonidhoo detention centre.**

Hassan Shakir, a journalist, was arrested in April and sentenced to six months' house arrest, apparently as a result of his writing for *Maavashi*, a magazine banned by the government before publication of its first issue. Four other prisoners of conscience continued to serve sentences of banishment imposed by police courts presided over by police officers. They had been among seven people sentenced in May 1990 to banishment for up to seven years for distributing leaflets criticizing alleged irregularities in elections held in 1989. Although police courts were abolished in 1990, the sentences passed by them still stand.

Twelve people were sentenced to prison terms of up to 15 years under the Prevention of Terrorism Act (PTA), which was applied retroactively. They included people arrested in connection with an alleged conspiracy to explode home-made petrol bombs during the Fifth South Asian Association for Regional Cooperation (SAARC) summit of heads of government in November 1990. Some of the prisoners were also accused of planning to fire marine signal

flares into the Presidential Palace. At the time of the SAARC conference two home-made bombs had exploded, causing minor damage but no injury. The government told Amnesty International that the "enormity of the crime planned remains unchanged and the effect on the people of such misdeeds urged the government to take action" (see *Amnesty International Reports 1991* and *1992*).

Towards the end of the year, the sentences of several political prisoners were reduced to terms of banishment or house arrest, and two of them were released as a result of appeals for clemency to President Maumoon Abdul Gayoom.

Little information was available on the procedures followed during the trials. Amnesty International's representatives were refused access to the courts to observe trials or to speak with judges.

Under the law, prisoners can be held in police custody for up to 45 days, in circumstances which may facilitate ill-treatment or torture. A prisoner held for questioning on Dhoonidhoo island, a detention centre run by the police division of the National Security Service, complained of prison conditions amounting to ill-treatment. He said that he had been held for over nine months in solitary confinement, and that for over 45 days he had been kept in handcuffs joined by a single hinge, allowing only extremely restricted movement.

Amnesty International called for the release of prisoners of conscience and sought information about legal procedures relating to their banishment or imprisonment and that of other political prisoners. In May Amnesty International submitted a memorandum to the government setting out its concerns about unfair political trials and the cases of individual political prisoners.

In November Amnesty International representatives visited the Maldives to discuss these concerns with government officials. They also discussed issues relating to judicial independence, legal representation for political prisoners and the retroactive application of penal law. They sought but were denied access to prisoners held in Dhoonidhoo detention centre and Gamadhoo prison, where most political prisoners sentenced under the PTA are held.

# MALI

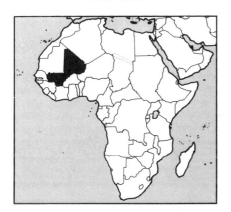

Several suspected opponents of the government remained in detention without charge or trial. The former President and other government officials were brought to trial on charges of murder and complicity to murder. Fourteen death sentences were passed and later commuted to life imprisonment. Several dozen members of the Tuareg community were extrajudicially executed by the army.

In January a new constitution was approved in a referendum and multi-party presidential elections were held in April. In June the transitional government, which had ruled Mali since the overthrow of a 23-year dictatorship in March 1991, handed over power to President Alpha Oumar Konaré and a civilian government.

Following a truce in February, the government signed a peace agreement on 11 April with the Azawad Unified Movements and Fronts, an umbrella organization of four Tuareg opposition groups. The government released 25 prisoners and the Tuareg groups released more than 30 captives. A commission of inquiry into human rights violations committed during the conflict of the previous two years, to be set up under the peace accord, was not known to have been established by the end of the year.

However, human rights abuses continued to be perpetrated by both the armed forces and by dissident Tuareg groups which did not agree with the peace accord. Between April and September about 60 people, mostly civilians, were reportedly killed either in attacks by Tuareg armed groups or in reprisals taken against members of the Tuareg and Moor communities

by the army and local people. Thousands of refugees fled into neighbouring countries.

Major Lamine Diabira, former minister of the interior, and seven other army officers arrested in July 1991 in connection with an alleged conspiracy to overthrow the government, were still held without trial at the end of the year, having been allowed to see their lawyers for the first time only in late 1991. Their cases were reportedly still under investigation by the examining magistrate. It was alleged that the real reason for their detention was because Major Diabira had sought the prosecution of officers he claimed were responsible for the killing of some 150 demonstrators in March 1991.

On 1 June the authorities announced that a plot by air force troops to overthrow the government had been foiled and the mutineers arrested. No names or numbers of detainees were given. They were not known to have been charged or released by the end of the year.

The trial of General Moussa Traoré, the former President, started on 4 June but was adjourned after lawyers withdrew from the court because of insufficient protection from angry spectators. It recommenced on 26 November and had not finished by the end of the year. Former President Traoré faced charges of murder and complicity to murder with three of his senior security officers and 29 former government ministers and officials of the former ruling party. The charges related to the killing of demonstrators by the army before his government was overthrown in March 1991. It appeared that further charges of corruption would be heard at a later trial. On 5 June, four children and the grandson of former President Traoré were released uncharged from house arrest and allowed to leave the country. However, the eldest son, who was charged in May 1992 with embezzlement of public funds, as well as the former President's wife and other relatives, all remained in custody.

In February, 13 men and a woman were convicted and sentenced to death for murder and complicity to murder after the hasty trial of 31 people on various charges in connection with the killing of a customs officer during disturbances in Yanfolila in January. Another 15 defendants were sentenced to prison terms and two were acquitted. They were convicted mainly on the basis of confessions allegedly given under duress after they were beaten in custody, and defence lawyers said that key witnesses had not been interviewed by the investigating magistrate. In April the Head of State commuted the death sentences to life imprisonment with hard labour.

Army reprisals against Tuareg civilians for attacks by armed Tuareg groups were reported up to mid-1992. In February the army was reported to have extrajudicially executed at least 25 civilians. In the Timbuktu Region soldiers reportedly killed 20 people, including 11 children, at Zouera near Bintagoungou, and five others, including three children, at the Imemalen Well near Farach.

On 16 May the army arrested and extrajudicially executed 10 Tuareg civilians in reprisal for an attack on Gossi a few days earlier by an armed Tuareg group which killed five people. On 17 May soldiers reportedly killed more than 20 Tuareg and Moor stockbreeders, including Mauritanian nationals, in encampments at Foïta, near the border with Mauritania. These extrajudicial executions were apparently in reprisal for an attack by an armed group believed to have entered Mali from a refugee camp in Mauritania.

Attacks by armed Tuareg groups on towns and villages in the north continued throughout the year, although it was not always possible to distinguish between armed attacks by politically motivated groups and banditry. Dissident Tuareg groups which opposed the April peace accord deliberately killed civilians and stole vehicles, on several occasions from foreign aid agencies and tourists. For example, in March an armed Tuareg group reportedly killed 18 civilians in a village near Tonka. In May an armed group took one person prisoner during an attack on Gossi and took three further captives in an attack on a bus on the Léré-Nampala road near the Mauritanian border. Several attacks in various parts of the country by Tuareg groups were reported in June in which eight people were killed. Members of the *Front islamique arabe pour la libération de l'Azawad* (FIAA), Arab Islamic Front for the Liberation of Azawad, one of the groups which signed the April peace agreement, were briefly detained by the Mauritanian authorities in July, apparently because they were suspected of involvement in attacks across the border into Mali

(see **Mauritania** entry). In July a Tuareg group reportedly killed one person and took two captives in an attack on Dioura in the Mopti region.

In August the government estimated that there had been about 40 attacks by armed groups since the April peace agreement. In October it said that there had been 120 attacks by armed groups since April but that the perpetrators could not always be identified.

Amnesty International urged the government to take action to halt and investigate alleged extrajudicial executions and to bring to justice those found to have been responsible for such abuses.

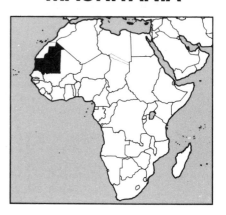

# MAURITANIA

**About 100 government opponents were detained briefly at the beginning of the year and were possible prisoners of conscience. There were reports of torture, and at least one prisoner died as a result. There were several killings by the security forces which appeared to be extrajudicial executions. The authorities took no action to account for more than 300 prisoners arrested in late 1990 who were believed to have died or been killed in detention.**

President Maaouiya Ould Taya was confirmed as head of state following presidential elections in January which were boycotted by one opposition party. Later parliamentary elections were boycotted by almost all opposition parties, notably the *Union des forces démocratiques* (UFD), Union of Democratic Forces.

The border between Mauritania and its

southern neighbour Senegal was reopened in May at one place, the Senegal river crossing at Rosso, and in November at other points, allowing some of the Mauritanians who had been expelled in 1989 and 1990 to return to their country (see *Amnesty International Reports 1990* and *1991*). However, in June some returnees were threatened by soldiers when they reached their villages of origin, prompting them to leave the country again. Several others were killed by security forces while crossing the Senegal river. Many black Mauritanians who had fled or been expelled to Senegal after April 1989 remained in Senegal, either because their identity cards had been destroyed at the time of their expulsion, preventing them from proving their Mauritanian nationality, or because they sought guarantees for their personal safety and compensation for their confiscated property before returning home.

On 26 January the paramilitary National Guard used tear-gas and rubber bullets to disperse a crowd which had gathered to hear the election results at the UFD headquarters in Nouadhibou, Mauritania's second largest town. The crowd retaliated by throwing stones. Three UFD members died as a result of rubber bullet wounds and many others were injured: no investigation was carried out into the deaths.

As many as 100 people arrested around the time of the presidential elections were possible prisoners of conscience. Most were arrested at their homes following the violent dispersal of the crowd at the UFD headquarters. Many were tortured to make them confess to possessing arms and to incriminate and reveal the whereabouts of other UFD activists. None was believed to have been questioned about specific acts of violence, although it was announced that at least 37 faced criminal charges. All were released by 5 February without being formally charged or tried.

In late June, 10 prominent members of the Tuareg ethnic minority including Malamine Ould Bady, a lawyer, were arrested in the capital, Nouakchott. They were apparently suspected of having links with the *Front islamique arabe pour la libération de l'Azawad* (FIAA), Arab Islamic Front for the Liberation of Azawad, a Malian armed opposition group composed of Tuareg and Moors which had reached a peace agreement with the Malian Government. They were detained without charge for a few days, apparently because they were suspected of involvement in attacks across the border into Mali.

In addition to the political detainees arrested in January, criminal suspects were also reported to have been tortured. In March N'diaye Abdou Oumar, known as "Kodda Dianga", was arrested by security forces while trying to cross the Senegal river and died after being beaten with the butt of a rifle. In August, following the murder of an Arab trader, the security forces detained all men aged between 18 and 70 from the village of Sory-Mallé. They were all black Mauritanians from the Halpulaar ethnic group (also known as Fulani). After questioning at the local school, 11 were arrested; some were later released, but at least four were transferred to the nearby town of Aleg, where they were charged with murder and remanded in custody. All four were reported to have been tortured. A fifth, Dia Hamath Atoumane, the 70-year-old brother of the village chief, reportedly died in Sory-Mallé on 24 August as a result of being beaten severely during interrogation. His relatives lodged a formal complaint about his death with the Procuracy but received no response.

Several people were killed by the security forces in circumstances suggesting they had been extrajudicially executed. There were at least four such killings on the Senegal river, which forms the frontier between Mauritania and Senegal. Two brothers crossing into Mauritania at Boghé were intercepted by police in February while the border remained officially closed. They were reportedly tortured and then thrown into the river. One of them, Oumar Diop, drowned. Later in the year, after the border was opened at Rosso, further killings were reported. For example, two Senegalese were shot dead in June by the National Guard, apparently as they crossed the river some distance from the official crossing point. No official inquiries were held into any of these deaths and no action was apparently taken against those responsible, suggesting that security forces along the border were able to act with impunity.

New information came to light about the gross human rights violations committed between 1989 and 1991 as local newspapers published photographs of execution victims. For example, in March three skeletons photographed in a ravine at Sory-Mallé were identified as those of the victims of extrajudicial executions carried out by the National Guard in 1990. Local human rights activists published information about 200 people who had been killed during the expulsions of black Mauritanians. However, the government took no steps to investigate past extrajudicial executions or to account for political prisoners who had "disappeared" in custody in late 1990 and 1991. Moreover, legal officials reportedly hampered attempts to initiate legal proceedings aimed at clarifying some of these "disappearances".

At least 339 political prisoners who had been among several thousand black Mauritanians arrested in late 1990 remained unaccounted for when the government announced the release of all political prisoners in April 1991 (see *Amnesty International Report 1992*). They are all believed to have died in police or army custody as a result of torture or to have been victims of extrajudicial executions. In early 1992 lawyers resubmitted a formal complaint to the State Prosecutor on behalf of nearly 200 families of the "disappeared", calling for those responsible to be brought to justice. The complaint had been previously rejected in September 1991 by the same official on the grounds that members of the armed forces could only be prosecuted following orders from the armed forces' Chiefs of Staff. However, the lawyers discovered that the Supreme Court had, prior to the 1991 rejection, advised the Minister of Defence that the Chiefs of Staff had no role to play in such prosecutions and that disciplinary proceedings should not be a substitute for criminal proceedings. The lawyers therefore resubmitted the complaint but were told by the President of the Special Court of Justice in October that his court could not examine the case because the court was being reorganized. However, he assured the lawyers that the case would be passed to the Avocat Général and then to an appropriate judicial body. No legal proceedings had begun by the end of the year.

Amnesty International appealed for information about those arrested following the January elections and urged that any held on account of the peaceful expression of their political views should be released. The organization also called for an inquiry into the death of Dia Hamath Atoumane

and other torture allegations. Throughout the year, Amnesty International also continued to press the authorities to clarify the fate of the more than 300 political prisoners who "disappeared" after their arrest in 1990, but the authorities did not respond to this or other appeals.

# MAURITIUS

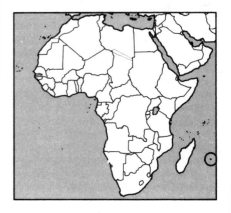

**There were reports that prisoners in police custody were beaten; one was reportedly killed. Death sentences against five men convicted of drug-trafficking were quashed and they were referred for retrial. One other death sentence was commuted.**

In February the Judicial Committee of the Privy Council (JCPC) in London, the highest court of appeal for Mauritius, ruled that a section of the Dangerous Drugs Act (1986) providing for the death penalty was unconstitutional. In April the National Assembly amended the law with the effect of restoring a mandatory death sentence for drug-trafficking.

In July Mauritius ratified the African Charter on Human and Peoples' Rights.

Two journalists were acquitted in February of charges which could have resulted in them becoming prisoners of conscience if convicted. Sydney Selvon, the editor of *Le Mauricien* newspaper, and Harish Chundunsing, then a reporter with *Le Mauricien*, faced charges of publishing or giving out false news information in connection with an article they had published in 1990.

There were reports of police ill-treatment of criminal suspects. In June Eddy

Labrosse died after he and another man were arrested by police in Pamplemousses and reportedly beaten. After an autopsy the police said that Eddy Labrosse had died as a result of injuries sustained in a road accident. An independent autopsy reported in October that Eddy Labrosse's injuries were incompatible with the police explanation for them. It was not clear to Amnesty International whether any investigation was undertaken.

In August Anil Imrith, a burglary suspect, was admitted to hospital following interrogation by officers of the Criminal Investigation Department (CID) at Vacoas. He alleged that he had been severely beaten on the feet in order to secure a confession. It was not clear to Amnesty International whether any investigation was undertaken.

In February the JCPC quashed the death sentences on three men convicted of drug-trafficking in previous years on the grounds that the law under which they were convicted was unconstitutional. An effect of the ruling was to render null and void the death sentences against two other men sentenced under the same legislation. Retrials were ordered in all five cases under legislation which provides for a maximum sentence of 20 years' imprisonment.

In May, following the recommendation of an advisory committee on the prerogative of mercy, President Cassam Uteem commuted the death sentence imposed on Ponsamy Poongavaram to life imprisonment. Ponsamy Poongavaram had been convicted of murder in 1987. At the end of the year, one person, Roger France de Boucherville, who had been convicted of murder, remained under sentence of death (see *Amnesty International Report 1992*).

Amnesty International urged members of the National Assembly to vote against amendments to the law that would reinstate the death penalty for drug-trafficking. The organization appealed for the commutation of all death sentences and for the abolition of the death penalty. In July Amnesty International representatives visiting Mauritius met President Cassam Uteem and government ministers to discuss human rights issues of concern to the organization.

# MEXICO

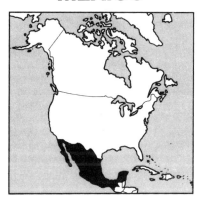

The widespread use of torture and ill-treatment by law-enforcement agents continued to be reported and at least one person died as a result of torture. Six prisoners of conscience, members of an indigenous community, were detained. Scores of people were arbitrarily detained and ill-treated by the security forces during land disputes and peaceful demonstrations. Little progress was reported in clarifying the whereabouts of hundreds of people who "disappeared" in previous years. Prison conditions continued to be harsh. At least one person, a member of an indigenous community, was extrajudicially executed.

The government adopted further measures intended to protect human rights. These included a law enacted in June which granted constitutional status and full independence to the National Human Rights Commission, and provided for the creation of similar offices in every state by the end of the year. The National Human Rights Commission continued to receive thousands of complaints of human rights abuses. It issued dozens of recommendations to the relevant authorities, but few of them were fully implemented.

Torture was frequently used by law-enforcement agents, particularly the state judicial police, throughout the country. Most of the victims were criminal suspects but some – including leaders of indigenous communities and human rights activists – were apparently targeted solely for their peaceful political activities. Torture methods reported included beatings; near-asphyxiation with plastic bags; hanging from the wrists for long periods; forcing

**208**

carbonated water with chilli pepper into the nose; burning with cigarettes; and psychological torture. Confessions extracted under duress continued to be admitted as evidence in courts, and scores of people continued to be imprisoned after convictions based solely on statements signed under torture. Official forensic doctors frequently failed to document cases of torture adequately, and medical treatment for detainees who suffered torture was frequently unavailable or inadequate.

Among the scores of cases reported was that of 17-year-old Pablo Molinet Aguilar, who was arrested without warrant in March in Salamanca, Guanajuato, by the state judicial police. While held incommunicado he was allegedly beaten, kicked, threatened with death and forced to sign a blank statement sheet, on the basis of which he was remanded in prison to await trial for murder. Two independent medical examinations confirmed that his injuries were consistent with the alleged torture. Despite this and other serious irregularities in the proceedings against him, Pablo Molinet remained in prison at the end of the year.

In April Enrique Ramos Dávila, a former policeman, died in custody in Saltillo, Coahuila, on the day of his arrest by the state judicial police. The authorities denied allegations that he had died as a result of torture and claimed that he had died of a heart attack. However, an inquiry by the National Human Rights Commission established that the cause of death was consistent with multiple trauma and asphyxiation. Seven police officers involved were charged with minor offences and taken into custody, but according to reports none had been convicted by the end of the year. Several other officers allegedly responsible remained at large.

In September Morelos Madrigal Lechino, a grassroots religious activist, was arrested by members of the Federal District judicial police in Mexico City. He was held incommunicado for two days. He alleged he was beaten, threatened with death and interrogated about his activities. In October Sabas Cruz Soto, a human rights activist, was detained without warrant in Mexico City by members of the Directorate of Protection and Highways police who allegedly beat him with pistol butts, kicks and blows. He was threatened with death for his human rights activities before being released on the same day.

Torture was also reported in prisons. In June Pablo Santoy and Francisco Pandilla, two inmates of the San Luis Potosí state prison, were accused by the prison authorities of planning an escape and were allegedly beaten, kicked and threatened with "disappearance" by the prison director. They were hung from the wrists overnight and then confined in punishment cells for three days, with no food, water, sanitary facilities or medical care. Following widespread complaints on their behalf, the prison director was removed in August, but to Amnesty International's knowledge, none of those responsible was brought to justice.

Very few of those responsible for torture and other human rights violations were brought to justice. For example, no action was taken by the Republic Attorney General's Office against those responsible for the torture of Amir Aboud Sattar in 1991 (see *Amnesty International Report 1992*), despite its own recommendation and that of the National Human Rights Commission that action should be taken.

Six prisoners of conscience were detained in January when state judicial police raided the community of La Trinidad Yaveo, Oaxaca. During the raid police officers extrajudicially executed one member of the community (see below). One Zapotec and five Mixe Indian activists were arrested without warrant, beaten, suspended by the wrists for long periods and threatened with death. Odilón Serafín, Abraham Prudencio, Efreín Prudencio, Alberto Hernández and Daniel García were forced to "confess" to a murder they did not commit and were imprisoned. Another activist, Agustín García, was also tortured but was released on the same day. The five were released in June, following national and international criticism of their detention. However, the police officers responsible for the torture and killing remained at large, despite official announcements to the contrary. Another eight Indian activists from the same community, imprisoned since 1990 for a murder they did not commit, were released in April.

Scores of people were arbitrarily detained and ill-treated by security forces in the context of land disputes and during peaceful demonstrations. In October the state judicial police forcibly evicted scores of Tzotzil Indian peasants from the community of Campo Alegre, Chiapas, and destroyed several houses. Men, women and children were ill-treated during the evictions and many suffered injuries. Fifty-eight people were arrested for a short period, but 20 were held for weeks. Also in October the state judicial police arrested 87 men, women and children when they violently dispersed a peaceful demonstration in Amatán, Chiapas, by Zoque Indian residents protesting against corruption of local officials. Most of those arrested were released on the following day but 27 remained in detention for nearly two weeks before being released uncharged after growing public protests at their detention.

Little progress was reported in investigations into hundreds of "disappearances" of political activists, most of which occurred during the 1970s and early 1980s. For example, the whereabouts of José Ramón García, who "disappeared" in 1988 (see *Amnesty International Report 1992*), remained unknown. In January Mario Rojas Alba, a former Congressman, accused several former Morelos state officials of responsibility for José Ramón García's "disappearance". He received anonymous death threats following his statements. He was attacked and seriously injured by unidentified assailants in February, as a consequence of which he and his family fled the country. In January the National Human Rights Commission published a report indicating that several former state officials were probably responsible for José Ramón García's "disappearance", and recommended that they should be brought to justice. At least three former officials were arrested and charged in connection with the case, but a former state police commander allegedly responsible for José Ramón García's "disappearance" remained at large at the end of the year. Those responsible for Francisco Quijano García's "disappearance" and killing in 1991 (see *Amnesty International Report 1992*) were also not brought to justice.

Police extrajudicially executed Tomás Diego García, a Mixe Indian, in January when they raided his house in La Trinidad Yaveo and arrested his brother and five other Indian activists involved in a peaceful campaign for their community's land. Those responsible had not been brought to justice by the end of the year. In October José Luis Rodríguez Morán, a teacher and union leader, was stabbed to death in Mexico City in suspicious circumstances. He had previously received death threats because of his activities on behalf of the Triqui Indians of Oaxaca state. The investigations into his killing continued at the end of the year. Those responsible for the killing of Víctor Manuel Oropeza in 1991 remained at large (see *Amnesty International Report 1992*) and the police officers allegedly responsible for the killings of Hector, Jaime and Erik Quijano Santoyo in January 1990 were not brought to justice (see *Amnesty International Report 1992*).

Prison conditions continued to be harsh, in some cases constituting cruel, inhuman or degrading treatment. Prisons were severely overcrowded and most had inadequate sanitary facilities. A large number of prisoners awaiting sentence had been held far beyond the constitutional limits for their detention. In July, five people were killed and eight wounded during an armed confrontation between rival gangs in the severely overcrowded state prison of Morelia, eight months after the National Human Rights Commission had recommended an investigation into alleged arms smuggling into the prison. In an effort to reduce prison overcrowding, a number of prisoners, particularly Indians, were granted pardons, were paroled or benefited from early release programs.

Amnesty International repeatedly called for full and impartial investigations into human rights violations in Mexico and urged the authorities to bring all those responsible to justice. In March it published *Mexico: Human rights violations against members of the Mixe and Zapotec indigenous community of La Trinidad Yaveo, Oaxaca*, and in July it published *Mexico: Human rights violations against Ch'ol and Tzeltal Indian activists*. In October Amnesty International published *Human rights violations against the indigenous peoples of the Americas*, which included concerns in Mexico.

In oral statements to the United Nations Commission on Human Rights in February and to the Working Group on Indigenous Populations of the Sub-Commission on Prevention of Discrimination and Protection of Minorities in July, Amnesty International included reference to its concerns about human rights violations against indigenous peoples in Mexico.

Amnesty International representatives

210

visited Mexico in February and August to investigate continuing reports of torture and other human rights violations, particularly against indigenous peoples. As a result of the representatives' findings, Amnesty International concluded that statements obtained under torture and other forms of coercion were still being widely used by the agencies in charge of criminal prosecutions to incriminate suspects. The representatives met the President of the National Human Rights Commission in Mexico in February and again in August to discuss the Commission's work. Amnesty International welcomed the Commission's activities but expressed concern about the frequent failure of the authorities to comply with its recommendations.

# MOLDOVA

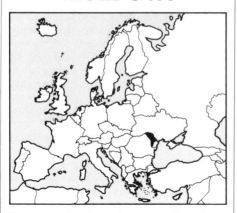

Government forces reportedly beat detainees from the self-proclaimed Dnestr Moldovan Republic (DMR) and extrajudicially executed at least one person. Fifteen people were awaiting execution at the end of the year. At least one political prisoner was said to have been denied access to a defence lawyer of his choice by the DMR authorities. Security forces under DMR control were alleged to have been involved in the abduction, torture and murder of non-combatant civilians.

Moldova became independent following the break-up of the Soviet Union. Headed by President Mirca Snegur, it joined the Conference on Security and Co-operation in Europe in January and became a member of the United Nations in March.

Armed clashes continued between the Moldovan authorities and forces of the DMR, an area in the northeast of the country opposed to calls for reunification with Romania. Hundreds of people, including civilians, were reported killed. However, the security situation had stabilized by the end of the year following the introduction of peace-keeping forces, including Russian troops.

In April the Moldovan parliament amended the criminal code to abolish the death penalty as a possible punishment for six peacetime offences. It was retained for premeditated, aggravated murder; rape with serious consequences or rape of a minor aged under 14; attempt on the life of a police officer; and for various military crimes defined as serious. Under the amendment women were exempted from the death penalty.

Government forces were said to have subjected detainees from the DMR to beatings and ill-treatment. DMR militiaman Vladimir Serdyukov, for example, alleged that he was detained in Bendery in June and subsequently severely beaten by Moldovan volunteers and police officers who carved three stars and the letter "V" on his body. Volunteer forces fighting for the Moldovan Government were also allegedly responsible for extrajudicially executing a man named Velichko and raping his wife in the Dubasari district in June.

Death sentences passed on 15 people had not been carried out by the end of the year owing to the lack of facilities. Previously, prisoners had been sent for execution to two neighbouring republics of the former Soviet Union.

At least one political prisoner, ethnic Moldovan Stefan Uritu, was reportedly denied access to a lawyer of his choice following his arrest in June in the DMR for alleged terrorist offences, which carry a possible death sentence. He was released pending trial in August. He and another man arrested on the same charge were reportedly beaten in custody, and a third was said to have faced mock executions.

Members of the police and so-called Republican Guard in the DMR were reported to have been involved in the abduction, torture and murder of civilians. Gheorghe Bejenari, for example, an ethnic Moldovan bus-driver outspoken in his opposition to the proclamation of the DMR, was reportedly detained in Dubasari in March by local police who were said to have told his wife that he would not leave their hands alive. His mutilated body was found in April.

Before Stefan Uritu's release Amnesty International urged officials in the DMR to ensure that he had adequate access to the defence lawyer of his own choosing in line with international fair trial standards. The organization also called on them to take immediate steps to initiate full and prompt inquiries into all allegations of torture and murder by security forces under their control; to make the findings public; and to bring to justice the perpetrators. The DMR public prosecutor replied that Stefan Uritu had himself initially refused a defence lawyer as he did not recognize the legality of the DMR investigatory body. The public prosecutor reported that an investigation was under way into one of the murders raised: the others, he said, took place in areas not at that time fully under the control of the DMR.

Amnesty International welcomed the abolition of the death penalty for a number of peacetime offences, and the reduction in its scope, but continued to press for complete abolition and publication of full statistics on its application.

# MONGOLIA

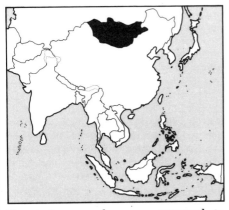

**Twenty-two people were sentenced to death and at least 11 executions were carried out.**

A new Constitution entered into force in February. It incorporates a number of human rights guarantees found in the principal international human rights instruments, and includes for the first time an explicit prohibition of torture. Elections in

June to a restyled 76-seat legislature were won overwhelmingly by the ruling Mongolian People's Revolutionary Party.

Mongolia retained the death penalty for eight peacetime offences. Official statistics indicated that 22 people were sentenced to death in 1992 and at least 11 people were executed. Execution is by shooting. The Justice Minister reported to the United Nations Human Rights Committee in July that preparations for a new criminal code envisaged a reduction in the number of capital offences.

Amnesty International continued to call on the government headed by President Puntsalmaagiyn Ochirbat to abolish the death penalty. In June Amnesty International published a report, *Mongolia: Continuing legislative reform*.

# MOROCCO AND WESTERN SAHARA

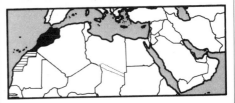

**Over 500 political prisoners, including at least 150 prisoners of conscience and possible prisoners of conscience, were serving sentences imposed after unfair trials in 1992 and previous years. Others were held without charge or trial. Three long-term prisoners of conscience were released. New reports of torture and ill-treatment of detainees held in pre-trial incommunicado (*garde à vue*) detention were received. Hundreds of Sahrawis and Moroccans who "disappeared" in previous years were believed to be still held in secret detention centres. Long-term "disappeared" and political prisoners released in 1991 continued to be subject to restrictions on their freedom of movement, association and expression. At least 150 people were under sentence of death, but no executions were reported.**

A new Constitution was promulgated in September after receiving an almost unanimous vote in a national referendum which was, however, boycotted by the main opposition parties. The Constitution, which refers to human rights in its preamble, allows the Prime Minister to appoint ministers.

A United Nations-sponsored referendum on the future of the Western Sahara, scheduled for January, had still not taken place by the end of the year.

Demonstrations and violent clashes between students and the police continued in many universities during the first three months of the year. Over 100 students, mostly members of left-wing or Islamic organizations, were arrested during and after the protests. There were further demonstrations in September and October in a number of towns in south Morocco and the Western Sahara in protest against falling living standards and the failure to reach a political settlement of the Western Sahara issue. Scores of people were said to have been wounded by police shooting during protests in Assa, Smara and Laayoune and over 100 were arrested. Dozens were reportedly held in prolonged incommunicado detention and ill-treated. Some were believed to have been charged with offences such as theft and damaging public property, but they had not been brought to trial by the end of the year.

At least 140 people were arrested for allegedly insulting sacred institutions or disturbing public order and sentenced to up to 10 years' imprisonment. They included prisoners of conscience and possible prisoners of conscience, who continued to be sentenced under broadly worded laws which permit the authorities to imprison people for the peaceful expression of their views. Among them were several trade unionists. One, Noubir Amaoui, Secretary General of the *Confédération démocratique du travail* (CDT), Democratic Labour Confederation, and a leading member of the main opposition party, the *Union socialiste des forces populaires* (USFP), Socialist Union of People's Forces, was convicted of defamation under articles of the Press Code commonly used to prosecute journalists. In April he was sentenced to two years' imprisonment by the Court of First Instance in Rabat in connection with an interview he had given to a Spanish newspaper. He was refused bail – which is usually granted, pending appeal, to those convicted under the press laws – and taken to Sale prison. He was later transferred to Kenitra prison where he remained held at the end of the year.

Over 500 political prisoners, including over 150 prisoners of conscience and possible prisoners of conscience, remained in prison at the end of 1992. Most were serving sentences imposed after unfair trials in previous years. Many had been convicted of offences such as conspiracy against the state after signing confessions which they alleged were extracted under torture. Among the prisoners of conscience were eight students, members of a left-wing tendency within the *Union nationale des étudiants marocains* (UNEM), National Union of Moroccan Students, who were tried and convicted in 1984, and 15 suspected members of *Ila'l-Amam*, Forward, who were sentenced between 1984 and 1987. Scores of other suspected members of left-wing or Islamic organizations convicted since 1984 on charges of distributing leaflets or disturbing public order were prisoners of conscience or possible prisoners of conscience.

Abdessalem Yassine, leader of the banned Islamic organization, *al-'Adl wa'l-Ihsan*, Justice and Charity, remained under house arrest without charge or trial at his home in Sale. Only his wife was allowed to see him.

Three long-serving prisoners of conscience – Ahmed Aitbennacer, Ahmed Rakiz and Abdalah Harif – were released on 15 January. They had been arrested in 1974 and 1975 and sentenced to between 30 years' and life imprisonment after an unfair trial of 178 left-wing activists in 1977 (see previous *Amnesty International Reports*).

Legislation promulgated in late 1991 to reform the law on *garde à vue* detention and improve safeguards for detainees (see *Amnesty International Report 1992*) failed, in practice, to protect detainees' rights. Although the six-day limit for *garde à vue* detention (for charges not related to state security) laid down in the law appeared to be respected more than in previous years, political detainees were still held incommunicado for longer than the maximum legal period.

For instance, scores of people of Western Saharan origin arrested during the year for political reasons or after demonstrations were reportedly held in prolonged *garde à vue* detention. Bella Ma' El Ainain, a bank employee from the Western Sahara, had been arrested in September 1991 after allowing a Swiss journalist to use the bank's fax machine to send an article to

Switzerland on the progress of the Western Sahara peace settlement. He was held for nearly four months without charge or trial before being released in January 1992.

Trials of political detainees continued to fall far short of minimum fair trial requirements set by internationally recognized standards and by Moroccan law. The most frequent abuses were the use of police statements allegedly extracted under torture or other coercion to obtain convictions and the refusal of the courts to investigate torture allegations. The courts also failed to address breaches of prescribed pre-trial procedures which had the effect of putting the defence at an improper disadvantage relative to the prosecution.

In one case, for example, at the trial of 35 students in April before the Fes Criminal Court, on charges including disturbing public order, the judge refused to order medical examinations, or even treatment, for some of the defendants who bore signs of torture. The defence lawyers withdrew from the case in protest but the trial proceeded: 33 of the students were convicted and sentenced to between two and 12 months' imprisonment. Two were acquitted.

Torture and ill-treatment of detainees remained common, particularly during the first 48 hours of incommunicado *garde à vue* detention. Methods included beatings, especially on the soles of the feet (*falaqa*), often while suspended in contorted positions; partial suffocation, frequently with rags soaked in salt water or chemicals; and electric shocks.

Many of the students arrested after clashes with the police in late 1991 and early 1992 alleged that they were tortured or ill-treated in *garde à vue* detention. For example, a student supporter of *al-'Adl wa'l-Ihsan*, Justice and Charity, who was arrested in late 1991 after violent clashes between Islamic and left-wing students at Oujda University, alleged that he was stripped naked and tortured with electric shocks and the "aeroplane" method (being tied and suspended in a contorted position, and then beaten). He was sentenced by Oujda Court of Appeal in January to 20 years' imprisonment after being convicted of involvement in homicide, kidnapping and causing explosions.

Hundreds of people of Western Saharan origin and about 100 Moroccans reported to have "disappeared" in custody in previous years were believed to be still held in secret centres or camps in Morocco. They included Abdelhaq Rouissi, a Moroccan trade union activist and former bank employee, who "disappeared" in 1964. He was reported to have been seen in secret detention, most recently at Ahermoumou military camp in 1989, the last indication of his whereabouts.

Most of the 260 "disappeared" Sahrawis who were freed from long-term secret detention in 1991 (see *Amnesty International Report 1992*) were kept under strict surveillance throughout the year and continued to be subject to restrictions on their freedom of movement, association and expression. None of them had received any official compensation for the long abuse of their rights: some, in fact, were said to have been required to move from their home regions to reside in the south of Morocco. No inquiry was known to have been held into any of the cases of long-term "disappearance", nor were those responsible for the "disappearances" identified or brought to justice.

The 30 surviving prisoners who were released in 1991 from the secret detention centre at Tazmamert (see *Amnesty International Report 1992*) also remained under close surveillance, with their freedom of movement and contact with others severely restricted. They were not given adequate medical care for serious illnesses caused by their prolonged imprisonment. By the end of the year, no inquiry had been initiated into their unlawful detention for up to 18 years, the inhuman conditions of detention in Tazmamert or the deaths of 33 of those who had been held there, including those who had died while still in detention long after their sentences had expired. The relatives of those who died had still not been informed of the causes of death nor had they been awarded any official compensation.

One death sentence was commuted. No new death sentences were known to have been imposed. However, about 150 prisoners remained under sentence of death at Kenitra Central Prison: 14 of them were political prisoners, including four possible prisoners of conscience.

Amnesty International welcomed the releases which occurred in 1991 and 1992 but expressed its concern to the government of King Hassan II about continuing reports of arbitrary detention, torture,

**214**

unfair trials and the death penalty. It called for a thorough and impartial investigation into all "disappearances", for the immediate release of the remaining "disappeared", and for those responsible for the "disappearances" to be identified and brought to justice.

In October Amnesty International published two reports, *Morocco: Continuing Human Rights Violations* and *Morocco: Tazmamert: Official Silence and Impunity*. No response was received from the government to any of the reports or communications sent to it during the year, and the organization's requests for access to the country for research continued to be denied.

In April Amnesty International submitted information about its concerns in Morocco and the Western Sahara for United Nations review, under a procedure established by Economic and Social Council Resolutions 728F/1503, for confidential consideration of communications about human rights violations.

# MOZAMBIQUE

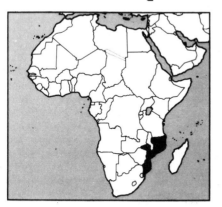

Scores of people were detained without trial on suspicion of committing crimes on behalf of the armed opposition *Resistência Nacional Moçambicana* (RENAMO), Mozambique National Resistance, before an agreement to end the 16-year conflict was signed in October. One person was acquitted of plotting to overthrow the government: the trial of 13 others had not concluded when a law passed in October granted amnesty to all political prisoners. Members of the security forces ill-treated civilians. One soldier was sentenced to a long prison term for the extrajudicial execution of captured RENAMO fighters. There were new reports of RENAMO soldiers mutilating and killing civilians.

A General Peace Agreement signed by President Joaquim Chissano and RENAMO's leader, Afonso Dhlakama, came into force in October. It provided for the release of all political prisoners and for fundamental human rights to be respected. It included a cease-fire and the confinement of both sides' troops to specified assembly areas in readiness for either demobilization or incorporation into a new national army. The agreement also provided for the return of refugees and for humanitarian assistance to those who had been displaced and reduced to starvation as a result of the 16-year conflict. Multi-party elections were to be held within a year. A United Nations Operation in Mozambique (ONUMOZ) was to monitor the agreement and chair the Supervisory and Monitoring Commission (SMC), which was responsible for implementing the agreement. Subsidiary commissions were set up to monitor the neutrality of the police and administration. The SMC was to reach decisions by consensus between the government and RENAMO – a practice which, in similar agreements in other countries, had prevented investigation of politically motivated killings and other human rights violations. The October amnesty law covered all politically motivated and military crimes committed during the conflict, including human rights violations committed by the security forces: this appeared to reduce still further any possibility that the authorities would account for the hundreds of prisoners who had "disappeared" since independence in 1975.

The cease-fire was violated within days of its entry into force when RENAMO forces occupied villages and government troops counter-attacked. Before the agreement there were reports that RENAMO soldiers abducted, mutilated and killed civilians. Victims included two people who had their hands cut off in Zambézia province in February and a Roman Catholic missionary who was killed in Nampula province in August. After the agreement there were reports of RENAMO soldiers beating civilians and abducting others whom they forced to act as porters.

At the beginning of the year scores of

people were detained without trial on suspicion of committing crimes on behalf of RENAMO. Most continued to be held until the October agreement, when the government released about 400 such people who had been arrested either in 1992 or in previous years, and was reviewing the cases of around 20 others to see if they qualified for release. The government said these were all the political prisoners it held. The releases were monitored by the International Committee of the Red Cross (ICRC). In contrast, RENAMO declared that it was holding no prisoners and that all captured government soldiers had joined RENAMO ranks. However, many prisoners remained unaccounted for, including prisoners taken by both sides during the armed conflict. They also included scores of government opponents who "disappeared" in detention in the years following independence in 1975 (see previous Amnesty International Reports).

Fourteen people who had been arrested in 1991 and accused of plotting to overthrow the government (see Amnesty International Report 1991) were brought to trial. Charges against one other person were dropped in January. Colonel-General Sebastião Mabote, a former army chief of staff, went on trial in August and was acquitted in September. He was tried by the Supreme Court because of his status as a Deputy in the Assembly of the Republic (Mozambique's Parliament). The trial of the other 13 before the Maputo City Court began in September but the defendants were released under the October amnesty law.

There were numerous reports of beatings or other assaults on civilians by soldiers, often to back up demands for money. In at least two cases, soldiers fired on protesters in questionable circumstances. In August four prisoners were shot dead and 13 wounded when soldiers opened fire to quell a riot by prisoners in Maputo Central Prison and another person was shot dead when soldiers suppressed a violent demonstration of war veterans near Maputo. An inquiry into the killings was initiated by the Maputo procuracy, but no findings were announced. However, one soldier was sentenced to 22 years' imprisonment by Zambézia Provincial Military Court in July for ordering the extrajudicial execution of six captured RENAMO fighters in September 1991.

Amnesty International appealed in August to President Chissano and to the RENAMO leader, Afonso Dhlakama, to include specific measures to protect human rights in the peace agreement. In February Amnesty International wrote to RENAMO about four people held by the group since 1988. RENAMO replied they would look into the cases but had provided no further information by the end of the year.

# MYANMAR
## (BURMA)

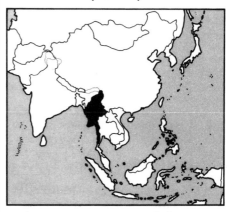

**At least 1,550 opponents of the government, many of them prisoners of conscience, were believed to be held despite the release of almost 1,300 others. Some were detained without trial, others had been sentenced after unfair trials. Gross and persistent human rights violations continued to be reported from all parts of the country, including arbitrary detention of civilians to serve as military porters, torture and extrajudicial executions.**

In April the ruling State Law and Order Restoration Council (SLORC) announced that it would release all prisoners detained for political reasons, other than those who posed a threat to national security. This was the first time it had acknowledged holding political prisoners. It also announced that it would hold a National Convention to establish principles for drafting a new constitution. In September the SLORC revoked Martial Law Orders 1/89 and 2/89, thereby abolishing military tribunals set up to try martial law offenders. In August Myanmar acceded to the four Geneva Conventions of 1949, which establish minimum humane standards of conduct in situations of armed conflict.

However, it was still not a party to the main international human rights treaties.

Despite these changes, Myanmar remained under martial law throughout the year. The SLORC, chaired by General Than Shwe, refused to convene the People's Assembly (parliament) elected in 1990 and continued to repress peaceful political activity and to restrict freedom of expression and association. The National League for Democracy (NLD), which had won the 1990 elections, was one of the seven remaining political parties which had not been banned.

Armed opposition against the government continued in several parts of the country, but violations of basic human rights by the military were not confined to those areas. Armed opposition groups also committed grave human rights abuses, including torture and summary executions of prisoners.

Thousands of government opponents were believed to be held, many of whom may have been prisoners of conscience. Amnesty International identified 1,550 political prisoners, including many prisoners of conscience, but believed that the actual number was far higher. Almost 1,300 political prisoners were released between April and the end of the year: only 66 of them were previously known to Amnesty International. Among those released were former Prime Minister U Nu and NLD leaders U Khin Maung Swe, U Chan Aye and U Soe Thein.

Some of those held throughout 1992 had been detained without charge or trial since 1988; others had been convicted under laws which criminalized peaceful political activity and allowed unfair trials. Among the prisoners were leaders and organizers of the NLD and most other opposition parties. Thirty-nine members of parliament-elect were still imprisoned at the end of the year. Buddhist, Christian and Muslim clerics, community leaders, university and high school students, writers, civil servants, doctors, lawyers and workers' leaders were among those imprisoned.

Prisoners of conscience included: NLD leader Aung San Suu Kyi, winner of the 1991 Nobel Peace Prize, who had been held under house arrest since 1989; Nai Tun Thein, a member of parliament-elect for the Mon National Democratic Front who had been detained since December

1991 and forced to sign a paper criticizing the Nobel prize award; U Hla Wai, an election candidate of the Democratic Party for a New Society, who was arrested on the eve of the May 1990 elections; and the Venerable U Kaweinda, a Buddhist monk.

Several prisoners of conscience arrested in 1991 were sentenced to prison terms during the year. Tin Moe, a writer and editor of a literary magazine, was sentenced to four years' imprisonment in June under the Publishing Act. Six university students were sentenced on unknown charges by military tribunals in July to prison terms ranging from six to 20 years. They included Zaw Min of the All-Burma Federation of Student Unions (ABFSU), who was sentenced to 20 years' imprisonment. The students were among about 900 arrested in December 1991 during demonstrations calling for the release of Aung San Suu Kyi (see Amnesty International Report 1992). It was unclear whether the others had been charged, tried or released.

Although military tribunals were abolished in September, hundreds of political prisoners sentenced by them after unfair trials remained imprisoned. They included prisoner of conscience Aung Din, General Secretary of the ABSFU, who was sentenced in 1989 to four years' imprisonment. To Amnesty International's knowledge, no one had ever been acquitted by a military tribunal.

Civilian courts also failed to meet international standards for fair trial. The independence of the civilian judiciary was undermined by intimidation by the military authorities. In January a judge in Pathein was convicted for his role in freeing up to 50 villagers who had been detained in the Ayeyarwady Delta. He was reportedly arrested by military intelligence officers while hearing a case in court and sentenced by a military tribunal the same day to six years' imprisonment. Several lawyers from Pathein were also arrested, including U Htun, U Tin Ngwe and U Tin Oo, apparently for acting on behalf of prisoners. They were reportedly still held at the end of the year, but it was not known whether they had been charged or tried.

Opposition activists and other detainees were routinely tortured or ill-treated in custody. Methods included sleep, food and water deprivation; the application of electric shocks to fingertips, toes, ear lobes or genitals; beatings with fists, boots or rifle butts; and the "motorcycle" – standing with arms outstretched and legs bent for long periods. At least six sections of the security forces were cited by former prisoners as responsible for torture, including the regular army, the police and the military intelligence service.

Hundreds of thousands of people were forcibly conscripted or seized by the military to serve as porters carrying army supplies, or as unpaid labourers building roads and army camps or working on commercial projects. Elderly men and women, schoolchildren and pregnant women were among those conscripted. In one incident in August, 300 porters, including 100 women rounded up from a village in Kayin State, were forcibly detained and sent to army camps in Kawmoora. Many people were seized at random, especially between January and April at the time of a major military offensive at Manerplaw. In previous years porters had come mainly from ethnic minority areas. In 1992 they were taken from almost any area of the country and from every ethnic or religious community, including the majority Buddhist Bamar (Burman), and were abducted from trains, ferries, buses, cinemas and city streets.

According to witnesses, hundreds of porters and labourers died from neglect and exhaustion. Others were shot or beaten to death by soldiers when they became too weak to carry their loads. Still others were killed for disobeying orders or trying to escape. Women conscripts were raped by soldiers.

On several occasions people who tried to evade conscription were extrajudicially executed. A father of five from Pruso town in Kayah State was reportedly shot dead in February when he tried to hide from approaching soldiers. In Christian areas, church leaders were said to be particularly targeted because they remained in their villages to protect local people when troops approached.

Members of the Muslim minority in Rakhine (Arakan) State, sometimes known as Rohingyas, were subjected to a barrage of human rights violations, leading to the flight of over 260,000 people to Bangladesh by July. Refugees said that the military had driven them out by destroying villages and mosques and arresting community leaders and members of political parties, especially the NLD. Witnesses testified that the security forces had forcibly conscripted many

Muslims as porters, and, in some cases, tortured and deliberately killed them. Several refugees described female relatives being raped and then killed.

Some Muslims were killed when trying to resist military demands. For example, a mother of six from Buthidaung township stated that her husband had been killed in January by the army. He was the village headman and had been unable to find any more porters for the army. When his corpse was found, his eyes had been gouged out and his body sliced open.

At least 20 Muslims were reportedly shot dead and as many drowned in February when security forces attacked a group of refugees trying to reach Bangladesh by boat. Some were killed by members of the security forces, others by civilian Rakhines whom the security forces did not attempt to restrain. The authorities denied the killings.

Other Muslims were killed because they were alleged members or supporters of insurgent groups. For example, Mohamed Ilyas, an elderly villager and NLD member, was reportedly beaten to death by soldiers in June. However, the level of armed conflict in Rakhine State was minimal.

In other parts of Myanmar, where armed opposition groups did confront the authorities, the population was consistently abused by the military during counter-insurgency operations. Ethnic minority communities were forced to move to "strategic hamlets" under strict curfews and rigid controls. Crops and villages were destroyed and expulsion orders warned that villagers remaining in their homes would be shot on sight. In March residents of 57 villages in Kayah State were ordered to abandon their homes and farms. Within three months more than 8,000 people had moved and thousands were confined in poor conditions in camps where deaths from malnutrition were frequent. Others were forced to do construction work for the army, during which many were beaten or shot.

In Kayin State, where the military launched a major offensive against the Manerplaw headquarters of the Karen National Union (KNU), whole areas were reportedly declared "free-fire" zones (where soldiers were authorized to shoot people at will). Refugees described dozens of extrajudicial executions of villagers between January and April, when the

**218**

offensive was called off.

In April the SLORC reached an agreement with the Bangladeshi Government to repatriate the 260,000 Muslim refugees from Rakhine State (see **Bangladesh** entry). The agreement, reportedly at the SLORC's insistence, excluded the United Nations High Commissioner for Refugees (UNHCR) from the resettlement process. In September over 40 refugees were returned by the Bangladeshi authorities without UNHCR monitoring. In October, 167 were returned under UNHCR monitoring, and in November almost 1,000 were returned: 165 of these were involuntary. In December almost 2,500 others were returned without UNHCR monitoring.

Armed opposition groups were also reported to have tortured, ill-treated or summarily executed prisoners. Evidence emerged during the year of executions in previous years by the KNU, the Democratic Alliance of Burma and the Kachin Independence Organization. In February the All Burma Students' Democratic Front (ABSDF – North) executed 15 alleged spies. One of them, Tun Aung Kyaw, was their former Chairman. The 15 were among 80 students detained in the second half of 1991 on suspicion of spying for the SLORC. The other 65 prisoners were held in harsh conditions, given inadequate nourishment, fettered and allegedly tortured. Fifty-five escaped in May, three reportedly died in captivity and the situation of the remaining seven was not clear. Amnesty International appealed to the ABSDF to end incommunicado detention of prisoners and to safeguard them from ill-treatment or execution.

Amnesty International repeatedly appealed to the SLORC to take action to stop violations of human rights. It called for the release of prisoners of conscience, for fair trials for political prisoners and an end to arbitrary detention, torture and extrajudicial executions.

In May Amnesty International published *Myanmar: Human rights violations against Muslims in the Rakhine (Arakan) State*, which documented the pattern of repression by the security forces. In October it published *Myanmar: "No law at all" – Human rights violations under military rule*. This report detailed gross and persistent violations of human rights in every one of Myanmar's seven political divisions and seven ethnic minority states.

Amnesty International welcomed the releases of prisoners of conscience between April and October, but expressed its concern about the continuing imprisonment of hundreds of other prisoners of conscience and possible prisoners of conscience. In September the organization wrote to over 20 governments worldwide calling on them to press the Myanmar Government to accept UNHCR monitoring of any repatriation of refugees from Bangladesh.

In oral statements to the UN Commission on Human Rights in February and to its Sub-Commission on Prevention of Discrimination and Protection of Minorities in August, Amnesty International included reference to its concerns in Myanmar.

# NAMIBIA

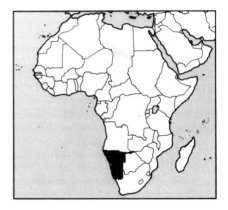

**There were several reports of torture or ill-treatment of prisoners by police. The authorities responded by ordering investigations. Little progress was made in clarifying the fate of hundreds of people who "disappeared" before independence in the custody of the South African authorities in Namibia or in detention camps run by the South West Africa People's Organisation (SWAPO) in Angola.**

Namibia became a party to the African Charter on Human and Peoples' Rights in September.

During the year there were several reports of prisoners being tortured or ill-treated. As a result of police investigations, seven cases of assault were lodged against seven police officers. One of the officers was suspected of assisting civilians who assaulted a youth whom they accused of theft in Khomasdal in May: the youth later died, apparently as a result of the assault.

The seven officers were suspended or transferred while their cases were referred to the Prosecutor General for a decision on whether they should face criminal charges. None had been brought to trial by the end of the year.

A dozen asylum-seekers were detained in late 1991 or early 1992 and held for several months: they feared repatriation to countries where they would be in danger of becoming prisoners of conscience or suffering other human rights violations. By the end of the year they had apparently all been released and none had been repatriated.

After Namibia's independence in 1990, the SWAPO majority government led by President Samuel Nujoma asked the International Committee of the Red Cross (ICRC) to trace those missing as a result of the conflict (see *Amnesty International Report 1991*). By the end of the year, the ICRC had received requests to trace over 2,100 people, the majority of whom were SWAPO combatants reported missing after military actions. The ICRC reported that it had been able to obtain information in some 320 cases, about 30 of which concerned people who had "disappeared" in SWAPO custody, and had informed relatives of the results. The fate of hundreds of prisoners who had "disappeared" or were killed in South African or SWAPO custody before independence remained unclear.

Amnesty International made inquiries about reports of torture, to which the government responded, and about the detained asylum-seekers.

# NEPAL

**Scores of political prisoners were reportedly detained without trial in police custody for up to several months. There were reports of torture by police of political and criminal detainees. Several people were killed by police officers in circumstances which suggested they may have been extrajudicially executed.**

Scores of opposition party supporters were reportedly arrested between May and July under the 1970 Public Offences Act (POA), which permits detention without trial for up to five months. They included Devi Lal Thapa, who was held for several days after his arrest at Jumla while peace-

fully demonstrating against price rises during a visit by the Prime Minister. Several members of the monarchist National Democratic Party were also reportedly detained for several days in May by police in Pokhara after canvassing during local elections. Fifteen members of the Communist Party of Nepal (United Marxist-Leninist), the main opposition party in parliament, were also reportedly arrested in May and detained for over three months, apparently without trial, after protesting about police action during demonstrations.

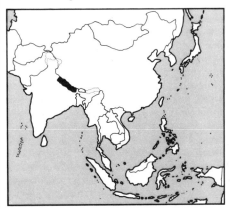

Torture of political and criminal detainees by police continued to be reported. Dilip Darewa, who had been arrested on a criminal charge in late 1991, reportedly displayed wounds on the soles of his feet, the result of his being beaten and burned in police custody, when he appeared in court in January. He was released in February. In Baglung district over 500 people were arrested following the murder of a policeman in January. Ten of them, including eight members of opposition parties, were held incommunicado, and allegedly forced to sign false statements under police torture. They were beaten on the face and body and in some cases subjected to other torture methods, including suspension from a pole, beatings on the soles of the feet, burning of the feet with flaming cloths soaked in kerosene, and having their bodies pierced with pins. When the 10 were formally charged in March, after up to 55 days in illegal police detention, three were unable to walk and had to be carried into court. They were remanded in custody in prison where seven remained without trial at the end of the year.

Five men arrested under the POA in February after a public protest were also

220

reportedly tortured by police in Kathmandu, the capital. They denied any involvement in the protest and were released on bail in March.

Several people were shot dead by police officers in circumstances which suggested that they may have been victims of extrajudicial executions. They included Tenzin, a Chinese national of Tibetan origin, who was shot dead by police in Solukhumbu district near the border with China on 3 January. Further killings occurred in Kathmandu and nearby Patan on 6 April when at least seven people were shot dead by police during a general strike against the government's economic policies. The killings occurred after demonstrations in support of the strike ended in clashes between police and demonstrators, but some of the victims had apparently not been involved in the protests. They included a seven-year-old boy. Human rights groups and some politicians alleged that the actual number of dead was higher than the official figure of seven. However, no official investigation was initiated into the circumstances of the killings or the number of victims.

In June Amnesty International published a report, *Nepal: a summary of human rights violations*. It described widespread human rights violations under the pre-1990 non-party system of government and continuing violations on a lesser scale since April 1990. The report made a series of recommendations to the government to increase legal and procedural human rights safeguards and to bring to justice perpetrators of human rights violations under previous and present governments. Throughout the year Amnesty International urged the government to publish and act on the reports of two commissions which had investigated torture, "disappearances" and possible extrajudicial executions before April 1990 (see *Amnesty International Report 1992*); to hold independent and impartial investigations into all post-1990 allegations of torture and extrajudicial or unlawful killings and bring those responsible to justice; and to ensure effective safeguards against human rights violations. In October the government informed Amnesty International that it had already implemented or was considering implementing several of Amnesty International's recommendations for increased human rights protection.

# NETHERLANDS
## (KINGDOM OF THE)

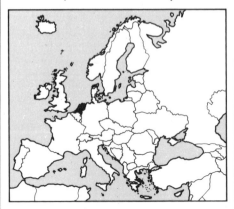

**There were further reports of torture and ill-treatment of prisoners in the Netherlands Antilles and Aruba, two Caribbean countries forming part of the Kingdom of the Netherlands.**

In the Netherlands Antilles a Commission of Inquiry, established by government decree, completed its report in August into allegations of unlawful violent behaviour by the police. It found evidence of unlawful use of violence by the police on every island except Saba. The violence mostly consisted of beatings with truncheons and, occasionally, fists; firearms were infrequently used. The Commission stated that neither disciplinary nor criminal action had been taken in obvious cases of serious police violence. One per cent of a representative cross-section of the entire population claimed to have been ill-treated by the police.

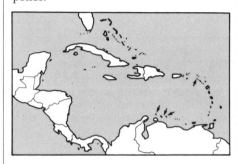

In June the Government of the Netherlands Antilles supplied further information on the cases of Henry K. Every, who died in custody in June 1990 (see *Amnesty International Report 1992*); Moreno Fabias, who required medical assistance after being beaten by police in May 1991 (see *Amnesty International Report 1992*); and Leroy Neil, who died of peritonitis in February 1991 while being interrogated by police in Curaçao. He had alleged that during a previous interrogation the police had forced a truncheon into his anus.

In July Cheroen Xavier Fluonia died in a police cell in Curaçao. According to the police, he had committed suicide by hanging himself. Amnesty International received reports that he had suffered substantial facial injuries consistent with allegations of ill-treatment before his death.

Benigno Guzman, a prisoner in Aruba, alleged that in August he had been kicked repeatedly in the stomach and beaten with a whip by prison guards, whom he identified. The day after the alleged assault eyewitnesses stated that they had seen injuries consistent with his allegations.

In June the Government of Aruba informed Amnesty International of the results of an internal police inquiry into allegations of severe beatings and other forms of torture and ill-treatment. In some cases the complainants had required hospital treatment (see *Amnesty International Report 1992*). The government stated that there was no basis for the complaints.

In October Amnesty International wrote to the Attorney General of the Netherlands Antilles about three cases of alleged torture and ill-treatment: the deaths in custody of Henry K. Every and Leroy Neil and the allegations of ill-treatment by the police of Moreno Fabias. Amnesty International considered that a full examination of the information had raised serious questions regarding the conduct and findings of the investigations into the two deaths and the decision of the authorities not to investigate fully the third case. The Attorney General was urged to investigate further certain specific points in the three cases. Amnesty International also wrote to the Attorney General requesting a thorough investigation into the case of Cheroen Fluonia, including the allegations of ill-treatment.

In December Amnesty International wrote to the Minister of Justice for the Netherlands Antilles regarding the report of the Commission of Inquiry into allegations of unlawful police behaviour. Amnesty International urged the government to implement the recommendations of the report and to introduce comprehen-

sive safeguards and remedies against torture and ill-treatment.

In July Amnesty International wrote to the Minister of Justice for Aruba welcoming draft legislation to establish a committee to deal with complaints against the police and requested further information on its powers, procedures and when it would start work.

# NICARAGUA

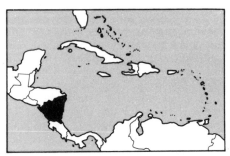

**At least five former *contra* rebels were reported to have been unlawfully killed by the police and army, although the circumstances were disputed. Eight members of the military escort of the head of the armed forces were implicated by a criminal court in the killing of a youth in 1990. Several detainees alleged that they had been tortured by the police. Dozens of deliberate and arbitrary killings by armed rebel groups were reported.**

Political polarization, violence by armed groups and deteriorating social and economic conditions remained as a legacy of the war which ended in 1990. President Violeta Barrios de Chamorro came under increased pressure from sectors of her ruling coalition party, the *Unión Nacional Opositora* (UNO), National Opposition Union, and from the United States (US) Government to reduce the influence of the opposition *Frente Sandinista de Liberación Nacional* (FSLN), Sandinista National Liberation Front. There was particular pressure to remove prominent Sandinista figures from senior posts in the police (*Policía Nacional*, National Police) and army (*Ejército Popular Sandinista* (EPS), Sandinista Popular Army). A conflict between the executive and legislature, provoked by confrontation between deputies of UNO, FSLN and *Grupo de Centro* (a breakaway UNO group), virtually paralysed the National

**222**

Assembly between September and December.

In the context of grave post-war problems, including demands for land and security by demobilized combatants and soaring levels of poverty and unemployment, there was continued violence by armed groups of former combatants and others, both politically and criminally motivated.

Groups of so-called *recontras* (former members of the *contra* or *Resistencia Nicaragüense*, Nicaraguan Resistance, which had fought the previous FSLN government) clashed with troops after carrying out occupations and attacks in the northern and Atlantic Coast regions. Demands for land and credit also motivated continued armed protests by so-called *recompas*, largely consisting of demobilized members of the much-reduced EPS. In March some *recontras* and *recompas* joined forces as *revueltos* and began a series of occupations of towns, road blocks, land take-overs and other protests. The army responded with force to actions by armed groups, with dozens of casualties resulting from the clashes.

The *Comisión Internacional de Verificación y Apoyo* (CIAV), International Commission of Verification and Support, a body of the Organization of American States set up to monitor *contra* demobilization, frequently acted as mediator in the conflicts. Governmental disarmament brigades collected thousands of weapons from groups which had agreed to disarm at the beginning of the year, often in exchange for payment, but armed clashes between *recontras* and the EPS escalated at the end of the year.

Deteriorating economic conditions led to strikes and protest action by students, former army officers, transport workers and others. Dozens were injured in violent clashes between police and demonstrators throughout the year.

Legislation was passed introducing reforms to the police, the Attorney General's Office and the Penal Code. The *Ley Orgánica de la Policía*, Constitutional Police Law, which aims to strengthen civilian control over the police, was passed in September and 13 senior police officials, including the Director of the National Police, were removed. This followed the suspension of US economic aid, partly on the grounds of alleged Sandinista control

of the security forces, and the publication of a report by the *Asociación Nicaragüense Pro Derechos Humanos* (ANPDH), Nicaraguan Association for Human Rights, demanding the removal of 26 senior National Police officials accused of human rights violations against former *contras*. ANPDH staff reportedly received threats from unidentified individuals after publishing the report.

Legislation creating the *Procuraduría de Derechos Humanos*, Office of the Human Rights Procurator, was passed in September but the office had not been established by the end of the year.

A package of amendments to the Penal Code, mostly regarding sexual offences, was approved by the National Assembly in July and became law in September. The amended Penal Code criminalized as "sodomy" the "induction, promotion and practice in scandalous form" of homosexual sex, punishable by up to three years' imprisonment. Amnesty International was concerned that this could lead to the imprisonment of people solely on the basis of their homosexuality, including the practice of homosexual acts in private between consenting adults. Such prisoners would be prisoners of conscience. An appeal challenging the law as unconstitutional was presented in November to the Supreme Court, which was due to make a ruling in early 1993.

At least five former *contras* were alleged to have been summarily killed by members of the police and army, although the circumstances remained disputed and unclarified. René Espinales Zelaya (known as Comandante Franklin II), was reportedly killed in an ambush by soldiers in Jinotega in June. Julio César Ochoa Mendoza (known as Comandante Matizón) was allegedly tortured and killed by troops in July as he was going to meet his mother in Zelaya Central. Other sources, however, claimed that both men had died in armed clashes. A Tripartite Commission consisting of government, CIAV and Roman Catholic Church representatives was formed in October to investigate killings of former *contras* since the end of the war. It had not published any findings by the end of the year.

In July a criminal court judge ruled that there was sufficient evidence to try eight members of the military escort of General Humberto Ortega, head of the armed forces, for the killing of Jean Paul Genie Lacayo, a

17-year-old shot dead on the Managua-Masaya highway in 1990 (see *Amnesty International Report 1992*). The judge ruled that the eight should be tried before a military court and that General Humberto Ortega and two army captains should be tried for covering up the killing. Amnesty International was concerned that, in view of indications of military obstruction at different stages of the investigation, the military court system did not offer sufficient guarantees of impartiality in this case. An appeal against the decision to transfer the case to military jurisdiction was lodged by Jean Paul Genie's father before the Court of Appeal, which upheld the judge's ruling. A further appeal was presented in November to the Supreme Court.

Exhumations continued at sites believed to contain the remains of victims of human rights abuses by government forces during the war. In April the ANPDH began exhuming the remains of seven people believed to have been extrajudicially executed by the army in 1985. However, no official steps were taken to investigate allegations of past abuses, whether by government or *contra* forces, nor to bring to justice those responsible, who were shielded from prosecution under amnesty laws passed in 1991.

Several criminal suspects were reportedly tortured in police custody. Miguel Lugo Reyes, a painter and decorator, was detained by police in February, accused of theft. He was taken to Nandaime police station, where he was reportedly beaten, kicked and denied food and drink. He was then held for three days by police in Granada where, according to fellow detainees, he was severely and repeatedly beaten. He was taken to hospital in Granada where he testified before a judge that he had been beaten by three police officials. A medical examination noted numerous injuries including severe head wounds, two fractured vertebrae and burns and bruises on various parts of the body. He died in hospital in Managua on 6 March. Investigations into his death by the *Inspectoría Civil*, the police monitoring body of the Interior Ministry, had not resulted in the prosecution of those responsible by the end of the year.

Several demobilized *contras* also claimed to have been tortured by police. Oscar Pérez Benavides was detained by police in Matagalpa in July. He was reportedly beaten and interrogated about his father, a local union leader. His sister, who tried to intervene on hearing his screams, was threatened by the police. Oscar Pérez escaped and a medical examination recorded injuries consistent with the ill-treatment he described. The *Centro Nicaragüense de Derechos Humanos* (CENIDH), Nicaraguan Centre for Human Rights, reported the case to the Interior Ministry but investigations were not known to have yielded any results.

Ill-treatment by police was also reported in the context of numerous strikes and demonstrations throughout the year. In January riot police arrested 32 workers of the *Empresa Nacional de Buses* (ENABUS), National Bus Company, during a demonstration outside the Transport Ministry. According to investigations by CENIDH, 15 showed signs of having been beaten on arrest. The police authorities claimed that several police had also been injured by protesters. CENIDH's call for an investigation remained unheeded. Police were also accused of ill-treatment in the context of forcible evictions from occupied property. In January Isidro Gonzalez Cisneros suffered severe cuts and bruises after being beaten with clubs by riot police who broke up a demonstration by residents of the Pedro Joaquín Chamorro settlement in Managua.

Dozens of deliberate and arbitrary killings by *recontras* were reported, mostly in rural areas in the north. In March FSLN activist Victor Manuel Martínez was killed by *recontras* at his home in Muelle de los Bueyes, Juigalpa, after receiving death threats. Relatives claimed to have been threatened by local police when they reported the killing. *Recontras* were reported to have killed a family of eight, including three children, in an attack on a hamlet in Rio Blanco in December.

A number of killings of former *contras* were attributed to *recompas* and individuals linked to the FSLN. *Recontra* commander Róger Benavides Castellón (Comandante Freddy) was killed in an ambush by *recompas* in Estelí in January. In November the president of an organization created to demand the return of property confiscated under the Sandinista Government to its former owners, Arges Sequiera Mangas, was killed at his home in León. The previously unknown *Fuerzas Punitivas de Izquierda*, Punitive Forces of the Left, later claimed responsibility for the killing. Initial investigations identified the killers as three

**224**

former army officers. Most other cases of *recontra* and *recompa* killings, however, were not thoroughly investigated by the authorities.

Amnesty International representatives visited Nicaragua in May to pursue the organization's concerns about political killings, torture and ill-treatment. The representatives met government officials, including the Attorney General and members of the *Inspectoría Civil*. In July Amnesty International wrote to the President about the amendments to the Penal Code, urging her not to ratify any legislation that could lead to the imprisonment of prisoners of conscience. Amnesty International also wrote to the government about its concerns regarding military jurisdiction in the case of Jean Paul Genie and the threats and harassment aimed at human rights workers. No substantive reply was received to any of these concerns.

In October Amnesty International published *Human rights violations against the indigenous peoples of the Americas*, which included concerns in Nicaragua.

# NIGER

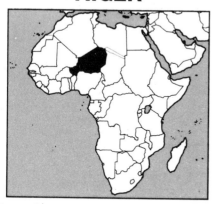

**More than 200 members of the Tuareg minority ethnic group were arrested and most were still held at the end of the year: some were possible prisoners of conscience. An army captain awaiting trial for killing Tuareg detainees in 1990 was released.**

A transitional period in the run-up to a multi-party political system, as agreed by a National Conference in 1991, continued throughout 1992. Amadou Cheiffou remained as Prime Minister and President Ali Saïbou continued as head of state but

with reduced responsibilities. A referendum on the Constitution took place in late November and parliamentary and presidential elections were due to be completed in January 1993.

Conflict continued throughout the year between the security forces and the Tuareg rebel organization, the *Front de libération de l'Aïr et de l'Azawad* (FLAA), Liberation Front of Aïr and Azawad. The FLAA killed or took prisoner dozens of members of the security forces and civilian officials, as well as killing or injuring people when seizing vehicles. Negotiations continued between the authorities and the FLAA, but a truce agreed in May was not effective.

A commission set up by the National Conference to examine past political crimes and human rights violations continued its work (see *Amnesty International Report 1992*). It undertook preliminary investigations into allegations of offences by officials, including torture, corruption and unfair dismissal. Cases were then passed to the transitional legislative body, the High Council of the Republic, to decide if those implicated should be prosecuted. In September, however, the President of the commission, Maman Abou, a Tuareg, fled the country fearing arrest after a large number of members of the Tuareg community were arrested.

The High Court of Justice, a special court set up by the National Conference to try former government and security officials, heard its first case. In November it sentenced two retired army colonels to 10 years' imprisonment after finding them guilty of killing Vice-President Sani Souna Siddo while he was in detention in 1977 on suspicion of involvement in an attempted coup. The killing was found to be an extrajudicial execution "carried out intentionally, with premeditation and without official orders". Although those convicted and sentenced by the High Court have no right of appeal, the Prime Minister pardoned both men a day later on the grounds of preserving national unity.

In June the former security adviser to the Head of State, Amadou Oumarou, known as "Bonkano" (see *Amnesty International Report 1992*), was released. The case against him had been passed from the commission to examine past offences to the High Council of the Republic. The Council had rejected it on the grounds that the only evidence against him concerned illegal enrichment, which had only recently become a criminal offence.

A large number of Tuareg were arrested during the year, often in apparent reprisal for actions by Tuareg rebels. Many appeared to be prisoners of conscience, arrested on account of their ethnic origin and having no connection with the Tuareg rebellion. In May the security forces arrested and ill-treated more than 50 Tuareg whom they held for about 48 hours when they raided an area of Arlit in the north of the country, looking for suspected car thieves. In July many Tuareg leaders were arrested and held briefly in the town of Abalak, after the discovery of a dead body near the gendarmerie headquarters.

More than 200 Tuareg were arrested by the army from August onwards and held outside of any legal framework. On 27 August a group of 50 soldiers arrested the Governor of Agadez and two of his colleagues the day after a police officer was killed by armed men, reported to be Tuareg. The soldiers were also protesting against the failure of the civilian authorities to deal with the increasingly violent rebellion by the Tuareg. In the next few days, the security forces arrested dozens of other Tuareg in northern Niger and in the capital, Niamey, and a joint command of the army, police and gendarmerie publicly announced their lack of respect for the official authorities. On 31 August Prime Minister Cheiffou stated that those arrested would be treated in accordance with legal procedures, effectively giving the government's approval to the action of the security forces. Arrests of Tuareg continued into October. Some 40 were released in December but more than 150 prisoners were believed to be still held; some were held incommunicado and uncharged in military barracks, but by the end of the year others had been questioned about possible links with the rebellion and transferred to ordinary prisons. No details about any charges were known.

Among those arrested were Mohamed Moussa, Minister of Transport; Akoli Daouel, founder of the *Union pour la démocratie et le progrès social* (UDPS), Union for Democracy and Social Progress, and current leader of the *Parti nigérien pour l'unité et la démocratie* (PNUD), Nigerien Party for Unity and Democracy; and many other members of the UDPS.

An army officer, Captain Maliki

Boureima, who was awaiting trial for killing Tuareg detainees in 1990 (see *Amnesty International Report 1992*), was released after junior officers took hostage a government minister and the President of the High Council of the Republic in February. The officers demanded improved living conditions, payment of salary arrears and the unconditional release of Captain Maliki. The authorities agreed to the material demands within a few days and in late March agreed to Captain Maliki's release, fearing further action by the army. His release appeared to signal an end to the attempts by the authorities to hold the army accountable for the extrajudicial executions of hundreds of Tuareg in 1990, and further angered and frustrated the Tuareg community. Although the National Conference had investigated and verified allegations of large-scale human rights violations against the Tuareg community in 1990, only Captain Maliki, who had publicly admitted to killing Tuareg detainees, had been arrested.

The FLAA, which continued to mount attacks throughout 1992, also committed human rights abuses. At least 14 people who were seized in January were still held at the end of the year. They appeared to be hostages. One hostage, Issoufou Wadin, a district administrator, was released in January with a demand that the government should withdraw all members of the security forces from northern Niger. By August the rebels had taken hostage at least 45 people, most of whom were officials. Most were believed to be still held at the end of the year but two died in detention in December. The rebels also killed over 20 officials and members of the security forces.

Amnesty International appealed to the authorities to release all those arrested purely on account of their ethnic origin and not known to have been involved in acts of violence. It also appealed to the government to guarantee the safety of all those arrested by the army and held in incommunicado detention outside of any legal framework from August onwards, and urged that all such prisoners should be tried promptly and fairly or released.

Amnesty International representatives visited Niamey in February to inquire about the activities of the commission set up to examine past political offences and the special court established to try former officials.

# NIGERIA

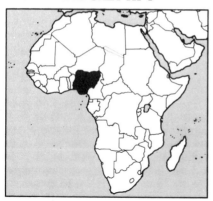

**Five prominent government critics were arrested and held incommunicado for several weeks before being released on bail; they were prisoners of conscience. Several people were arrested and four charged with subversion after protesting against the postponement of the return to civilian rule; they were prisoners of conscience. More than 240 Chadian nationals were arrested and held without charge or trial; over 200 were forcibly returned to Chad where dozens were reportedly tortured, at least three were extrajudicially executed, and about 40 died in harsh prison conditions. Nine army officers convicted in unfair trials remained held incommunicado, although 11 civilians held for almost two years in connection with the same case were released. No executions were known to have been carried out but at least seven death sentences were passed. Twelve death sentences were commuted. No action was taken against police involved in the extrajudicial execution of 80 villagers in 1990.**

Steep price rises led to widespread riots and demonstrations against government economic policies in May. Hundreds of people were arrested in Lagos and elsewhere and several deaths were reported. In addition, hundreds of people were killed in religious and ethnic violence in various parts of the country.

In the process of transition to civilian rule, due to be completed in mid-1993, elected civilian state governors took office in January. In legislative elections in July, contested by two parties created by the military government of President Ibrahim Babangida, the Social Democratic Party won majorities in the House of Representatives and the Senate over the National Republican Convention. In October the government postponed presidential elections due to take place in December 1992 after primary elections of party candidates were flawed by widespread corruption. It also banned all presidential candidates from further involvement in the elections.

Five prominent critics of the government were arrested in May and June. Dr Beko Ransome-Kuti, President of the Committee for the Defence of Human Rights and Chairman of the newly formed prodemocracy coalition, Campaign for Democracy (CD), was arrested at gunpoint by some 200 riot police at his home in Lagos on 19 May. Two other CD members – Femi Falana, President of the National Association of Democratic Lawyers, and Baba Omojola – were also arrested that day. After filing legal actions to have the detainees produced before the High Court, human rights lawyer and CD member Chief Gani Fawehinmi was himself detained on 29 May. Olusegun Mayegun, President of the National Association of Nigerian Students, was arrested two weeks later. He was reportedly beaten and kicked at the time of his arrest and during interrogation, and deprived of food for 10 days in detention.

The five were held incommunicado in Abuja, the new capital, despite several orders by the Lagos High Court requiring the authorities to produce the detainees in court. The Minister of Justice alleged publicly that the five had plotted subversion and had exacerbated recent civil unrest. They were finally brought before a magistrate's court on 15 June and charged with "conspiracy to commit treasonable felony", an offence which carries a maximum penalty of life imprisonment. On 29 June the five were released on bail and the case was adjourned in October to 1993. On 1 July the Lagos High Court ordered the government to pay Dr Ransome-Kuti 50,000 Naira (US$2,700) in damages for illegal arrest and detention.

In December four people in Kano, northern Nigeria, were arrested and charged with subversion after protesting against the postponement of the return to civilian rule. They included Wada Abubakar, a former deputy governor of Kano State, and Wada Waziri, an aide to one of the banned presidential candidates. Several members of human rights organizations which campaigned for a civilian transitional government were briefly detained.

More than 240 Chadians, some of them resident in Nigeria, were arrested in the northeastern city of Maiduguri between October 1991 and March 1992 and detained without charge or trial at a military camp. They were arrested at the request of the Chadian authorities who suspected them of supporting an armed opposition group which had clashed with Chadian government forces in Chad in January. Over 200 were forcibly returned to Chad in the following months, in secret and outside the terms of any legal procedure. At least three of them, including Goukouni Guet and other leaders of the opposition *Mouvement pour la démocratie et le développement* (MDD), Movement for Democracy and Development, were tortured to death or extrajudicially executed by the Chadian authorities. About 40 others died from thirst and exhaustion in March and April while detained in Chad. In July the Nigerian authorities arrested and forcibly repatriated two more Chadians and in November a further 15.

Eleven civilians who had been held for almost two years in connection with a coup attempt in April 1990 were released in March. Nine of them had been detained without charge or trial, apparently because they were related to people sought by the authorities (see *Amnesty International Report 1992*). The other two had been convicted with nine army officers after a grossly unfair secret trial before a Special Military Tribunal on charges of treason and concealment of treason (see *Amnesty International Report 1992*). The nine army officers continued to be held incommunicado.

The decline in reports of executions noted in 1991 continued and no executions were known to have been carried out in 1992. However, seven death sentences were reported, including those passed on three brothers convicted in July by a Robbery and Firearms Tribunal in Port Harcourt, southeastern Nigeria. New information was received about death sentences and executions in previous years. All the condemned prisoners were believed to have been convicted by Robbery and Firearms Tribunals, special courts whose procedures do not satisfy international fair trial standards and from which there is no right of appeal. For example, information

was received about four men who were executed publicly in their home towns in Imo State in 1990 and 1991, all for armed robbery, and five men who were executed at a military barracks in Ibadan in 1991.

In June death sentences imposed on 12 young men in 1988 were commuted to 10 years' imprisonment by the Lagos State authorities. One of the 12, Augustine Eke, was aged only 14 at the time of his arrest in 1984. Another had died in prison in 1990. The 12 were convicted by a Robbery and Firearms Tribunal after a trial which a senior Nigerian legal official has described as "full of procedural irregularities and overt bias against the convicts". The defendants stated that they had been beaten and threatened with death by the police while in pre-trial custody.

A further death sentence was passed in December in connection with violent clashes in Kaduna State in May between Christians belonging to the Kataf ethnic group and Muslims belonging to the Hausa community. Dozens of people were subsequently brought to trial before special courts – Civil Disturbances Special Tribunals which were established in 1987 and over which a judge presides. These courts had previously tried cases arising from religious and ethnic riots in northern Nigeria. Zamani Lekwot, a retired army general, and other Kataf leaders were detained without charge until 29 July when six of them were charged with unlawful assembly. They were acquitted on 18 August, but were immediately rearrested. Zamani Lekwot and six others were charged on 4 September with culpable homicide, which carries a possible death sentence, and other offences. In October they attempted to obtain a ruling in the High Court that their fundamental human rights were being denied because the special tribunal trying their case, whose members were predominantly Muslim and included no member of the Kataf community, was biased against them. However, the government promulgated a decree in December confirming that the tribunal's proceedings could not be challenged in the ordinary courts. In another case before the same special tribunal, a death sentence was passed on 4 December. Also in December, while one of the tribunal's members was absent for medical reasons, two defendants were sentenced to 18 years' imprisonment for unlawful assembly and rioting despite insufficient

**228**

evidence to support the prosecution's case. There was no right of appeal to a higher independent court – decisions of the tribunal can only be referred to the military government for confirmation or disallowal.

Prison conditions remained harsh, particularly for over 80 per cent of inmates who were awaiting trial. They were commonly held in overcrowded and insanitary cells, many for several years. According to official figures, 5,300 prisoners had died in 1991 from disease and lack of food and medical care.

In October the January 1991 findings of a judicial commission of inquiry into a police massacre were leaked to the press. Eighty demonstrators in Umuechem village, in Rivers State in southeast Nigeria, had been shot dead, victims of extrajudicial executions, and 500 houses razed in October 1990 when villagers protested at inadequate compensation for their land and environmental damage by a multinational oil company. The commission recommended prosecution of named police officers responsible for the attack, but its findings were not made public by the government and no police officers were brought to justice. The police unit was apparently disbanded following the shooting of another protester. However, no other action was known to have been taken by the authorities.

Amnesty International urged the government to release all prisoners of conscience and protested about its forcible return of Chadian detainees to Chad. It welcomed the release of 11 prisoners held in connection with the April 1990 coup attempt but called for the nine army officers still held incommunicado to be allowed to appeal to a higher court and to be given access to family and lawyers.

Amnesty International urged the government not to use the death penalty and appealed for the commutation of all death sentences.

# NORWAY

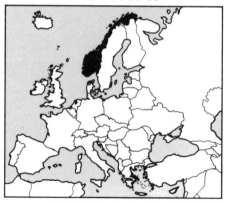

**Two conscientious objectors were imprisoned for their refusal to perform military service. They were considered to be prisoners of conscience.**

Jan Otto Nilsen had originally been granted conscientious objector status in 1982 on the grounds of his pacifism, but during alternative service he informed the authorities that he no longer considered himself to be an absolute pacifist. He stated that he could not perform military service while Norway was part of the North Atlantic Treaty Organization (NATO), whose strategy was based on nuclear weapons. A court in 1986 found that his newly expressed convictions did not fulfil the requirements necessary for alternative service; subsequently the Ministry of Justice withdrew his conscientious objector status. He was imprisoned from October to December 1990 for refusing to obey military call-up orders. Jan Otto Nilsen refused to respond to a further call-up for military service and he was imprisoned in June 1992 at the start of another 90-day sentence.

Kjetil Ramberg began serving a 90-day prison sentence in September after a county court ruled that he did not have a sufficiently "firm and unequivocal basic pacifist attitude" to obtain exemption from military service. He had declared his opposition to Norway's participation in NATO's nuclear strategy.

Amnesty International urged the immediate release of prisoners of conscience Jan Otto Nilsen and Kjetil Ramberg. The government replied that neither of them had fulfilled the conditions for exemption because their convictions lacked "firmness and strength".

# PAKISTAN

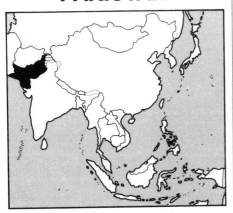

Scores of prisoners of conscience were held for their political activities or religious beliefs. Thousands of opposition party activists were arrested, many of whom may have been prisoners of conscience. Some were detained briefly, others repeatedly arrested on apparently false criminal charges. Many detainees were subjected to torture or ill-treatment. At least 15 detainees died in custody, allegedly as a result of torture. The security forces reportedly committed at least 20 extrajudicial executions. Over 130 death sentences were reported, most of them imposed by special courts which failed to meet international standards for fair trial. Nineteen executions were reported.

Political and criminal violence continued throughout the year, particularly in Sindh Province. The government of Prime Minister Mian Nawaz Sharif blamed the opposition Pakistan People's Party (PPP) for much of the violence, a charge which the PPP denied. PPP supporters and members of other opposition parties were systematically harassed through mass police round-ups and detentions.

During an "anti-crime operation" which began in late May in Sindh, the army reportedly committed numerous human rights violations, including extrajudicial executions. An ordinance issued in July by President Ghulam Ishaq Khan granted immunity from prosecution to members of the army for all acts undertaken "in good faith" during law and order operations. Hundreds of activists of the *Mohajir Qaumi Mahaz* (MQM), Mohajir National Movement, were arrested from June onwards, after the

army uncovered 23 cells in Karachi in which the MQM had allegedly tortured its opponents.

A bill providing for a mandatory death penalty for blasphemy against the Prophet Mohammed was adopted by the Senate in July. The National Assembly delayed its assent for more than the stipulated 90 days, causing the bill to lapse. It was unclear whether courts were legally bound to impose death sentences for blasphemy. A government order issued in October that personal identity cards should indicate an individual's religious affiliation led members of religious minorities to fear harassment.

The trials on charges of corruption of former PPP Prime Minister Benazir Bhutto continued. Her husband, Asif Ali Zardari, was acquitted in a murder case, but he remained in judicial custody on other charges.

Scores of prisoners of conscience were held on account of their non-violent political activities or their religious beliefs. Tahir Iqbal, a Christian held since December 1990 on apparently false charges of having used blasphemous language (see *Amnesty International Report 1992*), died in a Lahore prison in July in unclear circumstances. A court-ordered post-mortem had not been carried out by the end of the year. Another Christian, Gul Masih, was sentenced to death for blasphemy in November. He had been imprisoned in Sargoda, Punjab Province, since December 1991. The conviction was apparently secured solely on the basis of the complainant's testimony. Gul Masih's appeal before the Lahore High Court was pending at the end of the year.

Members of the Ahmadiyya community continued to be imprisoned solely for the peaceful exercise of their religious faith. In November, 10 Ahmadis of Chak village in Faisalabad district were sentenced to three-year prison sentences for having distributed invitations to a prayer meeting; one of them, Mohammed Ali, was given an additional three-year prison sentence for having made a call to prayer. Ahmadis were increasingly tried on blasphemy charges, both individually and in groups, but none of the cases had been completed by the end of 1992. In March, 20 members of the Ahmadiyya community in Kotri were arrested during the Friday prayer and charged with blasphemy and with propagating their

**230**

faith. They were released on bail after two weeks.

Two journalists – Mohammed Ishaq Tunio of *The Nation* and Shafi Bejoro of *Aftab* – were briefly detained and reportedly tortured by police in April because they intended to publish information on alleged vote rigging in a by-election.

G.M. Syed, the ailing 89-year-old leader of the *Jeay Sindh Mahaz* (JSM), Long Live Sindh Front, was held under house arrest from January under the Maintenance of Public Order Ordinance, after a speech in which he expressed his hope for an independent Sindh. Arrest warrants were later issued against eight other JSM activists, but their trial on sedition charges had not taken place by the end of the year.

Thousands of opposition party activists were detained during the year, many of whom may have been prisoners of conscience. About 1,000 PPP members were rounded up in late May in Sindh Province before a rally to protest against alleged vote rigging. In November thousands were detained before and during a PPP protest march on Islamabad. Among those arrested were 12 members of the non-governmental Human Rights Commission of Pakistan monitoring the demonstration. They were released after 30 hours, following appeals by foreign journalists and diplomats.

During the army operation in Sindh which began in late May, relatives and friends of MQM activists were reportedly arrested in place of suspects. In October the Chief Justice of Sindh ordered the release of the 70-year-old father of an MQM leader and reprimanded the police for arresting "relatives and friends of the nominated accused though no such law exists which justifies this action".

Most opposition supporters were released after a few days or weeks, but the practice of repeatedly bringing apparently false criminal charges against some opposition leaders persisted (see *Amnesty International Report 1992*). For example, member of parliament and former PPP provincial minister Pir Mazhar-ul-Haq had been detained on seven successive criminal charges in 1990: he was cleared of all but one charge for lack of evidence and was held under two preventive detention orders. In 1991, 10 further criminal charges were brought against him, five of which were dropped during that year. In January 1992, three co-defendants withdrew statements implicating Pir Mazhar-ul-Haq, and declared that these had been obtained "under duress, coercion and torture". Two further criminal charges were lodged against him in May and August; a detention order under the Maintenance of Public Order Ordinance was revoked in August. Pir Mazhar-ul-Haq was held on kidnapping charges from April to June and again for several days in September.

Many political prisoners were held in unacknowledged detention. Some were moved from one police station to another to make it difficult for their families to find them. In some cases police defied court orders aimed at tracing people held in unacknowledged detention.

Torture, including rape, and various forms of ill-treatment were frequently inflicted on political and criminal detainees to extract confessions, and in some cases to obtain information about suspected government opponents. For example, when Mushtaq Saigol, an MQM activist, and his sons were arrested in October, his wife was hit with rifle butts and threatened that her sons would be shot if she did not reveal the whereabouts of a particular MQM leader. During mass arrests of PPP demonstrators in November, several people were beaten by police and some were tortured in police custody. Salman Taseer, PPP Information Secretary, was allegedly hung upside-down for four hours and beaten in Dharampura police station in Lahore. Several journalists covering the demonstration, including Mariana Baber of *The News*, were severely beaten by police in Islamabad.

Although press reports of incidents of torture sometimes referred to "investigations", Amnesty International knew of no cases in which police or security force personnel were convicted of inflicting torture.

At least 15 detainees were reported to have died in custody as a result of torture. Mohammed Yusuf Jakhrani, President of the National Democratic Party, died in June in Pano Aqil cantonment near Kandhkot in Sindh Province after six days in detention. The police said that his death was due to heart failure, but his body bore extensive skin abrasions and burn injuries on the genitals. Ahmad Abdul Sajid, elder brother of MQM activist Ahmad Abdul Majid, was arrested on 15 October by police and paramilitary Rangers searching for his brother. On 5 November his family found his body in a charity trust in Karachi. It bore multiple injuries apparently inflicted by torture in custody.

Flogging continued to be imposed by the courts as a penalty for rape and drugs offences. In July a sentence of five years' imprisonment and 20 lashes, imposed on four men by a Special Court for Speedy Trial in Peshawar, was confirmed. There were new reports of the use of fetters on prisoners and detainees in police custody, in violation of the United Nations Standard Minimum Rules for the Treatment of Prisoners.

The security forces were reported to have committed at least 20 extrajudicial executions during the year. In February up to 12 people may have been killed when security forces opened fire on members of the Jammu and Kashmir Liberation Front who were marching peacefully to the cease-fire line between Pakistan and India. At least two were reportedly shot in the head.

During the "anti-crime operation" in Sindh Province, nine people were extrajudicially executed by an army patrol at Jamshoro. Initially, the army claimed the victims were "saboteurs" trained in India, but the local press presented contrary evidence. The army then admitted that they were tenant farmers caught up in a land dispute between local landlords. Several senior army commanders were removed from their posts and in October a major was sentenced to death and 13 others were sentenced to life imprisonment by a court-martial in connection with the incident.

At least 130 prisoners were sentenced to death, mostly for murder. Many were sentenced by Special Courts for Suppression of Terrorist Activities and by Special Courts for Speedy Trial.

At least 19 prisoners were executed, two in April and 17 in November. These were the first judicial executions reported since 1988, apart from one execution in a tribal area with a separate judicial system (see *Amnesty International Report 1992*). All but one of those executed, including a 17-year-old youth, had been sentenced by Special Courts for Speedy Trial, whose procedures fall short of international standards for fair trial. Six other convicted prisoners due to be executed were reportedly reprieved when relatives of the murder victims accepted compensation and, as permitted under Islamic law, granted pardon.

One of the men executed in April, Mehdi Khan, had been sentenced to death in 1988 by a military court which also failed to satisfy international standards for fair trial.

The Lahore High Court in January removed the President's power to commute death sentences under Article 45 of the Constitution, on the grounds that it contradicted Islamic legal provisions under which only the legal heirs of the victims of murder can pardon the murderer. Hearing appeals against the Lahore High Court's decision, the Supreme Court in July declared that it was beyond the powers of the Lahore High Court to decide on constitutional matters. The Supreme Court several times adjourned hearings on the propriety of public hangings, pending an assessment by the Council of Islamic Ideology.

In February Amnesty International called for a full inquiry into the killings of protesters at the Indian border and in May expressed concern about the reported detention and torture of an Indian diplomat. In June Amnesty International published a report, *Pakistan: Arrests of political opponents in Sindh Province, August 1990 – early 1992*, which documented systematic harassment of supporters of opposition parties since the dismissal of the PPP government in 1990. Amnesty International called on the government to respect the rule of law and to take action to stop the repression of nonviolent political activity. It also urged the government to ensure that the anti-crime campaign in Sindh Province would not be used to permit human rights violations. In July Amnesty International urged the government to institute an independent and impartial inquiry into the ill-treatment of journalists in April. It wrote to the government in August expressing its concern about the ordinance granting immunity from prosecution to members of the army.

In April, following two executions, Amnesty International appealed to the government to stop further executions, and in November expressed great concern about the large number of executions in Punjab.

**232**

# PANAMA

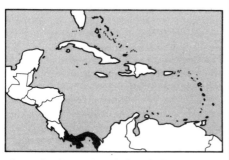

Three leaders of a disbanded paramilitary force continued to be held without trial on charges which appeared to be politically motivated. There were reports of ill-treatment of protesters and detainees by police following anti-United States (US) demonstrations. Prison conditions were reported to be harsh.

On the eve of a visit to Panama by US President George Bush in June, a US soldier was shot dead and another wounded when unidentified gunmen ambushed a US military vehicle. The next day, there was an armed attack on a US air force base by M-20, an armed opposition group. In October a bomb exploded near the office of the Attorney General. There were allegations that the M-20 had been responsible, but the group denied it.

Demonstrations organized by the *Movimiento de Desempleados Colonenses* (MODESCO), Colón Unemployed Movement, demanding jobs and development plans for the area resulted in violent clashes with the police in which one protester was killed and dozens were wounded and arrested. In July a MODESCO demonstration in Colón was violently dispersed by police, who fatally injured one woman, Marja Columba Calonge Ibarra, a mother of three, and injured several others. The police were alleged to have used excessive force in opening fire on unarmed demonstrators. The police version of the killing, reportedly contradicted by several witnesses, was that the woman had been hit by a ricocheting bullet. An investigation into the killing was reportedly initiated, but no results had been announced by the end of the year.

In June a former soldier was convicted of the murder of Father Nicolas van Kleef, a paraplegic Dutch priest, during aborted elections in May 1989 (see *Amnesty International Report 1990*). The soldier had reportedly entered Father van Kleef's vehicle and shot him in the neck while he was urging people to vote.

Three former leaders of the disbanded Dignity Battalions – Benjamín Colamarco, Arturo Marquínez and Enrique Thompson – arrested shortly after the US invasion of Panama in December 1989, continued to be held on vaguely defined charges which appeared to be politically motivated rather than for a specific criminal act (see *Amnesty International Report 1992*). No date for a trial had been set by the end of 1992. Over 40 other members of the administration and armed forces of former president Manuel Noriega remained in prison awaiting trial on charges ranging from corruption to murder.

Jaime Simons, former manager of the Savings Bank and a founder member of the *Partido Revolucionario Democrático* (PRD), Revolutionary Democratic Party, who had been arrested by US forces in December 1989, was finally charged with fraud after 22 months' detention. Jaime Simons, who had prostate cancer, reportedly asked to serve his prison term under house arrest but the authorities denied his request. By the end of the year he appeared to have been held longer than the penalty provided by law for the offence of which he was accused. His continued detention appeared to be politically motivated.

Police reportedly ill-treated protesters and detainees after anti-US demonstrations. In January Father Conrado Sanjur, a Catholic priest and coordinator of the *Coordinadora Popular de Derechos Humanos de Panamá* (COPODEHUPA), Human Rights Popular Coordination of Panama, was manhandled and two youths reportedly severely beaten by police during an anti-US demonstration. No investigation appeared to have been carried out into the incident.

At least 30 people, including some 20 minors, were reportedly arrested in June, at the time of US President Bush's visit to Panama, following an anti-US protest. The demonstrators reportedly threw stones towards the stand where President Bush was to speak, but were too far away to hit it. The police dispersed the demonstrators with tear-gas and birdshot, and the event was cancelled. According to human rights groups, only some of those arrested had participated in the demonstration and others were picked up near by. Many of those arrested were reportedly beaten upon arrest on the head, face, arms and legs. Víctor Manuel Cerda was reportedly beaten more severely, sustaining a serious arm injury, when police identified him as a member of MODESCO. Student Raúl de Gracia Guevara was wounded by birdshot in his foot.

Prison conditions were reported to be harsh because of severe overcrowding, dilapidated facilities, inadequate medical care and endemic violence, particularly in Modelo prison.

# PAPUA NEW GUINEA

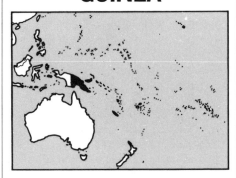

**Dozens of suspected supporters of the Bougainville Revolutionary Army (BRA), a secessionist group in Bougainville, were killed in extrajudicial executions by government forces; at least three others reportedly "disappeared". Torture and ill-treatment continued to be reported throughout the country. Serious human rights abuses, including the killing of prisoners, were reportedly committed by BRA members.**

General elections were held in June and Paias Wingti, head of the People's Democratic Movement, was elected Prime Minister in July. He vowed to revive the nation's economy, to tackle official corruption and to resolve the political status of Bougainville island, where an interim government, backed by the BRA, had declared independence in May 1990.

Armed conflict continued on Bougainville between the Papua New Guinea Defence Forces (PNGDF) and the BRA. There were persistent reports of PNGDF patrol boats shelling coastal towns and villages in the central and southern regions of Bougainville, causing residents to flee

their homes. In October the government announced a military offensive to recapture central Bougainville and PNGDF patrol boats shelled the island's capital, Arawa. Government soldiers were also reported to have burned houses and destroyed livestock belonging to suspected BRA supporters. In March and September the PNGDF carried out commando raids into the neighbouring Solomon Islands, ostensibly to prevent Solomon Islanders from supplying fuel and ammunition to BRA members. Following protests by the Solomon Islands, the PNG authorities acknowledged the raids but claimed they were unauthorized by the central government.

Despite an agreement signed in 1991 to restore essential services to Bougainville, delivery of food and medicine to the central part of the island continued to be obstructed by the PNGDF. In February BRA members impounded, then burned a ship carrying medical supplies to Bougainville, leading the government to intensify its blockade.

Dozens of people were reported to have been extrajudicially executed by government troops in Bougainville. Among the victims were at least three people reportedly killed when PNGDF troops strafed boats delivering goods to the island.

In May PNGDF troops reportedly entered Okogupa village in Aita and fired indiscriminately, killing an estimated 17 residents, possibly many more. Among those reported killed were village chief Silas Ausie, his wife and five children; and a man named Kaputoi and his family. Witnesses said the killings occurred while villagers were sleeping after anniversary celebrations marking the 1990 declaration of Bougainville's independence.

Two people were killed and a three-year-old girl wounded when PNGDF troops raided the Solomon Islands on 12 September. Those killed were Peter Kamaraia, a shopkeeper, and his sister, Jacinta Popo. Another man, Francis Beiaruru, was abducted after the killings and detained for several days during which he said he was questioned and accused of selling arms to the BRA, which he denied. The PNG Government condemned the raid, which it said was unauthorized. In October the government officially apologized for the troops' actions and said those responsible would be suspended and faced disciplinary action.

**234**

At least three people reportedly "disappeared" in military custody. Michael Vinias, Kevin Tabu and Richard Kikira were reportedly arrested on 29 August while travelling from the Solomon Islands to the Tubiana mission station in Bougainville with a boat-load of food and fuel. Military officials denied that the three had been detained by PNGDF soldiers on Torauto Island. There were unconfirmed reports that Michael Vinias and Kevin Tabu were subsequently killed and that Richard Kikira was taken to Buka Island and detained there.

Torture and ill-treatment by the security forces continued to be reported in Bougainville and throughout Papua New Guinea. In the Wakunai district of Bougainville, villagers were reportedly subjected to threats and beatings during May anniversary celebrations of Bougainville's 1990 declaration of independence, and two men were said to have had their fingers chopped off by soldiers. On mainland Papua New Guinea, police and military violence appeared to have increased during the election campaign. In July residents of Pempemeri and Gramaugle villages in Goroko province were reportedly threatened and beaten by soldiers after failed electoral candidates from the region had allegedly incited "tribal war". Up to 22 villagers were reportedly arrested and held incommunicado for four days, during which they said they were beaten, before being released without charge. The detainees subsequently filed a complaint with the police authorities but there were no reports of any official investigations being held by the end of the year.

Serious human rights abuses by the BRA were reported throughout the year. Civilians in various parts of the island reported being beaten and raped by BRA members, and others said they had been subjected to death threats and verbally abused. At least seven people taken prisoner by the BRA were reported to have been summarily executed. Anthony Anugu and six others were allegedly shot dead in April. The seven were apparently accused of betraying the BRA because they had sought to negotiate a separate constitution for south Bougainville with the PNG authorities.

In October Amnesty International expressed its concern to the government about human rights violations committed by the armed forces in Bougainville. It urged the government to initiate thorough and impartial investigations into human rights violations in Bougainville, and to bring suspected perpetrators to justice. Amnesty International also called on the government to ratify international human rights treaties and to permit international humanitarian and legal organizations to monitor human rights in Bougainville.

# PARAGUAY

**Allegations of torture and ill-treatment of criminal suspects, including juveniles, by police and prison authorities continued to be reported. An army colonel was arbitrarily detained after opening an internal investigation into corrupt practices by senior army commanders. Five former police officials were convicted of the death in custody of a teacher in 1976. Judicial investigations into other human rights violations during the previous administration were not completed. Judicial authorities discovered important new evidence of the torture, killing and "disappearance" of political prisoners during the past administration of President Stroessner.**

In June a new Constitution containing extensive human rights provisions was introduced. Among other safeguards, it guarantees the right to life and prohibits the death penalty for ordinary crimes. Also in June, Paraguay acceded to the International Covenant on Civil and Political Rights and the International Covenant on Economic, Social and Cultural Rights.

Renewed reports were received of the torture and ill-treatment of detainees, including minors, in police stations and detention centres. Although a number of formal complaints of torture were presented in the courts, in the majority of cases judicial authorities failed to conduct thorough investigations into such complaints and to bring those responsible to justice. A judicial investigation was opened into allegations that in April police officers had arbitrarily detained and tortured 16-year-old Ramón Melgarejo Ortega in the 26th police station in San Lorenzo on the outskirts of the capital, Asunción. According to Ramón Melgarejo's sworn statement, when he arrived at the police station he was blindfolded and handcuffed to a chair and a plastic bag was repeatedly placed over his head to the point of near-asphyxiation. He was interrogated about alleged thefts. The following day he was allegedly beaten and injured in his mouth when a police officer used pliers to grip and tear the tissue under his tongue. He was released without charge four days later. In October Ramón Melgarejo's mother presented to the court a petition on his behalf, alleging that her son had been harassed and persecuted by the police since lodging his complaint of torture.

No progress was reported in judicial investigations into previous allegations of torture of detainees in the San Lorenzo police station (see *Amnesty International Report 1992*).

In June at least 12 inmates of Tacumbú National Penitentiary, including a 16-year-old youth, were tortured and beaten by prison guards. They were then transferred with over 50 other prisoners to a remote army garrison known as Lagerenza in the western Chaco region. The prisoners were returned to Asunción weeks later after the Attorney General formally accused the prison authorities of acting unconstitutionally by denying the prisoners access to defence lawyers. On their arrival in Asunción, several prisoners required hospital treatment for injuries resulting from the beatings. Prisoners testified before the courts that the beatings had been carried out on the orders and under the direct supervision of the Director of Penal Institutes in reprisal for widespread internal disturbances in the prison days before. A judicial investigation was opened into the allegations of torture. The Director and four prison guards were arrested pending the outcome of the investigation.

Investigations which opened in August into allegations of widespread corruption, including alleged drug-trafficking, led to a major political scandal in which senior military commanders were implicated. Army Colonel Luis Catalino González Rojas, commander of the IV Infantry Division, was relieved of his command and arrested in September and held for several weeks after initiating an internal military investigation into corrupt practices by senior armed forces officials, including the army commander General Humberto Garcete. Colonel González was held in incommunicado detention in the barracks of the Presidential Guard for six days before being allowed access to a lawyer and relatives. Defence lawyer Hermes Rafael Saguier accused army commander General Humberto Garcete of responsibility for a machine-gun attack on his house shortly after he had presented a petition of *habeas corpus* on behalf of Colonel González. Military authorities failed to respond to requests from a civilian court judge that Colonel González should be presented before the court in response to the petition of *habeas corpus*. Charges of defamation and slander were brought against Colonel González but he was provisionally released when investigations in the civilian courts led to arrest warrants being issued against three senior army generals, including General Garcete. Amnesty International was concerned that the underlying motive for the detention of Colonel González appeared to be to prevent him proceeding with his inquiries. Colonel González reported receiving anonymous death threats following his release.

In a significant ruling, five former senior police officials were found responsible for the death under torture of teacher Mario Schaerer Prono in 1976 (see *Amnesty International Report 1990*). In May Pastor Coronel, the former head of the *Departamento de Investigaciones de la Policía* (DIP-C), Police Investigations Department, and three of his subordinates, Juan Martínez, Lucilo Benítez and Camilo Almada, were sentenced to 25 years' imprisonment for aggravated homicide and torture; former police chief General Francisco Brítez Borges was sentenced to five years' imprisonment for covering up the crime. Appeals against the convictions had not been resolved by the end of the year. There were few developments in dozens of other complaints pending before the courts for the torture, murder and "disappearance" of

**236** political opponents under the government of General Alfredo Stroessner. However, in December judicial authorities discovered extensive DIP-C documentation in a police centre on the outskirts of Asunción. The documents, which were impounded by a criminal court judge, were believed to contain information about the fate of dozens of political opponents who "disappeared" or were killed by DIP-C agents during the 1970s.

In February Amnesty International submitted a series of recommendations to the Constituent Assembly urging it to incorporate comprehensive human rights safeguards into the new Constitution.

In July Amnesty International wrote to the Interior Minister expressing concern at reports of the ill-treatment of prisoners in Tacumbú prison and urged the government to take all necessary steps to ensure the physical integrity of all prisoners. No reply had been received by the end of the year.

# PERU

At least 139 people "disappeared" and at least 65 were extrajudicially executed by the security forces. Widespread torture and ill-treatment were reported. Some 70 people were sentenced by military courts to life imprisonment after unfair trials. Two prisoners of conscience were incarcerated. Thousands of past cases of human rights violations remained unclarified. The main armed opposition group, the *Partido Comunista del Perú (Sendero Luminoso)* (PCP), Communist Party of Peru (Shining Path), arbitrarily and deliberately killed large numbers of civilians.

Internal armed conflict continued to afflict most of the country and large areas remained emergency zones under military control. Independent human rights defenders stated that they were unable to visit parts of the country for fear of attacks by the security forces or the PCP. An extensive pattern of human rights violations by the government's security forces was reported throughout the year. Widespread atrocities by the PCP were also reported and, on a significantly lesser scale, by a second armed opposition group, the *Movimiento Revolucionario Túpac Amaru* (MRTA), Túpac Amaru Revolutionary Movement. The PCP carried out deliberate and arbitrary executions of civilians; sabotaged public utilities, co-operatives and rural development projects; detonated powerful car bombs in urban centres; and threatened strike-breakers.

In January and February, in an attempt to strengthen civilian participation in counter-insurgency policies, Congress modified or repealed legislative decrees issued by the executive in 1991. However, on 5 April President Alberto Fujimori, with the full backing of the Armed Forces Joint Command, dissolved Congress, suspended constitutional rule, and set up an emergency government. The President also announced that the judiciary, Public Ministry, Congress and Constitution were to be comprehensively reformed. The judiciary and the Public Ministry were rendered inoperative for four weeks, during which complaints of human rights violations and *habeas corpus* petitions could not be filed. The dissolution of Congress meant that several commissions investigating human rights violations and political violence were forced to abandon their work.

From April President Fujimori and his Council of Ministers ruled the country by decree law. Decrees issued in April included the dismissal of the Attorney General, 13 Supreme Court judges and over 130 judges and prosecutors, and their replacement with appointees named by the executive.

Decrees issued in May and August widened the definition of "crimes of terrorism", accelerated judicial proceedings in such cases and lengthened prison sentences. The August decree defined the crime of treason and extended military jurisdiction to civilians accused of treason. The measures provided for secret trials. In July a decree penalizing "disappearances" was published, replacing a similar law issued in 1991 and repealed in May 1992.

In early May at least 39 PCP inmates and two policemen were killed during a police operation to regain control of two wings of the Castro Castro Prison in Lima, the capital. The authorities claimed the inmates died as a result of an armed confrontation or were deliberately killed by fellow inmates to prevent them from surrendering. PCP inmates subsequently claimed that at least 10 of the victims were killed after surrendering to the police.

Peter Cárdenas, of the MRTA, and Victor Polay, its leader, were arrested in May and June respectively. In September PCP leader Abimael Guzmán and members of the organization's central committee were arrested and charged with treason; scores of other PCP activists were detained in the following months. President Fujimori stated repeatedly that he favoured the death penalty for those convicted of treason.

From mid-September the government refused the International Committee of the Red Cross (ICRC) access to all prisons.

In response to international pressure for a return to democratic rule, elections were held in November for an 80-member legislative Congress charged with reforming the Constitution. The party political alliance *Nueva Mayoría-Cambio 90*, New Majority-Change 90, backed by President Fujimori, achieved an outright majority. Three major opposition parties refused to participate in the elections.

Of the 178 people known to have "disappeared" after detention by the security forces, 139 remained unaccounted for, 22 were later found dead, 16 had their detention acknowledged or were released, and one said he had escaped. Among the "disappeared" were 10 peasants from the department of Junín, who were detained in February by a civil defence patrol acting with the support of the army. The victims, seven men and three boys from the Paccha community in the province of Huancayo, were reportedly beaten, tied up and taken away by the patrol.

Between April and July Amnesty International documented 23 "disappearances" and three extrajudicial executions in the department of San Martín, most of which were attributed to soldiers stationed at the Mariscal Cáceres military base in Tarapoto city.

Lecturer Hugo Muñoz Sánchez and nine students "disappeared" on 18 July after reportedly being detained by soldiers on the army-controlled campus of the Enrique Guzmán y Valle Education University on the outskirts of Lima. The authorities claimed to have investigated the case and concluded that the 10 victims had not been detained. However, their whereabouts remained unknown.

In May, five police officers were charged with "violating personal freedom and abuse of authority" in connection with the 1991 detention and transfer into army custody of three officials and a peasant from Chuschi, Ayacucho department (see *Amnesty International Report 1992*). However, the authorities failed to initiate proceedings against soldiers alleged to have been responsible for their subsequent "disappearance".

A judge decided in August to close the case against four police officers charged with abuse of authority in connection with the "disappearance" in 1990 of Ernesto Castillo Páez (see *Amnesty International Reports 1991* and *1992*). An appeal against the decision remained pending.

Scores of people were reported to have been extrajudicially executed by the security forces. On 8 February, five peasants were killed when police opened fire on some 200 unarmed peasants as they marched to a small police station in the district of Chavín, Huari province, Ancash department.

On 17 March, three members of the *Alianza Política Izquierda Unida* (UNIR), Political Alliance of the United Left, were reportedly extrajudicially executed by hanging in the presence of witnesses. According to reports, they were detained in the village of Para, Lucanas province, Ayacucho department, by hooded men in civilian clothing acting under the orders of the military stationed at the Chaviñas military base. The victims were apparently accused of "subversion" and ill-treated before being killed.

Between August and October at least 19 university students in the city of Huancayo, Junín department, were found dead in circumstances suggesting they had been extrajudicially executed. A further seven students were reported to have "disappeared" during this period. All had allegedly been detained by the security forces in or near the city. In October the Attorney General appointed an *ad hoc* prosecutor to investigate the "disappearances" and the circumstances and manner in which eight of the students had died.

With few exceptions, the courts failed to bring to justice those responsible for human rights violations. In February a civilian court contested the jurisdiction of the military justice system over the trial of soldiers accused of murdering 14 peasants from the community of Santa Bárbara, Huancavelica department, in 1991 (see *Amnesty International Report 1992*). A decision on jurisdiction by the Supreme Court remained pending.

In March it was reported that a military tribunal had sentenced an officer to six years' imprisonment for the death of 30 of the 69 peasants killed in Accomarca, Ayacucho department, in 1985 (see *Amnesty International Reports 1986* and *1990*). The officer was said to have been conditionally freed pending an appeal against conviction. In September a sergeant accused of the massacre of 18 peasants from San Pedro de Cachi, Ayacucho department, was reportedly absolved by the Supreme Council of Military Justice of responsibility for the killings (see *Amnesty International Reports 1991* and *1992*). In December the Army Command published a communique claiming that a document publicly circulated by former vice-president Máximo San Román was forged: the document stated that soldiers had carried out the massacre of 16 people in Lima in 1991 (see *Amnesty International Report 1992*). However, *Sí*, a national magazine, subsequently published the testimony of an officer attached to the Army Intelligence Service confirming the army's involvement in the killings.

Torture and ill-treatment were frequently reported. In April, 15-year-old Olivia Pérez, who was seven months pregnant, was reportedly beaten by soldiers stationed at the Mariscal Cáceres military base in San Martín department. She subsequently lost her baby. In November members of the Lima Bar Association voted unanimously to condemn the "proven" police torture of a PCP leader and lawyer, Dr Martha Huatay, before her military trial on treason charges. Relatives and lawyers representing four active and retired army officers detained with 13 others following a coup attempt on 13 November against President Fujimori's emergency government claimed that the four had been tortured while in the custody of the army.

The systematic ill-treatment of hundreds of political detainees was reported from several prisons. In May, after the authorities regained control of two wings of the Castro Castro Prison, hundreds of men and women were transferred to other prisons and some 300 men kept in Castro Castro Prison. These and the transferred prisoners alleged that they were subsequently denied adequate clothing, food and medical attention. Those held in Castro Castro Prison also alleged that they were kept lying down in the prison yard for nearly two weeks and that many of them were severely beaten by armed guards on 22 May.

The procedures under which members of armed opposition groups were tried for treason by secret military tribunals fell short of international fair trial standards. Some 70 alleged PCP and MRTA activists, many of them leading members, were reported to have been sentenced to life imprisonment by such tribunals.

The authorities incarcerated two prisoners of conscience on false terrorism-related charges. In March Michael Soto Rodríguez, a medical student, was detained and charged with being a member of *Socorro Popular*, a welfare organization attached to the PCP. Amnesty International believes he was detained solely for giving medical attention to an alleged PCP member wounded in an armed confrontation with the police. In September Ayacucho-based journalist Magno Sosa was detained by the police and charged with having links to the PCP. Amnesty International believes Magno Sosa was detained for no other reason than his newspaper articles drawing attention to human rights violations by the security forces (see *Amnesty International Report 1992*). At least 16 other people were imprisoned during the year who appeared to be possible prisoners of conscience.

The PCP carried out scores of deliberate and arbitrary executions of civilians. Many of those killed had been previously tortured. Among the unarmed civilians killed were members of local authorities, aid workers, community leaders, peasants and town dwellers. On 15 February María Elena Moyano, a deputy mayor, was gunned down by members of the PCP and her body dynamited in Villa El Salvador, a Lima shanty town. Men, women and children were killed by PCP car bomb attacks on civilian targets in Lima. For instance, 25 people were killed in separate attacks on the headquarters of a television station and a residential street in June and July respectively. On the night of 10 October a PCP unit attacked the community of Huayllao, Ayacucho department, and massacred 47 peasants, including 14 children aged four to 15. The community had reportedly established a civil defence patrol but was said to have been armed with no more than five shotguns. On 18 December Pedro Huillca, Secretary General of the *Confederación General de Trabajadores del Perú*, General Confederation of Workers of Peru, was shot dead in Lima. *El Diario*, a clandestine newspaper sympathetic to the PCP, claimed the PCP had carried out the killing.

Amnesty International condemned such arbitrary and deliberate killings by the PCP in numerous publications, letters to the Peruvian authorities and in statements to the Peruvian press and on radio stations.

Amnesty International repeatedly appealed to the government to thoroughly and impartially investigate cases of "disappearance", extrajudicial execution, and torture and ill-treatment, and to bring the perpetrators to justice. The authorities replied on several cases, in most denying the allegations, but failed to investigate thoroughly thousands of past human rights violations or bring the perpetrators to justice.

In April Amnesty International expressed its deep concern to the President at measures taken by his emergency government which seriously undermined the protection of human rights. The organization called for the unconditional release of prisoners of conscience and investigated the cases of possible prisoners of conscience.

In May Amnesty International wrote to the President requesting a full and impartial inquiry into the deaths of PCP prisoners killed in Castro Castro Prison. The government replied that it had made public a complete list of the prisoners killed, and of those transferred to hospitals and other prisons. However, the government failed to initiate a full and independent inquiry into the killings and to supply information Amnesty International had requested on the fate of up to 130 PCP prisoners apparently unaccounted for after the operation.

In October Amnesty International published *Human rights violations against the indigenous peoples of the Americas*, which included concerns in Peru.

In October Amnesty International urged the President to ensure that the trial of PCP leader Abimael Guzmán would be conducted according to standards enshrined in international human rights law. In November the organization urged the President not to extend the death penalty, but to abolish it for all crimes. Also in November the organization publicly appealed to the government requesting guarantees for the physical safety of army officers detained after the coup attempt. In December Amnesty International stated publicly that it was concerned that procedures for the trials of alleged members of armed opposition groups fell short of international standards.

Amnesty International included reference to its concerns in Peru in oral statements to the United Nations (UN) Commission on Human Rights in February; to the UN Sub-Commission on Prevention of Discrimination and Protection of Minorities in August; and to the Sub-Commission's Working Group on Indigenous Populations in July. In April Amnesty International submitted information about its concerns in Peru for UN review under a procedure, established by Economic and Social Council Resolutions 728F/1503, for confidential consideration of communications about human rights violations.

# PHILIPPINES

**Scores of people were believed to have been extrajudicially executed and at least 16 people reportedly "disappeared" in police or military custody. At least 11 prisoners of conscience remained in detention throughout the year and possible prisoners of conscience were among around 475 other political prisoners. Some political detainees were reportedly tortured or ill-treated. Legislation proposing the restoration of the death penalty was debated by Congress but no vote was taken before the end of the year.**

The government continued to face armed opposition from the New People's Army (NPA), the armed wing of the Communist Party of the Philippines (CPP); the Moro National Liberation Front (MNLF); and other groups seeking independence for predominantly Muslim areas of Mindanao. The authorities publicly accused members of lawful political and social organizations of being members of armed opposition groups and labelled their organizations as "fronts" for the CPP/NPA. Armed opposition groups, particularly the NPA, committed abuses, including arbitrary killings, torture and hostage-taking.

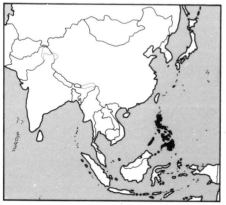

Fidel Ramos, a former Secretary of National Defense, was elected President in May general elections. He announced plans to restore political stability and introduced a series of peace initiatives. In August the new government issued guidelines for the bail, release or pardon of people detained or convicted on political charges. A number of high-ranking members of the CPP were temporarily released from prison. One alleged NPA leader, Rodolfo Salas, was granted an absolute pardon by the President in September. The offences covered by the guidelines included rebellion and illegal possession of firearms in furtherance of rebellion. In September the government repealed the Anti-Subversion Law (Republic Act 1700) which had outlawed the CPP, and in December the President announced that political suspects charged with common crimes would qualify for the amnesty. The government claimed that 349 suspected CPP/NPA members had been released by the end of December. However, independent human rights groups claimed that only 237 had been freed, the majority after dismissal of their cases or the granting of bail. Scores of military officers, who had been jailed for involvement in coup attempts against the previous government, were also provisionally released.

In September government representatives and leaders of the National Democratic Front (NDF), the umbrella political organization which includes the CPP, signed a declaration calling for a negotiated political settlement of the armed conflict. The same month rebel military officers agreed to participate in separate peace negotiations with the government. In October the MNLF indicated that it was open to negotiations if these were based on the 1976 Tripoli Agreement, which granted full autonomy to 13 Muslim provinces in Mindanao.

The Citizen Armed Force Geographical Unit (CAFGU) as well as unofficial vigilante groups engaged in counter-insurgency operations with the support or acquiescence of security forces. Despite considerable evidence of CAFGU involvement in human rights violations, a leading military official said in August that military training of CAFGU members had "corrected" this problem and the government proposed a substantial budgetary increase for the CAFGU in 1993.

Effective investigation of alleged human rights violations and related prosecutions continued to be obstructed by the security forces. Obstuction included intimidating judges, lawyers, witnesses and complainants; and refusing access to information, personnel or military premises. Investigations by the official Commission on Human Rights (CHR) continued to be impeded by cumbersome, lengthy procedures and by the CHR practice of placing the burden of proof on complainants, despite the risk of reprisals or the lack of resources at their disposal.

At least 60 people were victims of apparent extrajudicial executions by government and government-backed forces, many after being publicly accused of supporting the NPA. Those killed were members of farmers' or peasants' organizations, church workers, community workers, trade unionists and civilians living in zones of armed conflict.

In Zamboanga del Sur, human rights advocate Demetria Pedrano and her 63-year-old mother, Basilia, were shot and stabbed to death on 15 February by armed men believed to be members of a military-backed vigilante group. Demetria Pedrano was a church worker who had spoken out against human rights violations by pro-government vigilantes. Cosme Remontar, a farmers' organization member, was shot dead on 13 July in Guihulngan, Negros Oriental. According to witnesses, 11 members of the CAFGU and the Philippine National Police (PNP) arrived at his farm and said they were searching for his brother, an alleged NPA member. The witnesses reported that CAFGU members forced Cosme Remontar to kneel down before shooting him, and then hacked his body with a machete as he lay dying.

The CHR reported in March that an investigation into the killing of Edilberto Bensen (see *Amnesty International Report 1992*) had been suspended and the case dossier "archived". Edilberto Bensen, a trade unionist in Negros Occidental, had been killed in August 1991 along with his wife and daughter by armed men believed to be members of the Philippine Army. The CHR appeared to have accepted military claims that Edilberto Bensen was an insurgent rebel who had been killed by the NPA. The CHR provided no evidence to substantiate this claim and friends of the victims maintained that Edilberto Bensen was not an NPA member and suggested that he had been killed because he had resisted military pressure to join a militia group engaged in counter-insurgency activities.

Harassment of human rights advocates and others critical of government policy was widespread. Members of farmers' and fishermen's organizations were also particularly vulnerable, as were staff members of non-governmental organizations. Methods used included death threats, beatings and interrogation by military and military-backed forces.

Marcelo Fakilang, an outspoken critic of military human rights violations and an active member of the Cordillera People's Alliance, an organization working in defence of indigenous people's rights in the region, was threatened by a group of armed soldiers on 26 January at his home in Mountain Province. The soldiers fired guns in the air and reportedly threatened to blow up his house. The soldiers returned on 31 January and took Marcelo Fakilang to a village centre where he was beaten. The military had previously accused him of being a communist sympathizer and had alleged that he received a monthly allowance from the underground NDF, an allegation he vigorously denied.

At least 16 people reportedly "disappeared" after abduction or arrest by government or government-backed security forces. Domingo Limbangan, the vice-chairman of an indigenous people's association, and Ernesto Kalan, a community health worker, "disappeared" after arrest

on 4 August. They were reportedly woken at 6am by members of the 3rd Infantry Battalion of the Philippine Army, beaten and then questioned about their alleged involvement with the NPA for three hours before being taken to a local police station. Community workers were told at the police station that both men had been released at 2pm the same day, but neither was seen again.

Three people who reportedly "disappeared" during 1991 were found dead in early 1992. The bodies of Norberto Melanes and Julian Lingbawan were recovered from a pit in Tabuk, Kalinga-Apayao on 2 January. Both had been arrested by CAFGU members on 26 December 1991. In February relatives of Jerry Sabal, who "disappeared" in November 1991, were informed that his body had been found buried near the place where he was arrested.

At least 11 prisoners of conscience remained in prison in Cebu City. A twelfth, Rogelio Cinco, was released in July after serving more than four years in prison. The 12 were among a group of 25 farmers from Leyte who had been charged with rebellion in 1988 (see *Amnesty International Reports 1989, 1991* and *1992*). Despite a number of court hearings, no final verdict had been reached by the end of the year.

Over 100 people were arrested for suspected political offences, the majority under provisions of a July 1990 Supreme Court decision authorizing the arrest without warrant of suspects in crimes of rebellion or subversion (see *Amnesty International Report 1991*). Most were released after brief periods in detention. About 475 suspected and convicted NPA members remained in detention, among them possible prisoners of conscience. Most were accused of supporting the armed opposition and charged with illegal possession of firearms in furtherance of rebellion, or other criminal offences.

There were continued reports of torture or ill-treatment of political detainees. Pagnas Marcos, a farmer from Dupax del Norte, Nueva Vizcaya, reportedly died after being arrested and tortured by military personnel. According to reports, he and some friends were abducted by soldiers on 15 April and taken to a military detachment in Oyao district. They were accused of being NPA members and beaten severely. All were later released and Pagnas Marcos was taken, unconscious, to the local hospital where he died on 18 April. Military officers reportedly persuaded his relatives not to file formal charges against them and in May paid compensation to the family.

In July President Ramos called for the restoration of the death penalty. Several bills introducing the death penalty for "heinous crimes" such as murder, rape and drug-trafficking were filed in Congress. However, no vote had been taken by the end of the year.

Deliberate and arbitrary killings by the NPA continued to be reported. In March NPA members claimed responsibility for the killing of Eddie Villegas, a member of a vigilante group facing murder charges for the extrajudicial execution of Father Narciso Pico in 1991 (see *Amnesty International Report 1992*). In Cagayan, NPA members also claimed responsibility for the April killing of Leonardo Mamba, a congressional candidate in the general elections.

Military officials alleged that NPA members had tortured wounded soldiers after an ambush in Marihatag, Surigao del Sur, in February. An investigation team, composed of Department of Justice officials, members of the CHR and non-governmental human rights groups, concluded that the majority of the 38 soldiers killed had died of gunshot wounds. Exhumations revealed, however, that two of the soldiers had been shot and stabbed repeatedly, indicating that they had been killed after capture and that torture may have occurred.

Several people, including government officials and civilians, were reportedly taken hostage by the NPA and some hostages were released after negotiations with local authorities.

In Zamboanga, Mindanao, Muslim opposition groups were believed to have been responsible for the August bombing of a Roman Catholic shrine, which killed four people, and for shooting dead a Christian broadcaster and two others in September.

Throughout the year Amnesty International appealed to the government to conduct independent and impartial investigations of all reported extrajudicial executions and "disappearances" and called for those responsible to be brought to justice. It called for the release of all prisoners of conscience and for all other political prisoners to be given fair trials or released. It urged the government to dismantle militia forces, prohibit the use of vigilante groups in counter-insurgency operations and stop the practice of political labelling of real or suspected political opponents. It appealed to the government and members of Congress not to reinstate the death penalty. Amnesty International appealed to the NPA to cease the deliberate and arbitrary killings of non-combatants and to respect the principles of international humanitarian law.

An Amnesty International report, *Philippines: The Killing Goes On*, was published in February. It described a pattern of extrajudicial execution and provided details of 85 people believed to have been killed by government or government-backed forces between 1988 and 1992. The report also described a number of arbitrary killings apparently committed by NPA members. An international campaign was launched simultaneously to draw attention to the killings. During the same month an Amnesty International delegation visited the Philippines and met the Minister of Justice and other government officials. In May the Presidential Human Rights Committee, presided over by the Department of Justice, emphasized the positive aspects of government human rights initiatives but acknowledged continuing violations. In a June response to Amnesty International, the Department of Labor and Employment (DOLE) referred to government and military failure to provide accurate, timely information about reported human rights violations. The DOLE report also noted that judicial proceedings in human rights cases were subject to long delays and that convictions were rarely obtained.

In an oral statement to the United Nations (UN) Commission on Human Rights in February, Amnesty International included reference to abuses of human rights, including hostage-taking, by armed opposition groups in the Philippines. In August Amnesty International expressed concern about the extrajudicial execution by the security forces of members of tribal communities in an oral statement to the UN Sub-Commission Working Group on Indigenous Populations.

In February Amnesty International wrote to the NDF to request information about arbitrary killings allegedly committed by NPA members. In a reply, the NDF expressed its determination to protect human rights and stated that NPA combatants are required to study the principles of international humanitarian law.

# POLAND

A conscientious objector to military service who began serving a prison sentence in July was considered a prisoner of conscience. Two people were sentenced to death.

The lower house of parliament, the *Sejm*, adopted constitutional amendments in October. These gave the President a greater role in forming a government but restricted the President's authority to dismiss it. The amendments also empowered the government to make economic policy decisions by decree. The amendments came into force in November after President Lech Walesa signed them.

Roman Gałuszka, a Roman Catholic conscientious objector to military service, began serving an 18-month prison sentence in July. His application to serve alternative civilian service was rejected on the grounds that the Roman Catholic Church does not support conscientious objection to military service. In September the Military Chamber of the Supreme Court rejected an extraordinary appeal filed on Roman Gałuszka's behalf by the Minister of Justice.

One person was sentenced to death for murder in March and another in November. During the year information came to light concerning a death sentence passed in December 1991 for murder and rape and death sentences passed on four people during 1989. All these people were still on death row at the end of the year.

Amnesty International called for the release of Roman Gałuszka. The organization continued to call on the Polish authorities to commute all death sentences and to abolish the death penalty.

# PORTUGAL

**There were allegations of torture and ill-treatment by police and prison officers. Judicial and administrative inquiries into these allegations were frequently slow and inconclusive.**

Allegations of ill-treatment were made by criminal suspects and by people who were subsequently released without charge. They cited prison officers, officers in all branches of the police and in the *Guarda Nacional Republicana* (GNR), Republican National Guard. Some of the allegations referred to incidents in previous years.

José Paulo Ferreira Portugal was arrested by GNR officers on a street near Almada in August 1991. He had queried the action of a GNR officer who had fined him for a traffic offence. He claimed that approximately nine officers seized him, threw him head first against their jeep and assaulted him before taking him to their station and beating him once again. He was then taken in handcuffs to a hospital where a certificate was issued describing injuries to his head, jaw, eyes and back. He was subsequently charged with disobeying GNR orders and assaulting an officer. He made a formal complaint against the officers.

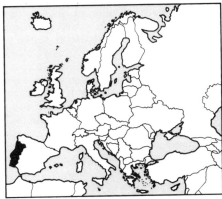

In December 1991 an officer of the *Polícia de Segurança Pública* (PSP), Public Security Police, in Setúbal stopped Alexandre Luis Marques Pires Gravanita, a Portuguese citizen born in Angola, and asked for his identity card. After examining the card, the officer ordered Luis Gravanita to accompany him to the police station where the officer allegedly kicked him, punched

**244**

him, and racially abused him. Eventually, details of his identity were taken and he was released without charge. He subsequently received hospital treatment for general cuts and bruising, especially to his face and right eye. He made a formal complaint against the officer.

Orlando Correia, a French citizen of Portuguese parentage, was arrested and imprisoned in September. On 9 September officers of the *Polícia Judiciária* (PJ), Judiciary Police, went to Guarda Prison to take a statement from him but he refused to comply unless his lawyer and an interpreter were present, as provided for by law. The officers then reportedly assaulted him before witnesses. He was later taken to the PJ offices where he claimed that he was verbally abused and beaten by PJ officers; a pistol was inserted in his mouth and he was tied, spread-eagled, to a railing. He was admitted unconscious to Guarda Hospital that afternoon. The hospital recorded bruising and scratches to his chest and back but a sworn statement from an eyewitness reported in the press alleged that there were noticeable injuries all over his body, that his lips were black and very swollen and that he had a large bruise over his left eye. On 14 September Orlando Correia made a formal complaint to the Public Prosecutor accusing the PJ officers of beating him, insulting him and threatening his life. The officers were reported as saying that these were self-inflicted injuries. His lawyer applied to the court on four occasions for a full forensic medical examination of his client but this was not carried out until 1 October. A disciplinary investigation was opened into his allegations.

Judicial inquiries, complemented by internal police and prison inquiries, were usually opened into allegations of ill-treatment. However, inquiries opened in previous years were often excessively long and inconclusive.

Isidro Albuquerque Rodrigues made a formal complaint in October 1990 alleging that PJ officers had beaten him, whipped him with a metal hose-pipe and forced a bottle into his anus (see *Amnesty International Report 1992*). Over two years later he had received no news regarding the inquiry into his allegations.

An inquiry into the alleged ill-treatment by the PSP in Sintra in July 1991 of Pedro Mariz Pires Neves Martins had not concluded by the end of the year (see *Amnesty*

*International Report 1992*).

There were also long delays in inquiries conducted by Military Tribunals. Domingos do Couto died in hospital in Chaves in August 1984. Four days earlier he had been arrested following an altercation with a GNR officer. He alleged that he was kicked, punched and beaten with truncheons in custody. The autopsy showed he had four fractured ribs, weals in the heart region and extensive bruising of the chest, apparently caused by blows from a truncheon. A complaint made to the Public Prosecutor by his family was passed to the GNR in November 1984 for action by the relevant Military Tribunal. After eight years there was still no result.

António Rodriguez Louro, a seaman, alleged that he was severely beaten by non-commissioned officers with a rubber hose-pipe in the Naval Prison of Alfeite in April 1991 (see *Amnesty International Report 1992*). At the end of the year there was still no news as to whether an inquiry, requested by his father, had ever been opened by the Naval Tribunal.

In June a court in Oporto convicted a PSP officer of causing bodily harm to a youth in October 1990 (see *Amnesty International Reports 1991* and *1992*). The youth had been thrown through a plate-glass door and required 59 stitches for injuries to his right arm. The officer was given a suspended sentence of six months' imprisonment and later amnestied. A second officer was acquitted.

A criminal judicial inquiry was still open into allegations that prisoners in the security wing of Linhó Prison had been ill-treated (see *Amnesty International Reports 1990*, *1991* and *1992*). An internal inquiry into allegations of ill-treatment made by prison inmate José Paulo Santos Silva in September 1991 said that his complaint was ill-founded (see *Amnesty International Report 1992*).

In April the Minister of Justice replied to Amnesty International about cases of alleged ill-treatment involving PJ and prison officers which the organization had raised with the authorities in April 1991 (see *Amnesty International Report 1992*). The Director General of Prison Services also replied on several occasions giving information on individual cases.

Amnesty International called on the authorities to establish serious and prompt inquiries into allegations of torture and ill-treatment and asked to be informed about the progress of such inquiries already under way.

# QATAR

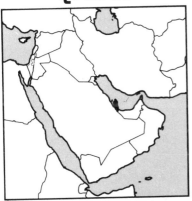

Four advocates of multi-party democracy were detained for periods of between five days and three months. All were believed to be prisoners of conscience.

'Issa Shahin al-Ghanim and Mohammad Salih al-Kowari were arrested in July and held in incommunicado detention, apparently without charge or trial, in Doha Central Prison. They were released in September and October respectively. They were among a group of 53 people who had signed a petition to the Amir of Qatar, al-Shaikh Khalifa Ibn Hamad Al-Thani, in late December 1991 seeking free parliamentary elections, a written constitution and the expansion of personal and political freedoms. Two other signatories were also held: 'Abd al-Latif Mohammad al-Nu'aymi, an official in the Ministry of Oil and Finance, was detained for five days in March; and Rashed Lamloum al-Musaifri was detained for 14 days in April.

Prior to their arrest in July, Mohammad Salih al-Kowari and 'Issa Shahin al-Ghanim were reportedly prevented from leaving the country and had their passports confiscated in May. They were arrested after sending a petition of protest to the authorities. Both had also reportedly refused to withdraw their signature from the December 1991 petition.

Amnesty International expressed concern about the arrests to the Amir of Qatar and called for the immediate and unconditional release of the prisoners of conscience.

# ROMANIA

Soldiers from a military police unit allegedly tortured and otherwise ill-treated members of the Roma community. There were also allegations of torture and ill-treatment by the police. The authorities failed to clarify a "disappearance" case. There was no apparent progress in the investigation into the killing of two demonstrators in September 1991.

In June a parliamentary commission of inquiry set up to investigate anti-government protests in September 1991 in Bucharest published its report (see *Amnesty International Report 1992*). It held the leaders of the Jiu Valley Miners' Free Trade Unions responsible for starting the events which led to violent clashes with the police authorities, during which at least four people died. Three members of the commission, representing the opposition parties, voiced a dissenting opinion.

After a new electoral law was adopted in July, presidential and parliamentary elections were held in September and October. President Ion Iliescu was re-elected and the Democratic National Salvation Front formed a minority government.

In July soldiers of a military police unit allegedly tortured and otherwise ill-treated members of the Roma community in Piaţa Rahova, in Bucharest, the capital. Following a dispute between a Rom and a soldier based in Rahova, 40 to 50 soldiers reportedly went to the market in this predominantly Roma suburb of Bucharest. They wore black masks and were armed with truncheons, *nunchakus* (weapons used in martial arts), chair legs and pick-axes and reportedly indiscriminately attacked Roma people. Mircea Gheorghe was allegedly hit with a stick on the head which made him lose consciousness. The soldiers continued to beat him despite bleeding from his head. Ion Constantin was hit with a rubber truncheon on the head and the back of the neck. Anişoara Duman and her child were beaten. According to one report, 13 people were injured in this apparently unprovoked attack.

There were also allegations of torture and ill-treatment by the police. For example, in May a civilian and two police officers broke into the home of Béla Tankó and allegedly beat him until he fell to the floor unconscious. Also in the house at the time was Filip Póra, whom the police reportedly beat after beating Béla Tankó.

In June Alexandru Tatulea was stopped near a Metro station in Bucharest by a police officer and a soldier. Alexandru Tatulea could not show them his identity card and was reportedly beaten by the police officer. When, as a result, Alexandru Tatulea fell to the ground the police officer took out a pistol and pointed it at his temple. Alexandru Tatulea moved his head and the police officer fired at point-blank range; the bullet entered beneath his left eye and exited behind his right ear. He survived the shooting but suffered paralysis of the left side of his face, a permanent disability with grave neurological complications. In October the police officer responsible went, together with four fellow officers, to Alexandru Tatulea's home and threatened him with bodily harm if he did not withdraw all accusations.

The whereabouts of Viorel Horia, a school pupil who was reportedly arrested and tortured following demonstrations in June 1990 in Bucharest, remained unknown (see *Amnesty International Report 1992*). Natalia Horia, Viorel's mother, reportedly came under pressure from police and other authorities while attempting to gain more information on the "disappearance" of her son. On one occasion, she was told in the Bucharest Police Department that Viorel had died on 15 October 1990 in Busteni, but that the body had already been buried. Her request to bring in an independent forensic expert to identify Viorel was rejected and this "discovery" was not mentioned again. During a meeting with an official of the Ministry of Foreign Affairs in June 1991 it was suggested that she was damaging the international reputation of Romania by maintaining contacts with

international human rights organizations. In the Bucharest Police Department, in February 1992, she was told by the officer who interviewed her that "if Viorel is not abroad and if he is not in a hospital with amnesia then maybe you have conspired in his disappearance".

No charges were brought in connection with the killing of Andrei Frumuşanu and Aurica Crăiniceanu during the demonstrations at Piaţa Victoriei in September 1991. A witness to the shooting of Andrei Frumuşanu reported seeing a military officer standing on the central balcony of the Government Building aiming a handgun at the demonstrators in the square. Andrei Frumuşanu was shot in the chest with a flare rocket and he died as a result of internal injuries. At approximately the same time Aurica Crăiniceanu was also shot in front of the Government Building. She died in the municipal hospital. An investigation into the deaths of Andrei Frumuşanu and Aurica Crăiniceanu was initiated. The Military Prosecutor reportedly told Andrei Frumuşanu's father that the identity of the officer who shot Andrei had been established and that he was of high military rank.

In July Amnesty International reiterated its appeal to the authorities to investigate fully and impartially the "disappearance" of Viorel Horia and to make public its findings. The organization also called on the authorities to ensure that Natalia Horia and others seeking to clarify the whereabouts of Viorel Horia were protected from harassment and intimidation.

In October Amnesty International called on the government to initiate an independent, impartial inquiry into the alleged torture and ill-treatment of members of the Roma community in Piaţa Rahova, to make public its findings and to bring to justice all those found responsible.

Amnesty International also called for full and impartial investigations into the deaths of Andrei Frumuşanu and Aurica Crăiniceanu. It urged the authorities to carry out an investigation into the torture and maiming of Alexandru Tatulea and to protect him from further harassment and intimidation.

In August the General Prosecutor informed Amnesty International that the police continued to investigate the "disappearance" of Viorel Horia. No other replies were received from the authorities.

# RUSSIA

**There were at least two prisoners of conscience, both conscientious objectors to military service. One possible prisoner of conscience was acquitted and released. At least 95 people were sentenced to death. Sixty death sentences were commuted and one execution was carried out. There were reports of inadequate legal protection for asylum-seekers arriving at Moscow airport.**

Following the break-up of the Soviet Union, Russia gained international recognition as an independent state under President Boris Yeltsin and took over the seat of the former USSR at the United Nations.

Work continued throughout the year on a new criminal code, with a draft in October envisaging a reduction in the scope of the death penalty from 15 peacetime offences to six, but it had not received parliamentary approval by the end of the year. In February a new law on the Procuracy provided for a stay on a death sentence if the Procurator General or his or her deputy lodged a protest against it. Previously, a death sentence, although suspended during an appeal, could legally be carried out before a judicial review of a protested sentence had been carried out. In May legal changes granted suspects the right to contact a lawyer from the moment they are detained, arrested or charged, a provision made under USSR law in 1989, and for the first time granted a person subject to arrest the right to challenge the legality of his or her detention before a court.

No legal provisions for a civilian alternative to military service had been introduced by the end of the year. At least two people, both Jehovah's Witnesses, served sentences for refusing their call-up papers. Dmitry Sokolov, sentenced to two years' compulsory labour in May 1991, was granted conditional early release in June 1992. He had previously been imprisoned

between 1988 and 1990 on the same charge. Each time his refusal had been because his religious beliefs forbade him to bear arms for a secular power or swear an oath of military allegiance. Oleg Lepin, also sentenced in 1991, ended his two-year term of compulsory labour in March.

Vladimir Mironov, a possible prisoner of conscience who had been sentenced to three years' imprisonment by a Moscow court in May 1991 for his homosexual activity (see *Amnesty International Report 1992*), had his sentence quashed on appeal in March. He had been sentenced under Article 121 of the criminal code, which punishes sodomy between adult males even if consensual, but a reinvestigation of his case found that his acts did not constitute sodomy. According to official statistics, 10 people were sentenced under this article in the first six months of the year, but stigmatization of offenders continued to make it difficult to obtain details on individuals or the circumstances in which the acts took place.

In May the Clemency Commission released death penalty statistics for 1991, reporting that 144 people had been sentenced to death. Of these 37 had their sentences commuted, 37 were granted clemency and 70 were executed. At that time the commission, which reviews all death sentences, had 308 such cases pending before it. In September the Ministry of Justice announced that 95 sentences had been passed in the first six months of 1992: one for an attempt on the life of a militiaman and the rest for premeditated, aggravated murder. According to the Clemency Commission, 60 death sentences were commuted during the year and one person was executed. A parliamentary proposal to include commutation of all pending death sentences in an amnesty in June was voted down.

Reports were received that Iraqi and Somali asylum-seekers who arrived at Moscow airport were not granted effective protection against being forcibly returned to their countries of origin. For example, Nabil Ali Hussain, an Iraqi, arrived in Moscow on 3 April after leaving Iraq without official authorization. He was detained at Moscow airport on 10 July as he tried to board a plane to the United Kingdom. Two other Iraqis, Samiya al-Khudri and her husband, Hasan, arrived in Moscow on 21 September from Jordan but were refused

**248**

entry. They returned to Jordan where they were also refused entry and were sent back on 2 October to Moscow, where they were detained. All three had connections with the Iraqi opposition and risked falling victim to human rights violations if returned to Iraq. They were believed to be still held at the airport at the end of the year.

Amnesty International called on the government to release all people imprisoned for their conscientious objection to compulsory military service, and urged the introduction of a civilian alternative of non-punitive length. It also sought from the authorities further information on possible prisoners of conscience said to be imprisoned for consenting homosexual activity between adults in private, and urged that the criminal code be amended so that such acts were no longer punishable.

Throughout the year Amnesty International urged the authorities to commute all death sentences and to impose a moratorium on death sentences and executions pending the review of the criminal code.

The organization urged that asylum-seekers at risk of human rights violations in their own countries, including the three Iraqis, be granted effective and durable protection against forcible return.

# RWANDA

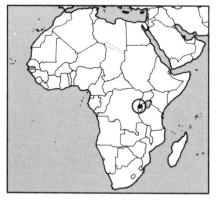

**Several journalists and others were imprisoned as prisoners of conscience: most had been released by the end of the year. Dozens of other political prisoners arrested in the previous two years were also released. There were new reports of torture and ill-treatment of detainees. Extrajudicial executions by members of the security forces and armed groups of** civilians who supported them continued to be reported. Dozens of cases of "disappearance" from previous years remained unresolved.

In April, after mass opposition demonstrations, Dismas Nsengiyaremye, the leader of the opposition *Mouvement démocratique républicain*, Republican Democratic Movement, was appointed as Prime Minister by President Juvénal Habyarimana. The new Prime Minister established a transitional government of national unity, comprising members of Rwanda's five main political parties. Stanislas Mbonampeka, a lawyer who had received death threats in early 1991 when he represented political prisoners, became the new Minister of Justice, but resigned in November in protest at what he said was lack of co-operation by members of the security forces with his ministry. The President's *Mouvement républicain national pour la démocratie et le développement* (MRND), Republican National Movement for Democracy and Development, retained control of other key ministries.

Armed conflict continued in the north between government troops, drawn predominantly from the majority Hutu population, and the *Front patriotique rwandais* (FPR), Rwandese Patriotic Front, an armed opposition group dominated by members of the Tutsi minority. A number of bomb explosions in the capital, Kigali, and other parts of the country killed several dozen people and injured many others, but it was not clear who was responsible. Nearly 30 civilians were killed and others injured by mutinous soldiers in the northwestern towns of Gisenyi and Ruhengeri; it was not clear whether any action was taken against the soldiers by the authorities. A new cease-fire between government and FPR forces was agreed in July but the state of siege declared in 1990 remained in force. Following the cease-fire, the government handed back 23 captured rebels to the FPR and the FPR released 11 captured government soldiers. In August a peace accord was agreed which provided for further negotiations leading to the formation of an all-party interim government in which the FPR would be represented. It provided also for the integration of FPR fighters into the national army, for the country's judicial and governmental institutions to be overhauled, and for the creation of a watchdog body to monitor human rights violations.

An agreement between the government and the FPR over the composition of an interim government and legislative body was concluded in December, but it was rejected by the MRND.

In February the government announced an amnesty for all those accused of political offences, which led to the release of 20 political prisoners and dozens of untried detainees. In September the government said that it would allow an international commission of inquiry to investigate human rights violations which occurred after an FPR attack in October 1990 (see *Amnesty International Report 1991*); this was due to take place in January 1993. The violations were believed to have included the extrajudicial execution of more than 1,000 Tutsi by government forces and armed civilians supporting them. The government also announced that there had been judicial investigations into mass killings committed since October 1990 by members of the security forces and groups of armed Hutu civilians.

Several journalists arrested after the military authorities issued a communique criticizing Rwanda's press in December 1991 were still held at the beginning of 1992. Most were released untried, but Jean-Pierre Mugabe, editor-in-chief of *Le Tribun du peuple* newspaper, was sentenced in February to four years' imprisonment by the High Court in Kigali. A prisoner of conscience, he was found guilty of publishing articles and cartoons which insulted the head of state. He was provisionally released in April pending an appeal hearing which had not taken place by the end of the year.

Two other independent newspaper journalists, André Kameya, editor-in-chief of *Rwanda Rushya*, and Théoneste Muberantwari, editor-in-chief of *Nyabarongo*, were arrested in February and accused of defaming the head of state. They also were provisionally released in April and had not been tried by the end of the year. Several journalists, one of whom remained in custody untried at the end of the year, were detained between September and November on charges of insulting the head of state. Janvier Africa of *Umurava* newspaper was arrested in September after he wrote an article which claimed that death squads were responsible for assassinations. He was still held at the end of 1992. Two of his colleagues were detained for five days in

October. Hassan Ngeze, editor of *Kangura* newspaper, was detained in November in connection with an article he published in mid-1992 accusing the Burundi authorities of perpetrating human rights violations against the Hutu in Burundi. He was released in November after reportedly being charged with insulting a foreign head of state. Another journalist and former prisoner of conscience, Vincent Rwabukwisi, editor of *Kanguka* newspaper, was due to be tried on state security charges (see *Amnesty International Report 1992*). However, the charges against him were apparently dropped as a result of the February amnesty.

Fidèle Kanyabugoyi, a Ministry of Public Works employee and member of a human rights group known as KANYARWANDA, was arrested in March. He had signed a statement on behalf of KANYARWANDA protesting against killings of Tutsi in Kanzenze district, south of Kigali, and had been compiling information about killings of members of the Bagogwe, a Tutsi clan, in 1991 (see *Amnesty International Report 1992*). A prisoner of conscience, he was charged with endangering the security of the state but was provisionally released in early April with restrictions placed on his movements. He was again interrogated in August but had not been tried by the end of the year. In August his wife and several other people were injured when his home was attacked by a group of armed men, one of whom was in military uniform.

At least two detainees who appeared to be prisoners of conscience were among nine Tutsi still held at the beginning of the year, apparently without charge or trial. They had been arrested in October 1991 in Kanzenze district by order of local officials, and were reportedly severely beaten at the time of their arrest. The authorities stated in December 1991 that Gisagara and Mushimire had been arrested for defaming the head of state. At the end of 1992 it was unclear whether they were still held.

There were new arrests of Tutsi suspected of supporting the FPR. They included Shabani Gasigwa and Evariste Sissi, a well-known businessman, who were arrested with six others during June: all eight were held without charge or trial for about three weeks during which they were beaten in a gendarmerie interrogation centre in Kigali. Evariste Sissi had previously been detained uncharged from October

1990 to early 1991. Shabani Gasigwa alleged that he had been beaten in detention to force him to make a false statement implicating Evariste Sissi. A third man, Ali Hitimana, reportedly needed intensive hospital treatment as a result of injuries sustained during interrogation.

At least 20 political prisoners who were serving sentences imposed after unfair trials in 1991 (see *Amnesty International Report 1992*) were released in the February amnesty together with untried political detainees. The 20 included Donatien Rugema and Charles Mukuralinda, who had been tortured under interrogation in 1990 and sentenced to death in early 1991.

There were new reports of extrajudicial executions by the security forces and armed groups of civilians who supported them. The latter reportedly included supporters of the MRND and a Hutu-based political party, the *Coalition pour la défense de la République*, Coalition for the Defence of the Republic. The victims were virtually all Tutsi who belonged to political parties which advocated negotiations between the government and the FPR. At least 150 Tutsi were reported to have been killed and many others injured by pro-government groups of armed Hutu in early March in Kanzenze district and surrounding areas. Among those killed was Antonia Locatelli, an Italian missionary, who was shot dead by a soldier on 9 March at Nyamata Roman Catholic church while trying to protect some Tutsi villagers. The authorities acknowledged that the missionary had been killed by a soldier but said she had been killed by mistake during a search for armed men and apparently took no action against the perpetrator. Nor was any official inquiry initiated into the other killings, although dozens of Hutu suspected of attacks on Tutsi were arrested.

The authorities failed to clarify the fate of dozens of people who "disappeared" from custody in previous years. They included eight Tutsi arrested in Kanzenze district in October 1991 (see *Amnesty International Report 1992*).

The FPR was also reportedly responsible for gross human rights abuses, including deliberate and arbitrary killings of civilians, particularly civilians displaced by the fighting. In February FPR fighters reportedly killed an 87-year-old French nun and some eight other civilians during an attack on a Roman Catholic convent and a health centre in Rushaki district. The FPR also shelled camps of displaced civilians.

Amnesty International appealed for the release of prisoners of conscience and for the fair trial or release of other political prisoners. It continued to press for information about the fate of prisoners who "disappeared" between 1990 and 1992, for impartial investigations into alleged extrajudicial executions and other human rights violations and for the introduction of safeguards to prevent their recurrence. It welcomed the government's decision to set up an international commission of inquiry to investigate the violations.

In May Amnesty International published a report, *Rwanda: Persecution of Tutsi minority and repression of government critics, 1990 to 1992*, and appealed to the new government of national unity to end the widespread persecution of the Tutsi. It welcomed the releases of political prisoners in February, but was concerned that those responsible for human rights violations continued to be able to act with impunity. Amnesty International urged the new government to take positive steps to prevent further human rights violations.

In an oral statement to the United Nations Commission on Human Rights in February, Amnesty International included reference to its concerns about human rights violations during internal armed conflict in Rwanda.

# ST CHRISTOPHER AND NEVIS

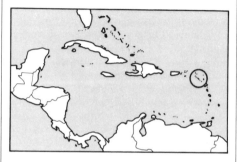

**Two prisoners scheduled to be hanged in what would have been the first executions since 1985 were granted stays of execution.**

Two men sentenced to death in 1991 for

murder were scheduled to be executed on 7 February. The day before, on 6 February, Bernard Richards and Ronald Browne were granted stays of execution. An appeal had been lodged against the dismissal of a constitutional motion that their rights under Article 7 of the Constitution (forbidding torture or inhuman or degrading punishment) would be violated if they were executed. The appeal was dismissed by the Court of Appeal in September. An appeal lodged in March in the Judicial Committee of the Privy Council (JCPC) in London, the final court of appeal for St Christopher and Nevis, was pending a hearing at the end of the year.

Amnesty International wrote to the Governor General, Sir Clement Arrindell, and the Prime Minister, Dr Kennedy Simmonds, in January. It stressed that the resumption of executions after seven years would be a retrograde step for human rights and urged the government to commute all death sentences. It urged the government to provide maximum safeguards for all prisoners facing possible death sentences. It expressed concern that the two men had not had the opportunity to submit their cases to the JCPC. It feared that they may have been unaware that they could appeal to the JCPC or that they could request financial assistance to pursue such an appeal.

Amnesty International welcomed the stays of execution and reiterated its call for the commutation of all death sentences.

# SAUDI ARABIA

**Over 50 people, many of them possible prisoners of conscience, were arrested and detained briefly for their religious or political activities: at least four were still held at the end of the year. Seventeen government opponents arrested in previous years, including six prisoners of conscience, were held without charge or trial throughout 1992, and at least five others continued to serve prison sentences imposed after unfair trials. New reports of torture were received and at least three detainees died allegedly as a result of torture or ill-treatment. Judicial punishments of flogging and amputation continued to be imposed. Sixty-six people were executed.**

In March King Fahd bin 'Abdul-'Aziz issued decrees as part of his promised political reforms (see *Amnesty International Report 1992*). One decree established a 60-member Consultative Council, the principal functions of which were to be advisory. Its members were to be appointed by the King, but this had not been done by the end of the year. Another decree envisaged the creation of local consultative councils in the Kingdom's 14 provinces. The King stressed that all the proposed changes were based on *Shari'a* (Islamic law as interpreted in Saudi Arabia) and that human rights would be respected.

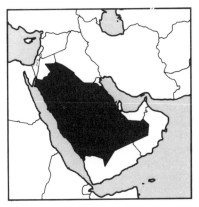

In September over 100 prominent religious scholars and university professors submitted a memorandum to the King entitled *al-Nasiha* (the Advice). The document criticized the Kingdom's foreign and economic policies as well as the alleged corruption of members of the royal family. It called for press freedom and meaningful political reforms. Several of the signatories were later prevented from travelling abroad by the authorities.

In January over 30 suspected opponents of the government, including possible prisoners of conscience, were arrested, principally in Riyadh and Qaseem. All were Sunni Muslims and suspected followers of *Salafiyya*, a fundamentalist Sunni Muslim doctrine. Among them was Ahmad al-'Abdani, a *Mu'athin* (caller to prayers in a mosque) from Riyadh. Most were released uncharged after being held for questioning for several days, but it was still not clear at the end of the year whether they had all been freed.

Between January and October, at least six other suspected opponents of the government, including possible prisoners of

**252**

conscience, were arrested in al-Qatif and other cities in Eastern Province. All were Shiʻa Muslims suspected of being supporters of the Organization of Islamic Revolution in the Arabian Peninsula (OIRAP). Three were released uncharged, but the others remained in detention, apparently without charge or trial, at the end of the year. Among those still held were Abdul-Khaliq al-Janbi and Mulla Turki Ahmad al-Turki, both students at King Abdul-ʻAziz University in Jeddah. They were arrested in October following an argument with a lecturer over texts which they perceived to be insulting to the Shiʻa faith. They were believed to be held in al-Mabahith al-ʻAmma Prison in al-Dammam.

In October at least 18 Korean and Indian Christians were arrested following a raid on their place of worship in Riyadh by members of the Committee for the Propagation of Virtue and Prevention of Vice, an official body which supervises the observance of *Shariʻa*. They were initially held at Suedi police station but were later transferred to Malaz prison in Riyadh. Among them was Sun-Keon Park, a Korean employee of the Saudi Ministry of Telecommunications. It was not clear whether any of the 18 had been released by the end of the year.

At least 17 government opponents arrested in previous years remained in detention, apparently without charge or trial. Six were prisoners of conscience: five students from King Saʻud University in Riyadh arrested in 1989 and one suspected OIRAP supporter arrested in 1990. Eleven were alleged supporters of *Hizbullah fil Hijaz*, Party of God in Hijaz, arrested in 1988 (see *Amnesty International Report 1992*).

Four other suspected *Hizbullah fil Hijaz* supporters continued to serve prison terms imposed after unfair trials in late 1989 or early 1990 (see *Amnesty International Reports 1989* to *1992*). Zuhair al-Safwani, a student and freelance journalist arrested in January 1991 and reportedly sentenced to four years' imprisonment and 300 lashes, also remained in prison.

Muhammad al-Fasi, a Saudi Arabian businessman, remained in unacknowledged detention at the end of the year. He had been arrested in Amman, Jordan, by Jordanian security forces in October 1991, apparently for speaking in support of Iraq during the Gulf War, and was later handed over to Saudi Arabian authorities (see *Amnesty International Report 1992*).

Information was received during 1992 about the release in 1991 of three prisoners of conscience, all OIRAP supporters arrested in 1990 (see *Amnesty International Reports 1991* and *1992*). At least two other prisoners of conscience who had been arrested in March 1991 were released uncharged in April 1991 and February 1992. They were among a group of six Shiʻa Muslims arrested between January and July 1991. At the end of the year, confirmation was being sought of the release of the remaining members of this group.

New reports of torture and ill-treatment of detainees were received. Among methods allegedly used were beatings, including *falaqa* (beatings on the soles of the feet) and sleep deprivation. Muhammad bin Fahd al-Mutayr, a bank employee, died in custody in April, allegedly as a result of severe beatings. He had been arrested a few days earlier following a robbery at his workplace in Riyadh. Zuhair Ibrahim al-ʻAwami, aged 18, died in mid-November, one week after his arrest. His body allegedly bore marks of severe beatings. ʻAbdullah ʻAbbas, a Ghanaian national, died in King Fahd Hospital in Jeddah in April several hours after his transfer from a deportation centre in the city where he had been detained for two weeks. Other detainees held with him at the deportation centre said that his legs and other parts of his body were swollen as a result of beatings by guards and that his urine was blood-stained. No investigation by the authorities into his death was known to have taken place.

New information was received during the year suggesting that scores of Iraqi refugees had been tortured or ill-treated while held in Rafha refugee camp and Artawiyya camp in 1991. The alleged victims were people who had fled from Iraq during and after the Gulf War or who had been captured and held as prisoners of war. The torture methods allegedly used included beatings, public floggings and rape. Reports of deaths as a result of torture were also received. Among the reported victims was Muhammad Khidhayer, who died in Artawiyya in September 1991 shortly after his arrest on suspicion of organizing a protest against camp conditions the previous month. In November and December the authorities transferred inmates from the Artawiyya camp to new facilities in Rafha, and by the end of the year almost all inmates had been transferred.

Between April and October, eight judicial amputations were carried out in Jeddah, Jizan and other cities. Among the victims were Filipino, Yemeni and Indian nationals. All had their right hands severed at the wrist after being convicted of theft.

During the year, 66 men were publicly executed by beheading. The victims were Filipino, Pakistani, Saudi Arabian, Sudanese and Yemeni nationals who had been convicted of murder, drug-trafficking, apostasy, kidnapping and sexual offences. Among them was Saddiq Malallah, a Saudi Arabian Shi'a Muslim who was reportedly beheaded in September after being convicted of apostasy. However, the details of the charges against him were unknown.

Amnesty International expressed concern to the authorities about the arrests of Christians and Sunni and Shi'a Muslims for the peaceful expression of their religious beliefs and called for the immediate, unconditional release of all prisoners of conscience, including those arrested in previous years. Amnesty International also urged the government to investigate deaths in custody and all torture allegations, and reiterated its opposition to the continued imposition of the death penalty and of the cruel, inhuman or degrading punishments of flogging and amputations. No response was received.

In July Amnesty International again indicated its wish to send a delegation to Saudi Arabia to discuss human rights violations with the government, but without response.

# SENEGAL

Government forces were alleged to have committed extrajudicial executions following an upsurge of violence in the Casamance region. Armed separatists in the region also reportedly committed serious abuses.

There was renewed fighting in Casamance during the last months of the year between government forces and armed separatists belonging to the *Mouvement des forces démocratiques de Casamance*

(MFDC), Democratic Forces of Casamance Movement.

Fighting broke out after the government of President Abdou Diouf announced in September that presidential and parliamentary elections would take place in early 1993 throughout the country, including in Casamance.

Government forces were alleged to have beaten and killed civilians and suspected supporters of the MFDC during counter-insurgency operations in Casamance but few details were available. The victims were said to include villagers in the Dioulolou area, who were briefly detained and beaten during army searches in October, and civilians at Bissiné village, five of whom were reportedly killed when soldiers attacked their village in late September or early October. The dead were said to include two children.

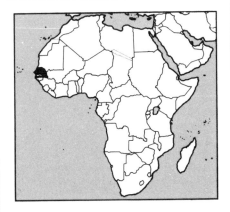

There were also reports of arrests of suspected MFDC supporters but none was known to have been brought to trial. There was concern that two suspected MFDC supporters apparently "disappeared" after they were detained in September. The two, Ibou Sagna and Famara Bodian, a Gambian national, were said to have been detained after an armed clash between government soldiers and MFDC separatists at Kaguitt. In other cases, suspected MFDC supporters were alleged to have been tortured while in military custody in Casamance. In several cases detainees reportedly had molten plastic dripped on to their skin.

Other suspected MFDC supporters were forcibly returned from Guinea-Bissau in October and detained. The exact number was unclear. Some were reported to have "disappeared" in custody and others to have been referred to the procuracy, but the

**254**

charges against them were not known. More than 50 were held in Ziguinchor prison at the end of the year. More than 10 other suspected MFDC supporters were also held in Ziguinchor prison, apparently after being referred to the procuracy. None had been brought to trial by the end of the year.

The government took no steps to investigate past human rights violations related to the Casamance conflict. Despite a statement in October before the UN Human Rights Committee, a body of experts which monitors implementation of the International Covenant on Civil and Political Rights, that a law of amnesty was not intended to absolve officials of responsibility for human rights violations, the authorities have continued to interpret the amnesty which it had granted in 1991 (see *Amnesty International Report 1992*) as conferring immunity from prosecution on members of the security forces and others who in the past perpetrated human rights violations.

The MFDC was also responsible for serious abuses, including deliberate killings of civilians, some of them because of their ethnic origin. More than 30 civilians, including children, were reported to have been deliberately killed by MFDC forces at Cap Skirring in October and at Pointe Saint-Georges in November, in some cases apparently because they came from outside Casamance. Boubacar Mané, head of the village of Bissiné, was said to have been executed by MFDC separatists in September or October after they accused him of assisting government forces.

When violence restarted in Casamance, Amnesty International began investigating reports of detentions, to establish if detainees were being dealt with in accordance with the law. It also investigated allegations that some prisoners or unarmed civilians had been executed extrajudicially. Confirmation, however, was not available by the end of the year.

# SIERRA LEONE

**After a coup in April, more than 150 people associated with the former government or suspected government opponents were detained without charge or trial: among them were prisoners of conscience. Most were still held at the end of the year. Torture and ill-treatment by the** security forces were reported before and after the coup, and about 300 Liberian nationals detained in 1991 were reported to have died in custody as a result of torture or neglect. Suspected rebels and people accused of supporting them in areas affected by armed conflict were tortured and extrajudicially executed by soldiers. Nine people were sentenced to death for murder. In December, 26 people accused of involvement in alleged coup attempts were executed after grossly unfair and hasty trials carried out in secret before a special court, and at least three others were extrajudicially executed.

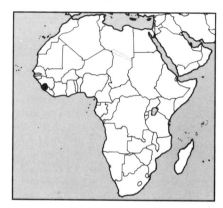

Armed conflict between the army and rebel forces in southeastern Sierra Leone persisted throughout the year. In mid-1992 the government estimated that more than 8,000 civilians and 125 soldiers had died since March 1991 when an invasion force from Liberia, led by members of the National Patriotic Front of Liberia (NPFL), captured villages and towns in Southern and Eastern Provinces. The rebel forces – principally Sierra Leoneans belonging to the Revolutionary United Front, a group in armed opposition to the government – were pushed back towards the Liberian border but again seized control of parts of Eastern Province from September. Government troops tortured and executed people suspected of supporting or assisting rebel forces and the rebels, for their part, tortured and killed unarmed civilians who refused to support them. Thousands of people fled as refugees to neighbouring Guinea or Liberia or sought refuge in other parts of Sierra Leone.

On 29 April the government of Major-General Joseph Saidu Momoh was overthrown in a military coup led by officers from the war front, who were subsequently joined by the security forces in the capital, Freetown. They proclaimed a National Provisional Ruling Council (NPRC), headed by Captain Valentine E.M. Strasser. The new military government suspended the October 1991 Constitution and declared a state of emergency. New and emergency legislation was introduced, giving the security forces unlimited powers of administrative detention without charge or trial, and specifically preventing challenges against such detentions in the courts.

On 7 December the NPRC promulgated the Treason and Other Offences (Special Military Tribunal) Decree, No. 12 of 1992, which established a special military court with the power to try any person involved in an attempt to overthrow the NPRC. The court comprised four army or police officers presided over by a senior armed forces officer, all appointed by the NPRC. No judicial appeal was allowed and all sentences had to be confirmed by the NPRC. The decree provided for a High Court judge to act as legal adviser to the special tribunal and for defendants to be represented by lawyers of their own choice. However, it specifically barred all other courts from questioning any decision of the tribunal or the confirming authority.

After the April coup more than 50 former government ministers and officials were detained. Former President Momoh sought refuge in neighbouring Guinea. Also arrested were people who appeared to have been detained solely because they were associated with or related to members of the former government. Some of the detainees were prisoners of conscience. All were held at Pademba Road Prison in Freetown and initially denied access to families and lawyers. Most were subsequently interrogated by a judicial commission of inquiry into the assets of former government ministers. Six were released uncharged in November and a further six in December, including three brothers of former President Momoh, although some were immediately restricted under house arrest and forbidden from communicating with other people. Many others had not been charged or brought to trial by the end of the year, although in a number of cases the commission had apparently found no evidence of corruption.

About 100 others were detained without charge or trial between May and December, and were believed to be still held at the end of the year. The reasons for their detention were not made known but they were believed to be held because of suspected opposition to the government.

Torture and ill-treatment of suspected rebels and their supporters, both by soldiers in the war zone and by security police, was common. Captives often had their arms bound tightly behind their backs with the result that many reportedly were paralysed and lost the use of their hands and arms. Of six captured suspects taken to Kenema in mid-March, for example, four were later released with burns and bruises on their bodies and serious injuries to their arms from being tied too tightly.

After the April coup there were further reports of soldiers beating, ill-treating and in some cases killing civilians accused of supporting the rebels. In one reported case in Koidu, Kono District, a boy was detained and badly beaten on 25 August and his mother later detained and beaten when she made inquiries about him. The new government reportedly punished some soldiers in such cases. In a well-publicized case, the government dismissed from office the Resident Minister for Southern Province, a senior army officer, after he ordered soldiers to beat a church minister unconscious in front of the Anglican Bishop of Bo on 29 August.

About 300 Liberian prisoners died in Pademba Road Prison as a result of torture or neglect in 1991 and 1992, according to 27 Liberians released from the prison in September. Nine of the 27 had been so badly treated in custody that they died in hospital in Liberia within a few days of their release. The Liberians had been arrested in March and April 1991 after the NPFL-supported invasion. Some were NPFL fighters captured in the war zone; others were Liberian nationals living in Sierra Leone. Survivors said they had been held in appalling conditions, in total darkness for the first four months, and denied adequate food and all medical attention. The security police reportedly tortured to death many of the 300, while the others died from malnutrition and disease. It was not clear whether Sierra Leoneans and other nationals also held at Pademba Road Prison since 1991 after being denounced as rebels – sometimes by personal or business rivals – were released in September. Their detentions, like those of the Liberians, had

**256**

been without any basis in law. They included Ishmael Mansaray, who reportedly died in detention in February, Ben Koni from Bonthe, Dauda Kamara and Santibi Kamara from Freetown, and two Ghanaians, Bruce Alphonso and Robert Cleur.

Government troops fighting rebel forces in the southeast were reported to have executed suspected rebels and their supporters after only the most perfunctory investigation and without any legal authority. Executions took place in public, in graveyards, on river banks and sometimes in the streets. Some of those executed were unarmed civilians, and all were denied the right to defend themselves in a court of law. In some cases, detainees were shot after they had been unable to prove that they were not rebels before unofficial investigation panels comprising military officers and local officials. None of the large number of rebels claimed to have been captured by the military authorities appeared to be held in detention centres or prisons: it was feared that they too had been executed extrajudicially.

Shortly after it came to power, the new military government offered an amnesty to all rebels who surrendered but, after rebel forces attacked Kono District, Eastern Province, in September, soldiers reportedly killed civilians accused of supporting the rebels. On 31 October, Sahr Songu-Mbriwa, a traditional ruler and former government minister, was reportedly flogged in public in Koidu before being tortured and killed by soldiers. Soldiers were reported to have carried out extrajudicial executions in public of two rebel suspects in Bo, Southern Province, in late October and of a rebel suspect in Koidu in early November.

On 18 February five men were sentenced to death after being convicted of murder. On 23 November three men were sentenced to death for aggravated robbery. All eight had been convicted by the High Court, Freetown, and appeals lodged with the Court of Appeal had not been heard by the end of the year. On 18 November a soldier was sentenced to death, without right of appeal, by a military court in Freetown. He had been convicted of an aggravated robbery in Koidu in September.

In December, 26 people were executed and at least three extrajudicially executed on suspicion of involvement in alleged coup attempts. On 21 November, 19 people had been detained on suspicion of plotting to overthrow the government. On 29 December the NPRC announced that a second coup attempt had been foiled the night before and the perpetrators arrested. On 31 December it announced that three alleged conspirators had been shot in cross-fire on 28 December and that 26 others had been sentenced to death: 16 men and a woman in connection with the alleged November coup attempt; and nine men for the alleged December coup attempt. It stated that the 26 had been convicted of treason by a Special Military Tribunal and their sentences confirmed. However, it later emerged that the sentences had been carried out on 29 December within hours of being confirmed and that the main evidence against them was their confessions and the testimony of an alleged co-conspirator. Those executed included nine civilians and 17 military and police officers.

Unoffical sources alleged that there had been no coup attempts, that no shooting or unrest had been heard in the area of Freetown where the government said the arrests took place, that some of those executed had not been tried at all, and that some had been tortured before being killed. At least two were alleged to have been killed before 28 December: James Bambay Kamara, a former Inspector General of Police and Minister of State, and Lieutenant-Colonel James Yayah Kanu, a former war commander. Both had been detained without charge or trial in Pademba Road Prison since the April coup. Those who were brought before the Special Military Tribunal received a hurried, secret and grossly unfair trial in which they were denied all rights of defence – neither defence lawyers nor the court's legal adviser were present. The homes and property of those executed were seized and plundered by the military.

Rebel forces were also responsible for gross human rights abuses. They tortured and killed suspected government supporters and the inhabitants of towns and villages which they attacked. Among the victims were traditional chiefs and Muslim businessmen. At Bunti, Kenema District, in mid-March rebels killed at least 20 and possibly as many as 50 people as they fled their houses, in one case setting fire to a house and burning alive a woman and her two children. Further rebel attacks on villagers were reported from Kailahun District in March and from Kono District late in the year. In October the rebels took control of Koidu, killing civilians who resisted and looting the diamond mines. In late October they took prisoner a foreign Red Cross worker and two Liberian nationals, who were held for over a month. In late November rebels beheaded a soldier they had taken prisoner near Koidu and cut off the hands of a civilian with him who was accused of assisting government forces.

In March Amnesty International representatives visited Sierra Leone and discussed the organization's concerns with government officials and others in Freetown and in Southern and Eastern Provinces. Amnesty International urged the government to halt extrajudicial executions and to order an immediate impartial inquiry into all reports of torture and killings by government forces. In April Amnesty International published a report, *Sierra Leone: The extrajudicial execution of suspected rebels and collaborators*, which described killings of prisoners, torture and illegal detentions by government forces and torture and killings by rebel and NPFL forces. The report called for the prompt introduction of measures to regulate and record the detention and interrogation of suspected rebels and their supporters.

After the April coup, Amnesty International called on the new government to release immediately any prisoners of conscience and to give all other detainees a prompt and fair trial or release them. It also called for all detainees to be allowed access to their families and lawyers and to be given medical care. In a response in September the government denied that the security forces had been responsible for extrajudicial executions or torture. It said that rebels who had responded to the government's amnesty had been screened at detention centres and released if found to have been coerced into joining the rebels. Detained former government officials found to be corrupt by the commission of inquiry would, it said, be "treated in accordance with the law" and, if found innocent, be released.

Following the December executions Amnesty International urged the government to give any other suspects fair and open trials and to commute any further death sentences.

In an oral statement to the United Nations Sub-Commission on Prevention of Discrimination and Protection of Minorities in August, Amnesty International included reference to its concerns about indefinite detention without charge or trial in Sierra Leone.

# SINGAPORE

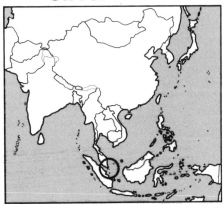

**Three former prisoners of conscience continued to be subject to government orders restricting their freedom of expression and association. Criminal offenders were sentenced to caning. At least seven people were sentenced to death and three were executed.**

The restriction order on Chia Thye Poh, a former member of parliament detained without charge or trial under the Internal Security Act (ISA) from 1966 to 1989, confining him at night to an offshore island (see *Amnesty International Reports 1991* and *1992*) was amended in November to allow him to live on the main island of Singapore. Restrictions on his freedom of association and expression continued to be imposed.

Restriction orders on two other former prisoners of conscience, Vincent Cheng and Teo Soh Lung, limiting their freedom of expression and association, were renewed in June. Vincent Cheng's order was renewed for a further two years and Teo Soh Lung's for one year. Similar restrictions on three other former prisoners of conscience were not renewed (see *Amnesty International Report 1992*).

Caning, which constitutes a cruel, inhuman or degrading form of punishment, remained a mandatory punishment for some 30 crimes, including armed robbery, attempted murder, drug-trafficking, illegal immigration and rape. In July Lee Seck

**258**

Hing, a car tyre dealer, was sentenced to three strokes of the cane and one year's imprisonment after being convicted of breaking the arm of another motorist. There was no information about the damages claim made in court in March 1991 by Qwek Kee Chong, a convicted prisoner, for "grievous injury" caused by caning (see *Amnesty International Report 1992*).

At least seven people were sentenced to death. They included Tan Chee Kwee and Joseph Soon Kim Liang who were sentenced to death in July by the High Court after being convicted of murder and robbery, and Mazlan Maidin whose death sentence imposed for murder was upheld by the Court of Criminal Appeal in October. At least three people were executed: all had been convicted of drugs offences. Tan Toon Hock was executed in February. Lim Joo Yin and Tan Chong Ngee were executed in April. Sim Ah Cheoh, a woman under sentence of death for the same drug-trafficking offence as Lim Joo Yin and Tan Chong Ngee, was granted clemency by President Wee Kim Wee in March and her sentence was commuted to life imprisonment. This was only the fourth such commutation in 30 years.

Amnesty International urged the authorities to lift the restrictions on the three former prisoners of conscience, to end caning and to commute all death sentences.

# SOMALIA

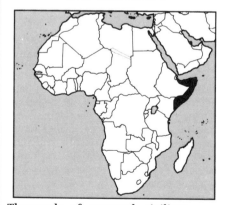

**Thousands of unarmed civilians were deliberately killed by political groups fighting in the civil war which had destroyed central government and fragmented the country since early 1991. Victims were apparently targeted on account** of their membership of a particular clan. Most captives were summarily executed. At least two political armed groups tortured and mutilated prisoners. Some of the other armed groups imprisoned civilian opponents.

The civil wars which began in early 1991, shortly after the overthrow by the United Somali Congress (USC) of former president Mohamed Siad Barre's 21-year dictatorship (see *Amnesty International Report 1992*), continued throughout 1992. Fighting was widespread throughout most of the country as different armed groups, generally based on particular clans or sub-clans of the Somali ethnic group, disputed control of different areas. Civilians not involved in the fighting, including children, were often deliberately killed because they belonged to an opposing clan. In the capital, Mogadishu, hundreds died and thousands were wounded in the first three months of the year during artillery shelling by two rival USC factions based on Hawiye clan sub-divisions, one loyal to Ali Mahdi, named in 1991 as interim President, and the other to General Mohamed Farah Aideed. The daily bombardment subsided in April 1992 when the United Nations (UN) negotiated a cease-fire. The city remained divided into areas held by these and other armed groups. In the absence of a recognized government or any central authority able to impose law and order, a high level of violence persisted throughout the year with killings, rape and looting committed by heavily armed gunmen belonging to these groups. Much of the killing was arbitrary and impossible to attribute to any organized force.

At least 300,000 people, mostly children, died of starvation caused by the fighting, breakdown of government, famine and obstruction of the flow of international relief aid. Nearly a quarter of the six million population fled the country. A large part of the famine relief supplies brought into the country was stolen at gunpoint by armed groups, some linked to clan-based political groups, who killed anyone presumed to be opposing them, including relief agency workers.

During 1992 the UN Security Council passed several resolutions on the situation in Somalia and sent 50 unarmed cease-fire monitors to Mogadishu in July, and 500 troops later to protect the distribution of relief food and medicines. Successive UN

Special Representatives for Somalia met the warring groups to try to secure relief channels and to seek political reconciliation. As the situation deteriorated, on 3 December the UN Security Council authorized a United States-led military operation to "establish a secure environment for humanitarian relief operations". The resolution referred to the threat posed by the crisis to international peace and security, and widespread violations of international humanitarian law, for which individuals who were responsible would be held accountable. "Operation Restore Hope" began the next day, with 28,000 US troops moving into Somalia and contingents from other countries following. It appeared to achieve its aim of reducing levels of violence by the end of December, and was due to give way to a UN peace-keeping operation when its objectives had been achieved.

In other parts of the south outside Mogadishu, there was fighting between different forces. In April the Somali National Front (SNF), comprising soldiers from former President Mohamed Siad Barre's army and members of his Marehan clan, advanced from Gedo region in the southwest towards Mogadishu. They were pushed back by General Aideed's forces and most fled to Kenya together with the former President. By October, however, the SNF had recaptured most of Gedo region. Both the SNF and USC forces killed, tortured and mutilated civilians of opposing clans. The SNF killed and committed gross human rights abuses against members of the Hawiye and Rahanwein clans. In the town of Bulohawo on the border with Kenya, General Aideed's forces rounded up members of the Darod clan-family (which included the Marehan and other clans) in April, and executed dozens of people, including children. They also publicly tortured and mutilated many civilians and raped women. Similar abuses were perpetrated by the SNF as it pushed the USC forces back. In a rare exception to this pattern of revenge killings, General Aideed's forces transferred to Mogadishu 300 Marehan clan members, including soldiers and civilians, whom they had taken prisoner, and allowed the International Committee of the Red Cross (ICRC) access to them.

In the southwest, control of the port of Kismayu fluctuated between opposed alliances centred on the USC and SNF respectively. Forces of the Somali Patriotic

Movement under Colonel Omar Jess, part of General Aideed's forces, reportedly killed over 100 Darod clan members in Kismayu in April in reprisal for a defeat in Gedo region. In August they abducted at gunpoint 11 Darod clan members whom the ICRC was protecting in Kismayu, including five Somali ICRC employees. They were never seen again and were believed to have been executed. Later, in early December, as US forces were about to take control of Kismayu, Colonel Omar Jess' forces massacred at least 100 and possibly many more members of Darod clans opposed to General Aideed. Those killed included clan elders, women and children.

The northeast, inhabited mainly by members of the Darod clan-family, was controlled for most of the year by the Somali Salvation Democratic Front (SSDF). A new political group, the Islamic Union, attacked Bosasso and Garowe in June, capturing many SSDF leaders. After brief but heavy fighting in which hundreds of fighters and civilian opponents were killed by both forces, SSDF forces regained control, defeating the Islamic Union force and freeing the imprisoned SSDF leaders. They reportedly pardoned captured Islamic Union fighters and allowed their leaders to leave the region.

In the northwest, the Somali National Movement (SNM), centred on the Issaq clan, headed a coalition of other clan-based groups in the former British Somaliland, which the SNM had unilaterally declared independent in May 1991 as the Somaliland Republic, although it did not gain international recognition. In January 1992 there were hundreds of casualties in fighting between armed groups belonging to two opposed Issaq sub-clans in the towns of Berbera and Burao. Political tensions and general insecurity and violence, erupting at times into sustained fighting, held back moves to establish a central government authority in the self-declared territory and obstructed development and relief activities.

Amnesty International was deeply concerned at the continuation during 1992 of a pattern of apparently uncontrollable gross human rights abuses. It was generally difficult to document specific cases, owing to the fragmentation of the country, the absence of public order and communications, and the general economic breakdown. It was often impossible to determine

**260**

who was responsible for the abuses, particularly since gunmen often appeared to operate independently of the main political factions.

After receiving details of killings of prisoners in the southwest, Amnesty International published a report, *Somalia: A human rights disaster*, in August. The organization appealed to all Somali armed political groups to halt the spiral of abuses and build respect for human rights. It called on their leaders and supporters alike to work to end the deliberate and arbitrary killings. It urged all forces to observe minimum humane standards, as set out in the Geneva Conventions, in particular to treat civilians and wounded or captured combatants humanely, and to prevent and punish extrajudicial executions, mutilation or torture. It also appealed to the international community to help in the search for effective solutions to end the horrendous cycle of human rights abuses in Somalia.

# SOUTH AFRICA

Hundreds of government opponents were victims of politically motivated killings carried out by the security forces or with their acquiescence. Some were assassinated, others killed in mass attacks on residents of black townships and squatter camps. The authorities announced various inquiries into these killings but rarely brought those responsible to justice. Some 500 people were detained under security legislation. There were new reports of torture and ill-treatment of prisoners, with at least 121 deaths in custody in suspicious circumstances. Over 400 prisoners remained under sentence of death but there were no executions.

A whites-only referendum in March resulted in a majority vote in favour of the reform process initiated by state President F.W. de Klerk's National Party government. However, the government and the African National Congress (ANC) failed to reach agreement at the Convention for a Democratic South Africa (CODESA) summit in May. In June the ANC withdrew from negotiations following the Boipatong massacre (see below), and launched a series of mass protest actions against the government, but direct talks between the government and the ANC were resumed in December.

There was a continued high level of political violence, particularly in Natal. More than 3,000 people were killed, many of them victims of security force action or fighting between supporters of the Inkatha Freedom Party (IFP), headed by KwaZulu "homeland" Chief Minister, Mangosuthu Buthelezi, and the ANC. The worst single incident occurred at Boipatong on 17 June, when 49 people, including children, were massacred, apparently by IFP supporters. Following this, the United Nations (UN) Security Council authorized the UN Secretary-General to deploy international observers to reinforce mechanisms established by the September 1991 National Peace Accord (see *Amnesty International Report 1992*). By December about 100 observers from the UN, the Commonwealth, the European Community and the Organization of African Unity were operating in South Africa.

The judicial commission chaired by Appeal Court Judge Richard Goldstone continued to conduct inquiries into incidents of political violence, ranging from armed attacks on black train commuters to the operations of covert military intelligence units (see *Amnesty International Report 1992*). However, in November President de Klerk rejected a request from Judge Goldstone for additional powers and resources to investigate the security forces.

Throughout the year new evidence of covert security force involvement in killings and other unlawful acts against opposition organizations came to light. The evidence implicated senior officers in the security forces and government ministers. However, the government enacted an amnesty law in November, effectively providing immunity from prosecution for human rights violators.

Some of those killed were victims of

attacks on black train commuters or on ANC-supporting communities by armed men believed to be operating from IFP-controlled hostels and acting with the acquiescence of the police. Others, including middle-level leaders of the ANC, the South African Communist Party (SACP) and the trade unions, members of the ANC's military wing and other returned exiles, were assassinated by hit squads composed of elements within the security forces or men acting with their acquiescence. In other incidents, local IFP leaders, members of the police force and white civilians were believed to have been killed by members of the military wings of the ANC and the Pan Africanist Congress of Azania (PAC).

Clear evidence emerged of direct security force involvement in extrajudicial executions. On 7 September, for example, 29 ANC supporters were shot dead and hundreds of others injured when members of the Ciskei Defence Force opened fire without warning on a peaceful demonstration. The Goldstone Commission's inquiry into the incident concluded that the conduct of the Ciskei soldiers was "morally and legally indefensible...[and] deliberately aimed at causing as many deaths and injuries as possible".

Further evidence implicating the military in assassinations and attempted assassinations emerged through inquest hearings. The inquest into the death of a human rights lawyer, Bheki Mlangeni, who had been killed in 1991 by an explosive device apparently intended for Dirk Coetzee, a former member of a covert police hit squad, revealed evidence of military intelligence and security police involvement in a further assassination attempt against Dirk Coetzee in 1992. Other evidence suggested that the police investigating Bheki Mlangeni's death had attempted to cover up police involvement.

In May newspapers published a secret military document which implicated the head of Military Intelligence and cabinet ministers in the 1985 assassinations of Matthew Goniwe and three other Eastern Cape political activists (see *Amnesty International Report 1986*).

During the judicial inquest into the 1989 assassination of human rights activist David Webster, evidence from former operatives of the covert military unit, the Civil Co-operation Bureau (CCB), and other witnesses appeared to implicate a former CCB

member. In November the Goldstone Commission seized documents from a secret military intelligence base. These revealed that the Chief of Staff of Military Intelligence had authorized the hiring in 1991 of the same man, a convicted double-murderer, to run a task force aimed at destabilizing the ANC and its military wing. Despite the commission's request for additional resources and powers to pursue its inquiries, President de Klerk ordered a military and a police general to lead the investigation. The police general, however, had been implicated in a previous cover-up of police and CCB involvement in hit squads. On 19 December President de Klerk announced that he had ordered the suspension or early retirement of 23 military officers for alleged involvement in illicit political activities, including murder. The list did not include key senior officers implicated in covert activities.

A member of a military battalion appeared in court charged with the murders of an IFP leader and four members of his family, who had been shot dead at their Natal home on 23 August by six men wearing security force uniforms. In November the Goldstone Commission released a report on East Rand violence, in which it concluded that the killing of 18 IFP supporters in Thokoza on 8 September 1991 had been planned and carried out by a police informer operating a "self-defence unit" in Phola Park, an ANC-supporting squatter camp.

In April the Natal Supreme Court found five police officers responsible for the 1988 murder of 11 people in Trust Feed, Natal. The presiding judge concluded that the main accused, a police captain then in charge of New Hanover police station, had ordered the killings at the behest of certain IFP officials and had himself shot two of the victims. The case also revealed an extensive senior police cover-up of the officers' involvement in the murders. The court sentenced the police captain to death and four "special police constables", who were found to have acted on his orders, to 15 years' imprisonment.

Witnesses, including a police constable, who testified to the Goldstone Commission about the Boipatong massacre said that they had seen security force armoured vehicles escorting and transporting the attackers, among whom were white men in camouflage uniforms. The majority of the

**262**

attackers came from a nearby IFP-controlled hostel, Kwa-Madala. The police denied that they had been forewarned of the attack or that their vehicles were present during the attack. However, the Commission had not produced its final report by the end of the year because it was still awaiting additional forensic analysis of the tapes of radio and telephone messages made in the police control room on the night of the massacre.

Approximately 500 people were detained for varying periods under security legislation. They included about 70 people held under the Ciskei National Security Act as the security forces sought out ANC supporters after the 7 September shooting of unarmed demonstrators. More than 100 people were detained under the Public Safety Act's emergency regulations following the 17 June massacre in Boipatong. In Bophuthatswana, over 100 students of the University of Bophuthatswana were detained on 18 September for refusing to disclose information relating to disturbances at the university. Most were released the same day, but seven were held for almost a month. After lawyers challenged their detention in court, the seven were charged under security legislation and released on bail.

Most detainees were not held for long periods. However, during the year a pattern emerged of prolonged detention without charge for months under "unrest areas" regulations declared in various parts of the country under the Public Safety Act. In one such case, Japie Maphalala was detained in June and held without charge until he was released, following intervention by his lawyers, in November.

At least 121 people died in police custody in suspicious circumstances. Some had been arrested for political reasons; others were criminal suspects. Jonas Kgosietsile, a mineworker, died on 20 January while held in indefinite, incommunicado detention at Phokeng police station, Bophuthatswana. He had been assaulted and tortured with electric shocks at the same police station two months earlier. According to an official post-mortem, he died as a result of a broken neck and internal bleeding. The police gave contradictory versions of the circumstances leading to his death. By the end of the year no inquest had been held.

In another case, Simon Mthimkulu was found dead on 16 July, two days after his arrest by police in Sebokeng township. A fellow detainee said the police had beaten and kicked Simon Mthimkulu during interrogation at Sebokeng police station and dropped a large stone on his ribs. The findings of a post-mortem by an independent forensic pathologist, Dr Jonathan Gluckman, were consistent with the witness's account.

In July Dr Gluckman told the press he had details of scores of deaths in police custody since the mid-1980s. Ninety per cent of these, he said, contained evidence that the police had killed people in their custody. The Minister of Law and Order responded to these allegations with an internal police investigation, the results of which were announced in November. The Minister dismissed the allegations as unsubstantiated. Following the publication of his concerns, Dr Gluckman was subjected to death threats and his office was placed under surveillance, apparently by the security authorities.

In October the government agreed for the first time to allow the International Committee of the Red Cross access to all detainees in police custody to examine conditions of detention and recommend possible improvements. Similar agreements had been negotiated earlier with at least three of the nominally independent "homelands".

While the authorities, in general, still failed to act effectively against police officers implicated in deaths in custody, there were several prosecutions arising from cases in previous years. In September, for example, the Pretoria Supreme Court convicted a police officer for the murder of Michael Nkabinde, who died in custody in November 1990. The police officer had continued to assault Michael Nkabinde even after he became unconscious. He was sentenced to nine years' imprisonment. Another police officer was charged with murder, after a 1991 inquest court found him criminally liable for the death of "Bongi" Nyokong, a schoolboy. In October another inquest court decided that the same police officer, together with one other, had unlawfully killed another detainee in 1990. Despite this, the police officer remained on active duty.

There were no executions during the year. In March the government turned down clemency appeals from 17 prisoners sentenced to death. However, five days later the Minister of Justice announced that all executions would be suspended pending agreement on an "interim bill of rights". At the end of the year at least 300 prisoners remained on death row in Pretoria Central Prison. Twelve prisoners remained on death row in the Bophuthatswana "homeland". Lawyers won a last-minute stay of execution for three of these prisoners, who were scheduled to be executed in November. Eighty-nine prisoners remained under sentence of death in the Transkei "homeland" where a moratorium on executions continued.

The Minister of Justice announced in March that the tribunal appointed to review death sentences imposed before July 1990 (see *Amnesty International Report 1992*) had completed its work in November 1991. The majority of the cases had been referred back to the Appeal Court. Amnesty International was not aware of how many of these resulted in commutations of the death sentences.

Throughout the year Amnesty International expressed its concern to the authorities about individual cases of human rights violations, including the torture and killing of detainees and extrajudicial executions by members of the security forces. In their responses, government officials denied that state agents had been negligent or responsible for political killings or other human rights violations and accused Amnesty International of bias. In June Amnesty International published *South Africa: State of Fear – security force complicity in torture and political killings, 1990-1992*. The report documented continuing security force involvement in extrajudicial executions and other serious human rights violations, and the authorities' failure in most cases to hold the perpetrators accountable or bring them to justice.

In an oral statement to the UN Commission on Human Rights in January, Amnesty International described its concerns in South Africa.

In August an Amnesty International observer attended part of the proceedings of an ANC commission of inquiry into reports of torture in its camps, in particular in Angola, during the 1980s. In November Amnesty International published *South Africa: Torture, ill-treatment and executions in African National Congress camps*, which documented evidence of torture and executions committed by ANC officials at military and prison camps, notably in Angola, Tanzania, Uganda and Zambia, on occasions with the active collaboration of agents of the governments concerned. Amnesty International urged the ANC to implement the recommendations of its own commission, which were made public in October, in particular by establishing a further and independent commission to establish the full truth of what had occurred and by compensating the victims. Amnesty International said that those responsible for torturing and killing prisoners should be brought to justice and never again be permitted to hold posts with responsibility for prisoners. The ANC announced that it had appointed an independent tribunal and would take Amnesty International's report into account in drawing up the tribunal's terms of reference.

# SPAIN

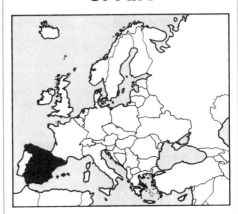

There were allegations of torture and ill-treatment by the security forces. Several inquiries opened into such allegations in previous years remained unresolved. Inquiries continued into killings in disputed circumstances of members of an armed Basque group by security forces. A conscript imprisoned for his conscientious objection to further military service was a prisoner of conscience.

Attacks by the armed Basque group, *Euskadi Ta Askatasuna* (ETA), Basque Homeland and Liberty, on the security forces and civilians continued throughout the year. Twenty-six people, including seven civilians, were killed in the attacks. People suspected of belonging to an armed group could still be held incommunicado for up to five days by judicial order – 48 hours longer than the legal limit for other suspects. They also continued to be denied the right to designate lawyers of their own choice.

Allegations of torture and ill-treatment were made following the arrest of approximately 50 people in a major security forces operation in the Basque province of Vizcaya between January and mid-May. Those arrested were suspected of belonging to or collaborating with the "*Bizkaia*" commando of ETA, which was accused of attacks on security forces and civilians. Thirty-two of them were held in extended incommunicado detention before appearing in the National Court in Madrid. Nearly all of them reportedly complained to the court that they had been hooded, blindfolded and forced to do exercises. Some detainees said they had been beaten and kicked and two alleged that they had been given electric shocks. Most of the women complained that they had been forced to strip and suffered persistent sexual insults and humiliations. Many of the detainees had visible cuts, bruises and other injuries when they appeared in court. Investigations were opened into some of the complaints.

Kepa Urra Guridi, arrested in January on suspicion of belonging to the "*Bizkaia*" commando, alleged he was beaten, kicked and punched by the Civil Guards on three separate occasions. A court doctor told the judicial inquiry that, on the day of Kepa Urra's arrest, he saw him lying unconscious on the floor of his cell, breathing very rapidly, and that he had marks on his face, eyes and wrists and was bleeding at the throat, nose and mouth. He was immediately transferred to hospital. Kepa Urra alleged that officers hit him in hospital and during his subsequent transfer to prison; forensic examinations recorded new injuries after his transfer to hospital. Nine Civil Guard officers were formally accused in connection with his complaint.

Allegations of torture and ill-treatment were also made by non-political suspects. In May eight members of a multinational rugby team were arrested in Benidorm. They alleged that officers of the Municipal Police had carried out a serious and unprovoked assault on them. The police claimed that the players were drunk, violent and had been vandalizing cars. The players

denied the charges and said they had been punched, kicked, hit with truncheons and menaced with firearms by the police. Two of them alleged that they had been beaten with truncheons while they were handcuffed and on the ground. The team's allegations were supported by photographic and medical evidence. An inquiry into their case was opened in court the day of their arrest.

In April, after a two-year judicial investigation, charges of ill-treatment were brought against 16 guards of the Modelo prison in Barcelona (see *Amnesty International Report 1991*).

In October five Civil Guards were found guilty of torturing Joaquín Olano in 1983 (see *Amnesty International Report 1984*). They were sentenced to between two and seven months' imprisonment, plus varying terms of up to seven years' disqualification from holding public office. The court found that the prisoner had been punched, kicked, hit with a telephone directory, hooded, partially asphyxiated with a plastic bag, submerged in water and given electric shocks. Two of the officers had been convicted in 1986 of torturing another prisoner. However, they did not serve their sentences, remained on active service and were pardoned in February 1991.

In September the Ombudsman urged the introduction of temporary, administrative suspension, during judicial inquiries, of officers accused of torture or ill-treatment. During the year officers sentenced on such charges remained on active service pending appeals and in some cases did not serve their sentences even after they had been made final. Some officers convicted of torture and ill-treatment were pardoned. Instances of recidivism occurred.

In July the Minister of the Interior released figures showing an increase in the number of Civil Guards and police accused of ill-treatment. In 1991, 171 judicial proceedings had been opened involving 392 officers accused of ill-treatment, 132 more than the previous year. According to the Ministry, two judicial proceedings, involving a total of seven officers, were also opened into accusations of torture during 1991.

In February Amnesty International sent an observer to the trial of Rafael Navarro Vacas, a police officer charged with the 1990 homicide of an ETA member, Mikel Castilló (see *Amnesty International Report*

AMNESTY INTERNATIONAL REPORT 1993

1992). He was acquitted. The court accepted that there was no forensic evidence to show that Mikel Castilló had been unarmed and also accepted police statements that he had been armed. The prosecution entered an appeal.

In June the National Court in Madrid sentenced two ETA members – Germán Rubenach and Juan José Zubieta – to 57 and 23 years' imprisonment respectively for the murder of a Civil Guard and the wounding of another in an exchange of gunfire in the Foz de Lumbier in 1990 (see *Amnesty International Reports 1991* and *1992*). The judicial inquiry into allegations of unlawful killing by the Civil Guard of two other ETA members was still open.

José Antonio Escalada, a conscientious objector to military service, was imprisoned while awaiting trial for desertion. He and fellow conscientious objector Manuel Blázquez Solís had spent three months in pre-trial detention during 1991 (see *Amnesty International Report 1992*). They had been charged with desertion after leaving the navy at the outbreak of the Gulf conflict. They applied for conscientious objector status on moral and philosophical grounds although the law allows the right to conscientious objection to be exercised only "until the moment of incorporation" into the armed forces. Hours before their release into provisional liberty in 1991 they had confirmed to the military authorities that they refused all further military service. Within a week new arrest warrants were issued against them. Both conscripts lived clandestinely while appeals against the warrants, including appeals to the Constitutional Court, continued. However, in June José Antonio Escalada was arrested during a routine identity check. In July the Constitutional Court ordered that the proceedings against Manuel Blázquez be suspended, pending its final decision on his appeal. José Antonio Escalada's release into provisional liberty in July was apparently a consequence of the court's ruling.

Amnesty International urged that all allegations of torture, ill-treatment and disputed killings be thoroughly and impartially investigated, and those responsible be brought to justice. The organization, emphasizing that individuals should be able to claim conscientious objector status at any time, appealed for the release of José Antonio Escalada and for all criminal proceedings to be dropped against him and Manuel Blázquez.

In an oral statement to the United Nations Commission on Human Rights in February, Amnesty International included reference to its concerns about torture and ill-treatment and killings by security forces in circumstances which were disputed or inadequately investigated in Spain.

# SRI LANKA

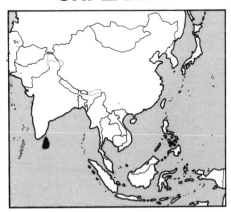

"Disappearances" and extrajudicial executions continued to be committed by government forces in the northeast, but at a lower rate than in the previous two years. In the south, human rights lawyers, trade unionists and others continued to be subject to intimidation, including death threats. Torture and ill-treatment of political and criminal prisoners appeared to be routine. Some 4,456 detainees were released, but at least 4,823 others continued to be detained without charge or trial under Emergency Regulations and the Prevention of Terrorism Act (PTA). Official investigations continued into a few cases of "disappearance" but no action was taken by the government to clarify the fate of tens of thousands who "disappeared" in the period up to January 1991. The secessionist Liberation Tigers of Tamil Eelam (LTTE) committed gross abuses of human rights.

Armed conflict between government forces and the LTTE continued in the northeast with heavy casualties reported on both sides. Control of much of the northeast remained uncertain: the government retained control of towns and most main roads, but fighting continued intermittently in rural areas. The Jaffna peninsula largely remained in LTTE hands, but government forces took over part of the peninsula and access was closed. Heightened tensions between the Tamil, Muslim and Sinhalese communities in the east were manifest in a series of communal attacks and counter-attacks.

The government of President Rana-singhe Premadasa took steps to implement some of the Amnesty International recom-mendations for human rights safeguards which it had accepted in December 1991 (see *Amnesty International Report 1992*). However, crucial procedural safeguards for the protection of prisoners had not been implemented by the end of the year and the state of emergency remained in force island-wide.

The mandate of the Presidential Com-mission of Inquiry into the Involuntary Removal of Persons was extended for one year, enabling it to investigate "disappear-ances" occurring from 11 January 1991 to 11 January 1993, and regional officers were appointed to transmit complaints of "disappearances" to the Commission. The Human Rights Task Force, established in 1991 to maintain a register of detainees and monitor their rights, opened several regional offices and established a 24-hour information service in the capital, Col-ombo. The United Nations (UN) Working Group on Enforced or Involuntary Disap-pearances visited Sri Lanka for the second time in October at the government's invita-tion.

Draft legislation to amend the funda-mental rights chapter of the Constitution, to create a new Human Rights Commission and to provide temporary death certificates to relatives of the "disappeared" as a basis for compensation payments, continued to be discussed. However, none of these pro-posals had been approved or implemented by the end of the year.

The LTTE committed numerous gross abuses of human rights, including the deliberate killing of hundreds of non-combatant Muslim and Sinhalese civilians, the arbitrary killing of civilians in bomb attacks on buses and trains, the torture and killing of prisoners, and abductions for ran-som. The LTTE executed several prisoners accused of being informers.

Extrajudicial executions were commit-ted in the northeast by military and an-cillary forces, police and home guards.

At Mandur, Batticaloa District, in April, a family of seven were among eight people killed by soldiers and members of the Tamil Eelam Liberation Organization (TELO), which operates alongside the army in the east. This followed the killing by the LTTE of two TELO members. The day after 10 senior army and navy officers had been killed by the LTTE on Kayts island in August, soldiers from Poonani camp killed 39 Tamil men, women and children at Mailanthanai, Batticaloa District, over 180 miles away, apparently in reprisal. At least 16 soldiers were remanded in custody fol-lowing an identity parade, but they had not been charged by the end of the year. Fol-lowing the extrajudicial execution of some 10 Tamil civilians by government soldiers at Velaveli, Batticaloa District, in October, the government said it would mount an inquiry, but no findings had been pub-lished by the end of the year.

In April, following an attack by the LTTE on Alanchipotana, a Muslim village in Polonnaruwa District, during which 54 Muslims were shot and stabbed to death, Muslim home guards retaliated by attack-ing Tamil villages, killing more than 80 Tamils. Police personnel did not attempt to prevent the reprisal attack. A committee of inquiry recommended a review of the home guard system – which had not been completed by the end of the year – and three home guards were charged with murder.

An inquiry into the reprisal killings of 67 civilians in June 1991 in Kokkadich-cholai (see *Amnesty International Report 1992*) found that the deaths had not res-ulted from cross-fire, as the military claimed, but from "deliberate retaliatory action" by the army. Twenty military per-sonnel were tried by a military tribunal. None was found guilty of murder. The lieutenant in charge was convicted of fail-ing to control his troops and disposing of bodies illegally at the site of the massacre; he was dismissed from the army. The 19 other military personnel were acquitted.

Scores of "disappearances" in military custody were reported from Batticaloa Dis-trict, and three in Amparai District from the custody of the Special Task Force (STF), a police commando unit. After 25 young men had been detained by the army in the Kiran area, Batticaloa District, in January and February, 11 were released and the military denied that it had detained the remaining 14. Two of the 14 were later found to be in detention and two more were released, but 10 boys and young men – including 12-year-old Manikkam Siventhiran – were not accounted for.

"Disappearances" were also reported following detention by Muslim home guards in Batticaloa District. Home guards detained 13 Tamil men, women and children near Thiyavaddavan in April. One boy escaped; the other 12 prisoners "disappeared".

In the south, several imprisoned *Janatha Vimukthi Peramuna* (JVP), People's Liberation Front, suspects were said by the police to have been shot dead during escape attempts or to have committed suicide. Emergency Regulations do not require that full, independent investigations be held into deaths in custody.

In the south, human rights lawyers, witnesses to human rights violations, journalists and trade unionists received death threats which they believed were made by government forces. Some lawyers refused to accept cases against security force personnel for fear of retaliatory action. Journalists critical of government policy were intimidated and attacked, including Yoonus, a newspaper cartoonist, who was physically injured and repeatedly threatened by people he identified as associates of a senior government minister.

Torture and ill-treatment of political detainees appeared to be routine in military, STF and police custody in both the northeast and the south. Members of TELO and the People's Liberation Organization of Tamil Eelam (PLOTE), both ancillary forces operating alongside the army, were also said to have tortured prisoners in the east. In Badulla and Nuwara Eliya Districts, torture of Tamil prisoners of Indian origin was reported in both military and police custody. Methods of torture included electric shocks; pouring petrol into prisoners' nostrils and then placing a plastic bag over their heads; suspending prisoners by their thumbs and beating them; beating with barbed wire; repeatedly submerging prisoners' heads in water while they were suspended by their ankles; and rape of women. Criminal suspects were also tortured: for example, a gem miner suspected of theft was beaten on the soles of his feet, suspended by his thumbs and beaten with clubs by Lunugala police in September.

Prisoners were subjected to other forms of ill-treatment. For example, prisoners, including a 73-year-old man apparently detained in place of his son, were held in chains at Pioneer Road police camp in Batticaloa. Severe overcrowding was reported from the sixth floor of Police Headquarters in Colombo, where political detainees had been held for more than a year in the custody of the Crime Detection Bureau.

According to official figures, 4,456 people detained in the south in connection with the activities of the JVP since their arrest in 1989 or 1990 had been released by the end of September. However, over 4,800 suspected insurgents remained in detention without charge or trial, including some who had been held for over three years. Emergency Regulations empower the authorities to hold suspects indefinitely under administrative orders; the PTA permits up to 18 months' administrative detention. In at least 120 cases, the Supreme Court awarded compensation to detainees who had been illegally detained.

According to official figures, in October 4,823 political detainees were being held under Emergency Regulations or the PTA: 1,523 in detention camps, 1,113 in prisons, 569 in police custody and 1,618 in rehabilitation camps, to which detainees deemed to have had minor connection with insurgent activity were referred. The number of prisoners held in army camps was not revealed. Of those held in prisons, 826 were said to be held in connection with the conflict in the northeast and 287 in connection with the southern JVP insurgency of 1988 to 1990. The majority of prisoners in detention and rehabilitation camps were Sinhalese.

In the south, hundreds of Tamil people were periodically rounded up in Colombo and screened for connections with the LTTE. These arrests were made by the police and by members of the Eelam People's Democratic Party (EPDP), an ancillary group which sometimes detained prisoners itself instead of handing them over to police custody. The EPDP has no known legal power to arrest and detain prisoners but has not been prevented from doing so by the authorities. Following the assassination by an LTTE suicide bomber of the Commander of the Navy in Colombo in November, over 3,000 Tamils were rounded up for questioning and hundreds were kept in detention. In Badulla and Nuwara Eliya Districts, dozens of Tamils of Indian origin

**268**

were detained without trial on account of their alleged connections with the LTTE. Hundreds of Sinhalese people suspected of connections with the JVP were also arrested and detained in the south.

The Commission of Inquiry into Involuntary Removals had completed hearings into six individual cases of "disappearance" in the two years of its existence; no decision was announced as to whether security forces personnel believed responsible for some of these "disappearances" would be prosecuted. Trials of several security forces personnel accused of human rights violations continued, but most had not reached any conclusion by the end of the year.

The LTTE also committed gross abuses of human rights. Among the thousands of prisoners believed to be held by the LTTE were police and military personnel, Tamils perceived as opponents by the LTTE, and Tamils and Muslims who were held as hostages for ransom. Some prisoners were reportedly tortured by the LTTE, which only rarely disclosed information about the whereabouts or fate of its political prisoners to their relatives. Those held for ransom included an 84-year-old Tamil man who was abducted by the LTTE in September, apparently because he had relatives living abroad who were presumed to be wealthy. In March, 12 of the 32 Muslim businessmen who had been held in Jaffna since 1990 were released, but the fate of the others was not known.

Executions of alleged informers by the LTTE continued to be reported. Prisoners sentenced to death in Jaffna were said to have been paraded in public before their execution. One witness described public executions of alleged informers carried out by the LTTE near Vavuniya.

Hundreds of non-combatant civilians in the east, particularly Muslims, were killed by LTTE forces. For example, in September, 22 people, most of them Muslims, were killed when a bomb exploded in a crowded market place at Sainthamaruthu. In October over 200 Muslim villagers were killed in an early morning attack on four adjacent villages in Polonnaruwa District. Sinhalese civilians were also killed in LTTE attacks in the east, such as at Kohongaswewa in Weli Oya, where 15 civilians were killed in October.

Muslims in the east continued to receive death threats from the LTTE, apparently in an effort to force them to evacuate their homes. Residents of Kattankudi, Batticaloa District, received such threats in November, for example.

Amnesty International expressed concern to the government that the Presidential Commission of Inquiry into the June 1991 extrajudicial executions at Kokkadichcholai would not subject the military suspects to cross-examination, and subsequently expressed concern that the suspects were to be tried by a military tribunal and not a civilian court. The government responded by sending Amnesty International a copy of the Commission's interim report. It also said it intended to establish a Human Rights Commission. The trial proceeded before a military tribunal (see above).

In April Amnesty International asked the government whether inquiries had been held following the discovery of 72 bodies on Mandaitivu island, Jaffna District. The victims were believed to have been prisoners, killed in the custody of the armed forces. The government later told Amnesty International that it had not been possible to investigate these deaths because of the security situation in the area.

In June Amnesty International published *Sri Lanka: Deliberate killings of Muslim and Tamil villagers in Polonnaruwa*, and asked the government for comments. The government sent Amnesty International a summary of the findings of the inquiry team it had appointed.

Amnesty International appealed to the LTTE to halt the killing of civilians. It also repeated its earlier appeals for prisoners to be protected against ill-treatment and hostages to be released.

In October, two Amnesty International representatives visited Sri Lanka to discuss with government officials, local human rights activists and others the implementation of the organization's recommendations for human rights safeguards and the current human rights situation in the northeast and south.

In an oral statement to the UN Commission on Human Rights in February, Amnesty International included reference to its concerns in Sri Lanka.

# SUDAN

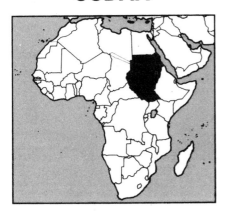

Hundreds of suspected opponents of the government, including dozens of prisoners of conscience, were imprisoned at any one time. Most were detained without charge or trial for weeks or months. Many political detainees were tortured, often in secret detention centres. Prisoners convicted of criminal offences were flogged. Hundreds of prisoners "disappeared" or were extrajudicially executed in the war-affected areas of southern and western Sudan. At least three prisoners were executed and at least four others sentenced to death. Both factions of the armed opposition Sudan People's Liberation Army (SPLA) were responsible for deliberate and arbitrary killings.

Gross human rights violations were committed in the context of continuing armed conflict in southern and western Sudan between the ruling National Salvation Revolution Command Council (NSRCC), headed by President Omar Hassan al-Bashir, and the SPLA. In the Nuba mountains of South Kordofan tens of thousands of Nuba civilians were displaced after their villages were deliberately destroyed by government forces. Between March and May, the government captured several towns held by the SPLA in southern Sudan, displacing tens of thousands of civilians. In July, after SPLA assaults on the government-controlled city of Juba, government forces demolished densely populated suburbs, rendering thousands of people homeless.

Outside the war zones, the authorities continued to detain and torture suspected opponents including members of banned political parties, trade unionists, civil servants, students, and people from southern Sudan and the Fur and Nuba communities. A state of emergency remained in force, effectively allowing indefinite administrative detention without charge or trial. There were fewer cases of long-term administrative detention in civil prisons, but hundreds of instances of detention without charge for periods of a few weeks to several months in secret detention centres known as "ghost houses". Many of the detainees were tortured and ill-treated. Although the government had said that detainees would be routinely referred to the judiciary, in practice most detainees were held exclusively on the authority of security agencies. In July, 110 prisoners were released in a presidential amnesty. More than half were military officers convicted of treason after unfair military trials over the previous three years.

At any one time hundreds of suspected opponents of the government, including dozens of prisoners of conscience, were in prison. Among the prisoners released during the year was Ahmad Osman Siraj, a prisoner of conscience and prominent critic of the government who had been arrested in 1990. He was released in July under the presidential amnesty. Eleven others convicted of treason with him after an unfair trial in December 1990 were also released. However, the fate of 28 soldiers arrested at the same time was unknown (see *Amnesty International Report 1992*).

Other prisoners of conscience arrested in previous years remained in prison throughout 1992. Among them was Mokhtar Abdullah Ahmad, a trade unionist and Communist Party member, detained without charge since August 1990. Also still held was 'Abd al-Rahman 'Abdallah Nugdallah, a former government minister and member of the Umma Party, who was sentenced to life imprisonment for treason after an unfair trial in October 1991 (see *Amnesty International Report 1992*). In July his sentence was commuted to 10 years' imprisonment.

Hundreds of members of banned political parties were arrested during the year. Tirab Tindal Sultan, a member of the Umma Party, was arrested in January with two other men and held uncharged until September. Members of the Democratic Unionist Party (DUP) detained in "ghost houses" included Mirghani Abdel Rahman Suleiman, a former government minister

**270**

who was arrested in March and released in November. Hassan Osman and two other men, all apparently suspected communists, were arrested in April for distributing a banned newspaper. They were still in detention at the end of the year. Thirteen members of the Ba'ath Arab Socialist Party were arrested in Khartoum in May; four were released in July, but the journalist Mohamed Sid Ahmad Atiq and eight others were held without charge or trial in a "ghost house" until their release in December.

Scores of trade unionists were arrested before elections to trade unions' councils in September. At least five were still held incommunicado at the end of the year. The majority, however, were released within three or four days. The authorities then made them report daily to security offices, where they were generally required to remain all day. This practice became common during 1992; hundreds of suspected government opponents were restricted in this way.

Hundreds of people suspected of supporting the SPLA were detained in western and southern Sudan, including scores of men from the Dilling area of the Nuba mountains. Ahmad Adlan Ibrahim, a teacher, was among at least five men who reportedly remained in detention at el-Obeid Prison at the end of the year, seven months after their arrest. In the south, at least 15 civil servants and local politicians were arrested in October in the government-controlled town of Malakal. Criminal charges were brought against five of them, eight were reportedly released uncharged in December, and two remained unaccounted for at the end of the year.

Torture and ill-treatment of political detainees was common in "ghost houses", in the security headquarters in Khartoum and in provincial security offices. Prisoners were beaten, whipped and forced to stand for long periods. Some were shackled and suspended from cell walls, sometimes upside-down, and then beaten on their testicles or kidneys. There were reports of prisoners being subjected to electric shocks.

Suspected government opponents arrested in the war zones were at particular risk of torture in military detention centres. For example, seven wounded SPLA soldiers captured in Juba in June were bound, suspended from the ceiling, beaten and had chilli pepper rubbed into their wounds before they were shot dead.

Cruel, inhuman and degrading punishments were imposed by the courts in northern Sudan. Unlicensed street vendors or people caught brewing alcohol – many of them displaced people from war zones – were frequently flogged in public after summary trials by Public Order Courts. In October eight men, including a former High Court judge, were publicly given 20 lashes in Khartoum for drinking alcohol.

At least one possible extrajudicial execution took place in Khartoum. In October Abu Bakr Mohy al-Din Rasikh, a known opponent of the government, was shot dead by a security officer in an apparently targeted assassination. The security officer was arrested by police but at the end of the year it was unclear whether he remained in custody.

There were dozens of reports of extrajudicial executions and "disappearances" of suspected SPLA supporters in the war zones. In February the government announced that Daoud Yahya Bolad, an SPLA commander from the Fur community who was captured in January, had been shot in Darfur while trying to escape. There were allegations that he had been extrajudicially executed. There were also many extrajudicial executions in the Nuba mountains. For example, in July troops were reported to have extrajudicially executed five men and a woman following an attack on the village of Oma.

After SPLA assaults on Juba in June and July, government troops arrested hundreds of southern Sudanese civilians, soldiers, policemen and paramilitary agents. Many of those arrested "disappeared": the majority were believed to have been extrajudicially executed. Following the first assault in June, 40 soldiers were extrajudicially executed after their commanding officer and several colleagues defected to the SPLA. After the second assault in July, around 200 unarmed civilians were reportedly killed by government soldiers during a house-to-house search of a densely populated suburb.

By the end of the year the government had failed to provide any information on the whereabouts of most of those arrested in Juba. However, officials admitted that Andrew Tombe, a Sudanese employee of the United States Agency for International Development, and Mark Laboke Jenner, who worked for the European Commission, had been executed in Juba in mid-August. Officials said they had been sentenced to death by a military court for treason, but there was no independent confirmation that they had received a trial, let alone a fair trial. In November the government established a committee chaired by a High Court judge to investigate the incidents in Juba in June and July. It had not made any findings public by the end of the year.

At least one man was executed for a criminal offence. Colonel 'Abd al-Rahim Mohamed Salih was executed by firing-squad in March after being sentenced to death in 1990 for embezzling funds from the army.

At least four people were sentenced to death for politically motivated offences. Nasr Hassan Bashir Nasr was sentenced to death for espionage by a military court in May. In September three men were sentenced to death by a criminal court in ad-Daien after being convicted of waging war against the state and illegal possession of firearms. One of the three, Zo al-Noon al-Tigani, was additionally sentenced to public crucifixion after death. It was not known whether they were executed, nor whether any death sentences were passed for ordinary criminal offences.

Both factions of the SPLA, which had split in two in August 1991, were responsible for gross abuses of human rights. In January, 40 prisoners arrested after disputes within the SPLA in previous years were released by the Torit faction, led by John Garang de Mabior, but at least 21 other prisoners were still held in June. In September, five of them were released after a mutiny: one, Malath Joseph Luath, was shot dead but the others escaped into Uganda where they were detained by the Ugandan authorities. The SPLA's Nasir faction, led by Riek Machar, was reported to be holding prisoners suspected of loyalty to the Torit faction but few details were available.

Both factions were responsible for deliberate and arbitrary killings and executions of prisoners. In January forces loyal to the Nasir faction raided the village of Pagarau in Bahr al-Ghazal and killed at least 87 civilians, including patients at a leprosy hospital. In May there were reports that Torit faction forces were responsible for the arbitrary killing of civilians of Toposa ethnic origin in villages around Kapoeta. In

September SPLA soldiers deliberately and arbitrarily killed four foreign citizens: three aid workers and a journalist. The Torit faction blamed mutineers but reports suggested that forces loyal to the leadership were responsible.

SPLA leaders of both factions executed their own soldiers. For example, in July the Torit faction was reported to have executed at least seven soldiers in Ikotos in Eastern Equatoria.

Amnesty International repeatedly appealed to the Sudanese government on behalf of prisoners of conscience, political detainees denied the right to a fair trial, victims of torture, "disappearance" and extrajudicial executions, and those sentenced to death. In some instances the government responded to Amnesty International's appeals, but not in a substantive manner.

In public statements in August the security authorities denied the existence of "ghost houses". In the same month an army spokesman denied that torture was taking place and said that any detainee was free to complain to the courts but that none had done so.

Amnesty International urged both factions of the SPLA to respect human rights. In June representatives of the SPLA Nasir faction visited the organization's International Secretariat and were urged to investigate allegations that their troops had committed deliberate and arbitrary killings and executed prisoners.

In March Amnesty International submitted information about its concerns in Sudan for United Nations (UN) review under a procedure, established by Economic and Social Council Resolutions 728F/1503, for confidential consideration of communications about human rights violations. In oral statements to the UN Commission on Human Rights in February and to its Sub-Commission on Prevention of Discrimination and Protection of Minorities in August, Amnesty International included reference to its concerns in Sudan. In March and October Amnesty International submitted information about violations of human rights guaranteed by the African Charter on Human and Peoples' Rights to the African Commission established under the Charter. In December the UN General Assembly adopted a resolution expressing deep concern at serious human rights violations in the Sudan and

272

called on the government fully to respect human rights. President Omar Hassan al-Bashir responded by dismissing allegations of human rights violations as "baseless".

# SURINAME

**An amnesty was granted to members of the military responsible for past violations of human rights and to members of armed opposition groups.**

A review of the 1987 Constitution was in progress. In March the National Assembly approved amendments to restrict the role of the army to national defence and to combating "organized subversion". As a consequence, members of the armed forces could no longer stand for public office.

Lieutenant-Colonel Desi Bouterse resigned from his post as Army Commander in November. He had effectively ruled Suriname from 1980 to 1987, when he was defeated in a general election, and had participated in a bloodless coup in 1990 (see *Amnesty International Report 1991*).

A peace accord was signed in August between the government of President Ronald Venetiaan and armed opposition groups. The main armed opposition group – the Jungle Commando – started operating in 1986 in eastern Suriname with the aim of overthrowing the military government then in power. Later, other armed groups emerged, some allegedly backed by the military. The conflict continued after the return to an elected government in 1988. Several previous attempts to end the armed conflict formally had failed.

A vital element of the August peace accord was the granting of an amnesty to the military and members of opposition groups for past actions. The amnesty cov-

ered human rights violations by the military, including extrajudicial executions, torture and detention without charge or trial, and abuses by opposition groups. There had been no thorough, independent investigation into human rights violations by the armed forces (see *Amnesty International Reports 1983* to *1989* and *1991*).

Amnesty International wrote to all members of the National Assembly in June about their review of the Constitution. The organization made a number of recommendations aimed at contributing to respect for fundamental human rights in Suriname. Amnesty International called for the Constitution to guarantee the rights to freedom of expression, conscience and religion. It urged National Assembly members to include safeguards prohibiting extrajudicial executions, torture and ill-treatment. Amnesty International pointed out that amnesties should not affect the investigation of past human rights violations and the bringing to justice of those responsible. The organization also called for the Constitution to incorporate the abolition of the death penalty, which had not been used for over 50 years under ordinary law.

# SWAZILAND

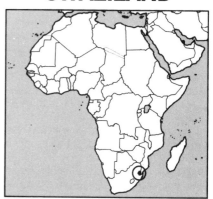

**The government announced that it intended to execute prisoners for the first time since 1983. At least six prisoners were believed to be under sentence of death at the end of the year, but no executions were carried out. A former prisoner of conscience was subjected to harassment.**

There was continuing pressure for reform of the *tinkhundla* system of indirectly elected government. Although political power remained in the hands of the monarchy, political parties, all of which were technically illegal, became increasingly active during the year.

In September the Minister of Justice announced that for the first time since 1983 prisoners who had been sentenced to death would be executed. At least six prisoners were believed to be under sentence of death at the end of the year, all of them convicted of murder, including at least two people sentenced in 1992. However, no executions were reported.

Ray Russon, a university lecturer and former prisoner of conscience, was arrested in April on charges of theft and released on bail. In September he was acquitted of at least one charge but reportedly faced further charges. These charges, as well as other harassment of Ray Russon and his family, appeared to be related to his advocacy of political change. In 1990 and 1991 he had been repeatedly arrested and either charged with treason or detained without charge.

The report of a judicial commission of inquiry into events at the University of Swaziland campus in November 1990, when at least 80 students required hospital treatment as a result of beatings by police and soldiers (see *Amnesty International Reports 1991* and *1992*), was submitted to the government but had not been made public by the end of the year.

Amnesty International called on the government of King Mswati II to commute the sentences of all those awaiting execution as a first step towards abolishing the death penalty.

# SWITZERLAND

**Scores of conscientious objectors to military service served sentences of imprisonment or compulsory work imposed by military tribunals. The death penalty was abolished for all offences.**

A national referendum held in May approved a proposal to amend the Federal Constitution to introduce a civilian alternative to military service. However, civilian service was not available to conscientious objectors during the year as the text of a law establishing its nature and length was still being drawn up.

In June Switzerland acceded to the International Covenants on Civil and Political Rights and on Economic, Social and Cultural Rights. In September an amendment to the Military Penal Code came into force, eliminating the death penalty from the Code and thus for all offences.

Scores of conscientious objectors were imprisoned although in several cantons there was a moratorium on implementing prison sentences imposed for refusing military service. Those sentenced during the year were tried under the amended Military Penal Code introduced in July 1991 (see *Amnesty International Report 1992*). Under its provisions refusal of military service remained a criminal offence. However, when a military tribunal concluded that a conscript was unable to reconcile military service with his conscience because of "fundamental ethical values", he was sentenced to a period of work in the public interest, and did not acquire a criminal record. The law provided for sentences of compulsory work ranging from one and a half times the total length of military service refused to two years. Sentences of compulsory work were not carried out until after 15 July when the relevant enabling legislation came into force.

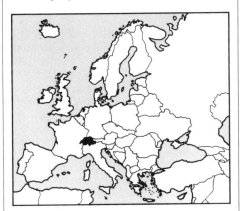

However, a number of conscientious objectors announced during their trials that they would not serve sentences of compulsory work. They did not consider that a sentence imposed by a military tribunal, following a trial for a criminal offence, constituted a genuine alternative civilian service.

For example, in February a military tribunal concluded that the sincerity of Nicolas Carron's Christian faith and non-violent philosophy was without question and that his refusal of military service was based on

**274**

"fundamental ethical values". Nicolas Carron, who had refused military service after completing initial military service training and seven refresher courses, rejected a sentence of compulsory work and started a two-month prison sentence in June.

Some tribunals apparently used a rather narrow interpretation of what constituted "fundamental ethical values" irreconcilable with military service. Conscientious objectors who failed to convince the tribunals that they qualified for a sentence of compulsory work and those who declared that they would not carry out such a sentence were liable to up to three years' imprisonment. In practice, sentences of up to 10 months' imprisonment were passed.

Some imprisoned conscientious objectors had been tried before the introduction of the amended Military Penal Code in July 1991. During the year Stefan Hasinger, who had refused military service on ethical and pacifist grounds but declared his willingness to carry out an alternative civilian service, served a seven-month sentence imposed in September 1989. The military tribunal had acknowledged the presence of certain ethical considerations, but had concluded that his reasons for refusing military service were predominantly egoistic and political.

Amnesty International appealed for the release of prisoners of conscience and expressed concern that under the July 1991 amendment to the Military Penal Code people continued to be punished for refusing military service on grounds of conscience. The organization welcomed the constitutional amendment establishing the principle of a civilian alternative to compulsory military service. It said this was a first essential step towards the introduction of a genuine alternative civilian service, outside the military system and of a non-punitive nature, available to conscripts objecting to military service on all grounds of conscience.

# SYRIA

**New arrests of political prisoners were reported and thousands of others, including prisoners of conscience, remained held. Some were serving prison sentences but the majority were held without charge or trial under state of emergency legisla-** **tion in force since 1963. Other political prisoners were held beyond the expiry of their sentences. Up to 1,500 political prisoners, including prisoners of conscience, were released. Torture was reported and two political detainees were alleged to have died as a result of torture and lack of medical care. Six people were executed.**

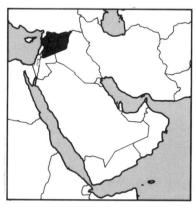

Hundreds of political detainees, including prisoners of conscience, were reported to have been transferred to prisons in or near Damascus in preparation for trial before the Supreme State Security Court. More than 150 appeared before the court. This apparently represented a shift in the policy of President Hafez al-Assad's government towards ending the long-standing practice of holding political suspects indefinitely without charge or trial. The Supreme State Security Court is a special court which does not conform to Syrian law relating to criminal procedure or international human rights standards for fair trial. By the end of the year, only one trial had been concluded.

Scores of new arrests of political suspects were reported and several thousand political prisoners, including at least 195 prisoners of conscience, remained held. More than 200 Syrian Kurds were reportedly arrested in October and November after the joint leadership of three Kurdish political groups in Syria issued a leaflet on 5 October to mark the 30th anniversary of a law which stripped tens of thousands of Kurds of their Syrian nationality. At least 30 of them remained in detention at the end of the year, including 'Ala'uddin Hamam Ahmad and Ibrahim Wiso Buzan. Most of the others were released after interrogation.

Ten of the 195 prisoners of conscience

were serving prison sentences of between five and 10 years, but the overwhelming majority of political prisoners, including prisoners of conscience, were detained without charge or trial.

The 10 sentenced prisoners of conscience were among at least 17 people arrested between December 1991 and January 1992 in connection with the Committees for the Defence of Democratic Freedoms and Human Rights in Syria (CDF), a banned voluntary organization (see *Amnesty International Report 1992*). The 17 were tried by the Supreme State Security Court between 29 February and 17 March. The trial was held mainly *in camera* and defence lawyers were reportedly denied prior consultation with the defendants. The evidence produced by the prosecution consisted mainly of confessions, said to have been extracted under torture, and copies of a CDF leaflet issued in 1991. Three of the 17 were acquitted and released. Four were convicted of withholding information by failing to inform the authorities about CDF activities. They were sentenced to three years' imprisonment, but were released in May. The remaining 10 were convicted of disseminating false information (in a CDF leaflet which criticized the government's human rights record and the procedure used for re-electing President al-Assad) and of receiving funds from abroad (reportedly referring to money sent to one of the defendants, Aktham Nu'aysa, by a brother in Europe). They were sentenced to between five and 10 years' imprisonment with deprivation of civil rights. No appeal was allowed as the Supreme State Security Court's decisions are final.

The several thousand other political prisoners included suspected members and sympathizers of prohibited organizations, members of professional associations and former government officials and their supporters. Virtually all were held without charge or trial. Some were arrested in 1992 but most had been held for many years.

Fourteen prisoners of conscience, all former members of the official Ba'th Party, including government ministers, continued to be detained without charge or trial (see previous *Amnesty International Reports*). All were reported to be in poor health. However, three others from this group of detainees, including Dr Nour al-Din al-Atassi, a former head of state, were

released during the year, reportedly because they were seriously ill. Dr al-Atassi died of cancer in December, three months after his release. Up to 40 other supporters of the official Ba'th Party, as well as members of *Hizb al-Ba'th al-Dimuqrati al-Ishtiraki al-'Arabi*, the Arab Socialist Democratic Ba'th Party, a prohibited political organization, remained in prison without trial. One of them, Ahmad Suwaidani, has been held since 1969 (see *Amnesty International Report 1990*). The others were arrested in the 1970s and 1980s.

At least 250 members and sympathizers of *Hizb al-'Amal al-Shuyu'i*, Party for Communist Action (PCA), including prisoners of conscience, remained in detention: they had been arrested at various times between 1980 and 1992 (see previous *Amnesty International Reports*). More than 150 of them were charged with membership of or links with a secret organization, the PCA, and brought before the Supreme State Security Court between July and December. They were represented by 12 lawyers chosen by their relatives, but the lawyers were said to have been denied access to the defendants before the trial. Access to the hearings was apparently limited to one family member per defendant. Some of the defendants were reported to have protested against their long-term detention without trial, their appearance before a special court, and the denial of their right to a fair trial. The hearings had not been concluded by the end of the year and were scheduled to continue in 1993 and to include the defendants in the case who had not yet appeared before the court.

About 12 other suspected PCA members were arrested during 1992, including Rozit 'Isa, who was arrested in February. She was held in incommunicado detention and her whereabouts were unknown. She had previously been detained between 1978 and 1980 in connection with the PCA. Her husband, Akram al-Bunni, has been detained without charge or trial since 1987.

At least seven members of Nasserist groups were imprisoned. Ahmed Ma'tuq, an employee of Damascus City Council, and Marwan Ghazi, owner of a publishing house, were arrested in March reportedly in connection with *al-Tanzim al-Sha'bi al-Dimuqrati al-Nasiri*, the Nasserist Democratic Popular Organization (NDPO), and held incommunicado. The others were believed to be held in 'Adra Civil Prison. They had been arrested between 1981 and 1987 in connection with *Hizb al-Ittihad al-'Arabi al-Ishtiraki fi-Suriya*, the Arab Socialist Union Party in Syria, and the NDPO.

Some 35 members of *al-Hizb al-Shuyu'i al-Maktab al-Siyassi*, Communist Party Political Bureau (CPPB), and dozens of members of professional associations were believed to be still held without trial. It was reported that some of these detainees were being interrogated in preparation for trial before the Supreme State Security Court, but none was known to have been tried by the end of the year. The CPPB members held included many of the party's leaders, including the First Secretary, Riad al-Turk, who has been held incommunicado since 1980. Detained members of professional associations were mainly doctors and engineers arrested in 1980 and 1981 following a one-day strike by various professional associations calling for political reforms (see previous *Amnesty International Reports*). The whereabouts of most of them were unknown.

Several thousand suspected members of the banned Muslim Brotherhood, *al-'Ikhwan al-Muslimun*, remained held. Most were arrested in the 1970s and early 1980s following violent clashes between the organization's armed wing and government forces (see previous *Amnesty International Reports*). Many were apparently not involved in violent activities and were arrested solely as suspected members or sympathizers of the organization. Others were said to have been arrested because of their family links to active members of the Muslim Brotherhood. All were believed to be held without charge or trial, and most of them were apparently denied access to the outside world. The fate and whereabouts of many remained unknown. For example, al-Hakam Karkoukli, a former student arrested in 1977, had not been seen by his family since 1979, when he was in al-Mezze Military Prison. Until 1990, when his family was told by former prisoners that he was being held in Saidnaya Prison, they had no knowledge of his whereabouts.

Scores of Lebanese and Palestinians arrested in Lebanon or Syria as suspected members of Lebanese and Palestinian organizations were held. Some were arrested in 1992, but the majority had been detained for years, some since the mid-1970s. The Lebanese detainees included Samih 'Abd al-Rahman Muneymana, a businessman who was reportedly abducted from West Beirut in June 1976. His whereabouts remained unknown until April 1992, when a former detainee informed his family that he was in a prison in Damascus. He was apparently suspected of having links with the pro-Iraq wing of the Ba'th Party in Lebanon. Among the Palestinian detainees was a 65-year-old woman, Shaykha Salim 'Abd al-Khaliq al-Hayek, and her daughter Yusra, held since 1986. They were arrested in Damascus reportedly on suspicion of having links with the Palestine Liberation Organization.

Other political prisoners continued to be held beyond the expiry of their sentences. Among them was Khalil Brayez, a former captain and intelligence officer in the Syrian army whose 15-year prison sentence expired in 1985. He was believed to be held in al-Mezze Military Prison.

Up to 1,500 long-term detainees, including some prisoners of conscience, were released during the year. Hundreds were released at the beginning of the year as a result of a presidential amnesty in December 1991 (see *Amnesty International Report 1992*) and 1,154 were released in April and December following two presidential amnesties. Among those released were Palestinians, Lebanese, and members and sympathizers of the PCA, CPPB, the pro-Iraq wing of the Ba'th Party and the Muslim Brotherhood. Also released were two Jewish brothers, Eli and Selim Swed, who were serving prison sentences (see *Amnesty International Report 1992*).

Torture of political detainees in incommunicado detention was reported. For example, two of those sentenced in early 1992 in connection with the CDF, Aktham Nu'aysa and Nizar Nayyuf, were reported to have been tortured in pre-trial incommunicado detention: as a result Aktham Nu'aysa was admitted to hospital. Independent observers at the trial said Aktham Nu'aysa was unable to walk into the courtroom unaided.

Two political detainees were alleged to have died in custody as a result of torture or ill-treatment combined with lack of medical care. Munir al-Ahmad, a poet and writer aged 60, died in January after six months in detention. Rif'at bin Ahmad Rajab, an electrician, reportedly died in 'Adra Civil Prison in April of a heart condition brought on by torture and lack of medical treatment. He had been detained as a suspected NDPO member since 1986. No inquiries into the two deaths in custody or other torture allegations were known to have been carried out by the government.

Six people were executed by hanging: four in April, one in August and one in November. Two had been convicted of murder and rape, three of murder, and one of murder and armed robbery. No details about their trials were available.

Amnesty International continued to call for the immediate and unconditional release of all prisoners of conscience, and for the fair and prompt trial or release of all political detainees. It welcomed the releases of up to 1,500 political detainees under presidential amnesties and asked the authorities for details of those released, but without response.

During the year Amnesty International urged the government to end the use of the death penalty and torture, and appealed for urgent investigations into new allegations of torture and the two deaths in custody.

Amnesty International made several appeals to the government to respect detainees' rights, in accordance with international standards, and urged the immediate and unconditional release of all those held solely for the non-violent expression of their beliefs. In March the Office of the Vice President told Amnesty International that the 17 CDF members tried before the Supreme State Security Court were being prosecuted not because they were members of the CDF, " ... but because of their involvement with an underground organization that adopts violence and terrorism as means to achieve its goals." However, no such charges were known to have been brought against any of the defendants.

In February Amnesty International sought authorization to send observers to the trial of the CDF members, but this was not granted. However, in December two Amnesty International delegates visited Damascus to observe the trials which were taking place before the Supreme State Security Court. The hearings were postponed before the delegates arrived, but they obtained information about the cases from government officials, the court judges, defence lawyers and relatives of some of the defendants. At the end of December, Amnesty International was studying the delegates' findings with a view to communicating its concerns and recommendations

about the proceedings to the government.

In July Amnesty International published a report, *Syria: Long-Term Detention and Torture of Political Prisoners*, which described the pattern of gross violations of prisoners' rights under state of emergency legislation.

In oral statements to the United Nations (UN) Commission on Human Rights in February and to its Sub-Commission on Prevention of Discrimination and Protection of Minorities in August, Amnesty International included reference to its concerns about detention provisions under the State of Emergency Law and the practice of indefinite incommunicado detention in Syria. In April Amnesty International submitted information about its concerns in Syria for UN review under a procedure established by Economic and Social Council Resolutions 728F/1503, for confidential consideration of communications about human rights violations.

# TADZHIKISTAN

**Unarmed civilians and Commonwealth of Independent States (CIS) military personnel were reportedly deliberately killed by members of the security forces and armed groups subordinate to the government. A political prisoner was denied adequate access to defence counsel.**

Tadzhikistan's independence, declared in September 1991, was recognized internationally following the dissolution of the Soviet Union. Tadzhikistan became a member of the Conference on Security and Co-operation in Europe in January and the United Nations in March.

In May, following protests in the capital, Dushanbe, President Rakhmon Nabiyev included opposition politicians in a coalition government. In September President Nabiyev was forced to resign and parliamentary speaker Akbarsho Iskandarov became acting Head of State. He was

**278**

replaced in November, with Imamali Rakhmanov becoming parliamentary speaker and Head of State.

In separate incidents in May, during armed conflict between supporters and opponents of President Nabiyev, nine reportedly unarmed demonstrators and two members of the CIS armed forces were said to have been deliberately shot dead in Dushanbe by members of the security forces loyal to the President. CIS armed forces were at that time maintaining a declared position of neutrality.

Armed conflict continued for the rest of the year, principally in the Kulyab and Kurgan-Tyube regions of southern Tadzhikistan. Armed groups were divided along both political and clan lines. Officials estimated that up to 20,000 people were killed and more than 420,000 people fled their homes in the conflict zones. There were reports of deliberate killings of unarmed civilians by the rival armed groups. In December, following the fall of Dushanbe to forces loyal to the administration of Imamali Rakhmanov, there were reports of the extrajudicial execution in the city of dozens of unarmed civilians suspected of supporting the opposition. Forces subordinate to the Ministry of Internal Affairs reportedly targeted for summary execution people from the Pamir and Garm regions of eastern Tadzhikistan as well as independent journalists.

Political prisoner Maksud Ikramov, a former mayor of Dushanbe who was identified with the opposition to President Nabiyev, was denied adequate access to defence counsel in the weeks immediately following his detention in March on corruption charges. Maksud Ikramov was released in October and the charges against him were dropped.

The death penalty remained in force for 18 peacetime offences. No death sentences were known to have been passed. Figures made available to Amnesty International during the year by the CIS Statistical Committee indicated that six death sentences had been passed in 1990 in Tadzhikistan and six in 1991. There had been one execution in 1990 and none in 1991. Execution is by shooting.

In June Amnesty International expressed concern to the government about the reportedly deliberate killing by members of the security forces of unarmed demonstrators and CIS military personnel

in May, and welcomed the establishment of an official commission to investigate these and other killings in Dushanbe. In December Amnesty International expressed concern about the reported extrajudicial executions of people from the Pamir and Garm regions and independent journalists. The organization called on the government to undertake a full and impartial investigation, and to take all measures necessary to ensure that forces under government control were aware of and conformed to international standards on the use of force. Amnesty International raised with the authorities the issue of Maksud Ikramov's access to defence counsel, and continued to press for the abolition of the death penalty.

# TAIWAN

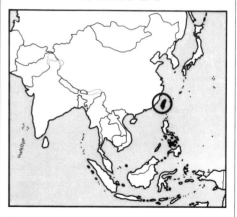

Ten prisoners of conscience and possible prisoners of conscience were released following amendment of the Criminal Code. At least 16 people were sentenced to death and five executions were known to have been carried out.

Article 100 of the Criminal Code, which covers offences against the internal security of the state, was amended in May with the effect that it may now be used to punish only those who engage in violent activities. Twelve political prisoners, including seven prisoners of conscience, were released as a result and over 240 other pending cases were dropped.

The National Security Law was also amended in July to provide that only those citizens who have resorted to violence against the state or travelled illegally to the People's Republic of China may in future be refused entry into Taiwan. Subsequently, 277 government critics resident abroad had restrictions on their return to Taiwan lifted. In July provisions banning the advocacy of communism or division of the national territory were removed from the Law on Organization of Civil Groups and the Law on Assembly and Demonstrations. Before the revision, it was an offence for any political organization to advocate the establishment of a Taiwanese state officially separate from China.

In February a regulation was introduced to punish prosecutors responsible for unlawful detentions. In April the Judicial *Yuan* (Council) and the Ministry of Justice ordered all judges and prosecutors to resign from their posts in political parties to safeguard judicial independence.

The Taiwan Garrison Command was formally disbanded in August; from its formation in 1958 until the lifting of martial law in 1987 it had been responsible for the arrest, interrogation and torture of hundreds of political prisoners, including prisoners of conscience; for conducting prosecutions in many cases; and for carrying out executions.

Four prisoners of conscience were released in May following the amendment of Article 100 of the Criminal Code provisions on internal security: they were Huang Hua, Kuo Pei-hung, Lee Ying-yuan and Wang Kang-lu. Six possible prisoners of conscience were also released following the amendment: Chiang Kai-shih, Chou Wu-chien and Hsu Lung-chun in May; Chen Cheng-ran, Lin Yin-fu, Wang Hsiu-hui in July. All had been arrested for supporting the formation of an independent Taiwanese state; three had also been convicted of illegally entering Taiwan in violation of a ban on their return (see *Amnesty International Report 1992*).

At least one political trial appeared to fall short of international fair trial standards. Chang Tsan-hung, who was accused of sedition and attempted murder, was sentenced to 10 years' imprisonment in June, reduced to five years under a 1988 Clemency Statute. The sole evidence against him was the "confession" of an alleged accomplice who had been interrogated under duress by the military authorities in 1977. In September the Supreme Court upheld Chang Tsan-hung's appeal on the grounds that there was no evidence to convict him and returned the case to the High Court for retrial. There were reports that Chang Tsan-hung did not receive adequate medical care in prison. The Taiwan High Court released him on bail in October, citing medical reasons.

The death penalty continued to be applied for a wide range of criminal offences. At least 16 death sentences were imposed, five of which were known to have been carried out. Amnesty International was concerned about ethical issues raised by the use of organs from executed prisoners for transplant operations, including the risk that the need for such organs might affect the timing of executions and that death row prisoners might become an accepted source of organs, which would impede reform or abolition of the death penalty laws. In June the legislative *Yuan* (Council) amended the law on corruption to remove the death penalty. In July it also amended the law prohibiting the use, manufacture and distribution of drugs and the law prohibiting smuggling to make the death penalty a discretionary rather than mandatory punishment.

In April Amnesty International wrote to Vice-Premier Shih Chi-yang urging him to ensure that the planned revision of Article 100 of the Criminal Code guaranteed freedom of expression and association. In June it wrote to the Minister of Justice expressing concern about the fairness of Chang Tsan-hung's trial and about his health. The authorities responded in August that Chang Tsan-hung's trial had complied with due process of law and that his applications for medical bail had been reviewed by a court. In October Amnesty International wrote to the authorities seeking clarification of the revisions of the laws under which prisoners of conscience had been detained and of the amended laws restricting the use of the death penalty. No response had been received by the end of the year.

# TANZANIA

More than a dozen supporters of opposition political parties were briefly imprisoned as prisoners of conscience. A prominent government opponent continued to face charges brought for political reasons. At least one prisoner was sentenced to death.

In February a presidential commission recommended the ending of the one-party state. In May both Union and Zanzibar parliaments endorsed legislation amending the Constitution to allow political parties in addition to the ruling *Chama cha Mapinduzi* (CCM), Party of the Revolution. Political activity continued to be restricted by regulations governing the registration of new political parties and the organization of meetings. New political parties were allowed to hold public meetings only if they were licensed by local government officials called Area Commissioners, the majority of whom were CCM members appointed by the central government. By the end of the year over 20 political parties had been registered.

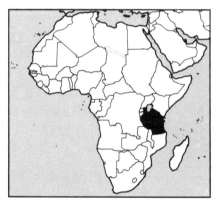

Early in the year, before the constitutional amendments approved in May, a number of non-violent opponents of the government were briefly detained, continuing the pattern of harassment of multiparty activists noted in previous years (see *Amnesty International Reports 1991* and *1992*). In February, 15 men were detained for 24 hours on Zanzibar, reportedly on suspicion of holding an illegal meeting. They included several men who were well-known for their opposition to the CCM, some of whom had been detained without charge or trial during 1990. The arrests followed a public announcement by Salmin Amour, the President of Zanzibar, that anyone found "instigating" people against the CCM would be arrested.

In July Christopher Mtikila and three other men were sentenced to nine months' imprisonment after holding a recruiting meeting for the Democratic Party in Dodoma. The meeting had been denied official permission and was illegal because the party was not then registered. In mid-September the four prisoners of conscience were released on appeal.

Seif Shariff Hamad, a former chief minister of Zanzibar and a leading Zanzibari nationalist, continued to face charges of illegal possession of government documents (see *Amnesty International Report 1992*). The charges had been brought in 1989 and Seif Shariff Hamad had been released on bail in December 1991. In December 1992 he petitioned the appeal court for the charges to be dropped. No decision had been reached by the end of the year.

At least one man was sentenced to death for murder. There were no reports of executions.

Amnesty International urged the government to release prisoners of conscience and appealed for the commutation of all death sentences.

# THAILAND

**Fifty-two unarmed demonstrators were killed, hundreds injured and scores "disappeared" when demonstrations were violently suppressed by the security forces in May; over 3,000 people, many of them prisoners of conscience, were briefly detained and many were tortured or illtreated. At least one prisoner of conscience was held throughout the year. Four Burmese nationals "disappeared" from police custody. At least two people were sentenced to death but no executions were reported.**

Elections were held in March. In April General Suchinda Khraprayun was appointed Prime Minister by the ruling coalition of five pro-military political parties. General Suchinda was Commander-in-Chief of the army and one of the leaders of the 1991 military coup that overthrew the previous elected government.

Protests at the appointment of General Suchinda, who was not an elected member of parliament, began in April and gathered strength through May. Major-General Chamlong Srimuang, a member of parliament and former governor of Bangkok, went on hunger-strike for several days and led numerous peaceful protest rallies. There were almost daily demonstrations of over

100,000 people in Bangkok between 4 and 10 May.

On 17 May an estimated 200,000 protesters tried to march towards Government House. They were met by armed security forces who used water cannons and truncheons in unsuccessful attempts to disperse them. Early in the morning of 18 May troops opened fire with automatic weapons directly on the crowd, killing several unarmed protesters and injuring dozens. The violence continued throughout the day; in the evening troops in full combat gear were filmed shooting directly into the crowd at head height. There were also widespread reports of people being deliberately shot by police and soldiers in side streets near the demonstrations. Dozens of people were killed, including possible victims of extrajudicial executions, and hundreds were injured both by gunshot and truncheon beatings. A state of emergency was declared in Bangkok and surrounding provinces.

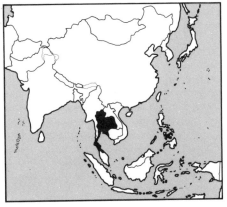

On the morning of 19 May troops stormed the Royal Hotel where demonstrators were seeking refuge. They kicked and beat dozens of the protesters as they lay prone on the ground. Between 2,500 and 3,000 people were arrested during the day, many of whom were reportedly beaten while being transported to detention centres. Peaceful anti-government protests spread to many other parts of Thailand.

On 20 May the constitutional monarch, King Bhumibol Adulyadej, appealed on television for General Suchinda and Major-General Chamlong to negotiate a settlement to the crisis. Major-General Chamlong and some 3,300 others were released from detention. General Suchinda promised to support a constitutional amendment requiring the prime minister to be an elected member of parliament and Major-General Chamlong publicly appealed for a halt to street demonstrations.

On 23 May General Suchinda announced a sweeping amnesty decree which apparently exonerated not only demonstrators but also members of the security forces who had perpetrated human rights violations. The decree was ruled to be constitutional by a Constitutional Tribunal in July. In October the newly elected House of Representatives unanimously overturned the amnesty decree. However, the new government again submitted the decree to the Constitutional Tribunal, which ruled in November that it was legally binding.

On 24 May General Suchinda resigned as prime minister and the state of emergency was lifted two days later. Compensation for victims of the violent suppression was ordered in late May. Interim Prime Minister Anand Panyarachan dissolved parliament in June and called elections for September. The elections were won by an anti-military coalition and Chuan Leekpai, leader of the Democrat Party, became Prime Minister.

According to official reports, 52 people were killed and 696 others were injured during the suppression of the demonstrations between 17 and 20 May, and 84 people "disappeared" after being detained. Unofficial sources, however, suggested the true number of "disappeared" was considerably higher. Troops fired directly at demonstrators on at least two occasions: at 4.15 am and at 10.30 pm on 18 May. Many of those killed or injured were shot in the back. There were also frequent reports of individuals being shot by members of the security forces in side streets in various areas of Bangkok during the series of demonstrations. Some of these reports were corroborated by forensic evidence showing that victims had been shot at point-blank range, and indicated that many of those killed may have been victims of extrajudicial executions.

At least 3,300 demonstrators were detained between 17 and 20 May, many of whom appeared to have been prisoners of conscience. Among the detainees were Major-General Chamlong and other demonstration leaders. Detainees were held in Bangkhen Police Academy, where witnesses saw prisoners being beaten by police commandos, and at Lad Yao Prison.

All were released uncharged by 21 May.

In the weeks after the military crackdown in Bangkok, pro-democracy activists received death threats and were harassed in other ways. For example, demonstration leader Prateep Ungsongtham Hata received letters and telephone calls threatening that her home and office would be bombed. An army spokesman denied that military hit squads were tracking the movements of pro-democracy leaders, but the military did not publicly condemn the death threats.

Two committees were set up by the government to investigate the events of 17 to 20 May and determine the whereabouts of the "disappeared". However, they were not given the power to subpoena witnesses and were therefore obliged to rely on the military officials and others involved to cooperate. Repeated but unconfirmed reports alleged that troops had removed the bodies of protesters and buried them at secret sites in military installations and elsewhere. Dr Pradit Charoenthaithawee, Rector of Mahidol University, who chaired a subcommittee to investigate the fate of missing people, received death threats after saying he had information about secret mass graves at military installations. The threats stopped once he resigned from the subcommittee.

The parliamentary and government committees found that military commanders had exercised poor judgment and used excessive force in controlling the demonstrations. Another committee set up by the Ministry of Defence to investigate the role of military commanders submitted findings to the interim Prime Minister in July. Several senior military leaders were subsequently transferred from their posts, as were commanders directly in charge of troops in Bangkok in May.

At least one prisoner of conscience, Chana Srikiatsak, was held throughout the year (see *Amnesty International Report 1992*).

A warrant was still being pursued for the arrest of prominent social critic Sulak Sivaraksa on charges of lese-majesty after a speech in 1991 in which he described members of the Royal Family as "ordinary people" (see *Amnesty International Report 1992*). He would be considered a prisoner of conscience if arrested.

In August the Criminal Court acquitted 13 members of the *Patiwat* (Revolutionary) Council charged with inciting unrest in 1989, including Prasert Sapsunthorn (see *Amnesty International Reports 1991* and *1992*).

Four Burmese nationals were reported to have "disappeared" from police custody in Ranong. Than Soe, Aung Kyaw and two others were arrested by police in May on suspicion of being illegal immigrants from Myanmar (Burma). The bodies of two unidentified people, believed to be those of Than Soe and Aung Kyaw, were later found outside Ranong: they bore marks of violent injury. No official investigation was known to have been carried out.

No further information came to light about the "disappeared" labour leader Thanong Po-arn (see *Amnesty International Report 1992*). A government-appointed committee concluded in August that there was no evidence that he was still alive.

At least two death sentences were imposed: one on a man convicted of murder and another for drug-trafficking. The death sentence on another man, Thonchai Tikham, sentenced to death for murder in 1988, was upheld by the Supreme Court in July: this was subsequently commuted to life imprisonment by a Royal Pardon Decree. Fifty other prisoners had their death sentences commuted to life imprisonment under a royal amnesty in August to mark the Queen's birthday. A total of 108 convicted prisoners were then reported to remain under sentence of death. No executions were known to have been carried out.

Ten Chinese asylum-seekers were detained and reported in August to be in imminent danger of being forcibly returned to China, where they would be at risk of serious human rights violations. Eight had been arrested in April on charges of illegal entry into Thailand. Li Maolong and Li Suwen were detained by police in Bangkok on 3 June as they prepared to hold a ceremony to commemorate the third anniversary of the Tiananmen Square massacre. All 10 were members of a dissident political group, the China Alliance for Democracy (CAD), and had been active in the pro-democracy movement in China in 1989. One of them, Lin Jingze, was forcibly returned to China in September. At the end of the year, Li Maolong and Li Suwen remained in detention but the fate of the others was not known.

Amnesty International appealed on 18 May for the release of Major-General Chamlong and other prisoners of conscience and for the government to instruct the security forces not to use unnecessary force against unarmed demonstrators. It continued to express its concern about the excessive use of force in suppressing the demonstrations and to appeal for prompt and thorough investigations. On 27 May it welcomed the release of some 3,000 people imprisoned for their peaceful political activity during the May demonstrations, and urged that no amnesty should be granted which would preclude the bringing to justice of those responsible for human rights violations.

Amnesty International representatives visited Thailand in June and met government officials to express concern about the human rights violations committed by security forces during the May demonstrations. Amnesty International urged the government to bring to justice those responsible for extrajudicial executions, torture and "disappearances", and to ensure that the amnesty decree issued by former Prime Minister Suchinda did not allow human rights violators to evade justice. Amnesty International welcomed the establishment of investigative committees, but urged that they should be empowered to subpoena witnesses, enter military installations and other official premises, and obtain all the information they required.

In October Amnesty International published *Thailand: The Massacre in Bangkok*, which described the May events and subsequent related human rights developments. It set out a series of recommendations for preventing such human rights violations in the future.

Amnesty International also urged the authorities to clarify the cases of "disappearance" of Burmese nationals; not to return the 10 Chinese asylum-seekers to China against their will; and to commute all death sentences.

# TOGO

**The authorities failed to take any steps to investigate past human rights violations or to bring those responsible to justice. Two armed forces officers suspected of opposition to the President were detained without charge and reportedly tortured. Opposition leaders were subjected to assassination attempts in which the army was implicated; two were killed.**

Political instability and violence intensified, with continuing rivalry between President Gnassingbé Eyadéma, backed by the army, and Prime Minister Joseph Kokou Koffigoh. Support for the Prime Minister was strongest in the south, while the President and the army were identified principally with the north. Prime Minister Koffigoh had been appointed by the National Conference in 1991 to head a transitional government until elections scheduled for 1992. After initially surrendering some of his power as a result of army action against him in late 1991 (see *Amnesty International Report 1992*), Prime Minister Koffigoh's authority was eroded further during 1992, with President Eyadéma regaining control of much of the machinery of government. This process culminated in an amendment to the draft constitution allowing President Eyadéma to stand for presidential election without having first to resign from the army. The transitional period was extended to the end of the year when elections, originally scheduled for early 1992, were again postponed.

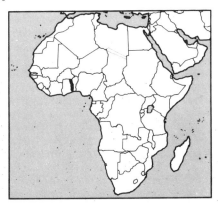

A new Constitution was endorsed by referendum in September. In October members of the transitional executive body were briefly taken hostage by the army until they agreed to unfreeze assets of the former ruling party led by President Eyadéma. Two lieutenants were excluded from the army, apparently for their role in the hostage-taking. A general strike which began in mid-November was continuing at the end of the year: it was called by the opposition to demand the resignation of President Eyadéma following his refusal to accept Prime Minister Koffigoh's decision to dismiss two ministers, both members of

**284**

the former ruling party, from his government.

Although substantial new evidence had come to light during 1991 about violations of human rights committed while President Eyadéma had been in power (see *Amnesty International Report 1992*), no steps were taken to investigate further the reports of arbitrary detention, torture and extrajudicial executions or to bring those responsible to justice. This lack of action, which amounted to granting impunity to soldiers and others responsible for human rights violations, was a direct result of the political situation, with supporters of the Prime Minister expressing fear that further investigations of reported violations might provoke the army to seize power. Army spokesmen described the reports of violations as fabrications and lies.

There were several reports of prisoners being tortured in military custody. In July Captain Esso Charles Pello, former head of the military intelligence service, was arrested in the capital, Lomé. He was apparently suspected of links with the President's political opponents and of having sensitive information about the role of soldiers in human rights violations. He was held incommunicado at the gendarmerie headquarters in the northern town of Kara, where he was reportedly beaten and tortured with electric shocks, and deprived of food until he went into a coma. Rumours then circulated that he was dead. The Presidency later circulated a letter signed by Captain Pello which stated that reports of his death were incorrect and that he had simply been transferred to a new posting in the army.

Another soldier, Corporal Nikabou Bikagni, was arrested in October by the gendarmerie in Aflao, on the border with Ghana. The Presidency reported that he had confessed to carrying weapons and explosives with a view to bombing civilian targets in Lomé. There were signs that his confession was made as a result of torture and that the real reason for his arrest was his perceived support for Prime Minister Koffigoh. A few days later his father and brother were arrested; they remained held without charge at a prison in Bassar, northern Togo, at the end of the year. Corporal Bikagni also remained in custody in Lomé.

Prominent members of the opposition faced a new pattern of assassinations and assassination attempts during the year, in which the armed forces appeared to be involved. In May four people, including Dr Marc Atipede, a leading government opponent, were killed, and another opponent, Gilchrist Olympio, was seriously injured when their motorcade was ambushed by gunmen in northern Togo while they were travelling to a political rally. Gilchrist Olympio, the son of a former president deposed by President Eyadéma and assassinated, was president of the *Union des forces de changement* (UFC), Union of the Forces for Change, a coalition of 10 opposition parties; Dr Atipede was the leader of one of the coalition parties. An inquiry into the incident was conducted by the Paris-based *Fédération internationale des droits de l'homme* (FIDH), International Federation of Human Rights, at the request of Prime Minister Koffigoh and a Togolese human rights group. The FIDH, whose representatives visited Togo in June, concluded that the army had probably planned and carried out the attack with the complicity of the highest levels of the army command. It found circumstantial evidence of soldiers' involvement in the incident, including the use of a type of automatic weapon used only by the army and the presence of certain senior officers in the area at the time. The army rejected the findings as a "tissue of lies".

In July another opposition leader, Tavio Amorin, was shot while walking in Lomé, reportedly by two people in civilian clothes. He died of his wounds two days later. Tavio Amorin chaired a Committee for Human Rights in the transitional executive body set up by the National Conference and was Secretary General of a new opposition coalition. Prime Minister Koffigoh's government suggested that a police identity card found near the scene of the shooting was evidence of security force involvement.

In continuing political violence later in the year, opposition figures and members of President Eyadéma's party were attacked. None of the attacks was the subject of official or independent investigations by the authorities. Although Prime Minister Koffigoh announced that the evidence gathered by the FIDH on the attempted assassination of Gilchrist Olympio was being transmitted to the procuracy, no further action was reported on the case. In relation to acts of political violence and reports of human rights violations in 1992, the procuracy appeared inactive and unable or unwilling to pursue an independent and impartial role.

In April Amnesty International published *Togo: Impunity for human rights violators at a time of reform*, which described past human rights violations, in particular those publicized during 1991. The report stressed the importance of impartial investigations of all reported abuses in order to establish the facts and provide appropriate remedies. It also urged the authorities to introduce a series of safeguards for human rights and warned of the dangers for human rights in the future if no action was taken.

The President's Office publicly denied that the human rights violations described in the report had occurred. Representatives of President Eyadéma repeated the denials during two visits to Amnesty International's International Secretariat and submitted a 39-page document disputing the accuracy of Amnesty International's information. This claimed that the findings of the official inquiry by the National Commission of Human Rights into the killings in 1991 were inaccurate and biased, and denied that officials were responsible for deaths of prisoners at Kaza detention camp in preceding years. However, its conclusions were not based on independent or impartial investigations. In September Amnesty International responded in detail to the document, observing that the controversy over some of the facts re-emphasized the need for a thorough and impartial investigation into past human rights violations.

During the year Amnesty International expressed concern at reports of torture and urged that independent inquiries be carried out into the cases of both Captain Pello and Corporal Bikagni. It appealed for Corporal Bikagni and his relatives to be released unless they were to be charged with criminal offences. The organization also called for investigations into the assassinations of opposition leaders, urging that all evidence implicating the army in extrajudicial executions be examined independently and impartially and that every attempt be made to hold soldiers accountable for their actions.

# TRINIDAD AND TOBAGO

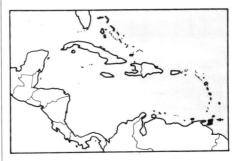

**285**

**Three prisoners were scheduled to be executed in November and two in December; the executions were suspended pending appeals. New death sentences were passed and over 100 prisoners were under sentence of death. A group of 114 people charged with treason were released. At least one person was sentenced to be flogged.**

The government of Prime Minister Patrick Manning, elected in December 1991, was "considering in further detail" the report of a Commission of Inquiry into the effectiveness and status of the death penalty. The report had been submitted to President Noor Hassanali in 1990 and its recommendations, which included executing prisoners who had exhausted their appeals, had been accepted by the previous government.

New death sentences were passed during 1992 and over 100 prisoners were under sentence of death at the end of the year.

Gayman Jurisingh, Peter Matthews and Faizal Mohammed were scheduled to be executed on 10 November and Brian Francois and Lal Seeratan on 8 December. These would have been the first executions since 1979. Lawyers submitted constitutional motions arguing that execution would violate their constitutional rights. The motion on the first three cases was dismissed by the High Court on 11 November. An appeal against this decision was heard by the Court of Appeal in December; a ruling was pending at the end of the year.

Daniel Pinto was granted clemency by President Hassanali in October on the recommendation of the Committee on the Prerogative of Mercy. His death sentence was

**286**

commuted to life imprisonment. In 1990 the United Nations Human Rights Committee, which supervises implementation of the International Covenant on Civil and Political Rights, had recommended that he should be released (see *Amnesty International Report 1991*).

Three men who had been sentenced to death for murder in 1989 were released in March. The Court of Appeal allowed their appeal on the ground that the judge had erred on various matters at their trial, including failing to warn the jury against over-reliance on identification evidence for a conviction.

In March the High Court heard the case of 114 people charged with treason, murder and other offences. In December 1991 the Judicial Committee of the Privy Council in London, the final court of appeal for Trinidad and Tobago, had ruled that they should have a new hearing in the local courts (see *Amnesty International Report 1992*). The group was involved in an attempt to overthrow the government in 1990 in which over 30 people had been killed during five days of confrontations. The group had taken 46 hostages, including the Prime Minister, who were released after the Acting President promised an amnesty to their captors. If convicted as charged, the defendants would have faced a mandatory death sentence. The court ruled in June that all 114 should be released and paid damages; it held that the amnesty negotiated with the group was valid. They were released on 1 July. The government appealed against the decision in August but the appeal had not been heard by the end of the year.

Corporal punishment (including flogging), which constitutes cruel, inhuman or degrading treatment, remained in force both as a penalty for criminal offences and as a disciplinary measure for prisoners. In May a man convicted of attempted murder was sentenced to 39 years' imprisonment and 20 strokes with the cat-o'-nine-tails (a device of nine knotted cords or hide thongs attached to a handle). It was not known whether this or other previous flogging sentences had been carried out.

In August Amnesty International wrote to Prime Minister Manning about the recommendations of the Commission of Inquiry into the death penalty. Amnesty International criticized several of the Commission's recommendations, noting testimony at the public hearings in which it was stressed that hanging is not a deterrent to murder. Amnesty International urged the government to commute all existing death sentences as a first step towards abolition. In September Amnesty International received an acknowledgement from the Prime Minister's office but no substantial reply had been received by the end of the year.

In November Amnesty International appealed to the government not to carry out the scheduled executions and to commute the death sentences. An Amnesty International representative observed the appeal hearing in December.

# TUNISIA

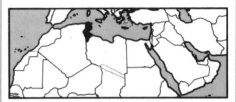

**Over 3,000 political prisoners, most of them suspected members of the prohibited Islamic *al-Nahda* organization, were serving sentences imposed after unfair trials in 1992 and previous years. Some were possible prisoners of conscience. Many had been held in illegally prolonged incommunicado detention before trial. Several government critics were prisoners of conscience; four were released before the end of the year. Reports of torture and ill-treatment of political detainees in police and national guard stations were widespread. One detainee was reported to have died in custody.**

The Law on Associations was amended by the National Assembly in March in such a way that, among other things, individuals occupying positions of responsibility in political parties may not at the same time belong to organizations or associations considered of a "general" nature. This led in May to the dissolution of the *Ligue tunisienne des droits de l'homme* (LTDH), Tunisian Human Rights League, for failing to amend its rules in accordance with the change in the law. The League had been critical of the government's human rights record.

In May President Zine El Abidine Ben Ali announced that he had asked the commission of inquiry into prolonged incommunicado detention and torture to report on the implementation of its earlier recommendations (see *Amnesty International Report 1992*). In response, the commission published a report in July: this stated that directives drawing attention to Tunisian law and international standards had been posted in every police station and that 116 police officers had been implicated in incidents of torture or ill-treatment. Amnesty International asked for further information, including the dates and details of alleged offences, but none was received.

Hundreds of suspected supporters of *al-Nahda* and dozens of members of the unauthorized *Parti communiste des ouvriers de Tunisie* (PCOT), Tunisian Communist Workers' Party, and other left-wing groups were arrested and held incommunicado in pre-trial (*garde à vue*) detention. Many were held for longer than the 10-day limit allowed by Tunisian law. Some were released uncharged, but hundreds, including possible prisoners of conscience, were sentenced to terms of imprisonment after unfair trials. For example, Abderrazak Hamzaoui, a student at Tunis University and a suspected sympathizer of *al-Nahda*, was arrested in September. He was held incommunicado for several weeks in Kasserine Police Station and inside the Ministry of the Interior, where he was allegedly ill-treated, and in Bouchoucha Police Station. Twelve Tunisian nationals who were arrested in Libya in January and returned to Tunisia in March were held in incommunicado detention for up to three months. Two of them, including Habib Khmila, were said to have been held in the Ministry of the Interior and tortured there.

The trials of almost all political prisoners fell far short of internationally recognized standards for fair trial. In many cases, defence lawyers complained that defendants had been held beyond the legal limit and tortured. Their pleas were ignored by the courts which failed to order appropriate investigations and readily accepted contested confessions as evidence of guilt. Several convictions were secured solely on the basis of *procès-verbaux* (police statements) allegedly extracted under torture during pre-trial detention and later retracted by defendants.

For example, Touhami Ben Boubacr Ben Zeid, a PCOT sympathizer arrested in February, was convicted of belonging to an unauthorized organization and distributing leaflets by the Court of First Instance in Grombalia, despite complaints by his lawyer that he had been held incommunicado in *garde à vue* detention beyond the 10-day limit and tortured. A prisoner of conscience, he was sentenced to eight months' imprisonment. The sentence was upheld by the Appeal Court in June. He was released in October, on expiry of his sentence.

A total of 279 alleged members of *al-Nahda*, including 56 *in absentia*, were defendants in two political trials which began in July and ended in August. Both trials took place before military courts and were unfair. The defendants, who had been arrested between October 1990 and September 1991, were accused of plotting to overthrow the government and other offences. They were divided, apparently without reason, into two groups and tried separately in the military camps of Bouchoucha and Bab Saadoun. Charges were imprecise and only a few of the defendants were charged with specific acts. Weapons, including guns and home-made hand grenades, were displayed outside the courtrooms but none of the defendants was confronted with a specific weapon. Almost all the defendants had been held incommunicado for weeks or months after their arrest and alleged that they had been tortured or ill-treated to force them to sign police statements in which they confessed to or implicated others in offences. These statements, which most of the accused retracted in court, formed the basis of the prosecution case. At least four of those arrested and questioned in connection with the alleged plot had died in 1991 in circumstances that suggested that torture had caused or hastened death. Some defendants still bore marks, which they said had been caused by torture, a year after their interrogation. Arrest dates for most of the defendants had been systematically falsified by police in an attempt to conceal illegally prolonged *garde à vue* detention. Many of the accused had had no access to a lawyer during up to 18 months' pre-trial detention. Lawyers did not receive relevant documents or their clients' files until a few days before the trial, and evidence which could have been favourable to the accused was withheld by the prosecution.

**288**

The verdicts were given in August: 45 defendants, including 24 *in absentia*, were sentenced to life imprisonment; 220, including 32 *in absentia*, received prison sentences of between one and 24 years; and 10 were acquitted. The charges against four defendants were withdrawn. The sentences were upheld by the Court of Cassation in September.

One prisoner of conscience was held throughout the year, but several others were released. Moncef Ben Salem, a university professor, continued to serve a sentence imposed in 1990 (see *Amnesty International Report 1991*). However, Mohamed Nouri, a lawyer sentenced in February 1991 for a newspaper article criticizing military courts, was released in March, seven months after completion of his sentence. He was the only political prisoner among 1,055 prisoners who were freed in an amnesty that month. Hamadi Jebali, who had received a one-year sentence in 1991 in connection with the same newspaper article, completed that sentence but received a further 16-year prison term in August after being convicted with others on charges including plotting to overthrow the government. Moncef Triki, a prisoner of conscience sentenced to 15 months' imprisonment in 1991, was released in October 1992. Beshir Essid (see *Amnesty International Report 1992*), who was serving a four-year sentence imposed in 1990 after he was convicted of defaming the President and other offences, was freed in a presidential amnesty in December.

There were numerous reports of torture and ill-treatment of detainees suspected of supporting *al-Nahda* and illegal left-wing parties in police stations and national guard centres throughout the country, as well as in the cells at the Ministry of the Interior. Torture methods used included beatings, especially on the soles of the feet; suspension by the ankles or in contorted positions, usually accompanied by beatings; electric shocks; and insertion of bottles into the anus. Sexual abuse by male guards was alleged by several women detainees, and psychological torture and the threat of sexual abuse to both men and women were also reported.

Noureddine Mabrouk, a teacher, was arrested in February in Bizerta and held in *garde à vue* detention for over six weeks. He was taken to Bouchoucha Police Station and the Ministry of the Interior and tor-tured by being beaten and suspended in contorted positions. He was tried in April and sentenced to a prison term of one year and 16 days for membership of an illegal organization and attending illegal meetings. The sentence was confirmed on appeal.

One detainee died in custody in circumstances where torture may have hastened death. Mouldi Ben Amor was arrested in December 1991 and held in prolonged incommunicado detention in Tunis. In January the authorities informed his family that he had died and allowed them to receive the body for burial. However, no medical certificate stating the cause of his death was provided, no inquest was held and the family were not allowed to examine the body.

The families of five supporters of *al-Nahda* who died in custody in 1991, reportedly after torture, were granted compensation by the government. However, no results of any inquiries into their deaths were made public. Amnesty International urged the reopening of inquiries into the deaths in custody in October 1991 of Faisal Barakat and Rachid Chammakhi. Eye-witnesses had reported that both detainees had been tortured in Nabeul Police Station before their deaths. An expert medical opinion was commissioned by Amnesty International in February on the official autopsy report on Faisal Barakat, said by the Tunisian authorities to have died in a road accident. This indicated that his death most probably had been related to an injury caused by the insertion of a foreign object into the anus and through the wall of the bowel. In response to this finding, the government stated in October that it would reopen the investigation into his death, but it was not known with what result by the end of the year. The government also stated that, at the request of President Ben Ali, the authorities were considering appointing an Ombudsman to monitor police registers and detention centres.

Amnesty International continued to express concern to the government about the prolonged incommunicado detention and alleged torture of suspected Islamic activists and other political detainees. The organization criticized the failure of the government to open investigations into the death in custody of Mouldi Ben Amor and to reopen the inquiry into the death of

Rachid Chammakhi. In March Amnesty International published a report, *Tunisia: Prolonged Incommunicado Detention and Torture*, and publicly urged the government to act immediately to end human rights violations. In October Amnesty International published a further report, *Tunisia: Heavy Sentences after Unfair Trials*, detailing the gross deficiencies of the trials of alleged *al-Nadha* members in July and August. Amnesty International urged the government to ensure that they were either retried in accordance with international fair trial standards, or released.

In late June an Amnesty International delegation visited Tunisia and discussed human rights with President Ben Ali and members of the government. The President assured Amnesty International of his own commitment to human rights and that alleged human rights violations would be investigated and the perpetrators brought to justice. Amnesty International also expressed concern that the amendments made to the Law on Associations were a violation of the right of freedom of association guaranteed in international human rights treaties to which Tunisia is a party. It also discussed recent difficulties experienced by the Amnesty International Tunisian Section. The President said that the section could import and distribute Amnesty International publications in Tunisia in accordance with the formalities required by Tunisian law.

In July and August Amnesty International observers attended the two mass trials before military courts of suspected members of *al-Nadha*.

In an oral statement to the United Nations (UN) Commission on Human Rights in February, Amnesty International included reference to its concerns about prolonged incommunicado detention and torture in Tunisia. In April Amnesty International submitted information about its concerns in Tunisia for UN review under a procedure, established by Economic and Social Council Resolutions 728F/1503, for confidential consideration of communications about human rights violations.

# TURKEY

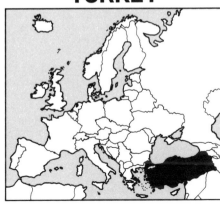

Scores of prisoners of conscience were detained briefly and several were sentenced to prison terms. Torture of political and criminal detainees continued to be a common practice in police stations and at least 13 detainees died in custody, allegedly as a result of torture. At least four people "disappeared". The number of alleged extrajudicial executions increased: there were more than 200 killings in the mainly Kurdish provinces of southeast Turkey in circumstances which suggested security force involvement. There were also allegations of extrajudicial executions during police raids on "safe houses" of armed political organizations. At least 120 people were killed in the southeast when police and gendarmerie officers fired on apparently unarmed civilians. There were more than 100 apparently deliberate and arbitrary killings of prisoners and other non-combatants by armed opposition groups.

State of emergency legislation was in force throughout the year in 10 southeastern provinces, where the eight-year-long conflict between security forces and the secessionist guerrillas of the *Partiya Karkeren Kurdistan* (PKK), Kurdish Workers' Party, grew fiercer in intensity. Over 2,000 people, including civilians, were killed.

In November a number of amendments were made to the Criminal Procedure Code concerning detention and remand procedures. The length of time during which common criminal detainees can be held in police custody before being brought before a judge was reduced to eight days and detainees were given the right to have a lawyer present during interrogation. However, the new measures do not apply to detainees suspected of political offences – those at most risk of torture – who may still be held incommunicado for up to 15 days (30 days in the Emergency Powers Region).

In December the European Committee for the Prevention of Torture (ECPT) announced that during a series of visits to Turkey over three years it had found extensive proof that "torture and other forms of severe ill-treatment of persons in police custody remains widespread in Turkey and that such methods are applied to both ordinary criminal suspects and persons held under anti-terrorism provisions". In Ankara and Diyarbakır police headquarters the ECPT discovered equipment apparently used for torturing suspects.

Scores of prisoners of conscience were held for hours or days after being taken into custody at public meetings and demonstrations. A few were sentenced to prison terms under various articles of the Turkish Penal Code (TPC). In May Ömer Okçu, who wrote under the pen-name Hekimoğlu İsmail for the daily newspaper *Zaman*, began serving three and a half months in prison following his conviction under Article 159 of the TPC for "insulting the armed forces". Also in May Sinami Orhan, editor of an Islamic political magazine, began serving four months in prison after being convicted under Law 5816 of publishing an article insulting the memory of Mustafa Kemal Atatürk. In May Sekvan Aytu, President of the Şırnak branch of the independent Turkish Human Rights Association (THRA), was taken into custody. He was held incommunicado for 15 days at Şırnak Police Headquarters, where he was reportedly beaten severely. He was charged with making separatist propaganda and membership of the PKK. However, he appeared to be a prisoner of conscience, imprisoned because of his work on behalf of the THRA. At the end of the year he was still in custody.

Torture by police continued to be reported from all parts of Turkey, particularly the major cities and the southeast. Men, women and children were tortured. Some were interrogated in connection with ordinary criminal offences. For example, Barbaros Göktaş, a waiter, was detained on suspicion of theft in January, and held incommunicado for more than a week at the Criminal Investigation Branch of Izmir Police Headquarters. He testified that he had been suspended by the arms, given electric shocks, and hosed with water at high pressure. He stated that police officers had forced the hose into his throat and turned the water on, squeezed his testicles and kept him naked and soaked with water in the cold for two days. When he complained to a judge that he had been tortured, the judge allegedly replied: "What did you expect, sweets?"

Detainees suspected of links with illegal armed political organizations were at particular risk of torture. Mehmet Polat, aged 15, was taken into custody when he took food to his uncle in police detention in Gaziantep Police Headquarters in February. He was questioned about his relatives' political activities. He said police blindfolded him, kicked him, beat his feet with a truncheon and applied electric shocks to his penis and his big toe. Nazlı Top, a nurse, said she was tortured for four days at the Anti-Terror Branch of Istanbul Police Headquarters while three months pregnant. She was detained in April on suspicion of taking part in an attack on a police minibus. She reported that during her interrogation, police ignored her requests to see a lawyer. She stated that they suspended her with her arms tied behind her and gave her electric shocks through her fingers and toes, and then through her nipples and sexual organs. They allegedly punched her all over, especially in the stomach, breasts and belly, raped her with a truncheon, and tried to rape her with a bottle. After 10 days in police custody, she was released without charge. The Forensic Medicine Institute issued a report stating that she was not injured, although an examination carried out by a doctor of the Turkish Human Rights Foundation the following day revealed injuries consistent with the allegations of torture. Nazlı Top made a formal complaint, but no charges had been brought by the end of the year.

During the year there were at least 13 deaths in custody allegedly as a result of torture. Tahir Seyhan, a member of *Halkın Emek Partisi* (HEP), People's Labour Party, died in April after four days' interrogation in incommunicado detention at Dargeçit Gendarmerie Battalion. The autopsy report registered the cause of death as brain trauma. A member of staff at the hospital where Tahir Seyhan died reportedly stated that he had been brutally tortured and that his body "was all in pieces". No prosecution had been initiated concerning his death by the end of the year. Miktat Kutlu, a bank clerk, was detained outside his home in Bismil in April and died approximately 24 hours later of a brain haemorrhage. Witnesses reported seeing Miktat Kutlu being beaten by the police both in the street and during interrogation in Bismil Police Headquarters. No one had been prosecuted in connection with his death by the end of the year.

There were also allegations of ill-treatment in prison. In April a group of unconvicted political prisoners arriving at Elaziğ E-type Prison were allegedly beaten on the hands. When they resisted having their hair forcibly cut, they were reportedly taken into the exercise yard in groups of three and again beaten, as a result of which one prisoner had to be taken to hospital. In September, at Buca Closed Prison in İzmir, prisoners who protested against a reduction in exercise periods by refusing to leave the exercise yard were reportedly beaten by more than 100 gendarmes and prison guards in the presence of the prison prosecutor and prison officials. More than 58 prisoners were injured, at least five seriously.

At least four people suspected of involvement with armed opposition groups "disappeared". One of them, Tuğrul Özbek, "disappeared" in October after a police raid on a house in Istanbul used by the illegal armed organization *Devrimci Sol*, Revolutionary Left. Three detainees testified that he had been detained and held at the Anti-Terror Branch of Istanbul Police Headquarters, but the police denied holding him. By the end of the year the authorities had provided no information on the whereabouts or fate of Tuğrul Özbek and it was feared that he may have died under torture.

The number of alleged extrajudicial executions increased. There were more than 260 "mysterious killings" in southeast Turkey, many of which were attributed to *Hizbullah*, (a local group apparently not connected to the Lebanese group of the same name). There was a striking degree of coincidence between the targets of the killings attributed to *Hizbullah* and the targets of police harassment, arbitrary detention, torture and other ill-treatment. There was evidence that the security forces had colluded in such killings, and may actually

have carried them out in some cases. Ramazan Şat was detained in Batman in March and interrogated for 12 days at Batman Police Headquarters on suspicion of harbouring members of the PKK. He later made a complaint of torture to the public prosecutor in Batman, and stated that the police had told him: "The next time we will not take you from your house. We shall kill you in the street when nobody is watching." Exactly three months later, Ramazan Şat was shot dead in the street by unknown assailants.

The targets of alleged extrajudicial execution included members of HEP, members of the THRA, and journalists. During the year 10 journalists were killed in southeast Turkey in circumstances which provoked allegations of extrajudicial execution. Musa Anter, a prominent Kurdish writer and journalist and founding member of the HEP, was shot dead in Diyarbakır by an unknown gunman in September. He had been imprisoned for his political writings and activities on numerous occasions over the preceding 50 years. Musa Anter had reportedly said that he was aware of being observed by the police from the moment he arrived in Diyarbakır a few days earlier to participate in a cultural event. He was shot in the outskirts of the city, not far from a police station and a police traffic control point. Three local newspaper reporters who went to the scene shortly afterwards were abducted at gunpoint, apparently by plainclothes police, and driven to a spot 200 kilometres away where they were released.

In Istanbul and Ankara there were allegations of extrajudicial executions during a series of police operations against "safe houses" used by *Devrimci Sol*. In May Songül Karabulut and Fikri Keleş were killed when police surrounded and fired on their apartment in Ankara. Witnesses agreed that a large number of police opened fire without adequate warning, that no fire was returned from the apartment, and that the suspects could have been arrested without loss of life.

At least 120 people were killed during the year in the southeast as a consequence of police and gendarmerie firing on apparently unarmed civilians. During disturbances in March on the occasion of the Kurdish New Year, 16 demonstrators were killed in the city of Şırnak when they refused to permit male police officers to search female demonstrators, and 19 reportedly unarmed demonstrators were killed by security forces in Nusaybin. In Şırnak, 22 civilians were killed in March and at least 15 in August when security forces fired at random on residential areas using tanks and mortars, apparently in reprisal for earlier attacks by PKK guerrillas.

A number of Iranian refugees and asylum-seekers in Turkey appeared to be at risk of forcible return to Iran. A group of 100 members and supporters of Iranian political opposition groups were rounded up by the Turkish authorities in January and driven to the Iranian border. Their forcible return was only prevented after the intervention of the Office of the United Nations (UN) High Commissioner for Refugees and a local branch of the THRA. Fears for the security of Iranian asylum-seekers were heightened in September when a protocol was concluded between the Governments of Turkey and Iran regarding border security and the activities of opposition groups.

During the year there were more than 100 apparently deliberate and arbitrary killings attributed to guerrillas of the PKK. Many of the victims were civilians, killed for allegedly assisting the security forces or passing information to them. PKK guerrillas also captured and then "executed" members of the village guard corps (a paramilitary force organized by the government to deny the PKK access to logistical support from the rural population). According to newspaper reports, in October PKK guerrillas reportedly entered the village of Cevizdali, Bitlis Province, and disarmed the village guards. Shortly afterwards, a small group of guerrillas on the far side of the village exchanged fire with reinforcements from a nearby security post. At the sound of gunshots, the main party of guerrillas reportedly opened fire on the assembled villagers, killing 37 people including children. Other armed opposition groups, including *Türkiye İhtilalcı Komünist Birliği* (TIKB), Revolutionary Communist Union of Turkey, and *Devrimci Sol*, carried out deliberate and arbitrary killings of alleged informers.

Amnesty International published reports summarizing the organization's concerns in May and November – *Turkey: Torture, extrajudicial executions, "disappearances"* and *Turkey: Walls of Glass*. The organization appealed for the release of prisoners of conscience. It called for thoroughgoing reform of detention procedures and repeatedly urged the government to initiate full and impartial investigations into allegations of torture and extrajudicial executions. An Amnesty International delegate observed a hearing of the trial of Sekvan Aytu at Diyarbakır State Security Court.

Amnesty International continued to raise concerns about the protection of Iranian refugees and asylum-seekers. The organization also sought assurances from the Turkish authorities that the new measures concerning refugees contained in the protocol with the Iranian Government would neither obstruct the individual's right to seek protection in Turkey, nor allow for the *refoulement* (forcible return) of any Iranian who risked serious human rights violations in Iran.

In oral statements to the UN Commission on Human Rights in February and to its Sub-Commission on Prevention of Discrimination and Protection of Minorities in August Amnesty International included reference to its concerns in Turkey. In April the organization submitted information about its concerns in Turkey for UN review under a procedure, established by Economic and Social Council Resolutions 728F/1503, for confidential consideration of communications about human rights violations.

# TURKMENISTAN

**At least 11 government opponents spent short periods under house arrest; they were prisoners of conscience. At least four death sentences were passed and at least four executions were carried out.**

Turkmenistan's independence, declared in October 1991, was recognized internationally following the dissolution of the Soviet Union. Headed by President Saparmurad Niyazov, Turkmenistan became a member of the Conference on Security and Co-operation in Europe in January and the United Nations in March. A new Constitution was adopted in May.

Eight members of the non-violent opposition *Agzybirlik* movement were placed under house arrest during the last week of October. All were prisoners of conscience. Ak-Mukhammed Velsapar, Khudayberdi Khalli, Nurberdi Nurmamedov, Klych Yarmammedov, Yusup Kadyrov, Aman Goshayev, Tuvak Takhatov and Akbabek Atayeva were released without charge after a few days. Sources suggested that they were detained because of contacts with Amnesty International representatives visiting Turkmenistan and because the authorities wished to prevent any possible disruption by the opposition of official celebrations of the first anniversary of Turkmenistan's independence declaration. Ak-Mukhammed Velsapar, Khudayberdi Khalli, Nurberdi Nurmamedov and Aman Goshayev were again put under house arrest briefly in early December, as were several others: they included Mukhamedmurat Salamatov, an independent newspaper editor; Amana Govshudova, a member of the unregistered Party of Democratic Development; and Shokhrat Kadyrov, a political scientist. All were put under house arrest to prevent them attending a human rights conference in Kyrgyzstan, and were released shortly after the conference ended.

The Turkmenistan Criminal Code retained the death penalty for 18 peacetime offences. At least four death sentences were passed and at least four executions were carried out.

Amnesty International called for the immediate and unconditional release of all those placed under house arrest. It continued to press for abolition of the death penalty.

An Amnesty International delegation which visited Turkmenistan in October was held for questioning by police and expelled from the country, officially because their visas were invalid. Amnesty International protested to the Turkmen authorities about the expulsion of its delegation, pointing out that the delegates' visas had been issued by the Embassy of the Russian Federation in London, which was empowered to issue visa documentation for all member countries of the Commonwealth of Independent States.

# UGANDA

Nineteen prisoners of conscience were freed; five after they were acquitted and the remainder after treason charges against them were dropped. Treason charges against more than 90 other people, including possible prisoners of conscience, were also dropped. However, at least 100 prisoners charged with treason remained in custody at the end of the year. At least 100 detainees remained in unlawful detention without charge or trial but over 150 others were released. Over 1,300 people sentenced in 1991 to prison terms after unfair military hearings were released. There were reports of torture and ill-treatment of detainees in military custody, and several detainees allegedly died as a result of torture. Several extrajudicial executions by government troops were reported. At least nine death sentences were passed by the High Court and at least one soldier was executed after an unfair military trial.

The government of President Yoweri Museveni continued to face armed opposition in the north and east, but on a smaller scale than in previous years. In the southwest military action against the armed opposition National Army for the Liberation of Uganda (NALU) was intensified. Rebel groups committed serious human rights abuses.

Steps were taken by the authorities during the year to curb human rights abuse; soldiers implicated in the killing of prisoners were arrested and prisoners arrested by the army were released. However, the government's National Resistance Army (NRA) continued to commit serious human rights violations.

**294**

In January treason charges against 14 northern political leaders, who were among 18 prisoners of conscience arrested in 1991, were dropped and they were freed (see *Amnesty International Report 1992*). The cases of the four others, who included Andrew Adimola, Vice-Chairman of the Democratic Party (DP), were referred to the High Court. A few days later the authorities arrested Robert Kitariko, the DP's Secretary General, and Ojok Mulozi, the party's Publicity Secretary, and also charged them with treason. In May, however, the High Court acquitted five of the six defendants. However, one, Tiberio Atwoma Okeny, leader of the National Liberal Party, faced a second treason charge with Irene Apiu Julu, a DP member of parliament. Within days these charges were also dropped and the two were freed.

In May the Inspector General of Government (IGG), Uganda's human rights Ombudsman, published the main findings of an investigation into the arrests of the 18 northern political leaders in 1991. The investigation found that the prisoners had been ill-treated and concluded that the arrests had taken place on the orders of the Minister of State for Defence, on the basis of insufficient evidence. In November the Minister was dismissed.

Since 1988 the authorities had used treason charges, which automatically preclude the granting of bail for 480 days, as a means of holding suspected government opponents for long periods without bringing them to trial. During 1992 a review of treason cases was initiated and charges against over 90 people were withdrawn. Among them were Joseph Lusse and eight others who had been arrested in late 1988 and held without charge until January 1990 (see *Amnesty International Report 1992*). The nine were released on bail in May 1992 and the charges against them were dropped in September. Also in September, 59 prisoners arrested in the north between March and May 1991 and charged with treason in October 1991 were released. Four prisoners arrested with them had died in custody during 1992 (see *Amnesty International Report 1992*).

At the end of the year over 100 prisoners charged with treason, some of whose cases were apparently still to be reviewed, remained in custody. They included 11 NRA soldiers arrested in January 1990 but not charged until March 1991.

At least 100 other suspected government opponents were held without charge or trial throughout 1992, but over 150 were released during the year. The vast majority of detainees had been arrested by the NRA, both in areas affected by armed opposition and in other parts of the country, often on the basis of little or no evidence.

Dozens of suspected opponents were arrested during the year and held in military barracks. In January, for example, Anthony Oracha, the Secretary of the West Acholi Cooperative Union in Gulu, and three of his sons were arrested by NRA soldiers and kept in army custody on suspicion of being rebels. All had been released uncharged by the end of the year. In February and March, 12 Sudanese refugees were arrested by NRA soldiers in Kampala and refugee camps at Adjumani in Moyo District. The 12 were held in Lubiri barracks in Kampala. They were not referred to court and no reason was given for their arrest, although it was apparently in connection with splits within the Sudan People's Liberation Army (SPLA), a Sudanese armed opposition group. Five were released in April but seven were held until August. Fifteen Sudanese asylum-seekers, including four prominent critics of the SPLA leadership who had escaped from SPLA detention in southern Sudan, were detained by the NRA in Arua in September but were released in November.

In June officials stated that there were 200 suspected government opponents detained without charge or trial in civil prisons. In August, 133 long-term detainees, some held since 1986, were released. According to the government, these prisoners represented the last "lodgers" – prisoners detained by the army in the war zones of the north and east and "lodged" in civil prisons. However, in September it emerged that seven "lodgers" were still in detention in Luzira. It was unclear whether the other 60 "lodgers" acknowledged to be in detention earlier in the year were still in custody in other prisons.

Over 100 other detainees, some arrested for political reasons, remained uncharged in military barracks at the end of the year. The majority were members of the NRA and former members of previous government armies. The authorities described the detainees as "army deserters" but they included suspected government opponents.

In August the authorities announced the pardon and release of 1,369 prisoners who in 1991 had been sentenced to terms of imprisonment for desertion from the NRA although they had not received a fair trial (see *Amnesty International Report 1992*). The prisoners, who included civilians, had been detained in mass round-ups during counter-insurgency operations in the north. In April the authorities promised to review their cases after a protest by 200 prisoners who said they were NRA soldiers who had been on authorized leave at the time of their arrest.

Torture and ill-treatment of detainees by soldiers were frequently reported and at least four detainees died allegedly as a result. In some cases those alleged to be responsible were arrested – but it was not known whether any soldiers had been tried by the end of the year. Former detainees at Lubiri barracks reported that prisoners were routinely beaten during their initial interrogation and as a form of punishment at the barracks.

In February Jimmy Okello, a police corporal, was reportedly beaten with a whip by an NRA officer at the time of his arrest in northern Uganda. He was then given 30 strokes of the cane by another soldier – a summary and unlawful punishment – before being set free. No action was known to have been taken to bring the soldiers responsible to justice.

In March a woman was beaten by soldiers after being detained at Kitgum Matidi in the north. She died shortly after her release. The Ugandan press reported that eight soldiers had been arrested and charged with her murder.

In April Alphael Moses Alungat died in military custody apparently as a result of torture. After his arrest in Atiri in Tororo District, he was bound by his wrists and ankles, hung upside-down from a tree and interrogated before a crowd of witnesses. Soldiers then took him away and two days later his relatives were told he had escaped. However, his body was returned to his family with an autopsy report attributing his death to a heart attack. A subsequent independent post-mortem concluded that he had died as a result of torture. Five soldiers were later charged with his murder.

Several extrajudicial executions by NRA soldiers in the north and east were reported, although significantly fewer than in previous years. In January soldiers searching for insurgents in Gulu District were said to have detained and then extrajudicially executed three men at an NRA post at Palenga. No investigation was known to have taken place.

In April NRA soldiers at Olelai in Soroti District reportedly extrajudicially executed John Otim and three other men and disposed of their bodies in a pit latrine. Two soldiers were arrested later that month in connection with the incident. In mid-May seven civilians were executed by NRA soldiers in Palebek, Kitgum District. In mid-July, 11 soldiers were arrested and charged with their murder.

In May the Attorney General announced at a press conference that a number of soldiers had been arrested in connection with past extrajudicial executions, including the killing of 69 youths in a railway wagon at Mukura in 1989 (see *Amnesty International Report 1990*). Among those he implicated was an officer who had remained at large until arrested in 1992 in connection with the death of Alphael Moses Alungat (see above). However, none of them had been brought to trial by the end of the year. In July 1989, immediately after the incident at Mukura, the authorities had similarly announced the arrest of soldiers. It appeared, however, that in practice soldiers often escaped prosecution.

At least nine prisoners were sentenced to death by the High Court for murder. The Supreme Court upheld death sentences against two men convicted of murder, bringing to over 50 the number of people under sentence of death in Luzira Prison whose sentences, which had been imposed by ordinary civilian courts, had been upheld on appeal.

One soldier, Stephen Egunyu, was executed in January on the day a Field Court Martial in Soroti District found him guilty of murdering a pregnant woman, an incident which had occurred the day before. He had no defence counsel or right of appeal. Over 100 soldiers were under sentence of death in Luzira after convictions by military courts in previous years.

Human rights abuses were committed by armed opposition groups, including deliberate and arbitrary killings, mutilation of captives and rape. For example, in May Uganda Democratic Christian Army (UDCA) insurgents abducted and killed three teenage girls in Gulu District. In the east,

**296**

rebels from the Uganda People's Army (UPA) killed several captured civilians during an attack on Bukudea town in Kumi District in which 12 people died. In September NALU rebels tortured and then killed civilians in attacks on villages in Kasese District in the southwest.

During the year Amnesty International urged the government to release prisoners of conscience, review the cases of all those charged with treason, and mount impartial and prompt investigations into reported extrajudicial executions.

In September Amnesty International published a report, *Uganda: The failure to safeguard human rights*, which recognized positive steps taken by the government since it took power in 1986, but highlighted the continuing pattern of extrajudicial executions, unlawful detentions, torture, misuse of serious charges such as treason, and the death penalty. It concluded that the government had failed to respond adequately to such violations and included a comprehensive set of recommendations aimed at stopping human rights violations. The report also described human rights abuses by insurgents. In a 15-page response issued in September, the authorities described Amnesty International's report as politically biased and out of date, but failed to address the substantive issues raised by Amnesty International.

In an oral statement to the United Nations (UN) Commission on Human Rights in February, Amnesty International included reference to its concerns in Uganda. In April Amnesty International submitted information about its concerns in Uganda for UN review under a procedure, established by Economic and Social Council Resolutions 728F/1503, for confidential consideration of communications about human rights violations.

# UKRAINE

**One known prisoner of conscience, a conscientious objector to military service, was held until March. At least four people were executed, and at least 13 people were believed to be under sentence of death at the end of the year.**

Ukraine gained international recognition as an independent state following the break-up of the Soviet Union. Headed by President Leonid Kravchuk, the country, already a member of the United Nations, joined the Conference on Security and Cooperation in Europe in January.

From February, for the first time, a civilian alternative to military service became available. However, it was open only to religious believers and its length was set at twice that for military service. In June the death penalty was abolished for two economic crimes, thereby reducing its scope to five offences, all involving the use of violence.

Prisoner of conscience Sergey Osnach was released in March from an 18-month sentence of compulsory labour imposed in June 1991 for his refusal on grounds of conscience to perform obligatory military service. Compulsory labour involved working under strict surveillance at a location determined by the authorities, with restrictions on freedom of movement. Unofficial sources reported that several dozen people who had been sentenced for refusing to perform military service on religious grounds were released in November.

At least four people were executed after their petitions for clemency had been turned down. All had been convicted of murder. At least 13 people were believed to be under sentence of death at the end of the year. No statistics were issued on the application of the death penalty, and the true number of death sentences passed and carried out was probably much higher.

Throughout the year Amnesty International urged the authorities to commute all death sentences and to publish comprehensive statistics on the application of the death penalty. The organization called for the release of Sergey Osnach. It called for the civilian alternative to military service not to be punitive in length and to be open to all those with political, ethical or other conscientiously held objections. No replies to any letters had been received by the end of the year.

# UNITED ARAB EMIRATES

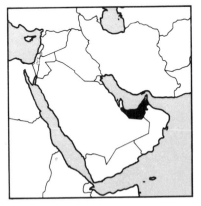

**Ten Indian nationals sentenced to six-year prison terms for allegedly insulting Islam were prisoners of conscience. Two Iraqi nationals who were detained without charge or trial for several months also appeared to be prisoners of conscience. One prisoner was sentenced to the amputation of his hand and two others to floggings. At least six people were sentenced to death but no executions were reported.**

Ten Indian nationals were arrested in June for their involvement in a play staged at the Indian Association in Sharjah in May. The play was considered to be insulting to Islam and the prophets Mohammad and Jesus. In October, eight actors, a video photographer and the President of the Indian Association were convicted of blasphemy by a Sharjah court and each sentenced to six-year prison terms followed by deportation.

At least two Iraqi nationals were detained without charge or trial during the year, apparently for political reasons in connection with the 1991 Gulf War. They were arrested on separate occasions when they tried to renew their residence permits. One was held from October 1991 to the end of February 1992, and the other was arrested in January 1992 and held in incommunicado detention for at least three months.

A Syrian national was convicted of theft and sentenced to the amputation of his hand by an Abu Dhabi court in July. In August a Ras al-Khaimah court sentenced a Pakistani man to a flogging of 60 lashes and four months' imprisonment and a woman, whose identity was not revealed, to 90 lashes and 18 months' imprisonment: both had been convicted of adultery.

In September the federal government introduced the death penalty for drug-trafficking. In October a Sharjah court sentenced three Pakistani nationals to death under the new law. Three people convicted of rape were sentenced to death: two in July and one in November. No executions were reported.

Amnesty International appealed to the Minister of Justice for the release of the 10 prisoners of conscience. It urged the government of President Shaikh Zayed bin Sultan Al Nahayan to commute all death sentences and not to widen the use of the death penalty. The organization called for punishments such as flogging and amputation to be replaced by an alternative form of punishment which does not amount to cruel, inhuman or degrading treatment. Amnesty International received a detailed response from the President expressing confidence in the death penalty's deterrent effect on serious crimes and questioning the effectiveness of alternative forms of punishment. He also gave assurances as to the fairness of appeals procedures in capital cases under United Arab Emirates law.

# UNITED KINGDOM

**The courts continued to review cases of alleged miscarriages of justice in England and Northern Ireland. Allegations of ill-treatment continued. Six people were killed in suspicious circumstances in Northern Ireland by security forces. Evidence of collusion between Loyalist paramilitary organizations and security forces in Northern Ireland was revealed in the courts and media. Armed groups arbitrarily and deliberately killed civilians in Northern Ireland and England.**

In Northern Ireland, violent conflict intensified as Republican groups and security forces clashed, and both Republican and Loyalist armed groups carried out torture and killings. Republican armed groups, notably the Irish Republican Army (IRA), which are predominantly Catholic, seek a British withdrawal from Northern Ireland. This aim is opposed by Loyalist armed groups from the Protestant community, notably the Ulster Volunteer Force (UVF) and the Ulster Defence Association (UDA) which acts under the name of the Ulster Freedom Fighters (UFF). In August the government outlawed the UDA following a wave of sectarian killings.

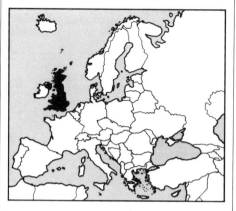

In June the Court of Appeal quashed the conviction of Judith Ward, who had been sentenced to life imprisonment for a 1974 IRA bombing in England on confession and scientific evidence which was later discredited. The court criticized members of the police, the prosecution, and psychiatric and scientific experts for failing to disclose key evidence during the original trial.

In July the Northern Ireland Court of Appeal quashed the convictions of three soldiers from the Ulster Defence Regiment (UDR), a regiment of the British Army recruited and based in Northern Ireland, and upheld that of a fourth. The "UDR 4" had been sentenced to life imprisonment in 1986 for the murder of a Catholic man. The Court of Appeal concluded that policemen had falsified interview notes and given untruthful testimony at the trial. The three had been convicted solely on the basis of confessions allegedly obtained through ill-treatment and coercion during incommunicado detention. The court upheld the fourth conviction on the grounds that there was sufficient other evidence of Neil Latimer's guilt.

People continued to be convicted in one-judge, juryless "Diplock Courts" in Northern Ireland on the basis of disputed and uncorroborated confessions. Courts drew adverse inferences against defendants for having remained silent during police questioning or at trial.

Police officers were committed for trial charged with conspiring to pervert the course of justice in the "Birmingham Six" and "Guildford Four" cases. The May Inquiry issued a second report in December recommending the establishment of an independent body to investigate alleged miscarriages of justice. The report concluded that the "Maguire Seven" had been victims of a serious miscarriage of justice. (See previous *Amnesty International Reports*).

In May the Director of Public Prosecutions (DPP) stated that insufficient evidence existed to bring prosecutions against any officers from the West Midlands Serious Crimes Squad. The squad had been disbanded in 1989 after allegations that some officers had fabricated evidence or committed perjury in order to obtain convictions. Twelve people investigated by the squad had had convictions for serious offences quashed since 1989.

There were frequent allegations that police and military patrols in Northern Ireland ill-treated people they stopped on the streets, and some allegations of ill-treatment at interrogation centres. Six members of the Parachute Regiment of the British Army were charged in connection with violence and assaults in the Tyrone area in April and May.

Allegations of ill-treatment by police in Britain were also made, among others by racial and ethnic minorities and by homosexuals; some victims were awarded civil damages.

Six civilians were killed in disputed circumstances by the security forces in Northern Ireland. Two soldiers were charged with murder after shooting Peter McBride, an unarmed Catholic, shortly after he was stopped and searched on 4 September. An investigation began into the killing on 25 November of Pearse Jordan by officers of the Northern Ireland police force, the Royal Ulster Constabulary (RUC). Eye-witnesses stated that Pearse Jordan, an unarmed IRA member, was shot dead without warning, after two unmarked police vehicles forced his car off the road.

Disputed killings that occurred in 1990 and 1991 remained unresolved. No trial had begun of security force personnel charged in 1992 with the murders of Kevin McGovern and Fergal Caraher and with the attempted murder of Míceál Caraher. The DPP decided not to prosecute undercover soldiers for the killing of John McNeill, Edward Hale and Peter Thompson, or police officers involved in the killing of Gerard Maginn (see *Amnesty International Reports 1991* and *1992*). An inquest held in April into the killing of UVF member Brian Robinson found that undercover soldiers shot him "at close proximity" while he lay on the ground (see *Amnesty International Report 1991*).

An inquest into the 1982 killings of Gervaise McKerr, Eugene Toman and Sean Burns began in May. An Amnesty International delegate attended part of the proceedings. After 18 days of hearings, the inquest was further delayed due to legal challenges concerning the withholding of documents from the inquest. The government issued Public Interest Immunity certificates which exempted from disclosure documents relating to the killings (see *Amnesty International Report 1989*).

Brian Nelson, a military intelligence agent who was also chief intelligence officer for the UDA, was convicted in January of four conspiracies to murder and 28 other charges. He was sentenced to 10 years' imprisonment. His duties for the UDA included obtaining information on Republicans and providing it to gunmen. At the same time he provided information about planned killings to army intelligence; it was alleged that 18 people were killed by Loyalists during this time. The government did not announce any investigation into revelations attributed to Brian Nelson about official collusion in the targeting of Republicans for killings.

In contrast, the government pursued with determination a Channel Four/Box Productions team over a television program, shown in November 1991, on alleged collusion. While rejecting calls for an independent inquiry, a barrage of other measures was taken to discredit the allegations and to require Channel Four to reveal its sources. It included unprecedented charges of contempt under the Prevention of Terrorism Act, and perjury charges (which were subsequently dropped) against the researcher of the program, Ben Hamilton.

In March the Isle of Man parliament voted to amend the Sexual Offences Bill to legalize homosexual acts in private between men over the age of 21.

By the end of 1992, Sikh asylum-seeker Karamjit Singh Chahal had spent 28 months in prison without charge or trial, challenging a deportation order issued on "national security" grounds. If deported to India, he feared torture (see *Amnesty International Report 1992*). A further judicial review of the refusal of his asylum application was pending.

Civilians in Northern Ireland were targeted by violent political organizations for their religion or their real or suspected political views.

During the year Loyalist armed groups claimed responsibility for killing 34 people, including 29 Catholic civilians. Five people, including a 15-year-old youth, were killed when UFF/UDA gunmen opened fire in a betting shop in a Catholic area of Belfast. A Catholic woman was shot dead by the UFF/UDA who wrongly claimed that her brother was a member of the legal Republican party, Sinn Fein. Among the victims of UVF shootings were an elderly couple and a Sinn Fein activist. Forty men were hospitalized after being shot in the limbs; others were beaten as punishment.

Twenty-nine people were reportedly killed in Northern Ireland by the IRA: nine members of the security forces and 20 civilians. A van carrying Protestant building workers on a government contract was blown up by an IRA bomb in January; eight workers were killed and six injured. Armed Republican groups subjected a number of people to punishment beatings and 36 men were shot in the limbs; the IRA ordered others to leave Northern Ireland or face torture. Four civilians were killed in IRA attacks in England. The Irish People's Liberation Organisation (IPLO), an armed Republican group, disbanded in November; it claimed responsibility for five deaths in 1992.

Amnesty International sent a delegate to the appeal hearing of the "UDR 4", which began in Belfast in May. Given clear evidence of police misconduct during the interrogation of all four men, and conflicting eye-witness accounts, the organization concluded that Neil Latimer's case should be the subject of further review.

In November Amnesty International sent an observer to the trial of seven men charged in connection with the 1988 "Casement Park" incident in which two armed plainclothes British army corporals,

**300**

who drove their car into Caoimhín Mac Brádaigh's funeral procession in Belfast, were dragged from the car by a crowd, beaten and later shot by two IRA members. Caoimhín Mac Brádaigh was one of three people killed three days earlier by a Loyalist who attacked the funeral of the "Gibraltar Three" (see *Amnesty International Report 1989*). Members of the crowd claimed that the sudden intrusion of the soldiers' car into the procession caused panic that another Loyalist attack was about to begin. By the end of 1992, a total of 41 people had been charged in connection with the incident and five people (none of whom was alleged to have shot the soldiers) had been sentenced to life imprisonment for murder. Amnesty International was concerned that in seven previous group trials relating to the Casement Park incident, many convictions had been based on disputed uncorroborated confessions, the drawing of adverse inferences against defendants for remaining silent, controversial video evidence and the disparate application of the "common purpose" principle.

In November Amnesty International produced a report, *Fair Trial Concerns in Northern Ireland: the Right of Silence*. The organization concluded that the Criminal Evidence (Northern Ireland) Order 1988, which allows the drawing of adverse inferences against an accused person for remaining silent in the face of police questioning or at trial, is inconsistent with the guarantees of presumption of innocence and the right not to testify against oneself or confess guilt. Amnesty International urged the government to repeal the Order.

During a visit to Northern Ireland in April, Amnesty International delegates found that the number of allegations of ill-treatment in interrogation centres had decreased significantly since August 1991, after international publicity and protest over reported abuse. The organization remained concerned that safeguards proposed by the government in 1991 had not been fully implemented, including statutory codes governing arrest, detention and questioning of suspects. A Commissioner to monitor procedures in police holding centres was, however, appointed in December. Amnesty International urged the government to reform interrogation and detention procedures.

Amnesty International investigated cases of alleged ill-treatment in Northern Ireland and Britain, including the forcible strip-searching of 21 Republican women prisoners in their cells at Maghaberry prison in March.

In August Amnesty International submitted written comments to the European Court of Human Rights in the case of Brannigan and McBride, which concerned the applicants' detention in Northern Ireland under the Prevention of Terrorism Act. Amnesty International emphasized that fundamental safeguards of prompt access to lawyers and judges are essential to ensure the prevention of ill-treatment, particularly during states of emergency.

Amnesty International observed the trial of Brian Nelson in January and the High Court hearing in the Channel Four case in July. In October the organization wrote to the government expressing concern that it had not taken adequate steps to halt collusion between members of the security forces and Loyalist armed groups in Northern Ireland, to investigate thoroughly and make known the full truth about political killings of suspected government opponents, to bring to justice the perpetrators, or otherwise to deter such killings. The government rejected this: it stated that although measures to prevent the disclosure of classified information had been taken, it would be impossible to prevent collusion or leakage of classified information, given the situation in Northern Ireland.

In February Amnesty International delegates visited the Isle of Man because of concern that existing legislation allowed for the prosecution and imprisonment of adult men for engaging in consensual homosexual acts in private. In March Amnesty International wrote to the Isle of Man Government opposing imprisonment on these grounds.

In July Amnesty International wrote to the government opposing Karamjit Singh Chahal's threatened deportation and expressing concern at his prolonged detention without charge or trial.

Amnesty International appealed for a halt to the deliberate and arbitrary killing, torture, and maiming of civilians by armed groups.

# UNITED STATES OF AMERICA

**Thirty-one prisoners were executed, more than in any one year since executions were resumed in 1977. More than 2,600 prisoners were under sentence of death in 34 states. Four states carried out their first executions in a quarter-century or more. All 33 conscientious objectors to the Gulf conflict adopted as prisoners of conscience were released after serving their sentences. There were reports of torture, ill-treatment and excessive force by police or prison officials. New appeals were lodged in the cases of several prisoners who alleged that their prosecutions were racially or politically motivated. Thousands of Haitian asylum-seekers were forcibly returned to Haiti without a hearing.**

In November Bill Clinton, a Democrat, was elected to succeed Republican George Bush as President of the United States of America (USA) in January 1993.

The USA ratified the International Covenant on Civil and Political Rights in June. However, it entered a large number of reservations in which it did not accept all of the terms in several non-derogable articles, including Article 6 on the right to life, and Article 7 prohibiting torture and other cruel, inhuman or degrading treatment or punishment.

Thirty-one prisoners were executed, bringing the number of executions since 1977 to 188. Arizona, California, Delaware and Wyoming carried out their first executions in 25 years or more (the first for 46 years in the case of Delaware). Texas had the largest number of executions; others were carried out in Alabama, Arkansas,

Florida, Missouri, North Carolina, Oklahoma, Utah and Virginia.

In February in Texas Johnny Garrett became the fifth juvenile offender to be executed in the USA since the death penalty was reinstated, in violation of international standards which prohibit the execution of people aged under 18 at the time of the crime.

Johnny Garrett was convicted of raping and murdering an elderly nun in 1981 when he was aged 17. He had been sexually and physically abused as a child and had sustained severe head injuries resulting in brain damage. He was described by a psychiatrist as "one of the most psychiatrically impaired inmates" she had ever examined and by a psychologist as having "one of the most virulent histories of abuse and neglect … encountered in over 28 years of practice". The Texas Board of Pardons and Paroles denied clemency despite appeals from the convent of the murdered nun and religious leaders.

At least six other prisoners suffering from mental illness, brain damage or mental retardation were executed, in violation of United Nations (UN) guidelines.

They included Ricky Rector, who was executed in Arkansas in January despite being severely brain damaged from shooting himself in the head after killing a police officer (the crime for which he was later sentenced to death) and subsequently undergoing a frontal lobotomy. The Supreme Court denied a petition for federal review of his mental competence to be executed.

Witnesses reported hearing loud moans from the chamber where Ricky Rector was executed by lethal injection, as technicians searched for nearly an hour to find a suitable vein in which to insert the needle.

Many of the executed prisoners had received inadequate legal representation at their trials, with court-appointed lawyers failing, for example, to present crucial mitigating evidence to the sentencing hearing, including a history of mental illness or abuse.

Roger Coleman was executed in Virginia in May for the rape and murder of his sister-in-law in 1982. The execution went ahead despite doubts which had been raised about his guilt. He had been represented at trial by lawyers who had never handled a murder or rape case before and who failed to investigate many points of

**302**

evidence. His appeal lawyers inadvertently filed an appeal to the state court one day too late, resulting in its dismissal on procedural grounds. The US Supreme Court dismissed his appeal in June 1991.

All 33 conscientious objectors adopted by Amnesty International as prisoners of conscience for refusing to participate in the Gulf conflict had completed their sentences and been released by the end of the year.

There were allegations of torture, ill-treatment or excessive force, including lethal force, by police or prison officials across the country.

In April, four officers of the Los Angeles Police Department (LAPD) charged under California law in connection with the beating of a black motorist in March 1991 (see *Amnesty International Report 1992*) were acquitted in a controversial jury decision which led to serious rioting in Los Angeles. The officers were later indicted on federal civil rights charges arising from the beating, trial of which was pending at the end of the year.

In July an inquiry into the Los Angeles County Sheriff's Department (LASD) conducted by Judge Kolts (the Kolts inquiry) found a serious problem of excessive force, including physical brutality and unjustified shootings of unarmed suspects by patrol officers as well as ill-treatment of jail inmates. The inquiry found that the lack of discipline in many cases and inadequacies in the investigation of complaints suggested that the department was "tolerant" of excessive force. It made a number of recommendations for improving the complaints and disciplinary process. The LASD accepted only some of the recommendations.

Trial in a civil rights action against Sheriff's deputies from the Lynwood police station, Los Angeles, was still pending at the end of the year (see *Amnesty International Report 1992*).

In July a juvenile court quashed the confession of a 13-year-old murder defendant who alleged he was subjected to electric shocks while being interrogated by Chicago detectives in September 1991. One of a group of teenagers arrested after a shooting, he was reportedly interrogated over a 24-hour period without a responsible adult present, contrary to state law and police guidelines relating to minors.

In March the Chicago police department concluded hearings into allegations that

three officers had tortured a murder suspect in 1982, but no result had been given by the end of the year. The department's Office of Professional Standards had recommended dismissal of the officers in 1991 after reinvestigating the allegations (see *Amnesty International Report 1992*).

In April Vaughn Dortch, an inmate of Pelican Bay Prison, California, suffered severe burns which required skin grafts after four guards and a prison medical officer allegedly forced him into a bath of scalding water while he was handcuffed, shackled and gagged. Several months earlier, lawyers had filed a civil rights action on behalf of Pelican Bay prisoners alleging a pattern of cruel treatment, including practices such as chaining mentally disturbed inmates to showers and toilets, shackling inmates for prolonged periods and the use of excessive force, including beatings. The outcome of this action and a criminal investigation into the April incident was pending at the end of the year.

David Carriger, an inmate of the Northwest Correctional Center, Vermont, was found dead in his cell in July after he had been involved in an altercation with guards. A prisoner alleged that he had been choked and beaten by guards and left unattended and shackled for an hour, despite being injured and apparently unconscious. Prison and civil liberties groups questioned the independence of an internal prison inquiry into the incident which found that no excessive force had been used; they claimed to have received numerous reports of beatings, medical neglect and other abuses at the prison and called for a full investigation into all these complaints. No further action had been taken by the end of the year.

There were complaints of ill-treatment of inmates at the Maximum Control Complex (MCC) of Westville Prison, Indiana, which opened in 1991 to house prisoners with serious disciplinary problems. Complaints included the lack of social contact between inmates, inadequate exercise, plus alleged beatings and inappropriate use of restraints.

In September and October three Native American inmates of the Young Adult Correctional Facility in Utah were confined to their cells for 24 hours a day and threatened with transfer to a maximum security prison when they refused for religious reasons to comply with an order to cut their hair. Amnesty International expressed the view that placing them in lockdown under the circumstances could amount to cruel, inhuman or degrading punishment.

A federal investigation into allegations of ill-treatment of prisoners at Montana State Penitentiary following a riot in September 1991 ended in October, when the US Justice Department reported that no criminal civil rights charges would be brought as it had found no evidence that guards had engaged in malicious or unjustified acts. A National Institution of Corrections inquiry had earlier reported serious abuses by guards following the riot.

The outcome of an administrative inquiry into complaints of ill-treatment of prisoners at two Connecticut prisons in January and April 1991 was still pending at the end of the year.

An order issued by President Bush in May allowed the US authorities to forcibly return to Haiti all Haitian asylum-seekers intercepted in international waters by the US Coast Guard, without giving any of them an opportunity to apply for asylum or attempting to examine the merits of their claims. By the end of the year, more than 25,000 Haitians had been returned to Haiti under this order. Since late 1991 Haitians intercepted at sea had been brought to the US naval base at Guantanamo, Cuba, where they were "screened" to determine whether they were at risk if returned to Haiti. At the end of the year, the legality of the executive order was being considered by the US Supreme Court.

In November, new arguments were presented in the case of Leonard Peltier, a leader of the American Indian Movement convicted of murder in 1977 (see previous *Amnesty International Reports*). Fifty-five members of the Canadian Parliament supported his appeal, contending that Leonard Peltier had been wrongfully extradited from Canada on false affidavits in 1976.

In June Amnesty International published a report, *USA: Torture, ill-treatment and excessive force by police in Los Angeles, California*. The report suggested that members of the LAPD and LASD regularly resorted to excessive force, particularly in black and latino neighbourhoods. It documented more than 30 cases involving physical brutality, unjustified shootings and the use of police dogs to inflict unwarranted injuries on suspects. The report acknowledged that some steps had been taken to address the problem of excessive force, including implementation of some recommendations made by an independent commission on the LAPD in 1991 (see *Amnesty International Report 1992*). Amnesty International's recommendations included incorporating UN guidelines on the use of force and firearms into police codes of practice, a review of the use of canine units and an independent oversight of complaints against both departments.

In July Amnesty International wrote to the LAPD asking to be informed of the outcome of an inquiry into the fatal police shooting of an unarmed black truck driver, John Daniels Jr, on 1 July. No response had been received by the end of the year.

In October Amnesty International wrote to the LASD and the Los Angeles Board of Supervisors, reiterating its concerns in light of the findings of the Kolts inquiry and urging full implementation of its recommendations.

During the year, Amnesty International wrote to the authorities about allegations of ill-treatment in prisons, including the burning of Vaughn Dortch and conditions in Pelican Bay State Prison; the death of David Carriger and the alleged ill-treatment and medical neglect of other inmates at the Northwest Correctional Center, Vermont; conditions at the MCC, Westville, Indiana; alleged abuses of inmates of Montana State Penitentiary and two Connecticut prisons in 1991 and the punishment of Native American prisoners who refused to cut their hair on religious grounds at the Young Adult Correctional Facility in Utah. Amnesty International also wrote to the federal authorities about the isolation of inmates in the maximum security K-Unit of Marion Prison; and it urged a review of a Washington State prison policy of intimate body searches of women prisoners by male guards. Amnesty International received replies from the prison authorities in Vermont, Indiana and Washington, denying ill-treatment or excessive force in the cases cited. The Warden of Pelican Bay Prison replied that a medical assistant involved in the bathing of Vaughn Dortch had been dismissed and that the other allegations were being investigated by the federal courts. Replies were also received from the Bureau of Prisons about K-Unit of Marion Prison, and from state and federal officials about Montana State Penitentiary.

Amnesty International wrote to the

Attorney General of Mississippi in November, urging that a full, independent inquiry be held into the death of a black youth, Andre Lamond Jones, found hanged in August in a Mississippi jail. Although his death had been ruled a suicide, no inquest was held and family and community members expressed concern about the circumstances. The Attorney General replied that extensive inquiries had been conducted into the case but gave no further information. Amnesty International continued to seek information on the case.

In oral statements to the UN Sub-Commission on Prevention of Discrimination and Protection of Minorities in August and its Working Group on Indigenous Populations in July, Amnesty International included reference to its concerns in the USA. In October Amnesty International published *Human rights violations against the indigenous peoples of the Americas*, which included concerns in the USA. In November Amnesty International published a report, *USA: Human rights and American Indians*. Cases described in the report included prisoners under sentence of death; allegations of ill-treatment; fair trial concerns in the case of Leonard Peltier and concerns surrounding the unsolved murder of an Indian lawyer, Julian Pierce, in North Carolina in 1988.

# URUGUAY

**Beatings and other forms of ill-treatment of criminal suspects by police continued to be reported. Judicial investigations into most reported human rights violations committed in recent years made little progress. The Inter-American Commission on Human Rights ruled that the 1986** Expiry Law which blocked investigations into human rights violations committed before 1986 was incompatible with the American Convention on Human Rights, and called on the government to investigate killings, torture and "disappearances" committed under the military government of the 1970s and early 1980s.

During the year there was a resurgence of clandestine armed groups allegedly linked to the military, which carried out several violent attacks, including bombings. Among the groups claiming responsibility were the *Guardia de Artigas*, Artigas Guard, and the *Comando Juan Antonio Lavalleja*, Juan Antonio Lavalleja Commando, which reportedly said it had been formed by 50 military officers, 15 of them on active duty. Among those whose property was attacked were former President Sanguinetti, the Commander-in-Chief of the Navy and a parliamentary deputy.

Uruguay ratified the Inter-American Convention to Prevent and Punish Torture in November.

New reports of ill-treatment of detainees in police custody were received. At least five of the victims were minors. In some cases, complaints were presented to the courts for investigation, but to Amnesty International's knowledge those responsible were not brought to justice.

Beatings were the most common method of ill-treatment, but other methods were also reported. One man arrested in Artigas in mid-1992 said that he had been deprived of food for three days to make him confess to a murder he had not committed.

In August a 17-year-old mentally handicapped youth shot in the leg as he attempted to flee from police was reportedly beaten on the injured leg while in police custody. His leg was fractured in three places but it was several hours before he received any medical treatment. Two 14-year-old youths arrested in Salto in August alleged that they were beaten on the chest and stomach and made to run around inside the police station. The head of police in Salto later made a public commitment to investigate the incident and punish those responsible, but it was not clear to Amnesty International whether any action was taken.

Little progress was reported in judicial investigations into cases of torture and ill-treatment which had occurred in previous years. In April the United Nations (UN) Committee against Torture recognized the government's commitment to abide by its international obligations but called on it "to prosecute cases of torture which were still outstanding".

In December, following the publication in a national newspaper of photographs claiming to show four detainees chained to their beds in punishment cells in Libertad prison, members of the Human Rights Commission of the House of Representatives visited the prison to investigate these claims, including the authenticity of the photographs, and other allegations of ill-treatment. Allegations were also received that excessive force had been used in a security operation in the prison shortly before the photographs were published. Prisoners said that a group of guards acting without the director's authority were responsible for the ill-treatment. The commission's report on its findings was due in early 1993. A judicial investigation was also initiated.

In its report to the UN Committee against Torture, the government stated that information about the death of 16-year-old Rafael Berón Charquero in Miguelete prison in 1991 had been passed to the judicial authorities, and that as a result of an administrative inquiry two special staff at the prison had been dismissed (see Amnesty International Report 1992). Lawyers acting on behalf of his family presented a civil suit for damages against the state, which was continuing at the end of the year.

In the case of Raúl González, who was shot dead by police in 1991 (see Amnesty International Report 1992), the state agreed to pay substantial damages to his family after acknowledging that one of its employees was responsible for his death.

No steps were taken to bring to justice those responsible for killings, "disappearances" and torture during the period of military rule from 1973 to 1985. In October the Inter-American Commission on Human Rights ruled that the 1986 Expiry Law (see Amnesty International Reports 1988 to 1992) was incompatible with the American Convention on Human Rights. Among other things, it violated the right to a fair trial and the right to court protection against acts that violate fundamental human rights. The Commission recommended that the government take measures to clarify the facts and identify those responsible for human rights violations during the period of military rule.

In May a judge ordered that a blood test should be carried out on a 15-year-old boy to ascertain whether he was the "disappeared" son of Sara Méndez (see Amnesty International Report 1992). Lawyers acting on behalf of the adoptive parents of the boy appealed against the judge's decision to order the blood test against the boy's will. The judge had ruled that under Uruguayan law a minor is not capable of acting "with mature judgement". The appeal was still pending at the end of the year.

# UZBEKISTAN

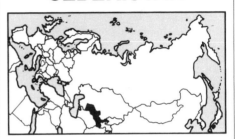

**Several prisoners of conscience were detained. Opponents of the government and independent journalists were assaulted by unidentified attackers, possibly with the complicity of the authorities.**

Uzbekistan's independence, declared in August 1991, was recognized internationally following the dissolution of the Soviet Union. Headed by President Islam Karimov, Uzbekistan became a member of the Conference on Security and Co-operation in Europe in January and the United Nations in March.

Prisoner of conscience Babur Shakirov was arrested in August and charged with "calling for the overthrow of the state and social order" under Article 60 of the Criminal Code. The charge related to his involvement in forming a non-violent social organization called Milli Mejlis, National Council. He had previously been a prisoner of conscience for 10 years under the Soviet government. In December, two other organizers of Milli Mejlis – Khazratkul Khudayberdi and Odanazar Arifov – were arrested on the same charge as Babur Shakirov. The same month human rights activist Abdumannob Pulatov was abducted by Uzbek security officials from a human rights conference in Bishkek, Kyrgyzstan, and forcibly repatriated to Uzbekistan where he was charged with "infringement upon the honour and dignity of the President" under the Criminal Code.

Short-term "administrative arrest", which can be imposed by a judge for up to 15 days without trial or right of appeal, continued to be used to detain people seeking to exercise non-violently their rights to freedom of expression and association. In April, for example, Yusuf Narov, a member of the opposition party *Erk* (Freedom), was placed under "administrative arrest" for five days for taking part in an unsanctioned demonstration. In July Mikhail Ardzinov served 10 days' "administrative arrest" in connection with his activities as deputy chairman of the Human Rights Society of Uzbekistan.

Pulat Akhunov, a probable prisoner of conscience, was sentenced in December to 18 months' imprisonment following conviction on criminal charges which had allegedly been fabricated to punish him for political activities. A deputy chairman of the officially registered opposition movement *Birlik* (Unity), he was arrested in July and charged with assault. Sources claimed that the alleged assault victim should have been serving a custodial sentence for rape and robbery at the time of the alleged assault, and had named Pulat Akhunov as his assailant at the prompting of police.

There were at least seven incidents of serious physical assault on opposition leaders or independent journalists by unidentified attackers. In June *Birlik* chairman Abdurakhim Pulatov needed emergency hospital treatment for skull fractures after four men attacked him and a companion with metal bars as they left an interview at a police station in the capital, Tashkent. It was alleged that local law enforcement authorities looked on while the attack took place.

The Uzbekistan Criminal Code retained the death penalty for 19 peacetime offences. However, senior officials stated in April that regulations introduced in December 1991 had reduced the number of offences which in practice still carried the death penalty to four: treason; premeditated, aggravated murder; murder of a minor; and aggravated rape. No death sentences were known to have been passed.

Amnesty International appealed for the release of Babur Shakirov, Khazratkul Khudayberdi, Odanazar Arifov and Abdumannob Pulatov. It sought further information from the authorities about the case of Pulat Akhunov. In July Amnesty International urged the authorities to ensure that the assaults on opposition figures and journalists were fully investigated and every effort made to identify and bring to justice those responsible. Amnesty International continued to press the authorities to abolish the death penalty.

In April Amnesty International representatives visited Uzbekistan for the first time. They met government ministers and other officials and discussed the death penalty and prospects for constitutional and legislative reform.

# VENEZUELA

Scores of people, including prisoners of conscience, were arrested during periods of suspended guarantees which followed coup attempts in February and November. The frequent use of torture by the security forces, sometimes leading to the death of the detainee, continued to be reported. Prison conditions remained extremely harsh. At least one person "disappeared". Dozens of people were extrajudicially executed by members of the armed forces.

On 4 February a faction of the army unsuccessfully attempted to overthrow the government of President Carlos Andrés Pérez. The coup leaders were arrested and at the end of the year 68 military officers allegedly involved in the coup attempt remained in prison. On 27 November a second coup attempt was foiled. Dozens of people were killed during fighting and at least 200 members of the armed forces and some civilians were arrested. On both occasions the government immediately suspended a series of constitutional guarantees for several weeks, including the right not to be arrested or imprisoned without warrant unless caught *in flagrante delicto*. In November it also imposed a curfew for five days.

There were widespread anti-government protests in March and April prompted by harsh economic conditions and dozens of demonstrations by students and others during the year. At least 15 people were killed by the security forces during the suppression of the protests.

During the periods of suspended guarantees the security forces carried out raids in several cities and detained hundreds of people for short periods, including prisoners of conscience. Those detained included student leaders, members of political parties and community activists.

Following the 27 November coup attempt, at least 200 members of the armed forces and some civilians, including prisoners of conscience, were arrested. They were charged with participating in a military rebellion and summarily tried by military courts in December. Most of the defendants were denied access to an independent lawyer.

During the periods of full guarantees, the police carried out scores of arbitrary arrests, particularly in the *barrios* (poor urban neighbourhoods). For example, in May the military intelligence agency *Dirección de Inteligencia Militar* (DIM) and the police intelligence agency *Dirección de los Servicios de Inteligencia y Prevención* (DISIP) arrested without warrant at least 27 student and political activists, among them former political prisoner Eder Puerta Aponte. Most were released hours later, but at least three were detained for more than two weeks without charge. Hundreds of other people were denied their right to a fair trial by being administratively detained under the *Ley de Vagos y Maleantes*, Law of Vagrants and Crooks, which permits administrative detention for periods of up to five years without judicial appeal or review. Most of those detained under this law are subjected to cruel, inhuman or degrading conditions in establishments which lack adequate sanitary facilities and detainees are frequently victims of torture and ill-treatment by prison wardens.

Torture and ill-treatment continued to be reported, usually during incommunicado detention, which is forbidden by the Constitution even when guarantees are suspended. Torture methods included beatings, near-asphyxiation with plastic bags, electric shocks and mock executions. Official forensic doctors often deliberately failed to document cases of torture adequately. Medical treatment for detainees who suffered torture was frequently unavailable or inadequate.

Among the dozens of cases of torture reported were those of 14 people, most of them students, arrested without warrant by the *Policía Metropolitana*, Metropolitan Police, when they raided a university campus in Caracas to disperse a demonstration in January. While in police headquarters the detainees were reportedly beaten, given electric shocks and threatened with death. One was released the same day but 13 were detained without charge in prison for almost two weeks. Those responsible for their alleged torture were not brought to justice. In February, 22 people, many of them students, were arrested without warrant in the town of Valencia, Carabobo, by the state police. The detainees, who were later charged with military rebellion, were held incommunicado for eight days, during which they were reportedly tortured with electric shocks, death threats and beatings. One of the detainees, Carmen Alicia Gómez Potella, who was four months pregnant at the time, had a threatened miscarriage as a result. Thirteen were released uncharged after one month and the rest two weeks later. None of those responsible for their alleged torture had been brought to justice by the end of the year.

In another case, José Blondell was arrested in March by members of the *Policía Técnica Judicial* (PTJ), criminal investigations police, in Caracas, and interrogated about an alleged murder. He alleged that he was repeatedly beaten with metal bars and nearly asphyxiated with a plastic bag. He was released uncharged after one week. He lodged formal complaints with the Attorney General's Office, but to Amnesty International's knowledge those responsible remained at large by the end of the year.

Several detainees died as a result of injuries sustained during torture. For example, in late May Rommer Figueroa Lizardi died reportedly as a consequence of

**308**

beatings and kicks by members of the *Guardia Nacional*, National Guard, who had arrested him earlier that day during a demonstration in Ciudad Guayana, Bolívar.

Prison conditions continued to be extremely harsh, in many cases amounting to cruel, inhuman or degrading treatment. Serious overcrowding, lack of security for prison inmates, the arbitrary use of punishment cells and poor sanitary conditions prompted protests in several prisons. In March at least seven prisoners were reportedly arbitrarily killed in the state prison of Valencia, Carabobo, known as *Máxima de Tocuyito*, when prison guards quelled protests about overcrowding and ill-treatment.

At least one person "disappeared" from custody. Hemelson Vertiz was arrested on 22 June by three uniformed men who identified themselves as members of the DIM in his home in Maracaibo, Zulia. His whereabouts remained unknown at the end of the year.

Dozens of people were extrajudicially executed by members of the armed forces. On 4 February three soldiers and four students suspected of having joined the rebel forces in the coup attempt were shot at close range in Valencia after they had been detained by members of the security forces. Those responsible remained at large at the end of the year. Other possible extrajudicial executions reported during 1992 included the killings of Naser Palmar and Pedro José Paz, two Wayúu Indians. They were killed by members of the presidential guard on 12 October and at least five other Wayúu were shot and wounded when their truck crashed near an official celebration attended by President Carlos Andrés Pérez in Paraguaipoa, Zulia state. Initial reports claiming that the Indians had made an attempt on the life of the President were later officially denied. Those responsible for the killings had not been brought to justice by the end of the year.

On 27 November at least 63 inmates of the *Retén de Catia* prison in Caracas were killed by members of the Metropolitan Police and the National Guard who raided the severely overcrowded prison to quell a reported escape attempt. According to reports, the security forces arbitrarily shot at the prisoners, many of whom were reportedly victims of extrajudicial executions. Forensic examinations reported that many victims had been shot in the back.

Those responsible had not been brought to justice by the end of the year.

At least 15 people were killed and dozens wounded during the suppression of anti-government protests by the security forces. On 10 March four people, three of whom were less than 15 years old, were killed in Caracas, reportedly as a result of excessive use of force, when the police fired at them with live ammunition. On 8 April three people died in Maracay when members of the state police of Aragua arbitrarily opened fire on protesters during a peaceful demonstration.

There were reports of dozens of killings by members of the security forces in the course of criminal investigations, particularly in the *barrios*, in circumstances suggesting that the killings were arbitrary and deliberate. Gabriel Antonio Martín Salaverría was shot at point-blank range by members of the Metropolitan Police. The police claimed that they shot him during an exchange of gunfire, but this was denied by several eye-witnesses, who also alleged that the police failed to provide emergency care for the wounded man who died hours later on 28 January.

Very few of those responsible for torture and other human rights violations were brought to justice, despite scores of complaints filed with the relevant authorities. For example, those responsible for the torture of Yorfán José Escobar Berrios and for the killing of Raúl Contreras in 1991 (see *Amnesty International Report 1992*), remained at large.

In May a military court absolved and released the 15 members of a military patrol accused of the massacre of 14 fishermen in 1988 (see *Amnesty International Report 1992*). An appeal against the decision was lodged by the victims' lawyers in July and the proceedings, which suffered a series of delays and contradictory rulings, were still continuing at the end of the year.

Judicial investigations into past human rights violations, including extrajudicial executions by members of the security forces and deaths in custody, continued to make little or no progress in the majority of cases. More than 200 cases of death and serious injury caused by members of the security forces reported in 1989 remained unresolved in the courts. During 1992 investigations into unmarked graves in Caracas were halted. Sixty-five bodies of people reportedly killed by the police and army during widespread disturbances in 1989, which had been recovered in 1991, remained unidentified (see *Amnesty International Report 1992*).

In February Amnesty International wrote to President Carlos Andrés Pérez calling for the adoption of effective measures to prevent human rights violations during the period of suspended guarantees which followed the coup attempt. In December the organization wrote to the President to express its concern about human rights violations reported after the 27 November coup attempt including the killings of prisoners in Caracas. The organization called on the government to adopt effective measures to bring those responsible to justice and to prevent further abuses.

In July Amnesty International published *Venezuela: Torture and other human rights violations*, which described the findings of an Amnesty International delegation which visited the country in May. The organization expressed its concern about extrajudicial executions reported in the wake of the coup attempt, continuing reports of torture and arbitrary killings by members of the security forces, and the failure of the courts to properly investigate complaints of human rights violations. Amnesty International repeatedly called on the government to bring those responsible to justice.

# VIET NAM

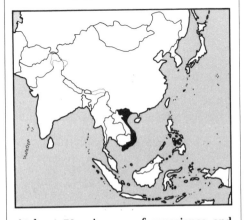

**At least 70 prisoners of conscience and possible prisoners of conscience remained imprisoned throughout 1992. Five prisoners of conscience were released, as were over 100 former officials and military personnel of the pre-1975 government who**

**had been detained without trial in "re-education" camps for up to 17 years. At least 20 suspected critics or opponents of the government were reportedly arrested during the year. At least 14 other political prisoners, including possible prisoners of conscience, were tried during the year; their trials appeared to fall short of international fair trial standards. Three people were reported to have been sentenced to death but it was not known whether there were any executions.**

In April the National Assembly adopted a new Constitution which introduced guarantees for fundamental rights, including freedom of expression, association and movement. Former General Le Duc Anh became President and Vo Van Kiet was re-elected Prime Minister following elections in July.

Five prisoners of conscience were released during the year. They were Le Van Tien, a writer, Thadeus Nguyen Van Ly, a Catholic priest, To Thuy Yen, a poet, Nguyen Khac Chinh, a lawyer, and Tran Xuan Tu, a Protestant pastor. However, more than 70 prisoners of conscience and possible prisoners of conscience remained in prison throughout 1992, including Dominic Tran Dinh Tu, an 86-year-old Catholic priest; Thich Tri Sieu, a Buddhist monk; Nguyen Dan Que, a doctor; and Tran Mai, a Protestant pastor. Tran Mai was reportedly arrested in October 1991 in Ho Chi Minh City, accused of "pursuing religious activities without permission" and using such activities "to fight the government". He was also accused of "abusing religious powers" and of having maintained links with overseas Christian organizations along with Pastors Dinh Thien Tu and Tran Dinh Ai (see *Amnesty International Report 1992*).

At least 20 suspected critics or opponents of the government were reportedly arrested in 1992. They included possible prisoners of conscience. Nguyen Si Binh, a nuclear engineer and businessman with United States (US) citizenship, was arrested with 16 others, including his sister and step-brother, in April and accused of attempting to overthrow the government. Nguyen Si Binh had reportedly returned to Viet Nam to do market research on behalf of some US companies. He and the others had not been tried by the end of the year. Nguyen Ly Tuong, a former parliamentarian and newspaper editor, was arrested

**310**

in June near the Thanh Da church in Ho Chi Minh City. Although not formally charged, he was apparently detained under Article 73 of the Criminal Code for alleged "actions aimed at overthrowing the People's Government". He had earlier been detained without trial in a "re-education" camp from January 1975 to February 1988.

Buddhist monks Thich Khong Tanh and Thich Tri Luc were arrested in October in Ho Chi Minh City and charged with "travelling without permission". The real reason for their arrests appeared to be their possession of documents signed and issued by Thich Huyen Quang, a Buddhist leader and prisoner of conscience held under house arrest in Quang Nghia village in Nghia Binh Province since 1982 (see *Amnesty International Reports 1986, 1987* and *1988*). Some of the documents, which were addressed to the Vietnamese authorities and distributed to Buddhist followers in Viet Nam and abroad, were critical of the government's treatment of and policies towards Buddhist monks and nuns. The documents urged the authorities to return all confiscated church properties and release all those, including monks, imprisoned or under house arrest for opposing government policies and regulations on religion. They also called for an end to divisions among Vietnamese Buddhists and urged the government to allow the Unified Buddhist Church (UBC) to function independently. Thich Huyen Quang and his followers are members of the UBC and oppose the government-sponsored Viet Nam Buddhist Church.

At least 14 critics or opponents of the government were tried and convicted in several trials under provisions of the 1986 Criminal Code. The trials appeared to fall short of international standards for fair trial in several respects, including the lack of independent legal representation. Doan Thanh Liem, a lawyer and a prisoner of conscience, was tried in May in Ho Chi Minh City. He had been arrested with several other people in 1990 for alleged espionage and involvement in the drafting of an unauthorized constitution (see *Amnesty International Reports 1991* and *1992*). He was sentenced to 12 years' imprisonment on a charge of spreading "anti-socialist propaganda", an offence under Article 82 of the Criminal Code. A co-defendant, Nguyen Tri, was sentenced to eight years' imprison-

ment at the same trial. Other opponents of the government were convicted of plotting against the government and sentenced to long prison terms.

It was reported in May that Doan Viet Hoat, an academic and a prisoner of conscience held since November 1990, and several others arrested with him, would be tried in Ho Chi Minh City. However, no date for the trial was given and it was not known to have taken place by the end of the year. Doan Viet Hoat had previously been detained without trial from 1976 to 1988 for peacefully expressing his political opinions.

More than 100 former officials and military officers of the former Republic of Viet Nam (RVN) were released between January and May. They had been held in "re-education" camps since 1975 under Resolution 49/TVQH, which provides for indefinite detention without charge or trial (see *Amnesty International Report 1992*). Those released reportedly included two former senior officials, eight former generals, nine former colonels and 11 former intelligence officers. Nguyen Thanh Long, a lawyer and a former officer in the Army of the Republic of Viet Nam (ARVN), was one of 38 prisoners released on 15 January. He had reported for "re-education" in June 1975 and had subsequently been held in a camp in Nam Ha, Ha Nam Ninh Province. Nguyen Kim Tay, another former ARVN officer who had been held since 1975, was released on 10 February along with 37 other former military personnel.

Three people were reportedly sentenced to death after being convicted of offences including murder, theft and arms trafficking, but it was not known whether there were any executions.

Amnesty International welcomed the releases of prisoners of conscience and long-term political detainees, but continued to press for the release of all prisoners of conscience and for the fair trial or release of political prisoners. Amnesty International also expressed its concern that the trials of some political prisoners may have fallen short of international fair trial standards.

In April Amnesty International published a report, *Viet Nam: Continued detention of members of religious organizations*, which expressed concern about the continued detention of people for the peaceful expression of their religious beliefs. In June Amnesty International published a further report, *Viet Nam: Arrests of political prisoners 1990-1991.*

In September the Vietnamese Government responded to a submission by Amnesty International concerning the case of Nguyen Dan Que (see *Amnesty International Reports 1991* and *1992*) to the United Nations Commission on Human Rights Working Group on arbitrary detention. The government wrote to the President of the Working Group denying that Nguyen Dan Que was a political prisoner and that he was being subjected to arbitrary detention. The government stated that he had been accused of "activities aimed at overthrowing the government" under Article 73 of the Criminal Code and had subsequently been tried and sentenced by a court of law in Ho Chi Minh City in November 1991. Amnesty International continued to appeal for the immediate and unconditional release of Nguyen Dan Que, whom it considered to be a prisoner of conscience held solely for the peaceful expression of his political beliefs and activities for the promotion of human rights.

# YEMEN

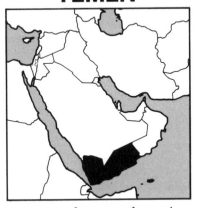

**Over 1,000 people, among them prisoners of conscience, were arrested following anti-government demonstrations, the majority of whom were released by the end of the year. At least 27 other government opponents, including two prisoners of conscience and several possible prisoners of conscience, were still held at the end of the year. Most had been convicted after unfair trials. Torture and ill-treatment of detainees were widespread and flogging continued to be used as a form of judicial punishment. Prison conditions were harsh. At least 16 people were killed in circumstances suggesting they were victims of extrajudicial executions. Several hundred cases of "disappearance" which occurred in previous years remained unresolved. Five people were executed and 31 other death sentences were ratified by the Presidential Council. Hundreds of other prisoners were believed to be under sentence of death.**

General elections scheduled for November were postponed until April 1993.

The Penal Code and the Code of Criminal Procedures of unified Yemen had not been promulgated by the end of the year and the legal systems of the former People's Democratic Republic of Yemen (PDRY) and the Yemen Arab Republic (YAR) remained separate.

One person arrested in April on charges of apostasy was a prisoner of conscience. 'Ali 'Abdul-Fattah Hashim, a school teacher, was held at Sana'a Central Prison; his trial had not been concluded by the end of the year.

Another prisoner of conscience remained under sentence of death after more than nine and a half years' imprisonment. Mansur Rajih, a member of the former National Democratic Front (NDF), the main opposition group in the former YAR, was arrested in July 1983. He was tortured during interrogation and convicted of a murder he did not commit after an unfair trial. His death sentence was pending ratification by the Presidential Council at the end of the year. It was not possible to confirm the continued detention of 'Ayesh 'Ali 'Ubad, another prisoner of conscience, and of 15 other suspected NDF members (see *Amnesty International Reports 1990* to *1992*).

In December over 1,000 people, including prisoners of conscience, were arrested following violent anti-government demonstrations in Ta'iz, al-Hudaida and Sana'a. The demonstrations were held in protest against rising prices of basic commodities and the government's general economic policy. The arrests were carried out by *al-'Amn al-Siyassi* (Political Security), *al-'Amn al-Markazi* (Central Security) and the army. Some of the detainees were arrested in their homes or in the street after the demonstrations had ended. Many of those held were students, but they also included civil servants, labourers and military personnel. The majority were released uncharged within days, but at least 50 remained in detention at the end of the year. Among them were Muhammad Yahya al-Sabri and Sarhan al-Muhayya, both officers in the air force, who were held incommunicado in the military intelligence detention centre in Sala in the city of Ta'iz. Many of the detainees were allegedly subjected to beatings and electric shocks.

Three people arrested after violent anti-government protests in Sana'a in 1991 (see *Amnesty International Report 1992*) were tried and sentenced to prison terms in March. Insufficient information was available to Amnesty International to assess whether they received a fair trial. Fourteen others arrested at the same time were released uncharged at the beginning of 1992.

At least 25 political prisoners, among them possible prisoners of conscience, continued to be held throughout the year. All were suspected members of the NDF who had been arrested between 1981 and 1989 in the former YAR. Two continued to be held without charge or trial and a third remained in Sana'a Central Prison despite having been tried and acquitted in 1988. Eight had been sentenced to prison terms or to paying *diyya* (a fine imposed in accordance with tribal tradition). Fourteen were under sentence of death following unfair trials. Those convicted had reportedly been denied prompt access to lawyers, been given inadequate time to prepare their defence and had been found guilty of murder, kidnapping and other charges on the basis of contested "confessions" and witness testimony. All the sentences were pending appeal or ratification by the Presidential Council.

In April and May, 27 other NDF members were released following a decision by the Presidential Council. Most had been sentenced to prison terms after unfair trials in previous years. Mahdi Naji al-'Awadi, an NDF member who had remained in custody although he had been acquitted when brought to trial in 1988, was also released in May.

Torture and ill-treatment of prisoners remained widespread. In one case at least 14 untried detainees were tortured in the Criminal Investigations Headquarters in al-Soor, al-Hudaida, between December 1991 and January 1992. They were allegedly arrested in connection with a land dispute but were tortured to force them to "con-fess" to having committed murder or to implicate others. Among them was Fatima Zayd Saleh 'Ali, a housewife who was detained with her two children. She suffered a broken arm and a fractured jaw as a result of repeated beatings, and was allegedly threatened with rape. While she was being interrogated, her one-month-old baby was left alone in the cold on the roof of the building. Three members of the group were still held at the end of the year; the remaining 11 were released uncharged in December.

At least five detainees were tortured in al-'Amri police station in Sana'a in December. Among them was 'Abo Muhammad Fath, a nine-year-old boy accused of theft, who was burned with cigarettes and beaten all over his body while suspended by the wrists from a high window. Following a strike by lawyers in protest against the abuses committed at the police station, the government ordered the release of the five detainees and the commander of the police station was arrested pending the outcome of a judicial investigation. Reports were also received of the torture and ill-treatment of Somali refugees, including the rape and attempted rape of five women in al-Hudaida Central Prison and of two others in Madinat al-Sha'b refugee camp in 'Aden.

The judicial punishment of flogging continued to be imposed. It was not possible to gauge the overall extent of its use in the country; however, between January and March, 77 prisoners were flogged in Sana'a and Dhamar Central prisons alone.

Conditions in prisons at times amounted to cruel, inhuman or degrading treatment. In May Suffyan Hammoud Muhammad 'Affan, a political prisoner, died in Ta'iz Central Prison; he had been held there for over nine years. Although seriously ill, he was apparently denied proper medical care during his imprisonment.

During the year several political activists were deliberately killed, apparently for political reasons. Those targeted were principally members of the Yemeni Socialist Party (YSP). Among them was Colonel Majid Murshid Sayf, a member of the Central Committee of the YSP. In June he was wounded after resisting attempts to abduct him at a military check-point in Sana'a. He was allegedly then taken to the headquarters of *al-Amn al-Markazi* in the city and killed. No investigation was known to have been held into his death.

In December at least 15 demonstrators were killed in Ta'iz and Sana'a during anti-government demonstrations (see above) in circumstances suggesting that some at least may have been victims of extrajudicial executions. According to reports, military and security forces brought in to disperse demonstrations did so using a level of force out of all proportion to any threat posed, including the firing of anti-aircraft guns and other heavy weaponry. The government subsequently listed the names of 12 people said to have been killed, but the real figure was believed to be higher. The official list did not include, for example, Hammud al-Halimi, a labourer who was killed in Ta'iz. A parliamentary inquiry into the killings was set up, but it had not been concluded by the end of the year. No judicial inquiry was known to have been initiated.

The fate of hundreds of detainees who "disappeared" in previous years in the former YAR and PDRY remained unknown, although Amnesty International received new information about hundreds of cases. Most had been detained in the 1970s or in January 1986 in the former PDRY but 11 had "disappeared" in the former YAR between 1978 and 1985 (see previous *Amnesty International Reports*). Those who had "disappeared" in the former PDRY included 'Abdul-Rahman 'Umar Baljun, a writer and General Director of Aden Television.

In May and December, five people convicted of premeditated murder were executed in Sana'a, Ibb and Hajja. Thirty-one other prisoners convicted of the same offence had their death sentences ratified by the Presidential Council in early December. Hundreds of other prisoners were believed to be under sentence of death.

Amnesty International urged the government to release unconditionally two prisoners of conscience, Mansur Rajih and 'Ali 'Abdul-Fattah Hashim. The organization also called for the fair trial or release of other political detainees and for judicial review of the cases of political prisoners sentenced after unfair trials. In March Amnesty International urged the government to establish an inquiry into allegations of torture of detainees at the Criminal Investigations Headquarters in al-Hudaida. In September the organization submitted details of 140 "disappeared" prisoners to

the government and again called for an independent inquiry to be initiated to clarify their cases. However, no such inquiry had been established by the end of the year. In December Amnesty International appealed to the government not to carry out the death sentences ratified by the Presidential Council.

In December the government reiterated its denial that political prisoners were being held in Yemen. It asserted that the officer responsible for the torture of detainees at the Criminal Investigation Headquarters in al-Hudaida had been "dismissed from his job and punished for the crimes he committed".

# YUGOSLAVIA
## (FEDERAL REPUBLIC OF)

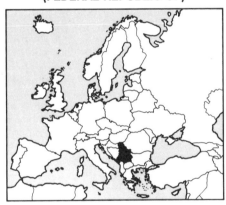

**In Kosovo province in the Republic of Serbia hundreds of ethnic Albanians were beaten or otherwise ill-treated by police; at least 16 ethnic Albanians died after being shot by police in disputed circumstances. Ethnic Albanians continued to be sentenced to up to 60 days' imprisonment for non-violent political activity. Ethnic Albanian political prisoners were convicted after unfair trials. In June and July four Croats were sentenced to death by a military court in Belgrade for war crimes.**

A new state, the Federal Republic of Yugoslavia, comprising the Republics of Serbia and Montenegro, was proclaimed in Belgrade on 27 April. This followed the break-up of the Socialist Federal Republic of Yugoslavia after the independence of three of its former republics, Slovenia, Croatia and Bosnia-Herzegovina.

Conflict in Croatia largely ended with the signing of a cease-fire which came into

**314**

effect in January. A United Nations (UN) peace-keeping force, known as UNPROFOR, was then established in the conflict zones in Croatia. In May the Yugoslav President Dobrica Čosić announced the withdrawal of Yugoslav National Army (JNA) troops from Bosnia-Herzegovina, but soldiers who originated in that republic were authorized to stay. Together with JNA arms and equipment they were effectively absorbed into the army of the self-proclaimed "Serbian Republic of Bosnia-Herzegovina", which by the end of the year controlled some 70 per cent of the territory of Bosnia-Herzegovina (see **Bosnia-Herzegovina** entry). In August the UN Commission on Human Rights appointed a Special Rapporteur to investigate the human rights situation in former Yugoslavia, and in October the UN Security Council set up a Commission of Experts to investigate war crimes committed in former Yugoslavia.

Ethnic tensions in Kosovo province in southern Serbia remained acute. Leaders of Kosovo's main ethnic Albanian political party, the Democratic League of Kosovo, demanded that Kosovo province be granted independence from Serbia. There were widespread protests by ethnic Albanians in September and October when secondary schools and university faculties remained closed to ethnic Albanian teaching staff and students who refused to accept Serbian educational programs. Ethnic Albanians continued to be dismissed, on political grounds, from their jobs.

Over 400,000 people, the majority Serbs from Croatia and Bosnia-Herzegovina, sought refuge in Yugoslavia. Thousands of Croats and Hungarians fled their homes in the Vojvodina province of Serbia after threats or the destruction of their property by members of Serbian extremist political parties, including Serbian refugees and Serbian irregulars. Similarly, thousands of Muslims left the Sandžak region after their homes, businesses or cars were destroyed by Serbian and Montenegrin political extremists and irregulars. By October the Conference on Security and Co-operation in Europe had established a long-term mission in Kosovo, Sandžak and the Vojvodina to monitor the human rights situation in these regions.

There were almost daily reports that ethnic Albanians had been beaten or otherwise ill-treated by police. Among the victims was Ismet Krasniqi from Peć, who was among a group of parents who in January protested against the Serbian curriculum followed by the Xhemail Kada primary school in Peć. He was arrested at the school by police who took him to a police station and beat him. Photographs and a medical report showed that he had sustained severe bruising to his buttocks, feet and hands, and that his left ear-drum had been perforated.

Ethnic Albanian sources alleged that in the period from 1 September to 10 October over 240 demonstrators had been beaten by police. The demonstrators had participated in protests against the closure of secondary schools and university faculties to ethnic Albanian students and staff who rejected the curricula laid down by the Serbian authorities. Several hundred others were beaten during similar demonstrations on 12 and 13 October. Among those severely injured were Sabrie Rrustaj and Samile Pupovci from Peć. Sabrie Rrustaj reportedly had her ear torn off and suffered a fractured arm; Samile Pupovci had her leg broken.

Conflict between police and ethnic Albanians resulted in the deaths of at least 16 ethnic Albanians in disputed circumstances. In one incident Bajram Hoxhaj, Muharrem Hysenaj and Hasan Hysenaj died after being shot by police in the village of Uče on 31 January. Ethnic Albanians alleged that police had arrested three school children and then opened fire on members of their families who sought their release. Police officers claimed that they had fired in self-defence after their patrol was fired at.

Ethnic Albanians continued to be sentenced to up to 60 days' imprisonment for the peaceful exercise of their right to freedom of expression. Among them were Fatmir Shala and Behadin Krasniqi. In July each received a 60-day prison sentence for sending a cassette tape containing greetings for broadcast on a local radio station in the neighbouring republic of Albania. In October Jahja Halabuku and Shukri Qerimi were sentenced to 60 days' imprisonment each for organizing demonstrations against the closing of education faculties to ethnic Albanians.

In October the district court of Peć convicted 19 ethnic Albanians of founding an illegal organization in order to obtain, by arms, the secession of Kosovo province from Yugoslavia. They were not accused of using violence and charges of terrorism against them were dropped during investigation proceedings. They received sentences of between one and seven years' imprisonment. The principal accused, Mentor Kaçi, reportedly admitted in court that he had bought a gun and revolver from a Swiss citizen and that he had tried, unsuccessfully, to buy arms in Albania. He and other defendants stated that they obtained weapons only for self-defence, in case the conflict in former Yugoslav territories spread to Kosovo. At the trial many defendants withdrew statements they had given during pre-trial proceedings, alleging that they were false and had been extracted under torture or threat of torture. Prison medical reports reportedly showed that Mentor Kaçi and several other defendants had suffered physical injuries as a result of ill-treatment following their arrest in late December 1991. Their lawyers had previously filed complaints that investigation proceedings had been carried out by police officers rather than the investigating judge. Their lawyers had also protested that they had been refused information about the charges against their clients and had been denied access to their clients until 19 January, though even then they had not been able to speak with them without supervision. Eight other ethnic Albanians accused of similar offences and their lawyers made almost identical complaints at a subsequent trial in the district court of Priština in October. Seven were convicted and received prison sentences of between two and six years, while one was acquitted.

The Constitution of the Federal Republic of Yugoslavia, promulgated in April 1992, abolished the death penalty and required that federal criminal law be brought into conformity with this by the end of 1994. Four men were subsequently sentenced to death by a military court in Belgrade. In June Martin Sabljič, Zoran Šipoš and Nikola Cibarič, all Croats from Borovo Naselje near Vukovar in Croatia, were convicted of armed rebellion against the Socialist Federal Republic of Yugoslavia and of war crimes against Serbian civilians in Vukovar. In July Zdenko Štefančić was convicted on similar charges. All four, together with co-defendants who received prison sentences, were released in August as a result of an agreement between the governments of Yugoslavia and Croatia to exchange prisoners of war according to

the principle of "all for all" and without conditions.

Amnesty International repeatedly urged the Serbian authorities to investigate cases in which police officers in Kosovo province allegedly beat or otherwise ill-treated ethnic Albanians. In June the organization published a report, *Yugoslavia: Ethnic Albanians – Victims of torture and ill-treatment by police in Kosovo province*, in which it documented, with medical reports and photographs, 15 illustrative cases. In September the organization received from the Ministry of Justice a briefing prepared by the Ministry of the Interior, which denied allegations of police abuses and claimed that police used physical force only in accordance with the law, that is, in self-defence. Despite medical and photographic evidence to the contrary, the briefing stated that police had never used physical force against Ismet Krasniqi. In August Amnesty International delegates attempted to observe the trial before a Belgrade military court of three Croats charged with war crimes against Serbian civilians and armed rebellion. The trial was postponed and the three men were released in a prisoner exchange later that month. Amnesty International expressed its concern about death sentences previously imposed on four Croats and about allegations that confessions made under duress had been used as evidence. It called for the commutation of their death sentences and an investigation into allegations of torture and ill-treatment.

In November Amnesty International wrote to the government expressing concern about human rights abuses committed by all parties to the conflict in Bosnia-Herzegovina (see **Bosnia-Herzegovina** entry). It said that the governments of the Federal Republic of Yugoslavia and of Croatia shared a heavy responsibility for abuses to the extent that they had supported politically and materially the various forces operating in Bosnia-Herzegovina. Amnesty International called on all parties to ensure respect for international human rights and humanitarian standards.

# ZAIRE

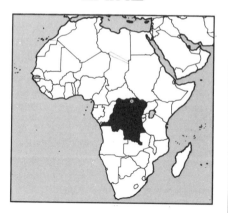

**More than 100 suspected opponents of the government, including prisoners of conscience, were detained during 1992. Although many of them were released, more than 70 were still held without charge or trial at the end of the year. About 30 soldiers, including one prisoner of conscience, were convicted unfairly by military courts. Torture and ill-treatment of detainees and government opponents were widely reported. Several dozen people "disappeared" after being arrested or abducted by armed men believed to be members of the security forces. Soldiers responsible for dozens of extrajudicial executions of civilians went unpunished.**

The Sovereign National Conference which began in August 1991 to review and reform Zaire's political system continued, despite objections by President Mobutu Sese Seko and his supporters. In mid-January Prime Minister Nguz a Karl-i-Bond stopped its proceedings, saying that it was too costly. He also said it was dominated by members of the Luba ethnic group, apparently because Etienne Tshisekedi, a Luba and leading opponent of President Mobutu, was favoured by the Conference to replace Nguz a Karl-i-Bond as Prime Minister. The Conference resumed in April following pressure on the government from a series of workers' strikes and demonstrations and from foreign governments.

Conference delegates opposed to President Mobutu accused him and his supporters of responsibility for the country's social and economic collapse and for gross human rights violations. Delegates loyal to President Mobutu pulled out of the Conference several times, claiming that the criticism was unjustified and defamatory. In May the Conference set up several commissions to investigate responsibility for crimes, including human rights violations, committed since President Mobutu came to power in 1965. The outcome of the investigations had not been announced by the end of the year.

In August the National Conference elected Etienne Tshisekedi, who had been imprisoned several times as a prisoner of conscience since 1980, to replace Nguz a Karl-i-Bond as Prime Minister. However, President Mobutu retained control over most state institutions, including some of the security forces, and refused to relinquish some of his powers as requested by the National Conference.

Political violence broke out in the country's southeastern Shaba region after the replacement of Nguz a Karl-i-Bond, as members of his Lunda ethnic group attacked members of new Prime Minister Tshisekedi's Luba community, killing dozens. Thousands of Luba left Shaba after their homes had been destroyed. The security forces did not intervene until several weeks after the violence had begun.

Following the January suspension of the National Conference, the security forces violently suppressed peaceful demonstrations calling for the resumption of the Conference. A peaceful march in Kinshasa on 16 February organized by lay Christian religious leaders was broken up using firearms, hot-water cannons, metal-tipped whips and tear-gas. At least 37 people were killed and dozens more injured. At least 50 demonstrators were arrested, including three Belgian missionaries. About 10 other demonstrators were detained during another protest on 1 March.

The detainees, all apparently prisoners of conscience, were released without charge by the end of April. The authorities refused to order a public inquiry into the security forces' behaviour on 16 February, claiming that their intervention was necessary because the demonstration was illegal.

Eight people preparing to welcome a delegation of French-based human rights activists were arrested at Kinshasa airport in December. The eight, all prisoners of conscience, included Mukendi wa Mulumba, a lawyer and adviser to Prime Minister Tshisekedi, and three security advisers to the Prime Minister. The eight

AMNESTY INTERNATIONAL REPORT 1993

were assaulted at the time of their arrest by troops loyal to the President, and were held incommunicado for three days until they were released without charge.

One other prisoner of conscience, Luc Mayolo Mokakoso, a lieutenant-colonel and army dentist, was held throughout the year. He had been arrested with several other soldiers in July 1991 and accused of plotting against the government, apparently because of their suspected links with opposition political parties. They were held at Ndolo military prison in Kinshasa where they were reportedly ill-treated and denied visits. Luc Mayolo Mokakoso's co-accused were provisionally released in mid-1992 and went into hiding in apparent fear of rearrest. He was tried by a military court in July 1992 and convicted of disobeying military orders by contacting politicians in order to form a political group within the army known as the Military Committee for National Salvation. He was sentenced to two years' imprisonment with hard labour.

Sixty-two soldiers arrested in January remained in incommunicado detention, without charge or trial, throughout the year. The authorities said they had committed criminal offences but others maintained they had been arrested on suspicion of sympathizing with opposition parties. They were transferred to Irebu military prison in Equateur region. At least two of them were later reported to have died from torture and lack of medical care.

Twenty-four soldiers were convicted in April by the Higher Court Martial in Kinshasa after an unfair trial. Four others were acquitted. They had all been arrested on 22 January after occupying a studio in Kinshasa's radio and television complex and broadcasting an appeal to President Mobutu's government to resign. They were held incommunicado at Kinshasa's Camp Tshatshi military barracks where they were reported to have been tortured. They had no access to legal counsel before their trial. The 24 who were convicted included 17 who the authorities claimed had escaped, and who were tried *in absentia* and sentenced to death for endangering the security of the state. There were fears expressed, however, that these 17 had been killed in custody before the trial and there had been no news of them by the end of the year. Of the 11 prisoners who appeared in court, seven were convicted and sentenced to prison terms of between five and 10 years.

Torture and ill-treatment of prisoners and other government opponents was reportedly widespread. For example, the soldiers tried in April told the court that while in custody members of the *Division spéciale présidentielle* (DSP), Special Presidential Division, had systematically tortured them to force them to confess and to implicate civilian political opposition leaders. They claimed that they had been regularly stripped and beaten with whips and gun butts. They were stabbed with bayonets and subjected to mock executions, and, in some cases, sexually assaulted. The court failed to order an investigation into the torture allegations and rejected demands by their lawyers that they should be examined by a doctor.

There were numerous reports of starvation and unsanitary conditions in Zairian prisons and detention centres. Dozens of prisoners were reported to have died in Kinshasa's Makala prison as a result of malnutrition and medical neglect.

In April and May there were reports of torture of civilians, including the rape of dozens of women, by members of the security forces during an anti-poaching operation around Salonga National Park, in Equateur region's Boende sub-region. Members of the security forces reportedly tortured men to force them to hand over property and to prevent them protesting about the rape of their wives or daughters. More than a dozen people were reportedly executed extrajudicially during the operation. Unarmed villagers were reportedly shot simply because they protested. Despite protests from local human rights groups, the authorities were not known to have investigated the reports or taken any action against the culprits.

Several dozen people, some of them suspected government opponents, reportedly "disappeared", especially in Kinshasa. They were reportedly abducted from their homes or on the streets by armed men in civilian clothes. For example, Jean-Marie Katonga Kabuluku, a former member of the National Assembly and a supporter of Etienne Tshisekedi's party, was reportedly abducted by unidentified men in January and had not been found by the end of the year. In July René Kanda, a resident of Kinshasa's Selembao zone, was seized by men in plain clothes carrying bayonets and handcuffs; his whereabouts remained

**318**

unknown. Appeals by human rights groups and relatives to the authorities to investigate these "disappearances" remained unanswered. The failure of the security forces to observe formal detention procedures made it difficult to identify those responsible for the abductions or to establish if the "disappeared" were in custody.

There were numerous reports of people being extrajudicially executed by soldiers engaged in looting or during reprisal attacks on civilians. In January soldiers in Kinshasa killed at least two people who apparently tried to stop them looting their homes. In mid-October several people were reportedly killed by soldiers on a looting spree in Mbandaka, the capital of Equateur region. In November soldiers near Likasi in Shaba reportedly executed extrajudicially about 10 villagers to avenge an army officer found dead in a village. The authorities failed to punish those responsible for these killings and for the killings of 37 demonstrators on 16 February, effectively condoning extrajudicial executions.

The United Nations (UN) Special Rapporteur on summary and arbitrary executions told the UN Commission on Human Rights in February that his investigation into an attack on students at Lubumbashi university campus in May 1990 (see *Amnesty International Report 1992*) had revealed that government troops had been involved and had killed students. He called for an official inquiry into the attack to be reopened, but the authorities took no action.

Seventeen soldiers convicted *in absentia* in April were still under sentence of death at the end of the year. A group of 24 others convicted of murder and robbery in 1989 were also known to remain under sentence of death. No executions of prisoners sentenced to death were reported.

Amnesty International protested at the killings of demonstrators in February, and other alleged extrajudicial executions. It called on the authorities to forbid the use of firearms and other lethal weapons by the security forces when lives were not at risk, and to investigate impartially reports of extrajudicial executions. The organization called for the release of Luc Mayolo Mokakoso and other prisoners of conscience and urged the government to account for prisoners and others who had "disappeared".

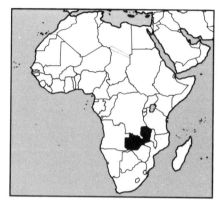

# ZAMBIA

**A number of foreign nationals, including refugees and asylum-seekers, were detained without charge or trial during the year. There were continuing reports of ill-treatment of prisoners. Several hundred prisoners remained under sentence of death, but none was executed and the government announced a review of the death penalty.**

A newly elected government headed by President Frederick Chiluba had taken office in November 1991, after the first multi-party elections in nearly two decades. The new government pledged to protect human rights. However, in August the Minister of Home Affairs stated publicly that the police and paramilitary Anti-Robbery Squads were authorized to "shoot to kill" armed robbers. The new government had been widely expected to abolish these paramilitary squads, which have been responsible for many killings, some of which may have been extrajudicial executions. Other government officials distanced themselves from the Minister's statement and the Attorney General stated that police were only allowed to use lethal force if criminals posed an immediate threat to life.

The year saw strikes and demonstrations by trade unionists and students protesting at government economic policies. In April and May police used tear-gas to disperse peaceful demonstrations by miners' wives and children. In October police shot dead a student demonstrator in Lusaka, the capital. Hundreds of students were arrested in protests throughout the year and charged with public order offences.

A number of asylum-seekers or recognized refugees were detained without charge or trial during 1992. In January some were arrested in the course of a round-up of more than 1,000 illegal immigrants. Ugandan asylum-seeker David Musinguzi was twice detained and threatened with deportation to Uganda where he appeared to be in danger of arrest for political reasons. He remained in detention at the end of the year.

A South African national, Katiza Cebekhulu, remained in detention throughout the year. He was one of the accused in a kidnapping and assault trial in South Africa involving Winnie Mandela. He had been smuggled into Zambia in February 1991 to prevent him from testifying in court. In May 1991 he was detained after giving a newspaper interview (see *Amnesty International Report 1992*). In April 1992 the chief immigration officer told a Lusaka newspaper that he had asked the Ministry of Home Affairs to release Katiza Cebekhulu since he was not an illegal immigrant. The legal basis for his continuing detention was unclear.

Another South African, Sipho Mbeje, was released from custody and deported in January. He had been abducted and assaulted by security officials of the African National Congress of South Africa (ANC) in 1989, then sentenced to two years' imprisonment on the basis of a conviction which was apparently unsafe. Sipho Mbeje appeared to have been imprisoned because of collusion between ANC and Zambian officials after he had resigned from the ANC over policy differences.

There were continuing reports of ill-treatment of prisoners. In February Musonda Mofya, a criminal suspect, filed a claim for damages against the police for torture which was alleged to have taken place in October 1991. Reports indicated that street children arrested for petty crime were often badly beaten by police or paramilitaries.

More than 200 prisoners remained under sentence of death, but no executions were reported. The government announced that it was undertaking a research project to solicit public opinion on whether the death penalty should be abolished.

Amnesty International sought information about the legal basis for the detentions of refugees and asylum-seekers and appealed to the government not to return David Musinguzi to Uganda against his will. The organization called for all death sentences to be commuted.

# ZIMBABWE

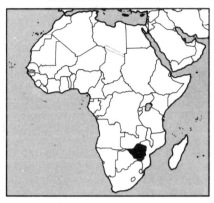

**Mass graves were uncovered which were believed to contain the remains of victims of extrajudicial executions by the army in the mid-1980s. The government failed to respond to calls for a full and impartial investigation. However, there were official investigations into a number of more recent deaths in custody and alleged extrajudicial executions or "disappearances". One prisoner died in custody during the year in unexplained circumstances. At least 12 prisoners were sentenced to death but there were no reported executions.**

The country was badly affected by the drought which prevailed across the whole of southern Africa, exacerbating an already precarious economic situation.

In the search for new sources of water to relieve the drought, mass graves were uncovered at various times throughout the year. These were alleged to contain the remains of victims of extrajudicial executions or "disappearances" in the western Matabeleland provinces between 1983 and 1985 (see *Amnesty International Reports 1984* to *1986*). During those years the army, notably the Fifth Brigade, was deployed against armed insurgents. Some of the sites where remains were uncovered, such as Antelope Mine near Kezi, had been described by eye-witnesses as the scenes of extrajudicial executions.

There were widespread public calls for the government to initiate a thorough and independent investigation into the graves

**320**

and the history of army abuses in Matabeleland. In particular, Zimbabwean human rights organizations called for the publication of the report of an official commission of inquiry into army abuses which was submitted to the government in 1985. However, the government did not publish the commission's report, nor did it initiate further investigations into human rights violations in Matabeleland.

In January and March two officials of the Central Intelligence Organization (CIO) were arrested and charged in connection with the "disappearance" in 1990 of Rashiwe Guzha (see *Amnesty International Report 1992*). However, in July Attorney General Patrick Chinamasa ordered that charges against the two should be withdrawn for lack of evidence, along with those against a former CIO official arrested in connection with the case in November 1991.

In October the Attorney General announced that he disagreed with an inquest verdict that an army officer, Captain Edwin Nleya, had been murdered (see *Amnesty International Report 1992*). Captain Nleya's body had been found on a hillside in Hwange in 1989, two months after he had disappeared from his unit. His family and some newspapers alleged that he was murdered because he had inside knowledge of military involvement in wildlife poaching. The Attorney General disputed this, saying the evidence supported the finding of an internal army investigation which concluded that Captain Nleya had committed suicide.

Also in October the Attorney General announced that two CIO officials were to be charged with the attempted murder of Patrick Kombayi, a prominent opposition candidate, in the course of the general election campaign in early 1990 (see *Amnesty International Report 1991*).

One prisoner, Miria Chizhengeya, died in police custody in Harare in June in unexplained circumstances. The authorities investigated a number of earlier cases of deaths in detention, holding inquests into some of them (see *Amnesty International Report 1992*). Some of the deaths were credibly attributed to natural causes. In one case, that of Clever Magwera, who died in police custody in Kadoma in March 1991, a police officer was charged in connection with his death. In a number of other instances where prisoners had died violent deaths, including the case of Shepard Chisango who died in military custody in June 1991 (see *Amnesty International Report 1992*), the authorities failed to provide satisfactory explanations.

At least 12 prisoners were sentenced to death in 1992, including Thembeni Joseph Moyo, who was aged about 17 at the time of the murder of which he was convicted. No executions were reported.

Amnesty International called on the government to initiate independent inquiries into several deaths in detention and possible extrajudicial executions. In a number of cases the organization received detailed responses from the government. Amnesty International also called on the government to publish the report of the commission of inquiry into the Matabeleland killings and to conduct further investigations into the newly uncovered human remains.

# APPENDICES

# AMNESTY INTERNATIONAL VISITS BETWEEN 1 JANUARY AND 31 DECEMBER 1992

| DATE | COUNTRY | PURPOSE | DELEGATE(S) |
|---|---|---|---|
| January | Bhutan | Discuss Amnesty International's concerns with government authorities | – Secretary General of Amnesty International<br>– Two staff members of International Secretariat |
| January | United Kingdom | Observe trial | – Staff member of International Secretariat |
| February | Mexico | Research | – Two staff members of International Secretariat |
| February | Georgia | Research/Discuss Amnesty International's concerns with government authorities | – Two staff members of International Secretariat |
| February | United States of America | Research | – Staff member of International Secretariat |
| February | Burundi | Research | – Two staff members of International Secretariat |
| February | Austria | Research | – Staff member of International Secretariat |
| February | Yugoslavia | Research | – Staff member of International Secretariat |
| February | Spain | Observe trial | – David Lachat (Switzerland) |
| February | United Kingdom | Research | – Koen de Feyter (Belgium)<br>– Staff member of International Secretariat |
| February/ March | Niger | Research/Discuss Amnesty International's concerns with government authorities | – Eric Gillet (Belgium)<br>– Staff member of International Secretariat |
| February/ March | Yemen | Research/Discuss Amnesty International's concerns with government authorities | – Two staff members of International Secretariat |
| February/ March | Philippines | Discuss Amnesty International's concerns with government authorities/Research | – Ligia Bolivar (Venezuela)<br>– Two staff members of International Secretariat |
| February/ March | Algeria | Research/Discuss Amnesty International's concerns with government authorities | – Two staff members of International Secretariat |
| March | Angola | Research | – Belisário dos Santos Jr (Brazil)<br>– Staff member of International Secretariat |
| March | Sierra Leone | Research/Discuss Amnesty International's concerns with government authorities | – Wesley Gryk (USA)<br>– Staff member of International Secretariat |
| March | Paraguay | Research/Discuss Amnesty International's concerns with government authorities | – Staff member of International Secretariat |
| March/April | Haiti | Research/Discuss Amnesty International's concerns with government authorities | – Michael Levy (USA)<br>– Two staff members of International Secretariat |
| March/April | United Kingdom | Research | – Stephan Parmentier (Belgium)<br>– Staff member of International Secretariat |
| April | Australia | Research/Discuss Amnesty International's concerns with government authorities | – Rod Morgan (UK)<br>– Elizabeth Funken (Germany)<br>– Staff member of International Secretariat |

| DATE | COUNTRY | PURPOSE | DELEGATE(S) |
|---|---|---|---|
| April | Israel/Occupied Territories | Research | – Staff member of International Secretariat |
| April | Kazakhstan | Discuss Amnesty International's concerns with government authorities/Research | – Secretary General of Amnesty International<br>– Two staff members of International Secretariat |
| April | Kyrgyzstan | Discuss Amnesty International's concerns with government authorities/Research | – Secretary General of Amnesty International<br>– Two staff members of International Secretariat |
| April | Uzbekistan | Discuss Amnesty International's concerns with government authorities/Research | – Secretary General of Amnesty International<br>– Staff member of International Secretariat |
| April | Armenia | Research/Discuss Amnesty International's concerns with government authorities | – Joseph Middleton (UK)<br>– Staff member of International Secretariat |
| April | Yugoslavia | Research | – Staff member of International Secretariat |
| April/May | Argentina | Research/Discuss Amnesty International's concerns with government authorities | – Two staff members of International Secretariat |
| April/May | Egypt | Discuss Amnesty International's concerns with government authorities | – Secretary General of Amnesty International<br>– Staff member of International Secretariat |
| May | New Zealand | Research | – Staff member of International Secretariat |
| May | Fiji | Research/Discuss Amnesty International's concerns with government authorities | – Staff member of International Secretariat |
| May | Nicaragua | Research/Discuss Amnesty International's concerns with government authorities | – Sebastian Brett (UK)<br>– Staff member of International Secretariat |
| May | Venezuela | Research | – Two staff members of International Secretariat |
| May | Kuwait | Observe trial/Discuss Amnesty International's concerns with government authorities | – Staff member of International Secretariat |
| May | United Kingdom | Observe appeal hearing | – Jill Heine (USA) |
| May | United Kingdom | Observe inquest | – Thomas Johnson (USA) |
| May | Turkey | Research | – Staff member of International Secretariat |
| May/June | Canada | Research | – Staff member of International Secretariat |
| May/June | Iraq | Research/Discuss Amnesty International's concerns with Kurdish authorities administering northern Iraq | – Staff member of International Secretariat |
| May/June | Cambodia | Discuss Amnesty International's concerns with government authorities/Research | – Deputy Secretary General of Amnesty International<br>– David Chandler (USA)<br>– Two staff members of International Secretariat |
| May/June | Equatorial Guinea | Research | – Miguel McVeigh (Spain) |
| May/June | Former Yugoslavia | Research | – Staff member of International Secretariat |
| June | Kenya | Research/Discuss Amnesty International's concerns with government authorities | – Two staff members of International Secretariat |

| DATE | COUNTRY | PURPOSE | DELEGATE(S) |
|------|---------|---------|-------------|
| June | Thailand | Discuss Amnesty International's concerns with government authorities | – Two staff members of International Secretariat |
| June | Algeria | Observe trial/Research | – Sheik Tarek (Yemen)<br>– Staff member of International Secretariat |
| June | United States of America | Research | – Staff member of International Secretariat |
| June/July | Romania | Research | – Charles King (USA)<br>– Staff member of International Secretariat |
| June/July | Tunisia | Discuss Amnesty International's concerns with government authorities/Research | – Secretary General of Amnesty International<br>– Two staff members of International Secretariat |
| July | Djibouti | Research/Observe trial | – Diabira Maroufa (Mauritania)<br>– Staff member of International Secretariat |
| July | Tunisia | Observe trial | – Jill Heine (USA) |
| July | Israel/Occupied Territories | Research/Discuss Amnesty International's concerns with government authorities | – Staff member of International Secretariat |
| July | United Kingdom | Observe court hearing | – Staff member of International Secretariat |
| July/August | South Africa | Research | – Staff member of International Secretariat |
| July/August | Former Yugoslavia | Research | – Two staff members of International Secretariat |
| July/August | Yugoslavia (Serbia) | Research/Observe trial | – Françoise Hampson (France/UK)<br>– Staff member of International Secretariat |
| July/August | Tunisia | Observe trial | – Ezzat Abdel Fattah (Canada) |
| August | Jordan | Research | – Staff member of International Secretariat |
| August | Mexico | Discuss Amnesty International's concerns with government authorities | – Emilio Mignone (Argentina)<br>– Staff member of International Secretariat |
| August/September | Colombia | Research/Discuss Amnesty International's concerns with government authorities | – Two staff members of International Secretariat |
| September | Guatemala | Research/Discuss Amnesty International's concerns with government authorities | – Francisco Ottonelli (Uruguay)<br>– Two staff members of International Secretariat |
| September | Brazil | Research | – Two staff members of International Secretariat |
| September | Bolivia | Observe trial | – Edgardo Carvallo (Uruguay) |
| September | Jordan | Discuss Amnesty International's concerns with government authorities | – Secretary General of Amnesty International<br>– Two staff members of International Secretariat |
| September | Chad | Discuss Amnesty International's concerns with government authorities/Research | – Ahmed Othmani (Tunisia)<br>– Two staff members of International Secretariat |
| September/October | Bangladesh | Research | – Two staff members of International Secretariat |
| October | Burundi | Observe trial/Research | – François Roux (France) |
| October | South Korea | Research/Discuss Amnesty International's concerns with government authorities | – Two staff members of International Secretariat |

| DATE | COUNTRY | PURPOSE | DELEGATE(S) |
|---|---|---|---|
| October | Maldives | Discuss Amnesty International's concerns with government authorities | – Javid Yusuf (Sri Lanka)<br>– Two staff members of International Secretariat |
| October | Azerbaydzhan | Research/Discuss Amnesty International's concerns with government authorities | – Joseph Middleton (UK)<br>– Staff member of International Secretariat |
| October | Turkmenistan | Research | – Joseph Middleton (UK)<br>– Staff member of International Secretariat |
| October | Lithuania | Research/Discuss Amnesty International's concerns with government authorities | – Marjorie Farquharson (UK)<br>– Staff member of International Secretariat |
| October | Latvia | Research/Discuss Amnesty International's concerns with government authorities | – Marjorie Farquharson (UK)<br>– Staff member of International Secretariat |
| October | Estonia | Research/Discuss Amnesty International's concerns with government authorities | – Marjorie Farquharson (UK)<br>– Staff member of International Secretariat |
| October | Romania | Research | – Staff member of International Secretariat |
| October | Japan | Research/Discuss Amnesty International's concerns with government authorities | – Staff member of International Secretariat |
| October | Brazil | Research | – Mariano Castex (Argentina)<br>– Staff member of International Secretariat |
| October | Jordan | Observe trial | – Safia Safwat (Sudan) |
| October | Turkey | Research/Observe court hearing | – Staff member of International Secretariat |
| October | Poland | Research | – Staff member of International Secretariat |
| October/November | Sri Lanka | Research/Discuss Amnesty International's concerns with government authorities | – Two staff members of International Secretariat |
| November | India | Discuss Amnesty International's concerns with government authorities | – Ian Martin (UK)<br>– Three staff members of International Secretariat |
| November | United Kingdom | Research/Observe trial | – Staff member of International Secretariat |
| November | Trinidad & Tobago | Observe trial | – Doodnauth Singh (Guyana) |
| November | Hungary | Research | – Staff member of International Secretariat |
| November/December | Peru | Research/Discuss Amnesty International's concerns with government authorities | – Rona Weitz (USA)<br>– Gonzalo Fernandez (Uruguay)<br>– Wolfgang Heinz (Germany)<br>– Staff member of International Secretariat |
| November/December | Egypt | Research | – Two staff members of International Secretariat |
| November/December | Cambodia | Research | – David Chandler (USA)<br>– Two staff members of International Secretariat |
| November/December | Former Yugoslavia | Research | – Two staff members of International Secretariat |
| November/December | Former Yugoslavia | Research | – Staff member of International Secretariat |
| November/December | Trinidad & Tobago | Observe trial | – Doodnauth Singh (Guyana) |

| DATE | COUNTRY | PURPOSE | DELEGATE(S) |
|------|---------|---------|-------------|
| December | Greece | Observe trial | – Staff member of International Secretariat |
| December | Algeria | Research/Discuss Amnesty International's concerns with government authorities | – Two staff members of International Secretariat |
| December | Yemen | Research/Discuss Amnesty International's concerns with government authorities | – Staff member of International Secretariat |
| December | Iraq | Research/Discuss Amnesty International's concerns with Kurdish authorities administering northern Iraq | – Staff member of International Secretariat |
| December | Syria | Research/Discuss Amnesty International's concerns with government authorities | – Imad Ali Hussein Sharqawi (Jordan)<br>– Staff member of International Secretariat |

**APPENDIX II**

# STATUTE OF AMNESTY INTERNATIONAL
## Articles 1 and 2

**As amended by the 20th International Council,
meeting in Yokohama, Japan, 31 August to 7 September 1991**

### Object and Mandate

1. The object of AMNESTY INTERNATIONAL is to contribute to the observance throughout the world of human rights as set out in the Universal Declaration of Human Rights.

   In pursuance of this object, and recognizing the obligation on each person to extend to others rights and freedoms equal to his or her own, AMNESTY INTERNATIONAL adopts as its mandate:

   To promote awareness of and adherence to the Universal Declaration of Human Rights and other internationally recognized human rights instruments, the values enshrined in them, and the indivisibility and interdependence of all human rights and freedoms;

   To oppose grave violations of the rights of every person freely to hold and to express his or her convictions and to be free from discrimination by reason of ethnic origin, sex, colour or language, and of the right of every person to physical and mental integrity, and, in particular, to oppose by all appropriate means irrespective of political considerations:

   a) the imprisonment, detention or other physical restrictions imposed on any person by reason of his or her political, religious or other conscientiously held beliefs or by reason of his or her ethnic origin, sex, colour or language, provided that he or she has not used or advocated violence (hereinafter referred to as "prisoners of conscience"); AMNESTY INTERNATIONAL shall work towards the release of and shall provide assistance to prisoners of conscience;

   b) the detention of any political prisoner without fair trial within a reasonable time or any trial procedures relating to such prisoners that do not conform to internationally recognized norms;

   c) the death penalty, and the torture or other cruel, inhuman or degrading treatment or punishment of prisoners or other detained or restricted persons, whether or not the persons affected have used or advocated violence;

   d) the extrajudicial execution of persons whether or not imprisoned, detained or restricted, and "disappearances", whether or not the persons affected have used or advocated violence.

### Methods

2. In order to achieve the aforesaid object and mandate, AMNESTY INTERNATIONAL shall:

a) at all times make clear its impartiality as regards countries adhering to the different world political ideologies and groupings;

b) promote as appears appropriate the adoption of constitutions, conventions, treaties and other measures which guarantee the rights contained in the provisions referred to in Article 1 hereof;

c) support and publicize the activities of and cooperate with international organizations and agencies which work for the implementation of the aforesaid provisions;

d) take all necessary steps to establish an effective organization of sections, affiliated groups and individual members;

e) secure the adoption by groups of members or supporters of individual prisoners of conscience or entrust to such groups other tasks in support of the object and mandate set out in Article 1;

f) provide financial and other relief to prisoners of conscience and their dependants and to persons who have lately been prisoners of conscience or who might reasonably be expected to be prisoners of conscience or to become prisoners of conscience if convicted or if they were to return to their own countries, to the dependants of such persons and to victims of torture in need of medical care as a direct result thereof;

g) provide legal aid, where necessary and possible, to prisoners of conscience and to persons who might reasonably be expected to be prisoners of conscience or to become prisoners of conscience if convicted or if they were to return to their own countries, and, where desirable, send observers to attend the trials of such persons;

h) publicize the cases of prisoners of conscience or persons who have otherwise been subjected to disabilities in violation of the aforesaid provisions;

i) investigate and publicize the "disappearance" of persons where there is reason to believe that they may be victims of violations of the rights set out in Article 1 hereof;

j) oppose the sending of persons from one country to another where they can reasonably be expected to become prisoners of conscience or to face torture or the death penalty;

k) send investigators, where appropriate, to investigate allegations that the rights of individuals under the aforesaid provisions have been violated or threatened;

l) make representations to international organizations and to governments whenever it appears that an individual is a prisoner of conscience or has otherwise been subjected to disabilities in violation of the aforesaid provisions;

m) promote and support the granting of general amnesties of which the beneficiaries will include prisoners of conscience;

n) adopt any other appropriate methods for the securing of its object and mandate.

---

**The full text of the Statute of Amnesty International is available free upon request from: Amnesty International, International Secretariat, 1 Easton Street, London WC1X 8DJ, United Kingdom.**

# AMNESTY INTERNATIONAL NEWS RELEASES 1992

**22 January**
**Haiti:** Amnesty International calls for international action on continuing human rights violations

**22 January**
**Israel and the Occupied Territories:** Amnesty International expresses concern about secret detentions in Israel

**30 January**
**Cuba:** Amnesty International urges government to halt executions

**5 February**
**Women:** Amnesty International calls for an end to rape and sexual abuse by government agents

**12 February**
**Haiti:** Amnesty International condemns return of Haitian asylum-seekers by United States authorities

**13 February**
**Algeria:** Amnesty International fears state of emergency may lead to a sharp deterioration in human rights

**26 February**
**Philippines:** Hundreds brutally killed by military forces since 1988, says Amnesty International

**4 March**
**Tunisia:** Thousands held illegally and tortured in the crackdown on Islamic opposition groups, says Amnesty International

**6 March**
**Malawi:** Amnesty International calls for an end to brutal punishments and unexplained deaths in prisons

**18 March**
Amnesty International representative visits **Algeria** for the first time since the state of emergency was declared on 9 February 1992

**19 March**
**Myanmar:** Human rights violations cause thousands to flee, says Amnesty International

**19 March**
**Yugoslavia:** Amnesty International reports further cases of extrajudicial executions and deliberate and arbitrary killings

**19 March**
**Malawi:** Amnesty International fears for bishops' safety

**23 March**
Human rights protection is an essential part of the function of the **Conference on Security and Co-operation in Europe**, says Amnesty International

**25 March**
**India:** Routine torture and rape by the police has led to hundreds of deaths, reports Amnesty International

**25 March**
**United Kingdom:** Amnesty International urges government to end legislation allowing imprisonment for homosexual acts on the **Isle of Man**

**27 March**
**India:** Amnesty International replies to the government's response to its report on torture, rape and deaths in custody

**8 April**
**Togo:** Amnesty International calls for thorough investigations into the April 1991 massacre by the security forces

**9 April**
**Cameroon:** Up to 70 deaths from malnutrition reported at a prison camp, says Amnesty International

**15 April**
**Sudan:** Torture and detention of government opponents continues despite government claims, reports Amnesty International

**15 April**
**Italy:** Amnesty International provides information to the United Nations Committee against Torture

**330**

**22 April**
**United States of America:** Amnesty International deplores "Urge to Kill" shown by the United States Supreme Court and California authorities in rushing to carry out an execution as soon as possible

**29 April**
**Sierra Leone:** Human rights abuses in a hidden war zone, reports Amnesty International

**30 April**
**Afghanistan:** Amnesty International calls for safeguards for prisoners

**30 April**
**United States of America:** Amnesty International calls for a full judicial inquiry into reports of routine police brutality by Los Angeles police officers

**6 May**
**Israel/South Lebanon:** Detainees tortured and isolated in the Khiam detention centre, reports Amnesty International

**7 May**
**Malawi:** Amnesty International calls for an inquiry into allegations of torture

**13 May**
**Angola:** Political killings continue despite peace agreements, reports Amnesty International

**13 May**
**Peru:** Amnesty International urges government to guarantee safety of prisoners

**14 May**
**South Africa:** New evidence of police and military complicity in human rights violations, says Amnesty International

**20 May**
**China:** Harsh repression leads to severe human rights violations in Tibet, says Amnesty International

**20 May**
**Thailand:** Amnesty International expresses concern about prisoners of conscience and the use of lethal force

**26 May**
**Algeria:** Amnesty International urges the government to end administrative detention

**28 May**
**Burundi:** Toll of extrajudicial killings reaches at least 1,000 – Amnesty International calls for inquiries into human rights violations

**2 June**
**Lesotho:** Amnesty International calls for action against police torturers

**3 June**
**Pakistan:** Government opponents face harassment through arrests, detentions and torture, says Amnesty International

**4 June**
**China:** Thousands remain in detention three years after the Tiananmen Square massacre, says Amnesty International

**4 June**
**Rwanda:** Amnesty International appeals for an end to the widespread persecution of the Tutsi people

**10 June**
**South Africa:** Abuses by the police and military threaten political reforms, says Amnesty International

**17 June**
**Nepal:** Amnesty International calls for further human rights safeguards

**18 June**
New **Secretary General of Amnesty International** appointed

**24 June**
**Greece:** Torture and ill-treatment continue in prisons and police stations, says Amnesty International

**26 June**
**United States of America:** Amnesty International documents the use of torture, ill-treatment and excessive force by police in Los Angeles, California

**1 July**
**Venezuela:** Amnesty International calls on the government to end torture

**9 July**
Amnesty International's annual report details human rights violations in 142 countries and highlights how governments let torturers and state assassins get away with human rights abuses

**22 July**
**Syria:** Political prisoners are still being detained and tortured despite mass releases, says Amnesty International

**24 July**
**Zimbabwe:** Amnesty International calls for an investigation into unexplained deaths linked to poaching

**5 August**
**Somalia:** A human rights disaster, says Amnesty International

**26 August**
**Haiti:** Human rights held to ransom by torture, arbitrary arrest and extrajudicial execution, says Amnesty International

**3 September**
**Malawi:** Mass arrests as police crack down on the "fax revolution", says Amnesty International

**9 September**
**Uganda:** Amnesty International calls for action to safeguard human rights

**23 September**
**Sudan:** Amnesty International reports on deaths and detentions as Juba is destroyed

**7 October**
Amnesty International calls for an end to centuries of human rights abuses against **indigenous peoples in the Americas**

**12 October**
**Kenya:** Amnesty International expresses concern about possible unfair trial procedures and death sentences in treason trial

**15 October**
**Former Yugoslavia:** Amnesty International fears escalation of ethnic conflict in Kosovo

**20 October**
**Tunisia:** Amnesty International calls for fair trial or release of 265 Islamic activists

**21 October**
**Children** around the world are victims of human rights violations, says Amnesty International

**23 October**
**Former Yugoslavia:** Amnesty International documents human rights violations in Bosnia-Herzegovina and Kosovo

**28 October**
**Myanmar:** Thousands of people are victims of human rights violations, says Amnesty International

**11 November**
**Turkey:** Amnesty International accuses the government of failing to tackle the deteriorating human rights situation

**13 November**
**China:** State violence and denial of basic freedoms underpin secret political repression of Muslims in central Asian region of Xinjiang, says Amnesty International

**27 November**
**Burundi:** Amnesty International calls for an end to impunity for security forces

**30 November**
**Liberia:** Amnesty International fears an increasing risk of human rights violations as conflict intensifies

**30 November**
**Iraq:** Marsh Arabs still persecuted – Amnesty International calls on the United Nations to monitor human rights on-site

**2 December**
**South Africa:** Amnesty International reports on torture and killings in African National Congress camps

**3 December**
**Djibouti:** Amnesty International criticizes convictions by security tribunal and appeals for release of prisoners of conscience

**9 December**
**China:** Torture on the increase, reports Amnesty International

**10 December**
**United States of America:** Amnesty International calls on the authorities to commute the death sentence against a prisoner scheduled to be executed in Virginia on International Human Rights Day

**15 December**
**Cuba:** Amnesty International calls on the authorities to release prisoners of conscience

# AMNESTY INTERNATIONAL AROUND THE WORLD

There are now more than 8,000 local Amnesty International groups in over 70 countries around the world. In 48 countries these groups are coordinated by sections, whose addresses are given below. In addi- tion, there are individual members, sup- porters and recipients of Amnesty International information (such as the monthly *Amnesty International Newsletter*) in more than 150 countries and territories.

## SECTION ADDRESSES

**Algeria:**
Amnesty International,
BP99 Garidi – Kouba,
16051 Alger

**Argentina:**
Amnistía Internacional,
Sección Argentina,
Avenida Colon 56, 6° Piso,
Oficina "A",
Córdoba 5000

**Australia:**
Amnesty International,
Australian Section,
Private Bag 23, Broadway,
New South Wales 2007

**Austria:**
Amnesty International,
Austrian Section,
Wiedner Gürtel 12/7, A-1040 Wien

**Bangladesh:**
Amnesty International,
GPO Box 2242,
Dhaka 1000

**Barbados:**
Amnesty International,
Barbados Section,
PO Box 872, Bridgetown

**Belgium:**
Amnesty International,
Belgian Section (*Flemish branch*),
Kerkstraat 156, 2060 Antwerpen 6

Amnesty International,
Belgian Section (*francophone branch*),
9 rue Berckmans, 1060 Bruxelles

**Bermuda:**
Amnesty International,
Bermuda Section,
PO Box HM 2136, Hamilton HM JX

**Brazil:**
Anistia Internacional,
Seção Brasileira,
Rua Vicente Leporace 833,
CEP 04619-032,
São Paulo SP

**Canada:**
Amnesty International,
Canadian Section
(*English-speaking branch*),
214 Montreal Rd, Suite 401,
Vanier, Ontario, K1L 8L

Amnistie Internationale,
Section canadienne (*francophone branch*),
6250 boulevard Monk,
Montreal, Quebec, H4E 3H7

**Chile:**
Amnistía Internacional,
Casilla 4062, Santiago

**Côte d'Ivoire:**
Amnesty International,
Section Ivoirienne,
04 BP 895, Abidjan 04

**Denmark:**
Amnesty International,
Danish Section,
Dyrkoeb 3, 1166 Copenhagen K

**Ecuador:**
Amnistía Internacional,
Casilla 17-15-240-C,
Quito

**Faroe Islands:**
Amnesty International,
Faroe Islands Section,
PO Box 1075, FR-110 Torshavn

**Finland:**
Amnesty International,
Finnish Section,
Ruoholahdenkatu 24,
SF-00180 Helsinki

**France:**
Amnesty International,
French Section,
4 rue de la Pierre Levée,
75553 Paris (Cedex 11)

**Germany:**
Amnesty International,
German Section,
Heerstrasse 178, 5300 Bonn 1

**Ghana:**
Amnesty International,
Ghanaian Section,
PO Box 1173, Koforidua E.R.

**Greece:**
Amnesty International,
Greek Section,
30 Sina Street, 106 72 Athens

**Guyana:**
Amnesty International,
Guyana Section,
c/o PO Box 10720, Palm Court Building,
35 Main Street, Georgetown

**Hong Kong:**
Amnesty International,
Hong Kong Section,
Unit C, Third Floor,
Best-O-Best Building,
32-36 Ferry Street, Kowloon

**Iceland:**
Amnesty International,
Icelandic Section,
PO Box 618, 121 Reykjavík

**India:**
Amnesty International,
Indian Section,
C10 South Extension Part II,
New Delhi 110049

**Ireland:**
Amnesty International,
Irish Section,
Sean MacBride House, 8 Shaw Street,
Dublin 2

**Israel:**
Amnesty International,
Israel Section,
PO Box 14179, Tel Aviv 61141

**Italy:**
Amnesty International,
Italian Section,
Viale Mazzini 146, 00195 Rome

**Japan:**
Amnesty International,
Japanese Section,
Daisan-Sanbu Building 2F/3F,
2-3-22 Nishi-Waseda, Shinjuku-ku,
Tokyo 169

**Korea (Republic of):**
Amnesty International,
706-600,
Kyeong Buk R.C.O. Box 36,
Daegu

**Luxembourg:**
Amnesty International,
Luxembourg Section,
Boîte Postale 1914,
1019 Luxembourg

**Mauritius:**
Amnesty International,
Mauritius Section,
BP 69, Rose Hill

**Mexico:** **333**
Sección Mexicana de Amnistía
Internacional,
Ap. Postal No. 20-217, San Angel,
CP 01000 México DF

**Nepal:**
Amnesty International,
PO Box 135,
Jamal, Ranipokhari,
Kathmandu

**Netherlands:**
Amnesty International,
Dutch Section,
Keizersgracht 620, 1017 ER Amsterdam

**New Zealand:**
Amnesty International,
New Zealand Section,
PO Box 793, Wellington 1

**Nigeria:**
Amnesty International,
Nigerian Section,
PMB 59 Agodi, Ibadan, Oyo State

**Norway:**
Amnesty International,
Norwegian Section,
Maridalsveien 87, 0461 Oslo 4

**Peru:**
Amnistía Internacional,
Sección Peruana,
Casilla 659, Lima 18

**Philippines:**
Amnesty International,
Philippines Section,
PO Box 286, Sta Mesa Post Office,
1008 Sta Mesa, Manila

**Portugal:**
Amnistia Internacional,
Secção Portuguesa,
Apartado 12081, 1057 Lisboa Codex

**Puerto Rico:**
Amnistía Internacional,
Sección de Puerto Rico
Calle Robles No. 54 – Altos,
Oficina 11, Río Piedras,
Puerto Rico 00925

**Sierra Leone:**
Amnesty International,
Sierra Leone Section,
PMB 1021, Freetown

**Spain:**
Amnesty International,
Sección Española,
Gran Via 6, 5° Piso,
Apartado de Correos 50.318
28080 Madrid

**Sweden:**
Amnesty International,
Swedish Section,
PO Box 27827,
S-115 93 Stockholm

**Switzerland:**
Amnesty International,
Swiss Section,
PO Box, CH-3001 Bern

**Tanzania:**
Amnesty International,
Tanzanian Section,
National Secretariat,
PO Box 4331, Dar es Salaam

**Tunisia:**
Amnesty International,
Tunisian Section,
Secrétariat National,
48 Avenue Farhat Hached, 3ème Etage,
1001 Tunis

**United Kingdom:**
Amnesty International,
British Section,
99-119 Rosebery Avenue,
London EC1R 4RE

**United States of America:**
Amnesty International of the USA (AIUSA),
322 8th Ave, New York, NY 10001

**Uruguay:**
Amnistía Internacional,
Sección Uruguaya,
Yi 1333 Apto. 305,
Montevideo

**Venezuela:**
Amnistía Internacional,
Sección Venezolana,
Apartado Postal 5110,
Carmelitas 1010-A,
Caracas

## COUNTRIES AND TERRITORIES WITHOUT SECTIONS
## BUT WHERE LOCAL AMNESTY INTERNATIONAL GROUPS EXIST
## OR ARE BEING FORMED

| | | |
|---|---|---|
| Albania | Gaza Strip and West Bank | Paraguay |
| Armenia | Georgia | Poland |
| Aruba | Grenada | Romania |
| Bahamas | Hungary | Russia |
| Benin | Jamaica | Senegal |
| Bolivia | Jordan | Singapore |
| Bulgaria | Kazakhstan | Slovakia |
| Cameroon | Kuwait | Slovenia |
| Central African Republic | Kyrgyzstan | South Africa |
| Colombia | Latvia | Taiwan |
| Costa Rica | Lesotho | Thailand |
| Croatia | Lithuania | Togo |
| Curaçao | Macau | Ukraine |
| Czech Republic | Malaysia | Yemen |
| Dominican Republic | Mali | Zambia |
| Egypt | Mongolia | Zimbabwe |
| Estonia | Namibia | |
| Gambia | Pakistan | |

Amnesty International groups in Sudan have ceased activities following the banning of all political
parties, trade unions and non-governmental organizations including the Sudanese Amnesty
International Organization,"under which the Sudanese groups were officially registered in Sudan.

# INTERNATIONAL EXECUTIVE COMMITTEE
Ligia Bolívar/Venezuela
Claudio Cordone/International Secretariat
Ross Daniels/Australia
Liz Jenkins/United Kingdom
Sofía Macher/Peru
Gerry O'Connell/Italy
Ahmed Othmani/Tunisia
Marie Staunton/United Kingdom

# SELECTED INTERNATIONAL HUMAN RIGHTS TREATIES

## (AS OF 31 DECEMBER 1992)

States which have ratified or acceded to a convention are party to the treaty and are bound to observe its provisions. States which have signed but not yet ratified have expressed their intention to become a party at some future date; meanwhile they are obliged to refrain from acts which would defeat the object and purpose of the treaty.

| | International Covenant on Civil and Political Rights (ICCPR) | Optional Protocol to ICCPR | Second Optional Protocol to ICCPR aiming at the abolition of the death penalty | International Covenant on Economic, Social and Cultural Rights (ICESCR) | Convention against Torture and Other Cruel, Inhuman or Degrading Treatment or Punishment | Convention relating to the Status of Refugees (1951) | Protocol relating to the Status of Refugees (1967) |
|---|---|---|---|---|---|---|---|
| Afghanistan | x | | | x | x(28) | | |
| Albania | x | | | x | | x* | x* |
| Algeria | x | x | | x | x(22) | x | x |
| Angola | x* | x* | | x* | | x | x |
| Antigua and Barbuda | | | | | | | |
| Argentina | x | x | | x | x(22) | x | x |
| Armenia | | | | | | | |
| Australia | x | x | x | x | x | x | x |
| Austria | x | x | s | x | x(22) | x | x |
| Azerbaydzhan | x* | | | x* | | | |
| Bahamas | | | | | | | |
| Bahrain | | | | | | | |
| Bangladesh | | | | | | | |
| Barbados | x | x | | x | | | |
| Belarus | x | x* | | x | x(28) | | x |
| Belgium | x | | s | x | s | x | x |

**AMNESTY INTERNATIONAL REPORT 1993**

| | International Covenant on Civil and Political Rights (ICCPR) | Optional Protocol to ICCPR | Second Optional Protocol to ICCPR aiming at the abolition of the death penalty | International Covenant on Economic, Social and Cultural Rights (ICESCR) | Convention against Torture and Other Cruel, Inhuman or Degrading Treatment or Punishment | Convention relating to the Status of Refugees (1951) | Protocol relating to the Status of Refugees (1967) |
|---|---|---|---|---|---|---|---|
| Belize | | | | | | x | x |
| Benin | x* | x* | | x* | x* | x | x |
| Bhutan | | | | | | | |
| Bolivia | x | x | | x | s | x | x |
| Bosnia-Herzegovina | | | | | | | |
| Botswana | | | | | | x | x |
| Brazil | x* | | | x* | x | x | x |
| Brunei Darussalam | | | | | | | |
| Bulgaria | x | x* | | x | x(28) | x | x |
| Burkina Faso | | | | | | x | x |
| Burundi | x | | | x | | x | x |
| Cambodia | x* | | | x* | x* | x* | x* |
| Cameroon | x | x | | x | x | x | x |
| Canada | x | x | | x | x(22) | x | x |
| Cape Verde | | | | | x* | x | x |
| Central African Republic | x | x | | x | | x | x |
| Chad | | | | | | x | x |
| Chile | x | x* | | x | x | x | x |
| China | | | | x | x(28) | x | x |
| Colombia | x | x | | x | x | x | x |
| Comoros | | | | | | | |
| Congo | x | x | | x | | x | x |
| Costa Rica | x | x | s | x | s | x | x |
| Côte d'Ivoire | x* | | | x* | | x | x |

| | International Covenant on Civil and Political Rights (ICCPR) | Optional Protocol to ICCPR | Second Optional Protocol to ICCPR aiming at the abolition of the death penalty | International Covenant on Economic, Social and Cultural Rights (ICESCR) | Convention against Torture and Other Cruel, Inhuman or Degrading Treatment or Punishment | Convention relating to the Status of Refugees (1951) | Protocol relating to the Status of Refugees (1967) |
|---|---|---|---|---|---|---|---|
| Croatia | x* | | | x* | x* | x* | x* |
| Cuba | | | | | s | | |
| Cyprus | x | x* | | x | x | x | x |
| Czech and Slovak Federal Republic | x | x | | x | x(28) | x | x |
| Denmark | x | x | s | x | x(22) | x | x |
| Djibouti | | | | | | x | x |
| Dominica | | | | | | | |
| Dominican Republic | x | x | | x | s | x | x |
| Ecuador | x | x | | x | x(22) | x | x |
| Egypt | x | | | x | x | x | x |
| El Salvador | x | s | | x | | x | x |
| Equatorial Guinea | x | x | | x | | x | x |
| Estonia | x | x | | x | x | | |
| Ethiopia | | | | | | x | x |
| Fiji | | | | | | x | x |
| Finland | x | x | x | x | x(22) | x | x |
| France | x | x | | x | x(22) | x | x |
| Gabon | x | | | x | s | x | x |
| Gambia | x | x | | x | s | x | x |
| Georgia | | | | | | | |
| Germany | x | | x* | x | x | x | x |
| Ghana | | | | | | x | x |
| Greece | | | | x | x(22) | x | x |
| Grenada | x | | | x | | | |

AMNESTY INTERNATIONAL REPORT 1993

| | International Covenant on Civil and Political Rights (ICCPR) | Optional Protocol to ICCPR | Second Optional Protocol to ICCPR aiming at the abolition of the death penalty | International Covenant on Economic, Social and Cultural Rights (ICESCR) | Convention against Torture and Other Cruel, Inhuman or Degrading Treatment or Punishment | Convention relating to the Status of Refugees (1951) | Protocol relating to the Status of Refugees (1967) |
|---|---|---|---|---|---|---|---|
| Guatemala | x* | | | x | x | x | x |
| Guinea | x | s | | x | x | x | x |
| Guinea-Bissau | | | | x* | | x | x |
| Guyana | x | | | x | x | | |
| Haiti | x | | | x | | x | x |
| Holy See | | | | | | x | x |
| Honduras | s | s | s | x | | x* | x* |
| Hungary | x | x | | x | x(22) | x | x |
| Iceland | x | x | x | x | s | x | x |
| India | x | | | x | | | |
| Indonesia | | | | | s | | |
| Iran (Islamic Republic of) | x | | | x | | x | x |
| Iraq | x | | | x | | | |
| Ireland | x | x | | x | s* | x | x |
| Israel | x | | | x | x(28) | x | x |
| Italy | x | x | s | x | x(22) | x | x |
| Jamaica | x | x | | x | | x | x |
| Japan | x | | | x | | x | x |
| Jordan | x | | | x | x | | |
| Kazakhstan | | | | | | | |
| Kenya | x | | | x | | x | x |
| Kiribati | | | | | | | |
| Korea (Democratic People's Republic of) | x | | | x | | | |

| | International Covenant on Civil and Political Rights (ICCPR) | Optional Protocol to ICCPR | Second Optional Protocol to ICCPR aiming at the abolition of the death penalty | International Covenant on Economic, Social and Cultural Rights (ICESCR) | Convention against Torture and Other Cruel, Inhuman or Degrading Treatment or Punishment | Convention relating to the Status of Refugees (1951) | Protocol relating to the Status of Refugees (1967) |
|---|---|---|---|---|---|---|---|
| Korea (Republic of) | x | x | | x | | x* | x* |
| Kuwait | | | | | | | |
| Kyrgyzstan | | | | | | | |
| Lao People's Democratic Republic | | | | | | | |
| Latvia | x* | | | x* | x* | | |
| Lebanon | x | | | x | | | |
| Lesotho | x* | | | x* | | x | x |
| Liberia | s | | | s | | x | x |
| Libyan Arab Jamahiriya | x | x | | x | x | | |
| Liechtenstein | | | | x | x(22) | x | x |
| Lithuania | x | x | | x | | | |
| Luxembourg | x | x | x* | x | x(22) | x | x |
| Madagascar | x | x | | x | | x | |
| Malawi | | | | | | x | x |
| Malaysia | | | | | | | |
| Maldives | | | | | | | |
| Mali | x | | | x | | x | x |
| Malta | x | x | | x | x(22) | x | x |
| Marshall Islands | | | | | | | |
| Mauritania | | | | | | x | x |
| Mauritius | x | x | | x | x* | x | x |
| Mexico | x | | | x | x | | |
| Micronesia (Federated States of) | | | | | | | |
| Moldova | | | | | | | |

AMNESTY INTERNATIONAL REPORT 1993

| | International Covenant on Civil and Political Rights (ICCPR) | Optional Protocol to ICCPR | Second Optional Protocol to ICCPR aiming at the abolition of the death penalty | International Covenant on Economic, Social and Cultural Rights (ICESCR) | Convention against Torture and Other Cruel, Inhuman or Degrading Treatment or Punishment | Convention relating to the Status of Refugees (1951) | Protocol relating to the Status of Refugees (1967) |
|---|---|---|---|---|---|---|---|
| Monaco | | | | | x(22) | x | |
| Mongolia | x | x | | x | | | |
| Morocco | x | | | x | s(28) | x | x |
| Mozambique | | | | | | x | x |
| Myanmar (Burma) | | | | | | | |
| Namibia | | | | | | | |
| Nauru | | | | | | | |
| Nepal | x | x | | x | x | | |
| Netherlands | x | x | x | x | x(22) | x | x |
| New Zealand | x | x | x | x | x(22) | x | x |
| Nicaragua | x | x | s | x | s | x | x |
| Niger | x | x | | x | | x | x |
| Nigeria | | | | | s | x | x |
| Norway | x | x | x | x | x(22) | x | x |
| Oman | | | | | | | |
| Pakistan | | | | | | | |
| Panama | x | x | | x | x | x | x |
| Papua New Guinea | | | | | | x | x |
| Paraguay | x* | | | x* | x | x | x |
| Peru | x | x | | x | x | x | x |
| Philippines | x | x | | x | x | x | x |
| Poland | x | x | | x | x | x | x |
| Portugal | x | x | x | x | x(22) | x | x |
| Qatar | | | | | | | |

| | International Covenant on Civil and Political Rights (ICCPR) | Optional Protocol to ICCPR | Second Optional Protocol to ICCPR aiming at the abolition of the death penalty | International Covenant on Economic, Social and Cultural Rights (ICESCR) | Convention against Torture and Other Cruel, Inhuman or Degrading Treatment or Punishment | Convention relating to the Status of Refugees (1951) | Protocol relating to the Status of Refugees (1967) |
|---|---|---|---|---|---|---|---|
| Romania | x | | x | x | x | x | x |
| Russian Federation | x | x | | x | x(22) | x | |
| Rwanda | x | | | x | | x | x |
| St Christopher and Nevis | | | | | | | |
| St Lucia | | | | | | | |
| St Vincent and The Grenadines | x | x | | x | | | |
| Samoa | | | | | | x | |
| San Marino | x | x | | x | | | |
| São Tomé and Príncipe | | | | | | x | x |
| Saudi Arabia | | | | | | | |
| Senegal | x | x | | x | x | x | x |
| Seychelles | x* | x* | | x* | x* | x | x |
| Sierra Leone | | | | | s | x | x |
| Singapore | | | | | | | |
| Slovenia | x* | | | x* | | x* | x* |
| Solomon Islands | | | | x | | | |
| Somalia | x | x | | x | x | x | x |
| South Africa | | | | | | | |
| Spain | x | x | x | x | x(22) | x | x |
| Sri Lanka | x | | | x | | | |
| Sudan | x | | | x | s | x | x |
| Suriname | x | x | | x | | x | x |
| Swaziland | | | | | | | x |
| Sweden | x | x | x | x | x(22) | x | x |

AMNESTY INTERNATIONAL REPORT 1993

| | International Covenant on Civil and Political Rights (ICCPR) | Optional Protocol to ICCPR | Second Optional Protocol to ICCPR aiming at the abolition of the death penalty | International Covenant on Economic, Social and Cultural Rights (ICESCR) | Convention against Torture and Other Cruel, Inhuman or Degrading Treatment or Punishment | Convention relating to the Status of Refugees (1951) | Protocol relating to the Status of Refugees (1967) |
|---|---|---|---|---|---|---|---|
| Switzerland | x* | | | x* | x(22) | x | x |
| Syrian Arab Republic | x | | | x | | | x |
| Tadzhikistan | | | | | | | |
| Tanzania | x | | | x | | x | x |
| Thailand | | | | | | | |
| Togo | x | x | | x | x(22) | x | x |
| Tonga | | | | x | | | |
| Trinidad and Tobago | x | x | | | | | |
| Tunisia | x | x | | x | x(22) | x | x |
| Turkey | | | | | x(22) | x | x |
| Turkmenistan | | | | | | | |
| Tuvalu | | | | | | x | x |
| Uganda | x | | | x | x | x | x |
| Ukraine | x | x | | x | x(28) | | |
| United Arab Emirates | | | | | | | |
| United Kingdom | x | | | x | x | x | x |
| United States of America | x* | | | s | s | | x |
| Uruguay | x | x | s | x | x(22) | x | x |
| Uzbekistan | | | | x | | | |
| Vanuatu | | | | | | | |
| Venezuela | x | x | s | x | x | x | x |
| Viet Nam | x | | | x | | | |
| Yemen | x | | | x | x | x | x |
| Yugoslavia (Federal Republic of) | x | s | | x | x(22) | x | x |

| | International Covenant on Civil and Political Rights (ICCPR) | Optional Protocol to ICCPR | Second Optional Protocol to ICCPR aiming at the abolition of the death penalty | International Covenant on Economic, Social and Cultural Rights (ICESCR) | Convention against Torture and Other Cruel, Inhuman or Degrading Treatment or Punishment | Convention relating to the Status of Refugees (1951) | Protocol relating to the Status of Refugees (1967) |
|---|---|---|---|---|---|---|---|
| Zaïre | x | x | | x | x | x | x |
| Zambia | x | x | | x | | x | x |
| Zimbabwe | x | | | x | x | x | x |

s – denotes that country has signed but not yet ratified

x – denotes that country is a party, either through ratification, accession or succession

* – denotes that country either signed or became a party in 1992

(22) denotes Declaration under Article 22 recognizing the competence of the Committee against Torture to consider individual complaints of violations of the Convention

(28) denotes that country has made a reservation under Article 28 that it does not recognize the competence of the Committee against Torture to examine reliable information which appears to indicate that torture is being systematically practised, and to undertake a confidential inquiry if warranted

# SELECTED REGIONAL HUMAN RIGHTS TREATIES

### (AS OF 31 DECEMBER 1992)

#### ORGANIZATION OF AFRICAN UNITY (OAU)
#### AFRICAN CHARTER ON HUMAN AND PEOPLES' RIGHTS (1981)

| | | | | | |
|---|---|---|---|---|---|
| Algeria | x | Gambia | x | Saharawi Arab | |
| Angola | x | Ghana | x |   Democratic Republic | x |
| Benin | x | Guinea | x | São Tomé and Príncipe | x |
| Botswana | x | Guinea-Bissau | x | Senegal | x |
| Burkina Faso | x | Kenya | x | Seychelles | x |
| Burundi | x | Lesotho | x | Sierra Leone | x |
| Cameroon | x | Liberia | x | Somalia | x |
| Cape Verde | x | Libya | x | Sudan | x |
| Central African Republic | x | Madagascar | x | Swaziland | |
| Chad | x | Malawi | x | Tanzania | x |
| Comoros | x | Mali | x | Togo | x |
| Congo | x | Mauritania | x | Tunisia | x |
| Côte d'Ivoire | x | Mauritius | x | Uganda | x |
| Djibouti | x | Mozambique | x | Zaïre | x |
| Egypt | x | Namibia | x | Zambia | x |
| Equatorial Guinea | x | Niger | x | Zimbabwe | x |
| Ethiopia | | Nigeria | x | | |
| Gabon | x | Rwanda | x | | |

x – denotes that country is a party, either through ratification or accession
This chart lists countries which were members of the OAU at the end of 1992.

#### ORGANIZATION OF AMERICAN STATES (OAS)

| | American Convention on Human Rights (1969) | Inter-American Convention to Prevent and Punish Torture (1985) | | American Convention on Human Rights (1969) | Inter-American Convention to Prevent and Punish Torture (1985) |
|---|---|---|---|---|---|
| Antigua and Barbuda | | | Haiti | x | s |
| Argentina | x(62) | x | Honduras | x(62) | s |
| Bahamas | | | Jamaica | x | |
| Barbados | x | | Mexico | x | x |
| Belize | | | Nicaragua | x(62) | s |
| Bolivia | x | s | Panama | x(62) | x |
| Brazil | x | x | Paraguay | x | x |
| Canada | | | Peru | x(62) | x |
| Chile | x(62) | x | St Christopher | | |
| Colombia | x(62) | s |   and Nevis | | |
| Costa Rica | x(62) | s | St Lucia | | |
| Cuba | | | St Vincent and | | |
| Dominica | | |   The Grenadines | | |
| Dominican Republic | x | x | Suriname | x(62) | x |
| Ecuador | x(62) | s | Trinidad and Tobago | x(62) | |
| El Salvador | x | s | United States of | | |
| Grenada | x | |   America | s | |
| Guatemala | x(62) | x | Uruguay | x(62) | x |
| Guyana | | | Venezuela | x(62) | x |

s – denotes that country has signed but not yet ratified
x – denotes that country is a party, either through ratification or accession
(62) denotes Declaration under Article 62 recognizing as binding the jurisdiction of the Inter-American Court of Human Rights (on all matters relating to the interpretation or application of the American Convention)
This chart lists countries which were members of the OAS at the end of 1992.

## COUNCIL OF EUROPE

| | European Convention for the Protection of Human Rights and Fundamental Freedoms (1950) | Article 25 | Article 46 | Protocol No. 6* | European Convention for the Prevention of Torture and Inhuman or Degrading Treatment or Punishment (1987) |
|---|---|---|---|---|---|
| Austria | x | x | x | x | x |
| Belgium | x | x | x | s | x |
| Bulgaria | x | x | x | | |
| Cyprus | x | x | x | | x |
| Czech and Slovak Federal Republic | x | x | x | x | x |
| Denmark | x | x | x | x | x |
| Finland | x | x | x | x | x |
| France | x | x | x | x | x |
| Germany | x | x | x | x | x |
| Greece | x | x | x | s | x |
| Hungary | x | x | x | x | |
| Iceland | x | x | x | x | x |
| Ireland | x | x | x | | x |
| Italy | x | x | x | x | x |
| Liechtenstein | x | x | x | x | x |
| Luxembourg | x | x | x | x | x |
| Malta | x | x | x | x | x |
| Netherlands | x | x | x | x | x |
| Norway | x | x | x | x | x |
| Poland | s | | | | |
| Portugal | x | x | x | x | x |
| San Marino | x | x | x | x | x |
| Spain | x | x | x | x | x |
| Sweden | x | x | x | x | x |
| Switzerland | x | x | x | x | x |
| Turkey | x | x | x | | x |
| United Kingdom | x | x | x | | x |

s – denotes that country has signed but not yet ratified
x – denotes that country is a party, either through ratification or accession

Article 25: denotes Declaration under Article 25 of the European Convention, recognizing the competence of the European Commission of Human Rights to consider individual complaints of violations of the Convention

Article 46: denotes Declaration under Article 46 of the European Convention, recognizing as compulsory the jurisdiction of the European Court of Human Rights in all matters concerning interpretation and application of the European Convention

* Protocol 6 to the European Convention on Human Rights: concerning abolition of the death penalty (1983)

This chart lists countries which were members of the Council of Europe at the end of 1992.

# OVERDUE REPORTS

## A) BY STATES PARTIES TO THE INTERNATIONAL COVENANT ON CIVIL AND POLITICAL RIGHTS

Governments that have ratified or acceded to the International Covenant on Civil and Political Rights (ICCPR) are referred to as "States Parties" to that treaty. Article 40 of the ICCPR requires States Parties to submit reports to the United Nations "on the measures they have adopted which give effect to the rights recognized [in the ICCPR] and on the progress made in the enjoyment of those rights". The reports are supposed to "indicate the factors and difficulties, if any, affecting the implementation of the present Covenant".

The initial report is due within one year after the ICCPR enters into force for the particular state; subsequent reports are due every five years. They are reviewed by the Human Rights Committee, the body of 18 experts which monitors implementation of the ICCPR.

The Human Rights Committee has repeatedly expressed concern about the non-compliance of states with their reporting obligations.

The Committee noted that there may be various reasons for reports being overdue, including a shortage of resources, the assignment of insufficient priority, and in some cases the reluctance of states to expose themselves to scrutiny.

The UN General Assembly has urged States Parties to the ICCPR which have not yet done so "to submit their reports as speedily as possible".

According to information provided by the UN Centre for Human Rights, as of 31 December 1992 the following states were at least one year late in submitting their initial, second or third periodic reports.

## INITIAL REPORTS

| State Party | Date due | Number of reminders sent |
|---|---|---|
| Gabon | 20 April 1984 | 18 |
| Equatorial Guinea | 24 December 1988 | 8 |
| Somalia | 23 April 1991 | 3 |
| Malta | 12 December 1991 | 2 |

## SECOND PERIODIC REPORTS

| State Party | Date due | Number of reminders sent |
|---|---|---|
| Cyprus | 18 August 1984 | 18 |
| Syrian Arab Republic | 18 August 1984 | 18 |
| Cook Islands (New Zealand) | 27 March 1985 | 7 |
| Gambia | 21 June 1985 | 16 |
| Suriname | 2 August 1985 | 15 |
| Lebanon | 21 March 1986 | 15 |
| Kenya | 11 April 1986 | 14 |
| Mali | 11 April 1986 | 14 |
| Jamaica | 1 August 1986 | 12 |
| Netherlands-Antilles | 31 October 1986 | 6 |
| Guyana | 10 April 1987 | 12 |
| Iceland | 30 October 1987 | 11 |
| Democratic People's Republic of Korea | 13 December 1987 | 10 |
| El Salvador | 28 February 1986/ 31 December 1988* | 8 |
| Central African Republic | 7 August 1987/ 9 April 1989* | 7 |

| | | |
|---|---|---|
| Gabon | 20 April 1989 | 7 |
| Congo | 4 January 1990 | 6 |
| Zambia | 9 July 1990 | 5 |
| Bolivia | 11 November 1988/ | |
| | 13 July 1990* | 10 |
| Togo | 23 August 1990 | 5 |
| Republic of Cameroon | 26 September 1990 | 5 |
| Viet Nam | 23 December 1988/ | |
| | 31 July 1991* | 8 |
| St Vincent and The Grenadines | 8 February 1988/ | |
| | 31 October 1991* | 8 |

## THIRD PERIODIC REPORTS

| State Party | Date due | Number of reminders sent |
|---|---|---|
| Libyan Arab Jamahiriya*** | 4 February 1988 | 10 |
| Iran (Islamic Republic of)*** | 21 March 1988 | 8 |
| Lebanon | 21 March 1988 | 10 |
| Bulgaria*** | 28 April 1989 | 7 |
| Cyprus | 18 August 1989 | 7 |
| Syrian Arab Republic | 18 August 1989 | 7 |
| Trinidad and Tobago | 20 March 1990 | 6 |
| New Zealand (Cook Islands) | 27 March 1990 | 6 |
| Gambia | 21 June 1990 | 5 |
| Mauritius | 4 November 1988/ | |
| | 18 July 1990* | 11 |
| Suriname | 2 August 1990 | 5 |
| Denmark | 1 November 1990 | 5 |
| Zaire | 30 January 1988/ | |
| | 31 July 1991* | 8 |
| Panama | 6 June 1988/ | |
| | 31 March 1992** | 4 |
| India | 9 July 1990/ | |
| | 31 March 1992** | 3 |
| Madagascar | 3 August 1988/ | |
| | 31 July 1992** | 6 |

\*     denotes that the first date is the original deadline and the second date is the extended deadline.

\*\*    these countries exceeded their original deadlines for submitting their third periodic reports by at least one year and exceeded their extended deadlines by at least five months.

\*\*\*   the State Party submitted single reports identified as second and third reports, but the Human Rights Committee normally treats such reports as second reports.

348

## B) BY STATES PARTIES TO THE CONVENTION AGAINST TORTURE AND OTHER CRUEL, INHUMAN OR DEGRADING TREATMENT OR PUNISHMENT

Governments which have ratified or acceded to the Convention against Torture and Other Cruel, Inhuman or Degrading Treatment or Punishment are referred to as "States Parties" to that treaty. Article 19 of the Convention against Torture requires States Parties to submit reports to the United Nations "on the measures they have taken to give effect to their undertakings [under the Convention against Torture]".

The initial report is due within one year after the Convention against Torture enters into force for the particular state; supplementary reports are due every four years and should cover "any new measures taken". The reports are reviewed by the Committee against Torture, the body of 10 experts which monitors implementation of the Convention against Torture.

According to information provided by the UN Centre for Human Rights, as of 31 December 1992 the following states were at least one year late in submitting their initial reports.

### INITIAL REPORTS

| State Party | Date due | Number of reminders sent |
|---|---|---|
| Uganda | 25 June 1988 | 6 |
| Togo | 17 December 1988 | 6 |
| Guyana | 19 August 1989 | 5 |
| Italy | 10 February 1990 | 2 |
| Portugal | 10 March 1990 | 4 |
| Poland | 24 August 1990 | 3 |
| Brazil | 27 October 1990 | 3 |
| Guinea | 8 November 1990 | 3 |
| Guatemala | 3 February 1991 | 2 |
| Somalia | 22 February 1991 | 2 |
| Paraguay | 10 April 1991 | 2 |
| Malta | 12 October 1991 | 1 |
| Liechtenstein | 1 December 1991 | 1 |

## C) BY STATES PARTIES TO THE AFRICAN CHARTER ON HUMAN AND PEOPLES' RIGHTS

Governments which have ratified or acceded to the African Charter on Human and Peoples' Rights are referred to as "States Parties" to that treaty. Article 62 of the African Charter requires States Parties to submit reports every two years to the African Commission on Human and Peoples' Rights, established under the African Charter to monitor implementation of that treaty, "on the legislative or other measures taken with a view to giving effect to the rights and freedoms recognized and guaranteed by the [African Charter]".

The Commission, composed of 11 experts, reviews these reports. According to the Secretariat of the African Commission, as of 31 December 1992 the following States Parties were at least one year late in submitting their initial or second periodic reports.

### INITIAL REPORTS

| State Party | Date due | Number of reminders sent |
|---|---|---|
| Benin | 21 October 1988 | 2 |
| Botswana | 21 October 1988 | 2 |
| Burkina Faso | 21 October 1988 | 2 |
| Central African Republic | 21 October 1988 | 2 |
| Comoros | 21 October 1988 | 2 |

| | | |
|---|---|---|
| Congo | 21 October 1988 | 2 |
| Equatorial Guinea | 21 October 1988 | 2 |
| Gabon | 21 October 1988 | 2 |
| Guinea | 21 October 1988 | 2 |
| Guinea-Bissau | 21 October 1988 | 2 |
| Liberia | 21 October 1988 | 2 |
| Mali | 21 October 1988 | 2 |
| Mauritania | 21 October 1988 | 2 |
| Niger | 21 October 1988 | 2 |
| Saharawi Arab Democratic Republic | 21 October 1988 | 2 |
| São Tomé and Príncipe | 21 October 1988 | 2 |
| Sierra Leone | 21 October 1988 | 2 |
| Somalia | 21 October 1988 | 2 |
| Sudan | 21 October 1988 | 2 |
| Uganda | 21 October 1988 | 2 |
| Zambia | 21 October 1988 | 2 |
| Chad | 11 February 1989 | 2 |
| Algeria | 20 June 1989 | 2 |
| Zaïre | 28 October 1989 | 2 |
| Ghana | 1 June 1991 | 0 |
| Burundi | 21 November 1991 | 0 |

## SECOND PERIODIC REPORTS

| State Party | Date due | Number of reminders sent |
|---|---|---|
| Benin | 21 October 1990 | 1 |
| Botswana | 21 October 1990 | 1 |
| Burkina Faso | 21 October 1990 | 1 |
| Central African Republic | 21 October 1990 | 1 |
| Comoros | 21 October 1990 | 1 |
| Congo | 21 October 1990 | 1 |
| Egypt | 21 October 1990 | 1 |
| Equatorial Guinea | 21 October 1990 | 1 |
| Gabon | 21 October 1990 | 1 |
| Gambia | 21 October 1990 | 1 |
| Guinea | 21 October 1990 | 1 |
| Guinea-Bissau | 21 October 1990 | 1 |
| Liberia | 21 October 1990 | 1 |
| Mali | 21 October 1990 | 1 |
| Mauritania | 21 October 1990 | 1 |
| Niger | 21 October 1990 | 1 |
| Nigeria | 21 October 1990 | 1 |
| Rwanda | 21 October 1990 | 1 |
| Saharawi Arab Democratic Republic | 21 October 1990 | 1 |
| São Tomé and Príncipe | 21 October 1990 | 1 |
| Sierra Leone | 21 October 1990 | 1 |
| Somalia | 21 October 1990 | 1 |
| Sudan | 21 October 1990 | 1 |
| Tanzania | 21 October 1990 | 1 |
| Togo | 21 October 1990 | 1 |
| Tunisia | 21 October 1990 | 1 |
| Uganda | 21 October 1990 | 1 |
| Zambia | 21 October 1990 | 1 |
| Zimbabwe | 21 October 1990 | 1 |
| Chad | 11 February 1991 | 0 |
| Algeria | 20 June 1991 | 0 |
| Zaire | 28 October 1991 | 0 |

# AMNESTY INTERNATIONAL
# 14-POINT PROGRAM FOR THE PREVENTION OF "DISAPPEARANCES"

The "disappeared" are people who have been taken into custody by agents of the state, yet whose whereabouts and fate are concealed, and whose custody is denied. "Disappearances" cause agony for the victims and their relatives. The victims are cut off from the world and placed outside the protection of the law; often they are tortured; many are never seen again. Their relatives are kept in ignorance, unable to find out whether the victims are alive or dead.

The United Nations has condemned "disappearances" as a grave violation of human rights and has said that their systematic practice is of the nature of a crime against humanity. Yet thousands of people "disappear" each year across the globe, and countless others remain "disappeared". Urgent action is needed to stop "disappearances", to clarify the fate of the "disappeared" and to bring those responsible to justice.

Amnesty International calls on all governments to implement the following 14-Point Program for the Prevention of "Disappearances". It invites concerned individuals and organizations to join in promoting the program. Amnesty International believes that the implementation of these measures is a positive indication of a government's commitment to stop "disappearances" and to work for their eradication worldwide.

### 1. Official condemnation
The highest authorities of every country should demonstrate their total opposition to "disappearances". They should make clear to all members of the police, military and other security forces that "disappearances" will not be tolerated under any circumstances.

### 2. Chain-of-command control
Those in charge of the security forces should maintain strict chain-of-command control to ensure that officers under their command do not commit "disappearances". Officials with chain-of-command responsibility who order or tolerate "disappearances" by those under their command should be held criminally responsible for these acts.

### 3. Information on detention and release
Accurate information about the arrest of any person and about his or her place of detention, including transfers and releases, should be made available promptly to relatives, lawyers and the courts. Prisoners should be released in a way that allows reliable verification of their release and ensures their safety.

### 4. Mechanism for locating and protecting prisoners
Governments should at all times ensure that effective judicial remedies are available which enable relatives and lawyers to find out immediately where a prisoner is held and under what authority, to ensure his or her safety, and to obtain the release of anyone arbitrarily detained.

### 5. No secret detention
Governments should ensure that prisoners are held only in publicly recognized places of detention. Up-to-date registers of all prisoners should be maintained in every place of detention and centrally. The information in these registers should be made available to relatives, lawyers, judges, official bodies trying to trace people who have been detained, and others with a legitimate interest. No one should be secretly detained.

### 6. Authorization of arrest and detention
Arrest and detention should be carried out only by officials who are authorized by law to do so. Officials carrying out an arrest should identify themselves to the person arrested and, on demand, to others witnessing the event. Governments should establish rules setting forth which officials are authorized to order an arrest or detention. Any deviation from established procedures which contributes to a "disappearance" should be punished by appropriate sanctions.

## 7. Access to prisoners
All prisoners should be brought before a judicial authority without delay after being taken into custody. Relatives, lawyers and doctors should have prompt and regular access to them. There should be regular, independent, unannounced and unrestricted visits of inspection to all places of detention.

## 8. Prohibition in law
Governments should ensure that the commission of a "disappearance" is a criminal offence, punishable by sanctions commensurate with the gravity of the practice. The prohibition of "disappearances" and the essential safeguards for their prevention must not be suspended under any circumstances, including states of war or other public emergency.

## 9. Individual responsibility
The prohibition of "disappearances" should be reflected in the training of all officials involved in the arrest and custody of prisoners and in the instructions issued to them. They should be instructed that they have the right and duty to refuse to obey any order to participate in a "disappearance". An order from a superior officer or a public authority must never be invoked as a justification for taking part in a "disappearance".

## 10. Investigation
Governments should ensure that all complaints and reports of "disappearances" are investigated promptly, impartially and effectively by a body which is independent of those allegedly responsible and has the necessary powers and resources to carry out the investigation. The methods and findings of the investigation should be made public. Officials suspected of responsibility for "disappearances" should be suspended from active duty during the investigation. Relatives of the victim should have access to information relevant to the investigation and should be entitled to present evidence. Complainants, witnesses, lawyers and others involved in the investigation should be protected from intimidation and reprisals. The investigation should not be curtailed until the fate of the victim is officially clarified.

## 11. Prosecution
Governments should ensure that those responsible for "disappearances" are brought to justice. This principle should apply wherever such people happen to be, wherever the crime was committed, whatever the nationality of the perpetrators or victims and no matter how much time has elapsed since the commission of the crime. Trials should be in the civilian courts. The perpetrators should not benefit from any legal measures exempting them from criminal prosecution or conviction.

## 12. Compensation and rehabilitation
Victims of "disappearance" and their dependants should be entitled to obtain fair and adequate redress from the state, including financial compensation. Victims who reappear should be provided with appropriate medical care or rehabilitation.

## 13. Ratification of human rights treaties and implementation of international standards
All governments should ratify international treaties containing safeguards and remedies against "disappearances", including the International Covenant on Civil and Political Rights and its first Optional Protocol which provides for individual complaints. Governments should ensure full implementation of the relevant provisions of these and other international instruments, including the UN Declaration on the Protection of All Persons from Enforced Disappearance, and comply with the recommendations of intergovernmental organizations concerning these abuses.

## 14. International responsibility
Governments should use all available channels to intercede with the governments of countries where "disappearances" have been reported. They should ensure that transfers of equipment, know-how and training for military, security or police use do not facilitate "disappearances". No one should be forcibly returned to a country where he or she risks being made to "disappear".

*This 14-Point Program was adopted by Amnesty International in December 1992 as part of the organization's worldwide campaign for the eradication of "disappearances". Similar programs are available on the prevention of torture and extrajudicial executions.*

# AMNESTY INTERNATIONAL
# 14-POINT PROGRAM FOR THE PREVENTION OF EXTRAJUDICIAL EXECUTIONS

Extrajudicial executions are fundamental violations of human rights and an affront to the conscience of humanity. These unlawful and deliberate killings, carried out by order of a government or with its complicity or acquiescence, have been condemned by the United Nations. Yet extrajudicial executions continue, daily and across the globe.

Many of the victims have been taken into custody or made to "disappear" before being killed. Some are killed in their homes, or in the course of military operations. Some are assassinated by uniformed members of the security forces, or by "death squads" operating with official connivance. Others are killed in peaceful demonstrations.

The accountability of governments for extrajudicial executions is not diminished by the commission of similar abhorrent acts by armed opposition groups. Urgent action is needed to stop extrajudicial executions and bring those responsible to justice.

Amnesty International calls on all governments to implement the following 14-Point Program for the Prevention of Extrajudicial Executions. It invites concerned individuals and organizations to join in promoting the program. Amnesty International believes that the implementation of these measures is a positive indication of a government's commitment to stop extrajudicial executions and to work for their eradication worldwide.

## 1. Official condemnation
The highest authorities of every country should demonstrate their total opposition to extrajudicial executions. They should make clear to all members of the police, military and other security forces that extrajudicial executions will not be tolerated under any circumstances.

## 2. Chain-of-command control
Those in charge of the security forces should maintain strict chain-of-command control to ensure that officers under their command do not commit extrajudicial executions. Officials with chain-of-command responsibility who order or tolerate extrajudicial executions by those under their command should be held criminally responsible for these acts.

## 3. Restraints on use of force
Governments should ensure that law enforcement officials use force only when strictly required and only to the minimum extent necessary under the circumstances. Lethal force should not be used except when strictly unavoidable in order to protect life.

## 4. Action against "death squads"
"Death squads", private armies, criminal gangs and paramilitary forces operating outside the chain of command but with official support or acquiescence should be prohibited and disbanded. Members of such groups who have perpetrated extrajudicial executions should be brought to justice.

## 5. Protection against death threats
Governments should ensure that anyone in danger of extrajudicial execution, including those who receive death threats, is effectively protected.

## 6. No secret detention
Governments should ensure that prisoners are held only in publicly recognized places of detention and that accurate information about the arrest and detention of any prisoner is made available promptly to relatives, lawyers and the courts. No one should be secretly detained.

## 7. Access to prisoners
All prisoners should be brought before a judicial authority without delay after being taken into custody. Relatives, lawyers and doctors should have prompt and regular access to them. There should be regular, independent, unannounced and unrestricted visits of inspection to all places of detention.

### 8. Prohibition in law
Governments should ensure that the commission of an extrajudicial execution is a criminal offence, punishable by sanctions commensurate with the gravity of the practice. The prohibition of extrajudicial executions and the essential safeguards for their prevention must not be suspended under any circumstances, including states of war or other public emergency.

### 9. Individual responsibility
The prohibition of extrajudicial executions should be reflected in the training of all officials involved in the arrest and custody of prisoners and all officials authorized to use lethal force, and in the instructions issued to them. These officials should be instructed that they have the right and duty to refuse to obey any order to participate in an extrajudicial execution. An order from a superior officer or a public authority must never be invoked as a justification for taking part in an extrajudicial execution.

### 10. Investigation
Governments should ensure that all complaints and reports of extrajudicial executions are investigated promptly, impartially and effectively by a body which is independent of those allegedly responsible and has the necessary powers and resources to carry out the investigation. The methods and findings of the investigation should be made public. The body of the alleged victim should not be disposed of until an adequate autopsy has been conducted by a suitably qualified doctor who is able to function impartially. Officials suspected of responsibility for extrajudicial executions should be suspended from active duty during the investigation. Relatives of the victim should have access to information relevant to the investigation, should be entitled to appoint their own doctor to carry out or be present at an autopsy, and should be entitled to present evidence.
Complainants, witnesses, lawyers, judges and others involved in the investigation should be protected from intimidation and reprisals.

### 11. Prosecution
Governments should ensure that those responsible for extrajudicial executions are brought to justice. This principle should apply wherever such people happen to be, wherever the crime was committed, whatever the nationality of the perpetrators or victims and no matter how much time has elapsed since the commission of the crime. Trials should be in the civilian courts. The perpetrators should not be allowed to benefit from any legal measures exempting them from criminal prosecution or conviction.

### 12. Compensation
Dependants of victims of extrajudicial execution should be entitled to obtain fair and adequate redress from the state, including financial compensation.

### 13. Ratification of human rights treaties and implementation of international standards
All governments should ratify international treaties containing safeguards and remedies against extrajudicial executions, including the International Covenant on Civil and Political Rights and its first Optional Protocol which provides for individual complaints. Governments should ensure full implementation of the relevant provisions of these and other international instruments, including the UN Principles on the Effective Prevention and Investigation of Extra-Legal, Arbitrary and Summary Executions, and comply with the recommendations of intergovernmental organizations concerning these abuses.

### 14. International responsibility
Governments should use all available channels to intercede with the governments of countries where extrajudicial executions have been reported. They should ensure that transfers of equipment, know-how and training for military, security or police use do not facilitate extrajudicial executions. No one should be forcibly returned to a country where he or she risks becoming a victim of extrajudicial execution.

*This 14-Point Program was adopted by Amnesty International in December 1992 as part of the organization's worldwide campaign for the eradication of extrajudicial executions. Similar programs are available on the prevention of torture and "disappearances".*

# SELECTED STATISTICS

### AMNESTY INTERNATIONAL MEMBERSHIP

At the end of 1992 there were more than 8,000 local Amnesty International groups in over 70 countries. There were more than 1,100,000 members, subscribers and regular donors in over 150 countries.

### PRISONER CASES AND RELEASES

At the end of September 1992 Amnesty International was working on 3,014 Action Files and cases featuring over 7,700 individuals, including prisoners of conscience and other victims of human rights violations. During the year action began on 629 new cases. A total of 1,041 cases involving the release of prisoners of conscience or those under investigation as possible prisoners of conscience was recorded.

### URGENT ACTION APPEALS

During 1992 Amnesty International initiated 585 actions which required urgent appeals from the Urgent Action Network. There were also 315 calls for further appeals on actions already issued. Members of the Urgent Action Network were thus asked to send appeals on 900 occasions. These actions were on behalf of people in 82 countries.

The 585 new actions were issued on behalf of people who were either at risk or had been the victim of the following human rights violations: torture – 213 cases; extrajudicial killing or "disappearance" – 112 cases; judicial execution – 87 cases; and harassment or death threats – 115 cases. In 26 cases prisoners were in urgent need of medical treatment. (These categories are not mutually exclusive; more than one concern may have been featured in an action.) Other actions were issued in cases of arbitrary arrest, prolonged incommunicado detention, detention without charge or trial, deaths in custody, amputations and *refoulement* (forcible repatriation).

### REGIONAL ACTION NETWORKS

Amnesty International's Regional Action Networks deal with human rights abuses in every country of the world. During the year 2,416 Amnesty International local groups participated in the Regional Action Networks, which worked on the cases of thousands of victims of human rights violations.

### AMNESTY INTERNATIONAL FUNDING

The budget adopted by Amnesty International for 1992 was £12,750,000. This sum represents slightly more than one third of the estimated income likely to be raised during the year by the movement's national sections. Amnesty International's national sections and local volunteer groups are responsible for funding the movement. There is no central fund-raising program and no money is sought or accepted from governments. The donations that sustain Amnesty International's work come from its members and the public.

### RELIEF

During 1992 the International Secretariat of Amnesty International distributed £247,343 in relief (financial assistance) to victims of human rights violations such as prisoners of conscience and recently released prisoners of conscience and their dependants, and to provide medical treatment for torture victims. In addition, the organization's sections and groups distributed a further substantial amount, much of it in the form of modest payments by local groups to their adopted prisoners of conscience and dependent families.

While Amnesty International's ultimate goal is to end human rights violations, so long as such violations continue it tries to provide practical help to the thousands of individuals affected by them. Relief is an important aspect of this work. Sometimes Amnesty International provides such assistance directly to individuals. At other times, it works through locally-based distributors such as local and national human rights organizations so as to ensure that resources are used as effectively as possible for those in most need. When Amnesty International asks an intermediary to distribute relief payments on its behalf, it stipulates precisely the intended purpose and beneficiaries and requires the intermediary to report back on the expenditure of the funds.

## DATE DUE

| | |
|---|---|
| | |
| | |
| | |
| | |
| | |
| | |
| | |
| | |
| | |
| | |
| | |
| | |
| | |
| | |
| | |
| | |
| | |

GAYLORD        PRINTED IN U.S.A.